D1238031

Gene Logsdon's
Practical Skills

Other Books by Gene Logsdon

The Farm Journal Almanac
Wyeth People
Two-Acre Eden
Homesteading
Successful Berry Growing
The Gardener's Guide to Better Soil
Small-Scale Grain Raising
Getting Food from Water
Organic Orcharding
Wildlife in Your Garden

Gene Logsdon's
Practical Skills

A Revival of forgotten Crafts, Techniques, and Traditions

Illustrations by Barbara Field

Photographs by Gene Logsdon,
Rodale Press Photography Department,
and Dennis Barnes

Rodale Press, Emmaus, Pennsylvania

Printed in the United States of America on recycled paper containing a high percentage of de-inked fiber.

Edited by Carol Hupping
Designed by Linda Jacopetti
Book layout by Lynn Gano
Editorial assistance by Cheryl Winters Tetreau
Copy editing by Cristina N. Whyte

Library of Congress Cataloging in Publication Data
Logsdon, Gene.
    Gene Logsdon's Practical skills.

    Includes index.
    1. Handicraft. 2. Do-it-yourself work. 3. Dwellings—Maintenance and repair. I. Title.
II. Title: Practical skills.
TT149.L64   1985   643'.7   85-8315
ISBN 0-87857-577-4   hardcover

2 4 6 8 10 9 7 5 3 1 hardcover

To my father, Gerald, who taught me some of this book and ingrained in me a great respect for the kind of people who could teach the rest of it.

CONTENTS

ACKNOWLEDGMENTS

I'm happy to have this opportunity to thank formally the people who have worked closely with me on this book. First of all, Carol Hupping, my editor, has been of inestimable value, not just in the ordinary work of handling semicolons and split infinitives but in suggesting worthwhile additions and making observations of a sound technical nature. She is no ordinary handler of split infinitives: One phone call interrupted her at work ankle deep in concrete as she and her husband poured a footer for an addition to their house.

So that I have the time to devote myself singlemindedly to writing, my own wife finds herself ankle deep on occasion in garden weeds or cow manure. While I split infinitives, she splits firewood. There are no words to thank her properly for the tranquility she brings to our home, without which I could not write.

Photographer Dennis Barnes provided needed photographs in subject areas we had all but given up hope of illustrating. More than that, his deep knowledge of working people and traditional skills time and again found me a source of information I might otherwise have missed.

Designer Linda Jacopetti took what at first glance looked like just a pile of manuscript pages and another of assorted art and photos and turned them into this—An honest-to-goodness book.

Barbara Field has enhanced my writing with her lovely illustrations.

Cheryl Winters Tetreau has been almost clairvoyant in the necessary task of routing manuscript pages and art proofs back and forth between writer, editor, and designer.

Tom Gettings, Bill Hylton, Mitch Mandel, and Phil Gehret have all made helpful suggestions and contributions.

INTRODUCTION

Cartoonists depict the birth of an idea by drawing a light bulb blinking on. In my case, the idea that eventually resolved itself into this book happened in exactly the opposite way. The fluorescent ceiling fixture above my typewriter blinked *off* as I was typing away one day. It made a little "poing" sound that I assumed was the last gasp of one of the bulbs. I stared up at the light. Actually, only one-half of the fixture had gone out—the two bulbs on the left side. The two bulbs on the right side still burned, fortunately for me. At the time, I did not think to wonder why both left bulbs had blinked off at the same time. I kept typing. About half an hour later, the two bulbs came back on again. A mystery. I could no more explain it than I could explain the inner workings of a mainframe computer. A little later, the bulbs poinged off again.

I decided to investigate. The first task was to remove the plastic cover from the fixture. I studied. I stared. I deduced. I contemplated. For the life of me, I could not see any way to remove it. There were no hooks, notches, latches, catches, turnbuckles, knobs, bolts, or anything that presented a clue to how the cover came off.

Undaunted, I fell back on my usual *modus operandi:* when in doubt, use force. I bent back the metal ends of the fixture and pried the cussed cover out, cracking it in the process. Removing a fluorescent bulb is not as cut and dried as it might seem, but nevertheless I accomplished this feat with little trouble. Naturally, there were no new spare fluorescents in the house, so I removed one from a fixture we rarely turn on, knowing it was in like-new condition. I put it in the socket where I had removed one of the wayward bulbs. Nothing happened. Hmmmmm.

Fortunately, a friend happened by my office about that time. He asked me why I was staring so disconsolately at the ceiling. I told him. He smiled indulgently. He owned apartments and so was an authority on changing light bulbs. First of all, he informed me (rather pompously I thought) that the way to remove the plastic cover was to grasp it at the sides with both hands, about midway between the two ends, squeeze inward, and then push it in one or the other horizontal direction. There was enough extra room for the cover to slide far enough to one end so the cover would slip out of the metal holder at the other end. I tried it. So simple. Yet how many people would know to do that?

Secondly, he continued, fluorescent fixtures like mine have the two bulbs on each side connected *in tandem* as any fool could see, ha ha. Therefore both bulbs had to be in place, and *both* had to be good ones, or *neither* would work. He slid a second bulb, robbed from the other fixture, into place, and both lights promptly poinged on. I felt worse than stupid. "Don't be embarrassed," he said cheerily. *"You'd be surprised how few people know that."* Right then and there, the vague outlines of this book began to form in my mind.

The vague outlines took a firmer grip on me an hour later, as I was again typing away. The two new bulbs poinged out again. Aha. Just as I suspected, my friend, the expert, didn't know it all, either. There were deeper mysteries involved than just changing bulbs. To make a long story short, several newly purchased bulbs and two trips to town later I learned that the problem was the ballast in the fixture. The word ballast has three definitions in my dictionary, none of which have anything at all to do with electric light fixtures. And my dictionary costs a good deal more than this book does. And if I knew then what I know now, I could have saved the cost of the electrician to replace it.

But I don't wish to give the impression that a book can take the place of professional know-how all the time. In attempting to write the *real* how-to about practical skills in this book, I soon learned why other writers have been smart enough not even to try. The inadequacies of the printed word to convey certain kinds of practical information were never more obvious to me than when trying to describe the finer points of butchering a chicken, or soldering and welding metals. Removing the lungs from the innards of a chicken, for example, is done blindly, the fingers searching out the ribs, then sliding between them and under the lungs to lift them out. How do you precisely tell, with word or picture, that which is done without the eyes? Even after cleaning at least 500 chickens,

I'm still getting defter at the job, but I cannot tell you how. You have to do it.

I say later on in this book that soldering is easy, but in learning how to solder a running seam, or lay a bead while brazing or welding, you have to learn the *feel* of the iron moving with the flow of the metal. Neither words nor pictures can instruct your hand to become one with that flow. Only by repetition does your soul finally perceive the soul of the metal and so the job becomes easy.

However, this doesn't mean that the written word is of no help at all. Even now, as you read this, you perceive the problem of learning skills. Knowing the problem is half the battle. Also, the written word can give you reassurance— the confidence that you *can* learn, which is the other half. Moreover, the written word can teach you other kinds of forgotten tricks, like making a wedge stick in tough wood by placing a pebble in the cleft of the split next to the wedge. Or breaking a large rock by star drilling a hole in it and filling the hole with water, which upon freezing, splits the rock.

Such skills were common knowledge hardly two generations ago, and their loss is evident in all the manual arts. In this age of specialization we have tried to avoid what the poet Gary Snyder so aptly calls the "real work"—the practical skills that are essential to the smooth execution of nearly all human activity. We have assumed that such manual arts are not worthy of artistic or scientific attention, but humdrum work to be assigned to the most mediocre minds or to an expert or to some automated wizardry (of which the computer is the latest fad to arise). I'll forego the long philosophical argument that suggests giving up our responsibility to the "real work" eventually makes us not free but slaves of a physically and economically debilitating technology. I'll just rest my case on the current situation: hardly anyone knows how to fix a leaky faucet anymore.

We complain about the shortage of good maintenance men, not realizing that there are plenty of them around, but they are kept too busy doing things we ought to be doing for ourselves instead of concentrating on really complicated repair work where they are needed. Then they make so much money doing our work for us that they can spend winters in Florida while professional people of a supposedly higher mentality (ha ha again) spend their spare time trying to figure out how the furnace works. We even find it amusing rather than pathetic when our Einsteins turn out to be too impractical to know how to balance a budget.

At a funeral a few weeks ago, I found a young apprentice mortician, tie askew and white shirt sleeves rolled up, sweating over the innards of a soft-drink dispenser in the lobby of the funeral parlor. Naturally, this great invention that is supposed to dispense food and drink automatically had broken down. It was Sunday and the serviceman who supposedly takes care of such matters wasn't available. Since people do die on Sunday, and grieving relatives get thirsty on Sunday like any other day, the intrepid young mortician was trying to fix the blamed thing. "Hardest challenge of my career so far," he said, ruefully. "Dad says if I can handle emergencies like this, I'll make a successful mortician." I was reminded of a similar experience. As a novice museum curator (far back in my checkered career), I found out that in reality I was a glorified janitor. I complained to the museum director that I had come there to learn how to run a museum, not be a maintenance man. "But my dear young man," he replied. "That's what running a museum is all about!"

The mundane and practical knowledge that keeps the world running—the ability of a society to maintain its technology—is what philosopher Eric Hoffer calls the first sign of a thriving culture. Even if robots ever do the most tedious tasks, we will have to look after the robots. Gary Snyder, the poet mentioned above, said it best: ". . . all of us will come back again to hoe in the ground, . . . or hand-adze a beam, or skin a pole, or scrape a hive—we're never going to get away from that [kind of work]. We've been living a dream that we're going to get away from it. . . .Put that out of our minds. . . .That work is always going to be there."

The wonderful part of the truth of Snyder's assertion is that, given a little knowledge and a little experience in the practical arts, that work can become a source of enduring satisfaction. Not to mention economy. And so, to this book.

PART I

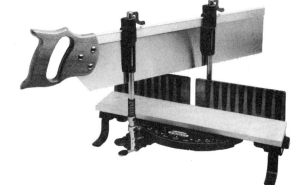

HOME IMPROVEMENT

CHAPTER 1

THE HOME WORKPLACE

Planning the Workshop

Eric Hoffer, the philosopher, said that a society could be judged on the quality of its maintenance and repair. In a society in decline or in chaos, nothing much works. The plumbing leaks, the railroad tracks deteriorate, cars and tractors stand idle for lack of qualified repairmen, and so forth. A home in disarray exhibits the same characteristics: peeling paint, stuck doors, cracked windows, leaky faucets, fences and gates falling down. But where a home is kept up neat and trim, invariably discipline and order reign in the lives of the owners. And someplace on the property there will be found a home workshop paying for itself many times over.

Most home workshops happen by accident, more or less. They are seldom planned into the construction of a house the way a kitchen or bedroom is. Within months, however, the need for a workshop impresses itself upon new homeowners. A basement area or garage corner is then pressed into use, and a vicious circle begins. The workshop space is inappropriate for one reason or another and so is not condu-cive to use no matter how much money is spent on tools. Unused, or used infrequently, the workshop does not justify putting more money into it. Not putting more money into it discourages use even more. The homeowner has money tied up in tools and then hires out for the repair work anyway.

Deliberately planning a room or building for a workshop may cost more money initially, but saves money in the long run. Although such a workshop will vary with the special interests of the home handyman or woman, there are basic considerations that apply to all.

Adequate space. A workshop specifically designed for repairing watches might get by in a 10 by 10-foot room, but for a typical home shop, a more or less squarish room of about 250 square feet is what I mean by adequate—say, a room 20 by 12 feet. But a room of 30 by 18 feet is much nicer and none too large if one contemplates a more or less full set of wood-working and metal-working tools some time in the future, in addition to the normal repair and maintenance tools, with ample room to work on the family car. (See The "Ideal" Workshop Plan, next in this chapter.)

Easy, direct access to outdoors. If you have to use the basement for a shop—and many of us do—that's better than nothing. But there are many advantages to a shop with easy outside access, especially if the workspace is rather small. If you are sawing a long board, you can carry it outside to turn it around, for one thing, or let it stick out the door while you work on it. You don't have to maneuver it down a narrow hallway and through a side door to get it in the shop. The door, incidentally, should be wider than a normal door so that if you build a cabinet or, say, a boat or other really big thing, you can get it out of the shop easily. A former garage or building with an overhead door the size of a garage door is ideal, so you can work on your car in the shop. With an outside wall, you can vent odors and dusts without saturating the whole house. You can also provide good ventilation at lower cost. An outside wall means windows, which make a workshop, psychologically, a much more pleasant place to work (more on that follows) and give you nice natural light.

Its own special place. Ideally, the workshop should be a workshop, not a combination of workshop and something else, such as food storage area, as my basement workshop was for years. You don't want sawdust drifting into the coils of your freezer, and you don't want flour from the grain mill drifting onto a freshly varnished tabletop. Sharing the garage workshop with automobiles doesn't work very well either. You look out there on a rainy Saturday and see that both cars have to be moved (out into the rain) before you can do anything. Besides, the bench upon which you left the lawn mower motor in thirteen parts has been taken over by flowerpots and a bicycle tire so that the thirteen parts are now scattered to the far corners. You will need half an hour for regrouping before you can begin to work. So you watch the football game instead. Just as all writers learn, you need to have a special place to do special work. When you go there, habit takes over and you move readily into the work at hand. I can't write at the kitchen table or in bed—I've tried. Neither can you do workshop work in temporary, makeshift, forever-changing environs.

The workshop must be comfortable. Otherwise, you will find tons of reasons not to go there and work. It must be heated in winter and at least endurably cool in summer. Metal rusts and wood warps in unheated rooms anyway, so controlling temperature and humidity is good business materially as well as psychologically. Basement shops have this one advantage—the cost of heating and cooling is much lower than in a garage or separate building.

A wood floor is best. Wood is much kinder to your feet, legs, and back than concrete, and so you will work longer. Dropped tools will not be broken or dulled so easily on wood, either. If you are stuck with concrete around your workbench, a covering of old, thick carpet is helpful.

The exception to having a wood floor is, of course, in a welding shop, blacksmith shop, or other type of shop where fire might be a hazard. In these cases a concrete, brick, or gravel floor is much preferred.

Good lighting. Trying to do shopwork in insufficient light is most irritating, especially after one has reached the age of bifocals. In addition to good overhead lighting, have a goosenecked lamp handy for close work.

A place for every tool and every tool in place. Cover the walls with plenty of Peg-Board and hooks. At a museum workshop where I was once employed, the curator spent several days painting the exact silhouette of each tool on the wall where it was supposed to be hung so that even careless dolts (like me) would be sure to get things back up in the correct place. I thought he was foolish for "wasting" all that time. But of course he saved hours and hours that we were previously spending trying to find where we had mislaid tools. And in the morning when he came to work, he could tell with one grim glance at the wall which tools I had not put back the evening before.

A pleasant place. The home workshop should not get associated in your mind with the grimmer atmosphere of your job world. It should be a place where you can relax, where you have that little inner satisfaction of knowing that you can quit any time you feel like it, or work as slowly as you are inclined. This kind of attitude will lure you more frequently into your workshop. Doesn't hurt to have a radio or TV there, too, so long as you do not try to watch a third-and-three situation on the four-yard line while running a board through a table saw. Also keep a comfortable chair handy. Sometimes you need to think before leaping into a project or a problem. A second chair might be appropriate in case a friend stops by to help you think.

The "Ideal" Workshop Plan

The plan shown here suggests a workshop in the best of all possible worlds. Though not extravagant, it is more than most of us can afford at the outset—or as a friend says, "If you can afford that much room and all those tools, you can afford to hire someone else to do the work." That's not necessarily true, but the point here is to suggest a really nice workshop toward which one can aim. It becomes more affordable if it is used secondarily as a garage, with the table saw (B) moved to the wall when not in use. A garage that doubles as a workshop is not ideal, as I said earlier, but a workshop that doubles as a garage is less objectionable. The ample space provided is primarily for car *repair,* not storage, and can be used to build a boat or restore an old car, buggy, or whatever. The

overhead door not only makes vehicle entrance and exit possible, but, as I mentioned earlier, it allows you to move large objects like cabinets and picnic tables in and out of the shop with ease. The door should fit tight and be as well insulated as possible.

Few home shop owners are ever going to want all the power tools shown or do work in all the areas provided. If, however, commercial labor continues to price itself out of the repair market, more people will use their spare time profitably in all these areas. Therefore, it could be wise to plan an all-inclusive workshop even though it may be years before you can equip it properly. Better "too much" room now than to have to build a new building later on to get more space.

In this so-called ideal situation, I've made an effort to keep the woodworking activities in

THE "IDEAL" WORKSHOP

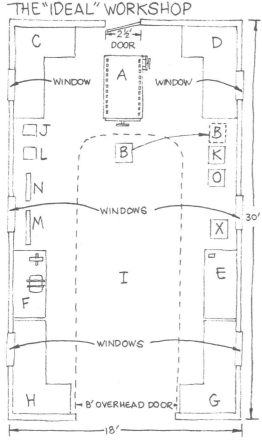

A: WOODWORKING BENCH
B: TABLE SAW
C: CARPENTRY CENTER
D: PAINTING – FINISHING CENTER
E: PLUMBING CENTER
F: SHARPENING-BENCH WITH HAND AND POWER BENCH GRINDERS
G: WELDING – BRAZING - SOLDERING CENTER
H: SMALL MOTOR – ELECTRICAL REPAIR CENTER

I: WITH TABLE SAW MOVED TO B AREA I (IN DOTTED LINES) PROVIDES ROOM FOR AUTO DURING REPAIR WORK (OR DOUBLES AS GARAGE)
J: POWER SANDER
K: BAND SAW
L: BELT SANDER– SHARPENER
M: LATHE
N: JOINTER- PLANER
O: DRILL PRESS
X: HEATER, SUCH AS WOOD STOVE

one half of the shop and the metal-working activities at the other end, as much as possible. Also, the "dirtier" power tools—sanders, planers, shapers, and lathe—are positioned as far from the painting center as possible. Volatile liquids should be stored in the paint center at the opposite end of the room from the welding area. I have positioned the stove or heater as close to the center of the room as possible and still far enough from volatile liquids to be prudent. But in a real situation, you might find another area better for a stove, or a totally different arrangement more practical. The purpose here is to *suggest,* and by suggesting, let you consider details you might not have thought of yourself.

Carpentry center (C). This is usually the largest part of the workroom and the best equipped—testimony to the fact that do-it-yourselfers work wood more than any other raw material because of its ease and versatility. Basic needs are a bench with a vise and the traditional hand tools: hammers, saws, planes, chisels, drills, squares, C-clamps, and so forth. As time and money permit, add small power hand tools like drills, saws, and sanders. And finally, for serious woodworkers, the heavier stationary power tools that provide professional accuracy and efficiency: table saw, band saw, drill press, jointer planer, shaper, and lathe. Woodworkers say that if you can afford only one big power tool, the table saw is the most versatile for the home workshop.

Painting-finishing center (D). This sounds like gilding the lily and is, in a way. If money were no object, you would have your painting center in another building altogether, to get away from dust, but that would be even more lily-gilding. Actually though, painting usually proves to be the most frequent activity in home maintenance. Cabinets to store brushes, scrapers, buffers, rollers, adhesives, paints, varnishes, thinners, removers, and so forth will be the first most-needed storage facilities in your shop. In this

Cutting Glass

There are always times around the house when the ability to cut glass for a windowpane or picture frame comes in handy. All of us have watched the hardware store proprietor cut glass with such a cool flourish that the job seemed almost magical. Trying to imitate him, flourish and all, we become all the more convinced of the magical undertones to the skill. When *we* first tap gently on the glass nothing happens. And when we tap a little harder, the glass eventually breaks, but not along the line we scored.

Is there a trick to cutting glass? Not really. But there are immutable conditions without which success seldom is achieved. First, you must cut glass on a level, smooth surface. Second, the straightedge or T-square, or whatever guide you use, must not slip even the least bit during the cutting. Some people nail brads and hold the straightedge solidly against them or put a strip of tape on the underside so the straightedge won't slip when held down tightly by hand. Third, the glass cutter should be sharp. Pros keep their cutters soaking in turpentine between uses. This prevents rust and seems to make the blade bite better into the glass.

To cut glass like a pro, set the straightedge firmly on the line to be cut and draw the glass cutter along it as if tracing a line with a pencil, only with much firmer downward pressure. Keep the pressure as even as you can. Start at the far edge of the glass, but do not bear down *over* the edge, as this can cause the edge to chip. Stroke across the glass and off the near end. *Do not rescore the line.* It only dulls the cutter and often prevents the glass from breaking evenly.

Next, lift the glass up, supporting both pieces, and gently tap with the cutter handle at both ends of the cut. Then tap on the underside along the outside of the cut. The glass will crack through the line but still

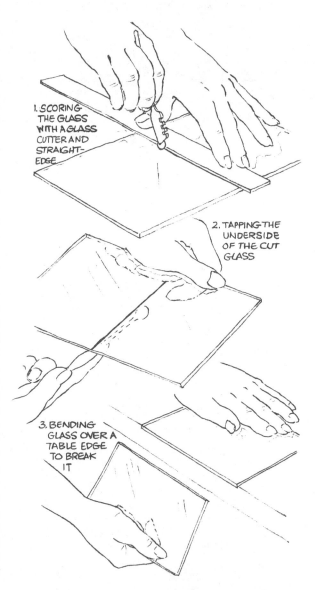

1. SCORING THE GLASS WITH A GLASS CUTTER AND STRAIGHT-EDGE

2. TAPPING THE UNDERSIDE OF THE CUT GLASS

3. BENDING GLASS OVER A TABLE EDGE TO BREAK IT

hold together. You can learn to see when it's cracked through. Now lay the glass back down with the cracked line at the exact edge of the table. Hold the glass down on the

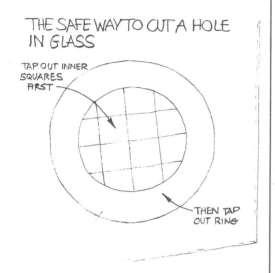

THE SAFE WAY TO CUT A HOLE IN GLASS

TAP OUT INNER SQUARES FIRST

THEN TAP OUT RING

table with one hand and grasp the waste extending out over the edge. Bend it sharply downward. It will part just as magically as if the hardware store proprietor were doing the job. If it doesn't, you are probably using a dull cutter. Practice on a narrow piece of glass first to get the feel of the cutting. The cutter should be putting a pronounced scratch in the glass. You can feel it biting in. If the cutter is sliding over the glass rather easily, like a skate on ice, it isn't sharp enough or you are not bearing down on it squarely.

Cutting a hole in glass without breaking the pane is safer if you follow a little trick—which Suzanne Beedell also describes in her book *Restoring Junk* (Macdonald & Co., London, 1970). Cut the outline of the hole you desire to make, then cut another circle about an inch, if possible, inside that one. Next, cut crosshatches in the inner circle, each about an inch square, if space allows. Use an older cutter to cross lines already scored, as this dulls a blade nearly as much as scoring down a line twice. Now tap out each square of the inner circle; then tap out the ring.

area, you will also keep putty and putty tools, wallpapering tools, and do glass cutting.

Welding-brazing-soldering center (G). Especially on the small country homestead where second-hand farm tools are the only affordable farm tools, welding your own repairs will pay great dividends over the years. The bench where welding is done should have a section of copper top, and where brazing is done, a brick top. Any noncombustible surface will do for soldering with a propane torch. (Although soldering irons and especially soldering guns appear to me much safer and handier than propane.) These soldering tools you will more properly locate at the electrical repair bench (H), where soldering or resoldering wire connections on household appliances is a frequent maintenance job. Hacksaw, tin snips, ball peen hammer, files, and wire brush are normal metal-working tools you will eventually need.

Electric welder or acetylene gas? For brazing, acetylene torches are most often used, although with special carbon arc torches you can now braze with an electric welder. As a novice at both types of welding, I prefer electric welding even though it is supposed to be more difficult to learn. I feel safer using electric arc welders than working with tanks of oxygen and acetylene gas. It depends very much on what you were raised up with: I fear gas stoves unnecessarily because we always had electric ones. I know gas stove lovers who fear electric stoves. But an electric welder can't flash back and burn in the feeder hose, requiring one to shut off the oxygen immediately to prevent a possible explosion. So if I ever get my own welder it will be an electric one. For minor brazing jobs, you can buy small tanks of Mapp gas, a type of acetylene that is handy and safer for the novice to use.

See *Make It! Don't Buy It* (edited by John Warde, Rodale Press, 1983) for a simple, clear discussion of welding and brazing equipment

Soldering Is Easy

Welding and brazing metals together looks difficult, and becoming expert at them is difficult. But an easy way to learn, or begin to learn, is to master soldering first, which is comparatively easy. In the process, you will get a lot of repair work done around the house. On the farm and homestead, for example, buckets are needed by the dozen and you will find, by and by, that metal ones are still the best for the money. But they have a nasty habit of springing leaks long before the rest of the vessel is worn out. You can easily solder such leaks before they become serious holes, and the buckets will last many years instead of the usual two. Loose handles on pots and pans can also be soldered (but aluminum takes a special kind of solder). And if you can solder, you can make almost any tin utensil you need with tin snips and a hammer, using one of America's most valuable yet free forms of metal: thrown-away tin cans.

Some tinsmiths still prefer the old traditional soldering iron with its comparatively large copper tip—the extra size of the tip was necessary to hold heat. Some roofers still prefer these traditional soldering irons for sealing seams on tin roofs. They have little gas "furnaces" to heat the iron. Today, the electric soldering iron and the soldering gun are generally used on all but heavier metal, which solders more effectively with a propane torch.

The simplest kind of soldering, for electrical connections or to plug a leaky bucket, employs soft solder. It comes as a bar or a coil of wire. In some cases the wire is hollow-cored and filled with the flux necessary for a strong bond. Rosin flux is used for soldering electrical connections only. Acid flux is used for joining tin, copper, and the like.

This solder melts very easily. But the soldering gun should not be used to do the melting *directly*, as most beginners try to do. Instead, use the gun or iron to heat the metal to be soldered. Apply the solder to the metal when the latter is hot enough to melt it. The solder will then flow over the metal around the tip of the soldering gun, which should be kept moving to draw the puddle of melting solder along the joint. If you are just soldering an electrical connection, there is not much movement, of course. Just heat and spot-dab a bit of solder to the preheated wire, and the solder flows over it, making a solid connection.

and many other home maintenance activities. Another book I've found helpful is *Complete Book of Home Workshops* by David T. Manners (Popular Science Publishing Co., Harper & Row, New York, 1969). But as far as learning the skills yourself, you just have to practice. I watched my father operate the electric welder for several years, and one day when he was gone and a piece of machinery broke, I just fixed it myself. My first welds were poor, but little by little, I learned.

Small motor-electrical repair center (H). There's no special reason these two should be grouped together. I do so because this bench usually has enough extra room to take a lawn mower apart and, if necessary, leave it there undisturbed when you can't get it reassembled right away. This is a great advantage of the commodious shop, or a shop with commodious bench space. You can have various projects in states of suspended animation while you wait for a new part you have ordered to arrive, or while you are out pulling the garden weeds, or playing golf, or whatever. Of course ample bench space may only lead to more procrastination, but that's a problem no shop, however equipped, can solve.

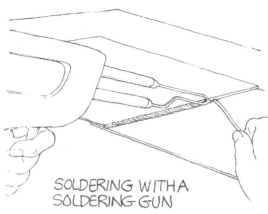

SOLDERING WITH A
SOLDERING GUN

pieces tightly together during soldering. Locking-grip pliers are a good tool for this. (In fact, locking-grip pliers are one of the most versatile tools you can own.) You'll probably have to move the pliers and solder a little at a time to avoid distorting the metal, and also because they will draw heat away so fast you'll find it difficult to melt the solder near the pliers.

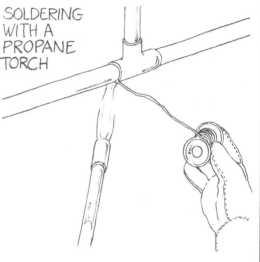

SOLDERING
WITH A
PROPANE
TORCH

Soldering in plumbing and on some sheet metal is done with a propane (or other gas) torch. Many times propane won't be hot enough for hard soldering or brazing.

In addition to getting the metal heated before soldering, a good bond requires that the metal be very clean. Burnish it with steel wool if in doubt. In joining a piece of metal to another, the seam lap or area of contact should be as much as you can manage—¼-inch minimum. Clamp the two

The Workbench

One of the first pieces of equipment you should furnish your workshop with is a wood-worker's bench, with at least one woodworking vise attached to it. Such a bench will be very handy for building the cabinets, shelves, and countertops in your shop. It will be the most-used "tool" in your shop for the rest of your life. Typically, workbenches are built against a wall and half their versatility is immediately lost. If possible (if room allows) situate the workbench so you can work *all around it.* That means putting it out toward the middle of the room, as

I have positioned it in my ideal workshop layout shown previously.

If you can afford a good European-style woodworker's bench (so-called), you will find it an excellent investment with its tail vise at one end and shoulder vise to one side, with tool tray alongside and perhaps drawers underneath. These benches are works of art, sturdily built of qual-ity hardwood; my only complaint about them is that the work surface is too small on the medium-size ones ($300 to $600) I can afford, and the largest, with about 13 square feet of tabletop, are quite expensive (around $1000). However, when you deduct the cost of the two vises—at

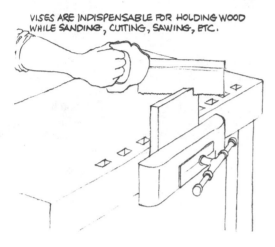

VISES ARE INDISPENSABLE FOR HOLDING WOOD WHILE SANDING, CUTTING, SAWING, ETC.

least one of which you will have to buy even if you build your own bench—the price is less heart-stopping. In any event, homemade, homelier benches modeled on these European beauties are not difficult to make and just as useful.

With one or the other vise and stops (often called bench dogs that fit into holes in the tabletop to hold objects against the pressure of the vise) you can hold almost anything made of wood, no matter what the shape, while you plane, sand, carve, chisel, sharpen, saw, nail, glue, drill, notch, rabbet, dovetail, mark, measure, mortise, and so forth. This ability to hold wood solidly while you work on it with hand tools is the whole secret (along with sharp blades) of efficient hand tool use. The workbench does the holding, leaving your hands free to put all your energy into the tool. Since the typical homeowner will and should rely mostly on hand tools rather than expensive power tools, the workbench and its vises pay for themselves a hundred times over in the course of a lifetime.

But if you shy away from spending that kind of money and don't have time to build such a workbench, any simple *but sturdy* table with a vise bolted to it will do. The vise should have a metal stop, or dog, on it that can be raised above the jaws of the vise so you can hold large flat

pieces tight against a block or stop on the tabletop (as in the drawing). You can have a very smooth bench surface without expensive hardwoods by covering your simple table with Masonite. When it becomes gouged, nicked, or punctured by too many nail holes, simply remove it and put on a new panel. The height of the tabletop should be about 34 to 35 inches from the floor, or if you are unusually short or tall, build the top to come up to your wrist when your arm is hanging loosely at your side. This way you can work over your table with the least amount of arm fatigue while exerting the fullest leverage and weight of your body on the work.

Although the tail and shoulder vises of a woodworking bench forestall the need for many auxiliary clamps, a few C-clamps of various sizes and a couple of bar clamps are still handy to have, and indispensable if you don't have vises. A type of bar clamp called a pipe clamp is the most inexpensive. You need buy only the two clamping parts and slide them on ¾-inch standard plumbing pipe of any length you desire. These clamps are great for holding any large object, like a chair, and you will find many other ways to use them. There are innumerable other specialized vises that you can buy if and when you need them.

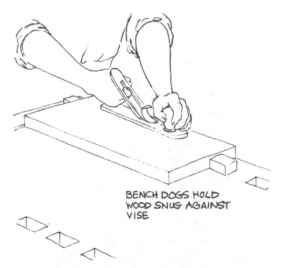

BENCH DOGS HOLD WOOD SNUG AGAINST VISE

The Uncommonly Common Hand Tools for Working Wood and Other Materials

The hand tools every household needs usually accumulate in the workshop in a haphazard manner. In a crisis, the homeowner rushes down to the hardware shop and grabs the first one of whatever he needs that meets his eye. This is not altogether a bad way to build a tool collection, since at least you do not have money invested in tools before you need to own them. But it not only leads to buying poor quality tools, but to using the wrong tool in hopes of saving a trip to the store. So the amateur carpenter tries to hand-rip a board (saw with the grain) using a crosscut handsaw that is too cheap to crosscut efficiently, let alone rip. This attempt at rip sawing does about as

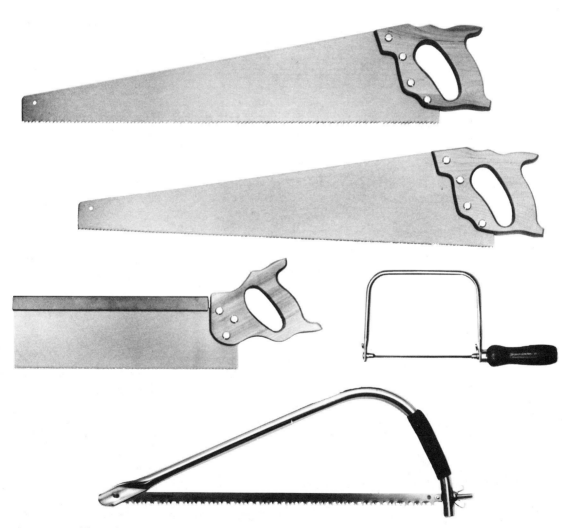

Top to bottom: ripsaw, crosscut saw, backsaw (left), coping saw (right), bow saw.

much good as if you cut notches in a ruler and tried to saw with it. The amateur carpenter then swears a thousand helldammits and buys a $750 power table saw he will never use enough to justify the cost. He will also carry with him for the rest of his life a prejudice against hand tools. Moral of the story: Use the right tool and buy the more expensive lines of hand tools rather than the cheapest. In hand tools the difference between happiness and rage is usually only a few dollars.

Saws. A 10-point crosscut saw makes a smoother cut but is a little slower than an 8-point. For ripping with the grain, buy a ripsaw, with a 6- or 7-point blade for a smoother cut. Ripsaw teeth are deeper and larger than crosscut teeth and are sharpened straight across rather than beveled like crosscut teeth.

For making angles on window sashes and frames, you will eventually need a backsaw or miter saw and a miter box. Unless you are very clever, you can't cut accurate angles with a cheap wooden miter box. But on the other hand, you do not have to buy the most expensive miter box either. A bow saw for cutting curves and inside holes of thicker woods and a coping saw for fine inside work both come in handy sooner or later.

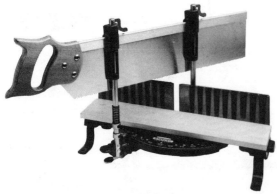

Miter box with 22" backsaw.

With all hand sawing, remember and respect the basics. Keep the blade sharp and let the saw do the work. Let it eat its own way into the wood. Don't push down on it.

Should you sharpen your own saws? I think not, unless you delight in learning such skills. If there is a good saw sharpener in your community—and there usually is—take your saws to him once a year.

Hammers. Watching a lifelong roofer hammer nails into a new roof he was installing, I was once again made aware of the limitations of books purporting to teach skills and the arrogance of writers who believe their books do so. Books, for example, talk about the various kinds of hammers—claw, tack, ball peen, framing, ripping, wood handled, steel handled, and so forth, as if all this is not readily discerned by anyone who can see, or explained in two minutes by the hardware store proprietor. What this old roofer was doing, however, was the important part of the story, yet rarely, if ever, written about. *Wearing gloves,* he would reach into his nail pouch, grasp six nails without looking, and by the time his hand had returned to the point where he was driving nails, his gloved fingers had automatically arranged the six nails in a neat row between his middle finger and index finger, heads up, palm of hand up. Then moving his hand wherever a nail was needed, he would drive each in turn through the metal panel, thumb far out of harm's way. Anyone who has worked on a roof in cold weather or smashed a thumb black and blue with a missed blow can appreciate the value of the roofer's skill.

I asked him how much his hammer weighed since the books make a great point of recommending 24- to 28-ounce hammers. He didn't know. I asked him if he preferred a well-curved claw or a straight claw, and he said it didn't make much difference, because if a nail was hard to pull out, you'd best put a little block of wood under the claw to increase the leverage of

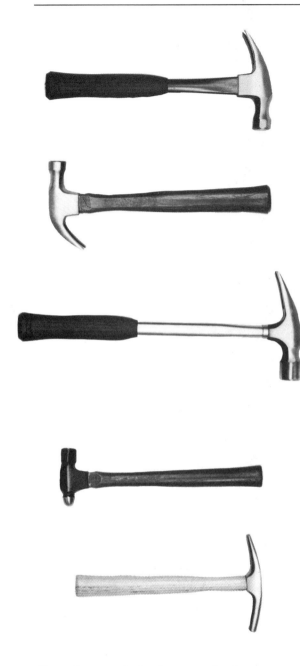

Top to bottom: ripping hammer, claw hammer, framing hammer, ball peen hammer, tack hammer.

the pull anyway. Did he like a wood handle or a steel one? Whichever one he picked up first. What was the most important thing a roofer needed to know? He thought about that one through several driven nails. Finally he replied, "When to quit." He was not speaking of age, or at least not of age only. "A roof in summer is the hottest place this side of hell," he explained. "If you don't get off and take a break about every hour you'll fall off and take a real break."

Measuring devices. Leonardo da Vinci said that genius is 99% hard work. By the same token, craftsmanship is 99% measuring accurately. Every shop needs a tape rule, a framing square, and a sliding bevel for transferring angles. Dividers for making circles, or taking measurements of cylinders, or dividing a given space exactly into two parts are also handy. A type of large framing square called a rafter square comes with a booklet that tells you how to use it to calculate rafter angles and other construction details. Carpenters like to say that if you know how to use a square you can do just about everything with it except paint a house. If a square is not square—like after you drop it or step on it—it is only trouble. The same is true of a level, of course. Both instruments should be checked against a known square or level surface.

Drills. A good electric drill is so versatile that every shop should have one. It should take preference over hand drills. Variable speed, reversible models are better choices. Buy a dowel jig for the drill that will let you center holes easily in board edges.

Chisels and knives. Perhaps the most versatile tool you can own is a good pocketknife. Carving knives (as small as pocketknives but not necessarily with folding blades) are considered very important tools by James Krenov, whose artistry in woodworking is recognized worldwide. He likes very small-bladed, comparatively large-

handled knives for delicate carving work. The ordinary shop owner can use plain old pocket-knives with various blades.

You need at least three wood chisels—a narrow-, a medium-, and a wide-bladed one for cutting mortises of different sizes. Chisel work is one of the most satisfying exercises in woodworking *if* the chisel is very sharp.

To make a square mortise hole in wood, first drill a hole so that there is empty space for the chiseled-off waste wood to move into. Other-

wise the chisel will tend to slant into the wood in the direction of the bevel, and not make a square side on the mortise.

When chiseling on a flat surface, always move with the grain, otherwise, the chisel may dig into the wood too deeply. Don't try to chisel away the waste wood by starting just at the line of the finished work. Rough out the waste wood first, always working *away* from your ultimate finish line. Then carefully pare down the last thin shavings to the finish line. Be patient.

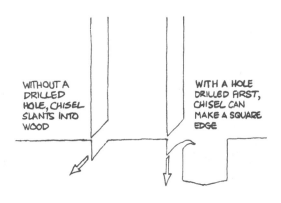

WITHOUT A DRILLED HOLE, CHISEL SLANTS INTO WOOD

WITH A HOLE DRILLED FIRST, CHISEL CAN MAKE A SQUARE EDGE

THE TRICK TO CHISELING A HOLE

Wood chisels, top to bottom: 1½'', 1¼'', 1'', ¾'', ½'', ¼''.

Much chisel work should be done only with the force of the hands, not by striking the chisel with a mallet. Tap, don't strike, when a mallet is necessary. You must learn to keep your eye on the chisel blade, not on your hands or your mallet or the butt end of the chisel.

In storage, keep chisels wrapped separately in some kind of box, not jumbled together or hanging naked on the wall. When out in the open, it's too easy to put a nick in the blades (which should be sharp enough to shave hair off your arm).

Planes. With a workbench capable of solidly holding down the wood you wish to plane, a block plane, jack plane, and jointer plane, costing in the aggregate under $200, will serve the typical homeowner almost as well as a $1500 power jointer planer. It just takes more skill and sweat. Woodworkers argue over the comparative advantages of wood planes versus steel ones, but good work can be done with either. With rabbet planes (the blade extends beyond the width of the plane) you can cut grooves and rabbets much like those you can cut with a power shaper, only, again, more sweat is involved.

The homeowner with only occasional planing work to do will be ahead of the game if he has his wood rough-planed or edge-jointed with

power tools at the lumberyard or a woodworking shop and then finishes planing with his own hand planes. Good hand planing requires practice. To joint an edge straight or a surface level, press slightly harder on the *front* of the plane as you begin a pass, evenly in the middle, and slightly harder on the *rear* of the plane as you reach the end of the board. Where high spots occur on the wood surface, as at a knot, plane that down first, then plane the whole surface. Otherwise, the plane will ride up over the high spot rather than level it. Use the long edge of a framing square or a straightedge laid on the board to discover very slight deviations from level.

When first beginning to smooth a board, you will find the chips from the plane will be short, sporadic, and uneven. The closer you get to level, the longer and more uniform the shavings will curl from the plane. If the plane blade leaves marks, the blade itself may not be level in the plane, or the corners may be a hair longer than the middle of the blade. If the blade is right, a somewhat *slanted* skimming pass will remove traces of scratches caused by the preceding pass. Only practice makes perfect. A good planing requires little or no follow-up sanding. In fact, sanding, however finely done, dulls the sheen of a planed wood surface.

Top to bottom: jointer plane, rabbet plane, jack plane, block plane.

CHAPTER 2

MAINTAINING AND REPAIRING

Applying Paints and Varnishes

Humans can't endure a plain unvarnished surface any more than they can endure a plain unvarnished truth. We have irresistible urges to decorate. A wall or table may be beautiful in its bare essence, but never mind. We will cover it with something whether it needs it or not. The silliest part of this compulsion is that the decorating fashion continually changes. One generation works hard painting furniture with gay colors; the next works even harder stripping off the paint and replacing it with stain and varnish. Eventually we institutionalize our manic desires. One *must* keep his shoes shined or be considered leprous; one *must* color her lips to be presentable.

If my mother and her sisters were an example (especially Aunt Bertha), the cause of "decoritis," especially that wild strain of it known as "painting fever," is rooted in an abhorrence of blemish and dirt. Walls, furniture, floors, ceilings, and so forth get smudged, nicked, gouged, scraped. Such imperfections can be scrubbed out or smoothed over to some degree, but not completely. Paint covereth a multitude of sins. Once painted, a surface shows up new

smudges, nicks, and scrapes more plainly, and so more painting is required. Aunt Bertha came to believe that painting was easier than cleaning, and at the time of her death, the woodwork in her house had well over an eighth of an inch of paint on it, a cross section of which looked like a rainbow. Each spring my mother was seized by the same delirium and tried to cover all wooden surfaces between the kitchen and the henhouse with a fresh coat of paint, enlisting the help of any unfortunate child in sight. Thus I grew up sprouting paint brushes from my fingers and hating the smell of linseed oil. Later, threats of starvation compelled me to take a job painting barns and houses, enabling me to this day to pass myself off as something of an expert on the subject.

Most of what you need to know about paints is right on the label of the paint cans and in the brochures your paint dealer is only too glad to give you. But this information assumes any human who has reached the age of reason understands the *technique* of painting. Not so. Human nature inclines us to one or the other of two opposing painting philosophies: dabbing

· 17

and sloshing. Dabbers dip their brushes barely into the paint and daintily daub a spot on the object being painted. Then they proceed to worry the spot with interminable strokes this way and that, as if they were trying to rub the paint back off the surface. Sloshers, on the other hand, plunge their brushes into the paint to the hilt, dribbling all along the journey from can to object, smearing what's left too thickly on the surface. The paint runs in rivulets down the wall, down the painter's wrist, down the side of the paint can, across the floor, and if the work day were longer, out the door and down the sidewalk.

Whether you are using a brush or a roller, the first lesson is to understand that your tool is not *just* an applicator. It is also a container. It holds a certain amount of paint that will properly cover a certain amount of surface. As you start to paint, you will quickly learn what that amount is, depending on the size of your brush and the kind of paint you are using. You then fix in your mind just about how far a brush-

Painting Wood

Some woods hold paint better than others. According to the USDA Forest Products Laboratory Wood Handbook No. 72, common woods are grouped into four categories of "paintability":

1. Woods that hold all types of paints well: all cedars, redwood, and cypress. However, these are woods that will endure well outside without paint or any preservative coating, so it is questionable whether one would be likely to paint them.

2. Woods that hold paint well if a primer is used: white pine, sugar pine.

3. Woods that hold paint well only with good priming coats, high quality finishing paint, and good maintenance: white fir, hemlock, spruce, lodgepole pine, ponderosa pine, basswood, cottonwood.

4. Woods that need specialized paints and primers to hold up well: Douglas fir, red pine, southern yellow pine, western larch, oaks, elms, maples, ashes, and in fact, most of the hardwoods. The general rule to follow is the denser the wood, the less it will "take" the paint.

But the overall, all-time, never-to-be-disputed fact of paintability is that paint will peel off wet wood, no matter how high the quality of the paint or the "holdability" of the wood. Even if the lumber used in house walls was kiln-dried, the paint may peel off if the house is not properly ventilated and there is excessive moisture being trapped in the walls and reabsorbed by the wood.

load will take you on the surface of the object being painted.

Following the old saying, "brush it on, brush it in, brush it out," is fine and dandy, but it doesn't really tell you how. First, dip the bristles of your brush into the paint about halfway, or a little less. Strike off the bristles on one side on the edge of the paint can, so that you don't dribble on the way to the surface being painted. In some cases, excess bubbles may form on the surface, especially with varnishes being applied to surfaces that will be finished super-smooth, as with fine furniture. These bubbles are coming from the paint or varnish dribbling back into the can when you strike off the bristles. If this problem arises, strike off your brush in another can, rather than back into the can from which you are dipping. (Another cause of excessive bubbling is painting or varnishing an object brought from a cold room to a warm one. Air in the cold wood expands in the warm room causing the wet finish to bubble. Let the wood warm up first.)

With a roller, dip into the rolling pan and run the roller around in the pan before moving to the wall being painted. If the roller skids or spatters excessively, you've got too much paint on it. Some paints spatter more than others. Some brands of the very same kind of paint spatter more than others. Even if your roller is not overloaded, it will spatter paint excessively if you push it too fast.

Do the nicks, crannies, corners, and edges first, then the more open spaces. In painting the open spaces last, you can meld the paint into the previously painted edges and corners, whereas reversing the order leaves noticeable daubings or lines of heavier application or brushmarks. Especially in rollering a wall, do the corners between two walls and between the wall and ceiling first, using the inexpensive flat little foam applicators available for this job.

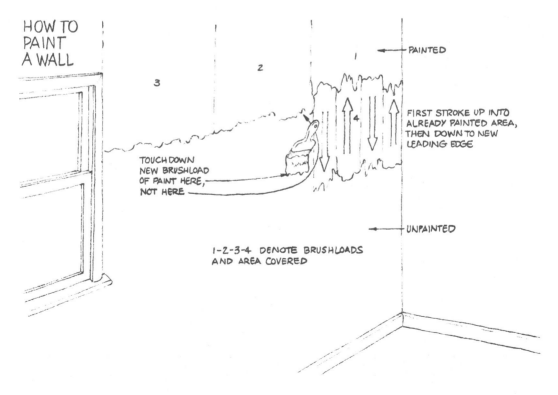

HOW TO PAINT A WALL

PAINTED

FIRST STROKE UP INTO ALREADY PAINTED AREA, THEN DOWN TO NEW LEADING EDGE

TOUCH DOWN NEW BRUSHLOAD OF PAINT HERE, NOT HERE

UNPAINTED

1-2-3-4 DENOTE BRUSHLOADS AND AREA COVERED

Then roll the paint into the corner margins left by the foam applicator, and the line between the two applications disappears. If you do the corners last, the trail of the foam applicator will be quite visible.

The main technique in painting with a brush, after the nooks and crannies are covered, is to lay on each brushload evenly and with as little effort as possible. In other words, don't spread the brushload any farther on the surface than you have to. Each brushload should be first touched down on the surface about halfway out from the leading edge of the area already painted and the new edge that will be formed when that brushload is adequately brushed out. The first strokes are made back toward the surface already painted, then the other way, advancing as far as the paint will carry (see drawing on preceding page). When the brush is empty of its load of paint, the final strokes before dipping again are from the new leading edge of the painted area, back across the painted area, gradually picking the brush off the surface as you stroke. This backstroke removes all brushmarks still remaining.

This technique might seem an overly precious attention to detail. But the tendency is to touch the fresh brushload of paint down right at the leading edge of the already-painted surface, and stroking only or mostly toward the unpainted area. This tends to leave a thicker "pile" of paint at the leading edge, which must be brushed out entirely in one direction, or twice as far as if the paint is first touched down a bit away from the leading edge and brushed out both ways. Once you become habitually adept at this procedure, you will find that you use fewer brush strokes, your arm does not tire as fast, and the work gets finished quicker.

Before quitting for the day, bring your painted area to some natural borderline. Never stop in the middle of a wall, board, or window sill. Invariably the stopping point will show. This is especially true of pigmented exterior oil stains. Even if you aren't quitting for the day, it

Cleaning Up

Most latex paints now used will wash out of brushes with soap and warm water. Varnishes, stains, and penetrating oils require a solvent (usually turpentine) to clean out a brush. For staining, cheap throwaway applicators are available to save the time and bother of trying to clean stains out of good brushes. After use, a good varnish brush ought to stand and soak in solvent for at least a day. (Read your labels—some kinds of bristles might dissolve in some solvents!) Never let the brush stand on its bristles, as they will often become permanently bent out of shape. Stick the brush handles through slits cut in a piece of cardboard, set the cardboard over the can of solvent and adjust the paintbrushes in the slits so that the bristles are submerged in the solvent, but not touching the bottom of the can. In a day or so, remove the brushes, shake out briskly, wipe as dry as possible, and wrap the bristles in a cloth.

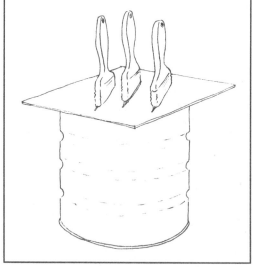

is best with these stains to do one whole board at a time, then go to the next.

Try always to hold the handle of the brush higher than the bristles, so that the paint doesn't run down onto the handle. This is not always possible, as, for example, when painting ceilings. This is where you learn to pay attention to how much paint your brush holds, and not to dip it too far into the paint can.

In painting around window glass or next to a surface of a different color or a baseboard next to carpeting, masking tape or a hand-held paint shield may ensure that you don't get paint where you don't want it. But painted tape can stick and be hard to remove, and hand-held shields usually pick up wet paint, which then is transferred to the area you are trying to keep paint off of. If you have a steady hand and learn how a paint brush works, you will rarely need a shield and won't need to tape around window glass when you paint the sash either. Taping is essential only when *spraying* paint.

The first requirement is a good brush. A nylon brush with the ends of the bristles split to a feathery taper (called split tip or exploded tip brush) is a good choice and readily available in paint stores. The very finely textured bristle ends allow you to lay down a smooth finish coat of paint. Even more important, the bristles hold together very well, but remain very responsive to slight changes in the pressure you apply on them. Many beginners think they should

LAYING A BEAD OF PAINT

use a very small (1-inch) brush on window sashes or other narrow pieces of trim. Seldom is this true. Very small brushes do not hold enough paint. Use a brush at least 2 inches wide, with a fine tapered-bristle edge. Then you can cover more area with each stroke. With a little practice, you can "run a bead" of paint along a window sash and never have a wayward bristle smear paint on the glass.

Though this is thought of as the most tedious kind of painting, learning the skill of running a bead is a satisfying and rather enjoyable task. Once learned, it saves lots of time, too.

With a fresh brushload of paint, struck off on one side (and in this case, dip the brush into the paint scarcely one-third of the way), set the brush on the sash or trim or edge about 1/8 to 1/4 inch away from the glass or whatever and press gently down on the brush in a way that keeps the bristles firmly grouped together, pushing them up very close, but not touching beyond the border of the area to be painted. At the same time, a little bead of paint will well up at the bottom corner of the bent bristles. Draw the brush along the edge, laying a firm, straight line of paint flowing out of that bead. As you draw the brush along, and the paint empties out

Painting around Hardware

Because the edges of hinges and other decorative hardware are seldom straight, it is very difficult to run a good paint bead along them. If you cannot remove such pieces from the object you are painting, you can cover them with petroleum jelly and then paint around them. After the paint dries, remove the jelly. Of course, take care not to smear the jelly on the wood to be painted because the paint won't adhere there, either.

of it, you will have to press down gradually a little harder and perhaps roll the brush slightly to force the paint to the edge where you are running the bead. Keep your eye glued right on that infinitesimal space between the bead and the glass, or whatever area you do not wish the paint to touch.

You will find that in time, you can lay down almost as fine a line as if you were using masking tape. When your bead skips a space, it is time to stop, go back and smooth out the paint you have laid down, but this time keep your brush far enough away from the edge so that there is no chance of touching the glass with your rapid smoothing strokes. Even in this kind of trim and sash work, it is better, whenever possible, to start each new brushload out from the leading edge of the painted area and draw your bead back toward the painted area.

Protecting Wood Outside

As a general rule (a phrase writers use when they know there are so many exceptions that the general rule is useless), paint is a decoration rather than a preservative. Paints do preserve wood but are no guarantee of protection. To protect wood against the insects that would eat it or the fungi that decay it requires materials like creosote, copper naphthenate, or pentachlorophenol (at 5% concentration in fuel oil). The last concoction can have dangerous toxic effects on people applying it without proper protection or on animals gnawing on it, and as a result, is to be used with caution, if at all, and never inside a house. In some states pentachlorophenol is not allowed, and at least one builder of log homes says his company no longer uses it, having found that simple raw boiled linseed oil is a satisfactory preservative on woods that are naturally resistant to decay.

The USDA Forest Products Laboratory (P.O. Box 5130, Madison, WI 53705) suggests the following mixture as a water repellent that

works nearly as well as a preservative above ground: For 5 gallons, mix boiled linseed oil and a solvent (turpentine or paint thinner) at a 3:1 ratio and add about half a pound of paraffin (up to a pound where moisture exposure is foreseen to be excessive).

Paint is a better outdoor wood protector than varnish—again, generally speaking. Varnishes, which are semiclear, allow ultraviolet light to penetrate the covering film and attack the wood. Hardwoods last longer under varnish than softwoods. Marine spar varnishes, thought of as the "best" for outdoor use, actually last no longer than newer phenolic-base and polyurethane varnishes. Ultraviolet inhibitors in varnishes protect the varnish but not the wood. In short, outdoor varnishes need to be renewed about every other year.

Woods That Preserve Themselves

Some woods will last for years without any preservative at all. The woods in the first two groups in the table below will last *above* ground, that is, not in contact with continual moisture (as *in* the ground) for many years unless attacked by insects. They will lose only about ¼ surface inch in a century from natural weathering.

The fungi that cause wood to decay must have proper temperature, oxygen, and moisture to survive. Wood submerged in water so air can't get to it will not rot. Wood dried to, and kept at, less than 20% moisture will not rot. The term *dry rot* is a misnomer. A dry-rotted board was at one time wet enough to rot, even if in its rotten state it is now dry. Rotting does not occur when the temperature is below 40°F. or above 105°F.

Some variation is experienced within strains of the same species, and in the age of the same strains, as in bald cypress. The huge trees of the virgin forest contained very dense heartwood not usually matched by the second growth and younger trees now being lumbered. That is partly why the siding of some very old barns weathers to a silvery grey and then seems to resist decay indefinitely.

Decay Resistance of Various Heartwoods

Very High	High	Medium	Low
Black locust	Arizona cypress	Bald cypress (young growth)	Alder
Osage orange	Bald cypress (mature growth)	Douglas fir	Ashes
Red mulberry	Black cherry	Honey locust	Aspens
	Black walnut	Longleaf pine	Basswood
	Catalpa	Slash pine	Beech
	Cedars	Swamp white oak	Birches
	Chestnut	Tamarack	Buckeye
	Junipers	Western larch	Butternut
	Mesquite	White pine	Cottonwood
	Pacific yew		Elms
	Redwood		Hackberry
	Sassafras		Hemlocks
	White oaks		Hickories
			Magnolia
			Maples
			Most pines
			Poplar
			Red and black oaks
			Spruces
			Sweet gum
			Sycamore
			Willows
			Yellow poplar

According to the Forest Products Laboratory, latex paints last longer than oil-base, the quality being equally good. All-acrylic latexes, applied in two coats over an oil-base or stain-blocking latex primer, lasted the longest in their tests. The reason is that latex paints are more flexible, stretching and shrinking with the wood, and so they hold up better even though they pass more water vapor than oil-base paints. However, oil paints adhere better to weathered wood surfaces. To ascertain whether latex is going to stick to a particular surface well enough, the Forest Products Laboratory passes on this trick: Clean a spot, paint it with latex, and let dry. Press a Band-Aid onto the paint then briskly snap it off. If the bandage lifts the paint, you need to clean the wood surface better or use an oil paint.

Comparatively new semitransparent outdoor stains are a compromise between paint and varnish, with the colors of the former and the more penetrating action of the latter. They usually contain a water-repellent preservative with color pigment added, and if brushed on, need to be applied very liberally in two coats. If they contain mildewcides like pentachlorophenol or copper naphthenate, obey all cautions on the label scrupulously. Penta is particularly hazardous.

Applying Wallcoverings

In the first place, it is best not to hang wallpaper with your spouse. The family that hangs wallpaper together may not stay together, no matter how fervently they pray together. Nevertheless, it is difficult to hang wallpaper alone (although my wife does it); so the first step for success is to get a helper. Pick one from among the calmest, coolest, most patient of your acquaintances. People who like to do things in a hurry need not apply. A good test for wallcovering aptitude is to have the prospective applicant wrap a gift. Good gift wrappers do not necessarily make good wallpaper hangers, but

bad ones are a disaster.

Directions that come with your wallpaper or that you get from your dealer will advise you on the particular circumstances of the covering you select, but as with painting, some of the fine points of technique are glossed over. The first important fact to keep in mind when approaching a wall with a strip of wet wallpaper smothering your face is that *most wall coverings stretch when wet.* A strip 2 feet wide will gain approximately an inch after glue has been applied to it or the preglued surface moistened. In measuring over from the corner preparatory to applying the first strip to a wall, that little bit of knowledge can come in very handy.

Wall coverings with glue already applied when you buy then are called prepasted wallcoverings in the trade. They need only to be soaked with water in special trays made for that purpose before being applied. Directions for each kind of covering will tell you mostly how to do this, but experience will prove that the directions can't be followed slavishly. Once we were instructed to allow 5 minutes after the wallcovering was moistened for it to "relax" before being applied. The covering relaxed so much it would not adhere to the wall after such a wait. Directions can't allow for all the varying wall situations the paper will be called upon to cover. You have to experiment a little.

You cut prepasted wallcoverings into the proper strip lengths, then roll them up again so that the exposed end is the top of the strip, and lay them, one at a time, in the water tray. You need a weight to stick inside the roll so it doesn't float and so you can unroll it without lifting the whole roll. The technique for applying is the same as for other wallcoverings (see drawing).

Prepasted coverings may seem handier, and in some cases they are, but many fabric-backed coverings are not available in prepasted form. So often you will find yourself applying glue to wallcoverings whether you prefer to or not. Actually, the job is not really any more difficult than wetting prepasted coverings. You need a table about 5 feet long, although a

HANGING WALLPAPER

smaller one will do. Usually you should glue two or three strips at a time and then apply them to a wall, since directions most often call for a short waiting period between applying glue and covering the wall.

Use a regular wallpaper glue brush to apply the glue. It is very important to cover every bit of the strip, especially the edges. Lay the strip to be glued on the table with one edge just over the edge of the table. Under the other edge place the next strip you intend to glue. In this way, you get no glue on the table as you brush it on. Glue on the table gets on the pattern side of the next strip. You will inadvertently get enough glue on the pattern side anyway, so take great pains to avoid this as much as possible and thereby shorten the task of sponging glue off the covering after it is on the wall.

Apply glue to the top portion of the strip and fold that portion over on itself, glue to glue. Then brush glue on the bottom portion and fold it over on itself. Important: The bottom portion that is folded over on itself *should be somewhat more than half* of the total strip, so that as you hang the strip, top portion first, you do not have to wrestle with any more wallpaper than absolutely necessary.

Okay? Now unfold the top portion of the strip and grasp it on both sides about a foot from the top, holding the strip out in front of you while lifting, so that the bottom portion (kept folded by the glue) swings clear of the floor. Most people cover walls from left to right, so the left side will be the one to butt against the previous strip. Your left thumb and fingers should hold the strip on the left side right at a point in the pattern that must match perfectly the same point in the pattern on the strip already on the wall.

Then, as you lift the strip to the wall, the first point of contact should be at your left thumb. Butt the edge of the strip against the edge of the strip already up, making sure the pattern at that point matches perfectly. *The left thumb and fingers anchor the paper there,* while the right hand sweeps upward, pressing the strip against the wall up to the ceiling. Then the right hand moves downward, pressing and smoothing the strip, keeping the left edge butted against the right edge of the previous strip. This is the crucial and only real skill in applying wallpaper—to get that first encounter on the wall in perfect alignment. This is where a helper comes in handy, helping you hold the paper up to the wall. Often you must pull the paper back off and try again. This is the critical time for marriages, when new four-letter expletives are invented because the old ones are not vile enough.

At any rate, with the top portion in place properly, you can then rest your weary arms a moment and relax before unfolding the bottom portion, pressing and smoothing it down to the baseboard. Wet wallcovering is stretchy and you can manipulate it one way or another a fraction of a millimeter as you press and smooth it on, so you can work the edge right up against the edge of the previous strip or in tight to a window frame or wall fixture. All air bubbles must be pressed out. The edges especially need to be pressed down firmly. There is a little seam roller sold for this purpose.

Getting Started

Walls are seldom if ever perfectly straight or plumb, but the edges where your strips of wallpaper meet must be kept as straight as possible, or the pattern will begin to zig when it should zag. However, by the time you paper around a room it is almost impossible for the pattern on the last strip to match the pattern on the first strip. So you should begin papering at a corner where there is a door adjacent on the opposing wall; then only on the small portion of wall above the door will the last strip meet the first strip. (See the drawing.)

Measure out from that corner the width of your strip, remembering that the strip will stretch a bit wider when wet than it measures when dry. You always want the covering to extend around a corner about ½ inch; so if the width of the strip before gluing is 2 feet, measuring out 2 feet will give you enough extra (when the paper is wet and stretches) to lap back around that first corner. Drop a plumb line (any weight on a string will do) where the edge of the strip will come. Mark the plumb line on the wall at top, at bottom, and at a couple places in between. With a ruler, draw the plumb line on the wall. Apply the first strip to that line.

In going around subsequent corners, always lap over about an inch. Then measure out from the corner and drop your plumb line again, as you did when starting. This keeps your strips vertically straight as you move from one wall to another. Your first strip on the next wall should lap back over the bit you carried around the corner. There's no way to avoid this lapping, and that is why you do it in the corner, where it is much less noticeable. A generous lap of ½ inch to 1 inch will stick better than a slim lap of ⅛ inch.

Directions usually advise leaving 2 extra inches of a strip at the ceiling and at the baseboard to allow for variations in height, especially in older houses. The excess is neatly cut off with a razor blade or any sharp tool knife after the strip is glued down. In newer homes you can almost always get by leaving only ½ inch to 1 inch excess at top and bottom. This saves possibly a whole strip, when you might otherwise end up with a long remnant that's not quite long enough for another strip.

Around Doors, Windows, and Fixtures

When going around the corner of a door or window frame, pretend at first that the frame isn't there. Just glue the strip at hand on the wall as best you can, letting the extra wall-covering flap over the molding of the frame. Press the wallcovering down as close to the frame as possible. Then with a scissors, cut a diagonal line from the edge of the covering that

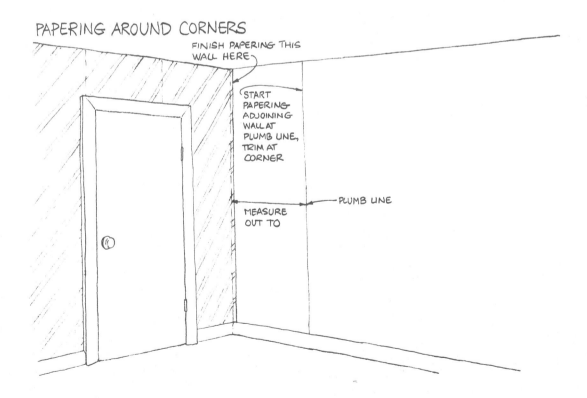

PAPERING AROUND CORNERS

FINISH PAPERING THIS WALL HERE

START PAPERING ADJOINING WALL AT PLUMB LINE, TRIM AT CORNER

PLUMB LINE

MEASURE OUT TO

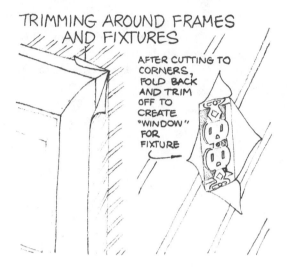

TRIMMING AROUND FRAMES AND FIXTURES

AFTER CUTTING TO CORNERS, FOLD BACK AND TRIM OFF TO CREATE "WINDOW" FOR FIXTURE

is extending out over the door or window to the corner of the door or window frame. (See the drawing.) That relieves the covering enough so you can then press it up tight against the frame both vertically and horizontally. Then cut off the excess with a razor blade or tool knife.

If there are thermostats, outlets, or other fixtures on the wall that can't be removed, stretch the covering right over them as tightly as possible. Then cut a slit in the covering about center to the fixture underneath, and make cuts to the four corners of the fixture. Press the wallcovering down around the fixture and cut off the excess as previously described.

Replacing Electric Plugs and Cords

It is arguable whether repairing small household appliances is worth the time and money. It is even more arguable whether you should invest in these gadgets in the first place. Some of them are just trash that pauses only momentarily in your house on an erratic flight from

factory to dump. But heaven knows what we'd do without toasters and sweepers and irons and so forth, *if* and when they are of good quality. (You are just donating money to some unworthy cause when you buy a $39.95 appliance that will last one day beyond the warranty when a $60.00 model that will last ten years is available.)

If you do have a good appliance and it suddenly quits working, don't begin to weep and gnash your teeth right away over the nine months it may take to get a new part. Nine times out of ten—well, seven times out of ten—the problem is in the electric circuit and is simple to fix. (The other common "problem" with appliances is a lack of proper lubrication maintenance.) You probably have a defective plug, corroded or loose terminal contacts, or broken wire in the cord.

Testing the Cord

You can't tell if an electric cord has a break in it just by looking. (Shorts in the line or plug are very noticeable, however, as are blown fuses, shocks, sparks, and burnt insulation.) Sometimes you can wiggle the plug or cord and make the appliance flicker on and off, in which case you know for sure your problem lies in the cord, not in the appliance itself. First, try spreading the prongs of the plug apart a little so they make better contact in the wall socket. If that doesn't solve the problem, remove the cardboard cover over the plug's innards and see if the wires are loose on the terminal posts under the two little screws in the plug. If the plug is okay, check the cord. Breaks usually occur right at the plug or where the cord enters the appliance, the two places suffering the most bending and stress. You can remove the cord and test it on a lamp or appliance you know works, but there is an easier way. What you need is an AC test lamp, an inexpensive and handy tool you'll find many

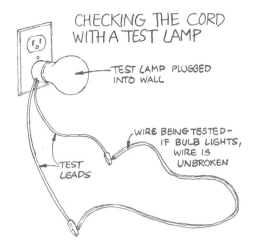

CHECKING THE CORD WITH A TEST LAMP

TEST LAMP PLUGGED INTO WALL

WIRE BEING TESTED — IF BULB LIGHTS, WIRE IS UNBROKEN

TEST LEADS

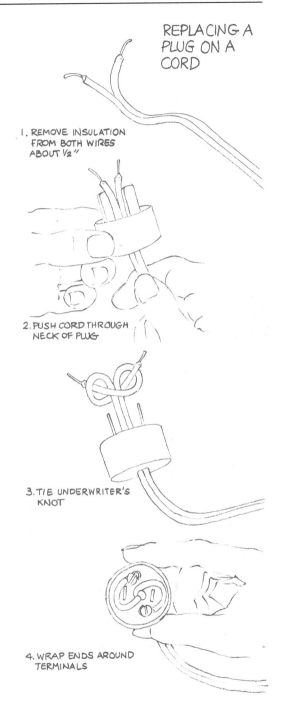

REPLACING A PLUG ON A CORD

1. REMOVE INSULATION FROM BOTH WIRES ABOUT ½″

2. PUSH CORD THROUGH NECK OF PLUG

3. TIE UNDERWRITER'S KNOT

4. WRAP ENDS AROUND TERMINALS

occasions to use. All repairmen carry one.

A test lamp consists of a small bulb in a socket with plug-in prongs at the base. Two wires run out from the side of the little lamp's base. The wires are called test leads. These two wires are not "hot" and "ground" wires as in a regular electric cord; they both connect to the same terminal in the lamp. (The lamp's ground wire is grounded inside the lamp.) Thus, the lead wires are really an extension of the same hot wire, and so one of them can be clipped or touched to one end of the wire and the other at the other end to test for breaks without causing a short. If, when the test leads are so applied, the bulb blinks on, then of course the wire is not broken; current is moving through it. Nevertheless, wiggle the wire a bit to make sure it is not partially broken.

Replacing a Plug

To put a new plug on a cord (or a new cord into a plug) you must remove the insulation from both wires about ½ inch back from the ends. Gently run a pocketknife blade around each wire until it cuts through the insulation. Then pull the bits of insulation off the end of the wires. Now push the cord through the neck of the plug. Tie a knot in the two wires called the Underwriter's Knot: make a loop of each wire and run each wire *through the other's loop.* The purpose of the knot is to prevent the wires from pulling loose from their terminals should someone jerk the cord or trip over it.

Pull the knot down snug between the two prongs, being sure you have left enough length above the knot on each wire so they reach around the terminals. Twist the strands composing each wire tightly together, then make a little loop of the wire ends and wrap each one clockwise around a terminal. It doesn't make any difference which wire goes to which terminal. As you tighten the screw, make sure all the strands in each wire are pressed compactly around the terminal, not sticking out to cause a possible short.

Some of the light-duty, low-wattage appliances and lamps have plugs that are supposed to be easier to connect to the cord. You don't have to strip insulation off the ends of the wires or screw them to the terminals. Instead, you stick the insulated wire ends into their respective slots or holes and close the plug. In one model, the prongs snap into position to close the plug; in another, a lever at the base of the plug snaps shut. But in either case, sharp prongs inside the plug pierce the insulation and make contact with the wires. Sometimes these prongs do not make good connections. If they don't, open the plug, cut off the present ends, reinsert the wires, and let the metal prongs take another bite into them.

Replacing a Cord in a Lamp

Everyone is more or less familiar with a lamp socket, into which the bulb screws. On the cover of the socket, you will always find the word PRESS embossed. Press hard with your thumb at that point and pull the socket cover

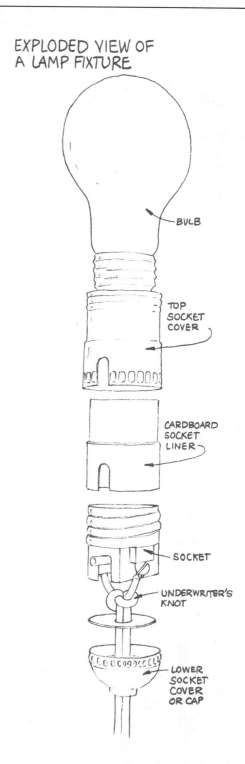

EXPLODED VIEW OF A LAMP FIXTURE

— BULB

— TOP SOCKET COVER

CARDBOARD SOCKET LINER

— SOCKET

— UNDERWRITER'S KNOT

— LOWER SOCKET COVER OR CAP

apart. (First, of course, you must unplug the lamp and remove the bulb and lamp shade.) There's a cardboard liner in the upper part of the socket cover. Inside that is the socket proper with the wires of the cord attached to the two terminals, as in the end plug on a cord (see the drawing).

In the rare event that the lamp cord needs to be replaced, loosen the screws on the terminal posts, untie the Underwriter's Knot (see the preceding item), and pull the cord out from the base of the lamp post. But *before* pulling out the cord, tie a strong string to the wire at the socket end, the string being at least as long as the lamp is high. Then when you pull out the cord, the string comes along down through the lamp post. Untie the string from the old cord and tie it to the new cord. Then, from the top of the lamp, pull the string and the new cord back up through the lamp. If you think about it, you'll realize there is no other easy way to get that new cord up through the lamp.

Proceed to attach the wires to the terminals as in the preceding item, snap the socket cover back in place again, and the job is finished.

Finding a Stud in a Wall

Some carpenters claim they can locate studs (the 2 by 4 kind in walls) by tapping on the wall with their knuckle or a hammer handle. On closer questioning, they admit that most of the time, or at least some of the time, they find a stud starting with this Sherlock Holmes method, followed by the seek-and-you-shall-find method. The grim truth is that, in searching for a stud, tapping can get you close, but a miss is as good as a mile. I have a hunch even Mozart didn't have an ear sensitive enough to recognize a change in tone of a wall tap from, say, ⅜ inch beyond the stud and dead center on it. Even after a stud is located, a good carpenter will often gingerly drive very small finishing nails in a few closely adjacent positions, to ascertain the exact edges of the 2 by 4 stud. Then he

knows where to drive in a nail dead center on the stud.

Strangely enough, few people seem to use stud finders which, with a magnet, find nails in the wall and thereby reveal the studs. This is so because even after the stud finder has located the nail, the careful carpenter will still want to explore with his finishing nail, to locate the exact edges of the stud. So he might as well use the Sherlock Holmes method to get the approximate location and then go to work with the finishing nail. Cheaper, too! In hunting studs, remember these points:

1. Studs are supposed to be 16 inches apart, center to center. They aren't always, my dear Watson, but usually.
2. Electric plug outlet boxes are always anchored on the side of a stud. You have to guess which side. But here is where tapping sounds can be of help. The deeper, more drumlike the sound, the farther away from the stud.
3. Baseboard can be a dead giveaway, especially if done in natural wood. You'll be able to see the nail holes even though they're filled with plastic wood. Often, you can find nail indentations even in painted baseboards. The baseboard is nailed to the studding. Elementary, my dear Watson.
4. Where sheets of drywall form the wall, the seam between two sheets, which must come together on a stud, are sometimes discernible. Either the builder did not adequately cover the seam indentation with joint cement and perforated tape, in which case the indentation still shows, or he may not have gotten the cement perfectly smooth and even with the rest of the wall. This is all easier for the discerning Sherlock to see if the wall is painted rather than papered. Look at the surface of the wall using several angles of light before giving up.

Deducing from these four criteria, one should be able to come within an inch of

CLUES TO FINDING THE STUDS

CENTER OF STUD SHOULD BE 16" OR 24" FROM CENTER OF NEXT

ELECTRIC BOXES ARE OFTEN NAILED TO THE SIDE OF A STUD (GUESS WHICH SIDE!)

LOOK FOR DRYWALL SEAMS ON PAINTED WALLS

LOOK FOR NAIL HOLES IN BASEBOARD

less than 50 pounds, and so you will not have to worry about finding a stud to fasten a hook to (see the preceding item). The common "picture hook," in its various sizes, will work quite well nailed anywhere on the wall. The picture hook consists of a nail that runs through eyelets in the hook-brace and then into the wall. The design of the little hook-brace is ingenious. It compels the nail to be driven in at an acute downward angle so that the nail head is slanted toward the ceiling. Then, when something is hung on the hook, most of the weight pushes against the wall, not down on the nail. This relieves the necessity of having the nail anchored solidly in a stud.

There are various sizes of picture hooks for various weight ranges. Up toward 50 pounds, the largest hook is necessary, and for that weight it should be nailed into a stud. But you can cheat in the 40-pound weight range by using

pinpointing a desired stud. Now explore with a small finishing nail. If you don't hit the stud, you don't have much to patch up, and you're surely not more than an inch away. Or two. Of course, if you want to avoid the studs, as you would for toggle bolts or molly bolts, which fasten just to the plaster board or drywall (see the next item), then you're "right on."

Obviously, it is easier to miss a stud than hit one, so going the toggle bolt route gives a better batting average. But for most objects you hang on the wall, a simple picture hook is all that is necessary and only rarely do you need a stud for it.

Hanging Things on Walls

In most cases the pictures and knickknacks you hang on your walls will weigh a good bit

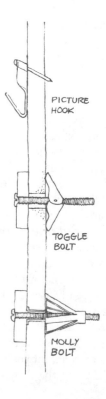

PICTURE HOOK

TOGGLE BOLT

MOLLY BOLT

two hooks adjacent to each other, thus avoiding the necessity of nailing into a stud. Paste a little piece of paper tape down and drive the nail into it to keep it from chipping the plaster.

Large mirrors, very large pictures, and other heavy objects (over 50 pounds) should be hung from picture hooks anchored in *two* adjacent studs. If the studs aren't positioned conveniently for the hanging, nail, or even better, screw a 1 by 4-inch board into two or three adjacent studs and hang the mirror or whatever on the board.

Toggle bolts and molly bolts are gadgets that can be used effectively between studs, too. Drill the proper size hole through the wall, shove the bolt into the hole, and tighten the bolt. The rear of these bolts expands and is drawn tight against the inner wall.

Adhesive hangers sound like a good idea in that they avoid holes of any kind. But often they either do not hold, or they hold too well. In the latter case they will pull plaster loose with them upon removal. They will not hold well if stuck to latex paint that is not *completely* dry.

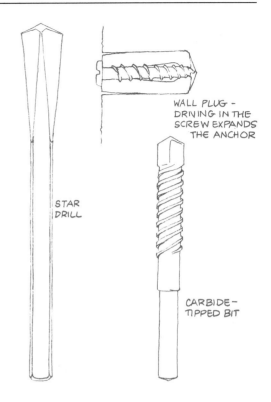

STAR DRILL

WALL PLUG – DRIVING IN THE SCREW EXPANDS THE ANCHOR

CARBIDE– TIPPED BIT

Drilling Holes in Cement

There are not too many houses, or barns for that matter, where you will need to fasten or hang things on cement walls, but when a hole in cement is necessary, the grand old star drill is the tool to make it with. Star drills look like foot-long punches, which is what they are, and they come in various sizes for various holes. The business end of the drill is a central point from which four sharp edges radiate back and away.

The key word is "sharp." Most of us who have had occasion to use a star drill have picked one up from Grandpa's toolbox and have found the tool dulled by use forty years ago. Beating on it with a hammer to try to make a hole is like trying to drive a fencepost through a sidewalk with a sledge. The only holes to appear are in the arms of the worker as the hammer bounces

off (or misses) the drill. The harder one pounds, the worse the injuries. The first time I used a star drill, I did not even realize sharpness was important, let alone how easily it could be accomplished on an emery wheel—or, if the drill was worn so far that sharpening was impossible, how much better off I would be to just go ahead and buy a new one.

With a sharp star drill, it is not necessary to beat the end of the drill mightily. A steady, firm rapping is all that is necessary, making sure that you *continually turn or twist the drill slightly with your holding hand as you pound.* You'll find that going into cement two inches or so to get an anchor solidly seated in the hole is not so difficult after all. Screws or bolts made especially for the lead anchors can then be threaded in to fasten or hang objects on the wall.

Another way to put a hole in concrete, or sometimes stone, is with carbide-tipped bits in an ordinary electric drill. There are also various cement nails available that will drive into cement for certain purposes, but these nails can break unexpectedly at the blow of a hammer and fly into your eye. Be careful.

Removing Furniture Finishes

Grandpa did a fair job of removing varnish from old furniture with lye water and a hose in the backyard. But we have easier and safer ways today. You can hand strip a piece yourself with one of many products available at any paint store, or if the furniture or woodwork is movable, you can take it to a professional furniture stripper. Professionals usually use a soak tank, dunking the piece of furniture into either a hot tank or a cold tank solvent. Or they might sit the piece of furniture in a large sink and spray on a finish remover with a pump in one hand and scrub off the finish with a brush in the other. Some of the removers used are strong concoctions that will literally eat a hole in your skin before you can get the stuff washed off and therefore should be used only by professionals adequately protected for the job.

The decision to take your piece of furniture to a soak tank should not be made lightly. While this is the easiest way to do the job and usually worth the cost, more delicate pieces, especially veneers and plywoods, might be harmed by the hot-tank treatment, and even in the gentler cold tank, the wood might be stained if left in too long. Glues have been known to come loose and window glazing compound can get eaten away. If in doubt, check with a woodworker before going ahead.

Quite often, if you decide to refinish a cherished heirloom or valuable antique, you will do it yourself using one of the paint and varnish removers on the market. These products work, but would work better if the solvent in them did not evaporate so fast. To solve this problem, lay on a thick coat of the stripping material and cover it with aluminum foil to keep the air off of it. Let stand a few hours—some say overnight—and then scrape off the old finish.

Make sure you remove all the remover after you strip the finish. Sometimes that takes a solvent like mineral spirits, or sometimes plain water, whichever the label indicates. Many people worry about raising the grain of the wood with water. If the water is removed quickly and the wood blow-dried with a hair dryer, the grain will not be affected. But raised grain is not that critical. You have to sand the piece anyhow.

When stripping, use scrapers first and then a brass wire brush to scrub out tiny cracks and crevices.

The fashion these days is not to try to remove *all* the old finish down to virgin wood, which is generally impossible with hand stripping anyhow. Rather, say craftspeople in my town, remove down to a base that retains the character, color, and some of the patina of the original finish, but is smooth enough that it looks freshly rejuvenated, while retaining the aura of its age. Not having to remove all the old finish relieves one of the hardest parts of the job.

After stripping, sand lightly with gradually finer grades of sandpaper. Then apply the new topcoat. It is generally not advisable to sand with steel wool before topcoating, as bits of the wool might remain on the surface and be cemented in by the next coat even if you've gone over the surface with a tack cloth between coats of finish.

The first rule to follow, if you intend to follow rules of fashion (which is certainly not obligatory), is to try to mimic the style of the period in which the furniture was made. Early American furniture was often finished to a soft dullness (if not painted). So to refinish an Early American dry sink, even of walnut or cherry, with a shiny lustrous surface would be in "poor taste." On the other hand, a Victorian piece should be as highly polished as you can get it.

By not removing all the old finish, you can usually go ahead and apply topcoats without worrying about primers, sealers, or fillers. What you use for topcoating is your choice (see next item).

The vogue is not to hide dents, scratches, nicks, or other injuries time has inflicted upon the furniture. Recently, in a furniture book, I saw a table made from old barn floorboards on which the trail of a spiked-wheeled wheelbarrow was clearly visible and lovingly preserved. But if you do wish to fill scratches, nailholes or small cracks, you can use wood filler, or better, use sawdust of the same kind of wood mixed with a bit of white glue (which dries clear). Dents can sometimes be raised by moistening the wood. Prick the dent in several places with a sharp nail point, then apply a drop of water or two. The water soaks into the wood, and the wood swells back to more or less its original shape. Another way is to put a moist cloth or paper towel over the dent and press down with a steam iron.

With newer furniture, and in some cases on older furniture, finishes can sometimes be removed without stripping solvents. Ordinary cabinetmaker's scrapers and shave hooks are used, though great care must be taken not to cut grooves into the wood. Using cabinetmaker's scrapers requires a little practice—and strong fingers. The scraper is held tightly in both hands and pulled toward the body, pressing down very hard but evenly on the wood surface. There are straight-edged scrapers for flat surfaces, and various curved and goosenecked ones for curved surfaces.

Applying Semiclear Stains and Clear Finishes

The purpose of a clear finish on wood is to enhance the beauty of the wood. If you don't want a clear finish you can use paint or apply many coats of a polyester-nitrocellulose lacquer to make it plastic-shiny like a lacquered piano. With the beauty of the wood the main goal, proceed to finishing it with great circumspection. My favorite quotation in this regard is from James Krenov, one of the world's foremost cabinetmakers. I think his book, *The Fine Art of Cabinetmaking* (Van Nostrand Reinhold Co., New York, 1977), is the best book ever written about cabinetmaking because on every point where my experience crosses his, I agree with him completely. In it he says: "Ash and elm . . . are nice woods and it is a shame to see them treated with oil or lacquer which turns them an unpleasant 'wet' yellow. Left natural, elm and ash are beautiful. . . . *Any* finish put on such wood will detract from rather than add to it."

There are other woods that are very beautiful to me (beauty is in the eye of the beholder) if left alone or just waxed lightly—walnut and cherry being among them. The wax to use is called Renaissance, much used by museums to protect and polish antique wood surfaces.

Obviously, stains don't appeal to me for hardwoods with any kind of character, but if you want to color the wood something more (or less) than it is, plenty are available. Before you do anything to the wood, it should be planed or sanded well because every saw mark or scratch from mistakenly sanding against the grain will show after a finish is applied. The most lustrous finish on wood is achieved by planing the wood without sandpapering at all or only *very* lightly after planing. A sanded surface, no matter how fine a grit is used, will not be as bright and clear as a perfectly planed surface, even with several coats of finish. But such hand planing is beyond the skill of most of us, so we use sandpaper.

Always sand with the grain. End grain (the cross-grain sawn edges of a board) should be sanded in only one direction, lifting the paper on the return stroke. Be careful not to round the edges of a board when sanding (unless you want them rounded)—use a sanding block or piece of wood with the sandpaper wrapped around it. A piece of felt between the wood and the sandpaper will allow you to do a better job. Electric belt sanders relieve the tedium, but be careful not to scratch the wood more deeply than you are sanding it. Never use a belt coarser than 100-grit. On a rough board, run a belt sander first about 45 degrees to the direction of the grain, then 45 degrees the other way. Then proceed straight with the grain, using finer grits of sandpaper (220- or 230-grit) till an eggshell surface is obtained. Oscillating sanders can scratch little circles in wood and are used most effectively between final coats of finish. Always blow dust off the wood before going to finer sandpaper.

Once you are ready to apply finishes to wood, eliminate all chance of dust. Old-time craftspeople would wet down their floors to keep dust out of the air during finishing. A separate room for finishing is most advantageous.

With a tack cloth or any lint-free cloth, moistened perhaps with a bit of turpentine (or a chamois with water), wipe off the wood. A steady room temperature of 75°F. is ideal.

The decision having been made to finish the wood with some kind of material, you will find yourself faced with myriad choices: oils, varnishes, shellacs, and lacquers of all types. The usual procedure is to stain the wood some awful color, apply filler paste, then perhaps a sealer, then a gloss varnish, and finally a couple coats of satin varnish. But filler paste to close open-grained hardwoods like oak and walnut is a pain to apply and not really necessary, except perhaps for a table or countertop you want to wipe clean with super-ease. Even then, an additional coat or two of the varnish will serve almost as well. Sealer, often referred to as sanding sealer, is usually recommended on labels, but it, too, is not really necessary and may give the finish a filmy appearance after a few years. Some of the newer polyurethane rubbing varnishes give a good finish without stains, fillers, and sealers. Some need thinning (one-to-one with mineral spirits); some are a paste—follow the directions. Apply lightly, about four coats. It takes a full 24 hours for a coat to dry.

Most woodworkers today generally prefer oils: linseed oil or Danish oils or tung oil. They are the easiest to apply, I think, and give excellent hand-rubbed results. A traditional saying in woodworking goes something like this: "Soak the walnut piece in warm linseed oil until it will take no more. Wipe off and let dry. Repeat that daily for a week, then weekly for a month, then monthly for a year, then yearly for the rest of your life."

The newer Danish resin-type oils go on with all the ease of linseed oil and produce a more durable finish. Tung oil doesn't darken the wood as much as Danish, but takes longer to dry. If open pores worry you, rub the oil (either Danish or tung) vigorously into the wood with a rag or 200-grit sandpaper and apply several coats.

If you don't quite want to shine your oil-finished wood "yearly for the rest of your life," you can, at any point, apply a coat of shellac over the oil and then wax it for a durable and highly polished surface without half the work of what is called "French polishing."

Now that the new brushable lacquers are available, lacquer finishing is more practical for typical homeowners. With other lacquers you almost need an air compressor and sprayer. Spraying is tricky. When you first spray a surface, it has a pebbly appearance—like the surface of an orange peel. On the next pass with the sprayer, you should add just enough lacquer so that the orange-peel surface changes to an egg-shell smoothness and then stop. Any more lacquer and it will run. Lacquers have the advantage of being very fast drying.

The things you *can* do with various finishes are almost limitless and it would be foolish to try to enumerate them all here. But listing a few things you shouldn't do is in order. The first one is just an opinion of mine, but I will quote again the renowned Krenov's words from the same book mentioned earlier. Other than oils, wax, and sometimes shellac, Krenov says:

I do not discuss other finishes simply because I know too little about them. I don't use them. The thought of lacquer and all sorts of synthetic solutions that seal the wood, that preserve it for eternity, or prevent it from drying, or assure absolute and complete protection against anything and everything—this is enough to keep me from these finishes and the attitudes they represent. . . . Many of the pieces I make are intentionally of wood that need not be sanded—or even finished at all.

Whatever your choice, the following points should be noted:

1. Don't use lacquer *inside* cabinets. The odor as years go by is rather offensive. Shellac has a pleasing odor, as do most waxes.
2. Don't use oil inside a drawer or bookcase or wherever cloth or paper is stored. Many oil finishes sweat on hot days and the cloth or paper will absorb them.
3. Linseed oil alone is not a particularly durable finish. To overcome this, the famous cabinetmaker Tage Frid teaches his classes this method: Mix raw linseed oil with turpentine (half and half) for a first coat. The next day, apply a coat of boiled linseed oil. After 2 or 3 hours drying, sand finely and wipe off. The following day, apply the last coat of half Japan drier and half-boiled linseed oil. When the finish gets tacky, rub across the grain, working the oil into the pores with a piece of burlap. Then wipe with a clean rag. Do only part of the piece at a time, since the point at which the finish gets tacky is unpredictable, but at that time, it must be rubbed. You can further polish the surface with steel wool and rottenstone.
4. Don't put lacquer on oil or varnish. It won't hold.
5. Don't use oil or shellac on top of varnish or it won't dry.
6. Oil won't protect the common wood stains used today.
7. Don't use liquid shellac after the date stipulated on the label or it may not dry—ever. Store shellac in glass or plastic only. Metal will cloud shellac.
8. Shellac dries fast and doesn't get air bubbles, but it does not repel water, heat, or alcohol. Not the way to finish a bar top.

Between finishing coats, whatever the material, the surface of the wood should be lightly sanded with very fine sandpaper or steel wool. A secret of some cabinetmakers who use

oscillating sanders on larger areas is to put a piece of an ordinary brown paper grocery sack in the sander instead of sandpaper. It buffs the finishing coats ultrasmooth without scratching.

Generally speaking, the more coats, the deeper the luster, but most of us are satisfied with three or four at the most. A high degree of polish can be obtained on varnish, lacquer, and shellac by rubbing the finish with pumice stone moistened with mineral oil, followed by sprinkling rottenstone over the surface and rubbing it with a piece of leather. Pumice and rottenstone are available from good paint and hardware stores or from innumerable mail-order catalogs that cater to woodworkers.

An acquaintance claims that the best finish for wood is the oil from human skin. He says wood rubbed frequently with the hands will continue to grow in beauty through the years. He smokes a pipe. He buys fairly cheap ones, and before smoking them, removes the finish from the outside of the bowl. He says the only difference between a cheap briar and an expensive one is that the cheap ones are heavily finished to hide imperfections in the wood. With the finish removed, the wood can breathe again, and he claims the pipe smokes much cooler. The continual handling the bowl receives puts on a beautiful nonsealing finish over the years. He also rubs the pipe bowl frequently against the side of his nose, where the skin secretes a greater quantity of oil.

In applying varnishes and lacquer with a brush, remember the admonition in Applying

Paints and Varnishes. Don't strike off the brush on the rim of the can because the varnish dribbling back into the can makes bubbles that your brush will transfer to the wood with the next dip. Strike the excess off the brush into another can or press the brush against the inside of the can you're using, so the excess runs down the can wall without making bubbles. Stroke your brush with the grain first, then against it, except for lacquer, which should not be back-stroked any more than necessary. Watch out for running. With clear finishes runs are hard to see—until they dry. Then you have to sand or scrape them out and brush again.

Regluing Rungs and Spindles on Chairs

Chair rungs and spindles frequently come loose on cheaper furniture because the wood shrinks in the socket, breaking the glue bond. But basically, the fault lies in the designs we persist in using in chair construction. A kitchen chair that has no arms to help hold the back spindles against the pressure of the person seated in the chair is an accident looking for a time to happen. Cheap imitations of Windsor chairs don't take into account the fact that the force of a person leaning back against the top rail of the chair is multiplied many times over at the point the spindles are joined to the seat. Likewise, the rungs (or stretchers) that connect the chair legs hold the legs only by the strength of the glue bond at the rounded tenon or dowel joint. To be structurally sound, the rungs should wrap around the *outside* of the splayed out legs, but this would result in design elements unpleasing to the traditional eye.

Thus and so, loose rungs and spindles are a condition of life, like death and taxes, until one can afford to buy really well-made furniture. And that may be never for most of us. The conventional way to glue those tenon joints

back into their mortise sockets is to clean all the old glue off the tenon and out of the mortise, reglue, and put the pieces back together again, holding them tightly with clamps until the glue dries. If clamps are not handy, chair rungs can be held together by passing a double rope or cord around the legs, and twisting the cords with a short stick, as in a tourniquet, until they are very tight. Then, turn the stick straight up and down so that it rests against a rung and cannot untwist.

If the chair rung or spindle has shrunk so it does not fit tightly in the joint, the glue will not hold for very long. Given another year of humid summer air and dry winter heat (particularly if you heat with a wood or coal stove), the wood could swell and shrink ⅛ inch or more, deteriorating the glue bond even more, especially with a little help from one of your heavier friends.

The best way to fix such a joint is with a blind wedge, if you can completely remove the rung or spindle or pry it far enough away from the chair leg or seat to work on the tenon. Cut a slot in the middle of the tenon end about ⅛ inch wide. (A table saw blade makes a slot about the right width.) Then fashion a little wedge to

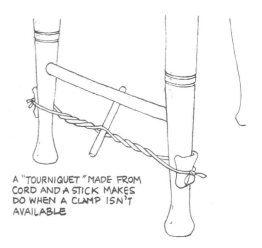

A "TOURNIQUET" MADE FROM CORD AND A STICK MAKES DO WHEN A CLAMP ISN'T AVAILABLE

Tightening Up a Table Leg

Table legs that splay outward slightly and are connected only to the apron under the table top can come loose and wobble. If you turn the table upside down, you will generally find that there are cross braces at each corner of the aprons. On better tables, these cross braces are dovetailed into the aprons, locking them solidly together. On such tables, there is usually a bolt and nut through the center of the brace and seated against the leg. Tighten this nut, and in most cases, your loose leg problem is solved.

If there is just a cheap glued brace connecting the corners, and the glue seal has broken, reglue, and then put a screw through the brace into each apron. If there are already screws holding the brace, they may merely need to be tightened.

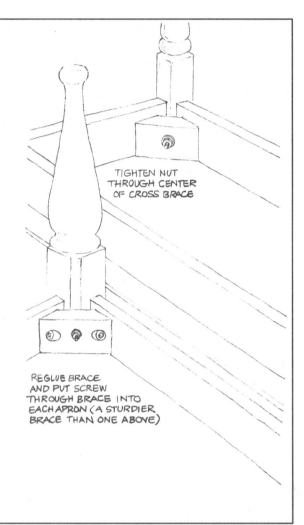

TIGHTEN NUT THROUGH CENTER OF CROSS BRACE

REGLUE BRACE AND PUT SCREW THROUGH BRACE INTO EACH APRON (A STURDIER BRACE THAN ONE ABOVE)

fit into the slot as wide as the tenon's diameter and as deep as the slot. The fat end of the wedge must be slightly thicker than the slot, so that it spreads the tenon when driven in, but not so fat as to split the tenon. Some people use the end of a clothespin for a wedge, but a wedge of ash or hickory is stronger. Push the wedge into the slot halfway, apply glue, and set the tenon (with wedge protruding) into its mortise hole. Then drive the rung into place, seating the wedge into its slot at the same time.

If the rung or spindle has remained solidly glued at one end and you don't want to loosen it to work on the other, you can wrap string tightly around the errant loose tenon, apply glue, and reseat it, hoping the string will take up the extra room. Another possibility is to use a "dowel lock." Glue the loose tenon back into its mortise hole as tightly as possible, then drill a small hole through the chair leg *and* tenon (never more than half the diameter of the tenon, so that the tenon is not weakened too much) and drive a dowel that fits very snugly into the hole. Apply glue to the dowel first, of course. After it is in place, sand off the ends and touch up with a stain the same color as the chair.

On a spindle-back chair, generally the spindles on the outside are the ones that loosen. If these go all the way through the seat and are already wedged, as is often the case, a metal shim driven along the side of the wedge, or a new wedge, should tighten up the joint, along with new glue.

If the tenon is broken off, don't despair—at least not immediately. Drill the old, broken tenon out of the mortise. Cut off the broken part of the tenon still on the spindle or rung. If the spindle or rung is not too small in diameter, you can drill a hole the same size as the mortise hole 1 to 1½ inches into it. Then cut a piece of dowel the same diameter as the hole and long enough to fit up into the hole with the same length protruding as the original tenon. Glue the dowel into the rung or spindle, then glue the new dowel-tenon into its mortise hole.

Sharpening Knives

Although techniques of knife sharpening may vary with the purpose of the knife and the preference of the person doing the work, the same basic principles apply. Before actual sharpening, you may have to reshape the knife, that is, put a new bevel on the cutting edge if it has worn away. This is called *grinding* although actually, unless you are making a knife from scratch, you are regrinding. The second step (the first step in most cases) is the actual sharpening, called *honing*. As a final step, the blade can be *stropped* to razor sharpness or *steeled* on a sharpening steel.

Grinding

Grinding, or at least regrinding, can be done by hand on coarse Carborundum whetstones, but generally either a power grindstone or belt grinder is used. The larger, slower-moving grindstones, either hand cranked or motorized, which run in a trough of water to keep the stone clean and cool, are much better for knives than the smaller, faster emery-wheel bench grinders. The latter easily overheat the blade and ruin the temper if you do not continuously dip the blade in water.

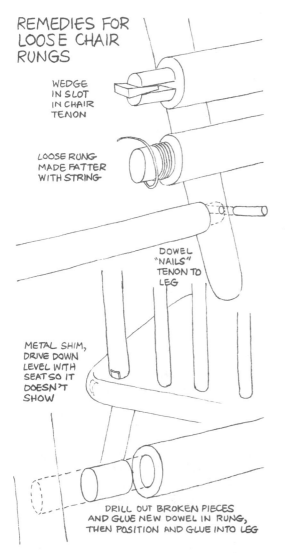

REMEDIES FOR LOOSE CHAIR RUNGS

WEDGE IN SLOT IN CHAIR TENON

LOOSE RUNG MADE FATTER WITH STRING

DOWEL "NAILS" TENON TO LEG

METAL SHIM, DRIVE DOWN LEVEL WITH SEAT SO IT DOESN'T SHOW

DRILL OUT BROKEN PIECES AND GLUE NEW DOWEL IN RUNG, THEN POSITION AND GLUE INTO LEG

In grinding, you must take into account the profile, width, and angle of the bevel. As to profile, knives destined to do heavy, hard chopping work are shaped slightly convex, while knives doing easier slicing work (as in the kitchen) are ground slightly concave, or hollow-ground. When in doubt, or for all-purpose knives, shape a straight profile, which is halfway between the two described. Hollow-ground is generally preferred in knives (convex blades are better for axes, hatchets, and meat choppers), since in repeated sharpenings, the blade does not tend to get fatter and therefore harder to sharpen. Hollow grinding is skilled work, done on a grindstone, taking out a little trough all along the blade right behind the cutting edge. The trick is not to take too much off of one side. This operation demands much practice on an

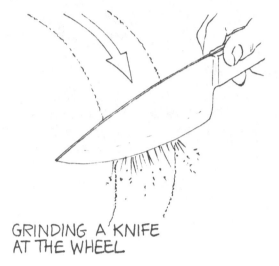

GRINDING A KNIFE
AT THE WHEEL

old knife first, but can be mastered in fairly short time.

The width of the bevel is usually about ⅛ inch, measured back from the cutting edge. Some knives—most pocketknives and whittling knives—do not have this secondary bevel at all and so hardly ever need regrinding. The angle of the bevel varies from about 18 degrees to perhaps 25 degrees on knives to be used to whittle hardwoods. Generally speaking, an angle of 20 degrees is adequate to cover most uses. The exact angle is not nearly as important as maintaining a *uniform* angle along the whole length of the blade. This is easier to do on a belt grinder than a grindstone because the belt is wider.

Present the blade to the grindstone or belt grinder just below the center of the wheel facing you, with the sharp edge *down.* The knife is usually held at right angles to the wheel, and in contact with the wheel along the whole grinding edge so that the wheel wears evenly and does not become rounded on the edges. Some people prefer to work on top of the wheel, with the sharp edge leading and the blade angled slightly across the wheel.

Occasionally, the wheel will have to be squared up and cleared with a dressing tool. Do not try to work with an uneven wheel or one

glazed over with metal filings. Keep the blade moving back and forth as you grind so the wheel doesn't dig in at any one spot. On a belt grinder use a 40-grit belt for heavier work, a 120-grit for lighter work.

On a belt grinder you can go on to the second step of actually sharpening by using finer grit belts (320) and finish off with a power stropping buffer.

Honing with a Whetstone

Most of us can't justify buying a grindstone for the occasional knife sharpening we need to do. So we use whetstones and sharpen by hand. With a little patience, just as keen a blade results. Honing on a whetstone is differ-

Honing a knife in preparation for a long day of butchering.

ent than honing on a belt grinder. The cutting edge of the knife is pushed *head-on* against the stone, avoiding some of the wire edge that develops when sharpening on a belt grinder where the blade is trailed away from the direction of the moving wheel. The whetstone should be anchored solidly on a bench so both hands can be used to hold the knife steady. Lay the blade at one end of the whetstone and tilt it up about 20 degrees. With one hand on the handle and the other on the tip of the blade, push the knife edge-first to the other end of the whetstone, drawing the blade across slowly as you go so that the whole blade is stoned at each pass. Turn the knife over and come back. Keep repeating, maintaining a constant angle. But this is only the way I do it. Some people like to do figure eights on the stone, and others prefer ovals to my straight back-and-forth motions. Instead of flipping the blade after each stroke, many people prefer to work one side at a time for all but the final, finishing work. This way they don't have to keep turning the knife over, which can be cumbersome and can make it tricky to keep a good angle. And some people feel more comfortable holding the whetstone with one hand and the knife with the other instead of using the two-handed method. To each his own.

The stone should be lubricated with honing oil or a mixture of light machine oil and kerosene (half and half) or, in some cases, water or saliva will do, depending on the kind of whetstone you have. (See the directions that come with yours.) Man-made Carborundum stones or natural "Arkansas" stones are available in several grades of fineness. Usually a stone has a coarse side and a fine side. Most of the sharpening is done on the coarse, finishing up on the fine. Whetstones are available from hardware stores and woodworking supply houses. One of the most complete sources for all kinds of sharpening tools is the mail-order catalog from Garrett Wade, 161 Avenue of the Americas, New York, NY 10013.

Stropping with Leather

To put a real razor edge on a knife after honing, strop it. Oiled leather is usually used for stropping, although old-timers use the toughened skin of the palms of their hands. In stropping, the action is opposite that of honing—the blade is trailed away from the stropping surface. (Stropping blocks are also available from Garrett Wade, but you can make do with an old leather belt.) Stropping removes any microscopic wire edge, and this action firms up the exceedingly fine edge that honing has put on the blade. Your knife is sharp if it will cut hairs off your arm or catch on a fingernail rather than slide over it.

To maintain sharpness, frequent stropping, or a bit of honing and stropping, will suffice. But most people who use knives a lot, such as butchers, prefer the sharpening steel to maintain sharpness because it is handy and, once mastered, fast. Butchers "steel" their knives after every few cuts, although this is sometimes done not for the knife's sake, but for a moment of rest or an excuse to tell a story.

Steeling

In using the steel, first draw the knife across it *slowly* until you understand what you are doing. Many people believe, after watching a butcher show off a bit, that the essence of steeling is to slash the knife back and forth across the steel with all the bravado of a conductor leading an orchestra, just because masters of the skill do it that way. More knives are dulled in the process than sharpened.

Knife against steel employs a honing action much like a knife against whetstone. The skill is to hold steel in one hand and knife in the other *at a uniform angle throughout the sharpening*—a 20-degree angle is adequate. Speed has nothing to do with it. Generally you draw the knife from heel to tip down the side of the steel away from your body, then the other side of the knife down the side of the steel facing you.

Since only experience enables a practitioner to maintain the angle well enough to sharpen the blade, various devices have been manufactured to lessen the margin of error. The best I have used (also available from

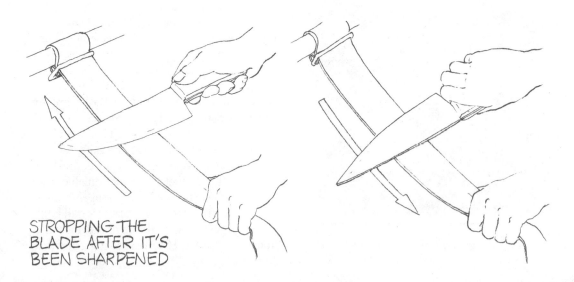

STROPPING THE
BLADE AFTER IT'S
BEEN SHARPENED

Garrett Wade and many other catalogs) is a pair of ceramic "steels" set at angles in a block of wood. If you hold your knife blade straight up and down and draw it down the two steels, first against the inside of one steel, and then the other side of the blade against the inside of the other steel, a consistent angle is maintained. This is true because it is easier for most of us to judge the perpendicular than the angle.

It goes without saying that all the sharpening skill in the world is wasted if the knife is cheap. It won't keep an edge and is worse than useless. With a good knife, time spent in sharpening is not lost, because a keen blade works faster and is vastly more enjoyable to use. The main reason hand tools have fallen out of favor around the house is because few people know how to sharpen them or understand the great difference sharpening makes.

Replacing a Ballast in a Fluorescent Light Fixture

If you have read the introduction to this book, you know that the hardest part of replacing a ballast is realizing you need to. New ballasts are available from your hardware or light fixture store. Be sure the package says, "Contains No PCB." There will be installation directions on the box and these are usually adequate as far as they go.

Actually, getting the cover off the light fixture is more difficult than replacing the ballast. (See the Introduction.) Then you have to remove the metal shield that covers the ballast and wires. It slips out of slots at the middle and ends of the shield. (This is the second hardest part of the job.) If the fixture is a four-bulb affair, there will be two ballasts inside. If a two-bulb lamp, one ballast. If two ballasts, you must ascertain which is defective. Easy. Follow the blue and red wires from the socket of the bulb that won't light back to their ballast. That's the bad one. Before going further, make sure the fuse to the fixture is switched off.

To remove the old ballast, cut the two blue, two red, and two yellow wires issuing from it. Cut them a few inches from the ballast. Be careful when you cut the yellow wires in a two-ballast fixture. The yellow wires from the other ballast pass right along the one you are removing, and you might confuse the two sets of yellows and cut the wrong ones. The black and white wires don't have to be cut. They connect to the black and white wires of the electric lead-in, the connection located under the little plastic caps (called Wire Nuts) you find there. Unscrew the Wire Nuts and untwist the wire that leads back to the defective ballast.

With all eight wires cut or disconnected, unscrew the bolt that holds the ballast in place, slide the ballast out of its slot, and remove. Put the new ballast in its place and rebolt.

The eight wires coming out of the new ballast are the same colors as those already in the fixture. All you have to do is connect the colors. The ends of the wires of the new ballast are bare about ½ inch. Remove the same amount of insulation from the ends of the wires you cut off. Run a knife blade lightly around the wire, cutting through the insulation, and then pull the piece of insulation off the end of the wire. Hold each pair of wire ends to be connected parallel to each other and twist *clockwise.* It is a good idea to twist the insulated parts around each other once or twice along with the bare parts. Use a pair of pliers to twist the bare ends tightly around each other. Then slip a Wire Nut over the bare connection and screw it clockwise until it is tight. The box in which the new ballast came should have six Wire Nuts in it to cover the connections. (The black and white wires already have their Wire Nuts.)

It is almost impossible, which means that it is possible, for an offbeat brand of ballast to have different colored wires than those on the new one. If so, there is always a diagram on the ballast showing which wire goes where.

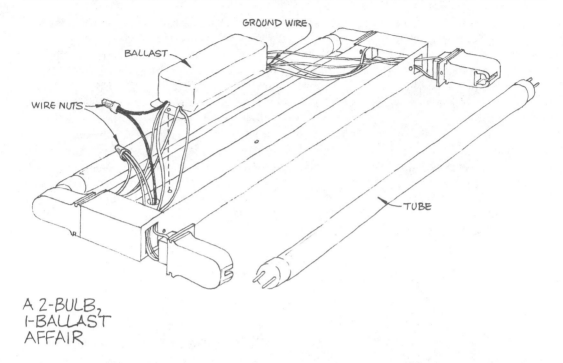

GROUND WIRE

BALLAST

WIRE NUTS

TUBE

A 2-BULB,
1-BALLAST
AFFAIR

Connecting all those wires looks like it requires a lot of skill, but anyone who is not color-blind can do it easily. If you have a small son watching, he will think you are brilliant. Whatever electricians charge for this work is too much. When finished, push the wires back up into the fixture and replace the metal shield. The directions call for removing the bulbs when replacing the ballast, so if you did, you must of course put them back in. I don't remove the bulbs, because in my opinion, putting them back in is the third hardest part of the job. The bulbs are 4 feet long with little prongs projecting from each end. The distance from the inside edge of the lip on each fixture end is 3 feet, 11½ inches. It is difficult (for me anyway) to get the bulb back up to the sockets. I've learned just to bend the fixture end out of the way a little, then slide the prongs of the bulb into the socket slots at each end just so, and twist the bulb gently to seat the prongs properly in the socket. This takes some fancy jiggling and

juggling. I much prefer the older incandescents, which simply screw into their sockets. And incandescents don't buzz like horseflies over your head the way fluorescents do.

The whole episode taught me something else. It is not a good idea to try to fix something up on a ceiling while wearing those half-size reading glasses. If you tilt your head back far enough to see through them to the ceiling, you are apt to fall off your chair.

Spouting Off about Spouting (and Gutters)

For every new convenience modern technology offers us, there is an equal and opposite inconvenience that we only learn about later. Aluminum is a good example. It is light so it is popular with those soft-muscled Americans who abhor physical labor. Aluminum ladders are easy to lift but dangerous and far inferior to wooden ladders. Aluminum roofing and gutters are light and easy to handle, but because the metal expands and contracts unduly and because it tears easily, it loosens in its nail holes, resulting in gutters that leak at the joints and roofing that leaks, tears, and blows off. In a village near my home, a lumber and construction business known for its integrity will not use aluminum roof panels or guttering, only galvanized steel. Since the latter now comes in maintenance-free baked-on enamel, too, there is hardly any good reason to use aluminum if you are building a new house. (The same lumber company won't sell aluminum ladders, either.)

That's my experience talking, the kind I'm sure the aluminum manufacturers would find hundreds of exceptions to. But, after six years, the aluminum guttering on my house had expanded and contracted enough to break the screws that held the joints together. Then it broke the caulking seal, and now the joints leak.

There are disadvantages to *any* kind of guttering—disadvantages that can be overcome only by the hard work of keeping gutters cleaned out. Gutters fill with leaves, tree seeds, and catkins that plug the little cage screens over each downspout, and the water overflows the gutters. Thinking to remedy that, manufacturers have marketed plastic and metal screens that clip over the top of the guttering to keep leaves out. But these work only partially on low-sloping roofs and hardly at all on steep ones. The screens get covered with debris from the trees, and in heavy rains, as much water cascades over the gutter as gets into it. In winter, the screens are covered with snow, which turns to ice in thawing-freezing weather, and if rain should fall rather than more snow,

the water flows over the gutter, not into it. Without the screen, the gutter can also fill up with ice and give the same unwanted result.

The moral of this story is: Clean out your gutters. Make sure the cage screens above the downspouts are not blocked with leaves. Even partially blocked, they back water up in the gutter which makes a little Riviera for mosquitoes.

Regardless of your efforts, downspouts will sometimes get plugged. A gentle tapping often loosens the blockage. Stick a hose up or down the spout as a next recourse. If all else fails, downspouts are fairly easy to remove, clean, and reinstall.

Remember that spring is just as bad as fall, if you have trees nearby. The winged seeds of maple and ash will plug a gutter worse than leaves, as will the catkins that fall from white oak trees. A cleaning in late fall for the leaves, and another in late May for the seeds and catkins will save you inundated sidewalks, wet basements, soggy yards, and brown streaks down the side of the house. As Confucius might have said: He who does not clean his gutters will have maple trees growing on his roof.

Minor Gutter Repairs

Because galvanized steel guttering is comparatively heavy, it is held by strap hangers that anchor up on the roof *under* the roofing. That makes it much harder to replace, since the roofing must be pried up to get out the old hangers or to put in the new. For this reason, aluminum might be the choice of the do-it-yourselfer. Installation is easier because the gutter hangers in this case fasten just to the facing board with little clips that extend over the top of the guttering. Aluminum or vinyl gutters may also be attached to the facing by long spikes driven into the ends of the rafters through the facing board.

In any case, replacing a length of guttering, aluminum or steel (or, for that matter, the new

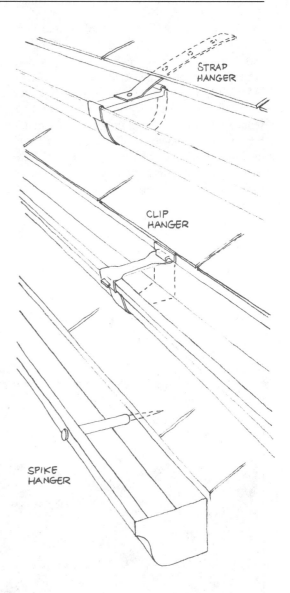

vinyl kinds), occasionally requires joining two pieces together. Directions that come with spouting tell you how to put on the end caps and the hangers. They also tell you what caulking to use (silicone rubber products are very good) but don't always speak clearly about the joints between two pieces.

The upstream piece should lap over the downstream piece about 5 inches, so that the water is running away from the crack. *Cut the rim of the top piece off* for 5 inches, so that the top piece will slide snugly into the bottom piece. To hold the two pieces of metal tightly together, professionals usually drill two holes about 3 inches apart into the front wall of the lapped pieces and insert screws. An installer once showed me an easier way that seems to work. On the back side of the lap, he cut off a ¼-inch piece of the remaining rim. Then (using tin snips) he cut two slots downward into both walls of the lapped piece, making the slots about ½ inch apart and 1 inch deep. Then with pliers he bent both pieces between the slots back and down tight—a sort of double tab that then held the two pieces of gutter firmly together at that point. On the front side he performed the same little operation, although cutting off that bit of the heavier front rim was more

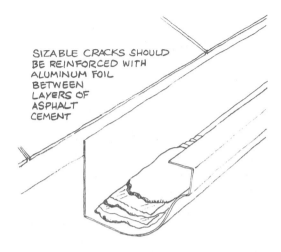

SIZABLE CRACKS SHOULD BE REINFORCED WITH ALUMINUM FOIL BETWEEN LAYERS OF ASPHALT CEMENT

difficult. The two tabs held the two lapped pieces tightly together. The caulking he had applied between the lapped pieces held a bond just as well as if screws had been used. On a house, he pointed out, one might prefer using screws over the tab method in front, for appearance' sake. (He was working on a barn.) But the small cut in the rim was hardly noticeable. This method works well especially with aluminum because the tabs will not come apart when the metal expands and contracts, while the screws (on my guttering at least) shear right off.

On old galvanized gutters, cracks, small holes, and joints can be sealed with ordinary asphalt cement. A large deteriorating section can (for a while) be healed by sandwiching two layers of heavy-duty aluminum foil between three layers of asphalt cement over the rusted out section. Try not to build up the patch too high in the gutter or it will act like a little dam holding water back—especially in guttering without much slope to it.

Plugging Roof Leaks

The roofing business is steady and profitable for a good reason: Most people don't like to

REPLACING A PIECE OF GUTTER

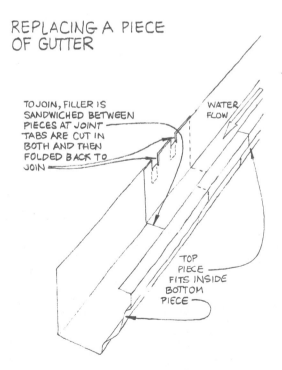

TO JOIN, FILLER IS SANDWICHED BETWEEN PIECES AT JOINT TABS ARE CUT IN BOTH AND THEN FOLDED BACK TO JOIN

WATER FLOW

TOP PIECE FITS INSIDE BOTTOM PIECE

climb around roofs and ought not to. And replacing leaking shingles or slates is sometimes a tricky business best left to professionals.

But there are a few easy things a person can do on his own roof is he is able to get up there. Wear shoes with rubber soles and heels or tennis shoes for safety. If you have a leak, check all the flashings first, no matter where the leak shows through below. Water coming through a roof will often run along a board a considerable distance before it drips down into the insulation and into the ceiling.

In the first place, all flashings ought to be painted regularly with a rust-inhibiting paint like Rustoleum (of course, if you've got fancy copper flashings, forget the Rustoleum). Many homeowners do not know this and are unpleasantly surprised ten years into a new house when the flashings have rusted out. New flashing comes with a coating that inhibits rust, but it wears off in seven years, or sooner.

But even well-maintained flashing is usually the source of leaks, if not because of cracks in the flashing itself, then because of cracks in the dried-up asphalt cement around it. Look around vent pipes, around chimneys, and in the valleys where two roofs meet. Put a new application on any suspicious-looking break in the old asphalt. Also check for cracks where the shingles have been bent over the roof peak. Another place you may have a leak and not know it is on *top* of the chimney around the flue liner. The masonry cement here may be cracked. If so, pile on the asphalt cement. Water running down through chimney-top cracks can filter right through the masonry joints of the chimney,

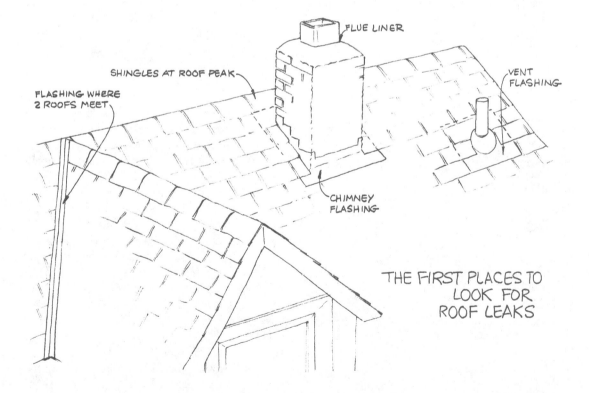

FLUE LINER

SHINGLES AT ROOF PEAK

VENT FLASHING

FLASHING WHERE 2 ROOFS MEET

CHIMNEY FLASHING

THE FIRST PLACES TO LOOK FOR ROOF LEAKS

down into the flue. Or it can filter out through the exterior of the chimney, carrying creosote from the smoke, making nice brown stains down the wall. This message comes to you courtesy of a man of experience whose chimney exterior is (was) white brick.

A roofing shingle that persists in curling up even when you paste it back down with a glob of roofing tar can be nailed down with a roofing nail, but it is not a good idea to put a nail in a roof anywhere it can't be lapped over with another shingle. If you are forced to so nail anyway, as you would be up on the peak, be sure to cover the nail head generously with roofing tar. Roofing tar covereth a multitude of sins.

A Homemade Radio Antenna

If you can no longer endure television, or when you are too blessedly busy to watch it, you might find radio a happy alternative. You can catch the news and weather, listen to music, and so forth, without missing a lick in your work. Animal scientists even claim that music in the barn keeps the cows contented.

The only problem is finding a station that broadcasts more than just jarring rock noises and endless advertising harangues. The FM stations geared to serving a quieter and possibly more thoughtful listener are few and far between and often have signals too weak to receive well, especially out in the country.

In most cases, there is a cheap and easy solution: a homemade, T-shaped, FM aerial. All you need are two pieces of standard 300-ohm TV and FM twin-lead aerial wire, one tacked horizontally to a board (or the wall) and the other connected to the horizontal piece leading down to the radio's FM aerial terminals. The length of the horizontal piece is somewhat critical if you are trying to boost the strength of one particular station. To determine that length,

divide the station's megahertz number on the FM band into 468; the answer gives the number of feet the horizontal piece of wire should be. Thus, if the station you want to bring in loud and clear is, let us say, 92 FM, 92 divided into 468 equals 5.08. Your aerial's horizontal arm should be 5 feet and approximately 1 inch. (Don't ask me why 468. That's the constant in the formula arrived at by TV engineers for designing antennae.)

Cut the horizontal length of aerial wire to the appropriate size. Cut through and strip off enough insulation at each end to bare the twin wires about an inch back from the end. Twist each set of wires together tightly and wrap in electrician's tape. You can solder the connection before wrapping, but that's not really necessary.

Next, find the middle of the length of horizontal wire and cut through *one* of the twin wires, removing and cutting away enough insulation to bare that wire an inch in both directions. This is where you will connect the vertical piece of wire, or tail, that leads back to the radio. Tape this connection, too, after twisting the wires of the tail piece to the horizontal piece.

Tack the horizontal piece to a light board or lath, and mount the lath on the wall or up in the attic—wherever you can obtain the best reception. You can put it on the roof, but in that case, you should add a lightning arrester for safety. It is easier, and usually effective enough, just to mount the aerial inside the house.

To get the best reception, the horizontal part of the aerial should be perpendicular to the direction of the radio station. The easiest way to do this is to position the aerial approximately perpendicular, say pointing north-south for an eastern station, and then, while listening to the radio, move the aerial back and forth to the position where reception is the most clear. The aerial picks up stations on both sides of the perpendicular—in this example, from both east and west.

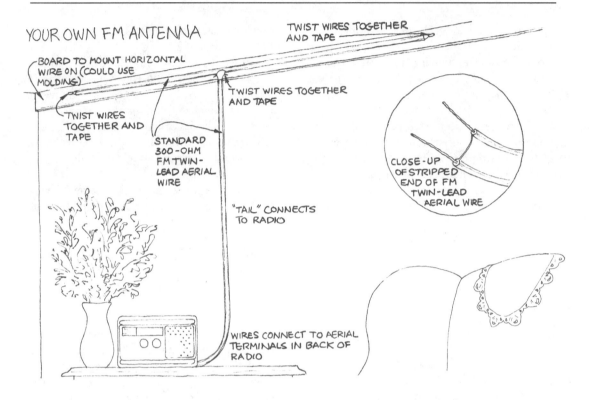

YOUR OWN FM ANTENNA

TWIST WIRES TOGETHER AND TAPE

BOARD TO MOUNT HORIZONTAL WIRE ON (COULD USE MOLDING)

TWIST WIRES TOGETHER AND TAPE

TWIST WIRES TOGETHER AND TAPE

STANDARD 300-OHM FM TWIN-LEAD AERIAL WIRE

CLOSE-UP OF STRIPPED END OF FM TWIN-LEAD AERIAL WIRE

"TAIL" CONNECTS TO RADIO

WIRES CONNECT TO AERIAL TERMINALS IN BACK OF RADIO

You can buy similar aerials already connected up properly, that is, both ends of the horizontal wire properly connected and encased in insulation, as well as the connection between the horizontal piece and the vertical tail. The horizontal piece usually measures 5 feet on these aerials, good for strengthening all the stations on the FM band somewhat, but not necessarily for zeroing in on any particular one.

We haven't even mounted ours on a board yet, but move it around the living room, depending on which station we are trying to pull. One station comes in clearly with the aerial draped east-west over a curtain hanger above a north window. Another comes in stronger when the aerial is spread out on the bookshelves in a north-south orientation. A third requires that my wife hold one end of the horizontal wire and I the other, while we sit on the couch. Well, it beats listening to rock and roll on the teeny-bopper stations.

Backyard Clotheslines

Most people would not want to be without their clothes dryer, but there's something lost for every gain. What you lose with a dryer, besides the money and the energy it costs to run it, is that heavenly fresh smell of clothes and sheets dried out in the fresh air and sunshine. For both economical and aesthetic reasons, folks with yards like to hang the wash out during the warmer months, even if it is more work.

For a clothesline, use nylon rope, not wire. The wire will rust and the clothes will get stained from it. The easiest way to erect a line is to tie the rope from tree to tree, if possible. Otherwise you have to set poles in the ground — and very solidly, since the weight of a line full of wet sheets is considerable.

Steel or wood posts are fine. If wood, use a kind that resists rot (see Protecting Wood Outside). Put the posts 3 feet in the ground and pour cement around them to a thickness of 3 to 4 inches. By notching a crossarm solidly in the top of each wood post, you can run two parallel lines. If using threaded pipe for a post, a T-union and extensions of pipe at the top will provide a sturdy crossarm.

How far apart the posts should be will depend, of course, on how much wash you need to dry at one time. The distance between posts should hardly exceed 40 to 50 feet, or the line will sag too much or get too heavy to prop up easily. The prop is a necessary addition to the line. It is set in the middle between posts to make sure a loaded line does not drag on the ground. The tops of the posts where the line ties on should be at least 8 feet from the ground. The prop should be about 10 feet long. A branch with a Y tip to accept the line (see drawing), or a 1 by 2-inch board with a V notch in one end will work fine. The prop is set under the line and, on a windy day, should be somewhat pointed toward the wind. The weight of the clothes will hold it up.

Where conditions are appropriate, a clothesline on pulleys is very handy and easy to put up. One pulley is set into a porch post or (ideally) an upper deck post and the other out in a tree in the yard. The Amish put the second pulley

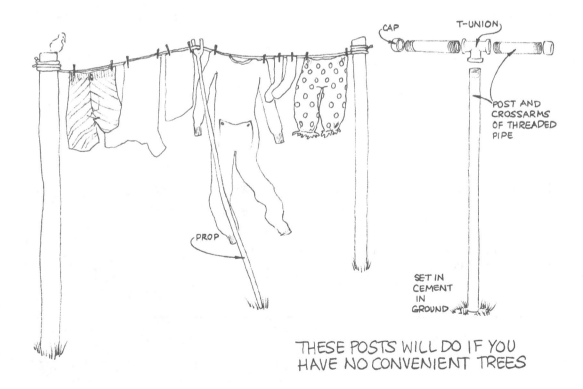

CAP

T-UNION

POST AND CROSSARMS OF THREADED PIPE

PROP

SET IN CEMENT IN GROUND

THESE POSTS WILL DO IF YOU HAVE NO CONVENIENT TREES

Washboard Secrets

Friends smile wanly when they see my wife's corrugated washboard in the sink. They wonder when we are going to go down to the "crick" and pound our clothes on the rocks. This is very funny, of course, but it reveals the modern ignorance about washing clothes that is becoming nearly universal. A washboard is still the cheapest and often the only way to get *dirty* clothes clean.

We have two washboards, actually, a "Silver King Top Notch" from the National Washboard Company of Chicago and Memphis, and a smaller "Dubl Handi" from the Columbus Washboard Company of Columbus, Ohio. There's another model of the Top Notch I'd like to own, which in addition to the usual message printed at the top—"Soap-Saving, Sanitary, Front Drain" as ours says—also carries this advice: "Do Not Rub Hard. This Board Will Do The Work." The corrugations on the board are zinc coated (brass is available) and are roughened by raised spirals, slanting in one direction on one corrugation and the other on the next corrugation and so forth. So when you push a dirty sock over the board, you push against a series of three different angled surfaces for triple scrubbing action. The smaller "Dubl Handi" ("packs easily in suit case or travelling bag," says the message at the top) has smooth corrugations for scrubbing more delicate fabrics, "ideal for silks, hosiery, and lingerie or handkerchiefs," the printed message informs us. My wife cautions either to buy the double kind of washboard or to buy one that is only rough-surfaced. The ones that are only smooth-surfaced are no good for dirty clothes, she says, and if the clothes aren't dirty, well,

throw them in the automatic washer. It does a real good job on clean clothes.

The proper use of the washboard involves setting it in a large sink, facing the scrubbing surface away from you, and leaning the top back into your waist. Take a really dirty sock (like one I've worn in the garden when hoeing and dirt has fallen into my shoes and I have ground the dirt into the sock) and wet it thoroughly. Rub a bar of soap against the wet sock or on the washboard until you have some working suds. Then scrub up and down against the washboard, turning the sock at every other scrub, until the dirt is gone.

My wife is the best advertisement the National Washboard Company ever had, if it is still in business. Believe me, she holds on to her washboard not for sentimental reasons. We bought her Top Notch when we married twenty-two years ago, and it has been used nearly every week since. It cost $1.45 and the frame is held together with dovetailed joints. We wouldn't part with it.

P.S. The only soap we've ever used on the board is a bar of Fels Naptha.

high on a nearby barn or shed wall, if no tree is available. Then one need carry the basket of wet clothes only to the deck or porch. Clothesline pulleys made for this purpose are available in many hardware stores and are preferred over smaller, cheaper pulleys with shallow grooves in the wheels. The rope comes out of the latter too easily.

A big hook screw is screwed into the deck post and another in the tree or whatever, and a pulley is attached to each hook. Then the nylon line is threaded through the pulleys. The knot joining the rope together again should be positioned on the lower rope and should be pulled up tight to the pulley where you begin to load on the wash. As each item of clothing is pinned on the rope, you pull the top of the line toward you, advancing the clothing on the bottom part of the line away from you. When the knot reaches the other pulley, the bottom of the line is fully loaded with clothing. To remove the clothing, reverse the procedure. When the deck is high enough off the ground, as is usually the case, no prop is needed.

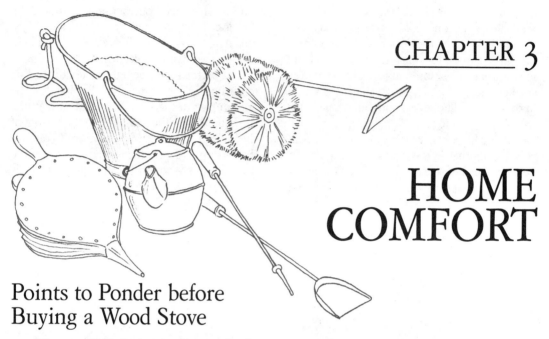

CHAPTER 3

HOME COMFORT

Points to Ponder before Buying a Wood Stove

How we decided upon the stove we finally bought for our house is a long story, but I can make it short. One, I could barely lift it off the floor; and two, my wife decided that it was the least ugly of the lot. I'll not mention the stove's brand name because, as I hope to point out, that is not by far the most important matter in selecting a stove. You won't believe me if I say that the two criteria above, bulk and beauty, are all you need to consider, so I'll make a short story a little longer. I'll explain—colored by my own bias, of course—the lessons all wood burners eventually learn in their quest for the "best" stove. I call them lessons in proper perspective.

Proper Perspective No. 1: There is no efficient wood- or coal-burning stove. All stoves lose at least half the convective heat up the chimney. Wood stove merchants do not dwell on this fact. They keep telling you that a fireplace loses 85% to 90% of its heat. They hope you won't ask about the 50% a stove is likely to lose no matter how great its "efficient" design is proclaimed to be.

Efficiency should not be your reason for selecting a particular stove, or selecting any stove, at least not in the literal sense of the word. Even if you have your own wood, the work and cost involved in cutting it will drive claims for money efficiency out of your head. Buy a wood stove for the only good reason: *It will keep you warm.* Central heat will not. I spent my childhood shivering on registers of a central hot-air furnace system; my youth shivering on the steam radiators of various educational institutions; and my young adulthood shivering under electric ceiling cable heat or beside oil-heated hot-water baseboard radiators. Only now, next to my wood stove, am I truly and comfortably warm.

Proper Perspective No. 2: A British thermal unit is a very small thing indeed. Under divine inspiration, wood stove merchants speak in Btus. Speaking in Btus, they can garble science every bit as profoundly as Pentecostals can garble the Bible while speaking in tongues. A Btu is the heat required to raise the tempera-

up to in twenty weeks of winter heating? About 700,000 Btus. Wow!

That's not really as wow as you think. Seven hundred thousand Btus equals about 50 pounds of hickory wood. That's a mighty wee pile of wood. The only thing baffled by talk of Btu saving is the unwary mind.

If I wanted to cheat when I sell wood, I could quite easily dump on an unwary soul a cord of pine for the same $85 I'd charge him for a cord of hickory. I would point out, in an awed tone of voice, that a cord of white pine contains 13 million—that's thirrrrteeeen mill-eee-yun—Btus. He'd be impressed and shell out the $85. What I wouldn't tell him is that a cord of hickory contains over 26 million Btus. That's perspective.

Proper Perspective No. 3: Everyone owns the best stove on the market. Ordinarily "asking the man who owns one" is a good way to learn what brand to buy. Not in wood stoves. For reasons that probably go far back in cultural history, every wood stove owner believes he is an infallible expert in the burning of wood. Therefore he could not, as a real American, have made a mistake in his choice of stoves. He will not admit to buying a lemon. If his stove has a fault, he won't say so.

Proper Perspective No. 4: It's not the stove that heats, it's the fire. A stove is a container that holds the fire so it doesn't burn the house down. Such an obvious fact only dawned on me slowly as I lay awash in the conflicting claims of two dozen manufacturers of expensive stoves. Then I became acquainted with a barrel that had a stovepipe in one end and a door in the other with a fire in the middle. It was heating a fairly large room in an uninsulated barn to a nice toasty warmth. The modifications that made the 55-gallon drum a stove cost $35. The stove wasn't much for looks, but as a heater, going on eight years, it worked just as well as the most sophisticated stove on the market.

ture of 1 pound of water 1°F. In other words, it takes bushels of them just to fry a hamburger. Keep that in mind when a stove salesman begins running along with a statement that sounds like this: "The system of baffles in our stoves is scientifically designed to direct the gases escaping from the burning wood back over the fire through a secondary combustion chamber where they are reignited, producing as much as 5000 more Btus of heat every day. These 5000 Btus just go up the chimney in our competitors' stoves." Accepting that to be somewhere in the neighborhood of truth (which you shouldn't), what do 5000 Btus per day add

The full import of the lesson I was learning did not become clear, however, until I saw my nephew's "Beast" in action. He built the Beast out of very heavy steel plate salvaged from the junkyard. Some of it was ⅜ inch thick and some as much as ⅝. There was nothing very subtle about the design—it looked like a Wells Fargo safe—but the Beast was the best stove I ever warmed myself by. I should say "is" because it is as indestructible and eternal as the mountains. The Beast needs a couple of hours after being fired up before the heat penetrates to the outer world, but half a day after the fire dies, you can still fry eggs on it. There is only one problem; it takes an elephant to move it.

So, to make a long story not quite as long as it could be, the Four Proper Perspectives led me, rightly or wrongly, to an inescapable conclusion: The more incredible the hulk, the better the stove. Since cast iron will hold more heat, pound for pound, than steel and radiate it for a longer period of time, I narrowed my search to cast-iron stoves, although steel stoves can be as good in quality as cast iron. I developed a habit of walking into a stove shop and hefting the stoves, totally ignoring all the sales pitches. I hefted rather than simply inquiring about the weight, because I wanted a stove I could move if I had to, but just barely. The stove I chose was the biggest one I could barely move. When my wife gave her imprimatur on its looks, our search was over.

Eight years later, I've yet to find a reason to regret my method of choosing a stove. A good draft, a well-insulated house, and seasoned firewood are more important to successful wood heating than a sophisticated, high-priced stove. Beyond that, beauty and bulk are the prime

Moving a Heavy Wood Stove

We move our wood stove out of the living room during the warm months. Our house was built before we understood that we were better off heating with the wood in our woodlot, and there is just no place a stove will "fit" into our house, which was designed for electric heat, except in front of the fireplace, using the fireplace chimney for a flue. The boss (my wife) does not, however, look kindly upon a wood stove in her immaculate, white-walled, light blue carpeted living room, and so we have reached this compromise: the stove goes out during the warm months. Besides, to give it a good annual cleaning, I like to take the stove outside, so I might as well leave it in the garage till fall rolls around again.

But the stove, as already mentioned, is a heavy brute, not designed to be carted about at seasonal whims. I used to invite friends over for an evening of frivolity and

considerations. The beauty (in the eye of the beholder) satisfies my wife, and the bulk keeps me warm 2 to 3 hours after the fire goes out, which (see the next item) saves wood, and if taken advantage of correctly, avoids heavy creosote buildup.

Minimizing Creosote Buildup

Very often you will read that burning green wood causes creosote buildup. That statement is not really true. Green or wet wood may smolder at such a low temperature that it indirectly causes creosote to build up overly fast in the chimney, but you can build up creosote just as quickly with very dry seasoned wood, *if you burn it at a very low draft.* The less air, or draft, you allow in your stove, the more creosote will form, because without oxygen, the fire cannot burn hot enough to burn up the gases that carry off the creosote. Just as night follows day, excessive creosote problems have followed in the wake of the so-called airtight stove. Always remember that *wood won't burn in a stove that is so tight air can't get in.* This should be obvious, but when you are being beaten over the head by sales talk that stresses the superior "efficiency" of airtight stoves, you come home with a terrible case of misplaced emphasis. You believe that the reason for "airtightness" is to see how long you can keep a piece of wood burning. So you turn the draft as low as possible without totally quenching the fire and brag to your fellow wood burners that an armload of wood lasts all night in your stove.

then just happen to remember that it was April, ha ha, and time for the stove to be exiled to the garage, and ah hah, four muscle-bound males just happened to be on the premises. Eventually, friends all found reasons not to accept any April invitations to our house.

So we began looking at dollies. Good ones, with good ball-bearing wheels and axles, are expensive. So my son, the man of all skills, made one: easy enough to make once we found a hardware store that carried good wheels. You want a hard rubber tread and a size of at least 3 to 4 inches in diameter—low enough to fit under the stove but with the wheels large enough to roll easily, even on carpet.

For the dolly frame, my son simply made a rectangular carriage big enough to hold the stove, out of 2 × 4s, half-lapped at the corners. (See the drawing.) The bolts that hold the wheels to the frame also hold the frame together.

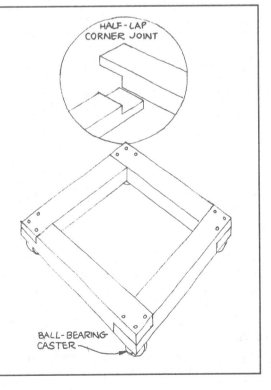

HALF-LAP CORNER JOINT

BALL-BEARING CASTER

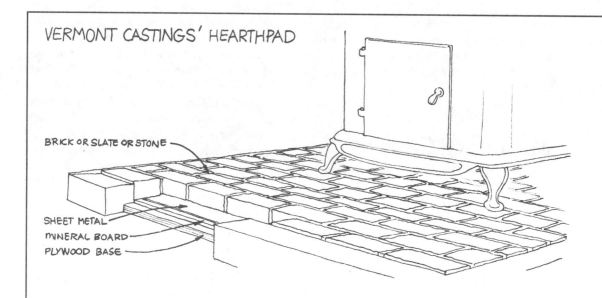

VERMONT CASTINGS' HEARTHPAD

BRICK OR SLATE OR STONE

SHEET METAL
MINERAL BOARD
PLYWOOD BASE

A Homemade Hearthpad

With modern, airtight stoves, the floor directly underneath the firebox can get hot enough to catch on fire if not protected. Wherever sold as an accessory, a bottom heat shield for the stove should be installed, and a good hearthpad put under the stove if the floor is of a combustible material. Portable hearthpads can cost $300 or more from a store, but you can make one for less that will work safely even if set on a wood floor or carpet, providing all safety regulations are followed.

A homemade hearthpad described by the *Vermont Castings Owners' News* is far superior to my homemade one, which also works well. Theirs calls for a base of ½-inch plywood, two sheets of mineral board (what we used to call asbestos plaster board), a piece of 24-gauge sheet metal, and a brick, slate, or stone top. Cut the plywood to the size you need, make a nice border for it of quarter round or stripping, and cut the mineral board to fit. (Wear an air filter mask when working with this material.)

All you really do with a cold, slow fire like that is transfer the unused heat of combustion from wood in the firebox to creosote in the chimney. And the low smoldering fire you are maintaining isn't heating the house very well, either. You finally learn to open the draft so the fire can burn hot and comparatively fast. Only a little creosote forms then, and even though the

fire probably goes out at 4:00 A.M., the house, if insulated properly, stays warm enough until you are ready to get up in the morning and rekindle it. By taking advantage of the hot radiating stove even after the fire has gone out, you also save on wood, especially in warmer spring weather when your heating needs are much less. You can fire up twice or thrice a day

Directions call for cementing the two sheets of insulating mineral board to the plywood and to each other, then the sheet metal onto this base. My experience is that the cementing is unnecessary. The top coverings call for mortar between the pieces, which I have found to be unnecessary, too. If you cement all these layers together, the pad is almost too heavy to lift. If a bit of hot coal ever did get into a crack, the steel and/or insulative board would be enough to protect the floor. But I suppose it's better to be supersafe.

With an extra bottom heat shield under the stove, as we have for our Defiant, we have minimal heat radiating to the floor to start out with. Our pad is ⅞-inch plywood, topped with two layers of asbestos padding, then a layer of slates off an old barn roof. It's attractive and simple, but safe only with a bottom heat shield attached to the stove, and stove legs long enough so the firebox is at least 8 inches off the floor.

All hearthpads I know about have mineral board—otherwise known as asbestos—in them. As long as you are not cutting it, and thus putting the dust in the air, danger is extremely remote. However, with a heat shield such as my stove is equipped, I am confident that the first hearthpad I described would protect the floor adequately with no mineral board in it at all, if the idea of asbestos bothers you.

and let the fire go out in between. If you learn how to start a fire easily (see Starting a Fire in a Wood Stove), this is not much of a problem. Otherwise, with the low, cool fire going continuously on those warmer days, you have creosote problems.

Three experiences convinced me of the truth of the above:

A Use for Creosote

When you clean creosote out of your stove flue, save some of it to use as a borer repellent. Steep the creosote in an equal amount of water for several weeks. Then around June 1, or earlier if you see the dark blue, orange-banded peach borer adults flying about, douse the lower trunks of your peach trees with the brew and leave a cindery, 2-inch-wide deposit of the creosote all around the trunk. This wood creosote remedy is helpful but not foolproof. With borers, nothing is.

Don't use commercial creosote from coal.

1. The first year I burnt wood from an old barn, I used timbers that had seasoned for forty years. But because I kept the draft low, I had an awful lot of creosote.

2. As a kid in my father's farm shop, I used to fire up an old stove that had cracks in it big enough for a sparrow to fly through. Because of the ample air to the fire, we never had a bit of creosote—although we almost burnt the shop down a couple of times. That is the real value of an airtight stove: You can keep a fire from getting *too* hot by shutting off almost all the air to a full load of wood. And in case of a chimney fire, if you shut off all the air, and if your flue has no leaks or cracks in it, you can control that danger to a considerable extent, too.

3. But the easiest proof is to watch what happens in an open fireplace. Creosote hardly ever becomes a problem there because of the abundance of oxygen to the fire. (Unfortunately, in an ordinary fireplace, you not only have a minimum of creosote buildup, you also have a minimum of heat.)

In a stove, you want to burn the wood hot, but of course not too hot. First, buy a surface thermometer for your stove top or the flue right above the stove. (Your stove dealer can instruct you on the best place to put the thermometer for your particular stove; if he is hesitant, take your business elsewhere, I say.) The idea is to get enough draft to your fire at each loading so that the temperature on the stove top or flue gets up to 550° to 600°F. Then damper the stove down so that it maintains a steady 350° to 400°F. Depending on the weather, your stove, your chimney, the wind direction, the size of your wood chunks, and other factors, the stove will heat up to 550°F. slowly or quickly. Some people burn a very hot fire every morning, after a night of lower fire, allowing the temperature to go up to 700°F. That way they burn out whatever bit of creosote formed overnight. But it is risky letting the stove get that hot. About 600°F. is safe—or whatever limits your particular stove manufacturer sets.

Another great aid in keeping the fire burning hot is to split your wood into rather small pieces, allowing only overnight logs to be more than about 4 inches in diameter. Also, softwoods will give you a quicker, hotter fire than hardwoods. The wood should be dry and seasoned, of course, but if pieces are small, you can burn *some* green with the dry with no problems.

If your thermometer shows that your stove temperature is under 300°F., you can be sure excess creosote is forming in the chimney—*except* when the fire has burned down to only glowing coals. Then usually, no problem. The worst creosote comes from chunks of only half-burned wood, smoldering away in the stove all day and night.

Some wood burners accept creosote as a part of their life, and rather than fiddle around keeping the fire going strong or not at all, take down their flue every two weeks and clean it. I'm not the type that works that way. I'd forget to clean the flue, or skip a week, and perhaps endure a chimney fire for my negligence.

A Homemade Power Drive Brush for Cleaning Creosote

The light, flaky creosote (the more dangerous kind because it ignites more easily) is relatively easy to clean out of a chimney. A worse problem is the hardcoat creosote—the liquid stuff that hardens to an almost glasslike surface. I vent my stove directly into a fireplace closed with a steel panel, and for reasons that experts could readily explain, I suppose, I get only a little ordinary creosote, but the smoke chamber above the fireplace gets glazed with the hardcoat stuff. If you have this problem, here's a way to solve it.

I bought a steel wire brush—the kind you put on a motor shaft or arbor for buffing work—and a 3-foot rod of threaded ½-inch steel. With two burrs and washers, I attach the brush to the end of the rod and secure the other end into my heavy-duty ½-inch drill. The chuck will hold the rod well enough, despite its length, but be careful not to exert too much pressure or you might bend the drill's drive shaft. Then I sit in the fireplace, wearing goggles, and push the brush up into the smoke chamber and buff away the creosote. Deposits in the fireplace itself I handle with the brush on a shorter rod.

Operating a Wood Stove Is an Art

"Never tinker with another person's stove." That's the veteran wood burner's way of saying that no two stove installations are the same, and therefore adjusting a stove properly varies from house to house and takes some learning. Of the many variables in operating a stove, here are the most important:

1. Height of the chimney.
2. Chimney capped or uncapped.
3. Flue size.
4. Insulation around the flue.
5. Material the chimney is made of.
6. Position of the chimney (exterior or interior).
7. Configuration of the flue (how many elbows and so forth).
8. Outside temperature.
9. Inside house temperature.
10. Outside air pressure.
11. Wind velocity.
12. Wind direction.
13. Humidity.
14. Density of the wood.
15. Size of the logs.
16. Moisture of the wood.
17. Size of the firebox.
18. Indoor ventilation.

Height of the chimney. Safety experts recommend that a chimney be 3 feet higher than the roof directly below it and 2 feet higher than any obstructions or roof peak 10 feet or less away from it. For a good draft, the chimney ought to be higher than any roof peak on the house; otherwise, the roof acts as an obstruction to the wind and can cause downdrafts in the chimney. Generally speaking, the taller the chimney, the better the draft, and where draft is continuously poor in the stove, the first suggested cure is to add a few feet on to the chimney. Short chimneys, only a story high on ranch-type houses, often have poor draft.

Chimney capped or uncapped. Caps on chimneys can keep birds and water out, but they will also influence the draft. On windy days, a cap may diminish backpuffing. Where there are two flues in the same chimney, side by side, the

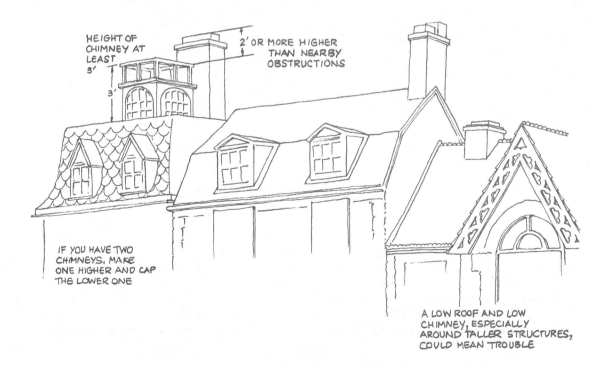

HEIGHT OF CHIMNEY AT LEAST 3'

2' OR MORE HIGHER THAN NEARBY OBSTRUCTIONS

IF YOU HAVE TWO CHIMNEYS, MAKE ONE HIGHER AND CAP THE LOWER ONE

A LOW ROOF AND LOW CHIMNEY, ESPECIALLY AROUND TALLER STRUCTURES, COULD MEAN TROUBLE

Chimney caps come in all shapes and sizes.

one not in operation can draw smoke down from the other. Lengthening the height of one by a few inches and capping the other can solve most of this problem. How necessary it is to keep water out of a chimney is debatable. Our builder put grooves in the masonry at the bottom of the flue to carry water running down the inside of the flue away from the fireplace and out weep holes at the lower chimney blocks. As a result, not much water ever gets into the fireplace from our uncapped chimney.

Flue size. The larger the flue opening, the greater the draft, everything else being equal.

An 8-inch flue is usually the minimum recommended.

Insulation around the flue. The warmer the flue, the greater the draft, so anything that influences flue temperature influences draft and varies the way the stove should be operated. For metal flues, the triple-walled kind should be used. A good masonry chimney is composed of an inner flue liner of vitrified tile surrounded by cement block or other masonry, with vermiculite between for insulation, then an outer shell of brick or stone to match the house.

Material the chimney is made of. Metal heats up and cools down quicker than stone, and so different fluctuating temperatures will influence the draft.

Position of the chimney. Traditionally, chimneys are positioned on the south side of the house to absorb the sun's rays and keep them warmer, thereby increasing the draft. That's still a good idea. But a better one is to put the chimney up through the center of the house to keep the flue warm all the time.

Configuration of the flue. The greater the number of bends, twists, turns, and horizontal stretches of the flue the less the draft. But with a good tall chimney, such configurations are not at all ruled out; some stoves draw well even with a dip downward in the flue. But all these configurations will dictate their own unique thermostat and damper settings.

Outside temperature. The colder the weather, the better a stove will draw, other things being equal. In warmish weather, stoves burn sluggishly with backpuffing and downdrafting that require variations in the normal way you operate your stove. Allow more air into the stove by opening the draft.

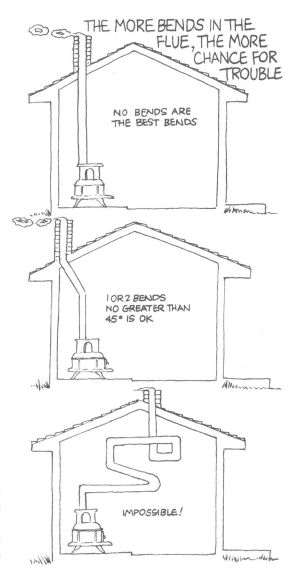

THE MORE BENDS IN THE FLUE, THE MORE CHANCE FOR TROUBLE

NO BENDS ARE THE BEST BENDS

1 OR 2 BENDS NO GREATER THAN 45° IS OK

IMPOSSIBLE!

Inside house temperature. Room temperature does not influence stove operation nearly as much as outside temperature, but the more nearly the two temperatures approach each other, the less the draft.

Outside air pressure. As the barometer falls, so does the strength of the draft. You can observe this phenomenon best in summer. When a low pressure area is approaching, you detect chimney odors in the house more easily even though you have no fire burning, because of downdraft in the chimney. With high pressure and fair weather, odors disappear up the chimney.

Wind velocity. If steady, a strong wind usually increases draft. But where roof peaks or trees make the wind swirl around, or the wind comes in gusts, downdrafting may occur. A roof cap may be the answer.

Wind direction. Backpuffing and downdrafts may only be a problem when the wind is in a certain direction.

Humidity. The more moisture in the air, the heavier the air, influencing draft. (See *Outside air pressure.*)

Density of the wood. The denser the wood, the more Btus of heat it contains, and burning it will usually require stove settings different from those you use when burning less dense woods. But just because a wood has more Btus than another doesn't mean the low Btu kinds cannot make a very hot fire. On the contrary, a stove full of light white pine kindling, given plenty of draft, will burn dangerously hotter *for a short period of time* than will a high-density wood.

Size of the logs. The size of the individual pieces of wood in a fire influences the heat of the fire. Although this fact seems to get short

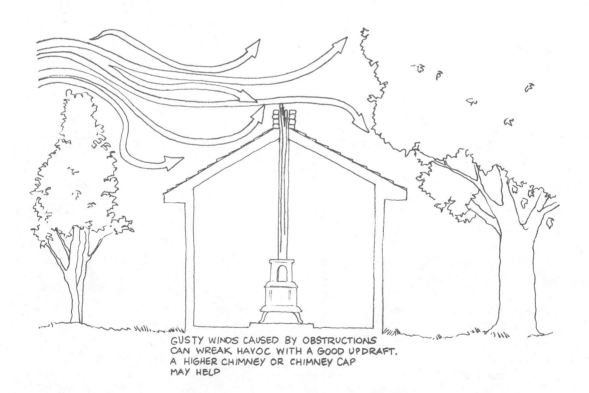

GUSTY WINDS CAUSED BY OBSTRUCTIONS CAN WREAK HAVOC WITH A GOOD UPDRAFT. A HIGHER CHIMNEY OR CHIMNEY CAP MAY HELP

shrift in most manuals, the difference is quite dramatic. If you have to burn wet or green wood, chop it into small pieces. Small pieces of wood burn faster than big pieces. The latter can cause creosote buildup no matter how dry it is (see Minimizing Creosote Buildup, earlier). One advantage of a small stove is that it forces you to use small pieces of wood and therefore maintain a hotter fire, which means less creosote.

Moisture of the wood. Dry wood obviously burns hotter than wet or green wood and therefore requires less draft.

Size of the firebox. Obviously, the amount of wood you can safely put into a stove dictates variations in the stove's settings.

Indoor ventilation. A modern home can be built so tight that the stove will not draw well. However, this is fairly rare and if it happens in your case, keep a window cracked. A house that tight with a wood stove in operation could be dangerous; carbon monoxide, a poisonous gas, could be the result. Homeowners occasionally install a vent directly from the outside to the fireplace or wood stove for better draft and to prevent drawing off of as much warm room air as might otherwise be going up the chimney. Experts debate the effectiveness of such vents, but if a house really is too tight, these vents seem justified.

A room air-to-air heat exchanger is another option. This simple, two-channel device allows fresh outdoor air to enter through one side and exhausts stale inside air through the other. Because the two channels are not open to one another but are adjacent, the warmer existing air loses some of its heat to cooler incoming air, effectively prewarming it. The result is ventilation without a lot of cold drafts.

Nobody can tell you how to work these variables into your own proper stove adjustments. It's an art. That's why humans come to have a rather personal relationship with their stoves.

(It's OK to talk to your stove until it starts talking back to you.)

Starting a Fire in a Wood Stove

Although it receives the least attention, the most irksome part of heating with a wood stove is starting the fire. Since my method of heating calls for starting the fire frequently or rekindling it fast, I experimented extensively so that I now have a way that is relatively easy. But I'm sure there are still others as well.

First of all, obviously, don't use green or wet wood. Living with a wood stove does not become a pleasure until the woodcutter gets two years ahead on his woodpile, with the wood split into smallish pieces—4 inches in diameter or less—so they can dry out well. Even in two years, oak may still not be as dry as it should be.

Next, keep on hand a supply of very dry, easily ignited kindling. Slivers of dry pine,

Homemade starter stick.

especially yellow pine, are best in my experience. I'm still using slivers of yellow pine barn siding I salvaged years ago. (Old barn siding is invariably yellow pine, although there's not enough of this splendid wood to use this way anymore. Yellow pine has a pitch or resin in it that preserves it and makes it burn quickly, too.)

Another good kindling is the traditional "starter stick," as shown in the photograph. A third type of good kindling is wood shavings from a drawknife, carving knife, or carpenter's plane.

With kindling at hand, you are ready to start the fire. Place two smallish pieces of stovewood in the firebox, leaving about 3 inches between them. The stovewood pieces should be *warm,* not just brought in from the cold. In the 3-inch space between them, put about five crumpled wads of paper and three pine slivers over them (or a shaved starter stick or two or three handfuls of shavings). Next, put two more pieces of warm stovewood on top of the first two, a little closer together, but still with a crack between them—about as wide as your finger. This space between the pieces of wood allows the first gush of flames from the kindling to sweep upwards, unimpeded along the inner faces of all four pieces of wood, creating a brisk draft that heats the wood to the kindling point quickly. Without the space between the stovewood pieces, the flame is half-smothered and balky.

Now light the paper, starter stick, or shavings. The usual end-loading wood stove requires you to start the fire at the front, which is the best place to start anyway. The draft will draw the flame in and up through the wood. If using paper and pine slivers, you may have to add two or three more wads of paper to the young flame before you hear the telltale crackle that says the wood has ignited. Add those wads right at the end of the wood closest to you. Don't try to push the paper into the space where the kindling is starting to burn. The draft will carry the flame

from the paper on into the wood.

Keep the stove door open a minute or two, or closed only partway to keep sparks from jumping out. Most airtight stoves don't allow in enough air in the early minutes of the fire, even with vents and damper wide open. But adjust to your situation. As soon as the kindling is burning vigorously, keep the door open just a crack or perhaps close it all the way if a wide-open vent and damper are providing enough air. (This will vary with the barometric pressure.) When the big pieces ignite, close the door but keep vents, damper, and so forth open until the stove thermometer indicates the fire is getting hot enough to burn without producing excess smoke. Leave the draft adjustments open fairly wide until the temperature rises to about 550°F. Then close down the draft so that the fire maintains a steady 350° to 400°F., or as your stove manufacturer recommends.

When a wood fire burns low, but has not gone out yet, many people just chuck in a couple more logs. They may smolder for an hour before really igniting. I invariably put in a few pieces of kindling and a wad of paper with

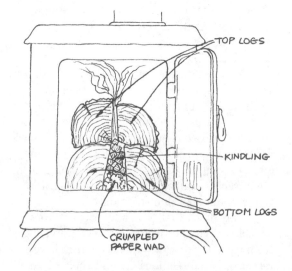

TOP LOGS

KINDLING

BOTTOM LOGS

CRUMPLED PAPER WAD

Ashes for Fertilizer

Wood ashes make a good fertilizer, being about 7% potash (with small amounts of various trace elements) and more than 50% calcium. Put them on the garden or around fruit trees. The recommended rate is 5 pounds per 100 square feet, but I usually put them on at twice that rate. Because of the high calcium content, ashes take the place of lime. The potash heightens the taste of the fruits and vegetables, encourges more vigorous growth and proper maturity, and helps balance organic fertilizers that contain more nitrogen than they do potash.

The ashes need to be saved in a metal container, since there will invariably be hot coals involved. And they must be kept under cover so rainwater doesn't leach out the nutrients in them. For the same reason it is best to apply them in spring shortly before planting, since nutrients from winter applications might wash away on frozen ground.

Some woods seem to produce more ashes than others. Burning white oak or beech, I do not have to clean out ashes nearly as often as when burning hickory or elm.

There are arguments pro and con on the subject of whether ash pans on stoves are advantageous. Stove makers who have ash pans on their stoves argue for the convenience; those who do not have ash pans say that the bed of ashes right under the wood retains more heat in the stove. Either way, the ashes have to be carried out. You can stick a coal scuttle's snout into the door of a nonashpan stove and scoop ashes carefully into the scuttle without spilling any on the hearthpad. The draft will carry the ash dust created back into the stove, not up to the ceiling, if you are careful with the scooping. Wear fireproof, heat-protective fireplace gloves in any event. Ash pans and coal scuttles full of hot ashes are hot.

Don't confuse wood ashes with coal ashes. The latter are not good for growing things.

the new logs to get them burning hot and bright in a hurry. There's less chance for creosote formation that way.

Getting the Most Heat from a Fireplace

You can coax more heat from a fireplace by the way you position the logs in it. Fireplaces are not very "efficient" in terms of convective heat, retaining hardly more than 20% of it even with a standard heat exchanger installed. But that measurement does not take into account radiant heat reflecting from the fire. If the burning logs are so positioned as to radiate heat outward into the room, they can keep you very warm and toasty indeed—at least on one side! If you sit before such a fire in a wing-backed chair, which shields the back of your neck from the cooler air being pulled toward the fireplace, the radiant heat will be quite effective.

The ideal is to keep a sort of wall of burning logs facing the front of the fireplace, stair-stepped from low in front to high in back. The closer to the front you can keep a nice cheery flame the whole width of the fireplace, the more heat it will radiate.

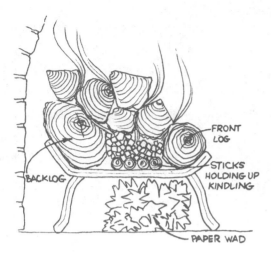

FRONT LOG

STICKS HOLDING UP KINDLING

BACKLOG

PAPER WAD

A Good Fire Makes All the Difference

There are surely a number of ways to increase radiant heat from a fireplace. Here is mine. This method makes for ease of starting the fire, too. First lay a backlog as large as you can handle on the andirons. If your fireplace has 2 feet of depth, a backlog 10 inches in diameter is not too large. Next, lay a small piece of wood at the front of the andirons, something about 3 inches in diameter. Between these two pieces of wood, lay a grate of sticks about 1½ to 2 inches in diameter, and on top of these, a good handful of twigs or kindling. On top of the kindling place two or three 3- to 4-inch diameter pieces, roughly stair-stepped back to the backlog. It is essential that there be cracks between the pieces for the flame to rise up through. If the sticks of wood fit too solidly against each other, the fire will smoke and smolder for awhile, not burn brightly and radiantly.

Next put a couple of wads of paper under the logs, make sure the damper is open, and light the fire. The flame will work up through the small sticks between the front log and the

backlog, ignite the kindling, and the kindling will ignite the middle pieces of wood. When they are burning brightly, you may want to add two or three more pieces of wood, depending on the size of your fireplace, so as to encourage a nice wall of burning wood facing the front of the fireplace. Except for the backlog, fireplace wood should not be too thick. Thinner pieces (4 inches in diameter) don't last as long, but produce a more flaming, radiant heat. Once a large bed of hot coals is achieved, however, thicker pieces will do all right.

In adding new logs to the fire, first pull forward the glowing ember logs in the fire (with a fireplace tool, of course) and put the new ones behind them. The fire in any fireplace tends to work its way to the back. You want to keep it as far forward as possible so the heat radiates better into the room. Eventually your backlog burns up, too, and its remains should be pulled forward and a new one inserted in the back. A new backlog added to a burning fire will have to be smaller than the first one because you can't get in close enough to the fire with a big, heavy backlog without singeing your eyebrows.

Let the ashes build up in your fireplace. They make something of a heat sink. You do not really need andirons to hold the fire above the ash bed, as some people believe. The wood will burn just as well resting on the ash bed as on andirons. But for *starting* a fire the andirons are handy. With the logs lying on them, I dig out a hollow in the ashes under them for the paper with which I start the fire. Flames coming up from below ignite the kindling quickly.

For pleasurable fireplace operation, use only seasoned wood. A backlog or front log can be somewhat unseasoned without adverse effects, but I don't recommend it.

Don't forget that a fireplace has a damper. Keep it open just far enough to produce a good cheery fire. Any more than that, and you are only drawing more warm air out of your room and up the chimney.

The Importance of Location and Air Movement

To get more efficiency from a fireplace, build it where it can't draw heat out of the entire house. Put it in a room that can be isolated from the rest of the house by closing a door. Then install an air duct directly from the outside to the fireplace. A simple 2-inch plastic pipe with a turn-off valve or a screw-on plug at the inlet (so mice or chipmunks don't crawl in) will do.

A fireplace so ducted gives more than average efficiency if placed in a basement or the lower level of a split-level home. Since warm air rises, a lower-level fireplace, especially if equipped with a steel-jacket heat exchanger like Heatform or Heatilator (there are many others), will push heat to the upper level faster than it draws warm air from above down. You can stand on the stairs from our lower level and feel the heat rising to the kitchen. In the terrible blizzard of 1978, before we had installed a wood stove on the upper level, we kept the lower level and the kitchen above it livable with the fireplace, even after four days of subzero temperatures without electricity or any other source of heat.

One last point. If your fireplace is equipped with a steel-jacket heat exchanger, you will get more heat out of it if you fill the fireplace adequately with fire. In other words, a small fire in a large steel jacket is no fire at all. A small fire won't allow enough heat to be generated so that the steel will heat up on all sides and begin to draw in cool room air in its lower vents and expel it warm from its upper vents. Thus, a smaller-size fireplace of this kind usually gives the typical homeowner more heat than a larger one, since the typical homeowner has neither the wood nor the inclination to build big fires. Many manufacturers of the newer fireplace inserts (which are really more stoves than heat

The Advantage of a Large Fireplace

While homeowners in many cases— especially if buying wood—are better off with a smaller fireplace, the homesteader who cuts his own wood may find the large fireplace in combination with a wood stove a money-saving duo, even if the fireplace is not so efficient.

The reason is simple. When cutting wood, every tree will contain a few knotty and virtually unsplittable chunks. Such chunks demand an expensive, heavy-duty mechanical splitter. (I've seen white oak knots that broke splitters rather than vice versa.) With a large fireplace, the woodcutter merely smiles at such chunks and relegates them to the fireplace, especially for backlogs. The time and energy saved not splitting these chunks makes the big fireplace quite "efficient" after all. The easily split wood goes in the stove, the hard stuff in the fireplace.

How large is large in this case? Our fireplace is 4 feet wide at the front, about 2½ feet deep, and 2½ to 3 feet tall, large enough to handle most knotty chunks. I wish it were a little bigger, to tell the truth. My father-in-law used to regale us about an aunt and uncle of his who lived in the mountains of Kentucky almost totally independent of the world. Their sole source of heat was a huge fireplace, into which they would *roll* backlogs they could not lift and which barely fit through the door. They did not want to split any more wood than they had to. They also did not believe in wasting matches. Perfection was striking one match in October every year to get the fire started and after that just poking a backlog into flame again every morning—until spring.

exchangers and are therefore somewhat more efficient) make much ado about the fans that hasten the passage of air through the vents. We have such fans in our heat exchanger and hardly ever use them. Natural convection moves the heated air in and out quite adequately.

Don't Overdo Insulation

The first house my wife and I bought had mushrooms growing on the rafters in the attic. So help me. That's why I like Charlie Wing's concise book *The Tighter House* (Rodale Press, 1981) about insulation. He stresses that one must not just lock out the cold air but must do so without trapping moist air inside. That house we bought was insulated well enough, but there was no vapor barrier in the walls or ceiling and only two tiny vents at the roof peaks at each end of the house. However, the shingle roof—asphalt shingles—made a marvelous vapor barrier; most roofing, except cedar shakes and tile, does. Warm air from inside the house meeting cold roof in the attic equaled condensation. To make matters extremely worse, the former owners had put a vent in the ceiling directly above the furnace, so that hot air could go directly to the attic—I suppose they thought that it would dry out the dripping attic space.

Most of the roof had to be replaced. But rather than tear out the inner shell of the house to install a vapor barrier, we had vents inserted in the soffit all around the outside of the house, plus a few of those globular vents on the roof itself. We, of course, plugged the vent above the furnace. Our problem was solved without a great expenditure of money.

The price was probably worth it in educational value. A house must breathe, even at the expense of superinsulation. If walls cannot breathe, paint won't hold on the outside (peeling paint is a good sign of too much wood-rotting moisture in the walls) and moisture caught and held in the insulation will eventually rot the studs. Crawl spaces under houses must have air circulation even at the expense of cold floors—which is one reason why a basement is superior to a crawl space. And if roofs can't breathe in some way, you can end up growing mushrooms in your attic.

Overenthusiasm in blocking out cold air from a house leads to other problems. Now, we're given to understand, pollutants from home heating systems, appliances, and other products used in the home are an increasing threat to health because houses are so tight the pollutants can't escape. I know of a house where a window has to be cracked to make the wood stove draw well.

Other folks say they have spent lots of money doubling and tripling the R-value of the insulation in their homes, but without gaining comparable savings in heat. What is generally the case in this situation is that "minor" heat leaks have been overlooked while an overall expensive insulation program was being followed. A little weather stripping and common sense might have saved more money.

The fancy front door on modern homes is almost always a very expensive proposition. It costs more than it's worth most of the time, and it becomes a hole in the wall in terms of heat loss. Unless you go to a great deal of expense to have a door custom-made, those wooden front doors will warp. They must endure Florida on one side and Alaska on the other and keeping them fitting properly is almost impossible. Weather stripping, dollar for dollar, will pay back far better than insulation in the walls and ceiling. But even good weather stripping isn't usually enough to block the howling blizzards of January. A storm door—the typical storm door you can buy now—is not very satisfactory either and too ugly for most folks to put in front of the fancy door. A vestibule is the proper solution, blocking the wind, providing an entrance way to doff boots, snowy coat, and umbrella. But the expense stops most people and the tacked-on look looks too tacked on.

The closest to an effective solution I know of—one we've adopted—is to seal off the door in the coldest weather and enter the house through the garage. I just taped the door shut. It looks ugly, but only for about twenty-five days of the year.

Living in a shaky old house one winter, we learned the value of a roll of tape. We taped around windows, doors, electric outlets, key holes—everywhere that could possibly have a leak to the outdoors. Tape does not have much R-value, but it kept the wind from blowing napkins off the table.

Attics are comparatively easy to insulate, so if you must oversplurge on insulation, here is the place to do it. Most heat loss is out of the top of a house. Infrared photography is the new way to check for heat leaks, but for the roof there's a much cheaper way. Watch your roof closely in the morning after a heavy frost or a snow. If there are sections of roof that haven't frosted

over, or from which the snow melts much faster than the rest of the roof, be assured there's a heat leak under that spot. That's how we learned we were losing heat through the trap door into the attic.

Running Water

Maude Opper is not the only one of my neighbors who does not have running water in her house, but she is perhaps the most striking of them all in the utter simplicity that permeates her life-style. None of these people are so poor that they could not easily afford the most modern indoor plumbing system available. They just prefer not to. Maude shrugs. "Oh, I never got around to it. Costs a lot of money and what do you have? Just worries about the pipes freezing up like everyone else was complaining about last winter." Maude's water system consists of a hand pump over the cistern outside and half a dozen 5-gallon white plastic buckets that she fills and carries into the house as needed. As did her parents before her.

She lives in only two rooms of the old house now, the kitchen to do some cooking in, to heat water on the electric range, and to do the laundry in the old Maytag washer. The other room is both living room and bedroom. Her bed edges up as close to the wood stove as possible on one side and her easy chair on the other. On the periphery of her living space there is a television set that she rarely watches: her one-word summation of television entertainment is rather unprintable. The old pictures, furniture, vases, and memorabilia that dustily clutter the room recall the '20s and '30s—a sort of bargain basement art deco. On a stool by the bed is a piece of soapstone. In the evening she sets it on top of the wood stove and when it is hot she takes it to bed to keep her feet warm. In the middle of the room is something that is an island unto itself, a sort of shining jewel in comparison with the surroundings: a neat, clean

---

It's More than Just the House That Needs Changing

The biggest question mark in your energy master plan is you. Two families, the same size, can live side by side in two identical houses, and the two household energy budgets can be as different as night and day. Consumption is dramatically affected by the way you operate your house, just as your gas mileage is affected by the way you drive your car. Do you linger around a wide-open front door saying good-bye to guests? Do you use a clothes dryer or a clothesline on a sunny day? Do you smoke enough to need a window opened to clear the air? Reducing total energy consumption requires a life-style audit, too.

Charlie Wing, in
The Tighter House

before passive solar heating became a common phrase, a farmer in Wisconsin we know cleaned out a gravity flow gasoline tank (cleaned it out *well,* I hope!), painted it black, and set it up astraddle an alleyway on the roofs of two close-standing sheds. On the spout he hung upside down a lidless soup can, the sides of which he had cut into strips, splaying the strips out so that they broke up the stream of water from the spigot and caused it to dribble showerlike upon him. In the morning he pumped the tank full and when he came in tired and grimy from the field in the evening, a hot, almost free shower awaited him in the privacy of the alleyway.

Years ago when the USDA really tried to help rural people, it published Farmers Bulletin 927, showing how to rig up a shower bath when running water was not available. A hook was screwed into the ceiling of whatever room or porch one might decide was the shower room. A small pulley was attached to the hook,

Maude Opper.

table, a typewriter, and several volumes of Maude's family genealogy that Maude has spent years compiling. The Lowmasters (her maiden name) trace their ancestry to Hohenzollern nobility in medieval Germany and she can prove it.

Most of us today not only find Maude's way of life unthinkable, but actually frightening. Yet there she lives, serene and satisfied, proof to anyone who cares to look that her way of life is certainly possible among the madness of the modern life most of us live. She fetches her water, walks to her privy, swings her ax, lifts her wood. Spurning such labor, we jog, press weights, go to unbelievably laborious substitutes for physical work to stay healthy.

There are cheap ways to enjoy home comfort without going as far as Maude does. Long

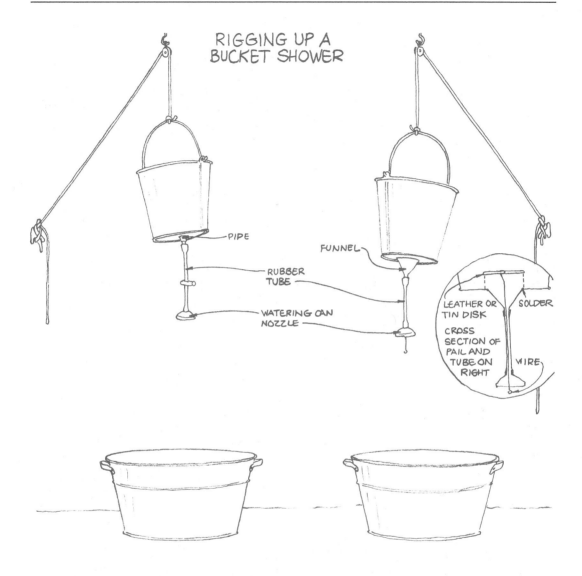

RIGGING UP A
BUCKET SHOWER

PIPE

FUNNEL

RUBBER
TUBE

WATERING CAN
NOZZLE

LEATHER OR
TIN DISK

SOLDER

CROSS
SECTION OF
PAIL AND
TUBE ON
RIGHT

WIRE

and a rope raised a 4-gallon bucket to any height the bather desired while he or she stood in a metal laundry tub underneath. For a shower head, a hole was cut into the bottom of the bucket and a 2-inch piece of pipe soldered into the opening. A watering can nozzle attached to a rubber tube, with the tube attached to the pipe, completed the rig. And how to turn on and off the shower? Simple. A clothespin clamped to the rubber tube!

Immediately, the human mind brought improvement to this crude design. To regulate the water better, a piece of 12-gauge wire could be run up through the tube and in this case through a common funnel soldered onto the bottom of the bucket, and then fastened to a disk of leather or tin (the lid of a tin can would work fine) by running the wire through the disk and looping it on the other side. The wire also had to be kinked right below the disk. By pushing up on the wire, the disk was raised and held open by the kink in it while one showered. When the disk was lowered over the hole, the weight of the water in the bucket formed a fair seal. But the clothespin was so much simpler.

The Hydraulic Ram

To walk into Henry Hershberger's house is to walk into the nineteenth century, although the house is brand-new. There is no electricity, no television, no record player. Kerosene lamps shed a soft warmth over the spare, plain lines of white plaster walls, grey wood wainscoting, and oaken floors stained only with linseed oil. The house is as quiet as a cloister. On the bench against the wall four children sit as round-eyed and naive as a primitive painting. Amanda, Henry's wife, crates brown eggs at the long kitchen table. Henry hunkers down on the open oven door—on a kitchen stove so massive it could heat that house and two more like it.

Hershberger is an Amish farmer and Amish minister, a man well thought of by his fellow church members even though he has recently been in jail. Or perhaps *because* he has recently been in jail. His beautiful new house, built much sturdier than most houses today, is the reason he was in jail. Hershberger would not apply for a permit to build the house. He said it was against his religion. He believes if people do not stand up against unnecessary regulation we will all soon lose our individual rights under the Constitution. He and his fellow church members are afraid that, as zoning regulations proliferate, their children will be denied the chance to build their homes on the ancestral farms. Hershberger is a latter-day Thoreau, willing to go to prison for what he believes.

But a community sense of justice and common sense brought such an outcry that he did not stay long in jail. The house is too well made. It transcends the political vipers of government regulation. It is framed with full-measure oak 2 × 4s. The exterior siding is redwood. The roof is channel drain metal. "We like the look of shingles," says Hershberger, "but shingles only last twenty years, you know."

Though there is no electricity in the house, there is running water. It comes from a spring by way of a hydraulic ram. It has been in operation for twenty-five years and with an occasional cleaning has never once given a moment's trouble.

Progress. If progress be measured in human enlightenment in the use of resources, the Amish are the most progressive people in society. Not every situation can be adapted to a hydraulic ram, but where it can be used it is a most effective answer to running water with the free natural power of gravity. The technology is so simple it defies belief. Water in a pipe running downhill compresses air in a chamber, which in turn pushes the water to an uphill reservoir. A ram is capable of lifting water ten to twelve times or more the original height of the water source. Thus a spring feeding into a pipe that falls 2 feet can create enough air pressure to push some of the water on up to a reservoir or tank 24 feet high.

The secret is in giving the falling water an abrupt ramming action against the air in the air chamber. If the descending water (in the "drive" pipe) flowed only gradually down to the air chamber, it would not create the ramming action needed to compress the air. To achieve this action, there is at the base of the drive pipe what is called an impetus or clack valve, out of which the descending water first squirts until the force of the falling water builds momentum and snaps the valve closed, sending the water pulsating sharply up into the air chamber and compressing the air. The air then rebounds, the valve in the chamber inlet closes, and the water is forced out the other side into the delivery pipe. When the air pressure has spent itself, the impetus valve opens, more water from the drive pipe flows down and snaps the impetus valve

THE SIMPLICITY OF THE HYDRAULIC RAM

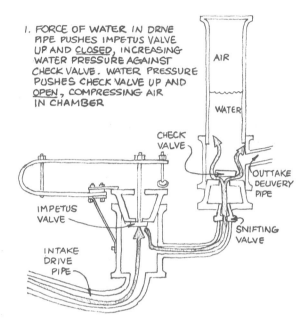

1. FORCE OF WATER IN DRIVE PIPE PUSHES IMPETUS VALVE UP AND <u>CLOSED</u>, INCREASING WATER PRESSURE AGAINST CHECK VALVE. WATER PRESSURE PUSHES CHECK VALVE UP AND <u>OPEN</u>, COMPRESSING AIR IN CHAMBER

AIR

WATER

CHECK VALVE

OUTTAKE DELIVERY PIPE

IMPETUS VALVE

SNIFTING VALVE

INTAKE DRIVE PIPE

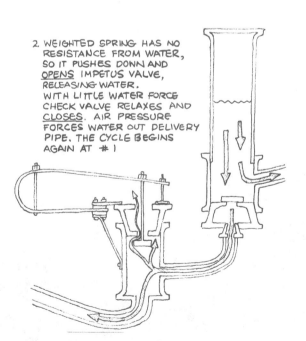

2. WEIGHTED SPRING HAS NO RESISTANCE FROM WATER, SO IT PUSHES DOWN AND <u>OPENS</u> IMPETUS VALVE, RELEASING WATER. WITH LITTLE WATER FORCE CHECK VALVE RELAXES AND <u>CLOSES</u>. AIR PRESSURE FORCES WATER OUT DELIVERY PIPE. THE CYCLE BEGINS AGAIN AT #1

closed and the process repeats itself, stroke after stroke. The key to success is that the outtake delivery pipe must be smaller than the intake drive pipe. The water in the drive pipe can force only a smaller part of itself up to a greater height. As long as the drive pipe is full of water, the ramming action will continue to repeat itself. A snifting or air valve beside the impetus valve allows a little new air to the chamber each time the impetus valve opens. Otherwise the air chamber would exhaust itself and eventually fill with water.

For success with a hydraulic ram, the following conditions must apply, according to early USDA bulletins:

1. There must be at least 2 feet of fall to the drive pipe and a flow of 1 gallon per minute from the water source.
2. The reservoir into which the water is pumped can't be more than ten to twelve times the height of the fall.

However, although these rules of thumb might be appropriate if you are going to try homemade versions of hydraulic rams, you can make do with 18 inches of fall. And with modern rams, you can lift the water considerably higher than the USDA recommendations. The *amount* of water available is more important to the amount and distance you can elevate, all else being equal, but the more fall you have the simpler your ram can be.

This is not the place to go into the complications of building a hydraulic ram. I don't know how and I believe earnestly that you should look at one in operation or one for sale before trying to build your own. *Producing Your Own Power* (Rodale Press, 1974) gives directions on building a ram, but it assumes the help of a professional machine shop anyway. Sources of hydraulic rams are: O'Brock Windmill Sales, Rt. 1, 12th St., North Benton, OH 44449; and Rife Hydraulic Engine Mfg. Co., Box 367, Millburn, NJ 07041.

PART II

HOME PRODUCTIVITY

CHAPTER 4

MAKING AND MAKING DO

Easy Things to Make from Sheepskins

A finished sheepskin makes the warmest of blankets or lap robes. A winter room a little too cool for comfort becomes toasty warm if you curl up in a soft chair and drape a sheepskin over you. Its insulative properties will amaze you. A sheepskin makes an attractive throw rug, comfortable to lie on in front of the fireplace. The wool won't wear out, although in time the hide might. A principal use for sheepskins is as bed pads. Long-distance truck drivers cover their truck seats with sheepskin—you know how uncomfortably sticky most auto fabrics are. Farmers often cure out a sheepskin and use it to cover a hard tractor seat. In this use, suppleness of the hide itself is not so necessary for rugs and seats, so a crude salt-tanning method works well enough.

A Simple Slipper

Sheepskin slippers are the most effective solution to cold floors you can find. And they are so comfortable that I wear mine in summer, too. In New Zealand, where sheep and wool are top commodities, the people long ago developed a way to make slippers fast and easy. What the slipper actually looks like is a sheepskin purse with an elastic top. You put your foot in the "purse," pull the elastic snug around your ankles, sew it together, and voilà! A slipper.

To make the purse the New Zealand way, first cut a piece of sheepskin large enough so that it extends about 2 inches in front of your toe and 2 inches behind your heel, and the two side edges, when folded together, extend about 2 inches above your ankle. Fold the piece together, then bend down 1½ inches of both top edges as if you were making a collar. Now sew up the front edge, being careful not to sew down the folded collar yet. Next, sew down the back (heel) edge halfway. Now push up the bottom half of the back to form a flat "heel"—an upside-down T with the seam above it—and sew it together. Next, sew down the edge of the collar on both sides and run an elastic string or ribbon through the tunnel you have created. Put

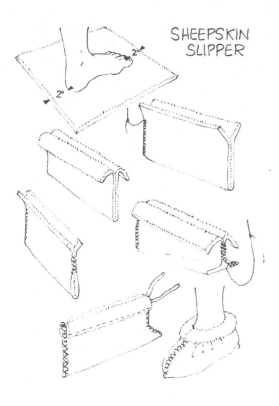

SHEEPSKIN SLIPPER

2"

2"

Improving Upon the Simple Slipper

Having made the crude New Zealand slipper, you will have proved one thing to yourself: Making footwear is not necessarily a craft beyond your ability. You can see that if you cut the front of the purse slipper more on a slant, instead of just sewing a straight-up seam, it would fit the front of the foot better. And that crude inverted-T heel seam can easily be improved on. Instead of just folding the seam to be sewn together, cut slits in the heel end so that the leather comes together neatly rather than folding over itself. There are two ways this is done, as the drawings here show you.

On to the Moccasin

The latter heel design approaches that of a regular moccasin. But look at the toe end of the slipper. Obviously, it is possible to flatten and streamline that part of the slipper still more by using two pieces of leather: a piece with a rounded toe end and a tongue piece above it, as in a moccasin or shoe. The two pieces can be laced together with nylon after punching holes along the edges of both. Then all you have to do is reshape the sides to a shoelike design and you are well on your way to becoming a cobbler.

Since the sheepskin will wear out (but not the wool), especially when subjected to the wear and tear of footwear, you will deduce that what your slipper needs now is a good leather sole. At shoe repair stores and even some shoe stores, you'll find a choice of leather and imitation leather soles for sale. Glue and stitch your slippers to the soles, and you have a crude but serviceable pair of moccasins.

You are now psychologically ready for a book like Christine Lewis Clark's *The Make-It-Yourself Shoe Book* (Knopf, New York, 1977). Making a neat fitted shoe, moccasin, or boot requires more practice, but essentially the skill involved is no greater than sewing a simple

your foot in the slipper, pull the elastic up snug, and sew it together. The purse will have roughly taken the shape of your foot and become a crude slipper.

Special flat needles for sewing leather are available from fabric shops. Most sewing machines can handle thin lambskins and some will sew thicker leathers. Many craft stores sell hand stitchers for leather, or you can ask your local shoe repairman where to find one. In working by hand, I suggest you get a leather punch or a leather awl and punch holes, then lace up the two pieces to be joined with nylon thread, using a blunt-end harness needle. In sewing sheepskin together, it is best to shear off the wool right at the seam to make the sewing easier.

garment, while the money your labor saves makes the work some of the most profitable of any home venture.

Mittens

By folding up a piece of sheepskin and sewing together the front and one side, you make a very comfortable pouch for a cold hand in the wintertime. Sew a loop at the open end to fit over the wrist and you have made what is called a hunter's mitt.

A regular mitten with a thumb piece is easily made from sheepskin, using the pattern on the next page.

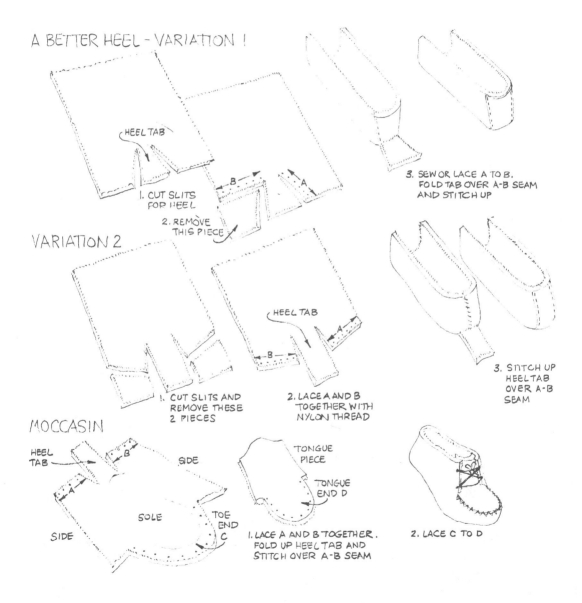

A BETTER HEEL - VARIATION 1

HEEL TAB

1. CUT SLITS FOR HEEL

2. REMOVE THIS PIECE

B   A

3. SEW OR LACE A TO B. FOLD TAB OVER A-B SEAM AND STITCH UP

VARIATION 2

HEEL TAB

1. CUT SLITS AND REMOVE THESE 2 PIECES

A   B

2. LACE A AND B TOGETHER WITH NYLON THREAD

3. STITCH UP HEEL TAB OVER A-B SEAM

MOCCASIN

HEEL TAB

B   A

SIDE

SOLE

SIDE

TOE END C

TONGUE PIECE

TONGUE END D

1. LACE A AND B TOGETHER. FOLD UP HEEL TAB AND STITCH OVER A-B SEAM

2. LACE C TO D

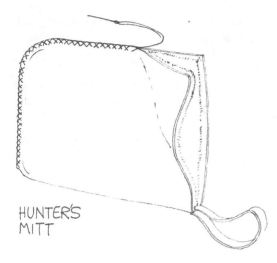

HUNTER'S
MITT

Start with a squarish piece of sheepskin that when folded over on itself is the right size to enclose your hand. Cut the sheepskin as shown by making two "arches," then make two cuts to form tab A that will wind up being the back of the thumb piece. Fold up tab A into proper thumb position. Cut thumb piece B out of another sheepskin scrap. Sew A to B but leave the dotted line open for the thumb. Sew the bottom of thumb piece B to the mitten, E to C and F to D. Now fold the mitten along the centerline, thumb out of course, and sew the outer seam. Your mitten is finished. To complete the pair, make a right-hand mitten by reversing the pattern.

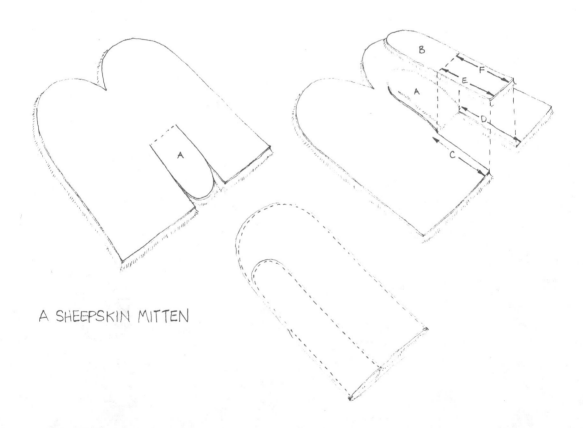

A SHEEPSKIN MITTEN

Dusters and Buffers

Strips of sheepskin left over from a bigger project make excellent shoe shining rags. And scraps tacked to the top of an old boom handle make a good cobweb sweep. No sheep*skin* is needed, but a generous tuft of long wool from a lanolin-rich fleece makes a perfect plant leaf duster. Wrap a few rounds of twine around one end to make a handle and a loop for hanging up.

Homemade Buttons

If you decide to make a vest or coat out of sheepskin (it's no more difficult than making a coat out of any other material once you've learned how to sew leather together as described here) you might want some unusual home-made buttons to sew on. Or you may want some buttons for other garments you are making. Wooden buttons are not hard to make, espe-

Sewing Leather on Your Sewing Machine

Although it may prove easier to hand-stitch heavy seams on boots, purses, or even coats with a glover's needle, you can sew most leathers on your sewing machine just about as easily as you can sew any other fabric. *But* you need a needle specially made for piercing leather. Such a needle has a wedge-shaped point, rather than a round one, so that it makes a clean cut in the leather. Ask for a leather-point needle—in sewing circles it is known as a 15 by 2 needle. For light leathers, use a size 11 needle; for medium-weight leathers, a size 14; and for heavyweight leathers, a size 16. Your own home-produced sheepskin, lamb-skin, or cowhide will usually require at least a size 14 and most likely a size 16.

You may need to adjust the pressure regulator on your sewing machine, too. With leather being thicker than other fabrics, the presser foot does not have to press down as hard. Loosen it a little so the leather slides through easily. Also, you may need to loosen the upper tension regulator. If the thread loops loosely on the bottom side of the seam, tighten tension; if it breaks or loops on the top side of the seam, loosen tension. A roller-type presser foot or a teflon-coated presser foot is recommended.

For thread, silk is the first choice because of its elasticity and tensile strength. But a subsilk or heavy-duty mercerized thread is adequate. (For hand stitching, the same recommendations apply, but on heavier leathers, run your thread through a cake of beeswax to make it slide through the leather more easily. For the heaviest hand-stitched seams, a waxed heavy linen thread is advisable.)

On your sewing machine run seven to ten stitches per inch as a rule of thumb. Lightest leathers can take as many as twelve stitches, the heaviest hardly more than seven or eight.

Lay your pattern on your sheepskin or cowhide, trace and cut it out as you would any other fabric. Follow instructions with the pattern as to the proper seam and seam allowance to make in each situation.

A book I have found very helpful for the true beginner is *How to Sew Leather, Suede and Fur* (Phyllis W. Schwebke and Margaret B. Krohn, Collier Books ed., Mac-Millan Publishing Co., New York, 1974). Don't let the out-of-date clothing styles put you off.

depth of well-finished wood. Once the button is shaped to approximate size, drill holes in it for the thread. Then finish sanding, so as to sand out any slight splinterings around the holes. You can, of course, carve little designs of whatever strikes your fancy on or into the buttons.

Handmade buttons can be made out of many natural objects, not just wood. For instance, acorn caps make very distinctive buttons. Just sand the point of the stem down smooth, drill in the button holes and spray with clear lacquer. Acorn cap buttons have to be removed before washing or dry-cleaning.

Walnut shell buttons are also very attractive, but they have to be removed before washing, too. Put the walnut in a vise, saw off desired thicknesses with a hacksaw, remove nutmeats if any, sand smooth, apply tung oil, and polish. The natural holes of the nut interior can be used to thread the needle through as you sew the button on.

Slices of horn or beef bone make pretty buttons. Cut with a hacksaw to desired thickness. If you are using a bone filched from the soup pot, clean and dry it first, of course. Drill holes, sand, and polish. If you have a power buffer, use it to polish the bone.

If you are a potter, you already know an infinite variety of buttons is possible from glazed and fired clay. If you know a potter, he or she might be glad to let you stick a handful of buttons into the kiln with a batch of pots, since the buttons don't take up much room. But it is quite possible, even for a beginner, to fire a few simple buttons in a hot open fire outdoors. Put the buttons in the center of the fire, pile on some wood, and see what happens after the fire burns out. In a kiln you can bisque-fire the green clay, then glaze and fire it again, or you can simply bisque-fire, then paint lightly with an acrylic color of your choice, and then spray clear acrylic finish on. This latter method would work better for crude, open-fire firing.

To form the button, make a ball of clay the desired size (only experimentation can deter-

cially larger, more expensive buttons. It's just that making them rarely occurs to us, and we are not aware how beautiful they can be when sanded and buffed to an ultrafine finish. Ordinary fine woods like walnut and cherry are more than adequate, but if you happen to have access to rare, exotic woods, you may be able to get small scraps very cheap, big enough for buttons. Teak, zebrawood, cocobolo, walnut burl, tiger maple, ebony, and other such woods are jewellike made up as buttons and bracelets— even as cuff links and earrings.

The easiest way (and for the very hard woods like ebony or lignum vitae, about the only practical way) is to form the button freehand on a power sander. Woods not so hard, like walnut, can be carved with a pocketknife and then sanded. The secret is to sand with finer and finer sandpapers so that the ultimate finish is so high it shimmers but still has the lustrous mine this, but about the size of a marble is usually right), press it out flat and round, and punch in holes with a needle. You can free-form any shape you desire and press into the soft clay any design—as from a woven fabric or a seashell or a glass pattern or a woodcut. After drying, the button is ready for firing.

Dyeing Wool: A Basic Method

The processes for dyeing any fabric are similar, so what you learn with one fabric is useful for others. Nevertheless, at home, wool, more than any other fabric, is the choice for dyeing. Animal fabrics take dyeing better. In the second place, wool is more universally available in all parts of the country and, all things considered, the easiest fabric to produce on your own place—by raising sheep. Most of all, wool is a fabric of highest quality, endurance,

warmth, and usefulness, and the easiest of all to spin into yarn.

Having said that, I must, however, add a caution. Dyeing is not the best way to use wool. To prepare wool for mordanting—the chemical treatment that makes the dye colors hold longer and brighter—you must wash out all the lanolin in the wool. As a result, some of wool's water-repellent properties are lost, and, because of the harshness of some mordant chemicals, perhaps a bit of the fabric's supersoftness. The *best* way to use wool, in my opinion, is in its natural colors: white, black, grey, brownish, and silver.

Mordanting wool can be done before, during, or after dyeing—or in some cases it is not necessary at all. But generally, when mordanting is required, it is done before dyeing, especially if alum is the mordant used. I think the beginner and the casual dyer should first experiment with dyes that don't need mordanting or use alum, the mildest of the mordants.

(continued on page 90)

Skeins of dyed wool drying in the sun.

Dyes from Right-Around-Home Plants

Nearly every plant material will yield some coloring for dye, but the favorites are those that give good bright colors, hold well, and produce unusual shades and hues. Most common dye plants produce "earthy" colors, quiet rather than garish. That is their charm—that and the fact that they hardly ever produce the same exact shade twice in a row. A natural vegetable dyed fabric is, essentially, one of a kind.

The following are common plants that you can expect to find in most American neighborhoods and that give good-to-exceptional coloring.

Violet, lilac, red-blue

Use fully ripened berries of the elderberry *(Sambucus canadensis)*. This tall bush with clusters of creamy white blossoms and then small black berries is familiar to everyone. Use the berries fresh or freeze them for year-round use. With alum as a mordant, the juice makes a violet color that holds fairly well. Even without a mordant, the red-blue dye persists, as anyone knows who has tried to wash the berry stains out of clothes.

Pokeberry or pokeweed *(Phytolacca decandra)* makes dull reds and purples with alum as a mordant. The color doesn't hold as well as elderberry. The seeds have a toxic substance in them, so be watchful if children are about. Birds eat the berries and the seeds pass harmlessly through them. I suppose the same could be true of humans, but caution is advised.

Chocolate brown, deep tan, tan

Black walnut hulls dye fairly well without a mordant. Fading eventually occurs, but the lighter brown that results is not at all unpleasant. We gather walnuts (for the nuts) when they fall from the trees in the autumn and scatter the nuts on the driveway where the car tires eventually squeeze off the hulls. The hulls turn black and make a deep brown dye. (You might like to know that fox and coon trappers use the walnut husk "dye" to de-scent their traps.) Butternut, a first cousin of black walnut, used to be commonly used for dyeing. In this case, the roots were used to make a warm brown color. Despite the official appellations of "blue and grey" in the Civil War, many Confederate troops wore uniforms dyed a butternut brown.

Red, cloudy red

Bedstraw *(Galium verum)* roots are dug in the fall and used fresh or dried. They make a dull red dye if used with alum. Bedstraw grows in a matted ground covering, the stems squarish and rough, slightly clinging to clothing. Branches grow from the main stem like spokes from a wheel. It begins to grow very early in spring, and patches of it are easy to spot by June, turning yellow and already dying.

Orange

Bloodroot *(Sanguinaria canadensis)* is a common white wildflower of early spring, growing in glades and open woodland. Break a stem and an orange liquid exudes. The roots are full of this liquid and are used to make the orange dye—a nice color that needs no mordant.

Onion skins produce a yellow-orange to burnt orange. My grandmother dyed Easter eggs with onion skins and got a deep mahogany none of us has been able to reproduce. The general theory around our house is that Grandmother's secret was using a rusty iron pot for simmering the dye and eggs.

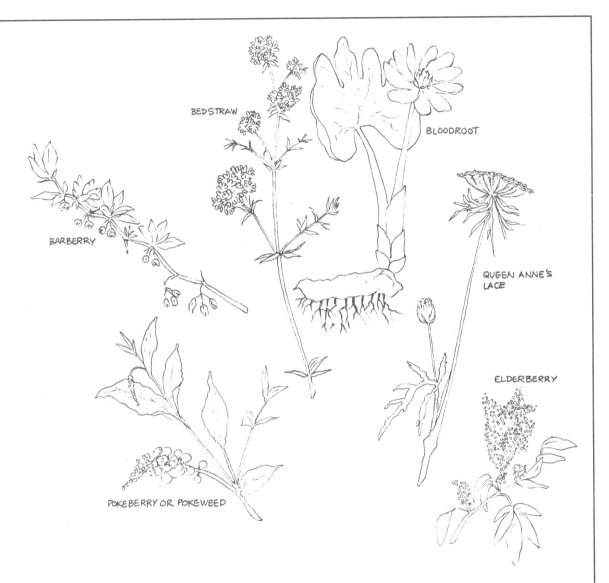

Unfortunately, in these modern times, no one has a rusty iron pot. They have either a nice, greased, seasoned pot or none at all.

Green

As common as the color green is in nature, one would think that a good green dye would be easy to come by. Not true. Hollyhock *(Alcea rosea)* leaves with alum as a mordant produce a pale green. Queen Anne's lace *(Daucus carota)*—flowers and stems—produces closest to a real green. Fresh lily of the valley *(Pyrola elliptica)* leaves give a so-so green.

(continued)

Dyes from Right-Around-Home
Plants—*Continued*

Yellow

This is the easiest dye color to find among native backyard plants. Zinnia blossoms with alum give a bright yellow that holds very well. The entire aboveground parts of goldenrod give a good yellow with alum, too. The inner bark of barberry *(Berberis vulgaris)* makes yellow without mordanting. Agrimony *(Agrimonia eupatoria)* is a common weed, blooming from July to September with small yellow flowers on a slender spikelike wand. Another telling sign of the plant is that on the main stem, large leaves are interspersed with smaller ones. With alum, the leaves and stems make a brassy yellow dye.

Tomato vines with alum make a pale greenish yellow—the same color the water gets when you wash your hands after picking tomatoes.

Surprisingly, a rather fuller range of colors can be derived from mushrooms than from ordinary plants, but most of the dye-rendering mushrooms are not common, or rather not commonly known. See the interesting book *How to Use Mushrooms for Color* (Miriam Rice and Dorothy Beebee, Mad River Press, Eureka, Calif., 1980).

Chrome and tin mordants are poisonous. All mordants should be treated with respect for safety. Alum is more readily available from builders' suppliers, if not pharmacies or chemical suppliers. Most of us live far from chemical supply houses anyway—another reason to favor nonmordanting dyes.

To prepare wool for mordanting, or for dyeing, you should wash it free of its lanolin (grease)—more so for mordanting dyes than for nonmordanting dyes. Wash wool gently with warm water (95°F.) and a gentle detergent. *Squeeze* out excess water. Never twist or wring wool. Rinse several times so that no soap remains. If mordanting is not going to take place immediately, hang the wool in the shade to dry.

To mordant wool with alum, use 4 ounces of alum for every pound of wool or 3 ounces if the wool is very fine and delicate like Rambouillet. Add to the alum 1 ounce of cream of tartar and 5 gallons of cold *soft* water; rainwater is best. Dissolve the alum and cream of tartar in a bit of boiling water, then stir in the cold water. Heat the water up slowly, adding the wool just as it begins to warm. The wool should be wet when put into the mordant. When the water comes to a boil, immediately lower the temperature and let the "stew" simmer for an hour. Let stand and then cool overnight. Next morning, rinse the wool and proceed with dyeing, or if dyeing is to be delayed, hang the wool out of the sun to dry slowly.

Preparing dyes is not at all an exact science. Plant materials even of the same species vary in their dyeing capabilities, depending on soil, season, and strain of species. It takes longer to draw dye out of roots than flowers. But the general idea is to extract a dye from a material by cooking it—and in all cases using soft water. Tough material, like roots, is presoaked overnight before cooking and often chopped up. Most directions call for soaking in about 2 gallons of water. Then strain out the dye material and put it in 2 fresh gallons of water—but save the old water, which you'll add later. Bring the new water and dye material to a boil slowly, then let simmer for an hour or more, as experience dictates. Softer materials from which dyes can be extracted more easily, such as leaves, blossoms, and berries, do not need presoaking. Put the material into 4 gallons of water (4 gallons is a favorite quantity for a dye bath). The actual amount of dye material to use per 4 gallons is not exact. Betty E. M. Jacobs, in her *Growing Herbs and Plants for Dyeing* (Select Books, Mountain View, Mo., 1982), says as sort of a general guideline that a pound of wool in 4½ to 5 gallons of water will require in dyeing material about a peck of flowers or a peck of leaves or a peck of stems chopped and crushed or a pound of berries or half a pound of roots or a pound and a half of bark.

Simmering time for frail blossoms may be only 15 minutes, for leaves 30 minutes, for berries 45 minutes. The tougher bark and root material, which you soak overnight, may need to simmer for 2 hours. In all cases, at the end of the simmering period, strain out the plant material, add the soaking water you've reserved, and let the water cool.

When the water is cool, wet the wool to be dyed, squeeze out excess water, put it into the 4 gallons of dye water, and slowly raise the temperature of the water. It should take nearly an hour to reach simmering temperature. Once simmering begins, the wool may absorb dyes from some materials in less than 20 minutes, but it can take over an hour to absorb dyes from other tougher materials. Stir and lift out the wool with a wood paddle to inspect it occasionally. You can add water to the original 4 gallons if too much steams away. When you have achieved the color you want, or as close to it as you are going to get, allow the water to cool with the wool in it until you can handle it with your hands. Then rinse in warm water, squeeze gently, roll in a towel for further drying, and hang in the shade to dry completely.

Making a Broom

As I have said previously about other projects (and will say many times before the last page of this book), my techniques are not represented here as the only way, or best way, to do the job. My hope here is not to make a champion broom maker or shoemaker or welder out of you, but just to acquaint you with enough information about the many facets of the complete home life so that you can orchestrate success and satisfaction from your life-style and become the Compleat Independent Homesteader, so to speak. The skill is in the orchestration, not so much in the individual playing parts.

One year I wanted to make brooms for Christmas presents. Since then, I've wanted to make a broom when one was needed, not to make a business or creative art out of broom making. The first one I made fell apart. But later ones swept out fireplaces well enough, and I could make one that would sweep a floor well enough should I need to. Heaven knows I can buy a better broom that costs less than the time it takes to make one. But a broom is something I *can* make for myself, and I have proved it by doing so.

First you have to grow the broomcorn. That's the easiest part. I got seed from Shumway Seeds, Rockford, Illinois, years ago and have saved my own seed from subsequent plantings ever since. Grow broomcorn just like any corn. Instead of having a tassel, the broomcorn stalk has a "brush," twenty of which (more or less) make a broom. The brush is actually a seed head, and you have to comb the seeds out of the fibers. This is really the hardest part of the job. A dog or horse comb works. A currycomb sort of works. Cut the brushes off first, each with about 6 inches of stalk. Cut them when still green, before they flop over out of shape too badly. Lay them in the sun to dry, turning them after a few days. If left in a pile, the brushes will mold quickly and easily. (You can leave more stalk on than 6 inches and braid the stalks together to make a handle for a short broom, instead of a stick handle, but this requires more skill.) With about twenty-five broomcorn tops or brushes ready, I next cut an ash sprout, shave the bark off smooth, and taper the end somewhat. I drive a small nail through the stick near the broom end, so that it sticks out about

diately wrapping the string around them several times. I've learned to cut one side of the stalk flat so it would fit more snugly against the stick. Then I select another ten or so brushes, longer than the first set, and bunch them around the stick a little higher up than the first bunch, lapping the stalks over the first set at the top. Then I continue to wrap the string around them, tying it as tightly as possible. Sometimes I've added a third bunch of brushes to make an extra fat broom. If so, I tie another string to one of the upper nails to wrap around the stalks temporarily.

With the broom all together, I soak the stalks in boiling water (or you can pour boiling water over them). This softens the stalks so they will bind tightly.

¼ inch on both sides. Up farther on the stick, where the stalks will extend to, I drive another nail through the same way but in the opposite direction. Then halfway between the two nails, I drive another nail through, in yet a different direction from the top and bottom one. Other than the bottom one, I'm not sure how necessary these nails are. I tie a string to the bottom one, to wrap around the stalks and hold them in place temporarily until I can put on the permanent binding. The other nails sort of hold the stalks in place and keep them from twisting when I tighten the binding.

With the string tied to the lowest nail, I select about ten brushes—the shortest ones—and bunch them evenly around the stick, imme-

To bind the stalks to the stick, hang a piece of nylon rope or strong twine to a solid hook or beam in the ceiling, or from a tree limb. Make a loop of the end that hangs down big enough to put your foot into. The loop should hang about 8 inches off the ground. Now, hold the broom horizontally in one hand, loop the hanging rope around the stalks *once* where you want to make your first binding—just up from the broom strands. Step your foot into the rope loop and push the loop toward the ground. The twist of rope will tighten around the broom stalks and actually help hold the broom, too, so that you can keep it more or less horizontal at waist height by clamping it between your elbow and body, leaving both hands free to wrap a strong piece of twine around the stalks right next to the tightening rope and tie it tightly. Release your foot pressure, move the rope another 4 inches or so up the broom handle, tighten the rope again, and tie around another piece of twine.

Two bindings are usually sufficient, though a third binding at the top of the stalks is best. The trick is to tighten the rope just as firmly as you can without twisting the stalks askew. When

the stalks dry, they harden and set in the bindings and seldom come loose. I switched from twine to wire on my third broom, which makes an even tighter binding because you can twist the wire very tightly with pliers. I like to use copper or brass wire because it twists easily and looks pretty, but these kinds of wire are comparatively expensive.

Wooden Combs

My son has been making wooden combs in his workshop. They are strikingly beautiful, and they do comb hair. They also make excellent letter or note holders on a desk. Much of the beauty comes from the wood itself. Since only scraps are needed to make the combs, one can use black walnut, rosewood, zebrawood, and other exotic woods without denting the pocketbook. Or one can use unusual woods generally available only in small widths or pieces, like pear, peach, and sassafras. The block of wood needed for a comb rarely exceeds 4 to 6 inches wide, 5 to 6 inches long, and ⅜ inch thick (never more than ½ inch thick).

The teeth must run in the same direction as the grain or they will quickly break off, but other than that, the design is up to you. Cut the teeth in the block first, then taper the block and teeth to the proper shape. You can cut the teeth with a table saw, handsaw, or band saw. The table saw makes it easier to cut straight and uniform teeth, since you can use the saw fence as a guide. But the saw kerf should be no wider than ⅛ inch and preferably smaller. Most table saw blades leave a kerf a bit large for a comb. My son uses a band saw because the blade makes a smaller kerf. But some skill is involved in making a band saw cut a perfectly straight line. A wavy cut shows up clearly in a comb.

At any rate, the comb's teeth should be ⅛ inch thick and the spaces between the teeth not more than that if the comb is to work well.

Pencil the saw lines in first. Or with a table saw, move the fence ⅛ inch over for each cut. Make the first cut ½ inch from the edge and proceed across the block to within ½ inch of the other edge. If you use a table saw, you will have to turn the block over and run the kerfs through the saw again to even up the end of the cut, since the circular blade cuts about ¼ inch more on the underside than the top side.

How far up toward the handle you cut the teeth is not critical. Teeth should be long enough to comb through the thickest hair, but the cuts should not proceed too far into the handle or they will weaken it or make it look out of proportion. Usually teeth are cut in various lengths, following the contour or curve of the handle (see the drawing), but they are seldom longer than half the length of the entire comb. This is, however, an arbitrary design feature.

With the teeth roughly cut out, shape the comb to a proper taper, from about ⅜ inch at the top of the handle to a point at the end of the teeth—but not too thin or sharp a point just yet. Sawing the taper is difficult, though a combination of sawing, whittling, and hard sanding will do the trick. A motor-driven belt sander makes the tapering easy work. Lay the comb on one flat side on the sanding belt and tip the handle slightly up as you push down. Keep checking the progress of the sanding. When one side is finished, turn the comb over and taper down the other side, ending up with a balanced taper on each side. Now sand in the bottom outside corner on both sides, to make those wide ½-inch outer teeth tapered inward and pointed (see the drawing).

Next comes the fine work of sanding the teeth smooth and semiround, with the ends coming to a rounded point. Put the comb in a vise, teeth up. (Clamp it between two other pieces of wood so you don't mar the comb with the vise jaws.) Using strips of sandpaper, work them between the teeth just as you do when flossing your own teeth. Don't sand too much or you will make the gaps too wide. At the very tip of the teeth, sand in to a firm but well-rounded point.

Sanding can be done on some belt sanders that allow you to slide the sanding belt out over the edge a couple of inches and operate the

sander that way. With the belt sticking out, you can slip the comb teeth in from the edge and, by tipping the comb ever so little one way and then the other, get the teeth nice and smooth. It takes a steady hand. And it is very easy to sand away too much wood, so be careful until you catch on to it. Upright sander-grinders with their narrow, vertical belts also work well for sanding comb teeth.

You can finish the wood any way you want, but beware of thick varnishes that might clot in the small spaces between teeth. Several rubbings of linseed oil is the best finish, in my opinion. If the comb is used regularly, it needs no finish at all; the oil from the user's hand and hair will add to the luster of the comb with the passing years.

An Old-Fashioned Whisk

Wooden whisks were used in Appalachia in former years (and still are used in Sweden) to stir soups and drinks, whip egg whites, even beat eggs, and break up curd during cheese making. Drew Langsner, well-known craftsman and homesteader, still makes wooden whisks and so can you. In addition to traditional uses, we find that small ones make excellent swizzle sticks.

Find a small tree in the woods that is going to be crowded out of its growing place and will die anyway. Any sapling that has limbs radiating off from the central trunk like spokes from a wagon wheel at set intervals up the trunk will make whisks—small whisks toward the top of the trunk, larger ones at the bottom. With a saw, cut the tree right below the set of branches you want to use for your whisk, then make a second cut right below the next set of branches above. The section of trunk above the radiating branches becomes the handle of the whisk. If you need only a small whisk, you need cut only the set of branches just down from the top of a sapling, and the tree will ordinarily grow a

WOODEN COMB

CAN BE INLAID OR EMBOSSED

CUT HANDLE TO ANY SHAPE DESIRED

⅜"

SAND OR CUT OFF BOTH SIDES

FRONT VIEW

NOT MORE THAN ⅛" SPACE

TAPER SIDE VIEW

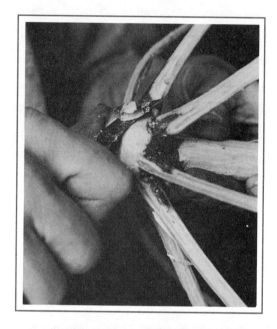

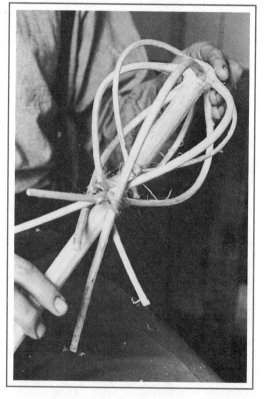

new top. The kind of tree that is almost always used is a white pine, which grows ideally for whisk making.

With pruning shears, cut the branches back to just a little longer than the "handle." Then with a pocketknife, scrape off all the bark and any resin that collects, especially right under the whorl of branches. Next, tie the branches while still green and supple up against the handle. Then let the whisk dry and set. In about two weeks, untie the branches from the handle and cut them back to the desired length. For a swizzle stick, this would mean cutting them back so they fit into a glass. For an eggbeater, you'd cut only a little off, so that the branches curve up gracefully half the length

of the handle, sort of like the blades of a metal eggbeater. Langsner says that by holding the handle of such a whisk between one's palms and rubbing briskly back and forth, the whisk will whirl rapidly enough to beat egg whites.

Stouter whisks, made from the lower whorls of branches on a pine sapling, make good hangers—for everything from pots to hats. Put a hole in the top of the handle from which to hang the whisk, and your hanger is ready for use.

Making Wooden Kitchen Spoons and Similar Utensils

There are only two little secrets to making spoons, ladles, and forks out of wood. The first is that you don't carve the spoon from a block of wood; rather, *you find a branch with a spoon in it.*

Nothing mysterious about that advice. A proper spoon or ladle must have a curve in the handle to be designed for easy use—those straight-handled wooden spoons you can buy cheap are almost unusable except to stir with. You might be able to steam bend a straight piece of wood to the proper curve, but that would be hard work. What you dare not do is cut the curve into a piece of wood *across* the grain. Such a spoon easily breaks. Therefore, when he is cutting firewood or when he is in the woods, a spoon maker keeps a sharp eye out for branches that have a natural curve in them to make the curved handle. It becomes, in fact, great sport to find the spoons in the wood.

Then there's the second secret. Having

WOODEN SPOONS "HIDDEN" IN TREES

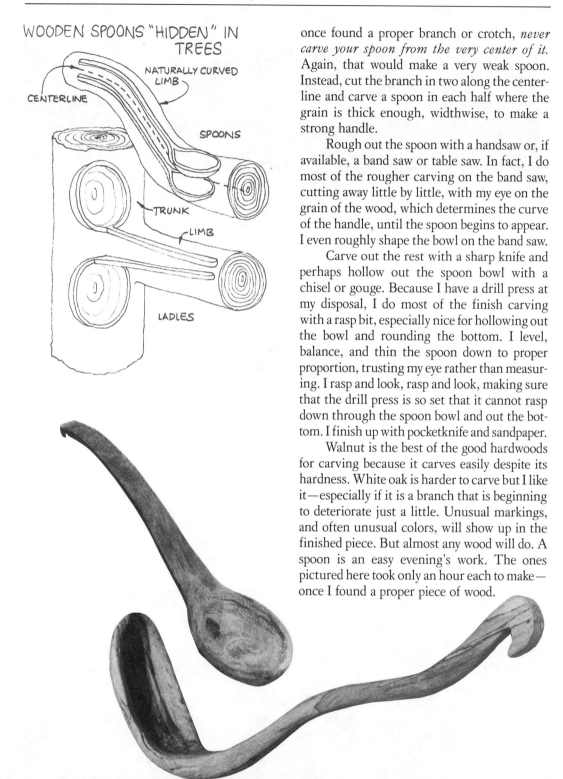

once found a proper branch or crotch, *never carve your spoon from the very center of it.* Again, that would make a very weak spoon. Instead, cut the branch in two along the center-line and carve a spoon in each half where the grain is thick enough, widthwise, to make a strong handle.

Rough out the spoon with a handsaw or, if available, a band saw or table saw. In fact, I do most of the rougher carving on the band saw, cutting away little by little, with my eye on the grain of the wood, which determines the curve of the handle, until the spoon begins to appear. I even roughly shape the bowl on the band saw.

Carve out the rest with a sharp knife and perhaps hollow out the spoon bowl with a chisel or gouge. Because I have a drill press at my disposal, I do most of the finish carving with a rasp bit, especially nice for hollowing out the bowl and rounding the bottom. I level, balance, and thin the spoon down to proper proportion, trusting my eye rather than measuring. I rasp and look, rasp and look, making sure that the drill press is so set that it cannot rasp down through the spoon bowl and out the bottom. I finish up with pocketknife and sandpaper.

Walnut is the best of the good hardwoods for carving because it carves easily despite its hardness. White oak is harder to carve but I like it—especially if it is a branch that is beginning to deteriorate just a little. Unusual markings, and often unusual colors, will show up in the finished piece. But almost any wood will do. A spoon is an easy evening's work. The ones pictured here took only an hour each to make—once I found a proper piece of wood.

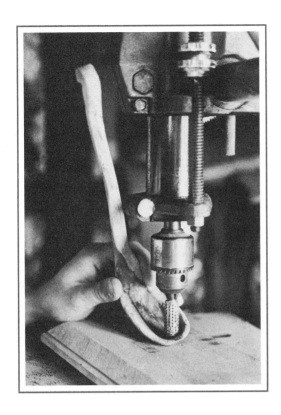

A Simple but Decorative Woodbox

It goes without saying that a wood-heated house needs a woodbox. But even in a house without wood heat, a woodbox makes very handy storage space—an excellent children's toy box, for example, or a place to put all those old magazines until you can get them to the recycling center.

A friend built ours in his carpentry shop for a Christmas present. It is made of rough cedar siding simply nailed together. Without any finish at all, the box has an antique look to it that fits in well with any interior. Only a minimal amount of sawing was necessary, holes needed drilling only for the bolts that hold the hinges and handle, and, best of all, very little sanding was necessary.

To build one like it, you need about 34 running feet of 1 by 12-inch cedar siding (that allows for a few inches of wastage—the dimensions can be changed to suit your own situation so long as an overall pleasing proportion is maintained), two strap hinges of a design that you like, and a handle to lift the lid with. Remember that a 12-inch width on a commercial board actually measures only 11¼ inches.

Back, front, and bottom boards all fit inside the side boards and so are nailed together. The top boards lap the sides ¾ inch at both ends. To make the box extra sturdy, two pieces of scrap lumber are positioned horizontally inside the box on both sides just below the lid, and the sides are nailed to them. A 1¼ by 22½-inch cleat can also be added to the bottom of each side board for extra support and to lift the box off the floor. The only least bit tricky saw cut is beveling the top edge of the top front board to 125 degrees to accept the lid flat against it.

Spinning and Weaving

Sometimes on a lonely country road one can drive into another century, a seeming dream world that won't go away no matter how many

WOODBOX

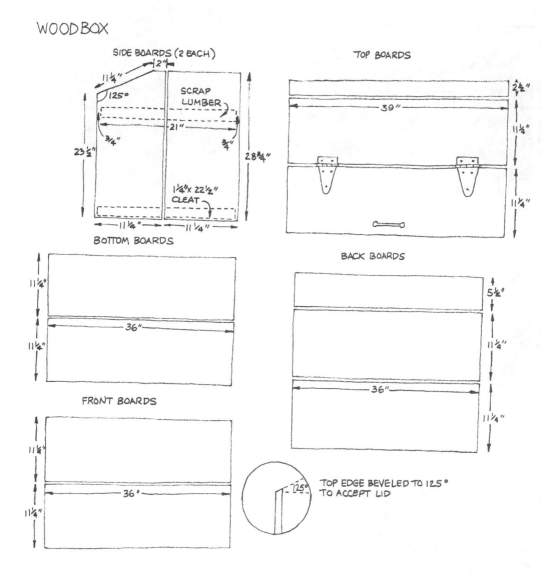

times you pinch yourself. Along such a road just east of the village of West Liberty, Ohio, past a sign that says Smuckers Arts, you will come to a building that looks as if it might once have been a chicken coop. There are indeed hens clucking in the dooryard. But from inside the building comes a sound steadily through the quiet warm spring morning—a sound stranger yet to the modern ear. *Chee-whack!*

Chee-whack! Chee-whack! It is the sound of the beater on a hand loom, as Isabel Smucker, at each pass of the shuttle through the warp threads, smacks the weft threads down tightly in place. She and her sister Christine, working nearby, are dressed in clothes not found in the avant-garde catalogs of 1985. They are clothes that, although new, come, like the sisters' lifestyle, from another time. And so does the honest-to-God castle that is, believe it or not, next to the little shop! Is it a dream?

The castle was built 100 years ago and is now just a stop on the tourist trail, but what the Smuckers are doing in its shadow is *living* tradition. They not only make the clothes they wear, sometimes completely from scratch— spinning, dyeing, weaving, and sewing the fabrics— but they also sell their startling creations to a growing clientele. Christine and Isabel are sharp businesswomen. Their romance with the past is grounded in everday practicality. The sound of their dooryard hens, the chee-whack of their looms, the quiet purr of their spinning wheels—these sounds were so common 100 years ago that they passed unnoticed. And the Smuckers see no reason why that could not be so again.

There must be more than 100 books in print on spinning, weaving, and the attendant skills of carding, sewing, dyeing, and knitting. What you learn from the books first is an impression that these skills are difficult to acquire. The typical response is to nod and exclaim out loud, "Oh my! How wonderful," while inside a little voice says, "but not for me." But before you read the books, before you take the detailed lessons, you should visit the Smuckers of this country so you can get a first-hand feel for these skills, and you'll soon see they are not so hard to learn. There are people similar to the Smuckers in every community, spinning and weaving fabrics of quality few can afford to buy, even if they can find them in stores.

Spinning and weaving can be slave labor, done, as they once were in factories, 12 to 14 hours a day—especially grueling when the profits went to someone else. But as a cottage industry, "the handwork involved can actually be therapeutic," says Isabel, weaving a linen hand towel with amazing speed. "You can listen to music, talk to visitors as I am doing to you, even watch television I suppose, although I don't. Spinning is especially restful, and that's the reason it is popular with so many people today."

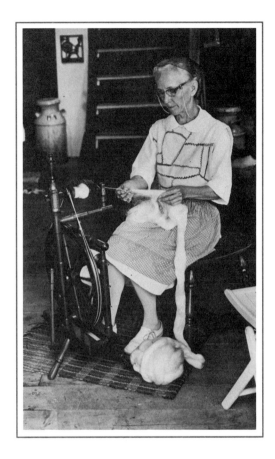

"The work is more of a joy to us," says Christine with a little smile. "It's the marketing that's the hassle. Making your *own* clothes requires simply a commitment to do so. There's nothing difficult or impractical about it. Just as the gardener commits time to his or her gardening, so the spinner and weaver commit time to fabric making. But even though now there is a much greater consumer interest in quality and handmade fabrics, making a business out of traditional home economies is still tough."

Tough, but possible. If you get good enough, business comes from the least expected sources. As a sideline, the Smuckers have produced on commission large tapestry wall hangings for churches and institutions.

Ralph Aling, way across the state of Ohio from the Smuckers, labored for years at the loom rather precariously, as far as profits were concerned. Then came an invitation from the Smithsonian to display his skills at a show there, and his handwoven rugs have sold well ever since.

But sheep raiser, spinner, and weaver Mary Stock says that spinning and weaving make sense as home industry even where one has neither the time, skill, nor inclination to make a business out of it. "Good, pure wool clothing won't wear out. You can hardly find it in a store. You can make at least one thing a year during the evening when you're relaxing."

Spinners and weavers are organizing in almost every community, as what seemed like a

fad a few years ago has grown and cemented into a movement. Within a few weeks of associating with such a group, you can have access to all the how-to information you need—in fact a great deal more than you need. As a start, subscribe to a magazine or two in the field of spinning and weaving. *Handwoven* is a good one. But first visit the spinners and weavers in your area. The first thing to learn is that everyone can master these skills. Just as everyone *did* 100 years ago. And the equipment is better today.

Making Soap

Not too much to my surprise, I figured out recently that our family (of four) spends about $150 on various soap products annually. Discussing this figure with my wife or daughter always turns into an argument about the definition of proper cleanliness, an argument I always lose. I doubt all that soap is necessary except to finance television shows. So I have spent some time investigating the possibilities of making soap at home—a routine chore years ago that a few independent souls still practice. As it turns out, making soap is not difficult, but even if you're spending $150 or more on the stuff, the homemade kind makes sense only if you do your own butchering or have it done where you can recover all the fat, or if you buy your meat as a hanging carcass with all the fat still on it. If, in addition, you heat with wood, then soap making is more or less a free by-product of these two practices. When you render hog fat into lard or beef fat into tallow, you are clarifying the fat, the first step in soap making. And the heat under the lard kettle (see Treasures in Wood in Chapter 11) is produced by those crotch pieces of wood you can't split and use in the stove. The wood ashes are the source of lye.

Soap is basically nothing but animal fat, water, and lye. Lye (potash, to be exact) can be made by pouring rainwater through wood ashes. Purchased lye, however, is relatively cheap, so don't let the fact that you may not be able to

make your own lye stop you. It's also called caustic soda and is usually found among the cleaning supplies in stores.

Good soap's secret is pure, nonrancid fat, properly clarified. (There are ways to make rancid fat usable but start out with the best foot forward.) A half-and-half mixture of hog lard and beef or mutton tallow makes the best soap, although small amounts of poultry fats and others can be used in the mixture. If you want to turn the waste cooking fats that accumulate in your kitchen into pure fats, further clarification is necessary. Remelt them and strain the liquid through two thicknesses of cheesecloth. Add an equal volume of hot water, stir, and bring to a boil. Remove from burner, and while still stirring, add 1 quart of cold water. As the mixture cools, the purest fat will rise to the top of the water and firm up. Scoop this off to use for soap.

Because soap making was always a farm activity, the USDA has excellent bulletins on how to do it, available through your local extension office. Lye makers often put soap-making formulas on their containers, or such formulas are available if you write to the companies. While there are endless variations in the kinds of soap you can make (and dyes and scents you can add), the basic soap-making process is fairly standard. The most common formula is based on the standard container of lye (13 ounces), 6 pounds of the clean fat, and 2½ pints of soft water. This makes 9 pounds of soap. Or if you want to experiment by making just one bar, you need 1 cup of clean fat, 5 teaspoons of lye, and ½ cup of soft water. You can add borax to make the soap sudsier (especially if you're in a hard water area). One-fourth cup of borax is added to the 9-pound formulation or 1 teaspoon for the one-bar formulation.

Since lye and fat have to be mixed together at rather precise temperatures, get the lye ready first. Dissolve the lye in the water in a glass or enamelware container. Never use aluminum because lye corrodes it rapidly. When you pour the lye into the water, the temperature will

General Household Soap

The ammonia in this recipe gives this soap a little extra cleaning action.

  3 pints cold water
  ¾ cup borax
  ¾ cup ammonia
  1 can lye (13 ounces)
  4½ pounds clean, strained fat (hog lard or beef tallow or a mixture of both)

Before you begin, read over the general soap-making directions in the main text, keeping in mind the safety precautions and proper equipment you'll need.

Put the water in a crock or other heavy-duty container that caustic lye won't harm. (If you're using tea to scent your soap, reduce the water by 1 to 2 cups—see below.) Add the borax and ammonia and stir until well dissolved. Then add the lye, being careful to keep your face away from the lye mixture to avoid inhaling the fumes that result from the reaction of the lye on the water mixture.

When the lye water has cooled to about 85°F., add the fat slowly and stir slowly and constantly until the soap is thick and smooth. Figure on anywhere from 10 to 30 minutes of stirring, and sometimes even longer.

At this point you should add any scents or dyes you plan to use—about 1 teaspoon of scent oil to every 1 to 2 cups of liquid soap. If you are using a strong herbal tea to scent your soap, use a cup or two for each batch of soap and add it at this time.

Then pour and stir the mixture into well-greased containers or into specially designed soap molds. Let the soap cool for a few hours, then cut into bars if you wish. The soap will be caustic for about three weeks, so you must allow it to cure for that long before you remove it from its mold and use it.

Lye from a Barrel

To make homemade lye, put a layer of gravel into a wooden barrel that has a hole in the bottom, then put a layer of straw over that, and then fill the barrel with fresh unleached wood ashes. Set a container (not aluminum) under the hole in the bottom of the barrel. The barrel should be tilted a bit so all the liquid collects at the exit hole. Pour rainwater over the ashes and straw-gravel filter. The process works much better if the water is boiled first. You have to experiment. It may take two days before the first bucketful seeps through, and while that bucketful will be strong enough, subsequent bucketfuls may need to be run back through the ashes again. The amount of water needed to charge the ashes at any one time depends on the size of the barrel or tub. Three gallons is about right (a standard bucketful) for a 55-gallon barrel. But charge with more water until the lye that comes out is too weak. Potash lye water has the right strength, say the old-timers, when a raw egg yolk will just barely float on its surface. Lye from wood ashes generally makes a softer soap than commercial lye makes (which is sodium hydroxide). But be aware that any lye is toxic—it will burn the skin if you splash some on you, and it can be fatal if swallowed.

shoot up due to chemical reaction. It will also give off harsh fumes. Work in a well-ventilated area and wear gloves, long sleeves, and long pants. For extra precaution wear safety goggles as well. Keep your head as far away from the container as possible and stir with a long-handled spoon or a stick. Let the mixture cool down to lukewarm—about 85°F.—before mixing with the fat.

Assuming that your lye water is ready, melt down your 6 pounds of clarified fat and then let it cool to about 110°F. Add borax now, if desired. Keep stirring the fat during the cooling period so crystals don't form. Next, pour in the lye water *slowly* while stirring *slowly.* If you speed up these steps, the fat may separate from the lye instead of combining with it. In about 15 minutes, the mixture should have the density of honey. If it doesn't in half an hour, the mixture may be too warm. (Combining fat at 110°F. with lyewater at 85°F. should result in a mixture with a temperature of about normal human body heat.) If the mixture is too lumpy, it is probably too cool. In the first case, set the container in cool water, in the second, in warm water. Keep a candy thermometer in the mixture to monitor temperature.

When the mixture is the density of honey, you can add scents and dyes now if you want. Adding salt to the soap mixture just before

pouring it into the mold will make it harden better. Don't add salt sooner, as that can make the mixture of fat and lye separate out, necessitating reboiling. Then it can be poured into molds. Cardboard or wood molds are fine. Whatever you use, the molds should be lined with wax paper or plastic wrap, or a wet, wrung-out cotton cloth, or petroleum jelly, to keep the soap from sticking. Cover the filled molds with a blanket or other insulating material so the soap stays warm for about 24 hours. During this time a chemical reaction is taking place that turns the lye, water, and fat into soap and glycerin, after which it can be removed from the molds and cut into bars. But let the soap age in a dry place for at least two weeks before using; until it has aged it is still caustic.

That's all there is to it, folks. A good way to cut soap is with a very thin piano wire or guitar string, cutting through with a sawing motion. If you cross the wire around the soap, the wire helps hold the soap cake while it is cutting through.

Soap making makes more sense, I suppose, as a fascinating hobby than as a practical homestead skill. If it appeals to you, get a good book, like Dorothy Richter's *Make Your Own Soap! Plain and Fancy* (Doubleday, New York, 1974). Not only are there many soaps you can make at home, using near-at-hand scents and dyes, but in the molding there is potential for artistic talent—and a beginning of a profitable cottage industry for you.

Making a Beeswax Candle

Candlemaking is one of the easiest skills to master and requires no expensive tools. Most candles are made of paraffin, but if you are going to go to the trouble of making your own candles, it is a pity not to use beeswax or bayberry, if at all possible. Beeswax requires no hardener to be added as in the case of paraffin, and it smells better. If you keep bees or know a beekeeper, you have a source of wax.

Growing Your Own Bayberries

Several shrubs or small trees of the *Myrica* family produce grey waxy berries, which have been used traditionally for making candles. The common bayberry grows mostly along the East Coast *(M. pensylvanica)* hardly ever more than 8 feet tall and usually shorter. A taller plant, the western bayberry *(M. californica)*, grows on the West Coast. The wax myrtle *(M. cerifera)* is native to the Southeast westward to Texas.

In addition to its value for wax, the bayberry is a good ornamental for poor, acid soil, to which it is adapted. In the garden or yard, grow it where azaleas and blueberries and other acid-loving plants do well. Soil pH for the bayberry should be 4.5 to 5.5, ideally. Less acid soil—beyond 6.0 pH—is not recommended for bayberry. The leaves last well into December, and the berries are very attractive to birds. Mulch with peat or oak leaves to increase acidity.

Traditionally, housewives made waxing pads for ironing by simply sewing up a handful or two of berries in a cloth bag. For candles, the wax was melted out of the berries by boiling in water, then kept liquid on a back burner of the stove. Every time the cook passed the stove, he or she would dip wicks hanging from an nearby dish towel rack into the wax, and so by the end of the day, the candles were made without too much fuss or extra work.

Bayberry is more difficult to come by. The wild bayberry, which gives the true scent, is protected by law in some eastern states where it grows. But nothing stops you from growing your own, if your soil is properly acid, and using the grey berries to make wax. You don't need to make a 100% bayberry candle. Just boil down a few berries to melt the thick wax coating. Then skim off the green scum that forms on top of the water and reboil what's left to a thicker wax to mix with paraffin or beeswax.

We save all the old wax when I replace combs in the beehives or from sections of chunk honey, and when the mood hits, hand dip a candle or two. Even if they aren't used for lighting, a beeswax candle is just the thing cobblers use for waterproofing thread for shoe repair or other uses. The method for making a beeswax candle is the same as for paraffin. We don't mix our wax with a hardener, and although I've not seen our candles drooping, some people like to mix in a little hardener with the wax anyway. I understand that about ½ ounce of stearic acid will do for each pound of wax. The wax is melted down in a container that stands in another container of water. Never try to melt down the wax directly over the stove burner. Wax is flammable or it wouldn't make a candle, right? If it starts to burn, smother it with a lid or baking soda.

Beeswax melts at 145°F. You can do it on the stove as described above, straining the melted wax through cheesecloth if it contains any impurities, or you can melt it in a solar heat collector. Beekeepers often build such a collector, a big insulated box with a glass front that tilts 40 degrees from horizontal and is positioned due south to catch the sun's rays in summer. Temperatures inside such a box can reach as high as 190°F. Old combs are rapidly melted down into metal pans in this arrangement. If cheesecloth is wrapped around the comb, dirt and other impurities are strained out as the wax melts.

For candle dipping, the wax must be kept molten, of course. You need a second container of cool water nearby, to cool the candle between dippings. Tie a weight to the bottom of the wick you are dipping so it goes down into the wax easily. A little steel washer works fine. After the first or second dip, pull the wick taut to straighten it. Each dip adds another layer to the candle, and so it grows fatter with each plunge into the wax. Lower the wick alternately into the cool water. To speed up the drying, wipe off excess

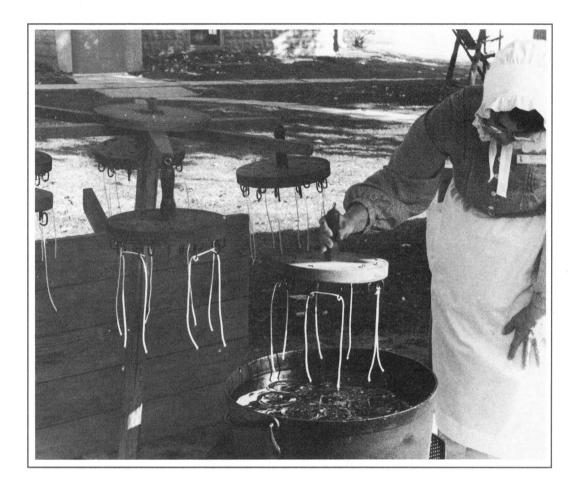

water with a paper towel. If the candle threatens to get crooked, roll it on a piece of wax paper on a level table surface to keep it straight. About thirty dips and the candle is finished, more or less, depending on what thickness you want to achieve.

The wax left over from dipping can be used for molded candles. Almost any container makes a mold—cardboard, tin—anything that results in an interesting shape. The mold ought to be smooth with no dents or nicks inside and, of course, not wider at the bottom than the top or the candle won't come out. Coat the inside

of the mold with cooking oil or silicone spray so the candle won't stick. If the candle does stick, heating the mold (if it is metal or glass or some other noncombustible material) will cause the candle surface to melt a bit and it will slide out. For cardboard molds, the heat of the wax should be just barely above the melting point. In a metal mold, wax temperature can be as high as 190°F.

Getting the wick anchored in the mold before pouring in the wax can be tricky. The mold needs to have a small hole in its center at the bottom, through which the wick is run and

A Wooden Candle Mold

For a Christmas present, my son made an altogether untraditional candle mold for me out of walnut wood. It works like a bullet mold, two halves of the mold hinged together, with special orifices to hold the wick. Close up the mold, pour wax into the top opening, allow cooling, open the mold and the candle is ready. The mold has to be greased or oiled beforehand, so the wax doesn't stick. It makes a nice decoration for the living room when not in use.

tied. Then pull the wick taut from above and tie it to a little stick or pencil laid across the open top of the mold. A bit of putty around the wick where it comes through the bottom of the mold will keep the hot wax from running out. Another method is to anchor a plastic straw in the center of the mold, then after the wax has cooled, pull out the straw and insert the wick in the hole it left. When the wick is lighted, it quickly melts wax down, filling the hole around it.

Simple Toys

The toys most of us really remember playing with as children weren't really toys but things we turned into toys. My earliest recollection is a matchbox of multicolored and multisize rubberbands I played with by the hour when I was about two. I don't know why they fascinated me, only that they did. Even the match-

box was a wonder—the way it slid so neatly open and closed.

My next favorite toy was a big tin box full of all kinds of buttons that my mother gave me occasionally after I was old enough not to try to eat them. I sorted buttons by size and shape and color for hours—my first crude notion of what would later help me understand the idea of classification by genus and species.

At the age when children like to have a playhouse or any small place to hide in or feel secure in, corn shocks in my father's fields were the perfect answer. They looked like tepees. We could push aside the stalks tied upright together and hollow out a room inside. When my children were that age, I shocked the sweet corn stalks after harvest in the garden into a tepee. The kids discovered it without my saying anything and spent hours in this playhouse that cost me nothing.

Marble Raceway

My favorite all-time toy when I was nine years old was the living room floor and a handful of marbles. In our old farmhouse, the floors were far from level. A marble would roll down one side of the living room, gaining speed, and then gradually slow down as the floor sloped up the other way. The marble would come to a halt near the far end. The space between the baseboard and the carpet (which in those days was laid only to within about a foot of the baseboard) formed a perfect raceway. I'd let gravity fuel the marbles down the "track" and bet on which marble would win. If one rubbed on the carpet side or even the baseboard side or hit an obstacle I might place on the track or get boxed in by slower marbles as in a real race, then the others had a good chance of rolling the farthest before coming to rest at the far end.

This game is so much fun that you might want to build a raceway that easily duplicates the down and up slope of our old farmhouse

MARBLE RACEWAY

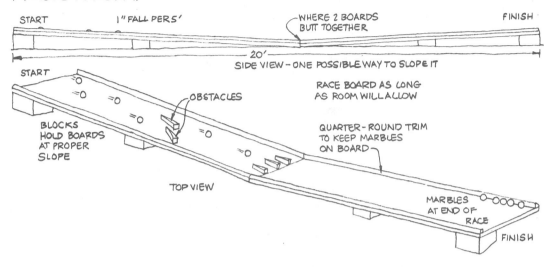

START   1" FALL PER 5'   WHERE 2 BOARDS BUTT TOGETHER   FINISH

20'

SIDE VIEW – ONE POSSIBLE WAY TO SLOPE IT

START

OBSTACLES

BLOCKS HOLD BOARDS AT PROPER SLOPE

TOP VIEW

RACE BOARD AS LONG AS ROOM WILL ALLOW

QUARTER-ROUND TRIM TO KEEP MARBLES ON BOARD

MARBLES AT END OF RACE

FINISH

floor. If your family room is 20 feet long, you can use two 1 by 12-inch boards each 10 feet long, or use Masonite of that width and length instead. (The Masonite can be bent slightly to put tilts into the raceway.) The slope you give your track is somewhat optional. The first portion of the course, for example, might be sloped and the rest level, if the course is long enough so that the marbles' momentum is naturally stopped before they reach the end of the course. Obstacles can be put on the track to slow or divert the downward progress of the marbles and make the race more interesting. Both edges of the race board need to be framed with quarter-round molding to keep the marbles on the track. When you have the boards sloped and tilted properly, in order to keep them that way, blocks should be nailed to the underside of the boards. The boards can be butted against each other and require no special connection. Occasionally an enthusiastic player will bump the track apart, but it can be realigned manually.

Burdock Basket

Children today have wonderful building toys like the Lego plastic building blocks that fasten together to make any shape the imagination can inspire. An adequate substitute is the

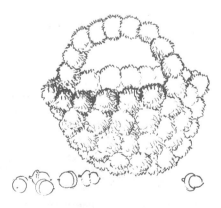

BURDOCK BASKET

burs from a common weed, burdock, which looks like rhubarb because of the size of its huge leaves. On a spike on top of the plant, seed burs form toward late summer, and they catch on clothing, sheep's wool, and in hair. The burs also stick to each other easily if squeezed together gently. Yesterday's children used the burs to form all sorts of fanciful shapes. A tiny basket, complete with a usable handle, was a favorite. In the baskets we often carried our favorite acorn "tops" for spinning. Red oak acorns are best for spinning, at least in our area, because the stem of the acorn is usually straight and long enough to manipulate between thumb and forefinger.

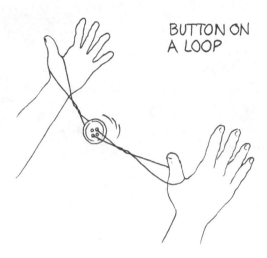

BUTTON ON A LOOP

Button on a Loop

Another homemade toy that will charm a child now as in times past is made from a button and a loop of string. We called it a buzz saw, because the button, by the action of the string, whirls like the blade of a cut-off saw. You need a large button with two or four holes in it. Run the piece of string, which should measure about 3 feet long, through one hole in the button and then back through its opposite hole. Next, tie the two ends of string together to make a continuous loop. Hook one end over one thumb and the other over the other thumb. Jiggle the button down to the middle of the string. Now twirl the button around in the air by revolving your thumbs so that the double strand of string wraps around itself several times. As the string wraps around itself, pull outwards gently with both thumbs, tightening the string. Immediately let the string slacken a bit and then pull out tight again. It takes a bit of practice, but very soon the twistings and untwistings of the string will start the button turning like a little flywheel, and its speed will increase as you rhythmically pull out and let up on the string. Soon you'll have the button humming prettily. (If the button is of a material you can notch around the edges, you can run

the humming button against a hard surface and create a tremendous racket that will drive parents crazy.)

Tube Sled

Sometimes you can buy a used tractor tire inner tube from a junk yard or farm machinery dealer for a few dollars. Patch any holes, fill with enough air so that it doesn't give too much, and you have yourself a very exciting sled that won't hurt you or anyone else if you have a collision or upset going down a snowy hill. Some tubes slide better than others for mysterious reasons, so you may want to experiment with more than one.

Hoop and Push Stick

As kids we rolled hoops with a T stick by the hour. An old steel wheel or steel ring of about a foot to 18 inches in diameter works best, but they are hard to find, even in junkyards. You can use a bicycle wheel so long as you cut out the spokes with a wire cutter. The push stick is a 3-foot lath with a short 6-inch piece of lath nailed crossways at one end. Start the wheel rolling by running it down the lath, then run along, "pushing" the wheel by exerting just the right amount of pressure behind it with the crosspiece of the push stick, at just the right height on the wheel. You can chase the wheel around the block till you run out of wind. When you get good, you can make it jump low obstacles. Careful, though. As you run along, the action of the stick on the wheel sort of hypnotizes you, and you may forget to watch where you're going. Hold the stick out to your side a bit so that if you run it in the ground you don't jab yourself with the other end.

HOOP AND PUSH STICK

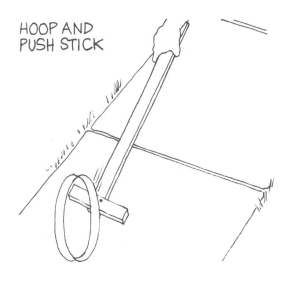

Grass Whistle

The simplest (and loudest) whistle requires only your hands and a strong blade of grass. Choose a blade about ¼ inch wide, although one a little narrower will work well, too. Hold it vertically and as taut as you can between your thumbs, which you hold as you see them in the drawing. You'll notice that even when your thumbs are tight against each other there is a slot below the knuckles. The grass blade should stretch down through that slot tautly, the edge

GRASS WHISTLE

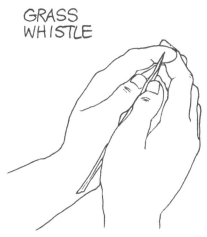

facing you. Cup your hands behind your thumbs to create a sort of noise chamber. Place your thumbs against your mouth and blow hard through the slot. The whistle varies with the kind of grass you use and how tightly you hold it. Often, you can simulate the distress cry of a rabbit or the hunting cry of a hawk or the cry of a baby crow and lure curious birds close to you.

Twig Whistle

A twig whistle is made in early spring when the bark is still loose enough to slip on the wood. Willow wood is ideal, but other woods also work. Cut a twig about 6 inches long, free of knots or side twigs. The twig should be about ¾-inch in diameter. The fattest end is your handle.

Cut out a narrow ring of bark about 2 inches from the fat end (more if your twig is longer than 6 inches). Then, with your pocket-knife handle, knock on the skinnier portion of the twig all around, until the bark begins to loosen. Then twist the bark and slide it off the twig, being careful to keep it all in one piece. Put the bark back on and cut a slant onto the skinny end, starting about 1 inch back from the

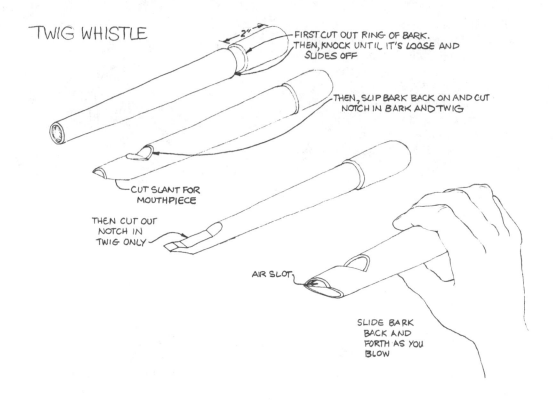

TWIG WHISTLE

FIRST CUT OUT RING OF BARK. THEN, KNOCK UNTIL IT'S *LOOSE* AND SLIDES OFF

2"

THEN, SLIP BARK BACK ON AND CUT NOTCH IN BARK AND TWIG

CUT SLANT FOR MOUTHPIECE

THEN CUT OUT NOTCH IN TWIG ONLY

AIR SLOT

SLIDE BARK BACK AND FORTH AS YOU BLOW

end. Cut through bark and wood as shown in the drawing. This is your mouthpiece. Next, cut a notch on top of the whistle about ½ inch in from the mouthpiece. The notch is cut to the middle of the twig, straight down on the back side, slanted about the same degree as the mouthpiece is slanted on the front side. Now slide the bark off again and slice out the top half of the twig, beginning at the notch and back for about 1½ inches. Cut just a thin sliver off the top from the mouthpiece end to the notch. Replace bark and blow. If it doesn't whistle, slice off another thin sliver above the mouthpiece.

Butcher Blocks

Nothing is handier in the kitchen than a table a bit lower than counter level with a hardwood top you can slice foods on. Hundreds of butcher block designs have emerged over the years, having in common a very hard wood for the slicing area and a height of about 30 to 35 inches—low enough so that the arms fall to a comfortable position for slicing, chopping, kneading, and so forth on the table.

The traditional butcher block was in most ways the easiest to make. It was simply a thick slice from a large log—cut long enough so that when stood on end the "stump" approached a height of 30 inches, or perhaps a little shorter. (People were shorter in those days than they are now.) Sycamore was the preferred wood because it did not crack and check as badly as other woods as it dried. I say "as badly" because it is almost impossible to dry out a thick log piece slowly enough so that it does not crack at least a little around the outside. Because of the cellular structure of the log, it almost *has* to crack as it shrinks from drying.

A Block from a Log

A friend who made a log chunk butcher block out of red oak learned about peripheral cracking the hard way, but the cracking that took place after the block was ensconced in his kitchen did not at all detract from its beauty and had no effect at all on its use, since the central cutting surface was unmarred. He filled in peripheral cracks with wood filler.

His block (see photo) measures about 20 inches thick. He drilled holes deep into the bottom of the block with an old-fashioned breast drill and inserted legs. Braces from leg to leg ensure stability for the heavy block of wood.

Drilling the holes up through that hard red oak was extremely hard work, the owner admits. Just as attractive a block might have been forthcoming if he had just cut the log piece long enough to stand firmly and evenly on its own end at the proper height. With the bark removed, the natural undulations of the tree trunk can be as pleasing to the eye as carpentered legs.

Constructing a Butcher Block

Should you want to make a butcher block of sawn, finished lumber and do not have much in the way of woodworking tools, here is an easy and attractive design to follow. Its simplicity makes it advantageous when you want to give a local lumberyard the dimensions to cut from your wood so you can assemble your butcher block at home.

First make the cutting board itself, gluing up strips of hardwood, then cutting, planing, or sanding to the proper dimensions. You can buy a cutting board if making one appears too difficult. In any event, use a hardwood—birch is a good choice because it is usually available and is not as porous as white oak. An inch and a half is a good thickness. When the block wears down on one side, it can be turned over and in this way last at least a lifetime.

The size of the block determines the length of the four apron boards that fit around it, mitered at the corners. The four legs are 3 inches square at the top to give a pleasing proportion (see the drawings on the next page). Beginning 6½ inches down, the legs taper on the two inside edges to a 2-inch square dimension at the bottom. The apron boards are 1-inch thickness, 8 inches wide, and are glued and screwed to the legs, leaving 1½ inches (the thickness of the cutting board) sticking above the legs. Next, with apron and legs attached, nail or screw two rails to the inside of the legs.

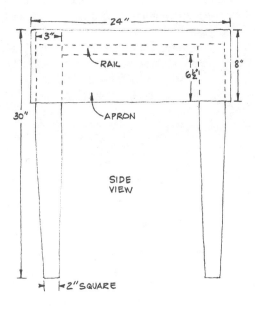

SIDE VIEW

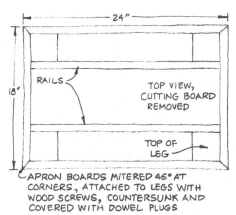

TOP VIEW, CUTTING BOARD REMOVED

TOP OF LEG

APRON BOARDS MITERED 45° AT CORNERS, ATTACHED TO LEGS WITH WOOD SCREWS, COUNTERSUNK AND COVERED WITH DOWEL PLUGS

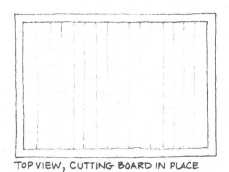

TOP VIEW, CUTTING BOARD IN PLACE

The rails run lengthwise and even with the tops of the legs and the ends of the rails butt up against the inside of the apron at both ends of the table. The cutting board sits on these rails, flush with the top edge of the apron. It should fit very closely. If you have a sander or power plane, it is a good idea to make the cutting board just 1/16 inch larger than it should be and then sand or smooth to a glove-tight fit. The cutting board then does not have to be glued or screwed down, but can be lifted out for cleaning or for turning over.

Apron and legs can be finished any way you desire, but the cutting board should be given a coat or two of vegetable oil only. It is important that it be kept clean—food particles embedded or sticking to the wood and spoiling could become a source of odor problems, not to mention food poisoning.

Making a Patchwork Quilt

You know you are getting old when you can remember when patchwork quilts were actually used to keep people warm in bed, not hung on walls for decorations. The one I slept under as a boy was a crazy quilt design of hundreds of fabric scraps, some velvet, on a black backing.

The patchwork quilt may be thought of as art today—and often quite expensive art—but it was born out of a very practical and pragmatic necessity. When fabrics were laboriously woven together on kitchen looms or bought dearly from early factories, no scrap was ever thrown away. "Use it up, wear it out; make do or do without" was the virtue people lived by, and when the scraps of clothing could be used no other way, they could be sewn together into a large spread. If two other layers of cloth were sewn together with it, the result was a very effective insulating blanket. The blanket became known as a quilt when the three layers were

stitched together; a comforter when tied together with yarn.

In the Amish community near Pfeiffer's Station, Ohio (a crossroads marked by a store that is no longer open for business), I watched an elderly Amish lady quilt. She lived in a tiny two-room addition to a large house, connected by a sort of covered walkway, the sides of which were lined with slabwood for the little stove in her kitchen. A pot of stew simmered on the burner. Occasionally she would rise painfully from her quilting frame and chuck a piece of the wood into the stove. Then she would toddle on arthritic bones back to the quilting frame, all the while laughing and dickering with a client who had come to order a quilt. The quilting frame was the roller type—the unquilted portion of the quilt rolled up on one side, the finished portion rolled up on the other, with just enough working space stretched between the two rollers so she could easily reach the center of the large quilt. There was room for at least two more quilters, but the old woman worked alone in her tiny bedroom. A line of prayer books, all in German, rested on a stand by the bed. She had a tiny garden outside, a few chickens, some pet cats. She was the last of her immediate family and had come to live out her days here with more distant relatives. But she could still take care of herself. Still pay her own way.

She did not quilt as much as formerly. Her fingers hurt and her eyes were failing, she told the visitors. They would have to be patient if they wanted a quilt. I watched the old woman's hands, porcelain smooth and white, carrying on their own activity on the quilt as if they had a life of their own. Her right hand stitched away on top of the stretched quilt, her left hand underneath, feeling the needle come through the backing at each stitch. Yes, sometimes she did prick her finger. That's why she kept that finger taped. She could still feel the needle through the tape, but the tape prevented her from sticking herself and staining the backing with blood. (If you do get a spot of blood on the backing, dab it immediately with saliva, she said, and rub out the stain before it sets.)

Her stitch was marvelously fine and even, having been repeated who knows how many times in the last seventy years. (She did her first stitch when six years old, and at ten, she says, could run a straight ¼-inch seam allowance by eye. She made twelve stitches to the inch—stitching that would not loosen or unravel in a lifetime of laundering. She threaded about 20 inches of thread into the needle, pulling a couple of inches through the needle's eye, and tying a knot down at the other end of the single strand. She used ordinary thread that she slid across an old stub of beeswax candle to coat it so that it would slide easily through the fabric and not twist up. (Commercial quilting thread coated with silicone is preferred by most quilters, but you can buy little bars of tailor's beeswax to use in place of the candle stub.) She was careful always to thread the needle *before* she cut the thread from the spool, ensuring that she would then stitch in the same direction the thread came off the spool, because sewing *with* the natural twist of the thread rather than against it keeps the thread from twisting and knotting up.

To begin, she dipped her needle through the top fabric and into the middle layer of batting and then out through the top again, pulling the end knot up snug against the quilt top. With a sudden little jerk, she then popped the knot on through the top, hiding it from

---

Quilting a Legacy

I think the urge to make things is very primitive—in fact, prehuman. There are little primates called lemurs that have scent glands, and as they go along from tree to tree, they leave little puddles of aroma saying to the next lemur to happen along, "I exist! I've passed this way!" Sometimes I see myself that way, going through life trailing quilts and pillows and things. They're nonverbal, they don't have to be explained, they just exist, and the fact that they exist proves that I exist. Perhaps someday people will see them and think, as I do when I see antique quilts now, "Some human being whose name I'll never know imagined this just this way, in these colors and no others, and then made it with her own warm living hands." Don't misunderstand me; I don't make quilts as a hedge against death. What I like is the general sense of continuity, the fact of communication between humans who know nothing about each other and who weren't even on earth at the same time. I don't make anything of it. I just like it.

Beth Gutcheon, from *The Quilt Design Workbook.* Copyright © 1976 Beth and Jeffrey Gutcheon. Reprinted with the permission of Rawson Associates.

---

view. "Good quilting looks as if it is all done with one continuous thread," she explained. Next, she began the quilting stitches, picking up three stitches on her needle before pulling them tight, then three more, on and on until only a small length of thread remained on the needle. Then she pushed the needle through the top (always with a thimble on the middle finger of her stitching hand), into the batting, and back up through the top again, then making a backstitch under just one strand of the top fabric, down into the batting again, back up, another backstitch like the previous one, and then cutting off any extra thread that remained sticking out. Then she threaded on another 20 inches of thread and began quilting again at the point where she had left off her last stitch. No unique or hard-to-learn skill was involved, only a close attention to detail and a certain peaceful commitment to the work. She was secure in that commitment. In our society she would no doubt be in a "rest" home, a burden on herself if not on society. In the Amish way, she went, instead, about her work, smiling almost continuously, with purpose in her life. Because she was willing to stitch a million stitches over, willing to accept the discipline of everyday work rather than let a machine send her to an early grave, people sought her out. She was still needed. She was still happy.

The Design

The actual quilting, as described above, is only the last step in making a patchwork quilt. One must first sew together the patches that are cut from scrap pieces of cloth. Although scraps of worn clothing can be and are used, anything worn too badly would be a poor candidate for the quilt pieces. But in most American closets there is hanger upon hanger of clothing that has never worn out, but has simply been dated out of fashion, and that is perfectly fine to cut up and use in quilts. The best scraps are those left over from making new clothes.

All scraps, especially from new cloth, should be laundered to remove excess dyes before you use them. Use only colorfast fabrics, since bleeding or fading can ruin a finely composed design.

Design books and quilters' manuals will provide patterns galore, both traditional and modern. Try something simple the first time, or after studying the classic patterns, design your own. Something as personal as a handmade quilt seems to me to deserve a homemade design, even if it ignores some of the accepted

fashions in the quilting community. Whatever design you choose, be sure to draw it out to scale on graph paper first. Ascertain the size of your quilt. If it is to cover a queen-size bed, measure the bedspread on a bed of that size. You can cheat in quilting and add a wide border of other material around the edges to drape down over the box springs. This is all up to you. It might be best to make a baby quilt first and do a full-size treasure only after you've had the practice.

A patchwork quilt design is composed of pieces of different fabrics, colors, and shapes that are arranged geometrically, usually into square blocks. The basic design units are often sewn together into blocks, the blocks sewn together into strips, and the strips sewn together into the completed quilt top. It is of utmost importance that the scrap pieces be cut accurately so that they will fit exactly against each other, square and true. To assure this, quilters cut out cardboard templates of each of the basic geometric shapes and use these templates to trace the shapes onto the scrap pieces. A hard lead pencil is usually used to mark, and a very sharp pair of scissors should be reserved for the cutting. Some quilters cut out several pieces at a time, which requires pinning all the corners of the geometric shape and an extremely sharp pair of scissors, so there is no slippage during cutting and therefore no distortion.

If you are a beginner, you will not only need a template to trace out the pieces, but you may also want to use a second template to mark the seam lines on the pieces. A seam allowance of ¼ inch on every piece is always used in quilting. Professionals may be able to sew this seam by eye, but to get good alignment it is better to mark the seams until you have had plenty of practice. To do this, make a second template, ¼-inch smaller all around than the first, and place it carefully on the back side of each cut-out piece; then draw a line around it with a hard pencil.

Sewing the Quilt Together

After you have your pieces cut out according to your graphed plan, you can begin sewing them together. Put two adjoining pieces together, right sides facing each other, and align the two seam marks. Sew them together, by hand or with a sewing machine (purists insist by hand), then proceed to sew on the next adjoining pieces until the square block is formed. Some quilters iron down the seam allowances underneath after each piece is sewn on; others wait and iron down the seams after the block is completed. Continue in this fashion until you have all your blocks. Then sew blocks in strips, and finally, sew the strips together until you have sewn together the entire quilt top.

Now cut your backing and middle layer. The middle layer, which is batting, can be cotton or perhaps a polyester blend, or an old cotton blanket, as in the old days. Wool is not so good unless all the top quilting is wool, too, because wool demands different laundering practices than other fabrics. A cotton blanket is better, but it, too, will tend to knot and lump inside the quilt like wool does over time, unless quilting seams are never more than 2 inches apart. Most quilters today much prefer polyester batting especially made for quilting. It is lighter and easier to work with, they say. Get the good kind, labeled "bonded" or "needlepunched."

A cotton bedsheet makes good backing for a quilt. It irons smoother and flatter than blends or synthetics, and so there is less chance of racking or getting it crooked in relation to the top.

Arrange the three layers on top of each other on the floor in their proper positions. Baste them together with a contrasting color thread, making inch-long stitches so that the layers lie flat and stay together while you quilt

it. Basting is usually begun in the middle, with diagonal lines radiating out to the sides all around. Starting in the middle means that you'll have less danger of getting wrinkles or puckers in the surface of the quilt.

Quilting

After the basting is completed, the quilt is ready to frame. Some quilters prefer the little hoop frame that holds a small portion of the quilt tight while that section is being quilted. Others prefer the larger roller type that I described earlier. Either is much preferred over the frames

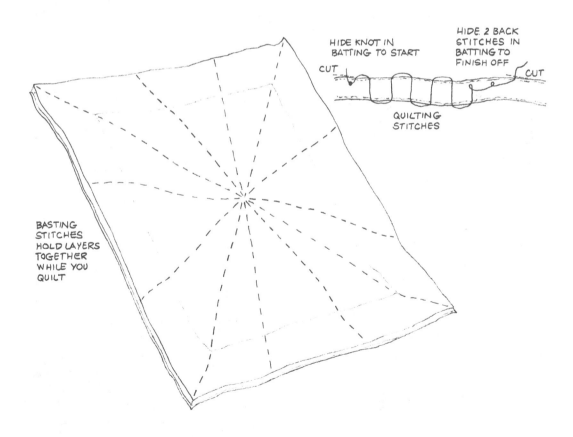

HIDE KNOT IN BATTING TO START

HIDE 2 BACK STITCHES IN BATTING TO FINISH OFF

CUT

CUT

QUILTING STITCHES

BASTING STITCHES HOLD LAYERS TOGETHER WHILE YOU QUILT

that stretch the whole blanket out, as shown later for tying a comforter, unless you are only going to make baby quilts or several people are quilting at a time. The quilt should be stretched tight in the frame, but don't overdo it. If you are using polyester batting, the quilt will retain the puffy, quilted look without the extra stretching that is necessary if a cotton blanket is being used for batting.

Where exactly you run your quilting stitches is somewhat arbitrary. Often, the stitching parallels the seams holding the pieces together, about ¼ inch away. But not every piece seam needs to have a line of quilting stitches beside it. In fact, with polyester batting, quilting lines can be as much as 8 inches apart, although the more quilting, the better the quilt and the longer it will last. Sometimes quilting is done in diagonal lines, evenly spaced across the entire quilt, disregarding the design altogether. Or instead of diagonal lines, joined semicircles or arcs are sewn over the whole quilt; this is called the teacup design. Other times, especially on an appliquéd quilt or one combining appliqué and patchwork, where there are comparatively empty areas between design features, the quilting will be done in artful floral patterns to enhance this "open" space.

Along with the amount of quilting done, the value of a quilt depends on the fineness of the stitching. Hand stitching done evenly at twelve stitches per inch or more is considered far more beautiful than machine stitching, which generally runs ten stitches per inch and, though faster, is often more difficult to do well on a large quilt. To keep a tight stretch and to prevent bunching at the sewing machine, a special overhead arm attachment is now used to do quilting on sewing machines. The result is adequate, and certainly very satisfactory for warmth, but lacks the artistic quality of a well-made, hand-stitched quilt. And the machined quilt does not command a third of the price of a handmade one, even if it's well made.

Finishing

After the quilting is finished, trim and bind the edges. There are many ways to do this. For example, you can tuck or pleat in the corners as you do for hooked rugs. (See Latch and Hook Rugs.) But I think the nicest way to finish off the quilt is to miter the corners, because you wind up with a very neat-looking binding that is beautifully squared off at each corner.

To begin a mitered binding, cut or buy a binding strip 3 inches wide and longer than the length of all four sides added together. You want one long strip, even if that means sewing several smaller strips together. Iron out one edge of the right side of the strip. Then pin the right side of the strip (so the ironed edge is out) to the edge of the quilt, through all four layers. Sew this strip ¼ inch in from the edge, right to the first corner, as shown in the drawing.

Now turn the strip to form a right angle to the sewn edge, so that you form a diagonal fold at the corner. Maintaining that fold, fold the strip back on itself and lay it along the edge of the next side of the quilt. The corner of the strip should be right at the corner of the quilt. Begin your next stitch right at this corner, being sure to loop your thread over the folded corner. If you look at the drawings, you'll see what I mean.

Continue sewing and folding and sewing again all around the quilt. When you're through, fold the strip over to the back of the quilt, smoothing out the corners. Then hemstitch around the edges and slipstitch the mitered corners.

There are many variations and additions to the quilting steps I've described. Today's quilts tend to use very sophisticated and detailed designs calling for many small pieces. The more pieces, the more time involved in the making, and the more skill required to keep them all aligned. One need not strive for such sophistication. The main goals on the practical

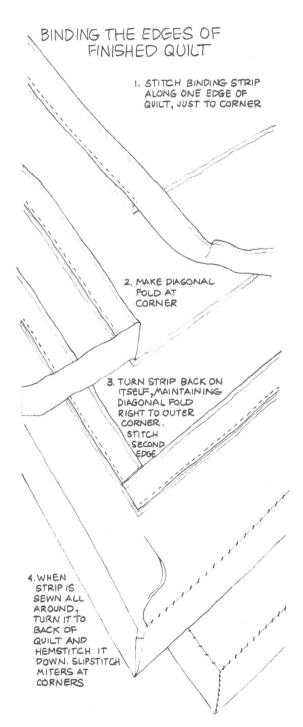

BINDING THE EDGES OF
FINISHED QUILT

1. STITCH BINDING STRIP
ALONG ONE EDGE OF
QUILT, JUST TO CORNER

2. MAKE DIAGONAL
FOLD AT
CORNER

3. TURN STRIP BACK ON
ITSELF, MAINTAINING
DIAGONAL FOLD
RIGHT TO OUTER
CORNER.
STITCH
SECOND
EDGE

4. WHEN
STRIP IS
SEWN ALL
AROUND,
TURN IT TO
BACK OF
QUILT AND
HEMSTITCH IT
DOWN. SLIPSTITCH
MITERS AT
CORNERS

homestead are to make use of scraps that might otherwise go to waste and to supply your family with adequate bedclothes at low cost but high value. Even a simple design, if made well by hand, can mean a quilt worth several hundred dollars—and at the rate quilts are going, an investment that will increase in value and be treasured by your grandchildren.

Making a Comforter

A comforter is a fast way to make a quilt. Instead of fastening the three layers of fabric together with close, fine stitching to last a lifetime or two, you tie or stitch the layers together at rather infrequent intervals. Don't make your ties closer than 2 inches or farther apart than 7 inches. This method of making a three-layered blanket is used especially where the middle layer of batting is quite thick and therefore not amenable to close, fine quilting. It is also a good method when the batting is wool or down or feathers, all materials that you don't want to just toss in the washing machine very often, if ever. In these cases, the comforter should be tied together so the ties can be cut, the covering of the comforter removed and washed, and the tying redone.

At Rastetter's Woolen Mill (at the intersection of State Routes 39 and 62, Millersburg, Ohio) Tim Rastetter, along with his grandfather, Ralph Aling, turns raw wool into batting on a 120-year-old carding mill, as the family has done for over 100 years. He makes wool comforters on order, or you can still send in raw wool in exchange for carded wool, get credit for your wool, and make your own comforter. (There are at least two operations like this in the talking stage in other parts of the country and if the cottage wool industry continues to grow, there will be small mills dotted all over the countryside to serve you. Check with people in your own area who are active in the cottage

wool industry for small wool processing plants. Two examples: Shippensburg Woolen Mill, 13 N. Washington St., Shippensburg, PA 17257, custom makes 100% woolen blankets for sheep-owning customers. Bartlettyarns, Inc., Harmony, ME 04942, takes wool in exchange for finished yarn at a good savings over commercial yarn.)

Most often Rastetter's customers today simply buy their comforters already finished, without bringing in wool for exchange. Rastetter puts a cover of cheesecloth around the wool batting, then covers the whole thing with a removable flannel coverlet, which has a zipper at one end. The entire flannel is tied down in proper comforter style, so the wool does not bunch up inside. He recommends not washing the wool ever, but cutting the ties, slipping off the flannel cover and washing it alone, only airing the cheesecloth-covered wool batting. Washing would bunch the wool out of shape over time, but by washing just the cover the batting will only have to be removed and recarded once every twenty years or so to make it smooth again. Since there is nothing warmer for the weight than a wool comforter, except a down comforter (also available at Rastetter's), the infrequent removal of the flannel is well worth the work.

Putting It Together

Without a carding mill to make wool batting, most people make their comforters with washable cotton batting—usually one or two old blankets—but you can use regular quilting bat-

ting if you prefer and put the three layers together permanently as in quilting. The top fabric can be, and often is, made up of the same kind of patchwork scraps as in a patchwork quilt, but it may be a cotton print or solid flannel or even a sprightly colored sheet. The bottom layer or backing is usually a sheet. Slippery fabrics are not used for backing because the comforter would be inclined to slide off the bed too easily.

If quilt stitching is used, the stitches should be much farther apart than in regular quilting, following any design that seems appropriate to the quilter. Tying is more popular for comforters and much faster. Regular cotton yarn is most often used. Thread about 3 feet of yarn into the shortest needle you have with an eye big enough to accept the yarn. Pull the yarn

CUT THREAD BETWEEN KNOTS

TYING A COMFORTER

through until it is double, but don't tie the ends. Where the first tie-down is to be made in the comforter, push the needle clear through all three thicknesses and pull the double thread through until only about 2 inches remain above the top of the comforter. Then push the needle back up through the comforter right next to the first stitch, pull tight, then back down and up again, pulling tight, and then tie a square knot tight down against the fabric. Some quilters make only one pass down and up through the comforter before tying, but two passes are much better. Don't snip off the yarn after the tie, but continue to the next tie-down and repeat the first step. Only when you run out of thread should you take up scissors and cut the yarn midway between the ties. This is much faster than cutting after every tie, and you don't have to worry about pulling the loose end of your yarn all the way through the fabric as you begin every tie-down.

If your comforter has a patchwork design, as it most often will in the frugal household, then the design of the patches should decide

where the tie-downs should go, perhaps at every corner of a block. But wherever you put them, they should be in a regular pattern with the ties close enough together to keep the batting from bunching—2 to 7 inches apart, as mentioned earlier. If the comforter has just a random print design or is a plain solid color, find a large piece of cardboard, punch holes in it in a grid pattern satisfying to your eye, and use it as a template to mark the tie-downs on the comforter.

You can hold the comforter in a hoop frame or in a roller, just as you would use when quilting, but for simple tie-downs, a larger flat, rectangular frame is more practical if you have the room. A very simple frame can be made quite fast with four 1 by 4-inch boards, long enough to frame the largest comforter you ever intend to make. Then all you do is arrange the boards to the proper size for the comforter you are making, then clamp the boards at the corners with C-clamps, and set the frame up on four chairs, one at each of the four corners.

You can baste the layers together before stretching or stretch them as evenly over each other on the frame as possible, thumbtacking

TEMPLATE FOR MARKING TIE-DOWNS

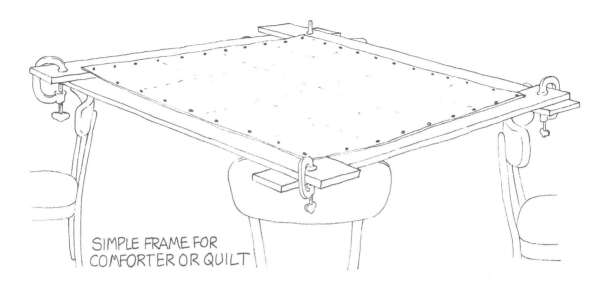

SIMPLE FRAME FOR
COMFORTER OR QUILT

them down in either case. You don't have to stretch the whole quilt at once. Because the boards are easily adjustable simply by loosening the C-clamps and moving them in or out, you can change size easily and even do a fairly good job of keeping the comforter evenly tight all the way around—but it takes a person at each clamp to do it. More elaborate frames are rather easily made, involving more permanent and fixed supports than the four chairs, but for a comforter, this makeshift frame does the job.

When finished, you can trim the edges and bind them in any number of ways, such as the one I describe for finishing off a quilt in the preceding item, or the way one might bind a hooked rug, in Latch and Hook Rugs.

Braiding Rags into Rugs

One way to change rags to riches is to make rugs out of them. Rag strips can be braided, then the braids sewn together into round or oval rugs.

Braided rugs are usually made out of wool for long life—strips torn from old clothing.

You can also buy wool scraps from mill outlets. If you do not have enough wool for a rug, you can braid denim and wool—two of the cables in the braid being denim, one being wool. Denim is preferable to other nonwool fabrics because it is so strong. In this case, instead of braiding all three cables alternately around each other as in ordinary braiding, the wool cable is twisted alternately over and under the two denim cables so that the woolen one is always on the outside of the braid. The result is a wool-covered, denim-cored rug.

The most time-consuming part of making a braided rug is in tearing the strips of wool from old clothes, first removing lining, buttons, zippers, etc. Strips are usually about 1¼ to 1½ inches wide, a little wider for thin fabrics, a little narrower for thick ones, so that when the edges are turned in, the resultant cables of both thin and thick fabrics are of about the same fatness. Some beginning braiders sew the edges down after folding them in, for easier braiding, or they pin them temporarily together, removing the pins just ahead of the braiding. But neither practice is necessary. An experienced

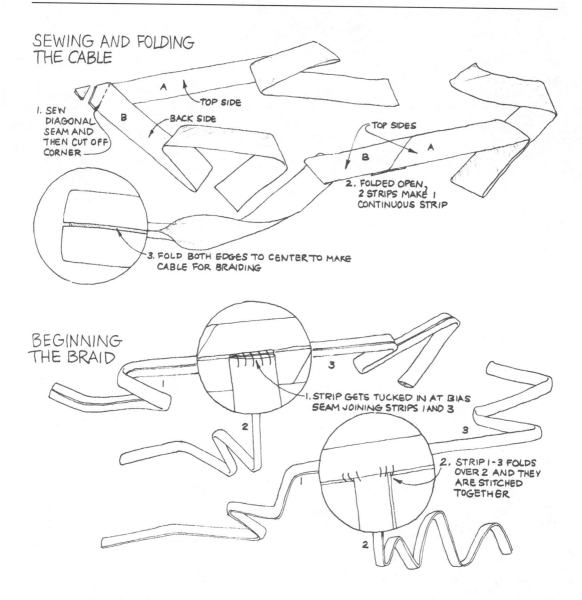

SEWING AND FOLDING
THE CABLE

1. SEW DIAGONAL SEAM AND THEN CUT OFF CORNER

A
TOP SIDE
B
BACK SIDE

TOP SIDES
B
A

2. FOLDED OPEN, 2 STRIPS MAKE 1 CONTINUOUS STRIP

3. FOLD BOTH EDGES TO CENTER TO MAKE CABLE FOR BRAIDING

BEGINNING
THE BRAID

1
3
2

1. STRIP GETS TUCKED IN AT BIAS SEAM JOINING STRIPS 1 AND 3

3
1
2

2. STRIP 1-3 FOLDS OVER 2 AND THEY ARE STITCHED TOGETHER

braider learns how to fold in the edges of the strips and hold them folded until they are braided securely together.

Before you begin braiding, sew the strips together with a bias seam. To do this, place the end of the strip to be added over the end of the first strip at right angles to each other (forming an L) with the top side of one facing the top side of the other. Stitch a diagonal seam across both, as in the drawing, and cut off the outer corner. When the joined pieces are opened, they form a continuous strip with a bit of overlap that will be hidden in the braid. After joining many such strips together, roll them into balls.

will be inclined to curl rather than remain flat. The first few feet are usually sewn together rather than laced. Use a large needle and heavy-duty thread and sew through the folds of the two inside loops until you sew all around the second row, then begin lacing.

On an oval rug, the first stretch of braid determines the shape of the rug. If you know

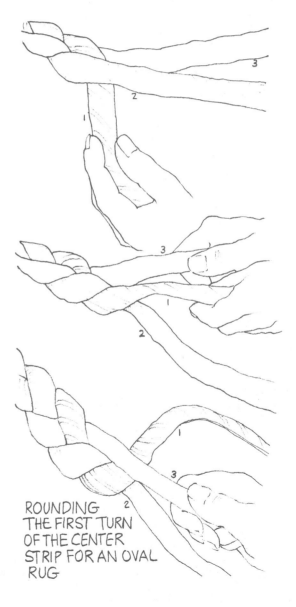

ROUNDING THE FIRST TURN OF THE CENTER STRIP FOR AN OVAL RUG

To begin braiding, sew the left- and right-hand strips together and then sew the middle strip to them at right angles, forming a T, as in the drawing. Assuming the left hand strip is 1, the middle, 2, and the right hand, 3, begin by folding 3 over 2, then 1 over 3, then 2 over 1, then 3 over 2, and so forth in the usual braiding method. As you braid, you also fold in the edges of the strips. Always keep the open side of the folds *to the center* as you braid, so that they are braided in and don't show.

If making a circular rug, you simply wind the completed braid around itself and lace the sides together with a double strand of carpet thread or string and a blunt needle, lacing back and forth through the loops of the braids and pulling them snug, but not too tight or the rug the finished size you want, you can calculate the length of that center braid so the rug comes out right. Subtract the length from the width of the finished size. Thus a 9 by 12-foot rug would require a center strip of 3 feet of braid. To go around the sharp corners in those center strips, you make a corner in the braid, which is simple to do. Again with left, middle, and right cables numbered 1, 2, and 3, to make a turn to the right, 1 goes over 2, and then 3 goes over 1. Pull the entire braid around to the right a bit and then bring 1 over 3 and continue regular braiding. Sew and lace together just as in a round rug.

You can choose your fabric colors to make a regular pattern, but if you are limited to whatever rag scraps you happen to have, don't be dismayed. Some of the most spectacular braided rugs are made up of random selections of scraps, with no attention being paid to pattern or regularity of color.

When you get within about 20 inches of the end of the rug, start cutting the strips to a narrower taper, so that the braid gets smaller and smaller and can be blended into the outer-

FINISHING OFF THE BRAID

TO FINISH OFF, CUT STRIPS TO NARROW TAPERS, FOLD AND BASTE INTO CABLES. THEN BRAID AND TUCK ENDS IN BRAID LOOPS. SEW TO SECURE

most full braid instead of coming to an abrupt end out on the edge of the rug where it would be quite noticeable (see the drawing).

Latch and Hook Rugs
Latch Hooking Rugs

Walter Kail is gone now, but Berenice, his wife, has many memories of him in her neat white farmhouse down the road from our place. For years, Walter spent his evenings on his farm making latch-hook rugs, and it is hard to walk anywhere in the house without stepping on one of them. He worked on the enclosed porch on the south side of the house, where he could keep an eye on the cows. He made one original contribution to the art of latch hooking rugs. To keep a rug from sliding off the little table where he worked on it, he weighted it down with a huge iron ring—the kind used to hitch railroad cars together. While he made rugs, Berenice worked on her needlepoint or quilted or sometimes hooked a rug the old-fashioned way. They never had a television set in the house and Berenice still doesn't. She keeps on quilting and sewing and if she looks up at anything at all, it is at the iron ring still on the table. Its nearness draws Walter to her mind.

Walter's biggest and best rug is a pictorial scene taken from a photograph of him and Berenice standing by the white picket fence in the yard with the red barn in the background. He sent the photograph to Shillcraft's (500 N. Calver St., Baltimore, MD 21202), a craft supplier that specializes in converting pictures to rug designs, putting the design right on the canvas mesh rug backing, coded to the proper colors. All Walter had to do was latch hook the right colors of wool pieces into the canvas mesh. It took him the better part of two winters of spare time to finish it.

The art of latch hooking rugs is in the design and color choices. The hooking itself,

Berenice Kail.

especially latch hooking, is a mechanical skill easily learned and perfected by the time you have tied in a hundred pieces of yarn. All that is required is a tool called the latch hook, the canvas mesh backing, and thousands of pieces of wool yarn, each 2 inches or so long. The general rule of thumb is that the yarn pieces should measure ½ inch longer than two times the desired length of the rug pile. A usual length of pile is ¾ inch, which requires a 2-inch length of yarn. You can use cotton or acrylic yarn, but I think it would be silly to do so. As long as you are going to spend the time to handhook a rug, use the best yarn, wool, even if it is more expensive. Wool rugs wear forever, are fairly fireproof, resist dirt, and the pile

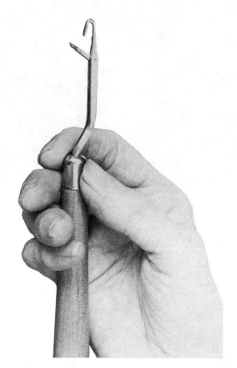

A latch hook.

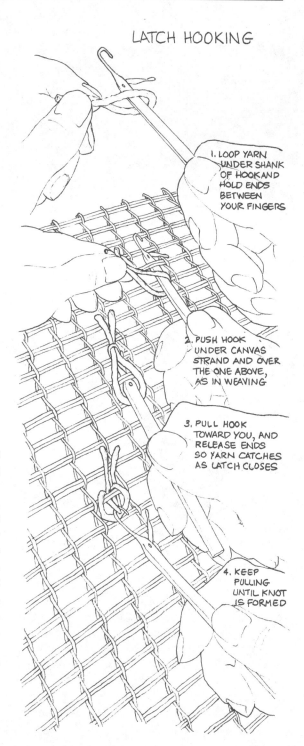

LATCH HOOKING

1. LOOP YARN UNDER SHANK OF HOOK AND HOLD ENDS BETWEEN YOUR FINGERS

2. PUSH HOOK UNDER CANVAS STRAND AND OVER THE ONE ABOVE, AS IN WEAVING

3. PULL HOOK TOWARD YOU, AND RELEASE ENDS SO YARN CATCHES AS LATCH CLOSES

4. KEEP PULLING UNTIL KNOT IS FORMED

springs back up after being walked on. If you're just learning to spin your own yarn, those first lumpy stretches are best used for a rug.

In latch hooking, unlike regular hooking, the yarn pieces are *tied* to the horizontal strands of the canvas mesh backing. The tie is accomplished swiftly and easily by the latch hook. To begin, lay the canvas mesh (whose cut edges have been covered with masking tape to prevent unraveling) on the table in front of you in a roll so that what will be the top side of the rug faces the tabletop. Unroll the canvas backing toward you and bend back the edge to the first horizontal strand that you intend to tie yarn to. This is usually about five strands in from the edge. Now you are ready to start. Hold the latch hook in your right hand (if you are right-handed), hook and latch side up, and put a piece of yarn

Backing for Berenice's rugs.

under the shank of the hook just up from the handle in the bend of the shank and hold it there between the thumb and forefinger of your left hand. Now push the hook *under* the horizontal strand you intend to tie the yarn to, and over the next strand above it. Slide the hook on forward until the latch passes under the horizontal strand. Then pull back slowly, while at the same time releasing your grasp on the yarn ends. The open latch will catch on the horizontal strand and start to close as you pull back. Proceed very slowly now until you learn how and study the drawings. Continue pulling the latch hook back out of the canvas mesh. The hook will pull the doubled yarn through its own

loop and make a knot. The knot is made so fast you will have to repeat the maneuver several times slowly to see how the simple mechanical manipulation works.

Though simple, the action is hard to describe in words even after having done it thousands of times. None of the descriptions in manuals were of much help to me, and I have read some directions that were actually confusing. Probably the best thing you can do is to have someone show you how to do it, and then use the drawings here as reference as you do it on your own.

The only trick, or skill involved, is learning to keep the two yarn ends in every tie even. One end should not be longer than the other. To achieve this evenness, learn to hold the yarn piece against the shank at the beginning of the tie with exactly the same length on either side. Practice makes perfect.

Old-Fashioned Rug Hooking

The latch hook knot allows the pile of the rug to stand up better and so latch hooking can produce a deeper, plusher rug than plain hooking can. However, the old-fashioned rug hooking is a process more adaptable to the homestead situation. Although you can buy wool strips for hooking, regular hooked rugs can be made out of any woolen scraps available, all torn into strips about ⅛ inch wide. All you have to buy is the hook, which is like a latch hook without the latch. Even the backing can come from your place, if you happen to have some old burlap sacks or homespun. Both are tough enough and widely meshed enough to be used for hooked rugs, and were for centuries. You are, however, advised by most experts to buy the commercial burlap sold by hooked rug suppliers. The mesh is a bit wider and more evenly spaced for easier hooking, and the burlap is heavier for long wear.

Small rugs can be hooked in your lap, but for larger ones, the work is easier if you have a wood frame to stretch the burlap on tightly and tack down. You can make a frame as described in the item on making comforters. Or you can buy a canvas stretcher cheap at a craft shop. You need only a small frame to stretch part of the rug you are working on. To stretch the burlap so it has no wrinkles in it, tack it at one corner of the frame and pull that side tight to the adjacent corner. Tack there and run tacks every 2 inches between. Pull tight and tack to the next corner. Then fill in with tacks every 2 inches, as along the first side. Next, go down to the last untacked corner and pull tight both ways. Tack that corner and then fill in tacks all around, pulling taut and tacking alternately, first on one side and then the other.

Hooking is basically pulling up loops of thin rag or yarn through the holes in the burlap. The hook is pushed through the top side with one hand. The other hand below the burlap feeds the yarn or rag strip onto the hook by feel—you can't see through the burlap. The hook goes down through the burlap easily enough, but you have to turn the shank sideways to enlarge the hole to pull it back up through with the loop of rag or yarn. Pull loops up about ¼ inch, depending on the fabric you are using, and twist the hook to release it from the loop. Then push down through the next hole in the backing for another grab of yarn. Depending on the thickness of the material, you may or may not have to skip a space occasionally. If pulling a loop through every space in the burlap produces too much tightness, skip a space every other or every third one and see how that goes.

Designs are usually put right on the burlap with crayons of the colors you want to use. You can hook in a straight line across, from right to left if you are right-handed, left to right if you are left-handed, or you can hook more randomly, going in all directions from a starting point. Or you can hook in curves. Practice makes perfect. It is generally easier to hook in the outline of a design and then fill in the middle. Both ends of a length of hooked yarn or rag must be pulled up through the burlap and cut to match the height of the loops.

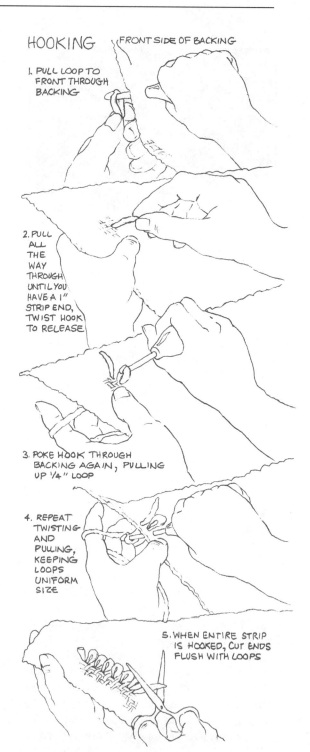

HOOKING — FRONT SIDE OF BACKING

1. PULL LOOP TO FRONT THROUGH BACKING

2. PULL ALL THE WAY THROUGH UNTIL YOU HAVE A 1" STRIP END, TWIST HOOK TO RELEASE

3. POKE HOOK THROUGH BACKING AGAIN, PULLING UP ¼" LOOP

4. REPEAT TWISTING AND PULLING, KEEPING LOOPS UNIFORM SIZE

5. WHEN ENTIRE STRIP IS HOOKED, CUT ENDS FLUSH WITH LOOPS

In hooking rag strips, the hardest part of the job is making the strips. The prime purpose of a hooked rug in early days, as with quilts, was to use accumulating scraps of wool and old woolen clothing. After removing nonwool parts of such clothes, the woolen parts are torn (start with a scissors cut) into 2-inch strips, then cut into narrower strips—about ⅛ inch for thicker types of fabric like flannel, ¼ inch for lighter weight cloth. If a strip is difficult to pull through the burlap, it is too wide. Professionals use a mechanical cutter that cuts cloth into many strips at a time.

Binding the Finished Rug

If you've used masking tape on the rough edges of the canvas, remove it before binding the rug. Then, cut a piece of binding tape (cotton twill is the most popular kind) equal to the length of the perimeter plus about 6 inches. (Two-inch binding tape will give the rug extra strength, but 1-inch tape is more readily available.) Pin the tape on the front side of the canvas as close to the hooked stitches as possible and sew it, easing the tape around the corners. Once you've got it all sewn on, cut the excess canvas about 1 inch out from the binding stitches. Then turn the tape out and around the canvas to its back side. Stitch the binding right through the canvas, folding in the corners to form a pleat, which can be sewn down, if you wish, so that it will be smooth and flat.

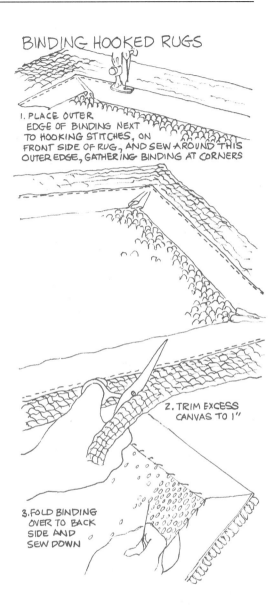

BINDING HOOKED RUGS

1. PLACE OUTER EDGE OF BINDING NEXT TO HOOKING STITCHES, ON FRONT SIDE OF RUG, AND SEW AROUND THIS OUTER EDGE, GATHERING BINDING AT CORNERS

2. TRIM EXCESS CANVAS TO 1"

3. FOLD BINDING OVER TO BACK SIDE AND SEW DOWN

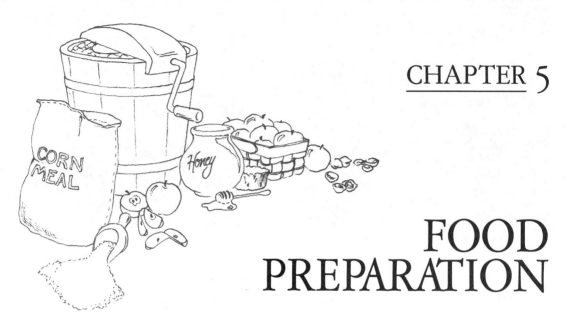

CHAPTER 5

FOOD PREPARATION

Handling Milk from the Cow to the Refrigerator

I would like to avoid the argument over pasteurized versus unpasteurized milk. If you do not know the source of your milk and therefore are unsure of how it is produced, you are probably better off with the pasteurized kind. If you produce your own milk and do it properly, you do not have to pasteurize it and are in fact sacrificing some of the milk's nutritive value by doing so. Home pasteurizers are available, however. Milk processed through them tastes cooked to me, and the cream tends to coagulate into globules your children will probably find offensive. To each his own. I've been drinking unpasteurized milk for the better part of fifty years with no ill effects.

Milk, especially if consumed unpasteurized, must be handled with utmost sanitation. Start off with a healthy cow. She should be checked by a veterinarian every year for brucellosis and tuberculosis, just as all cows are in commercial herds. It is believed that these diseases can be passed on to humans in the milk if it is not pasteurized. There have (but very rarely) been problems with campylobacter and salmonella traced to bad milk, which pasteurization and cleanliness might have avoided. But many, many more people are poisoned by salmonella-infested potato salad than milk, and I have not noticed any rush to pasteurize potato salad yet. The truth is that the big milk processors capitalized on our obsessive fear of undulant fever to get rid of the competition they once felt from small, on-farm raw milk producers selling direct to consumers. Only a few states allow the sale of raw milk today, although most Grade A dairymen and their families drink it themselves, and considerable bootlegging of raw milk goes on in the country.

You can, however, legally drink your own raw milk. The biggest danger in doing so today is antibiotic contamination, which pasteurization does *not* clean up anyway. If you need to use antibiotics on a cow with mastitis, the milk should be discarded for 72 hours thereafter. The way I raise my two cows (see Chapter 9) I've been fortunate enough not to have any diseases that require antibiotics so far, so I do not have this problem.

Milking

Cows should be kept reasonably clean. In summer when they are on pasture, this is usually quite easy, requiring only an occasional brushing of the hind quarters and udder and a perfunctory washing of the teats. In winter, however, the longer hair on the cow's back legs occasionally becomes matted with manure or straw, and even a clean cow will have dandruff, tiny flakes of which fall in the milk bucket. Brush the cow before each milking. Wash the udder. Currycomb the back flanks, or the whole cow, once a week. Once or twice in midwinter, on a warmish day, I wash the cow's tail and

entire hind flanks with warm water and soap. Keep the cows bedded with fresh straw. Clip off the bottom 6 inches or so of tail that drags in the manure.

When cows are on fresh, lush pasture in May and June, the milk often has a grassy taste. To avoid much of that, bring the cows in from the pasture 2 hours before milking.

You can milk a cow from either side, whatever she is used to. I milk from both sides, as my cows are extremely tame. I begin "pretend" milking long before they calve the first time, so there is little training or "breaking" that needs to be done when they freshen.

In milking, make yourself comfortable, so that the job is relaxing, not tense. The milk stool needs to be just the right height to allow you to reach the teats on the other side easily, but not so low that you have difficulty holding the bucket between your knees *off* the ground. The stool height will depend on your own arm and leg length. Do not be afraid to get up close to the cow. A difference of just 2 inches or so too far away will make the job twice as difficult as it need be.

I stick my head right into the cow's flank and make sure my knee (the left one if I am milking on the cow's right side) is between her leg and the bucket. If she lifts her leg, she hits my knee first. I also have developed an automatic response to a cow's kick—my left arm goes immediately against the leg (sometimes without even letting go of the teat), stopping the kick before it really starts. This won't work on a really mean kick, but my cows like me, and they do not kick mean even if they have a sore teat.

But the point I wish to make is that you need to sit yourself in *close* to the cow to use knee and arm in these ways. And you are actually safer from a kick than if you sit back away from the cow and try to lean gingerly forward. You are then unbalanced and cannot control the bucket you have gripped (or should have gripped) between your legs. Being able to

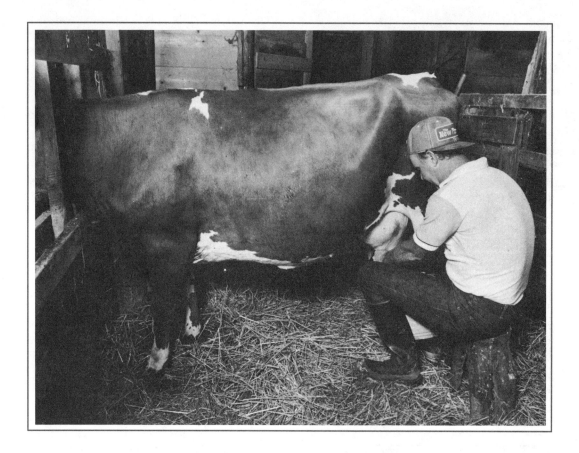

move the bucket with your legs slightly one way or another to accommodate back or front teats is helpful.

Never let the bucket sit on the floor, since it is easier then for a fidgety cow to flick a bit of manure from her hoof into it. Make sure your arms are free of hay chaff that might fall into the milk. Milk buckets that have lids with only a small opening help immensely in keeping dirt out.

No one can tell you how to milk. You have to do it. Grasp the teat in your fist and squeeze from the topmost finger down. With practice that sequential squeezing becomes almost one simultaneous squeeze. Eventually you can learn to milk with thumb and only three fingers or

thumb and two fingers or even thumb and forefinger only if you prefer—or must on a short-teated cow. You do not have to milk the cow out completely if she has a calf nursing. The calf will do it. If not, you must remove all the milk or you'll be setting the cow up for mastitis or she'll begin to dry up. To milk out the last bit, I grasp each quarter of the udder in turn with my left hand and squeeze gently while squeezing the teat with my right hand. This is faster than trying to "strip" each teat.

Straining and Cooling the Milk

The quicker you can get the milk to the house and cooled, the less chance of picking up odors and the better it will taste. I strain the milk first through two thicknesses of cotton cloth—an old-fashioned cotton diaper to be exact—into a big graniteware pan. I place a plastic sack (a Ziploc freezer bag) of ice in the pan so the milk cools rapidly. Then I wash and brush the milk bucket in cold water before any milk has a chance to dry and stick on the stainless steel. Then I rinse out the diaper-strainer cloth. Later, when the plastic sack of ice has melted, I remove it and pour the milk into bottles through a funnel into which I insert a regular milk strainer pad. Pads are available from milk equipment suppliers—we get ours from the local cheese plant, which keeps them on hand for its Grade B milk producers. Before throwing the pad away after straining, rinse the milk out of it, or it will begin to stink in the wastebasket.

Then I wash all the utensils in warm water, soap, and a dash of 5% chlorine (regular washing bleach): bucket, strainer cloth, funnel, graniteware pan, and plastic sack. The sack then goes into the freezer until it's needed. A sack lasts about a month before it begins to leak and has to be replaced.

The bottles of milk are kept in the refrigerator, of course. When the cream rises, we ladle it off, or siphon it off with a basting syringe. The cream is what we are really after since it transforms fruit and cereal and desserts into heavenly delights and makes wonderful butter, which I tell you about a bit later.

Cottage Cheese

My mother-in-law could not understand why we were having trouble making cottage cheese. "Easiest job in the kitchen," she sniffed. "That's why everyone used to make it." Yet, we had followed directions in several cookbooks to the letter, or so we thought, and the result was a cottage cheese that chewed like an all-weather tire. "You probably heated it too long," mother-in-law opined.

I told her, step by step, how we made the cheese. She kept interrupting, like a good mother-in-law should. The conversation went something like this:

ME: First we took the cream off the milk, then warmed the skimmed milk up to room temperature (it had been in the refrigerator) and let it set for 24 hours to clabber. We didn't have any cultured buttermilk on hand, so we added rennet—a fourth of a tablet to the gallon of milk we were doing. (Half a cup of buttermilk per gallon or 4 tablespoons of fresh, unflavored yogurt are the alternatives.)

SHE: Well, you've got good raw milk, don't you? Don't need any rennet or anything else to make raw milk clabber, unless the cow's been on antibiotics recently. Just pasteurized or store-bought milk needs that stuff. (We learned later she was right.)

ME: When the milk congealed to a jellylike consistency, we ran a knife down through it to the bottom of the pan, crisscrossing both ways to cut the curd into about 1-inch squares to release more of the whey.

SHE: Hope you were using an enamelware pan. That or stainless steel is best since whey is slightly acid. (We used a large crock dish, but I decided not to tell her that.)

ME: Then we set the crock, er, pan of cut curd into a larger kettle containing water heated to about 120°F. and let the cheese rise slowly to that temperature, using a kitchen thermometer in the cheese as a guide and stirring very gently so as not to break up the curds.

SHE: Oh, that way's too much trouble. The old-fashioned way was to pour boiling water right into the curd, stirring it in gently until the temperature of the cheese gets to 110°F. Then just pour the whole business into a cloth bag, and hang it up outside where the cats can't get to it, and let it drain all day. Simple.

ME: Well, as I was saying, we heated *ours* up to about 120°F. and held it there for 25 minutes like the book says—

SHE: Humpf. No wonder it was rubbery.

ME: —and then we poured it off into a colander lined with two layers of cheesecloth to let the whey drain out. Then we washed the curds twice, first in lukewarm water, the second time in very cold water, using twice the volume of water to cheese.

SHE: All that work. We just brought ours in after it dripped in the bag all day and added cream and milk and maybe a little salt to taste. Half a cup of cream per pound of cheese. And then we ate it.

ME (Trying to show a little expertise, too): Well, one thing. Once you add the cream and milk, the cheese won't store for long, even in the refrigerator.

SHE: Yea, but it tastes so good a batch gets eaten up in a hurry anyway.

Obviously, there is more than one way to make cottage cheese. With a little experience, you should be successful one way or the other. There's more than one way to eat the stuff, too. My favorite is to put a layer of it over fried potatoes and onions.

Cottage cheese will take freezing well for at least three months, but it is better to compress it into a cake first. Put the chilled but unwashed curds back in cheesecloth and press them gently into a ball. Then with a flat object—a pan bottom or platter will do—press the ball into a flat disk about an inch thick. Leave in the refrigerator overnight and then wrap in a suitable container (aluminum foil is fine) and freeze. Upon thawing, the cheese can be crumbled or sliced.

Easier Homemade Butter

We almost gave up trying to make butter on our own. Following instructions in various cookbooks, we did not have the success we wanted. When the butter would "come," which it sometimes stubbornly refused to do, it would turn rancid or at least get too strong for our tastes within a day or two. We followed instructions closely. The cow was not eating anything that would give the butter a strong taste. We did not use cream more than four days old, but, as the books recommend, we "ripened" it before churning, that is, let it set out at room temperature until it is just beginning to sour. We suspected this was part of our problem, since we did not like sour cream butter, but sweet cream butter.

We followed temperature guidelines closely: cream should be 52° to 60°F. for summer churning and 58° to 66°F. in winter. Still, it was a struggle to get butter and a bigger struggle to get it eaten before it became rancid. We wanted to blame our blender, but when we learned that a churn may take half an hour to make a batch of butter, we were less than enthusiastic to spend the money or the time if the results weren't going to be any better than what we already had achieved.

This spring, when our cow was fresh and giving far more milk and cream than we could use, my wife decided to try once more to make good butter, experimenting this time, rather than following the conventional rules. She decided to try to make butter in the little electric food processor, which I had bought one Christmas in a moment of weakness and which we rarely used after the first faddish fervor. The processor had a stirring attachment with two S-shaped blades that were much larger than blender blades. What would it do?

It made butter in effortless ignorance of the rules. We poured into it a little over a pint (all it could handle at one time) of very heavy cream *straight out of the refrigerator,* and in 5 minutes there was almost half a pound of butter slopping around in the buttermilk. This was fresh, sweet cream, hardly 48 hours old, about the time it takes for Guernsey cream to rise. In fact, our cream gets so heavy it hardly pours, which might be part of the reason the processor makes butter out of it regardless of the rules. But my wife's theory is that the blades of the processor whirl so fast that they actually heat the cream up to the temperature at which the fat globules separate out into butter. Whatever the reason, this method is certainly the easiest way we've found to make butter.

The rest of the operation is conventional. We pour off the buttermilk (save it for pancakes and other delights—see the box), then rinse the butter right in the processor with ice water. Three rinsings with the processor on for about 10 seconds each and the water clears up, indicating most of the buttermilk is washed out. Then we put the butter in a bowl and press and squeeze and work out every last drop of buttermilk with the back of a wooden spoon. (We make the spoons too, see the item on wooden spoons in Chapter 4). The round spoon bottom avoids the inclination to squish the butter out too thinly, which can make it greasy.

This sweet butter has a very delicate taste, perhaps not strong enough for some but much preferable to us than sour cream "ripened" butter. Even without refrigeration, it stays sweet for several days. We add just a bit of salt to it—not as much as most directions call for. Just to make sure we have no problems with rancid butter, we divide a batch up into pats of the size we consume in about three days, then freeze the extra pats until needed. "They" say butter will keep well in the freezer, if wrapped carefully, for as long as three months, but we can't verify that, since it never lasts that long around here.

Our Favorite Ice Cream

There is no argument when it comes to taste, of course—to each his own. But I sigh in distress every time I look at what most cookbooks would have you believe is old-fashioned, homemade ice cream. Almost all the recipes nowadays call for cooking the ingredients. What results should be called frozen ice cream custard, and if the modern Twinkie generation has convinced you that ice cream must be oily smooth (pasty) and stick cloyingly to the roof of your mouth, then cook those ingredients in all good faith and enjoy the results. But if you want real old-fashioned *ice* cream that has a satisfyingly

---

Buttermilk, the Baker's Secret

Discerning cooks will tell you that the flakiest, lightest biscuits, muffins, pancakes, and quick breads are made not with milk, but with buttermilk. This is because the lactic acid in buttermilk reacts with the alkaline baking soda to produce a gas that causes the dough to rise beautifully. Buttermilk reacts nicely with yeast, too. Use it in place of the water or milk in whole grain breads and you'll be giving the yeast extra rising power that will make these heavier breads lighter.

Be aware that homemade buttermilk varies in acidity and is unpredictable in its rising power; you'll never be quite sure what you can expect when you use it with baking soda in a recipe.

Buttermilk from butter making isn't the same as the kind you can get in the dairy case, which is really skim milk that's been inoculated with a bacteria culture. You can make your own cultured buttermilk from homemade buttermilk, or even from plain milk, by mixing a quart of it with a cup of commercial buttermilk. Or you can use some freeze-dried culture (read the directions on the package) and incubate it, just as you would when making yogurt, by letting it sit undisturbed in a warm place for 8 hours. A temperature of 90° to 115°F. is about right, and a gas oven with its pilot light on, a warm wood stove, or a warm radiator would probably provide the gentle heat the culture needs to grow.

---

granular texture to it and a sharp, intense, noncustardy taste—vanilla that tastes like vanilla, not oily vanilla; chocolate that tastes like chocolate, not greasy chocolate; and peach that has peaches in it, not just an orange shade of peaches—then don't cook the ingredients. Save yourself the work and the waste of energy. And save yourself the worry about chilling the ingredients before churning the ice cream.

When you finally find a recipe for "uncooked" ice cream it surprisingly does not include eggs. We always include eggs in our ice cream. Here's our recipe—the way Grandma made ice cream back in the days when Grandpa would cut a cake of ice off the horse trough, smash it up in a burlap grain sack, and use it to freeze a gallon or two for an ice cream party.

Handcranking does not add flavor to the ice cream, but only whets the appetite so the ice cream tastes better. An electric churn is not really an improvement, however. Those motors do wear out, but the handcrank, not in a lifetime. Moreover, the electric motors tend to stall when little chunks of ice around the turning ice cream container wedge tight. This can be exasperating and can be avoided only by using machine-crushed fine ice. We found switching to a handcrank model to be more practical. And having expended the energy of cranking, I feel justified in eating an extra bowl of the result.

Uncooked Ice Cream

This recipe makes 1 gallon of ice cream. It is not efficient to use smaller churns; it takes the same amount of time and energy to handcrank a gallon size as a 2-quart size.

4 eggs
2½ cups sugar or 1¼ cups honey
4 cups heavy cream
6 cups milk
2 tablespoons vanilla extract
½ teaspoon salt

Beat the eggs until thick, add sweetener gradually, then add other ingredients, mix well, and pour into the churn.

Pack the space around the ice cream container with crushed ice and salt, 3 parts ice to 1 part salt, in layers, first filling the bucket about ⅓ of the way with ice, then a sprinkling of salt, then another ⅓ layer of ice, another sprinkling of salt, and a final ⅓ layer of ice and sprinkling of salt.

Crank for 10 to 15 minutes. The crank should be getting hard to turn, but do not worry if your ice cream is not as solid as you'd like when you are finished. It will cure, or solidify, to the proper state after a few hours in the deep freeze, or left in the churn with more ice packed around it, and the whole covered with a burlap sack or similar cloth for added insulation.

Beyond Vanilla

For chocolate ice cream, add a half cup of unsweetened cocoa to the ingredients, first making a paste of it with a little milk.

We like to make fruit ice cream, such as peach or strawberry, by making vanilla and then, when it is about half churned, opening the container and stirring in the slightly mashed fruit. If you just drop in whole berries or slices of peach, they tend to turn into just icy chunks, not really blending into the ice cream.

Some ingredients like grated or chopped chocolate chips, for example, we stir into the ice cream *after* it is made. Before the ice cream ages a bit in the freezer, it is gooey enough that, as we dip it out into pint and quart containers, we can easily stir in such ingredients. This method works well for nuts, especially for making butter pecan ice cream. Sauté the broken pecan meats in a skillet in butter (*not* margarine) for about 5 minutes, stirring constantly. Dip out the nuts and let them drain and dry on paper towels for another 5 minutes. Then, as you dip the ice cream into containers, add the nuts. The amount depends on your taste. About 6 cups of pecans is normal for a gallon of ice cream. Hickory nuts, or even black walnuts, can be used this way very gratifyingly.

Butchering a Chicken

Butchering anything is disagreeable work. But if a person is going to eat meat, he can hardly avoid the work just for that reason and not be a hypocrite. And because chickens are the one animal eminently practical for all homesteads (even the smallest), knowing how to butcher them can be a very handy skill to acquire. Once the technique is learned, the time involved is fairly little. My wife and I can kill, scald, and butcher four chickens in half an hour, if we're in a hurry.

There are other ways to do it, but I kill chickens by chopping their heads off on a stump. I use a regular ax, not a hatchet, as the heavier tool does the job quickly and more accurately, and the poor animal is dead, as far as anyone knows, instantly, without pain. Nevertheless, it will jump around a lot and bruise the meat after decapitation, so for a few seconds I continue to hold it, with both legs and the wing tips grasped together in my left hand, after delivering the death blow with the ax in my right. If you do not hold the wings, too, they will flap uncontrollably. I stick the chicken, neck down, in a bucket, so the blood does not spray on me. It is necessary in butchering anything to get a good "bleed," and decapitation does that as well as the more surgical methods of just cutting the veins in the throat.

Plucking

The next step is to scald the feathers off. Again, there are other ways to remove feathers, but I can assure you my way is the best way for the homeowner with just a few chickens. Theoretically, the water should not be quite boiling—about 180° to 190°F. is just right. But we let the water come to a boil, then let it sit a bit. Our water is usually a bit too hot, and it cooks the skin a wee bit, but this is no problem other than the skin might tear in the defeather-

ing process. A bit of torn skin is no catastrophe either, and eventually you will learn to avoid it. I like to start with the water a bit too hot, so that if we are butchering four or more chickens at once, which we usually do, the water will not be too cool by the time we get to the last one. Better too hot than not hot enough.

Slosh the chicken around in the scalding water for about 20 seconds (less in very hot water, more in not-so-hot water), making sure the water soaks through the feathers to all the skin. Then let the water drain out of the feathers a few seconds and lay your chicken in a pan or bucket or on a sheet of paper while you pluck the feathers. The wing and tail feathers have to be pulled off, sometimes rather forcefully, but the rest of the feathers can practically be rubbed off with the heel of your hand. I generally strip down the thighs first, then pull the wing and tail feathers, then rub down the back, and then the belly and inside of the wings. I do the neck last. With practice you can get 90% of the feathers off in a few seconds. The last 10% takes a bit longer. The hairy pin feathers and the stout feather sheaths that did not come off with the plucking can be scraped with a knife later. My mother used to singe off the hairs that remained after scalding in the time-honored way—over a candle, a kerosene lamp, or with a burning piece of newspaper—which is a good way to set your own hair on fire.

You can scald the lower legs and feet and peel the skin off easily enough. We did so when I was a child, even though there was little meat on the legs. In these days, when we think we are richer, we give the feet to the dog, though this may actually be more economical, since if he is eating chicken feet, he is not eating store-bought dog food.

Cleaning

The plucking finished, the chicken carcass is ready for the actual butchering. Make yourself some kind of work table about waist high and put a pan or bucket under the edge where you will be working. (I use a step of the stairs going up to our outdoor deck.) Set the chicken on its back on a clean piece of paper. A grocery sack is fine; newspaper is not because the print comes off on the chicken skin. Cut off the lower legs first—they are sticking up in your way. Press the heel of the knife blade into the leg joint while bending down the leg with your other hand. The joint will snap open and you can easily cut down between the bones, severing the leg.

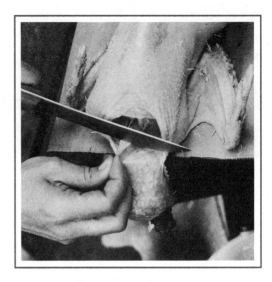

Lifting the skin as shown keeps you from cutting through the crop itself.

Push the knife between the joints—don't try to cut through the bone. Snap the leg backward as you push the knife through.

Next, turn the chicken around, still on its back, so its neck is over the bucket below. The bulge under the skin at the base of the neck is the crop, and it is full of whatever the chicken had been eating. Cut the skin open over the crop. Be very careful because it is easy to cut into the crop, and then the contents spill messily down the neck. (If that happens, don't panic. Clean the mess out and pour a little water over it to flush the grain, digestive fluids, or whatever, into the bucket.) I pinch the skin over the crop between my left forefinger and thumb and raise it up (see photo), slicing horizontally and very shallowly through the raised skin. With a slit of an inch or two made, I use my fingers to peel back the rest of the skin and pull the crop out and down, slicing behind it with the knife as I pull crop and windpipe down the neck and into the bucket.

Now turn the chicken around again, on its back still, with the back end facing you. Spread the legs apart with your left hand, and cut crosswise toward the head just under the breast-

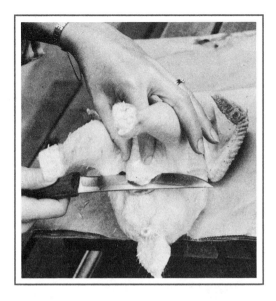

Slice straight in or slightly upward. Don't cut down or you will cut into the intestine.

the original slit, and come down in a similar fashion on the other side, passing in under the anus till I meet my first cut. If you have cut correctly, you will not have punctured any intestine.

Now lay the knife down, grasp the chicken across the breast with your right hand, and reach your left hand into the interior cavity of the chicken until you feel the oval gizzard—about the size of a large egg. Grip the gizzard and pull out and down. With the gizzard and part of the entrails hanging outside the chicken, reach in again and gently grasp the liver and pull it out, too. Cut the gizzard off and lay it aside. Cut the liver out, being sure to remove the gallbladder (that green gland you see in the middle of the liver), and lay it aside. Now pull the entrails on down into the bucket. The last to go will be the intestines right at the anus, and

bone and slightly upward. Do not cut down or even straight in horizontally or you will cut into the intestines nestled inside (see photo). The slit should extend across the chicken from side to side. There will usually be a layer of fat under the skin, and you will have a hard time knowing when you have cut into the interior of the chicken far enough, but not so far as to cut an intestinal lining. If you do cut through an intestine, don't panic. The mess will clean up.

Next, punch the knife straight downward at one end of the slit you made, holding the knife *perfectly vertical,* and cut between the entrails and the flesh. With an up and down motion, like using a jigsaw, cut through the skin and fat layer down past the pelvic bone, staying as close to it as you can, down around the anus. As you come around the anus, your knife should come down from its vertical position to almost horizontal as you cut under the anus and the intestine just inside it. Halfway past the anus I stop, go back to the other end of

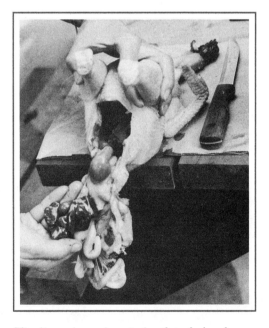

The liver, shown here in hand, is dark red, with the dark green gallbladder in its center. After the liver is removed, entrails go into the waste bucket.

you may have to loosen these gently so that the whole falls into the bucket cleanly—without a speck of manure getting on the carcass. If the latter does occur, no sweat. Just wash it off.

The heart, lungs, and probably part of the esophagus will still be in the chicken. The heart comes out easily. The lower esophagus, which looks something like the heart, needs a hard pull. The lungs lie over the rib cage and are a bit tricky to remove. Feel the rib cage with your fingers, then slide one finger between two ribs at the deepest groove, *under* the soft cushiony mass of lung, and the lung will pop loose, at least it will on older chickens. This technique works better if you slide your finger between the ribs from the outside toward the center of the chicken. On younger chickens, the lungs sometimes seem to get lost, and you have to look up in the chicken several times to find them. With practice though, you can remove them quickly by feel only. The light pink color

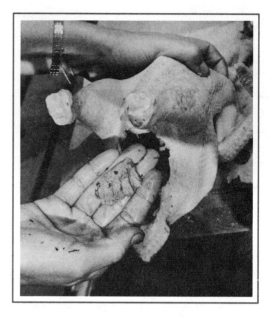

There are two pale-pink lungs, one on top of each rib cage.

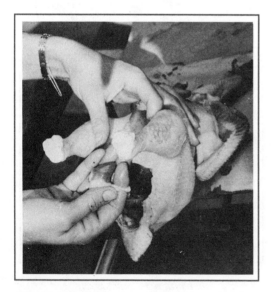

The heart is easily recognizable—it is red and heart shaped. A bit of pale fat always clings to it.

of the lungs distinguishes them from other vital organs.

I clean everything out of the inside of the chicken. Some folks I know prefer to leave the kidneys in along the back because they like the taste of them. To each his own.

The next step is to turn the chicken over and cut the oil sacs off the tail. About 1 inch forward of the tail, cut in about ¼ inch and then down toward the tail, pulling on the flap of skin you have cut with your other hand. The idea is to cut under the oil sacs, but the first time (and many other times) you will no doubt cut right into them. You'll know because the sacs are yellow and exude a yellowish liquid. Tradition says a chicken should not be cooked unless these sacs are removed and as far as I know, everyone follows that tradition.

You still have the gizzard to clean out. It is full of half-digested food. The ideal method is

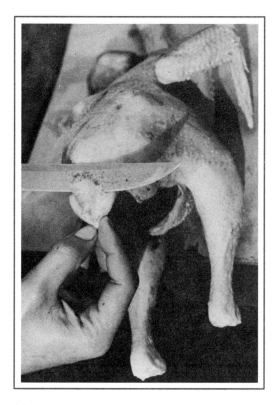

The sac contains a yellow fluid—try not to cut into it.

pouch off the inner gizzard lining (see photo). Then I wash off the gizzard.

In putting the finishing touches on a butchered chicken, my wife scrapes or picks off any bits of feather missed, and cleans out any particles of windpipe, esophagus, or lung I might have carelessly left inside the chicken. She washes the carcass well, inside and out, cuts off the neck to freeze separately, but does not cut up the rest of the chicken before freezing it. In cleaning up the chicken, she is, as old farmers say, very persnickety. There is no untidy speck of anything left on the carcass. For example, on the last joint of the wing, there is a tiny clawlike appendage left over no doubt from the long-ago evolutionary era of pterodactyl flying reptiles. She cuts this tiny claw off. Why? She shrugs. She has no reason. The claw to her is unseemly, that's all.

to slice into the edge of the gizzard but not through the inner pouch containing the digesting food. Once you have an opening of about an inch into the gizzard lining that surrounds the pouch, use your fingers to peel the gizzard away from the pouch. Housewives of my mother's generation prided themselves on their ability to get the pouch out without breaking it. They would say they'd get a new dress for every unbroken pouch.

But especially on young fryers, this pouch tears so easily I don't even try to remove it in one piece—what would I do with a new dress anyway? I simply cut the gizzard open, and then, holding it over the waste bucket, peel the

Skilled butchers can peel out a whole pouch intact, but we just cut it open, scrape out most of the waste, and then peel off the remaining pouch.

A Simple Chicken Catcher

To butcher a chicken, first you have to catch it. Unless you take it off the roost at night, this first step in butchering should not be taken for granted. You can chase the chickens around the coop trying to corner one, raising dust and pandemonium, stumbling, perhaps falling among the squawking biddies. Each subsequent attempt at capturing becomes more difficult as the chickens get wilder and warier. Both you and your flock get bruised and hypertensive in the process.

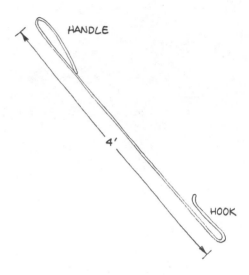

There is a time-honored, easier way. Cut a piece of heavy wire about 4 feet long. No. 9 will do, but heavier stuff is better if you can find it. Bend one end around into a longish loop for a handle and bend the other end into a hook shaped like the one in the drawing. The width of the hook at the closed end should be about the width of your little finger or the approximate width of a chicken leg, opening wider at the mouth of the hook. Then all you do is walk quietly to within striking distance of your unsuspecting feathered friends, hook a leg, and, all in one motion, pull the chicken toward you. While keeping tension on the leg with the hook, grab the leg with your free hand. Works like a charm.

A Traditional Family Hog Butchering

On the two days following Thanksgiving every year, the Dave Pahl family, friends, and neighbors near Kirby, Ohio gather to butcher hogs—using the traditional methods the Pahls have followed for generations. Even the timing is traditional. Experience shows that in this region the last week of November and the first week of December most generally provide temperatures low enough to cool the meat naturally overnight, but not so cold as to freeze it. Without an artificial cooler available, this is all-important. Pork not properly cooled before processing will taste rank and strong, a common failing of home-butchered hogs.

The morning of the first butchering day, all is ready for the slaughtering. The hogs are penned in the barn. The fires roar under the great black iron kettles, used the first day to boil water for scalding off the hogs' hair. A hay wagon, wheels blocked, and with a 55-gallon barrel tilted at a 45-degree angle and chained to the edge of the wagon bed, serves as the scalding platform.

The hogs are shot with a .22-caliber rifle. By mutual and seemingly unspoken consent, certain men have certain jobs, according to their demonstrated skills. One of Dave's grown sons does the shooting. As he aims, older men voice, as they do each year, the traditional

advice: "Wait till the pig looks at you before you pull the trigger"—a graphic way of insuring that the bullet aimed between the hog's eyes will indeed hit the brain, dropping the animal instantly, rather than veering off to the side of the brain.

The rifle cracks, the hog drops, stunned into a brief motionlessness. Swiftly a man jumps forward, with a sticking knife in hand. Before the hog can start kicking in its death throes, he slashes open its throat about 3 inches ahead of the end of the breastbone, then plunges the knife down inside and back slightly under the breastbone, moving the knife rapidly back and forth at its farthest penetration, until a gush of

Kettles are ready for the scalding.

blood indicates the main arteries from the heart have been severed. It is important to the quality of the meat that the animal bleed out as completely as possible.

A steel hook is inserted into the dead hog's mouth, and two men drag the carcass from the shooting pen and roll it onto the hydraulically operated manure scoop on the Pahl's tractor—one of the few modern conveniences they use in butchering. The scoop is raised, and the tractor takes the hog across the barnyard and deposits it on the scalding platform.

The Scraping

Meanwhile, boiling water from the kettles has been carried by bucket to the scalding barrel. Cold water is added, too, if necessary, to bring the temperature down to about 155° to 165°F. If the water is too hot, or gets below 140°F., the hair will not scrape off easily. Two men, each holding a back leg, dunk head and forequarters of the carcass into the barrel, sloshing and rolling it around for a good soaking, pulling the carcass up and "testing the hair" to see if it comes off easily, usually giving it a second or third dunking before they are satisfied. Then the carcass is pulled out, the steel hook inserted again into the hog's jaw, and the hindquarters dunked. When the whole carcass has been scalded, it is pulled out flat on the wagon bed, and five or more men and boys scrape off the hair and dead skin layer. The workers scowl when one of the hogs is brown-haired. "Black and brown hogs never scrape as easy as whites," one says.

(A homesteader, butchering just one or two hogs, can just as well skin them rather than go to the trouble of scalding and scraping off the hair. The objection to skinning is that too much fat is left on the hide, and so less lard can be rendered. But my own experience indicates that if one skins carefully, there is still plenty of fat on the carcass to make a quantity of lard

sufficient for a family's normal needs.)

Speed is essential in the scraping, and the men work feverishly before the hot skin can cool, which could make the hair more difficult to remove. Scraping with the bell scraper is done in the direction the hair lies. Around the feet and head, where there are many wrinkles and indentations, knives are used rather than the bell scraper. When the men are finished, the hog is doused clean with cold water. Then the hide is gone over with knives, as if shaving, to remove any of the top dead skin layer that still remains.

The carcass is then transferred, again via manure scoop, to where actual butchering takes place. To hang the carcass on the tripod scaffolds, the underside of the two back feet are cut open, revealing the tendons located there from which the hog will hang on the scaffold hooks. First the butcher slices through the skin in the center of the foot from the hoof up toward the hock about 3 inches. When he cuts in about ½ inch, he can see the tendon below. Then he cuts deeply on each side of the tendon, and with finger or knife, makes an opening under it to receive the hook.

The scaffold is laid flat out on the ground, the one back leg in one direction, the other two legs in the opposite direction. The scaffold is raised by pushing up the back leg while another man blocks the front legs to keep them from sliding. When the scaffold is raised part way, the hog, still on the manure scoop, is hooked by the back leg tendons to the two hooks on the front legs. Then the scaffold is raised on up and the hog hangs free, its nose just off the ground. (A hog can be hung up by any number of other ways—on a gambrel or single tree—raised by chain hoist or block and tackle, for instance.)

The Butchering

First the head is removed and hung up to cool on the fence, to be dissected into headcheese meat the next day, kept away from the chickens, dogs, and cats.

The carcass is now cut open and the entrails removed. To do this, Dave Pahl first makes a shallow cut with his knife all the way down the carcass belly, from hams to throat. Then, with his knife at the point where the hog was first stuck for bleeding, he cuts upward through the breastbone to the rib cage following his scored centerline.

Next, Pahl goes back up to the top of his original scoring line to open up the abdomen. This must be done carefully, so as not to cut into any intestines lying just beneath the skin. First he cuts through the skin at the top of the abdominal cavity between the hams where there is a bit of a hollow space inside. Then he puts his knife hand into the hollow space with the knife blade pointed outward and slanted slightly upward. He begins cutting down the carcass through the skin with the heel of the knife, the hand that grasps the handle also holding the intestines back away from the knife blade. In this way, he proceeds all the way down to the chest cavity.

Now he goes back up where he started, between the hams, and, staying in the exact center of the carcass, cuts down between the pelvic bones. When he can't cut any farther, he knows he is against what is called the aitchbone at the end of the spinal column. Because the legs are spread wide apart on the scaffold, there is quite a bit of tension on the aitchbone, and it parts rather easily when Pahl puts his knife against it and bumps the end of the handle with the palm of his other hand. (He must be careful so that the knife does not plunge on through and hit the bladder.)

If the hog is a male, Pahl next cuts the penis loose from the skin, but leaves it attached to the internal organs. Then he goes back behind the hog, cuts around the rectum, and ties the intestine closed just back of the anus with a piece of twine to forego any spillage. Then, going around to the front side of the carcass, he pulls the whole loosened business down to where the rest of the entrails are hanging, using his knife to sever any membranes, still holding these internal organs to the wall of the carcass.

The entire entrails are now ready to be removed. Pahl sets a tub beneath the carcass. So as not to tear any of the intestines, he holds them up with his left hand, while loosening and pulling them down and away from the carcass wall with the other. The weight of the entrails is considerable. As they sink lower and lower, the diaphragm appears, and Pahl cuts through it to the backbone and then around each side; the entrails fall free into the pan.

He cuts out the liver from the pan full of organs, discarding the gallbladder. Then he cuts out the heart. Heart and liver are hung up on the barnyard fence to chill and dry.

Stripping offal from the intestines.

The Pahls save the small intestine for sausage casing in the traditional way. After the intestines are separated from the ruffle fat in which they are nestled (they are just pulled apart), the long coils of intestine are taken to the butchering shed (or to the kitchen if no butchering shed like the Pahls have is available). Women traditionally "clean the guts," that is, strip out the contents of the intestines by hand. The female Pahls still do this unpleasant task. My hunch is that women traditionally have been assigned this task because they have more intestinal fortitude (pun intended). Once the

Turning the intestines inside out to make sausage casings.

Headcheese

To make the headcheese, clean and cook the decapitated heads. Some people remove the ears, but most include them in the headcheese. Remove the face hairs from the hoghead by singeing them with a blowtorch. Then remove the teeth and jaw. Cook the rest of the head until the meat falls easily from the bone. Then grind the meat and stuff it into the cleaned stomach and tie the stomach shut. Then it gets smoked. Store the meat in a dry place until you want to slice to serve.

intestines are stripped out, they are scraped on a wooden board with the back edge of the knife. They must also be turned inside out so the mucous lining of the gut can be scraped off on the wooden board, too. To turn the empty intestine inside out requires a neat trick; its original discoverer is lost far back in the misty regions of folklore. The end of the intestine is turned up, as a cuff on a pant leg. When the cuff is sufficiently deep, it is filled with water, the weight of which will pull down the intestine as the "cuff" is lifted, effortlessly turning the intestine inside out (see photo). Once cleaned, the intestines are called casings and are kept in lukewarm water till sausage stuffing the next day.

The Pahls also save the stomach for its traditional use as a container for headcheese, which they call "swagamauger," a corruption of a German word no one seems to know how to spell, but which amounts to smoked headcheese. A slit of about 4 inches is made through the stomach lining, and the contents are carefully worked out and discarded. Then the stomach is turned inside out and placed in scalding water to loosen the inner lining so that it can be removed easily by scraping and washing. The stomach is then kept in lukewarm water until it is filled with the headcheese next day.

The final operation on the hanging carcass is cutting it in half. Starting at the top, Pahl saws straight down the exact middle of the backbone, cutting the carcass completely in two. Then, as a final touch, he loosens the leaf fat on the interior carcass wall, holding the loose flap of it in his left hand and "fisting" upwards with his right to break it loose where it is attached just below the last rib. The removal of the leaf fat hastens cooling. The split carcasses then hang all night to cool.

Cutting the Meat

By the next day, all the body heat is out of the meat and it is ready to be cut up and processed in various traditional ways. The work is more relaxed and pleasant now, more time for talking and joking, more time to pass the traditional bottle of whiskey around the cutting table. The Pahls' butchering shed is long and narrow, a wood stove at one end, the corner opposite the stove taken up by the sausage grinder and stuffer. A long table runs the full length of the building and around it the workers stand, cutting up the meat, trimming the cuts, and cutting the trimmings into pieces small enough to fit into the grinder and the fat into chunks for lard rendering. Along the wall is a band saw for cutting up pork chops and a power slicer for the bacon—the only two tools not strictly traditional.

The Pahls cut up the carcass mainly in the usual way. If you must cut up a carcass without first observing a veteran do it, avail yourself of a chart found in many publications, like *Stocking Up* from Rodale Press (1977), which shows the main divisions into which a half carcass of pork is cut. One of the best books available on the subject is *Butchering, Processing and Preservation of Meat,* written back in 1954 by a USDA employee, Frank G. Ashbrook. Much of the

Everybody gathers around the table for cutting up the meat.

material comes from USDA bulletins. The book has been published most recently by Van Nostrand Reinhold Co. (New York, 1955). This latter book has some good (however grisly) photos of butchering cattle, lambs, and game animals, as well as hogs, poultry, and fish.

The sides of pork are unhooked from the scaffolds, carried to the butcher shed, and laid on the long table, skin side down. The shoulder is cut off first, on a straight line from between the third and fourth ribs at the top down to just behind the leg. An older, more experienced man does this work, the younger ones watching, learning. The cuts are made with a knife and when bone is encountered, the handsaw is brought

Sawing off the shoulder.

into play. The saw is never forced but is allowed to work its own way through the bone.

With the shoulder cut off from the carcass, the butcher then removes the neck bone from the shoulder and trims the latter neatly of all scraps, rounding the fat along the edge. He may or may not, depending on which particular family the shoulder belongs to, further cut it widthways along the blade bone, removing the upper third as a butt or blade roast, leaving the remainder of the shoulder as what is called a picnic shoulder. The fat may or may not be cut off the butt roast depending on its use. (If you are going it alone without experience, visit your local supermarket with an eye to what the different cuts of pork look like. Don't be fearful. Remember that meat is meat no matter how you cut it, and if you make a mistake according

to the normal way of cutting up meat, you can still cook and eat your mistakes.) Finally, the butcher cuts off the foot and lower leg just above the knee joint.

Next, he cuts off the ham from the center portion of the carcass. He positions his saw about 3 inches or three fingers in front of the aitchbone at the end of the spinal column, with the saw at right angles to the leg sticking out beyond the ham. Then he cuts straight through on that angle. Next, he cuts off the foot and lower leg just below the bottom of the hock joint. Finally, he trims off loose pieces of meat on the ham and rounds off the fat edge, nice and neat.

Now he turns his attention to the middle section, which must be separated top from bottom horizontally. The top is called the loin section; the bottom is called the belly or bacon section. To divide them, he cuts straight across the deepest part of the curves in the ribs. This involves starting rather high on the first rib, leaving lots of rib on the belly piece, very little on the loin piece, then sawing in a more or less straight line across the rib cage, each rib on the loin side getting progressively longer and on the belly side, shorter. Once through the ribs, he continues his cut with a knife, severing the two sections.

Then he turns the belly piece over and strikes it with the back of a hatchet to loosen the ribs. Turning the belly over again (skin side down), he cuts out the ribs, starting from the front end and slicing horizontally right under the ribs while lifting them away from the meat with his other hand. The soft cartilage tips of the ribs are left on the belly. What is removed becomes the spare ribs. The belly slab remaining is the bacon slab after trimming off fat on all sides until a good red streak of meat can be seen in the edge.

The butcher now moves to the loin section. Under the backbone on the back part of this section lies a strip of red meat more or less separate from the rest. This is the tenderloin, the choicest meat on the hog. The Pahls, again following tradition, cut this out to be roasted or pan fried fresh—the customary noon dinner on butchering day and alone worth all the work.

Next, the butcher cuts off the back fat from the loin piece, leaving about ¼ to ½ inch of fat on the loin. Dave Pahl then cuts the loin up into pork chops on the bandsaw, perhaps saving part of it for a choice roast.

Meanwhile, the younger workers around the table have been cutting the red meat trimmings into pieces small enough to fit into the sausage grinder, and the fat into chunks about 2 inches square for lard rendering. When there are enough fat trimmings for a batch of lard, they are dumped into the black kettles and the fires stoked up again, slowly at first until the fat begins to melt. The back or external fat is put in first and, when it is about half cooked out, the internal or "lean" fat as the Pahls call it, is added in, since it cooks down much quicker. They also toss in the pig tails to cook—the children look forward to eating them while the cracklings are being pressed out later.

The Lard Making

The lard kettles have to be stirred almost constantly with long wooden paddles to keep the fat from burning. In a couple of hours the pieces of fat have shriveled and cooked down to a golden-brown color, and when they will not float anymore, the lard is rendered. Liquid lard and crisp fat chunks, now called cracklings, are dipped from the kettles after a bit of cooling and are poured into the lard press and then strained through two layers of cheesecloth. The cracklings are then pressed to get out the last bit of lard. The dry cracklings are considered a delicacy by some, and the kids gnaw on their now-cooled pig tails with gusto. (At some family butcherings, a bit of lard is left in the kettle, and several quarts of popcorn are poured in. At first the corn pops and flies everywhere but very

quickly a top layer of popped corn forms and holds the popping kernels underneath in the kettle. Everyone gorges on popcorn, which country folk believe tastes much better popped in lard than in butter.)

The lard is strained into crocks, covered as tightly as possible after cooling, and stored in the cellar. In taking lard out of the crock, I was instructed, always keep the surface level so air has less chance of penetrating the lard and hastening rancidity.

The Sausage Making

While the lard is being rendered, another group is busy making sausage in the butchering shed. The meat trimmings are piled into batches on a table with a certain amount of fat that only preference and experience can dictate, each pile salted and peppered in turn and then ground. The Pahls do not put other spices in their sausage, believing the fresh sausage, well made, needs no other flavoring. Rosy Pahl, Dave's wife, panfries several patties of the first grinding and passes them around for everyone's approval as to the amount of fat, salt, and pepper that have been put into the mix. Everyone nods. The tasting is more of a ritual. Everyone knows that Grandma (Mrs. Alice Pahl) never misses in her sausage mixes.

The ground sausage then goes into the sausage stuffer or press, and the cleaned casings are slipped over the spout, where the sausage squeezes from the press. While one person screws the press down, another feeds the casings on the emerging meat, tying off each casing as it comes to an end, and starting another over the long round sausages.

Grandma keeps a sharp eye over all the operations. She is a marvel, helping tirelessly wherever she is needed. I ask her how many hogs she has helped butcher in her lifetime. "About ten every year," she replies. "And how many years would that be?" I ask. Her eyes

Pressing sausage.

twinkle. "Now that would be tellin', wouldn't it?" she answers. She admits to having been married sixty years, so I figure she has butchered at least 600 hogs and made over a mile of sausage—and cleaned the casing for most of it.

"You raise your own meat, you do your own butchering, you save some money," says her son, Dave. "And when you have the family working all together, there's some fun in it, too." Not to mention fresh tenderloin and lard-crust pies.

Butchering Beef and Lamb

Butchering is a learn-by-doing preceded by a learn-by-watching lesson. If you have read the preceding item on butchering hogs, you under-

stand what must be done to cattle and sheep, too, since the operation is essentially the same. I refer you once again to Frank Ashbrook's fine book, *Butchering, Processing and Preservation of Meat* for the details. The main difference is that cattle and sheep are skinned, and the fat is not rendered for lard (although it might be for soap tallow). Beef animals are skinned with a skinning knife, while lambs are skinned mostly by separating the hide from the flesh and fat with one's hand, or more properly, one's fist. With the fist, the skinner pushes the lamb flesh one way while with his other hand, he pulls the hide the other way. The reason this method is used is because it is very easy to cut through the hide with the knife and ruin it for use as a full sheepskin. However, having skinned a few lambs, I would advise you to keep your skinning knife handy, since fisting alone leaves too much fat and flesh on the hide. If you are very careful, you can skin with the knife without scoring the hide, at least when the flesh won't come loose easily by fisting.

Skinning Beef Carcass

The old saying, "there is more than one way to skin a cat," comes to mind. The idea is to get the skin off in one piece and, if you are a beginner trying to do the job from the written word only, I don't see too much purpose in getting precious about the minor details of an expert job. On a beef carcass, imagine a zipper running down the middle of the animal's belly and down the undersides of the legs. When you skin out the hide, what you will do is "unzip" it along these lines and peel it back and off. The carcass is positioned on the ground, propped up straight on its back, with appropriate blocks on both sides. Slit through the skin along the imaginary zipper lines, starting at the back legs, then down the belly and then the front legs. Cut back under the hide along both sides of the slits. When you have enough skin loose to hold in the fingers of the other hand, do so, pulling the hide away as you cut it loose from the fat and flesh beneath. Use a skinning knife with a curved blade for faster work with less chance of cutting through the hide. Skinning out the legs (first) is slow going, but once you start down the flanks, the work progresses more rapidly. You learn to hold the skin in one hand, pulling away gently, and *press* the skinning knife against the line where hide is separating from flesh. You press or push the knife rather than slice with it, and once the art is learned, the hide seems to fall away effortlessly.

Obviously, with the carcass on its back, the back is the last portion of the hide to come off. When all else is skinned, the carcass is raised gradually on the gambrel by block and tackle or chain hoist—the back feet hooked to the gambrel by the tendons in the same way hogs are hooked to the scaffolds (see A Traditional Family Hog Butchering in this chapter). Expert skinners then rip off the hide from the back

ridge, rather than use the knife. You may find it more practical just to continue skinning with the knife.

Without help from an experienced skinner, I don't think you should try to do a professional job. Don't try to skin out the head. You won't use it for leather (or sheepskin in the case of lamb) anyway. The same with the legs. You will no doubt trim off the scraggly leg scraps anyway. And in the crotch, just "unzip" the skin around both sides of anus and sexual organs. What you want to save is the large back flank sections in one intact skin. And if you do score a hole in the hide, it is not automatically ruined. The sheepskin I use for a lap robe has a hole in it, but it is no less a lap robe for it.

Skinning Lamb Carcass

A lamb is hung up on gambrel or scaffold to skin. Whether you "fist" out the hide or skin

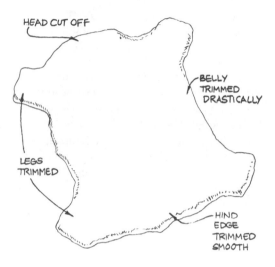

HEAD CUT OFF

BELLY
TRIMMED
DRASTICALLY

LEGS
TRIMMED

HIND
EDGE
TRIMMED
SMOOTH

it with a knife, you proceed more or less as when skinning a calf. But start at the top (rear legs as the carcass hangs) and bring the back down with the rest of the hide. Don't worry about the head—cut it off before starting to skin if you are following my directions. As I said about the beef hide, you will no doubt trim off the scraggly edges of your sheepskin where you skinned around tail and legs, since you are not working for a commercial tannery where every little bit counts. For the same reason, you needn't worry about breaking the leg joint and leaving it exposed on the carcass to prove the meat is lamb and not old ewe. You know what you have.

The hide, when finished, should look something like the drawing above when you have trimmed the edges.

Butchering

From a practical point of view, you may never be faced with the need to skin your own lamb or beef. Home butchering of these animals is not as widespread as with hogs, for

some good reasons. The main one is that both beef and lamb should cool and age at least a week before being cut up and frozen. Few homes have coolers large enough to accommodate hanging carcasses, and outside cooling is risky. Will the weather turn too cold or too warm in that length of time? Few people want to bother with the heat lamps and blankets that I use. Actually, ten days of aging is not too long, and don't let a custom slaughterhouse proprietor (or a university expert) tell you differently. (He doesn't like to clog his cooler space with carcasses that long.)

Al Kin, nationally known Corriedale sheep breeder down the road from us, serves his own lamb at his annual auction and it is always delicious without the least hint of an off-muttony taste. I asked him why. He said he believed the secret was in the aging—that twelve days was about right! Mature beef that is not allowed to age at least a week is not going to be particularly tender no matter how it was fed, in my opinion.

At any rate, lambs are usually ready for butchering in summer, and so home butchering is ruled out unless you have a walk-in cooler. In taking your lamb to the custom slaughterhouse, be sure to impress upon the operator that you want to save the sheepskins, asking him as sweetly as you can to try very hard not to score a hole in them. Pick up the skins right after butchering and prepare them or send them off for tanning.

For beef, we have discovered a convenient compromise between doing the butchering ourselves and hauling the critter to a slaughterhouse. There is, in our area, a traveling butcher—most areas have one. He brings his mobile butcher shop to our place and does all the work from slaughter to processing, even wrapping the meat in paper ready for us to put in the deep freeze. He comes first to butcher the animal, which we hang in the garage to cool and age. A week later he returns with his wife to cut up the meat. Occasionally (we butcher beef in early

Why Cornmeal Is So Practical as a Home-Produced Flour

Maize or corn is as American as rice is Oriental, and there is a certain irony to the fact that we have come to consider bread from wheat as our "staff of life." Corn bread was far more a staff of life in Colonial America— pioneers lived the first several generations without wheat at all in many instances, and memoirs of those days attest to the fact that without "Indian corn" many early settlers would have starved to death.

As a grain for a home food system, corn is still much more practical than wheat or any other small grain. First of all, as the pioneers quickly learned, it is dependable. Except in the extreme North, where the growing season is not long enough, maize suits our American climate, and despite bugs and blights, it generally produces better in bad years than any other field crop. Moreover, corn is extremely versatile. It not only makes meal for batter or bread, it can also be pickled for relish, flaked, parched, popped, roasted, or boiled as sweet corn, fried, made into hominy, or converted to oil or starch. The husks have been used as mattress filling, braided into mats and horse collars. The cobs make smoking pipes, bedding, insulation, even corn-cob jelly. The stalks and leaves make good fodder for animals.

Nutritionally, wheat and other small grains are supposed to contain more protein than corn, but the difference is often slight, and getting slighter now with the development of high lysine corn. Grind a few soybeans in with your cornmeal, and the protein content may equal or exceed wheat. Actual protein content in any grain varies with the fertility of the soil and in some cases climate. Wheat averages about 13% protein; corn 9.5%. But corn on highly nitro-

December or late February) I have to use heat lamps around the carcass to keep it from freezing during the week of aging. But I've learned it takes quite cold weather to be a real threat. Even with 20°F. nights, the meat will not freeze in the garage if wrapped in blankets.

The advantages of using a traveling butcher are many. Not having to find someone with an adequate truck to haul the steer away is advantage enough in my opinion. In addition, you can watch the butcher at work and learn much, much more than I can put into words here. You can dictate exactly how you want the meat cut, for example, how thick you'd like your steaks. You know you are getting your own meat, and all of it. The cost is reasonable. Our butcher charges $35 for a hog or lamb and $75 for beef.

Choosing a Kitchen Mill for Cornmeal and Other Grains

A friend of ours has occasionally ground cornmeal in an old coffee grinder. Early settlers, lacking any other tool, grated their corn across a piece of tin in which they had punched holes—the rims of the upraised hole edges acting as a grating surface. The Hemmingers have a sleek, electric Meadows 8-inch stone mill, acquired some years ago when they were grinding their own grains and selling them commercially to a local bakery. Schertzer uses a little Lee hand grinder that clamps to a table edge. Newcombe has an ancient restored Eureka commercial stone mill that runs off a 6 horsepower gas engine. I have a C. S. Bell No. 2 steel buhr, handcranked mill. The moral of this story is that since we all appear satisfied with our lot, choice is mostly a matter of personal preference and situation.

Most stone mills won't grind oily beans. Steel buhr mills will, but won't grind grain flour as fine as stone mills. Those are the two generalities. My family and I run wheat flour through our steel mill twice. It is still not as fine as the finest wheat flour but it is good enough for our tastes. On the other hand, our mill gums up with soybeans after a couple of cupfuls, even though it is supposed to handle them. (A handful of corn or wheat will usually clear the buhrs.) There is a mill on the market with interchangeable steel and stone buhrs, the Corona King Convertible. From my experience, if I had to make a choice between stone or steel, and I was only going to grind grains, I'd get a stone mill. If I wanted to grind roots, bones, and other weird materials (I use my Bell, for example, to knock sunflower seed meats out of the hulls), I'd buy a steel buhr mill.

ing to Frank B. Morrison's classic *Feeds and Feeding* (Morrison Publishing Co., Ontario, 1961). In either case, the protein in the two grains is not enough that they can be fed to animals without supplemental protein. And in the case of humans, the point is moot, since we derive our protein largely from other sources anyway.

But the main reason cornmeal is more practical as a home-produced flour is because corn is so much easier to grow, harvest, and process with simple hand tools than is wheat or other small grains. It is far easier to harvest 20 bushels of corn by hand than 5 bushels of wheat. The ear of corn is a marvelous invention—the cob being a convenient "handle" by which 750 or so kernels of corn can be picked off the tall stalk, dried, stored, and eventually shelled off. This advantage is especially significant where corn is raised in relatively small quantities for animal feed—the homesteader with minimal equipment can easily harvest as much as an acre of corn but lacks any really practical small threshing machinery for an acre or two of wheat. Corn grown strictly for a family's own eating purposes can be harvested rather painlessly with your two bare hands. (See Tools for a "Handcrafted" Corn Crop in Chapter 10.) Even in the grinding, corn is easier. Although some connoisseurs of corn bread like their flour ground very fine in a stone mill, most of us are content or even prefer the toasty grittiness of cornmeal ground a bit coarsely in a steel buhr mill.

Varieties? Each to His Own

The variety available in corn species can make home grinding an adventure in food discovery. Jim and Mary Hemminger, who farm near Monroeville, Ohio, and who eat a diet based on grains and beans, prefer old harder flint corn for meal. They grow the Longfellow variety. "Flint corn makes a sweeter and tastier meal than dent corn," says Mary. She reinforced her argument by passing me a plate full of flint corn bread, making me an instant convert.

genous soils may contain as much as 12% protein, while wheat may contain as little as 10% in the climate of the Pacific Northwest, accord-

Newton Schertzer, a gardener near Upper Sandusky, Ohio, dotes on corn bread and mush, and, after much experimentation, now prefers dried sweet cornmeal. "You have to dry it real hard or else the meal sticks to your teeth," he says. "I put it in a pan over the furnace during the winter." He also claims that yellow popcorn flour makes excellent corn bread and hoecakes. (Popcorn, according to Morrison, cited earlier, is on the average about 3% higher in protein than regular field corn and therefore nearly equal to wheat.)

The last time I visited Ersel Newcombe in Crestline, Ohio, he was grinding both his own white field corn, which he had brought north with him from West Virginia, and yellow field corn. "Folks always say white corn tastes better than yellow," he told me, "but to tell you the truth, with my eyes closed I can't tell any difference."

Gary Nelson, a Minnesotan writing in *Organic Gardening* magazine in April, 1978, reported that his favorite cornmeal is that which he grinds from his own Black Mexican sweet corn, an ancient variety that turns from purplish white to black at maturity and makes a purplish-hued flour!

I, myself, have always used my open-pollinated Reid's Yellow Dent for meal. What I have learned is that new corn (this year's crop) always tastes better than old corn (last year's crop). The animals know that, too, and always eat more eagerly when I start feeding them the new corn. Also, if corn is left on the cob until right before grinding, it maintains its fresh taste longer than if shelled and stored.

Drying

Corn for meal should be harvested and dried in the traditional manner, either shocked and then cribbed or allowed to dry in the standing stalk and then cribbed to finish drying. (See Tools for a "Handcrafted" Corn Crop in

Modern corn dolls date back to American Indians, who honored them in annual corn harvest feasts.

Chapter 10.) This kind of natural drying is safer than drying with artificial heat in commercial dryers, where sometimes the corn gets too hot and the nutritive value decreases. A small amount of corn can be dried by the oldest method of all—hanging it by the husks in the attic or other dry, rodent-free place. Corn can be braided together by the husks into garlands or clusters for decoration and then used as needed, as one would with braided onions. Use the French braiding method, adding in a new ear husk with each twist of the braid.

Popping Corn

I used to be so uninformed about the finer things in life that I thought everyone popped corn the same way. Or at least popped corn according to the same general theories.

Oh my, no. Popcorn lovers are a very opinionated clan. My brother-in-law, Otto Binau, who claims he could not survive, or at least not survive watching television, without popcorn, grumbled to his wife for ten years that despite everything he tried, the corn no longer tasted as good as it did when he was a youngster. He finally decided the fault was in the popper. He gently persuaded his mother to root around in her cupboards until she found the pan she had used in years long gone to pop corn.

There is nothing special about the pan. It is in fact just a plain old lidded pan with a handle ample enough to allow for some good healthy shaking to keep the kernels from burning while they are heating up prior to popping. Otto operates his pan under the theory that electric poppers make the corn pop tough because they heat up too slowly. With his trusty pan, he allows the oil to heat up on the bottom until it starts to smoke a wee bit, then he pours in the corn. Because the pan and oil are preheated, he says, the corn pops much quicker than in an electric popper. But what fascinates me is the way he scoops off the popped corn as his pan fills and gets the pan back on the burner with hardly a pause in the popping or with hardly one errant kernel exploding across the kitchen. And when popping slows to a final sputter or two, he does not linger over the stove waiting for the last bang. "Makes the corn tougher if it stays hot too long," he says.

This is all in accord with what the old-timers maintained. But they *always* use lard for oil (Otto will settle for corn oil) and salt the popcorn before eating, but decline butter. Lard and salt on popcorn makes a vastly superior snack, so I have often heard in the houses of my neighbors.

I happen to be a butter man myself. In fact, I sometimes suspect I eat popcorn only as a guise to satisfy my craving for butter. I watch people out of the corner of my eye who do not put butter on their popcorn. Such niggardliness could indicate a character who might not always tell everything he knows when selling a used car. So much do I like buttered popcorn that I have renounced all oils, including lard, because of the additional calories. There was a time when any cooking oil in the popper was all right with me. Then I advanced to peanut oil and then to olive oil when I felt really profligate. All were fine, but they conflicted with the amount of butter I wanted on my corn. So when the new air poppers came on the market, which suspend the kernels in air until they pop, doing away with the need for any oil, I bought one, despite my pious aversion for electrical gadgets. Incidentally, not all air poppers are created equal. From my experience so far, I advocate only those that have a separate receptacle for butter, allowing you to add the amount you wish.

The corn from this kind of electric popper seems to me to be just as tender as that from homespun old pans. I have a hunch that tenderness has more to do with variety of corn or moisture content of kernel, although even the experts do not agree. In some ways, white—so-called hull-less—corn is tenderer than yellow, but it also pops smaller and less fluffy than a good yellow hybrid. This tends to confuse the issue of taste quality and leaves the matter up to individual preference. We like Burpee's hybrid Creme-Puff, which approaches Orville Redenbacher's best "gourmet" corn.

Given any good hybrid popcorn, or perhaps even a selected nonhybrid, the only secret to good popped corn is getting it to, and keeping it in, the proper moisture range—about 14% moisture give or take a percent or two. If corn is too moist yet, it won't pop well—giving off loud, promising explosions but only small and tough results. If too dry, the popping is softly

muffled, and the final product will be more burnt than popped. Ohio State home economists say that to maintain moisture in corn, it should be shelled when dry and stored in sealed glass containers in a cool place or refrigerator. But Orville Redenbacher, quoted by Michael Lafavore in the October 1983 issue of *Organic Gardening,* says that corn will pop much better if brought to room temperature before popping.

In our experience, popcorn is rather easily kept at proper moisture. We leave it in the field or garden on the stalk until October, when it is mature and nearly dry. Then we pick it, tying two or three ears together by the husks and hanging them on a wire in the unheated garage for complete drying. By December the corn is down to the optimum 14%, I would guess, or maybe a little drier. But because of the humid climate of the eastern United States, it reabsorbs moisture during wet weather the way wood does and does not get too dry. We start using it about Christmastime, taking down and shelling only two ears at a time—what we eat at a setting—and putting any extra from the two ears in the refrigerator until next time. We have not in many years had any trouble popping the corn, even though it hangs in the garage sometimes for over two years before being popped. And what we hold over in the refrigerator pops OK, too. Corn that gets too dry can be remoistened by sprinkling with water and putting it in a glass jar or plastic container for a few days. Go easy on the water or the corn might mold.

Practical Wild Foods

Harlan and Anna Hubbard live on the bank of the Ohio River near Milton, Kentucky, in the house they built themselves years ago. They are my heroes, not so much because they have learned to live such a serene and gentle life without even electricity to be dependent upon, but because they do so rather elegantly. To live as simply, yet as comfortably as they manage, requires tremendous knowledge and mastery of

Harlan Hubbard.

Harlan paints and does some occasional writing, all of which brings in a small amount of cash. But most of the time he and Anna are busy with the daily activities of producing food, shelter, and fuelwood from their woods and gardens.

Their approach to wild foods is characteristic of their approach to other aspects of subsistent living: They do not spread their efforts too far over an array of exotic possibilities the way Euell Gibbons was wont to do. They do not dabble, or rather they dabble only for recreation. In their "business" of homesteading, they concentrate on the few tried and true sources of food that will net the most results for the least amount of time. A trotline on the river is busy providing fish while they are busy doing something else. They can turn even carp into a delicacy by smoking it. Instead of just cussing

the homesteading arts. I asked Harlan once why he didn't write a book detailing exactly how he and Anna provide for themselves without sinking into the kind of servitude modern society imagines life would be like without modern conveniences. He smiled. "Such a book would be too tedious for the modern reader. No publisher would want to print it."

So he and Anna go on living their own quiet way, although now in their eighties they have a younger man who comes to help out when needed. Anna likes to play the grand piano they brought down the mountainside using a team of horses (there is no real road to their house). She plays the cello, too, and Harlan the violin. When they need to go to town for the few supplies they cannot produce themselves, they go across the river in their rowboat. Mostly they go to the library for a new supply of books.

Anna Hubbard.

groundhogs in the garden, they eat them. Anna makes good tea from readily available plants: spicebush, stinging nettle, sassafras, and pennyroyal, to name a few. Cream of nettle soup is a favorite dish. The salad they served me on my visit several years ago contained not only the standard Bibb lettuce from the garden, but fresh violets (blossoms and all), some slices of Jerusalem artichoke, and sliced daylily shoots (which they also fix like asparagus), the whole sprinkled over with crumbled black walnut meats. That's what I mean by elegant. For berries, they don't spend too much time trying to grow much in the garden, since wild blackberries are so abundant nearby, and the gooseberries they allow to grow almost wild bear without any care at all.

Even with more domesticated foods, the Hubbards strive for this kind of efficiency. Harlan's usual breakfast is a mixture of wheat and soybeans (half and half) that he grinds to meal himself, then cooks in a Dutch oven converted to a double boiler over the fireplace. The gruel cooks while he does morning chores. "But you can just let it sit there and simmer for use at any time of day," says Anna. "You don't have to bother with it much."

Getting good food without bothering too much is one of the keys to a good quality of life on a busy homestead. The following list of wild foods, learned by the Hubbards and my own family, meets that criterion.

Black Walnuts and Other Wild Nuts

Gathering nuts is the most rewarding way to supplement home food supply from the wild. The gathering is pleasant work; the food is a good source of protein. Black walnuts "crack the fastest" as we say, meaning that of all the wild nuts, you can work up a pint of walnut nut meats quickest by hand cracking. However, most nut gatherers prefer hickory nuts and pecans to walnuts and butternuts because the former are less messy and taste better. Wild

hazelnuts rank fifth because they usually do not produce as abundantly as the top four and taste quality is lower. Beechnuts have an excellent taste but are too small and too difficult to crack to be practical to harvest.

Before gathering any wild nuts, crack a few from each tree to see if they are good. Out of ten, five or more should be good before gathering is practical. If black walnut meats are dark-skinned, or if there is a noticeable amount of a pinkish-orange fluid around the nut meats, the nuts will not keep in storage and usually do not taste very good. The nut meat should have a light tan or ivory skin color. This is also true of hickory nuts. Hickories are usually infested with hickory shuckworms that eat the nut meats and then bore a hole out through the nut—usually after you gather it. Use the same five for ten rule for wormy hickory nuts. Some trees some years are infested worse than other trees other years. The nut meats in hazelnuts sometimes do not develop, and the nuts are hollow. This is also true of beechnuts.

Where there are many nut trees in the woods, be selective. Some trees have nuts that crack easier than other nuts of the same tree species, that taste better or that have larger amounts of meat to shell. Size alone is not always a good indicator. A smaller thin-shelled hickory nut may crack out more kernel than a larger, thicker-shelled one. The very large "bull" hick-

---

Nut Butters and Oils

Hickory nut butter or black walnut butter makes a good sunburn lotion. Mash and liquidize the nuts in a blender or food processor. Or do as the Indians did, pounding the nuts and then boiling them in water until the oils melt and float to the top of the water. Skim off and cool. What results is a very good and rare cooking oil.

ory nuts usually do not have the taste of the smaller normal-size ones from shagbarks. Some shagbark hickories have very thin-shelled nuts, but they will not crack out whole halves like a good shagbark will. Taking time to sample the nuts from various trees will make the harvest much more worthwhile. And once you locate the good trees, they will consistently reward you, year after year. Or I should say every other year, since most wild nut trees usually follow a year of heavy bearing with a year of light

bearing. Our family has names for the best hickory trees in our woods—"Big White," "Long One," "Little Whole-Halver," and so on. In looking for nuts, favor open woods or meadow trees. Nut trees of all kinds produce better if not crowded by other trees.

Black walnuts fall from the tree in their green outer husks, which then proceed to rot and turn brown, with the nut remaining intact within. The trick is to remove that fleshy husk without getting the brown stain on your hands,

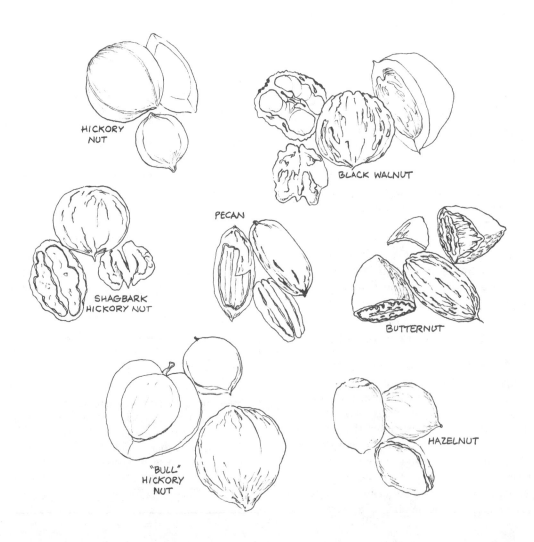

HICKORY NUT

BLACK WALNUT

SHAGBARK HICKORY NUT

PECAN

BUTTERNUT

"BULL" HICKORY NUT

HAZELNUT

a stain exceedingly difficult to remove. That's why it makes such a good dye. The best way we have found is to gather the walnuts when the husks are still solid and green and then run over them with a car. Some folks nail together a wooden trough in which they put a few nuts in at a time, and then run over them with the car tire, but this is needlessly elaborate. Just dump the nuts on the driveway and the car, in its comings and goings, will squish the nuts out of the husks. The husks will shrivel and dry, and you can pick up the nuts (with gloves on) without much mess. The nuts can be spread out to dry further in some sheltered place, then stored in baskets or boxes in a cool, dry building.

Butternuts can be harvested the same way. The husks are sticky but not as staining.

Hickory nuts and pecans either fall free from their husks or the husks can be easily pried loose after the nut matures. The nuts should be spread out and dried for about a month. During this period, the little white maggots in any of the infested nuts will bore out and gather in the bottom of your drying containers or crawl out across the floor. Don't be alarmed. They won't hurt you. Sweep them up and feed them to the chickens or put them in your bird feeder.

Hazelnuts, which are better known to some as wild filberts, are cracked out just like the tame ones, preferably with a nutcracker. We think they taste better if roasted first, like a chestnut. My sister sprinkles the crumbled nuts over breakfast rolls she bakes.

There are various crackers on the market for black walnuts and hickory nuts. (C. E. Potter Co., P.O. Box 930, Sapulpa, OK 74066 sells the Potter Walnut Cracker, which, according to manager Jim Oare, is the granddaddy of them all: "It will crack any nut the Dear Lord has provided with ease and good meat recovery.") But most of us end up using a hammer and a big rock. Experiment in your cracking. Try hitting the walnut on the end, on the flat side, and on the edge side. Different nuts from different trees crack out better, depending on where they are struck. With hickory nuts, always strike on one of the edge sides. The nut is then apt to crack apart in a way that allows you to take out the two whole halves intact. Otherwise, a nutpick is necessary to pry out pieces of nut meat. Keep a pair of nipping pliers handy. Often you can nip off a bit of shell with the pliers, thus freeing a whole half without further cracking. In event, crack out a panful of nuts, then pick out the nut meats. That's faster than taking one at a time through the entire process. With practice, you can easily crack and pick out a pint of nut meats during an evening session in front of the television set, although it is more entertaining to just sit around and talk while you crack.

It is sad that in discussing wild nuts, I can't say much about the American chestnut, which once produced as much protein per acre for man and animal as a crop of corn—and on poor soil, too. But chestnut blight has all but obliterated the tree from the wild. In some parts of its former geographical range, sprouts continue to grow and sometimes produce nuts from old stumps, but seldom with crops practical for harvest. (Robert Wallace, at Chestnut Hill Nursery, Rt. 3, Box 477, Alachua, FL 32615, is selling the Dunstan Hybrid chestnut, a cross between American and Chinese chestnut. The Dunstan Hybrid derives from a large American chestnut found healthy in a grove in dead and dying chestnuts in 1953 near Salem, Ohio. It appears to be very resistant to blight, and its nut is of good quality and taste.)

Blackberries and Other Wild Berries

Blackberries and their close relatives, dewberries, are the most practical wild berries to gather, both for taste and abundance. In their natural range, you can pick a gallon of them in half an hour, so my mother- and father-in-law

STINGING NETTLES

A Natural Berry Remedy

From very ancient times, blackberry roots and leaves, dried and powdered, have been used as relief from diarrhea with positive results. Even eating the berries can help. And by seeming coincidence, the berries are ripe at the time of the year when other fruits and vegetables eaten in quantity can cause diarrhea.

---

say, who once depended on wild blackberries as an important source of supplemental income on their farm. I will always remember my mother-in-law for her answer to my question about whether she thought work on the old-fashioned farm was "back-breaking drudgery," as the literary mythmakers of the early twentieth century have so often written. "Oh, no. We lived very well, especially when I was young and farming was done with horses and we had little expense for outside supplies. *The grocery always owed us money.*"

Wild raspberries, in years when they are plentiful, are worthwhile to pick, although they are not as large as blackberries and so pick slower. Tea from raspberry leaves is rich in vitamin C. Blueberries, in their range, are also very practical. Many wild patches are still harvested commercially.

When picking berries, especially blueberries, hang your picking basket or bucket from your neck or belt so that both hands are free. Most often you will want to hold the stem in one hand while picking the berries with the other. Much practice will teach you how to strip a handful of berries off at a time without mashing them. Be careful of the thorns—especially on gooseberries.

Nettles

The stinging nettle *(Urtica dioica)* is a most interesting wild plant. First of all, the stem is covered with tiny stinging hairs, painful and itchy when you brush bare skin the wrong way against them. The irritation goes away in a minute or two, but one wonders how man ever decided to try to eat a plant so offensive to his skin. Once cooked, of course, the hairs are of no threat. The plant can be cooked just like spinach or cooked with soup stock to which cream and lemon juice is then added to taste, as in cream of nettle soup. But the shoots must be gathered early, and only the top 3 or 4 inches of the plant is used. If the nettles cook up stringy, you have waited too long.

Interestingly, in the Middle Ages, nettle fibers were used for weaving. The dried leaves make a good herbal tea—nettle is rich in vitamins A and C and protein. Old herbals recommend a strong brew of the tea as a cure for dandruff. The plants make a relatively rich nitrogen mulch. The roots of nettle provide a good yellow dye.

The plant is found in rich, moist, shady woodland most often. It grows 15 to 30 inches tall, has leaves ovalish to heart shaped, deeply toothed and 5 inches long by 3 inches wide, with fingerlike clusters of tiny green flowers. But botanical descriptions like that won't identify it very well for you. Once you get stung by it, as all woodland rovers sooner or later do, you'll remember what it looks like. *A Field Guide to Wild Flowers of Northeastern and North-Central North America* by Roger Tory Peterson and Margaret McKenny (Houghton Mifflin Co., Boston, 1968) is the best reasonably priced guide to identifying plants that I have found.

Dandelions

Nearly everyone knows dandelions, although few people eat them, preferring to work twice as hard growing less savory and less nutritious greens in the garden. The only problem with dandelions is that their season of good taste, like that of stinging nettle, is quite short—in the early cool part of spring before hot weather turns them bitter and before the blossom stems emerge from the crown. Gather the plants carefully so they will be easier to clean in the kitchen. Slice off the root below the crown, lift the plant, separate the lower soiled and/or dead leaves from the rest of the plant, and cut them off as you cut off the remainder of the root. Clean off your knife after each slice in the ground so that the next cut will not transfer dirt to the plant. Check for slugs and insects hiding in the base of the leaves.

Forcing Dandelion Roots

Very tasty and delicate dandelions can be enjoyed all winter by forcing the roots in a warm, dark cellar. Dig the roots in late fall before the ground freezes and plant them in soil in a bucket or other container. If you dig up a good clump of soil with the roots, that will suffice. Keep the soil quite moist, never letting it dry out. Before long, pale yellow new plants will emerge.

This kind of forcing works well for pokeweed, too, but remember—the roots themselves are poisonous. Rhubarb will force easily, too. Once the rhubarb roots have been forced, they will seldom, if ever, continue to grow if planted out in the garden again. But usually after a number of years, a rhubarb plant should be dug up and the roots divided, anyway. The extra roots can then be forced.

In the kitchen, wash the plants, then wilt them by blanching them quickly in a bit of boiling water. Mix in vinegar, bacon bits, and chopped boiled eggs. Eat while still hot.

Other Wild Greens

Gather violets in the same way you gather dandelions to mix with lettuce or other fresh salads. Several sprigs of yellow wood sorrel (*Oxalis* species), with its piquant lemony taste, will also perk up a salad. Or sprinkle with the powder of dried wild gingerroot (*Asarum canadense*).

Another wild green practical enough that it is sold commercially comes from certain ferns. The unfurling new branches growing from the old crown—referred to as crosiers because their shape is similar to a bishop's staff—taste as good as asparagus. Pick the "fiddleheads" when they are about 6 to 8 inches

DANDELION

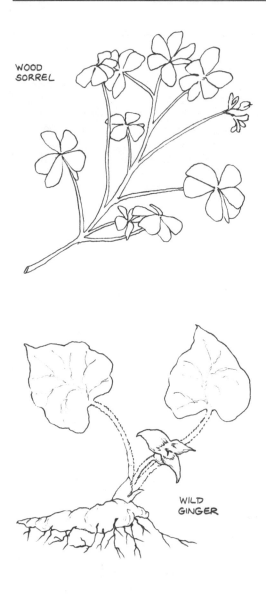

WOOD SORREL

WILD GINGER

The other two are best known in the northeastern quarter of the nation.

One of the most practical and popular greens, pokeweed *(Phytolacca americana),* is actually poisonous in part. The roots, fruit seeds, and the old stems and leaves are quite dangerous when they turn purplish red, yet traditionally, people have learned to eat the fresh spring growth with gusto. The shoots are picked when

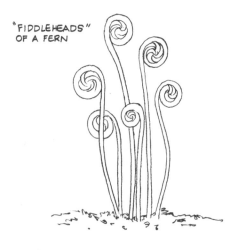

"FIDDLEHEADS" OF A FERN

high. Brush off the hairy coating before boiling or steaming them.

The genuine fiddlehead is *Osmunda cinnamomea,* according to the veteran hunters, but the Ostrich fern, *Pteretis pensylvanica,* is also used, as is *Pteridium aquilinum,* common bracken or brake. The latter grows in one species or another over most of the United States.

about 4 inches long. The little developing leaves are stripped off, the stalks boiled once, and then again in new water, and fixed like asparagus. "Poke" is particularly beloved in the South, where it is often grown in gardens.

Watercress *(Nasturtium officinale),* if you are fortunate to have it growing naturally in your area, and even more fortunate, in a reasonably unpolluted stream, is also most practical to gather and exceedingly delicious to eat. Gather in winter and spring when little else green is available. In warmer weather it turns bitter. I like it best as a fresh salad with a dressing of 2 parts French dressing to 1 part catsup and a dash of steak sauce and/or lemon juice.

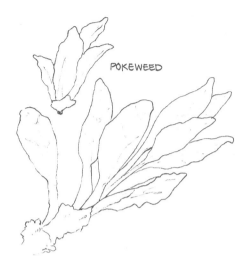

POKEWEED

WATERCRESS

Mushrooms

Again, because they are often plentiful, easy (or pleasurable) to gather, and delicious to eat, the commoner mushrooms are practical fare for busy homesteaders. Morels in spring, common field mushrooms and puffballs in the fall, oyster mushrooms throughout the year, and shaggymanes of the inky cap family are all widely distributed and their identification easy to master.

Morels (*Morchella* species) generally resemble pieces of sponge, although some have long stems and very little body, while others are almost all body and very little stem. Hunting them is a very popular sport in Michigan and many other areas, like my own. Some kind of morel grows everywhere, and you should have no trouble finding someone to teach you to identify them. (Books are of limited help in the case of mushrooms.) Fry morels in butter and a light dusting of your own cornmeal, freshly ground.

The common field mushroom (*Agaricus campestris* and closely related species) is the same fungus that is grown commercially. The mushrooms favor pastures where the soil has not been disturbed by cultivation but has been liberally fertilized by livestock manure. They grow in September and October, sometimes in fairy rings, usually with caps of about 2 to 3 inches in diameter, but sometimes with huge umbrellas 6 or more inches in diameter. They are best if eaten while still in the "button" stage or just as they are beginning to open. These mushrooms are white to brownish on top with *pink* gills. In the button stage, they can be confused with poisonous mushrooms that have

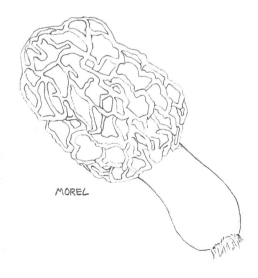

MOREL

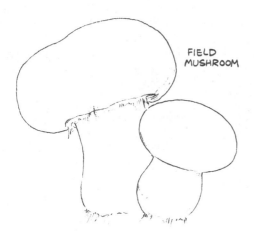

FIELD
MUSHROOM

white gills. (Not all white-gilled mushrooms are poisonous, but tradition in our area teaches us that "only with gills of pink and skin that peels" should the field mushroom be eaten.) Sauté. So delicious are they that you will eat too many as I do and ruin your desire for mushrooms until spring.

Puffballs are highly prized by some fungus lovers. The giant kind *(Calvatia gigantea)* and the baseball-sized *(Calvatia cyathiformis)* are both edible. Slice and fry in butter—they're very rich. The flesh should be firm and pure white at the best eating stage. The skin varies from white to brown. The powder from dry dead puffballs has several reputed benefits— everything from an ability to stop bleeding to curing cancer.

Field mushrooms on a forest floor.

OYSTER MUSHROOM

Shaggymane in a suburban backyard.

PUFFBALLS

Oyster mushrooms *(Pleurotus ostreatus)* grow in tiers on dead or dying wood. They are white to ivory to very pale grey in color, the gills underneath pure white and even edged, not saw-toothed. They, too, are quite easy to get to know, and similar mushrooms are not poisonous anyway. They grow commonly on elder, aspen, elm, some kinds of hickory, and many other woods. You may find a clump of them on a stick of firewood in your wood pile. If so, keep the piece of wood. Generally, the mushrooms will continue to grow from it for several years. Sometimes oyster mushrooms will grow in winter if temperatures are in the mid-40's. Sauté them.

The shaggymane *(Coprinus comatus)* is apt to grow in your yard, especially if the soil has been disturbed and moved around in the construction of a foundation. The mushroom is often found along new highways for the same reason. When fresh, it is tall (2 to 6 inches), slender, more white than grey, and definitely white when compared to other inky caps. It quickly turns grey to black and liquidizes and so should be eaten soon after picking. It tastes good only when young. Once you identify a shaggymane it is hard to confuse it, even with its relatives, which aren't always safe to eat. But the first time, let an expert guide you. Color plates in books are not always accurate.

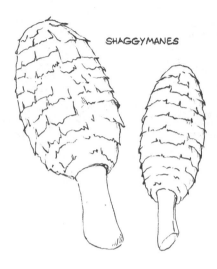

SHAGGYMANES

Meat

The most practical wild food is from animals, though this is the food source most often neglected in books on wild foods. Eating wild rabbits, squirrels, groundhogs, and raccoons seems distasteful, even to those who are gulping down steak and hamburger every day. As civilization "advances," that part of its society that eats meat tends to restrict itself to fewer and fewer species of animals, which is quite wasteful. Earlier societies ate many more kinds of meat than we do today: In medieval Europe all manner of birds and small game were kept in captivity for meat, occupying various niches in the food web and so brought to the table with far more efficiency than our cows and pigs fattened at such horrendous costs of energy and soil.

Almost all small wild animals are perfectly good to eat, although the smaller they are, the less the efficiency in butchering time. Even so, farmers I knew in Minnesota back in the 1950s responded to the explosion of the red-winged blackbird population, which was threatening their corn, not by whining to the government for a subsidy, but by eating the little creatures. I never ate one, but I was assured that blackbird breast is a gourmet delicacy. One well-aimed shotgun blast could bring down a half-bushel of them, too. This is considered by the hoity-toity as barbaric. The hoity-toity prefer that the Army Corps of Engineers poison millions of blackbirds off their winter roosts.

The only special knowledge you need to remember when preparing groundhog, raccoon, opossum, muskrat, deer, and all fur-bearing animals (at least to my knowledge) is that they have scent glands that will taint the taste of the meat if not removed. These scent glands are located under the forelegs and sometimes also near the rump along the spine. They are round or bean shaped, about the size of a pea (larger on deer, of course) and reddish or shiny looking (light yellow on a muskrat). Try not to cut into these while butchering or let them come in contact with the meat, and in any event, remove them before cooking the meat. If you are unsure of what is or is not a scent gland, just clean the carcass of all suspicious lumps and you'll be OK.

I skin all these small animals approximately the same way. I hang them up by the back legs with stout string and proceed just as if I were skinning a hog—as I described in A Traditional Family Hog Butchering. I cut the skin down the inside of the back legs, then work it or "peel it" down off the carcass, pulling with one hand, cutting between hide and flesh with a knife in the other. Sometimes you can just strip the hide off once you are well started, especially with rabbits. In the field with another hunter or at home with a helper, I skin a rabbit by cutting through the skin at the middle of the carcass and then peeling it both ways in two parts, one back over the hind legs, the other down over the front legs. (The head is cut off before skinning.) With this method, when I skin down to the last joint of the legs, I cut off the lower leg with a hoof trimmer or nipping pliers.

I open the carcass down the belly, much as

I described for a hog earlier in this chapter, and remove the innards. Inspect the liver of wild rabbits closely, even if you don't intend to use it. If it has whitish cystlike spots on it, the animal may have tularemia, which infects humans as "rabbit fever." Discard the animal and disinfect your hands immediately. Careful rabbit hunters carry Lysol with them to wash their hands if they should happen upon this problem. We were always taught never to shoot or at least butcher a wild rabbit that did not run vigorously when we jumped it, as such a rabbit might be sick with tularemia. I doubt that this is necessarily a safe way to diagnose the disease. On the other hand, I often wonder about the precautions that are so bandied about. How many rabbits I have seen, dead and alive, and how many rabbit hunters I have known, but not once a case of tularemia. Writers, to cover themselves, must overemphasize safety. But only in some areas. If writers in the field of automobiles or football followed the same cautionary compulsion, their readers would long ago have fled from cars and gridirons, which claim many thousands upon thousands more victims than the poor cottontail rabbit has done in a million years.

Bad experiences with eating wild animal meat is almost always traceable to careless handling: The carcass was lying around too long before gutting or wasn't bled well or was cooked too soon after the animal was killed. At a coon hunter's banquet I once attended, the meat was, believe it or not, half rotten. Fixed with the same care you'd roast a chicken, coon meat can be excellent.

Fish

Careless handling also results in fish that tastes like cod-liver oil. After catching a fish, try to keep it alive until you are ready to clean it, either in a bucket of water or strung up in the water in which it was caught. If you can't do

that, pack it in ice. In any event, do not delay the cleaning for long. Bleeding a fish can be done by pulling out its gills completely, but I generally just cut the whole head off right behind the gills. Then I cut a slit straight down the belly to the anus and strip out everything with my finger. First, however, before beheading the fish, I remove the scales by scraping them with a knife blade or fish scalers, holding the fish by the head.

If you do not have ice and your freshly caught fish dies, and you will not get it to

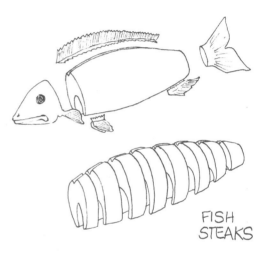

FISH STEAKS

FILLETING A FISH

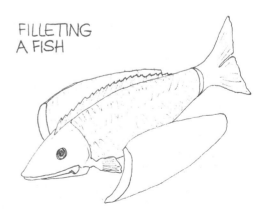

Your Own Honey

I hesitate to describe the way I produce the 8 to 10 quarts of honey we eat every year (we use honey, maple syrup, and sorghum molasses for sweeteners but seldom use honey in cooking or baking). I ignore almost all the rules in bee books about producing honey, and I have done so for eight years without any ill effects at all. Commercial beekeepers will say I've just been lucky, and I suppose to some small degree that's true. But you, too, can easily be that lucky while reducing the complications of beekeeping to a very simple, low-cost, and low-labor activity.

The reason I can ignore the "right" ways of beekeeping is that I allow the bees to perform their natural functions as naturally as possible in the domesticated environment I provide them. Bees in the wild take care of themselves quite

---

Filleting Fish

Begin by making a cut right behind the gills, from the top to the belly, being careful not to slice so deep that you puncture the belly cavity. Then slice along the backbone, from the gills to the tail. The knife should just be touching the bones; you can tell because you can feel them.

Now angle the knife and slice the entire side off, just above those bones that you can feel with the knife.

Turn the fish over and repeat the process to remove the second fillet.

Then skin the fillets with a slight sawing motion of the knife, cutting from the tail end toward the head end. Grasp the skin while the knife slices it away from the flesh so that you can see what you're doing and guide the knife along.

---

refrigeration for some time, clean the fish and wrap it in green leaves (burdock is best not only because the leaves are large, but because they stay exceptionally cool if kept moist).

Some fish are bonier than others. Some have tough dorsal fins that should be cut out. Cut a wedge shape down on either side of a fin and lift it out of the carcass. If it's a big fish, it can be cut crosswise into steaks. If the fish has many fine bones branching off the spine or backbone, it can be filleted. Filleting takes some practice, some trial and error. It is not necessary on some catfish, such as bullheads, nor on most commercial sea fish. Baked whole, a trout's bones will strip out fairly well, like a bullhead's. Bass and pike, in my experience, are notorious for being bony so filleting is in order, even though it is wasteful of some of the meat.

well, and so long as there are places for them to live and nectar for them to gather, they go right on living, even though individual colonies occasionally die out.

The "right ways" that I more or less ignore are the necessary steps the beekeeper must attend to when he is *manipulating this natural bee activity for the highest possible honey production,* that is, when he or she wants to produce enough honey to make the operation *commercially* profitable, possibly even as a way to make a living. Almost all how-to books consciously or unconsciously assume this kind of profitability as the ultimate purpose of home-based work: If the work is cottage industry, then it must make dollars and cents in the so-called real economic world. This assumption even insinuates itself occasionally into how-to gardening books even though the salvation of gardening is that it is a *noncommercial* type of agriculture. The reason I harp and carp on this point is because the very essence of traditional skills and crafts is the avoidance of and freedom from the profit motive. My bees do not make money for me. But being free of the time and equipment I'd need to manipulate them to "profitability," my bees certainly do not lose money, either. The 10 quarts of honey would cost us, retail today, about $40. We bought a $150 extractor, an extravagance already paid for out of that yearly honey income. We've bought little else except honey frames and wax foundations and the usual veil, gloves, and hive tools. I made the hive bodies or received them free from other beekeepers simply by being patient and alert.

There are always bees in hives for sale in the fall in rural newspapers, or to be had for free from someone who went into the bee business for money and lost interest, or from swarms free for the capturing. Hardly a year goes by that I am not called to capture a swarm, usually by a frantic homeowner scared to death of the bees, although when swarming, bees seldom if ever sting. I got my start with a colony owned by a man who found he was becoming dangerously allergic to bee stings. He had three hives. I knew nothing about bees (still know very little). I called a beekeeper. Would she help me get the three hives in exchange for two of them? Gladly. The owner graciously gave us the hive bodies and supers (hive boxes), too (all were in bad shape). We wrapped up the hives in burlap sacks (I watched) and carted them off in a pickup truck. I was in the bee "business." The old saying is that you have to move a colony either just a few feet, or you have to move them a few miles so that the bees will not return to their old location. We were beyond the 3-mile limit, so no worries.

I put my hive up on bricks and doused the bricks with used oil to discourage ants from raiding the hive. I cleaned and refurbished the honey supers that I would eventually add on top of the brood chamber. I must confess that in eight years I have never looked into the brood chamber. To be quite honest, I've been afraid to

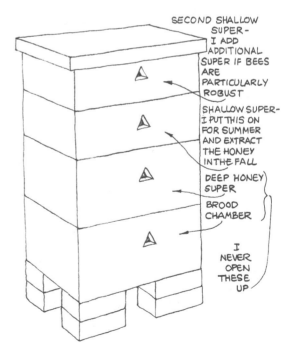

SECOND SHALLOW SUPER—I ADD ADDITIONAL SUPER IF BEES ARE PARTICULARLY ROBUST

SHALLOW SUPER—I PUT THIS ON FOR SUMMER AND EXTRACT THE HONEY IN THE FALL

DEEP HONEY SUPER

BROOD CHAMBER

I NEVER OPEN THESE UP

root around down in there and get on a first-name basis with the queen, or do any requeening or such complicated maneuvers. My theory is that she will do her job if I just don't bother her too much. And I never have. Every June I add a shallow super over the original brood chamber and original deep honey super that I never monkey with. In recent years I've added a second shallow super. In late October I take off this top super and remove the honey. Next June I put it back on again. That is the entire extent of my beekeeping efforts.

What happens, of course, is that when the colony gets overcrowded, because I do not add more supers in the summer, they swarm. The commercial beekeeper goes to great lengths to avoid swarming, so that hive population increases and produces more honey. I welcome swarming. It is the bees' *natural* way to increase themselves. The old queen and old bees leave the hive. A new queen and new workers build up in the hive—renewing the vigor of the colony, and, I'm now quite sure, helping to avoid diseases and other problems that come with the unnatural buildup of huge colonies.

The reason my careless beekeeping methods work is because there is always plenty of honey in the hive for the bees. I'm convinced that feeding them sugar water is not a healthy substitute.

But since I've never taken very good care of the hives (I don't even insulate them for protection in our often subzero winters), I've believed that sooner or later my hive *would* develop problems—at least needing the brood chamber cleaned or replaced. Rather than do that, and also so that I would have to take even less honey out of the one hive, I started a second by capturing a swarm (see the box, Capturing a Swarm of Bees) that issued from the first one. Now, if something goes haywire in the first hive, I will simply destroy it, clean out the brood chamber, and start a new hive from another swarm from the newer colony. But nothing has gone haywire in eight years, as I've said, and the

two-hive arrangement works well for me. When production is down in one due to a recent swarm, production seems to be up a little in the other. So now I'm preparing a hive to start a third colony, after which I will (I tell myself) destroy the oldest one right after it swarms, since two healthy hives is all I wish to keep.

My two hives are not up to professional standards. In one there is no hive cover under the lid as the books say is necessary. One hive has a queen excluder over the brood chamber; the other does not. In neither of these cases does there seem to be any difference in bee activity or honey production. I don't have a proper bee entrance on either hive—just a little piece of wood to block part of the entranceway so the bees have less doorway to defend in case of intruders. Ants try to get in the hives (which are not up off the ground far enough) but when I've watched an ant raid, it always seems to fizzle. The bees carry the ants away as fast as they try to come in. I suppose some day I will get wax moths, but not so far. There's a buckeye tree nearby, the pollen of which is supposed to be poisonous to bees (although the honey bees make from it is OK), but this has seemed to pose no threat either. I continue to operate on the theory that the bees know what they are doing.

I have no very professional way to remove the supers and frames full of honey. I wear protective clothing and use a smoker, of course, puffing smoke all over myself, as well as at the entrance to the hive before I pry off the lid. I puff more smoke over the exposed frames, but not too much. Too much just upsets the bees. I've never found an easy way to drive the bees down into the hive farther, since I have no air blower. I merely pry up a frame at a time, shake the bees off of it, or brush them with my gloved hand (I have no bee brush, either), and carry the frame back to a pan or bucket sitting beyond the range the bees consider their own private territory—about 30 feet away. Then I go back and take out another frame, and so on until the super is empty. Then I lift off the empty

Capturing a Swarm of Bees

If you decide to start beekeeping by capturing a swarm, have your empty hive, smoker, and veil ready at all times. After you have informed local beekeepers and everyone else that you are looking for a swarm, you will almost surely get more calls than you want. But if you follow my advice, be patient and choosy. I believe you should wait for a swarm that is clustered close to the ground. Those high in a tree are too difficult to capture. Banging on a pan will not bring them down after they have clustered, although strange as it seems, there are beekeepers who insist a swarm in the air can be brought down by this ancient custom. Also if there is a hive of bees in a house or building, leave their removal to experts, I say. Such bees are usually not swarming but are a working colony, and they will not take kindly to capture the way a swarm will. In these cases, you can often get a beekeeper, for $20 or so, to capture the swarm for you (or move the housebound colony).

A swarm you can reach from the ground is fairly easy to coax into a super. Set the super on the ground next to the swarm and take the lid off. Bend over the branch the bees are clustered on (or cut it off) and gently shake and brush the bees over the super and in front of it. Keep your smoker handy but use it sparingly. Swarming bees rarely sting. I was scared to death the first time I hived a swarm. They were on a fence post, and the best I could do was brush them into a cardboard box and then pour the full box over the open super. Don't waste time trying to locate the queen. She's down in the middle of the cluster and is difficult to pick out. Usually she crawls right on in the hive with the other bees. You will soon be able to tell, because if she inadvertently crawls under the super or is still back on the post or wherever the clus-ter formed, the bees will come out of the super and crawl or fly around aimlessly and eventually back to wherever she is. When I had most of the bees in the super—don't try to get all of them—I closed it up and carried it back to the stand I had prepared for the occasion. I was amazed at how easy the undertaking had been. And more than anything else, the adventure cured me of being overly afraid of bees. After you have raked fistfuls of them into a box right under your nose, they just don't ever seem so awesome again. Bystanders will think you tremendously courageous or possessed of some gift. They will never believe that bees in swarm are so gorged with honey they hardly ever think about stinging.

A swarm of bees.

A Bee-Hiver

A very old tool can be helpful in capturing a swarm. It is called a bee-hiver and is easy to make. Take an 18 by 14-inch board of regular ¾-inch thickness. (This size of board fits easily inside a super.) Drill about half a dozen holes in the board, sized to accommodate a corncob tightly. Make a sort of hood on the board by nailing another small board, 3 or 4 inches wide and 14 inches long, at one end of the bigger board, with two little triangular wood braces at each side to strengthen the connection between the two boards and to complete the hoodlike structure. (See drawing.) Then nail or bolt a long handle to the back of the hood. The handle can be from an old broom, or even better, a longer piece of 1 by 2-inch lumber. Stick corncobs through the holes you have made in the original board. The tool is now ready for use.

Lift the hood up to the swarm and gently work it in amongst the bees. Or tap the branch they are on with it. Invariably, the bees will begin to crawl onto the corncobs, which have a very nice texture for them to hold onto tightly. When the swarm has clustered onto your bee-hiver, lower it to the ground, lay it flat, and set the super over it. The bees will go up into the frames and then you can set the super back on its base.

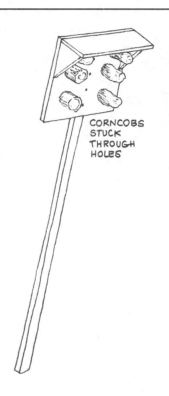

CORNCOBS STUCK THROUGH HOLES

The original use of bee-hivers was more to lure a swarm than to capture one. Two or three were kept stuck into the ground at a slight angle in the vicinity of the beeyard. When a swarm left a hive, it would most often alight on the bee-hiver.

super and put the lid back on the top of the super below.

Then I carry the pan full of frames to the house. The bees remaining on the frames I can now brush off with impunity and they fly away. There's always a couple that get crushed in this transfer. Back at the hive you should be very careful to try not to crush a bee. This can arouse coworkers. But never panic! I've injured bees at the hive, without disaster. I puff a lot of smoke if they start up that certain angry kind of buzzing you soon learn to recognize. I've only been stung twice in eight years.

The caps have to be cut off the combs. We don't have an electric decapper either, but use a butcher knife, the blade kept reasonably hot by dipping it into hot water now and then. The hotter the blade, the easier it cuts through the combs in the decapping process. It's a messy job no matter what, and you should put down newspapers everywhere, because no matter how careful you are, honey will drip on the floor, you will step on it, and then track it elsewhere.

Some of the frames are filled with sheets of foundation wax reinforced with wires that run through them; other frames have wax sheets that are not reinforced. The former are stronger and better, but with the latter, we can cut out large squares of comb honey. I use these unreinforced sheets for comb honey rather than fussing around with the little boxes and special supers used for production of comb honey in commercial apiaries. I first read about this in the books by Ormond and Harry Aebi, *The Art and Adventure of Beekeeping* and *Mastering*

Capping combs.

the Art of Beekeeping, which are, in my opinion, the two best and most readable books on bees (the former now published by Rodale Press, 1983, the latter by Unity Press, 1980, now out of print). The sizes of the squares, once cut from the frame, are just about right to fit on a saucer. We put a piece of wax paper over each square, so they are protected until they are eaten.

The frames with the "windows" cut out for comb honey can be put back in the hive, and the bees will fill them in with comb and honey again so that I can extract the honey from them. If I want more comb honey, I cut out the entire comb in the frame, rather than leaving enough margin around the "windows" for the bees to work from, and I put a new sheet of foundation wax in the frame.

Most of our honey gets extracted in our stainless steel extractor. This operation is very simple. Two frames that have been capped are placed in the wire basket inside the extractor (one at each end). A few twists of the hand crank begins the centrifugal force that throws the honey out of the outside combs of each frame. Then the frames are turned around, the process repeated, and the other sides of the combs emptied. The honey flows slowly down the sides of the extractor to the bottom and then is drawn off through the spigot into jars. Bits of comb wax in the honey float to the tops of the jars and can be skimmed off. The only honey that we strain is that from the comb cappings taken off in the decapping.

In some frames, the honey is occasionally of such poor quality that it crystallizes right in the comb, something none of the books warned us about. As far as we can learn, this is honey from certain wild weeds and flowers. You can't do much with it, and the taste is not very good, so we put it back for the bees to eat. We also put back the cappings and old combs and the bees clean up every bit of honey on them. We then use the wax for an occasional candle or to coat thread for sewing or for grafting. Fortunately,

Some Bee Wisdom

Since there is almost always some grain of truth in the most ridiculous of folklore, I have often wondered about the ancient superstition that when someone dies in the family (i.e. who has been caring for the bees) the bees have to be told. Although literally the notion is ridiculous, I have a hunch it began as a sort of clever or droll way to underline the much less ridiculous belief that bees know their keepers quite well and even distinguish friendliness in humans from fear, if not dislike. This kind of differentiation is well documented in animals, particularly dogs, so why not in so intelligent a being as a honeybee? The hive I started from the swarm I captured has always been friendlier to me than the other hive. Or perhaps I unconsciously am more comfortable around this hive, and so the bees respond in kind. In any case, folklore that teaches us, however drolly, to treat bees as if they were almost human is not ridiculous in the least.

Locate hives in an area where they are protected from harsh winter winds, but where in summer they are shaded in the afternoon. Nearness to water is not as important as some books insinuate. Bees can get plenty of water from dew. But it is important to have your hives located near nectar sources. The farther a bee has to fly for nectar, the less nectar it can gather. Bees are in bad humor on cool days when they can't find much nectar, but when there is a good flow of nectar, as from an apple tree in full bloom, you can brush the bees in the blossoms without fear. They are too happy to sting. Around the hive, however, try not to get between the hive entrance and the airways the bees generally travel. Approach the hive from the rear.

To lessen the danger of being stung when working around the hives, as in mowing grass and the like, hang a piece of your clothing—any cloth with your scent on it—close to the hive so that it flaps in the wind. The bees get used to this "intruder" in their midst and are less wary when you walk close. Don't wear perfume, after-shave, or anything of that sort around bees; they'll go right for you, thinking you're a big, juicy flower.

that poor-quality honey is a rarity, and in most years we don't find any of it in the frames. The best source of good honey in my area is now soybeans, vast acreages of which are a great boon to beekeeping, so long as the crops aren't sprayed with lethal insecticides.

But the honey is different every year. Some years it tends to crystallize in storage more than in other years. Some years it doesn't crystallize at all. When it does, we put a quart as needed in a pan of water and set the pan on the wood stove. It takes about half a day to melt the honey back to a clear liquid.

Apple Drinks and Foods

Although apples aren't quite as American as corn, they are almost as reliable in our climate and even more versatile. The busy homemaker could quite practically depend upon apples for a family's only fruit, and because of the number of varieties and the many ways apples can be processed for food, they never bore the taste buds. Apples can be eaten fresh, canned, sauced, buttered, dried, baked, spiced, and candied. Earlier generations spent many a long winter evening playing euchre and pinochle

while devouring huge bowls of popcorn and pans of apple slices, or when the fresh apple supply ran out, strings of dried apple slices, or "schnitzes," as we called them.

Country people, at least in our neighborhood, no longer are as sophisticated about apples as their ancestors. They don't plant whole orchards full of Pumpkin Sweet just for apple butter, nor do they insist on Duchess apples for pie and Old Virginia Winesap for sauce. Gone is the tradition of mixing 1 part pear juice (perry) to 3 parts apple juice to make what was considered the best cider of all.

But a group of us down our road are headed in that direction. Ever since we all, as by some common impulse, planted little orchards and then went together to buy a hand-cranked apple press, we no longer talk about cider in the singular, but rather about various ciders we have known. The excitement of working with any biological process is that the outcome is never quite precisely predictable. Each year, each variety, and each tree has its own unique individuality when it comes to cider, and this is what makes cider making fun. (I have a friend who claims he can not only distinguish differences in the eggs his ten hens lay, but insists that the eggs from one of the hens actually taste better than from the others.)

As we take turns at the cider press, the discussion often becomes esoteric, if not downright peculiar. One of my sisters prefers a cloudy cider, heavy enough, she says, "so that you can almost feel the apple's fruit cells on your tongue." Everyone seems to understand this description except me. This same sister has experimented with as many as seven different apple varieties in her cider and now believes that the best mixture is about equal parts of Yellow Delicious, Jonathan, and Red Delicious, substituting Winesap if Jonathan is not available. But then she adds, "Go easy on the Red Delicious and heavier on the others." Red Delicious is too bland to make good cider by itself, but she likes it added to the cider. Another member of our Cider Society dismisses Red Delicious altogether, believing that an equal amount of any yellow apple and a tart red apple makes the best cider. Still another says, after much experimentation, that Jonathans alone make the best cider, so long as they come from the particular Jonathan tree in her orchard!

There are, of course, hundreds of older varieties once considered "the best" for cider—which leads to the inescapable conclusion that good cider lies on the tongue of the taster.

Among the things we have learned about making cider, one is this: you will be able to squeeze with a hand-operated press just as much juice out of a basket of ground-up apples filled to only about two-thirds full, as from a basket crammed full. It means the difference of a little over 3 gallons per bushel of juicy apples versus a little less than 2½ gallons.

We strain the apple juice twice, once as it comes from the press, a second time when pouring from the collecting container into jugs or barrels. We strain through a double layer of cheesecloth. Don't fill the container clear to the brim and don't cap it tightly, as the juice will soon start to work even in the refrigerator. Let it stand for a day and then slowly pour off the cider, being careful to leave the bottom inch of dregs in the container. These cloudy, heavier dregs will seldom strain out otherwise. Most important of all if you intend to freeze the juice for winter use, is to freeze it *immediately,* before it starts to work. If you don't, the thawed cider will have a bit of an off-taste to it.

Most of us prefer cider when it is in the "beady" stage—when it has begun to ferment, but is still quite sweet, and so we do not put preservatives in the juice. Usually this beady stage occurs about a week after squeezing in normal fall weather. If the weather is quite warm, the cider will turn hard very fast, sometimes so fast that it actually sours rather than becoming good hard cider or good vinegar. That's why I prefer not to make cider until the last week in October, at the earliest. The slower the apple juice ferments, the better the cider, in my opinion. A small amount made earlier can be kept in the refrigerator in warm weather.

When cider is meant to ferment into hard cider and then into vinegar or applejack, the juice should be stored in a wooden keg, ideally a whiskey keg known not to have been contaminated with any nonfood liquid. Fill the keg with water first so the wood swells and closes any leaks. Then drain. Prop the barrel on its side, bunghole up, and insert a wooden spigot tightly in the hole at the end of the barrel. Fill the barrel through the bunghole.

Vinegar

To make vinegar, just let the cider age naturally. If mother of vinegar is available from someone who has a good batch of vinegar brewing, put a pint or so of it in with the cider to hasten fermentation. But unless cold weather freezes the hard cider and stops fermentation temporarily, vinegar will result with or without mother. Sometimes wild yeasts colonize the cider and ruin the taste of the vinegar, but not usually. It goes without saying that any preservative added to cider will keep it from turning to vineger. If wine is added that has had preservative added (and most cheaper wines have), this will also stop the fermentation process.

Passing on the Mother

An old tradition in our area is to give newlyweds a barrel of vinegar, which, if properly cared for, is supposed to last them a lifetime. Here's how: Whenever taking an amount of vinegar from the barrel, add an equal amount of water. Why this works I'm not scientist enough to know, but I have heard of several barrels of vinegar that have lasted twenty years this way before the fermentation power (or the mother, as it is often called) of the liquid is exhausted.

This practice is very ancient, described in the 1616 edition of *Maison Rustique,* compiled by Charles Estienne and John Liebault: "Vinegar is made in this manner: You must cut these apples into gobbets and leave them in their peeces for the space of three dayes, then afterwared cast them into a barrell with sufficient quantitie of raine water, or fountaine water, and after that stop the vessell and so let it stand thirtie daies without touching of it. And then at the terme of those daies, you shall draw out vinegar, and put into them againe as much water as you have drawne out vinegar."

Hard Cider and Applejack

Hard cider requires an acquired taste to enjoy, in my opinion. The old traditions say that intoxication by the hard cider route results in a very mean drunk, which is why New England early on tried to regulate its production. I don't like the stuff myself, although I will confess to a certain fondness for applejack, which in our area is really apple wine.

To make it, add 3 pounds of brown sugar and a cup of raisins to each gallon of fresh cider. The liquid is allowed to ferment just like any wine. The hole in the barrel (or jar) in which it is fermenting is stoppered with a plug that has a hole in the center through which a length of tubing runs from inside the barrel to a glass of water on top of the barrel. The gases escape from inside through the tubing and bubble up in the glass of water. The water keeps air from getting down through the tubing into the barrel. In due course apple wine results; it is called applejack around here.

Real old-time applejack requires one more step, however. If the barrel of apple wine is allowed to freeze in winter, the contents turn to any icy slush, having too much alcohol to freeze solid. Then a red-hot poker is thrust through the slush, melting a hole in it. The unfrozen alcohol in the slurry then drains into the hole and is drawn off. The result is probably about 120-proof liquor. An easier way, so I'm told, is to fill gallon jugs three-quarters full with the apple wine and set them in the freezer until the contents are soft-frozen. Then turn the jug upside down over another container, and the alcohol—really a kind of apple brandy—will drain out. Supposed to be very good—if you like brandy.

Applesauce and Apple Butter

Grandmothers used to boil down fresh apple juice to a syrup they used then to flavor

HARD CIDER, LIKE WINE FERMENTS IN AN AIR-FREE CONTAINER. THIS SETUP LETS GASES OUT WITHOUT LETTING AIR BACK IN

The traditional way of making apple butter—a full day over an outdoor fire.

pies, especially mince. But the more common ways of processing apples was, and still is, to make applesauce and apple butter. For both processes, I don't think the old ways are the best ways. Our Cider Society has found faster methods, thanks to new kitchen tools.

For applesauce, cook the apples whole in a bit of water until they are soft. For McIntosh and McIntosh-types of apples, this takes only about 15 minutes, same as for Yellow Transparent apples. (However most of us no longer like the early green apples for sauce, but rather for the first apple pie of the year.) Then just run the

whole apple through one of the Squeezo or Victorio handcranked strainers now on the market. The sauce is neatly separated from skin and seeds—no peeling, no slicing required. Sometimes the apples are dirty and need to be washed first. One of my sisters has even invented a faster way to do that. You won't believe this, but she runs them through a partial cycle in the dishwasher (without detergent).

There's a faster way to make apple butter, too, compared to the old all-day cooking arrangement. To make a batch, slice the apples but do not bother peeling them. Add half as

Traditional Apple Butter

5 pounds cooking apples
7 cups water
2 cups apple cider
1 teaspoon ground cloves

1 teaspoon allspice
1 tablespoon cinnamon
½ teaspoon nutmeg

Wash and quarter the apples. Put them in a large, heavy pot with the water and apple cider. Cook for about 15 minutes, or until the apples are soft. Press the apples through a sieve or process in a food mill to make about 2 quarts of apple pulp.

Put this pulp back in the pot, add the spices. Bring to a boil and cook gently for a few hours, until thick, stirring frequently so that the butter doesn't stick and burn.

Can or freeze for long-term keeping.

You can make pear butter the same way, using ginger to spice it.

Butters and sauces can either be canned or frozen.

much cider as apple and cook for about an hour, until the apple slices are very soft. Then run the whole business through a Victorio or Squeezo, which separates the skins from the pulp. Then add your spices: cinnamon, cloves, a bit of nutmeg. Cook for about another hour on a low flame, stirring often, until the butter blobs off a spoon rather than runs off, like a syrup. Then if you wish to make the butter perfectly smooth, whirl it in a blender for a few seconds.

Dried Apples

Apple slices can be dried in the oven, in solar heaters, under cheesecloth on a roof, or wherever. (Traditionally, little effort was made to protect the drying fruit from insects, since the belief then was that the bugs, by sucking out the liquid, hastened the drying.) Another way is to string the apple slices with needle and clean white yarn and hang the strings in a hot attic space.

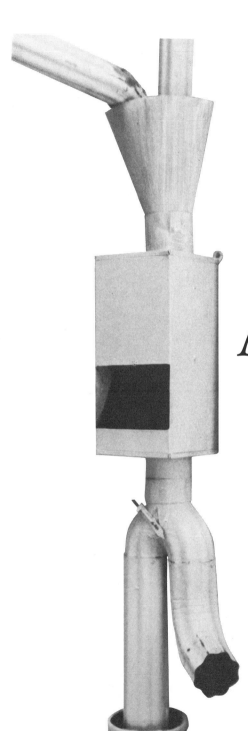

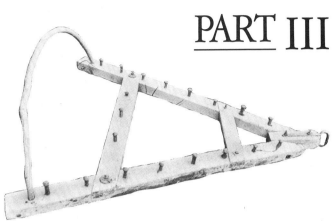

PART III

IN THE YARD AND GARDEN

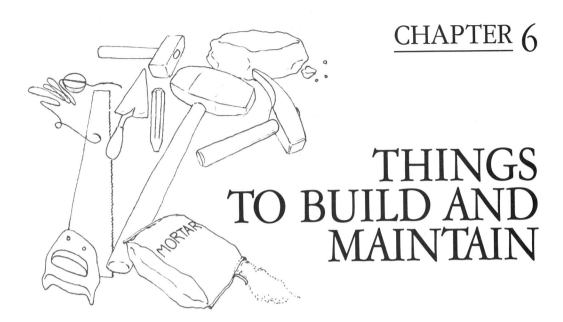

CHAPTER 6

THINGS TO BUILD AND MAINTAIN

The Anatomy of a Homestead Landscape

I am always struck by the simple attractiveness of the Amish home where we have our sorghum pressed and cooked into molasses. Its very plainness, like Shaker furniture, is its beauty. There is some lawn around the house, but not much. Fences and gates, of woven wire and 1 by 6-inch boards, respectively, are strictly of no-nonsense utilitarian design. Gardens are extensive but heavily in favor of food. The flowers are grown in the rows with the vegetables in accordance with old traditions of companion planting, not just for pretty. The orchard extends in a narrow band along the south of the house and barnyard, the trees protected by rings of fencing so the sheep that mow it and eat the windfalls won't gnaw on the bark. The driveways are of gravel. There are sidewalks but only what is necessary from driveway to front door and from back door to barnyard and privy. There is no attempt, or not much, at purely decorative landscaping. The hand pump and windmill are not decoration but necessity. The

montadale sheep are allowed occasionally into the yard to keep the grass smooth and low, not just for whimsy. The noises they make, as well as their appearance, are certainly far more pleasant than those attributes of noise and metal that characterize a riding mower. The house itself is straight, cleanly rectangular, again like Shaker furniture, evocative of a peace, security, and spiritual freedom one does not feel in the presence of bay windows, split levels, and large but forever empty foyers.

While most homesteaders today may not wish to live like the Amish, they will find life much easier if they *begin* to build upon that kind of model rather than the typical suburban landscape, with its extensive, machine-manicured lawns, ample patios, and exotic ornamentals. They must begin yard and garden design with an eye to practicality and achieve beauty as a reward.

The first order of business around the homestead landscape is to control mud, that is, to be able to move about without sinking to your knees in the stuff and leaving, by late spring, great yawning ruts or jagged paths across dooryard or barnyard. Between February and May in my part of the country you cannot *drive* to the barn even with a horse, without gravel lanes. No sod will endure frequent traffic—even of human feet. So one must figure where to place driveways and sidewalks leading to the barn, to the woodshed, to the mailbox, and so forth. If you don't want lanes, you must learn to get all the work that requires horse or tractor or truck done when the ground is dry or frozen and move only on foot in mud time—with big boots.

Fencing is the next consideration. Even if you never intend to graze sheep on your lawn, you will want to fence it to keep out livestock that occasionally escape their lots—yours or your neighbors'. There is no sound more sickening than mud sucking at the hooves of a herd of cows stampeding across your lawn in March. And in many cases, you will want the chickens running loose in the barnyard, but rarely in the dooryard. If you have an orchard, it will be a great advantage to fence it so that you can let chickens and livestock in there regularly to keep windfall fruit cleaned up, a great aid in minimizing orchard insect pests.

The wood pile's place in the landscape should be as close to the house as possible if wood is used regularly for heating, no matter how much its presence there violates the more sensitive tastes of the *House Beautiful* crowd. A well-stacked rick of wood is a thing of beauty in itself (and if not well stacked will soon fall over from frost heaving). Unfortunately the panels of corrugated tin most of us use to cover the ricks are anything but beautiful, but will have to do until a proper woodshed can be built.

The kitchen garden should also be located as close to the house as possible, handy for a last-minute gathering of salad greens. The root cellar, if not an integral part of the house cellar, should also lie close by so that in preparing a meal, you need not bundle up in winter as you would for a long trip to the barn.

Just as the woodshed has come back into favor in many households, so could the summer kitchen of the preelectric era. The summer kitchen usually was an annex to the main kitchen, a roofed step or two from the back door. The idea was, of course, to do the summer cooking where it did not heat up the whole house. If you have electricity, but not air-conditioning, a summer kitchen is still a great idea when it's time to can tomatoes, beans, and peaches—always in hot August.

The orchard should, ideally, be closer to the barn than the house so that livestock can be turned in and out conveniently. An apple tree under which sheep stand all day to escape the hot sun always produces bountifully. The scuffling hooves of the sheep "cultivate" the ground under the tree, and the sheep's manure fertilizes it wonderfully.

When a privy is planned, locate it handy to the house. We have a theory in our family that some of our constipation problems trace back to the time, when as children we hated the long, cold trek to the privy and put it off as long as possible. A well-made privy (see A Practical Privy, which follows) should never cause a problem of seepage into groundwater, but nevertheless, shallow wells should not be dug nearby or downslope from either privy or barn.

TYPICAL TRADITIONAL MAINE FARMSTEAD

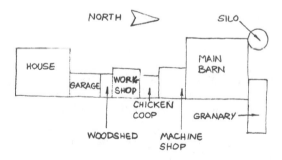

An 1880s Farmstead in Union Springs, New York

This is the layout of a 60-acre 1880s farmstead taken from Vol. IV of *Rural Affairs* by J. J. Thomas (published in 1889). The farmstead is at the edge of the village of Union Springs, New York. Obviously, the residence belonged to a somewhat wealthier-than-average farmer. The plan shows how nicely the various traditional functions of the old farms could come together in a pleasing landscape. Strangely, there is no indication in the layout, nor in the more detailed plans of the farmhouse itself, of a privy or bathroom of any kind. I assume that in those sensitive Victorian times it was not seemly to mention such matters. But from some clues given in the text, I believe the left side of the woodshed was indeed a privy.

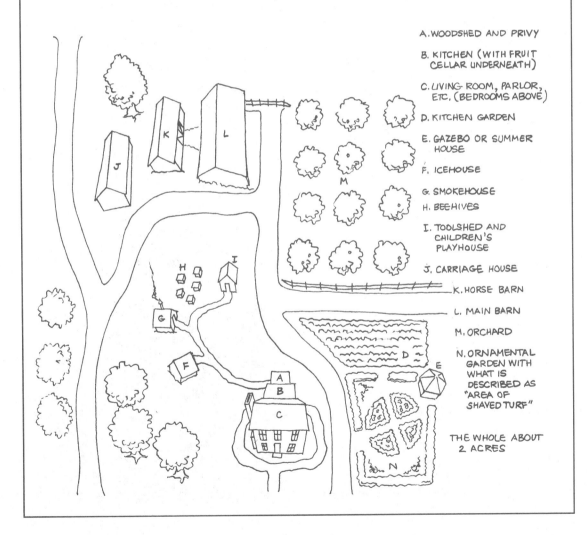

A. WOODSHED AND PRIVY

B. KITCHEN (WITH FRUIT CELLAR UNDERNEATH)

C. LIVING-ROOM, PARLOR, ETC. (BEDROOMS ABOVE)

D. KITCHEN GARDEN

E. GAZEBO OR SUMMER HOUSE

F. ICEHOUSE

G. SMOKEHOUSE

H. BEEHIVES

I. TOOLSHED AND CHILDREN'S PLAYHOUSE

J. CARRIAGE HOUSE

K. HORSE BARN

L. MAIN BARN

M. ORCHARD

N. ORNAMENTAL GARDEN WITH WHAT IS DESCRIBED AS "AREA OF SHAVED TURF"

THE WHOLE ABOUT 2 ACRES

Barns and various barnyard buildings will be discussed in Part IV, but note well here that, ideally, the barn should be downwind and downslope from the house. Thus, if your prevailing winds are westerly, the barn should be eastward of the house. However, this is very much a matter of custom. There are plenty of homes in Europe where people still live above their livestock or at least in houses directly connected to their barns. Where barns are cleaned as fastidiously as the Swiss and Austrians once cleaned theirs as a matter of course, there is no more odor or fly problem in the house than there is in the typical American house whose typical American barn is situated 75 yards away. The traditional barn in Maine is connected to the house by a series of sheds so that a person can walk from one to the other under roof. If you do not have a woodlot or a really good shelterbelt of trees to protect a homestead in winter, this Maine design is still very practical anywhere north of the Ohio River.

Many other small buildings dotted the landscape of the traditional homestead, giving it a pleasing attractiveness while serving practical functions. The icehouse that stood near the house may be gone forever, although its return might be more practical than we imagine (see Icehouse Coolers later in this chapter), but the smokehouse, the toolroom-workshop where all manner of repairs were made, and summer house or gazebo, are as useful today as ever. And with some innovative thinking, the old summer kitchen mentioned earlier might be converted with a large, long firebox and chimney into a maple syrup-sorghum molasses boiler (see Multiple Uses of Backyard Barbeques later in this chapter) used also to heat water for hog scalding (see A Traditional Family Hog Butchering in Chapter 5). The unit could be converted into a Hahsa-type furnace similar to the kind made today in which the furnace is in a shedlike structure separate from the house, with pipes that carry heat into the house during winter; they are supposed to be supersafe.

A Practical Privy

Until a few years ago, anyone in our neighborhood who burned wood to heat his house was looked upon as being too poor or "too tight" to switch to more modern heating systems. Now that we are being forced to pay some of the true cost of our extravagant use of fossil fuel, wood heat looks more up-to-date all the time. (The only sad part of this revolution in public opinion is that while thousands of rural people have purchased wood stoves, hardly one in ten of them has taken the first step toward planting more trees.)

Privies are in exactly the same situation that wood stoves were in a decade ago. Only someone too poor or too tight would still use one, so public opinion would have it, since we are not yet forced to pay the full cost of the

Handling and Composting Human Wastes

Take the following precautions with composted human waste:

1. Its use should be confined to fertilizing the soil in orchards and to the culture of upright berry bushes (e.g., raspberries), corn, and other plants, the edible portion of which is well above the surface of the soil.

2. If you farm, you can use privy compost on pasture, allowing some time for the material to settle into the soil before you allow your animals to graze.

3. Any fruit, berry, or vegetable that may accidentally touch the ground should be cooked.

4. After tilling the soil, thoroughly wash your hands before harvesting the fruits.

5. Human waste should be used only after it has been composted and thoroughly aged.

6. Do not rely upon an isolated bacteriological examination. It takes but a single contribution by a carrier to contaminate the feces being collected.

7. Be extremely careful about personal hygiene when working the compost pile. If possible, a set of clothing should be reserved for use when working the pile. The shovel (or fork) used to move the waste should be reserved solely for that job.

8. Until the compost process has been completed—at least six to eight weeks—the pile should be sealed from the environment. It should be protected from rainfall, and no seepage should be allowed to escape. This precaution is especially important if the operation takes place on a hillside.

[By Clarence Golueke; reprinted from *Organic Gardening and Farming*, December, 1973.]

waste water and pollution from our so-called sanitary flush toilets. As Wendell Berry, the Kentucky poet, essayist, and farmer, has so aptly written in *Organic Gardening and Farming* (December, 1973) in an article about his privy: "In order not to be confronted and offended at home by our 'bodily wastes,' we contrive to swim in them on our vacations."

As long as the Environmental Protection Agency allows rural people to get by with inadequate septic systems, then the privy will not make a comeback. But once country people are faced with the choice of spending big bucks such as my family and I have had to spend to build and maintain a septic system that sends out water clean enough "for minnows to live in" (so the EPA claims), then a good composting privy will look sensible again. Such privies could even be sensible for very small villages that cannot afford the expensive sewage disposal systems the EPA wants them to build. The only problem is that environmental officials listen to water quality experts who are in the hip pockets of the engineering firms who make the big bucks building the expensive sewage systems. They don't want to hear about solutions that won't make money for anyone except the homeowner. As a result, one such village near us continues to flush its septic sewage into a stone quarry lake that people swim in.

The problem with privies is human nature, and in a certain sense, most of the technology we have invented lately embraces mere gadgets that are supposed to solve the failings of human nature but which do so only for a while. The privy demands a certain amount of attention and discipline. Samuel Crapper's flush toilet seemed to absolve us of that need for discipline. But in the long run, it is more difficult to exercise the much-needed discipline of saving water in the bathroom than summoning up the energy to clean out the privy.

Most of us over fifty can remember growing up in a culture where privies (along with the bodily functions that were taken care of there) were considered to be outside the pale of good Christian living. As a result, I grew up in a house that was routinely scrubbed so clean you could eat off the floor, yet our cows defecated in far cleaner surroundings than we did. If we had lavished a fraction of the time and money on the privy that we later spent on the bathroom, I have not the slightest doubt every farm would still sport an elegant outhouse. And the creeks which now carry away effluent from ill-kept septic tanks would still be clean enough to swim in.

The Two-Holer

The best privy I have used lately is one that was built on a steep hillside at a friend's farm. One enters the privy on the uphill side and cleans out the compost chamber from the back door at the lower downside level. The composting chamber is walled with cement blocks that are waterproofed inside and out to prevent seepage in either direction. Over the chamber is the privy proper, which consists of two toilet holes on a bench 16 inches above the floor. Both holes are covered with regular bathroom toilet seats and lids. The windows are screened, and the wooden walls and floors fitted together well enough so that flies cannot get in as long as the door is closed and the toilet lids are down. In eight years of visits to this privy I've never noticed much unpleasant smell, even though there is no vent out of the lower chamber to carry odors away. To put it bluntly, any bathroom in use, even with exhaust fans, stinks no less than this privy. As a carpenter said while building the bathroom onto our farm home when I was a kid: "I don't know as I'd call it progress. We used to make sauerkraut in the house and have the bathroom outside. Now we've just switched around."

A large container of wood chips, sawdust and/or wood ashes are kept on hand in this privy, a quart canful dumped down the hole after each use. Only one hole is used at a time, until the pile of waste below that hole has built up to about 2 feet. Then everyone switches to

the other hole. When the pile under the first hole has stood two to three weeks, it is turned over and shoveled ahead in the chamber to make a new pile. Fresh sawdust or peat moss is then placed on the chamber floor where the pile once stood, along with a bit of earth and lime. Meanwhile, the pile of waste under the other hole has been building up and after it stands for two weeks or so (while the first hole is again in use), it too is shoveled forward in the chamber into another pile. Eventually there are four piles in the chamber, one new, one two weeks

A two-holer of a different sort.

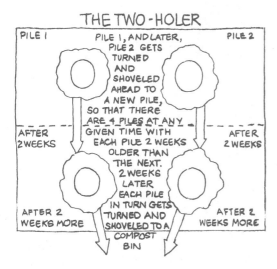

THE TWO-HOLER

PILE 1

PILE 1, AND LATER, PILE 2 GETS TURNED AND SHOVELED AHEAD TO A NEW PILE, SO THAT THERE ARE 4 PILES AT ANY GIVEN TIME WITH EACH PILE 2 WEEKS OLDER THAN THE NEXT. 2 WEEKS LATER EACH PILE IN TURN GETS TURNED AND SHOVELED TO A COMPOST BIN

PILE 2

AFTER 2 WEEKS

AFTER 2 WEEKS

AFTER 2 WEEKS MORE

AFTER 2 WEEKS MORE

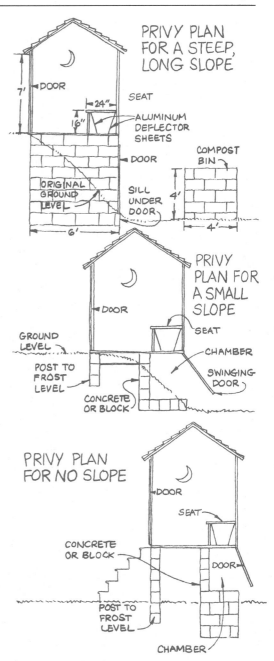

PRIVY PLAN FOR A STEEP, LONG SLOPE

7' DOOR — SEAT — 24" — 16" — ALUMINUM DEFLECTOR SHEETS — DOOR — ORIGINAL GROUND LEVEL — SILL UNDER DOOR — COMPOST BIN — 4' — 6' — 4'

PRIVY PLAN FOR A SMALL SLOPE

DOOR — GROUND LEVEL — SEAT — CHAMBER — POST TO FROST LEVEL — CONCRETE OR BLOCK — SWINGING DOOR

PRIVY PLAN FOR NO SLOPE

DOOR — SEAT — CONCRETE OR BLOCK — DOOR — POST TO FROST LEVEL — CHAMBER

old, one four weeks old, and one six weeks old. (The drawing shows this simple sequence.) The oldest is then shoveled out into a wooden compost bin, which is 4 feet high by 4 feet wide. The material further composts in the bin for six to nine months, or until the owner wants to use it for fertilizer around trees, shrubs, and other ornamentals. The rotation of the piles in the chamber is then continued.

By the time a pile has composted six weeks in the chamber, the toilet paper has mostly decomposed and the waste has no more odor than barn manure. The work involved, says the owner, is about an hour a month. Our fancy agitating septic tank costs about $100 a year to maintain, so that hour is worth about $9, not to mention the value of the fertilizer produced. You can see why I am going to build a privy.

The Tub and Wheelbarrow Approach

Another good privy I've used is inside a small bank barn that is there primarily for wood storage. The privy room is out over the basement part of the barn. The owner keeps a large tub on an old wheelbarrow under the toilet hole. He throws plenty of wood ashes down the

hole after each use. When the tub is full, he carts it out to a spot in his woodlot and dumps it in a long, continuing windrow. He mixes many leaves in the windrow with the tubfuls. In about a year, the material at the end of the windrow where he first started has composted suitably for use as fertilizer. Of course, he does not use the composted manure where it might come into contact with edible vegetables.

This privy has a vent (a length of roofing downspout) from right below the toilet more or less horizontally out to the barn wall, but there are no screens on the window. I doubt either is necessary. There isn't much odor or flies anyway. What's more, a wren built a nest right above my head where I sat on the toilet—a bathroom accessory even the richest king cannot buy.

The Multibin Method

If you do not have a hillside in which to incorporate a handy compost chamber under the privy, you'll have to alter your design. The building will need to be raised above ground level, with steps up to the door, so that you can get enough space under the privy for the manure to pile and begin composting. You will also need several outside composting bins. After the manure stands aging in the privy for two to three weeks, shovel it out into one of the bins, then in a couple more weeks shovel it into a second bin. At least the first bin ought to be covered so that not too much rain gets in, which might more or less drown the pile and hamper aerobic decomposition. The closer you follow good composting procedures, the better (and quicker) will your end product be. You can add other kitchen and garden "wastes" to the manure piles, and occasionally mixing in a layer of dirt helps. Always sprinkle some finished compost back into the other piles as bacteriological "starter."

Septic Tank Principles

In many instances, especially out in the country where houses are not close together, and where the soil is deep enough to absorb the effluent without leaching into groundwater or oozing back to the surface, the septic tank is a suitable way to dispose of human waste. In fact, the soil is thereby enriched. As Erma Bombeck has noted, the grass over the septic tank is indeed always greener.

The septic tank is a very simple device and works when managed right because of a natural phenomenon: bacteria literally eat the solid waste, converting it to liquid and gases. The whole secret is to keep those bacteria working hard. In other words, don't flush down the toilet or the sink any materials that contain bacteria-killing chemicals. Only white toilet paper is recommended, since dyes in colored papers often interfere with bacterial action. In a healthy septic tank (well, healthy for the bacteria) solid wastes coming in form a thick crust or scum on top of the liquid, and this crust remains more or less stable year in and year out if it is not disturbed, as bacteria continually reduce the bulk of the solids by 90% or more.

If a septic tank is not burdened beyond its capacity, it can go thirty years without a cleanout. When cleaning is done every three or four years, it is done either unnecessarily, or because a family is using more water or flushing down more waste and garbage than the system can handle. Grease and fats from the kitchen, for example, do not get broken down like excreta does and really should not go into the septic system at all. Nor should most laundry soaps.

How It Works

The traditional septic tank is made of reinforced concrete and has two chambers, although one-chambered tanks with proper baffles to keep the floating crust away from inlet and outlet work just about as well. (In most areas, septic tanks are severely regulated, so you will have to consult with health inspectors, and they will tell you exactly how a septic tank needs to be designed to meet the regulations of your area. You won't have much choice in the

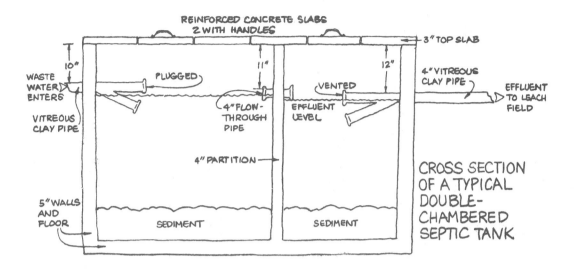

REINFORCED CONCRETE SLABS
2 WITH HANDLES

3" TOP SLAB

WASTE WATER ENTERS

10"

PLUGGED

11"

VENTED

12"

4" VITREOUS CLAY PIPE

EFFLUENT TO LEACH FIELD

VITREOUS CLAY PIPE

4" FLOW-THROUGH PIPE

EFFLUENT LEVEL

4" PARTITION

5" WALLS AND FLOOR

SEDIMENT

SEDIMENT

CROSS SECTION OF A TYPICAL DOUBLE-CHAMBERED SEPTIC TANK

matter.) Waste from the house empties into the larger of the two chambers, where the encrustation forms on the surface, and then, ideally, only a relatively clear liquid trickles over into the second chamber, settles out, and then trickles on out through solid header pipe to perforated pipes that distribute the effluent over the leach field.

Laying in a System

A 600-gallon or 800-gallon capacity tank is usually standard for the typical family. The leach field on the average takes 300 feet of perforated pipe, usually broken up into runs of about 50 feet each. But all this can vary with area and soil type.

A few calculations do not vary and need to be kept in mind, even if you are only going to oversee a backhoe operator doing most of the installation. The flow of effluent through a septic tank system is by gravity, so the grade of the pipes going in and especially going out of the tank should not be too great. Wastewater coming into the tank should come at a fairly slow trickle so as not to disturb the top crust—certainly never with more fall than 10 inches in

10 feet and preferably much less than that, but not less than 2½ inches per 10 feet. The septic tank itself should *not* sit level but should be tipped to allow at least 2 inches of fall from inlet to outlet. The distributor pipe that conveys the effluent to the various lines of perforated pipe needs to be exactly level so that all the lines are equally fed.

The grade of the perforated pipes in the runs should be very gradual, not more than 4 inches per 100 feet in most recommendations. With a steeper grade, the effluent will run too rapidly over the weep holes in the pipe and run out only or mostly down at the end of the lines. If, on the other hand, there would be no grade at all, the effluent would tend to run out rapidly at the start of the pipes.

Another reason for not putting much grade into the system is to keep the leach field as close to the surface of the soil as is possible. That leaves more soil below to absorb the effluent and puts the field up where more rapid evaporation can take place, and where the fertilizer value of the effluent is more readily available to plants.

One more caution: Solid plastic pipe now used for septic tanks often warps into a slight curve if left lying on an uneven surface in

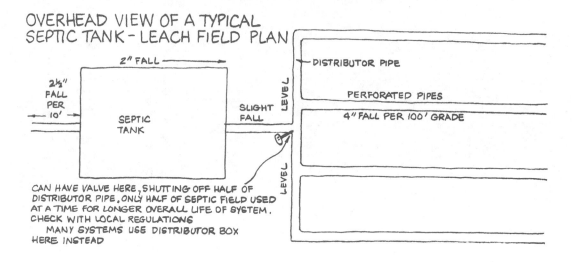

OVERHEAD VIEW OF A TYPICAL
SEPTIC TANK - LEACH FIELD PLAN

storage. When you lay the pipe, eye it up and keep the curve to the side, not up or down, which would cause problems with the grade. Perforated pipe has to be placed holes down, so try to avoid pieces with bad warps in them. Fill in with gravel around the pipe before filling the trench with dirt.

In some cases where a leach field is very difficult to make (in the woods) or where there is not sufficient room for a leach field at all, the EPA has given approval for agitator-aerator septic tanks, which have a chamber where the solid wastes are more or less constantly stirred, and the effluent is run through a gravel filter and aerated back over the filter a second time. These systems are quite a bit more expensive to buy and to operate than ordinary septic tanks, but, when they are working properly, result in an effluent clean enough to empty into streams.

A Practical Cistern

Where well water is not conveniently available in the country or is so hard that it rusts the plumbing out in only a few years, a cistern is not the old-fashioned impracticality most of us moderns believe. A neighbor, Gerald Frey, who is in the construction business, just finished building himself a new house. He equipped it with a large cistern—not difficult for him to do since he is one of the few builders I know who still builds cisterns commercially. "We don't get too many calls anymore, except from members of our own family. We've all been brought up on cisterns and much prefer the taste of rainwater."

Although a good cistern costs as much as a well, Frey points out that from then on the savings are all on the side of the cistern: no water softener needed, no monthly charging with salt. The cistern pump is far cheaper to run than a well pump. Rainwater requires less soap to get a clean wash and glistening hair. Clothes are not stained yellowish as from hard water. And corrosion from rainwater is far less than from hard.

A cistern can be built of any material that can be sealed against leaks, and in any shape. Frey builds round cisterns out of brick. His is large—14 feet deep and 19 feet in diameter. The wall needs to be only one brick thick because the earth has the same effect on a round form as a roof has on an arch—the harder the earth pushes in, the tighter the wall. The bricks are then plastered on the inside and then to insure against leaking, a coat or two of masonry paint is applied over the plaster. The

first row of bricks is laid right on the hard clay ground; 14 feet down no footer is needed on the hard clay because there will be no frost heaving that far below the surface. The concrete floor of the cistern is poured (4 inches deep) *after* the walls are up. That anchors the bottom of the wall solid. "I don't like to lay the bricks right on top of the concrete," explains Frey. "I'm afraid the pressure might crack that juncture between wall and floor and spring a leak."

Frey employs two different filtering systems. He makes (and sells since they are not commonly available anymore) a tin box that fits on the side of the house. The downspouts from the roof feed into the box. Inside there is a screen of hardware cloth, positioned on a slant, with an opening to the outside of the box at the bottom of the slant. Water falls right on through the slanted screen, but leaves and other large pieces of debris roll down the screen, out the exit and onto the ground. A metal plate at the exit slot swings outward so the dirt can fall out, but not in, and so birds cannot get inside. A second, horizontal screen at the bottom of the box catches smaller debris. Below the filter box, the water enters an upside-down Y junction, where by shifting a deflector pipe, the water can be diverted out on the ground (or into a barrel) or allowed to go on into the underground tile that takes the water to the underground concrete filter box on its way to the cistern.

After a period of dry weather, when some dirt is bound to gather on a roof, the first few minutes of rainwater is customarily deflected away from the cistern until the roof is washed off. Some cistern users save no water that falls in May, June, July, or August—"save water only in the months that have an R in them," the old saying goes. The reasoning behind this practice is that warm summer water is likely to become stagnant in the cistern. Frey agrees that snow-melt water is the best for cistern water, but his

Cistern downspout system, complete with slanted hardware-cloth screen in box.

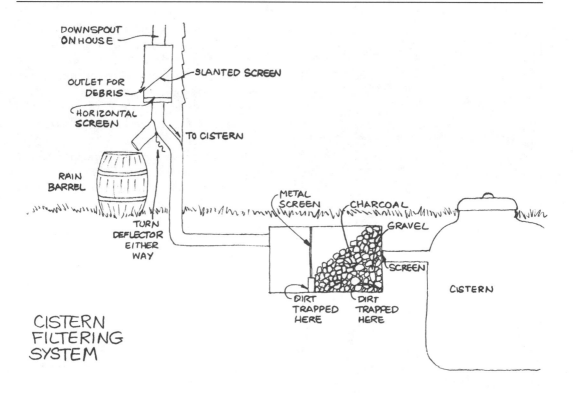

DOWNSPOUT ON HOUSE

SLANTED SCREEN

OUTLET FOR DEBRIS

HORIZONTAL SCREEN

TO CISTERN

RAIN BARREL

TURN DEFLECTOR EITHER WAY

METAL SCREEN

CHARCOAL

GRAVEL

SCREEN

DIRT TRAPPED HERE

DIRT TRAPPED HERE

CISTERN

CISTERN FILTERING SYSTEM

family saves summer water, too, because they use water up relatively fast. With a good filtering system, they have not experienced problems with stagnant water.

The underground filter box is divided into two compartments, the first taking up about one-third of the box. The downspout feeds into this compartment, which is separated from the rest by a metal screen. The screen sits up on a raised base off the floor so water flowing through it must rise to a certain level first. The partition below the screen acts like a trap. Dirt in the water waiting to flow through the screen settles out there.

On the other side of the screen is a section of charcoal, taking up another one-third of the box, and behind that a section of gravel. Water is purified by the charcoal and further filtered by the gravel. The outflow pipe is also screened, or the water might wash gravel on into the cistern.

The pipe is up off the floor of the filter box about 8 inches. This allows water to gather in the gravel below the outlet and again trap out any dirt that might remain in it. The filter box must be cleaned and recharged about every five years.

Filtering water into a cistern is not a standard procedure. There are many methods different from Frey's. In one kind, the filter box is a very elaborate affair, made up of three compartments about 10 inches square and 5 feet deep. Water enters the first compartment and rises *up* through the second compartment, through layers of gravel, charcoal, and sand, then into a third compartment where it goes back down again through three more layers of sand, charcoal, and gravel, and then out to the cistern. The drawback in cold climates is that the outlet is already 5 feet below ground level, and so the cistern must be even deeper.

A rare type of filter divides the cistern

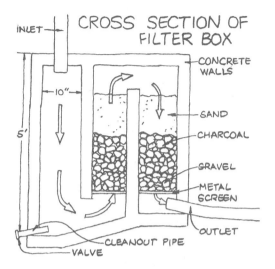

CROSS SECTION OF FILTER BOX

INLET

CONCRETE WALLS

SAND

CHARCOAL

GRAVEL

METAL SCREEN

OUTLET

CLEANOUT PIPE

VALVE

10"

5'

driveways. In those saner days, the road noise was pleasant: a peaceful clip-clop of horse hooves, perhaps punctuated by the jingling of harness bells; the friendly halloo of a neighbor passing by; children laughing on their way from school. Lest you think I romanticize out of a sentimentalism for a past I never experienced, I only wish everyone could have shared with me the evenings a few years ago when I sat on the porch of Miles Fry's lovely farm home near Ephrata, Pennsylvania, and listened to the Mennonite horse and buggies crossing the covered bridge and passing the house. The days when everyone traveled that way were saner times and bred saner people. That covered bridge, for example, which served the neighborhood well over 100 years, was later burned down by vandals.

itself with a brick wall. The brick, being porous, filters the water. Another cistern design incorporates a filter box full of sharp sand, and two well points stuck into the sand draw off the water and relay it to a tank in the basement.

A final caution: it is best not to build a cistern or filter box close to a tree. The roots might wreck it.

Laying Out and Maintaining Country Lanes

For peace and privacy, the country dweller often buys, or builds, a house far back off the road—as far back as he can afford to bring a lane to. In these days of roaring trucks and huge tractors, not to mention the ear-splitting babel of motorcycles, snowmobiles, and recreational vehicles, living back off the road may be a way of preserving sanity, but it means a long lane to maintain and keep open in winter.

Traditionally, most rural people built their homes close to the road so as to contend with the least amount of snow and mud in their own

The Roadbed

In planning lanes and driveways over a couple hundred feet long, understand that unless you are very rich, you will have to be satisfied with some sort of gravel topping. Blacktop makes a splendid all-weather road, but it is too expensive for most of us. Even a gravel lane can become costly, so you should get an estimate from a bulldozer operator experienced in that line of work as part of your house-building budget. Because soil varies from place to place, no general rule serves all situations, but usually you will want to remove about a foot of soil, some of which can be used on the shoulder slopes at the lane edges and some to fill in particularly low spots. Replace the soil with crushed rock or stones of about fist size—at least a foot deep. Over these put a 5 to 6-inch layer of smaller-size stone or gravel, approximately 1 to 2-inch pieces, and then, according to personal preference, perhaps a thin layer of stone dust or very fine gravel to make a hard-packed surface. Your nearby stone quarries will have suggestions on the best kind of material to use in your area. In Florida, very attractive and serviceable driveways are made of crushed oyster shells—expensive, but not as expensive as they would be in Iowa.

Grading

On level land, and especially in low, poorly drained flat land, the roadbed should be at least 6 inches to a foot higher than adjacent soil. However, don't make the road any higher than necessary; otherwise, slipping off of it in winter becomes a hazard.

And remember to observe closely the direction of runoff water, since your roadbed will act as a small dam across any waterway. In this case you will need to install a culvert to drain the water under the lane, or it will stand on the uphill side and make a little mosquito bog out of whatever is growing there now. Generally, an

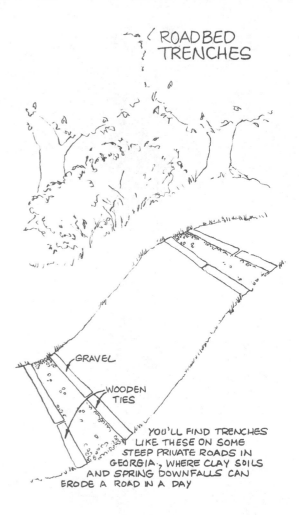

ROADBED TRENCHES

GRAVEL

WOODEN TIES

YOU'LL FIND TRENCHES LIKE THESE ON SOME STEEP PRIVATE ROADS IN GEORGIA, WHERE CLAY SOILS AND SPRING DOWNFALLS CAN ERODE A ROAD IN A DAY

8-inch culvert suffices in such cases, although if you have to cross a ditch of any well-defined size, it will take a much larger one and require the advice and assistance of experts.

In general, avoid going straight up hills, trying as much as possible to build the lane somewhat at an angle to the main slope of the hill. Cutting a lane into the side of a hill may require laying up stone into a terrace on the uphill side. A terrace on the downhill side to

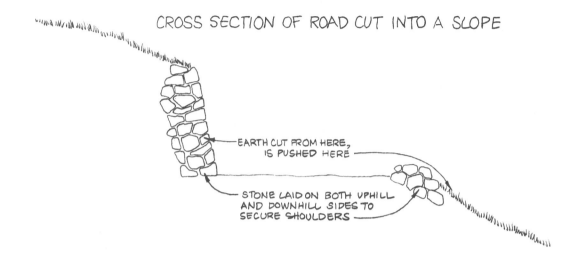

CROSS SECTION OF ROAD CUT INTO A SLOPE

EARTH CUT FROM HERE,
IS PUSHED HERE

STONE LAID ON BOTH UPHILL
AND DOWNHILL SIDES TO
SECURE SHOULDERS

hold the shoulder from washing away might also be necessary.

Make sure you do not inadvertently slope your lane, however slightly, down into your garage, or water will, of course, flow right in during heavy rains.

Cutting into the Road

The entrance of your lane to the public road requires some particular attentions. First, you should contact the county highway department, which may supply and install (usually not free of charge) a culvert of the proper size in the road ditch your lane crosses. Ditches along roads are not just places to get stuck in, but are there to drain water away. This would seem perfectly obvious to anyone living in modern society, but many farmers evidently do not know that since they regularly run their big plows at fields' edges, right down into the ditch, filling it with dirt. Then they wonder why water lies there in springtime.

If you have a choice of various entrance locations into your property, choose one that commands a good view of the road when you are sitting in your car ready to pull out of your lane, so that you can see oncoming cars, and they can see you, too.

Do not put your mailbox directly across from your driveway entrance, especially if you have daughters of dating age. I can guarantee you that their boyfriends will back out of the lane at night and eventually knock over the mailbox, if you don't do it yourself first. You would be smart to put the mailbox a few feet down the road from the lane.

Incidentally, there are road-running vermin that like to knock over mailboxes with pickup trucks. There are two ways of counterattacking. One is to put in a solid cement post halfway to China and then paint it to look like a frail wood post. The other way, which I have grudgingly adopted, is to put the post in very loosely and prop it solid enough to please the mailman, with little stakes driven in around it. Then, when the vandals have passed by, just pick up the post and stick it in its hole and jam the stakes around it again. Since snowplows sometimes inadvertently hit mailboxes, the latter method is no doubt saner. The former might even be illegal, a possibility that does not keep me from imagining the pleasure I'd get seeing vandals smash into it.

A Tool for Leveling Gravel Lanes and Clearing Snow

As traffic passes back and forth over a gravel lane, the tires dig out the gravel and push it to the sides and the center. Unless the stones are scraped back level, the lane eventually becomes rutted. In earlier times, some farmers owned heavy land graders equipped with dozerlike blades that they used to make lanes and keep them level. But few were available even then, having been made originally for use on public roads and inherited by farmers when better road-grading machinery came along. Today's tractor-rigged scrapers do not do as good a job, but are still adequate for lane maintenance and pushing aside moderate amounts of snow. But a cheaper tractor "attachment" that you can make does nearly as good a job—a heavy, wooden, triangular frame that you simply drag behind your tractor, truck, or horse.

Use full 2 by 10-inch hardwood boards for the triangle, if you can get them, probably as rough lumber from a sawmill. If not, buy the heaviest hardwood 2×10s you can find at the lumberyard. (You can use wider boards or thicker ones, but if you go much narrower than 8 inches wide, the drag will not be very effective for snow removal.) The two long sides can vary in length from 10 to 15 feet. The only critical measurement is that the rear or base of the triangle be as wide as your lane is, usually 8 feet.

Where the two long boards meet at the point (or front) of the triangle, bevel the inside edges so they will fit flush against each other. It is not necessary to do fine workmanship here—just bevel roughly with a chain saw.

Next, cut a third piece of 2×10 as long as your lane is wide to form the base of the triangle. Connect its ends to the side boards. Again the inside edges of this short board will have to be beveled to fit flush against the side boards. (See the drawing.) Spike all three corners together.

Next, drill a hole just in back of the front point of the drag through the middle of both side boards that is big enough to accept a $\frac{7}{8}$-inch rod or larger. Get a threaded rod of that dimension long enough to go through both boards. Bolt the rod tight, using large washers ahead of the nuts. This rod helps hold the point together better and acts as the hitch for the drag.

Next, nail some 1-inch boards over the top of the drag to hold about 400 pounds of

No Trespassing

Friends of mine have discovered that if you have a country place back off the road that you cannot live in regularly, a strong, padlocked gate or chain does discourage vandals. The road-running, beer can slinger's courage diminishes in direct proportion to the distance he must walk away from his wheels. A gate won't stop an all-terrain vehicle, of course, but a woven wire fence across the front of the property will. A farmer I know devised another method after the beer can–slinging bunch drove one too many times through his cornfield. He laid old spike-toothed harrows in the grassy ditch—spikes up—and calmly called the sheriff while the vandals sat helplessly in their tire-punctured four-wheel drives.

Maintenance

A gravel or crushed stone lane requires continual maintenance—a new coating of gravel every other year or so. A lane will need leveling as tires work the gravel out of the lane tracks. (See the box here for a leveling tool you can make.) The amount of new stone and how often you must add it will depend on your soil type.

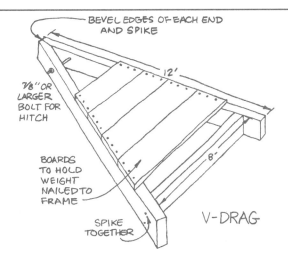

BEVEL EDGES OF EACH END AND SPIKE

12'

7/8" OR LARGER BOLT FOR HITCH

BOARDS TO HOLD WEIGHT NAILED TO FRAME

8'

SPIKE TOGETHER

V-DRAG

weight—concrete blocks, bags of dirt, or a couple of portly uncles. Your drag is ready to go to work.

Hitch it to the tractor or truck with enough chain so that the angle of pull is as straight forward as practical—a short chain will tend to lift the point off the ground, which you want to avoid as much as possible.

To level the gravel, straddle each shoulder first with the drag and then go down the middle. Repeat several times if necessary.

For snow removal, the drag works well on snow about 6 inches deep or less, and if there is no high bank of snow already on the edges of the lane. Go straight down the middle of the lane, and you'll push the snow to either side the way a V-shaped snowplow works. If there is a slight bank of snow at the edge, sometimes you can straddle the shoulder on both sides to push part of the bank farther from the lane, then go down the middle several times to clear the lane. But in deep or heavy snow the drag is not too effective. It is ideal in climates that usually have moderate snowfalls that often melt before the next storm moves in.

Where I live we can go down 30 feet and not hit a rock; gravel lanes seem to keep on sinking no matter how many years you add new stone.

Off the Beaten Lane

In planning lanes back through woodland or fields, which you will not usually gravel but use only when the ground is dry and solid enough to support travel, circumspection will pay off. Note where the land dries up quickest in spring, both in woodland and field. If you can map out a lane that sticks to these naturally drier areas, you can add another month onto your use

of them in spring and fall. But invariably you will be forced to traverse these lands when they are a bit muddy and, if in so doing you wear a few mud holes in the lane, they can be filled with large flat stones embedded in and covered by crushed stone dust from a quarry. In woodland, discipline yourself to walk rather than ride in muddy weather or wait until the ground is frozen—especially on sloping land. In the soft forest, it is extremely easy to start a tire rut that will turn into a washout in hard rains.

To get to the back of my farm, I must drive up and down a fairly steep but short hill. I have found that by planning my trips better, I can eliminate half of them. I never drive in the same tracks every time, but vary them up and down the hill so that the grass does not wear out in one place and start a gully.

A Score or More Uses for Stones and Rocks

Our visitor from the city laughed when he saw the stone slab on a nearby farmer's corner post. He assumed that the farmer was naive enough to think the rock would hold the post in the ground against the yearly heaving of freeze and thaw. I didn't know whether to embarrass him by pointing out his mistake or not. I decided not to. He was not a person who was ever going to need to know the significance of the stone anyway. So in my contrariness, I replied in a way that would only reinforce his folksy image of farmers. "I don't worry about my posts coming out of the ground because I only set them in the dark of the moon," I said, enjoying the studious way he avoided a "knowing" smile.

The rock slab on the post was adding years to the post's life by protecting its endgrain from rainwater seeping in and rotting it. We often cover corner posts by nailing on a piece of tin, but a handy flat rock is certainly as effective. And a hundred times more enduring. (Rocks also protect other fence designs, like the Virginia zig-zag rail fence, which makes use of two flat rocks at each corner to keep the wood up off the ground and away from moisture.)

Not that we don't use rocks to hold posts down sometimes. If a wire fence dips down into a sudden depression and then back up again, stretching the fence tightly will tend to pull the post in the low area right out of the ground. A rock on top of or wired to the post can supply just enough weight to hold the post down. A discarded cement block, although it isn't much to look at, works well in this capacity, too.

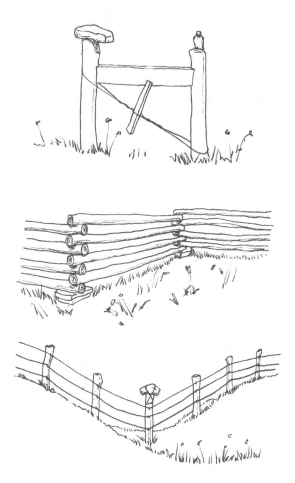

Fences

Rocks and stones around the homestead are free for the picking up, and so the traditional mind finds many uses for them in place of materials that would otherwise have to be bought. Instead of filling in around a gatepost with concrete, you can set the post with two big rocks positioned as in the drawing on the next page and make it just about as solid.

In this part of Ohio, you can find a large, flattish rock (once called the "deadman") buried a foot or so beneath the surface, 8 to 10 feet away from old corner posts. Its purpose was to

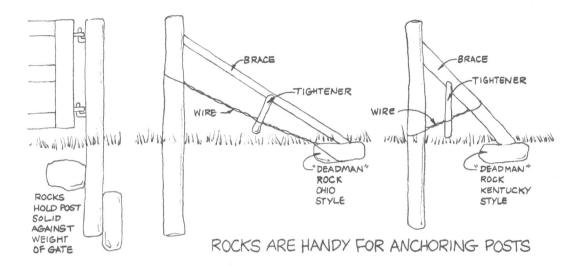

ROCKS ARE HANDY FOR ANCHORING POSTS

act as a foundation for the corner post brace and at the same time provide an anchor for the wire that ran around it and around the corner post; the wire, when twisted tight, held brace, rock, and post solidly together. In other parts of the country, as in Kentucky, a deadman is used in a slightly different kind of corner post brace (see the drawing above).

Gates

A rock's weight can be used to advantage in making a self-closing garden gate when forgetful children (and adults) leave the gate open, allowing in dogs and chickens. Hinge a gate of any design that suits your eye to one post, with the horizontal boards extending past the post on the other side, so the door can swing only one way — out. Then attach one end of a rope or chain to the outer edge of the gate and the other end to the inside of the gatepost. Tie a rock in the middle of the rope or chain, with enough sag in the line so that the rock hangs down about a foot from the ground. When the gate is swung open, the rope or chain tightens to a somewhat more horizontal level. When the gate is released from one's grasp, the weight of the rock pulls the gate back shut.

In keeping with the times, one more often finds a heavy gear from an old piece of farm machinery used today as the gate's counterbalance.

Another traditional gate design uses a counterbalancing rock in an even more unique and charming way. The top bar of the garden gate extends back behind and over the top of the

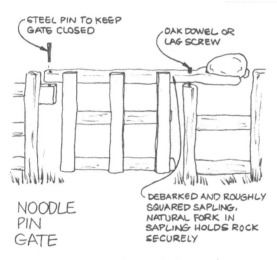

NOODLE
PIN
GATE

STEEL PIN TO KEEP
GATE CLOSED

OAK DOWEL OR
LAG SCREW

DEBARKED AND ROUGHLY
SQUARED SAPLING,
NATURAL FORK IN
SAPLING HOLDS ROCK
SECURELY

done more often can only be explained by our habit of buying instead of making do. Such headstones would certainly save money. We use boulders as markers for historical monuments now, and often as "signs" to identify a homestead.

Rocks line country drives, not just for decorative curbing, as urban passersby assume, but to keep careless drivers off lawns in mud time.

The weight of rocks also makes them handy for anchors to hold small boats against the current. If you lose one, another is easy to come by, although properly shaped rocks, smaller in the middle than at the ends, are not always easy to find. But in New England a real "kellick," as it was called, employed a bit of flat board and a long Y-shaped branch forked over the rock for an anchor.

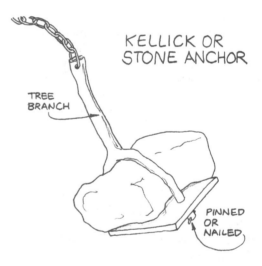

KELLICK OR
STONE ANCHOR

TREE
BRANCH

PINNED
OR
NAILED

post to which it is hinged. The hinge is a simple but heavy oak dowel or iron lag screw driven into the top of the post through a hole in the top bar. A rock half or more the weight of the gate rests on top of the extension of the top bar. The gate will swing open and close with ease if the hinge is kept well greased. This kind of gate is called a noodle-pin gate.

Headstones, Curbs, and Anchors

I have seen large, strikingly shaped boulders used for gravestones, and why this is not

Rock Gardens

The rocks in rock gardens are not always just decorative, either. They absorb the sun's heat to protect nearby plants on cooler nights, and they preserve moisture beneath them. If you lay a rock in your lawn, you will notice that the grass grows taller and greener right next to it in early spring and late fall.

Walks and Patios

One of the most common uses for rocks is to make sidewalks. Nice, flat flagstones are often chosen, laid atop 4 to 6 inches of gravel or sand, with mortar filling the cracks between the rocks. But even roundish rocks can make a sidewalk, so long as they are laid in a bed of concrete. The effect created is that of a cobblestone road, the rocks sticking up slightly above the concrete. If the concrete between the rocks is kept slightly higher in the middle of the walk and all seams in the concrete "T" into the edges of the sidewalk, water will not stand on it.

The advantage of a cobblestone type of sidewalk is that any size or shape of rock can be used. Put the flattest side up and dig out the gravel or sand to accommodate the varying bulk of the rocks. In fact, having a rock every square foot or two that penetrates deeper than 6 inches will make the sidewalk stronger.

My father-in-law built a walk out of rocks he hauled in from his creek. These particular rocks were about a uniform 4 to 6 inches in thickness, resulting in a surface that was bumpy rather than flat. While not immediately perceived as good sidewalk material, the rocks made a very attractive path.

In most cases, rocks or flagstones laid in sand will make a cheaper sidewalk and one just as enduring as one made from concrete alone or concrete and rocks. Concrete will invariably crack in the North from freezing and thawing, unless the soil is excavated down to below the usual frost depth or unless a generous amount of steel reinforcing is used. Rather large expanses, as in patios, need both kinds of freezing protection. Stones laid without mortar in or on a sand bed 4 to 6 inches deep (from which topsoil has been excavated) heave a bit from freezing and thawing but stay put indefinitely, and you don't have to worry about cracking mortar.

Generally, additional sand is sprinkled on

top of the walk after it has been laid, and this sand is swept into the cracks or is hosed and then swept. Some grass and weeds eventually grow up through the cracks. Sprinkling dry cement on the walk and sweeping and hosing it into the cracks is often done, but though it hardens, this kind of mortar eventually (usually quite soon) cracks and crumbles, and the weeds grow up through it. Salt water and an occasional weeding will control the problem. People in their fifties in my area remember that as children one of their summer jobs was scratching and digging the weeds out of the cracks of such sidewalks with an old knife.

Whether using mortar or sand, the rocks at the edges of the sidewalk should be large or deep enough so they don't work loose. Smaller stones, or bricks along the edges, need to be protected by a deeper curbing, or they work loose. Old railroad ties serve this purpose nicely, so long as you sink them about halfway in the ground. You might also want to drill some holes partway in the ties and drive spikes right through them, about 3 inches into the ground. Not much will move them then.

If you have access to a large amount of smooth rocks from egg to fist size, you can turn a drab cement patio or walk into a very attractive design. First pour the concrete slab in sections—better to do no more than about 12 square feet at a time.

In the North, the concrete ought to be 4 inches thick on a bed of gravel at least that thick, with reinforcing wire laid down before pouring the concrete. When building my patio, I went to the added safeguard of digging a 6-inch diameter hole down 2 feet at 6-foot intervals to be filled with concrete as a sort of foundation to protect against the heaving caused by freezing and thawing. (The patio cracked anyway, but only in one place.)

Level off the wet concrete in the usual way with a floater, then put on a layer of the egg-to-fist-size, smooth stones and with a board, press them down into the concrete. Then, with your wooden floater, work over the surface until you have pushed the rocks down and brought up enough concrete to cover them, making sure the surface stays level all the while.

Have a push broom and hose handy. After the concrete has set about an hour, spray a small section of the surface and brush with the broom. If your brushing dislodges the stones, the concrete hasn't set long enough.

Keep testing. As soon as your spraying and brushing test reveals a nice pebbly surface of stones firmly set in the concrete, quickly clean off the entire slab, spraying and brushing.

You won't believe how beautiful a walk or patio such a simple trick will result in. The more colorful the rocks, of course, the more delightful the result, but almost any smooth, smallish rocks will produce a handsome surface. It is also possible to add larger smooth rocks occasionally too, giving the surface even more character.

Breast Walls

Stones of nearly any size or shape can be used effectively in terraces, or breast walls, as they are commonly called. One needs to worry only about the outer face of the wall, because all irregularities are buried into the earthen side. Even an amateur can build a professional breast wall because of this, if he or she remembers to keep the wall slanted, or canted, in toward the uphill bank of earth behind it—and if he or she occasionally inserts a rock twice as long as the rest, the extra length running back into the earth for greater stability.

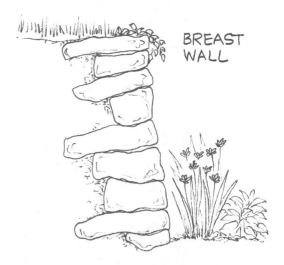

BREAST WALL

Drains

Stones can be used to drain wet holes in gardens, lawns, and fields through various applications of what is generally referred to as the "French drain." The idea of such a drain is to use a pocket of rocks like a sieve to draw water

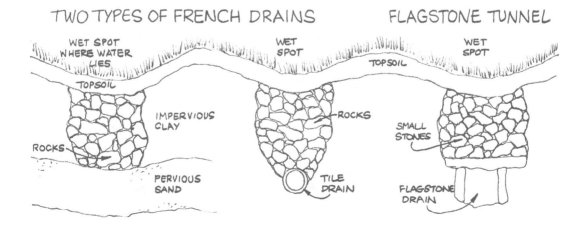

TWO TYPES OF FRENCH DRAINS   FLAGSTONE TUNNEL

WET SPOT WHERE WATER LIES

WET SPOT

WET SPOT

TOPSOIL

TOPSOIL

IMPERVIOUS CLAY

ROCKS

ROCKS

PERVIOUS SAND

ROCKS

TILE DRAIN

SMALL STONES

FLAGSTONE DRAIN

through impervious topsoils into more pervious soils, or into a drainage tile or ditch. Farmers in our neighborhood still use this ancient kind of drain—in fact there has been a resurgence in its use due to soil compaction problems from heavy modern equipment. The advantage of French drains over open-catch basins is that you can farm or garden right over the former.

Sedimentary rocks that break or split into large, flattish flagstones can be used in place of drainage tile, just as they were for hundreds of years in Europe. Such drains can last for centuries before becoming plugged with dirt. All it requires is digging a ditch (2 feet deep is minimum) on a grade, as one would with field tile, then building a three-sided flagstone tunnel in the bottom of the ditch. Cracks between the stones due to irregularities of shape will allow water from the soil above into the drain.

With precisely the same design, an enduring culvert can be built for use, for example, under a lane, saving you the considerable cost of a metal culvert.

Pond Banks

Rocks make an attractive and usually necessary protective face for pond banks. Even a small backyard pond will generate enough wave action to eat away at the banks, causing them to cave and slide into the water. On large ponds, protective rock is called riprap and is hauled in by the truckload. In a small backyard pool, you can arrange rocks by hand more artistically in any design that strikes your fancy, so long as your riprap slopes away from the water from bottom

to top, rather than leaning in toward the water. Riprap has the added advantage of discouraging weeds in the shallow water near shore.

Dry Stone Walls and Fences

Where a great amount of rocks are strewn over fields, stone fences and walls are quite practical even today, mostly because of the traditional rule of work that makes seemingly slow-hand methods very efficient indeed: "You never do just one task at a time." In this case you can simultaneously clear the field for easier cultivation and build a fence—a fence that will, incidentally, last forever. As good-quality woven wire fencing increases horrendously in price, that old-time efficiency looks better every year.

Building stone walls gives me another chance to elucidate the attitude this book takes regarding tradition, and which I think you should take in your home life. Don't overdo the traditional methods, just because they're traditional. If there is a genuinely better modern way, you'd be a fool not to leave tradition behind. Stone fences make sense for the reasons I mentioned above, but the traditional methods of moving these rocks off the fields to the fence site are practical only if you are gearing your life to horse farming. If you have a tractor, you probably have a hydraulically operated scoop for it (now available on even garden tractors). There is no handier modern tool for the homestead. Instead of using a stoneboat and those outrageously laborious methods given

· 213

in some books for moving heavy rocks onto a stone wall, simply pry the rocks into the tractor scoop, drive to the wall, and let hydraulic power lift them to precisely the height at which you are working.

Frost Protection

In seeking advice about building dry stone walls, you will quickly learn that more art than science seems to be involved, and the artists are far from in agreement on technique. In Walter Needham's and Barrows Mussey's lovely *A Book of Country Things* (The Stephen Green Press, Brattleboro, Vt., 1965), Needham says that his grandfather dug a ditch down to subsoil to start a stone wall and then put into this rather shallow trench very large stones first. But in J. J. Thomas' 1889 *Rural Affairs,* the author admonishes: "These trenches . . . should be

deep enough to be below frost . . . and may be filled with such small stones as cannot be used in the wall; large ones will never do." And finally, in two recent issues of a country magazine I've been reading, writers with stone wall experience asserted that dry stone walls could be built right on the surface, or at least no more than a few inches below ground surface, and that frost heaving would not be significant. One of these modern writers said that damage from frost heaving could be repaired fairly quickly, if it did occur.

I have myself built only two small stone walls, but I'm an unwilling expert on the damage frost heaving can cause. I can only view with suspicion anyone who minimizes that damage. At least in our heavy soils, Mr. Thomas' advice, above, is the only safe course to follow. However, I once examined, stone by stone, a fairly new dry stone wall in Maine. Little effort

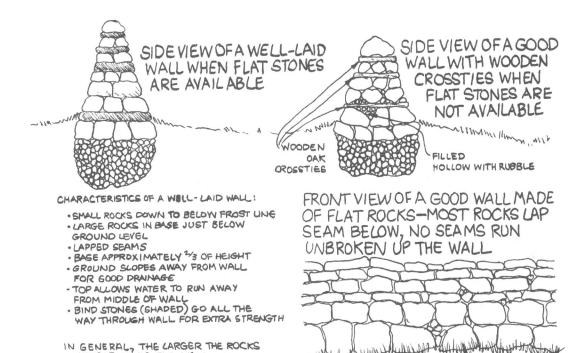

SIDE VIEW OF A WELL-LAID WALL WHEN FLAT STONES ARE AVAILABLE

SIDE VIEW OF A GOOD WALL WITH WOODEN CROSSTIES WHEN FLAT STONES ARE NOT AVAILABLE

WOODEN OAK CROSSTIES

FILLED HOLLOW WITH RUBBLE

CHARACTERISTICS OF A WELL-LAID WALL:

- SMALL ROCKS DOWN TO BELOW FROST LINE
- LARGE ROCKS IN BASE JUST BELOW GROUND LEVEL
- LAPPED SEAMS
- BASE APPROXIMATELY ⅔ OF HEIGHT
- GROUND SLOPES AWAY FROM WALL FOR GOOD DRAINAGE
- TOP ALLOWS WATER TO RUN AWAY FROM MIDDLE OF WALL
- BIND STONES (SHADED) GO ALL THE WAY THROUGH WALL FOR EXTRA STRENGTH

IN GENERAL, THE LARGER THE ROCKS THE STRONGER THE WALL

FRONT VIEW OF A GOOD WALL MADE OF FLAT ROCKS—MOST ROCKS LAP SEAM BELOW, NO SEAMS RUN UNBROKEN UP THE WALL

had been made to give it a frost-proof foundation, but it sat on well-drained light soil in which huge boulders of bedrock rose occasionally to the very surface. It would probably take an earthquake to shake loose this wall, even though it has no foundation of its own.

Laying Stone

This wall also demonstrated the only piece of traditional advice that I believe applies to all dry stone walls: "Every rock should touch as many other rocks around it as possible." In other words, the more snugly the rocks fit against each other, the more solid the wall. Add to that the admonition that the base of the wall be slightly wider than the top. A wall 4 feet high will hold cattle, so following the rule of thumb that the wall should have a base two-thirds the height, a base 2 feet, 8 inches wide

will suffice for that cattle-proof wall. If you have lots of rocks to play with, you will find that it is much easier to build up a 4-foot wall by starting with a base as much as 3 feet wide, especially when you have to use many roundish field stones. The flatter your stones, the more narrow and more vertical you can make the wall. But traditionally, the base of dry stone walls was never less than 2 feet wide.

As you build, the third rule of thumb comes into play: Whenever possible, lap the gap between rocks with the rock above. Save larger flat rocks for "bind stones" or "stretchers" to fit clear through the wall from side to side, lapping all the cracks directly below them. Lacking such flagstones for binding in the wall, old-timers often used wooden boards of a durable wood like red oak for bind stones. Because such boards stayed relatively dry, they lasted for many, many years.

Capping the Wall

One generally envisages the "perfect" dry stone wall as being level on top, capped by the flattest flagstones available. However, it is really better to tilt the top flagstones so as to encourage water to run away from the wall rather than down into it. Dome-shaped or rounded triangular rocks make good caps for directing water away from the wall, too, and they should be bulky and heavy enough so cows won't push them off the wall. On shorter stretches of dry stone wall used decoratively in the home landscape, it pays to cement the gaps between the cap stones to keep water out of the wall.

Mortared Stone Walls for Gardens

A dry stone wall will never do around a garden, in my opinion. It will draw chipmunks who can work much mischief in the garden. Other potentially harmful wildlife can easily climb a dry stone wall—I'm thinking mainly of woodchucks. To make the wall as smooth, vertical, and inaccessible as possible means using mortar.

Using mortar does not mean you can lay the wall up carelessly and depend on the mortar to glue the rocks together. Mortar doesn't really do that. When dry, it simply acts as a support for the rocks' downward gravitational force. It makes perfection of that old saying I quoted earlier—that all rocks should touch all other rocks around it in as many places as possible. The mortar makes them all touch in all places. But the mortar has only a bit of adhesive strength, and so rocks may break loose if the seams between them are not lapped properly, or if the wall is built out of plumb.

You can lay up rock and then mortar between them as you go, or you can build forms in which to pack rocks and pour in mortar a course at a time, or a whole wall at a time. The latter seems easier and faster, especially with roundish rocks difficult to lay up without support to hold them in place. But forms, even small slipforms, involve time and money in building. Also, even in putting rocks in the form, you need to take the time to lap seams and lay in bind stones to make a strong wall. Furthermore, it is difficult to know what your finished wall is going to look like when working in a form—all you can do is put flat sides of rocks against the inner wall of the form and hope they will show to good advantage when the form is taken away.

But if your only goal is to have a smooth-faced wall using as many rocks as possible to substitute for more expensive concrete, forms will provide it. Most of the old barns in eastern Minnesota have lower walls built this way. Full forms were built, and the whole wall poured at once, with men dropping granite rocks, as many and as large as possible, into the soupy concrete. With a large work force, massive walls could be thrown up in a day, and the result not all that unattractive, especially after half a century of weathering brought more of the granite rocks near the exterior surface of the wall into view.

Slipforming

One method of slipforming a rock wall requires the construction of form sections in matching pairs. One section is set upon the foundation, wired and braced together, and when it is full of rocks and cement, the second is placed on top of it and filled with rocks and concrete. When the first course is sufficiently dry, usually in a few days, the lower form section is taken apart and set on top of the upper section, wired and braced together again and rebolted to the section below it, and so on until the wall is finished. The operation is not as easy as it sounds, however, especially at the corners where both walls need to rise together and some adjustment in the forms must be made to accommodate the corners. And it almost always takes two people to slip the forms up. To deal with the corners, you can make special corner forms, or the corners can be laid up without forms with what squarish rocks are available.

Usually, slipforms are not more than 8 feet long and about 20 inches high, for ease of

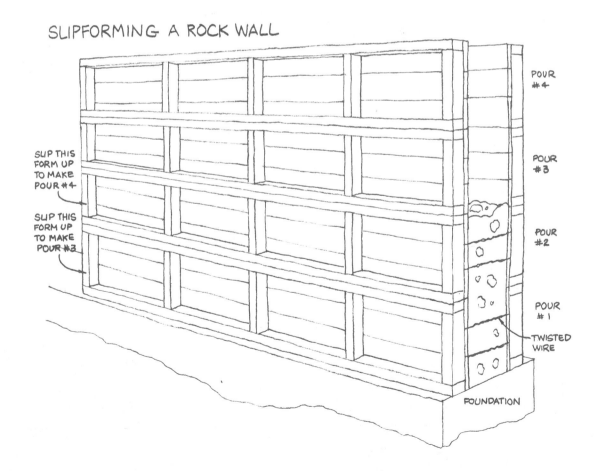

SLIPFORMING A ROCK WALL

SLIP THIS FORM UP TO MAKE POUR #4

SLIP THIS FORM UP TO MAKE POUR #3

POUR #4

POUR #3

POUR #2

POUR #1

TWISTED WIRE

FOUNDATION

handling. The facing can be 1 × 4s or exterior plywood, backed by 2 × 4 studs with 1 × 4s nailed to top and bottom. Holes evenly spaced in the 1 × 4s allow bolting two forms together. Provision must be made to keep the forms from sliding down the wall when top braces across the wall are removed before the next form is put in place. A nail here or there, driven through the facing when the cement is still wet, will do the trick, and the nails can be easily pulled back out with a claw hammer when the form is moved, so long as they are not driven flush with the wood.

For a more complete explanation of this method of slipforming, see *Build It Better Yourself,* by the editors of *Organic Gardening and Farming* (Rodale Press, 1977).

There are other ways to contrive a slipforming operation, as with squared posts along the wall-to-be, holding 2 by 12-inch (or whatever) facing planks. The posts are anchored in the ground at the bottom, of course, and wired and braced together at the top. The planks are toenailed lightly to the posts to make the form. The bottom plank is released after the concrete has set, and the plank is slid out past the posts and reinserted above the top planks.

Laying Up Mortar

Despite the fact that Helen and Scott Nearing have made the slipforming technique famous throughout the homesteader world, I think you are better off to lay up mortared walls

Cutting or Dressing Rocks to a Particular Shape

In laying mortared walls, you should try to find a rock of the right shape to fit a particular space. If your pile of rocks is limited, you can't always do that, and so cutting or breaking a rock to shape becomes necessary. A mason's hammer, a stone chisel, and a sledgehammer come in handy for dressing rocks. In general, the idea is to chisel out a rough groove perhaps ½-inch thick along the line where you want the rock to break, then deliver a sharp blow with the mason's hammer or sledgehammer while praying for good luck. Some kinds of rock will break fairly predictably along the incised line. Most igneous rocks like granite will not break so conveniently, and you might just as well lay such a rock on a solid base and smash it with the sledgehammer, hoping it will shear off in flat planes you can use. Wear eye protection for this kind of work.

The secret of breaking to shape those rocks that only want to splinter (if they

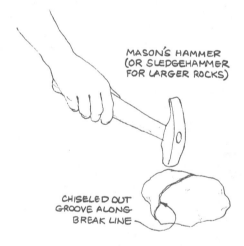

MASON'S HAMMER (OR SLEDGEHAMMER FOR LARGER ROCKS)

CHISELED OUT GROOVE ALONG BREAK LINE

break at all) is to have a very solid edge upon which to lay the rock. A length of railroad track resting on a concrete foundation is ideal. Lay the incised line on the track, give the rock a sharp blow, and it is more likely to break the way you want it to. It's the same principle as that involved in cutting glass.

without forms. By the time you get a 4 by 8-foot square section up, I can just about guarantee you that you will have learned how to use even roundish rocks in the wall, so long as you have plenty of squarish or rectangular ones for the corners and to carry the bulk of the wall.

You will find that you need lots of little wedge-shaped rocks to chink up the spaces between the bigger ones and make them set solid in the fresh mortar. When you are finished with a section and before it gets completely dry, tuck-point in more mortar in the seams. Hose and brush off the film of mortar that gets on the rocks. You can raise the wall only about a foot a day or the weight of more rocks might squish loose the lower ones before the mortar sets. But this is true of slipforming, too.

Use regular masonry sand and mortar. For a white mortar you can use white portland cement and white sand. You can get a nice contrasting black mortar by mixing lampblack into ordinary grey cement. Use string and plumb lines to guide you in keeping the wall plumb. Learning to lay up walls without forms allows you great freedom—you can lay up curved walls, leave little alcoves in the wall (as for a fireplace wall), or let particularly flat rocks stick out of the wall for shelves, which is also handy in a house wall, or even in a garden.

A Stone Gatepost

If the idea of putting up a whole wall scares you, you might first want to try a smaller

---

A piece of angle iron on a solid foundation will work, too. Sometimes just by pecking away at the edge of a rock with a stone hammer you can nibble the rock down to the size and dimensions you desire.

The more you work, the more you will learn the secrets of the fracture planes of your native rocks. And fitting proper pieces into a wall is very satisfying and therapeutic work—if you aren't in a hurry. Stone masons are never in a hurry. They take their time and the results last for centuries.

Big Boulders

To split a large boulder you want to remove from a field or the basement hole you are digging, you can use dynamite. The proper way is to place the explosive *on top* of the boulder, then pack a blob of mud over it. The natural force of dynamite is downward, especially with the addition of the mud cap. Old-timers used to say if you wanted to prove that fact, look at the tragic consequences of setting off a firecracker in the

open palm of your hand versus letting it explode in your hand with a piece of paper covering it. In the first case, you are quite likely to injure your hand; in the second case you are quite likely to lose your hand. I prefer illustrating the lesson on rocks.

Once I spent several hours ignorantly digging a hole down under a huge boulder in a Minnesota field. In the bottom of the hole I put two sticks of dynamite and lit the fuse. The explosion barely budged the big rock. An old farmer advised me to put half a stick on top of the rock with a mud cap over it instead. In the subsequent explosion, the rock broke into four pieces, each manageable enough to be dragged from the field. I was 2 hours and a stick and a half of dynamite smarter.

An even slicker way to split a rock, another old-timer tells me, is to drill a hole in it with a star drill (or the new carbide masonry drills) about 8 inches deep, wider at the bottom than the top, if possible. Then fill the hole with water on a very cold night. The freezing water will crack the rock.

L-HINGES ARE MORTARED IN PLACE

BARS SLIDE INTO RECESS IN BETWEEN STONES

project, in which case I suggest stone gateposts. With flattish rocks you can lay up a post quite easily, starting 2 feet in the ground and mortaring as you go. Remember to lap the gaps. A 2-foot-square or at least 18-inch-square post is better than a skinnier one. L-type post hinges can be imbedded in the mortar at the proper locations—the farther the shank runs back into the mortar, the better. Bars that slide into pockets between stones keep the gate secure when it is closed.

Multiple Uses of Backyard Barbecues

Until I saw how an Amish acquaintance designed, built, and operated his sorghum molasses cooker, I didn't realize how easily the backyard barbecue can be modified for uses other than a simple cookout. His cooker was a long (about 8-foot) masonry firebox with a chimney at one end and a door at the other. With a large metal pan in place over the firebox, the Amishman had actually converted it into a stove. He regulated the fire by how far he left the door ajar, and the draft created by the chimney at the other end drew the heat across the bottom of the evaporator pan evenly. He stirred the sorghum with a wooden paddle, dipping off the

greenish foam as it formed on the surface. The whole "barbecuer" was housed in what was really a woodshed, with most of the room taken up by neatly stacked firewood. Although rarely used as such, the cooker could double as a maple syrup evaporator.

It didn't take much imagination to understand that such a setup was practical for any backyard where home production of food was an integral part of the life-style, with or without the woodshed built around it. Not only could sorghum molasses and maple syrup be processed, but also apple butter, lard, and other cooking jobs. What's more, without too much modification, meat could be smoked too, all while enhancing the barbecue's usefulness for outdoor cookouts. This setup could also be used to dry fruit.

The Structure

Picture the simple outdoor "fireplace" used mainly in the country for burning trash—and for cookouts on Sunday. Double the outside dimensions from the typical 3 by 4 feet to make it 3 by 8 feet or perhaps 4 by 8 feet. Exact size is not critical, since you can set any smaller-size evaporator pans in, or on, or next to, a metal cover over the firebox. Now envision a chimney: Ten feet high is enough, although if your evaporator is enclosed in a shed, the chimney should rise 3 feet above the roof at one end of your rectangular firebox, with a metal door at the other end. (See the drawing.)

The inside of the firebox should be lined with firebrick or other heat-resistant masonry; ordinary concrete blocks will crack if directly subjected to high temperatures. The outside can be any stone, brick, or cement block (preferably one of the more decorative kinds).

Clay flue liner in the chimney is not necessary, but since only a few sections of it are needed in the rather short chimney, the added expense is probably worth it. You can buy cement chimney block made to receive clay flue

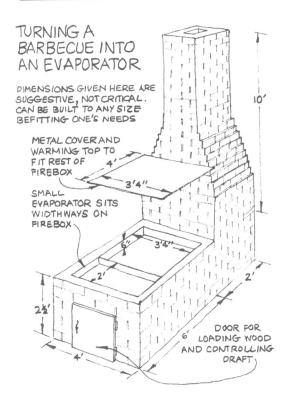

TURNING A
BARBECUE INTO
AN EVAPORATOR

DIMENSIONS GIVEN HERE ARE
SUGGESTIVE, NOT CRITICAL.
CAN BE BUILT TO ANY SIZE
BEFITTING ONE'S NEEDS

METAL COVER AND
WARMING TOP TO
FIT REST OF
FIREBOX

SMALL
EVAPORATOR SITS
WIDTHWAYS ON
FIREBOX

10'

4'

3'4"

6"   3'4"

2'

2'

2½'

6'   DOOR FOR
LOADING WOOD
AND CONTROLLING
DRAFT

4'

liner; it is easy for an amateur to lay up. If the cement block is then faced off with brick, you have a very handsome (if expensive) barbecue. Needless to say, the whole structure must rest on a solid foundation down to below frost line. If you use the chimney for smoking meat, you may wish to cap it, or at least have a piece of metal handy so you can set it on bricks over the chimney hole to keep out rain.

Pans

Now all you need is a cover over the firebox and you're in business. Exactly how you will design your cover will depend on what you intend to do with the barbecue. You can set a pan on the firebox large enough to cover it completely, or you can design a flat metal cover with holes in it to receive whatever size pans or pots you wish to set in it. Or, although pans will not heat up as quickly nor as evenly, you can set them on top of the metal cover. Or you can use a pan that covers a portion of the firebox and cover the rest with a piece of sheet metal.

In any event, the pan and/or cover should be of 12-gauge soft steel, available at any metal-working shop. That's about 3/32 inch thick. This will work fine for the metal door on the front of the firebox, too. A metalworking shop will be glad to make a pan for you to your specifications. My sister had a nice one made for the maple syrup she boils down every spring. Her pan is quite small, designed to sit on her old gas stove in the garage.

The size of your pan will be dictated by the amount of sap or whatever you intend to boil down. For the average family's backyard ventures, a pan that covers the whole firebox is considerably larger than necessary. One 2 feet wide and just long enough to stretch over the width of the firebox is plenty. Then you need enough sheet metal to cover the rest of the firebox, upon which you can set other pans of sap for prewarming.

Commercial pans, especially for sorghum, have baffles in them, and a spigot at the lower end to keep the operation going at a continuous pace, juice in one end, finished product coming out the other. But for the backyard, a batch at a time is fast enough, and you can pick up the smaller pan and pour out what you can't dip out. (When working around hot pans like this, it is a good idea to have a pair of heat-protective fireplace gloves to wear.)

You will find other uses for your "outdoor stove." You can cook down apple butter on it. If you do, be sure to make your pan out of steel or stainless steel or use a cast-iron pot. Don't use an old aluminum pan. Besides the more likely possibility of scorching in a thin aluminum pan, the acid in the fruit will chemically react with aluminum, creating aluminum oxide, which isn't good for you. You'll have a similar reaction with the iron in a cast-iron pot, but the iron (ferrous oxide) will do you no harm. Your

A Meat Smoker

If you want to give your evaporator or cooker or barbecue—whatever you have decided to call it—another use, it can be made into a meat smoker by putting a metal door on the front of the smoke chamber at the base of the chimney. With a bar or two inserted into the mortar joints right below the beginning of the chimney flue, you can hang meat in the smoke chamber and smoke it nicely. If this is a main purpose of your barbecue, you will want to make it at least a full 4 feet wide, so that the smoke chamber will have enough room in which to hang two hams and two sides of bacon.

A barbecue can be used for both hot-smoking fresh meats to be eaten right away and cool-smoking for cured meats. The proper temperature for cool-smoking is about 90°F. and for hot-smoking, 130°F. You will find it convenient to drill a hole in the smoke chamber door to insert a thermometer so you can regulate your fire properly.

We hot-smoked poultry in a barbecue pit that didn't have a chimney, building a very small fire at one end and placing the meat at the other (6 feet away). We put a sheet of corrugated metal roofing over the barbecue to contain the smoke and heat. An ordinary cooking thermometer stuck down through a hole in the roofing panel next to the meat took the guesswork out of the job.

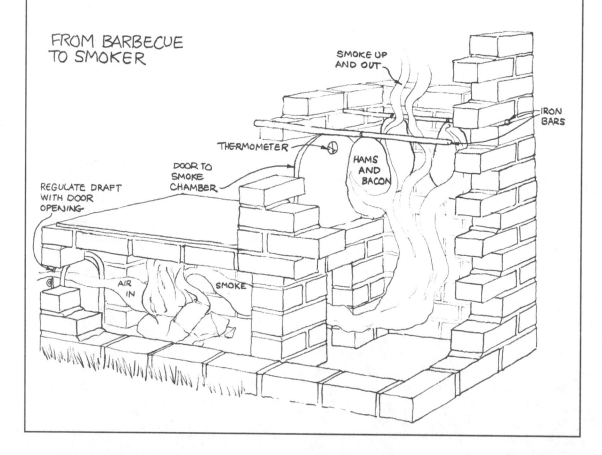

FROM BARBECUE TO SMOKER

SMOKE UP AND OUT

IRON BARS

THERMOMETER

DOOR TO SMOKE CHAMBER

HAMS AND BACON

REGULATE DRAFT WITH DOOR OPENING

AIR IN

SMOKE

"stove" will be adequate for cooking down lard, too, and in fact you can do your canning on it if you want to keep all that heat out of your kitchen in August.

For apple butter and lard, carve yourself a wooden paddle of suitable size for the almost constant stirring that will be necessary sometimes. For sorghum, you need a screen skimmer with a handle on it for skimming off the green foam.

A Roof Overhead

Obviously, building a roof over the barbecue and a patio around it (if not an entire building) will greatly enhance its use—no summer cookout need be canceled because of rain. More importantly, it is not much fun to boil off maple sap in the rain. But if you're not inclined to build a roof, you can devise a temporary cover above the evaporator pan with another piece of sheet metal.

Taking a cue from the Amish, I think the way to justify a really Cadillac barbecue is to build a woodshed (which most of us need) and "just happen" to make it big enough for a barbecue. Model it after the sorghum boiling sheds of southern Indiana—poles around the sides supporting a roof to keep off rain, while allowing cooling and ventilating breezes through the structure that is uninhibited by walls.

A Practical Backyard Pool

Gene and Evelyn Long built an earthen pond in their lawn, which draws wildlife to their property. The pond is also a very pretty ornamental jewel in their landscape and serves as a swimming pool for their grandchildren.

"I knew our clay subsoil would hold water pretty well," says Evelyn, "and I knew I could handle the overflow with a gravity drain to the field behind the house. So I just stuck a stake in the wettest spot of the lawn and told the backhoe operator to go to work."

What resulted was a more or less kidney-shaped pool of about 600 square feet of surface

water, 5 feet deep at the center, rising to about 6 inches along the shoreline. On the upper end of the pond where the bank is highest, Evelyn had several truckloads of sand dumped for a bit of beach. Along the bank, on either side of the beach, she had crushed rock riprap hauled in. In the shallow water along the shores, she covered the pool bottom generously with pea gravel—small, rounded pebbles that are easy on bare feet. At the lower end of the pond, the lawn comes right down to the water, so that Gene can mow almost to the water's edge.

The pond teems with fish. Flocks of birds habitually flit along the shoreline during the summer. White water lilies come up and bloom every year without care, even though they aren't supposed to be hardy enough to survive our winters without special protection. A pile of large rocks at the lower end of the pond serves as housing for salamanders and other amphibians. Small as it is, and surrounded by human activity, the pond still lures in wild ducks during migration. One year a muskrat took up residence.

To keep the pond water clear of too much algae, Evelyn treats it annually, but very sparingly, with copper sulfate. She puts the crystals in a burlap bag which she then draws slowly through the water with a length of nylon rope from several different shoreline locations. If algae start growing again in late summer, she spot-treats it rather than redoing the whole pond. She keeps other pond weeds, like cattails, under control with hand weeding.

In hot, dry weather, the well pump sends a steady dribble of water into the pond, as much to aerate it as to maintain normal water level. An overflow pipe makes sure the pond never gets too full.

The Longs figure that over fifteen years they have spent about $3000 on the pond—an average of about $200 a year—most of that was for the original excavation. "And we've got our money back many times over in the pleasure the pool has provided," says Evelyn.

You should have no trouble disposing of the excavated dirt, should you decide to build a

Stocking a Warm-Water Pond

Much controversy still exists over what species of fish and how many ought to be stocked in an artificial pond, particularly a warm-water pond. (A warm-water pond is an artificial pond fed by surface runoff water rather than cold springwater. Trout and other cold-water fish will not survive in a warm-water pond. Bass, bluegills, and catfish will.) The root of the controversy rests on the question of how much "management" a pond owner is going to exert over his fish population. State and federal recommendations are made on the usually correct assumption that most pond owners are not going to take the time and work necessary year in and year out to control fish populations and, more importantly, do not intend to feed the fish supplementally. Federal and state biologists therefore recommend stocking rates that come closest, in their experience, to providing a pond with a supply of fish, and hopefully a balance of fish, eating only what the pond provides naturally in the way of food.

That being so, the most common stocking rate recommended for warm-water ponds is 100 largemouth bass fingerlings and 500 bluegill fingerlings per acre of surface water. Sometimes the recommended rate is 1000 bluegills to 100 bass or 400 bluegills and 100 redear sunfish per 100 bass. In ponds larger than a ½ acre in size you can add 100

pond like this. There is a constant demand for fill dirt. Or you might have a good use for it right on your own place, for a rock garden, or for extra dirt over a root cellar.

Three Backyard Ideas for the Kids
A Sandbox

Some of the most enduring toys you can give your children are the simplest and cheapest.

channel catfish per acre to the stocking mixture. For ponds a ½ acre or smaller, many fishery biologists are now recommending either the bass-bluegill mixture *or* 200 channel catfish at the per-acre rate, not both.

Why largemouth bass, bluegills, and channel cats? Bluegills eat the insect life that lives on the plankton in the pond, and the bass prey on the smaller bluegills as well as their own offspring. Ideally, the two will work out a balance of population beneficial to the pond and to each other. Every conceivable combination of fish has been tried; none work as well as this one. Other kinds of bass will not forage the bluegills hard enough. Other kinds of sunfish, especially the green sunfish, multiply too fast. Perch and pike will live in farm ponds but not easily or well.

Catfish like farm ponds; they eat food the bass and bluegill would let go to waste. Channel cats are the best choice, as they do not muddy the water and will hardly ever reproduce in a pond, hence will never overpopulate. Overpopulation is the bane of farm ponds. Fish rarely starve to death when a pond becomes crowded, but they do not grow. You get a multitude of small fish, less fun to catch and tedious to clean for supper. Better that the channel cats get fished out and replaced every three to four years than to have them overpopulate, like bullheads and crappie are almost sure to do. The trouble is, the bass/bluegill population

will get out of whack, too. The number one problem in most farm ponds is too many bluegills, no big bass. The main reason this happens is that in the first two years, the owners fish too much and after that, not enough. Water biologists have worked out a simple but strict regimen for harvesting bass and bluegills, which, if followed, will provide good fishing indefinitely, they say, without further stocking or supplemental feeding. Their regimen goes like this:

1. The first year after stocking bass and bluegill fingerlings, return all fish caught to the pond.

2. The second year, fish out 80 pounds of bluegill per acre but throw all bass caught back into the pond. (Incidentally, always handle fish with wet hands, as the slimy protective coating on a fish may come off on dry hands.)

3. The third year, and thereafter, take out 80 pounds of bluegill per acre and 20 to 25 pounds of bass per acre. However (and this is the real tricky part of management), bass caught between 12 and 15 inches in size should always be returned to the water, as this size largemouth bass prey most voraciously on the bluegills. Smaller or larger bass can be kept.

[By Gene Logsdon; reprinted from *Getting Food from Water* (Rodale Press, 1978).]

A sandbox is a good example. Sand is cheap, though hauling it is not. If you can move a pile of it yourself, your out-of-pocket cost won't be more than $5. (The first time I built a sandbox I hauled sand by the sack in the trunk of the car.) A box is not really necessary for a sandpile, although without one a relatively small sandpile will eventually get scattered around too much and your "pile" will slowly disappear. Four boards nailed together or four small logs positioned into a square corral or a rectangular

row of large rocks or a few courses of flat stones or a border of those leftover cement blocks you don't know what to do with all work fine to contain a sandpile within its boundaries—not counting what the kids carry into the house in their shoes. However you make your sandbox, one thing's for sure: it will bring hours and hours of enjoyment to your children.

A word of caution: cats love to use sandboxes for litter boxes. If there are roaming cats in your neighborhood or on your farm (and where

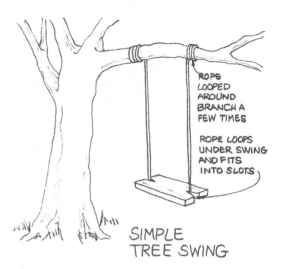

ROPE LOOPED AROUND BRANCH A FEW TIMES

ROPE LOOPS UNDER SWING AND FITS INTO SLOTS

SIMPLE TREE SWING

aren't there?) you may wish to cover the sandbox with a sheet of plastic when the kids aren't using it.

A Tree Swing

A tree swing is another favorite childhood toy that won't empty your wallet. An old tire suspended by a rope from any handy tree limb serves the purpose. But a swing more comfortable to sit in can be made with a wooden board seat notched at each end to fit over a looped rope hanging from the tree. This kind of notched seat is better than a seat with holes drilled through it for the rope. In the latter case, the rope has to be threaded through the holes before being tied to the tree branch, or two

separate ropes have to be suspended from the branch and knotted under the holes at precisely the right height so the seat is level. This is not easy to do even when the branch is perfectly horizontal, which it seldom is. With the slotted seat, you tie both ends of the rope to the branch, then adjust the slotted board seat in the loop of the rope. Use nylon rope for longer life, and if the rope has been outside through the winter—the usual fate of swings—test it for rottenness or replace it as a matter of course. In tying the rope to the branch, loop the rope around the branch a couple of times after making the knot. This prevents the rope from slipping and rubbing back and forth against the branch as the swing swings; such slippage might otherwise quickly wear the rope through. Choose a good, stout horizontal limb and cut off lower branches the swinging rope would strike.

Wading Pool

A small child needs supervision in the shallowest of pools, but the danger of drowning in a foot of water is very minimal if there is a watchful older eye about. The cost is considerably more than a swing or a sandbox, but

Sapling Pole Swing

Folklorists have documented an early American child's swing made not of rope or chain, but of sapling poles. The saplings are attached to a horizontal pole by bending the shaved top of the saplings into loops or by using iron straps bent into loops, with the loops held in bent position by pins or nails.

The horizontal pole, by which the swing was suspended, was lodged in convenient crotches of two close-standing trees. If the trees did not have properly positioned crotches, a Y-shaped sapling pole might be cut, braced, and tied against the tree trunk to hold the horizontal pole.

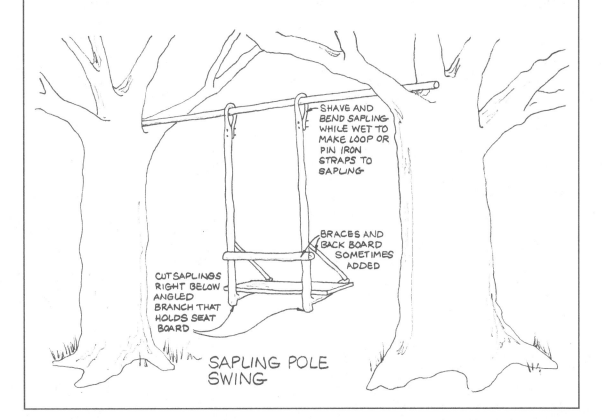

SHAVE AND BEND SAPLING WHILE WET TO MAKE LOOP OR PIN IRON STRAPS TO SAPLING

BRACES AND BACK BOARD SOMETIMES ADDED

CUT SAPLINGS RIGHT BELOW ANGLED BRANCH THAT HOLDS SEAT BOARD

SAPLING POLE SWING

not so much really if you do the work yourself. In terms of childhood delight, every penny is worth it.

Wading pools always remind me of how resourceful my mother was when we were kids. Heaven knows we didn't have a wading pool (we spent days wading in the creek instead), but she contrived to supply us with one anyway. In a tiny village near our farm was a small, lovely park, the money donated by a wealthy local patron. In the park was a large shallow concrete pond, I think more for ornament than for children to wade in, since I rarely saw anyone in it except our family. On hot summer afternoons, Mother would drive to the park and read a book while we played in the pond. This was part of

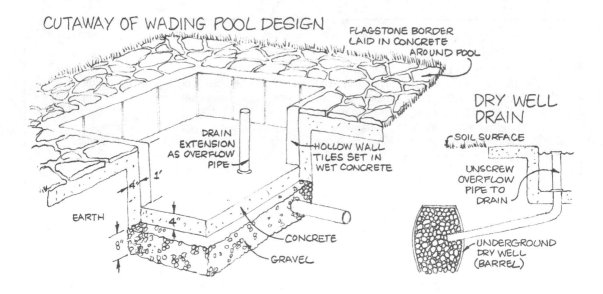

CUTAWAY OF WADING POOL DESIGN

FLAGSTONE BORDER LAID IN CONCRETE AROUND POOL

DRAIN EXTENSION AS OVERFLOW PIPE

HOLLOW WALL TILES SET IN WET CONCRETE

EARTH

4" 1'

4"

8"

CONCRETE

GRAVEL

DRY WELL DRAIN

SOIL SURFACE

UNSCREW OVERFLOW PIPE TO DRAIN

UNDERGROUND DRY WELL (BARREL)

our summer routine. We took it for granted. Only years later did I realize that in those happy hours we were living like the wealthy, surrounded by beautiful landscaped plantings and swimming in what amounted to our own extravagantly expensive private wading pool. Twenty years later I returned to the park and went straight to our old "swimmin' hole," only to find it gone. Park caretakers explained that it had become a nuisance, constantly being fouled by vandals with beer cans and broken bottles and other debris.

So civilization continues its slow downward spiral. The area has not increased in population, so we cannot blame the vandalism on that, as is commonly done. There is no escaping the sad fact that for whatever reasons, there is less discipline and responsibility instilled into people today. The first signs of a decaying society. The riffraff shall inherit the land and then starve on it.

Lining the Pool

A small backyard wading pool is easier to build than it sounds. If the pool is to be 1 foot deep—and that's deep enough—you need excavate only 2 feet or less, if the top of the pool extends above the soil surface a bit. Put down 8 inches of gravel and pour on it a 4-inch slab of concrete, heavily reinforced with steel rod and/or mesh. Darrel Huff in his solid book (no pun intended) *How to Work with Concrete and Masonry* (Harper & Row, New York, 1968), says that even in cold regions, no more footing than that is needed. This could very well be true, since the gravel will cushion the heaving movement of freeze and thaw, and the small reinforced pond will move up and down without cracking. But if I lived in the far North, I would consult with local builders and get their opinions. Anyhow, with the concrete floor still wet, set into it a wall of those foot-square hollow wall tiles. Bricks or other wall masonry material can be used, but the foot-square tiles are easier because you're laying up fewer pieces overall. Set them at least 1 inch into the wet concrete, and about 4 inches out from the earth wall of the excavation.

In a day or two, when the concrete has set up, mix more and fill in the space behind the tile walls all around. In this way you get an attractively faced concrete wall without using forms. You can fill the hollow tile with cement, too, for added strength if you wish. Around the edge of the pool and extending over the top of the tile wall, you can pour a concrete slab at the same time you pour the wall, or you can lay flagstones of some kind. The kids will be slopping in and out of the water making a lot of mud otherwise.

If you're pouring the concrete in hot weather, keep wet cloth or plastic on the fresh concrete so it doesn't dry too fast. It's a good idea to fill the pool at least partially after the concrete has cured, let it stand a few days, and then flush that first water out and refill. This flushes away alkalies in the new cement that are harmful to fish and, while not particularly so for children, won't do them any good, either.

Drainage

Because a wading pool needs to be drained and cleaned occasionally through the summer, it should be located so that you can drain it by gravity—either underground drainpipe or siphon. The underground pipe is best, which means a drain in the pool floor. A 1½-inch pipe is drain enough for a small wading pool. Be sure the floor slopes toward it. You can plug it with a standard pipe plug, but a better idea is to screw an extension into it that rises up above the water level or right at the level so it can act as an overflow. But more important, you can then handily unscrew the extension of pipe to drain the pool rather than having to grope around underwater trying to find and unscrew the plug. And because it's visible at the water surface, no one is going to unknowingly jump on it or run into it.

A nice added touch for a wading pool is to situate it, when possible, above a garden or orchard plot so the water can be used for irrigation when the pool needs emptying. When you can't get sufficient grade to drain your in-ground pool, alternatives are to build it more or less aboveground or rely on the old dry well

idea. In the latter case, the pond is piped into an underground pile of rocks, usually placed in the ground inside a barrel that has no bottom but a lid on top. Water seeps away as it would in a septic tank field or a French drain (see A Score or More Uses for Stones and Rocks earlier in this chapter).

Food Storage Structures

Traditional methods seldom die never to return. It just takes time for the reasons why they were once practiced to reassert themselves. Just when the root cellar sounds about as old-fashioned as a Model T (which was not traditional and so could go out of style forever), it springs back up again under modern guise. Root cellars can keep certain foods fresh all winter without any energy use at all. Bob Oldham

in Ohio (and others, I'm sure) is selling a prefabricated root cellar as a sideline to his precut concrete septic tank business. Sales have not been exactly brisk because most of the people who would appreciate a root cellar are long since gone. (If you want to learn about the practicality of root cellars in detail, read Mike and Nancy Bubel's book *Root Cellaring* [Rodale Press, 1979].) Oldham's prefab cellar can be installed in a hillside, in a pit, or in a surface mound of dirt. The joints are sealed with butyl rubber to provide watertight installation.

I gained an appreciation of root cellars from one in Minnesota in which I stored many a bushel of potatoes. It was not in a hillside location, but rather dug into a very sandy knoll above a stream. Groundwater was never a prob-

lem because of the sandy soil. Steps led down about 8 feet to the cellar. The entrance was double-doored for extra insulation. A vent in the outer door that could be closed let in air, and another vent in the ceiling at the far end of the storage room allowed a flow of cool air through the room when outside temperatures were in the 30's and 40's. At such times, the inner door could be left ajar. Storage space was about 15 feet wide, 25 feet long, and 8 feet high. The arched concrete roof was covered with about 18 inches of sod. In winter, we would add a thick covering of cornstalks or straw as extra protection from temperatures that routinely fell to −20°F. The floor was gravelly sand. Shelves lined the walls and filled the middle, with a narrow aisle between.

Fruit and Vegetable Storage

Commodity	Place to Store	Storage Temperature (in °F.)	Humidity
Late cabbage	Pit, root cellar	32	Moderately moist
Carrots and other root crops (beets, parsnips, turnips, etc.)	Pit, root cellar; or in garden where they grew, heavily mulched	32	Moist
Cauliflower	Root cellar	32	Moderately moist
Late celery	Pit; or roots buried in a bucket of soil in root cellar (6 to 8 weeks)	32	Moderately moist
Endive	Roots buried in a bucket of soil in root cellar	32	Moderately moist
Onions	Cool, dry place (root cellar OK, but often too moist for long storage)	32	Dry
Parsnips	In garden where they grew, heavily mulched; or in root cellar	32	Moist
Peppers	Unheated basement or room (2 to 3 weeks)	45 to 50	Moderately moist
Potatoes	Pit or root cellar	35 to 40	Moderately moist
Pumpkins and Squashes	Home cellar or basement	55	Moderately dry
Sweet potatoes	Home cellar or basement	55 to 60	Moderately dry
Tomatoes (mature green)	Home cellar or basement (4 to 6 weeks)	55 to 70	Moderately dry
Apples	Fruit storage cellar	32	Moderately moist
Grapes	Fruit storage cellar (1 to 2 months)	32	Moderately moist
Oranges	Fruit storage cellar	32	Moderately moist
Pears	Fruit storage cellar	32	Moderately moist

Getting the Temperature and Humidity Right

Root cellars tend to be too warm rather than too cold for most of the food traditionally stored in them. Ground temperatures are about 55°F. normally, and for some vegetables and most fruit, especially apples and potatoes, a temperature in the mid to upper 30's is best. The trick is to open the root cellar to cool air as soon as night temperatures fall into that range in the autumn, then close up the cellar when the outside temperature warms up during the day. Until this kind of cool weather comes, it is better not to store those commodities that need 35° to 40°F. temperatures. Therefore, delay root crop harvest as long as possible. Store *late* cabbage, cauliflower, celery, and apples. Pumpkins, squashes, and sweet potatoes, which like a 55°F. temperature, store fine in a root cellar at ordinary ground temperature (and for that reason are better off in a regular cellar where that temperature is normal).

A thermometer is a must in a root cellar to guide your venting procedures. Don't worry if you can't achieve exact temperatures and humidity as recommended. Without doubt your potatoes and onions will begin to sprout toward spring anyway, if not sooner. We always turned cabbages upside down (with the roots still attached) in the root cellar because that was the tradition we were taught. I've not seen that advice in print and do not know if it makes that much difference. The floor of the root cellar was sand, which kept the humidity a little higher than if the floor were concrete. This helped the potatoes, but not the onions, which nevertheless were mostly usable until the very early perennial onions started growing in the garden. For better air circulation it turned out best to store various crops in bushel or peck baskets rather than in larger bins. We set the baskets out from the wall a few inches for the same reason.

Pit Root Cellars in Barrels and Drums

For small amounts of produce, a pit dug into the ground, in which barrels or drums are buried, suffices as a "poor man's root cellar." Borrowing the idea from Harlan Hubbard, I buried a couple of 30-gallon steel drums in the earth, the brims sticking above the soil surface about 3 inches. I use them mostly for potatoes, but beets, carrots, and other root crops also store well this way. Onions do fairly well, although the air in the drums is usually a bit too humid for them. I use these 30-gallon drums rather than the standard 55-gallon kind because it is too difficult to reach down to the bottom of the latter. I bury the drums straight up, not tilted as

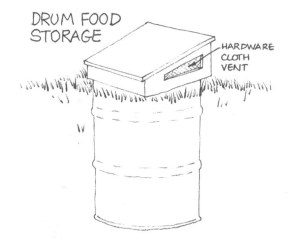

DRUM FOOD STORAGE

HARDWARE CLOTH VENT

you see pictured so often in books. I pack the potatoes in layers, alternating with clean dry straw, and I try to keep any potato from touching the ones next to it. No bruised or cut potatoes go in.

Harlan built wooden frame tops for his drums that look like little shed roofs, with hardware cloth vents in the sides for air circulation. Venting is important but I've gotten enough air to my drums by sticking twigs about the thickness of matchsticks (small enough so no mouse can squeeze through) between the metal lids and the brims of my drums. I weigh down the lids with rocks, then cover with a foot or two of leaves when the weather turns sharply cold. Even in the coldest weather, nothing has ever frozen in the drums.

An amusing incident occurred when I installed my drums, and it will provide a lesson for you as it did for me. I buried the drums at a high location at the edge of the lawn and I thought this would solve any water problems. I filled dirt in loosely around them, sat the lids in place over them, and went to bed. That night heavy rain fell. The sight that greeted me next morning was that of two drums on top of the ground! Water had oozed in around them, filled the holes, and floated the drums to the top. I had to do the job over again. But the second time I tamped the dirt in *well* around them and ran water from the hose to settle the dirt even better. Then, just to make sure, I put heavy rocks on both drums until the soil had settled in tight around them.

A Fruit Room

You will notice in the chart Fruit and Vegetable Storage that the guidelines suggest not a root cellar but a *fruit* cellar for apples and other fruit. Although experienced root cellar devotees often store fruit and vegetables in the same room (the Bubels, for example, say that in relatively small amounts there's no problem),

the traditional view is that apples will take on offensive odors from root crops and cole crops in the storage cellar. Also, stored apples give off ethylene gas, which can cause potatoes to sprout faster. In the latter 1800s and early 1900s when the techniques of "natural" refrigeration were reaching their peak just before the introduction of iceboxes and electric refrigeration, fruit was not only stored separately from vegetables, but the most advanced technology had concluded that it should be stored *aboveground,* in heavily insulated buildings. Farmers found that they could more easily keep apples in the proper temperature range (mid-30's) aboveground than contending with the average 55°F. in-ground temperature. The secret was in using late varieties of fruit (which keep better anyway) that did not have to be harvested until fairly cool nights arrived.

These storage houses were called cold-air houses and have enough practical potential to reconsider today. The walls of the cold air house were double, with a *foot* of space between them that was filled with sawdust. Floor and ceiling were also double with 8 to 12 inches of sawdust for insulation. Windows were double-sashed with outside shutters to close off both sunlight on warmish days and bitter cold on January nights. Sometimes there were vents in the floor and near the ceiling, but all vents had to have the capability of being closed up tight, usually with tight-fitting wood blocks.

As soon as cool nights arrived in the fall, the house was opened up to take advantage of lower night temperatures. In daytime, it was closed up tightly. There were two thermometers, one near the floor and one near the ceiling. By assiduously taking advantage of nighttime temperatures, the room, by the middle of October, became quite cool and by wintertime went down to the high 30's. From then on until spring, one had only to keep the fruit from freezing, which, early accounts say, was rarely ever a problem. The insulation, plus the sunlight through the windows, plus the opening of vents on thawing days, kept indoor temperatures above freezing. Since pears were often kept in closed drawers out of the light and apples packed in barrels and bedded in sawdust or chaff, slightly below freezing outside temperatures did not affect them. (Timothy chaff was considered the best packing material for apples, a useful plant unfortunately ignored too much today.)

The interior arrangement of a fruit room might be shelves down the middle with a 2½-foot aisle all around. If the shelves were 5 feet wide to allow easy reach to the middle from either side, the room would be 9 feet wide and as long as desired. More often, there were shallower shelves along each wall, fitted with drawers in which pears were kept. Two sets of shelves or bins 4 feet wide for apples were in the center of the room, with an aisle between and on each side. The room was about 16 feet wide, but few families today would need anything approaching that size.

With today's advances in both materials for, and knowledge of, insulation, a fruit room would be most practical for northern regions. The secret, say the old-timers, is to try not to enter the building except when the temperature is in the 28° to 42°F. range, and then to close the door quickly behind you. Store only fruit in good condition and use the apple varieties that begin to turn bad first. If fruit shrivels from being too dry, set pans of water under the shelves. (An acquaintance of mine solved the problem of shriveling apples by storing them in a belowground well pump house and letting the water drip a bit, more or less continuously. Another used to store apples in a springhouse dug deep underground, where water ran continuously.)

When it is all said and done, the most important ingredient to success in fruit storage is variety. Winter pears such as Kieffer will keep so well in any cool storage that they will hardly soften enough to eat until taken into a warm, dry room to ripen up. For apples, Winesap,

Storing Fresh Grapes

Accounts in old farm magazines from the 19th century tell of keeping grapes in cold storage much longer than the USDA recommends. For success, only grapes of the highest quality were used, dead ripe but not overripe. Small or sour grapes from crowded vines didn't contain the quantities of sugar and juice, so tradition says, that would resist drying up, rotting, or freezing. When the grapes reached the right degree of ripeness, which was when the *stems* turned from green to brownish or at least dark green in color, the bunches were picked and packed carefully in boxes. No trace of dew could remain on them. The boxes were not to be of pine because it imparts a piny taste to the fruit. And bunches were not to be packed so tight as to squash any of them.

In closed wooden boxes, the grapes wouldn't freeze unless the temperature dropped below 28°F. Any fairly dry storage room where the temperature could be kept at or a little above that level could result in grapes keeping until spring, so 19th-century farmers said. Isabelle was the variety named for storage, but I assume that any Concord-type grape will do. The catch is that, at least in our country, there are many strains of Concord, or more correctly many strains of purple slip-skin grapes on old farms and homesteads—all of which are called Concord. Some are better than others in size and taste, so keeping quality would vary, too.

Yellow Newtown, Northern Spy, Rhode Island Greening, Roxbury Russet, Smokehouse, Winter Banana, and Arkansas Black all keep well. Your best bet is to inquire at some length in your own neighborhood about old varieties still growing that are known for good-keeping quality and graft scions from these trees to your own (see Grafting Skills Anyone Can Learn in Chapter 7). They have stood the test of time in your locality and that's what you want, no matter what name the apple goes by.

Icehouse Coolers

The ultimate cold-storage facility in the days immediately preceding modern refrigerants was a room built onto the old-time icehouse, and cooled with ice from it. Such a cooler was considered too expensive even in the 1800s just for fruit, but where dairy products and meat needed to be kept in high quality, this kind of cooler with its "built-in" icebox for perishables could keep food as cold as GE's finest.

It was not, of course, nearly as convenient as today's refrigerator or walk-in cooler. However, the word convenient tends to vary in meaning with its relation to profits or savings, and if electricity continues to mount in cost, the traditional icehouse might suddenly become "convenient" again, just as the wood stove has. Popular wisdom would have us believe that people will not do "backbreaking" or tedious work if there is any alternative, but the truth is that where good money is to be made, there is no such thing as backbreaking work in the colloquial language. If money can be saved harvesting ice again, people will harvest it. (Icehouses and ice harvests are by no means long-gone activities. For one example from Woodruff, Wisconsin, see "Ice Harvest" by Peter Maller in *Farmstead* magazine, Vol. 10, No. 6, 1983.)

The Icehouse

In some ways the best icehouse is the cheapest. All that is required is a foot of sawdust on all sides of the stack of ice including the top and bottom, excellent venting over the top of the ice, and good drainage beneath, without letting warm air back to the ice stack. The cheapest shell of a building around such an

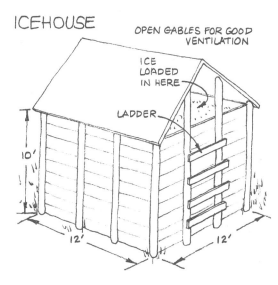

ICEHOUSE

OPEN GABLES FOR GOOD VENTILATION

ICE LOADED IN HERE

LADDER

10'

12'   12'

CONSIDERATIONS:

- SIMPLE POLE CONSTRUCTION
- BOARDS NAILED ON INSIDE
- ROOF <u>NOT</u> NECESSARY
- SITS ON SANDY KNOLL FOR GOOD DRAINAGE – OTHERWISE TILE NECESSARY TO DRAIN WATER
- CAN BE DESIGNED MUCH FANCIER IF DESIRED

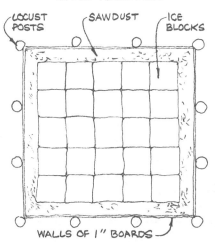

SIMPLE FLOOR PLAN

LOCUST POSTS   SAWDUST   ICE BLOCKS

WALLS OF 1" BOARDS

insulated and ventilated stack will keep the ice as good as the most expensive, and a roof is of no real need except to keep the sawdust on top from blowing away. Many icehouses in fact had no roofs, although without one the sawdust on top should be 2 to 3 feet deep. Sawdust is the best insulation for the money available, but other materials are possible. Chopped straw or chaff works, but only at twice the thickness of sawdust.

The cheapest icehouses consist of poles in the ground with inch-board walls nailed to the interior sides of them. Although on a high, very gravelly soil, a floor may not be necessary, in most cases joists are laid and floor boards rest on them loosely, or are nailed down with cracks between to let melting water through. Treated lumber was used (a century ago crude oil and whitewash were used to protect the wood). The floor was covered with a foot of sawdust, with some pains taken to pack it level, but raising the surface slightly higher near the walls toward the top layer. Then, as the ice and sawdust would settle after filling, the ice blocks would be forced in upon themselves rather than settling apart and opening cracks between the blocks of ice where air might circulate and increase the rate of melting. If the soil under the icehouse was not sandy or gravelly, tile drainage was installed to carry away the water, in some form of culvert drain.

The ice blocks usually were cut about 8 to 10 inches thick and 2 feet square, weighing 150 to 200 pounds, although they could be smaller or larger, so long as they were all the same size so they would stack tightly and evenly. A ground-level door or opening was used for bringing in the ice, then closed up until the ice inside was used down to that level again. The same with second-story doors or openings. Ice was best removed from the top only, digging aside the sawdust and then replacing it over the new ice.

As each layer of blocks was stacked, a foot of sawdust was packed around the outside, between the ice and the walls. Another trick was to pack a little snow between the ice blocks, which kept them from freezing together. Over the top, a foot or more of sawdust was added. If there was a roof, large vents (often doubling as entrance doors) were built into the gable ends, since good ventilation is the most important key to holding ice through the summer, strange as that may seem. If the building could be built in the shade of trees, all the better.

Sometimes a tight floor was installed with a drain to carry away water. So that warm air would not travel back up the drain to the ice, the pipe emptied into a water trap, or had a curved trap in it like the drain under a sink.

Double-walled icehouses were often built, but they kept ice no better and in some ways were less desirable. It was still necessary to pack about 4 inches of sawdust between ice and wall, even though the double wall might be filled with a foot of sawdust, because it was essential that there be no cracks or crevices around the ice itself for air to circulate. So as long as one was packing 4 inches, he might as well be packing 12. Also, because of the moisture constantly about, the sawdust in time rotted, even inside the walls. On a small icehouse in particular, a single wall was better.

A vast improvement was a brick or masonry wall to withstand the constant moisture. But build such a substantial icehouse only after you learn from experience how much ice you need to store. Old accounts say that a stack 8 by 10 feet wide and 7 feet tall will last a family's needs, but that if a cooler were attached, three times that much was required—say a 12 by 12-foot stack 10 feet high. Don't forget to add in the foot of space for sawdust between wall and ice.

The Cooler

The cooler added on to the icehouse was also well insulated, with double walls filled with sawdust and a double door, like the fruit rooms I described earlier, possibly with shuttered, double-paned windows. Against the partition dividing the icehouse from the cooler sat a large icebox with a metal chute atop it that ran up the top of the wall. A block or two of ice was broken and dropped into the chute from above every morning or as needed. At the bottom of the chute were two registers or vents exactly like those found on some wood stoves today. As soon as the ice in the chute had lowered the chute temperature to near freezing, the vents could be opened and, with a thermometer at floor level and another at ceiling level, the temperature of the cooler could be regulated with rather remarkable accuracy to between 35° and 45°F., just by opening or closing the vents.

At the same time, the metal bottom of the chute became ice-cold, and the cold air sank into the icebox beneath it, which was double-walled and insulated. Temperatures remained there as cold as in any modern refrigerator so long as there was ice in the chute. Melting water from the chute could be piped to a pan in the lower chamber of the icebox, or more often, into a larger tub or trough sitting alongside the icebox next to the partition. This pipe had a trap in it, too, to keep warmer air from drifting back into the chute. When the ice level in the icehouse got so low the pieces of ice could not be thrown into the top of the chute, ice blocks were carried around into the cooler from outside and loaded in from a door halfway down the chute.

Feeding ice into the chute every day was of course an "inconvenience," although for the farmer going to the barn daily, the chore added only a few minutes to the daily routine, or for the housewife, the work was no more "inconvenient" than tossing wood in the stove in winter. Nevertheless, much experimentation was done to avoid the job. Instead of the ice chute, ventilators were built into the bottom and top of the partition between icehouse and cooler. Cold air entered at the bottom vent and exited at the top. The cooler's temperature could

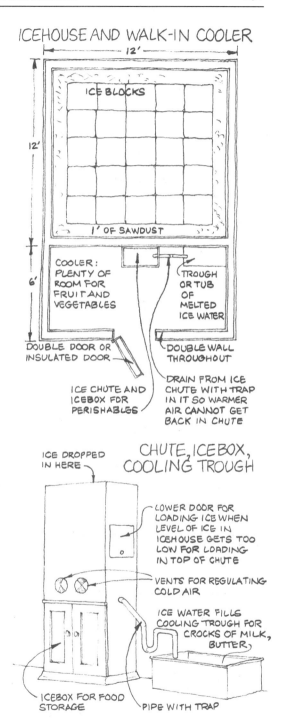

ICEHOUSE AND WALK-IN COOLER

|← 12' →|

ICE BLOCKS

12'

1' OF SAWDUST

COOLER: PLENTY OF ROOM FOR FRUIT AND VEGETABLES

6'

TROUGH OR TUB OF MELTED ICE WATER

DOUBLE DOOR OR INSULATED DOOR

DOUBLE WALL THROUGHOUT

DRAIN FROM ICE CHUTE WITH TRAP IN IT SO WARMER AIR CANNOT GET BACK IN CHUTE

ICE CHUTE AND ICEBOX FOR PERISHABLES

CHUTE, ICEBOX, COOLING TROUGH

ICE DROPPED IN HERE

LOWER DOOR FOR LOADING ICE WHEN LEVEL OF ICE IN ICEHOUSE GETS TOO LOW FOR LOADING IN TOP OF CHUTE

VENTS FOR REGULATING COLD AIR

ICE WATER FILLS COOLING TROUGH FOR CROCKS OF MILK, BUTTER,

ICEBOX FOR FOOD STORAGE

PIPE WITH TRAP

Harvesting Ice

The problem with trying to consider seriously labor-intensive energy sources like icehouse coolers is that our memories of them—in this case the ice harvest—are tinged either with too much sentimentalism or too much realism. The last ice-harvest operations were, for the most part, *commercial* operations for which a great amount of ice had to be cut and hauled and stacked away, often into three-story houses where horses and ropes and pulleys were necessary to slide the ice high into the loft. Thus, older people who lived and possibly worked on dairy farms before electric refrigeration remember the work connected with the ice and thank their lucky stars for electricity.

But a family supply of ice to supplement or take the place of the ordinary kitchen refrigerator is not that much of an undertaking. In a 12 by 12 by 10-foot stack of ice there would be approximately forty-five blocks, 2 feet square by 8 inches thick. Even without the big gas-powered saws used to cut blocks of ice forty years ago, forty-five blocks is not that big of an undertaking. And as homesteaders have learned, you can use a chain saw to cut blocks of ice, if you clean the water and slush out of the chain gear and oil it well after the day's work is finished.

One tool that is indispensable is a pair of ice tongs to lift the blocks with. Ice tongs are fairly indestructible, and old ones are commonly found at farm sales. Your hardware store may even know of sources for new ones (ask them to look through their wholesale catalogs from the large hardware distributor Belknap's in Louisville, Kentucky). Timber-carrying tongs, used around lumberyards, are much like ice tongs and are still available (one source is Nasco, Fort Atkinson, WI 53538). Or get a blacksmith to make you a pair. They are quite simple in construction, the two curved, pointed hooks joined at the handle in such a way that the harder you pull or lift on the handle, the more firmly the hooks bite into the ice.

Long poles to push the floating blocks

Cutting river ice.

be kept low enough in this manner, but at a much greater use of ice, since direct venting to the icehouse caused the ice to melt much faster.

If the best minds today were turned to the task of modernizing the principles of icehouse cooling, we might be pleasantly surprised at the results both in convenience and savings in energy, not to mention safety. Chlorofluorocarbons from refrigerants are the single most devastating chemicals responsible for the deterioration of the ozone layer in the upper atmosphere that shields us from ultraviolet radiation.

Lest you doubt the icehouse-cooler principle works in practice, we still use the method when we make homemade ice cream. The ice in the outside of the freezer transfers its coldness to the cream inside. The oak-paneled, metal-lined iceboxes that sat in the kitchens of my of ice to shore are also sometimes handy. The poles used for this purpose in the old days had steel points and a sort of hook that could be used to pull the block as well as push it.

It's best to harvest ice when the temperature is well below freezing—about 20°F. is ideal. If the ice is melting, it is slippery, increasing your danger of falling in the water below. Blocks of such ice more easily freeze together in the icehouse, too, although as mentioned earlier, putting a bit of snow or sawdust between the blocks will solve that problem.

Some folks make or buy hauling sleds for their snowmobiles. These could be well utilized in hauling the ice, a few blocks at a time, back to the house—thereby justifying the money so extravagantly spent on such vehicles.

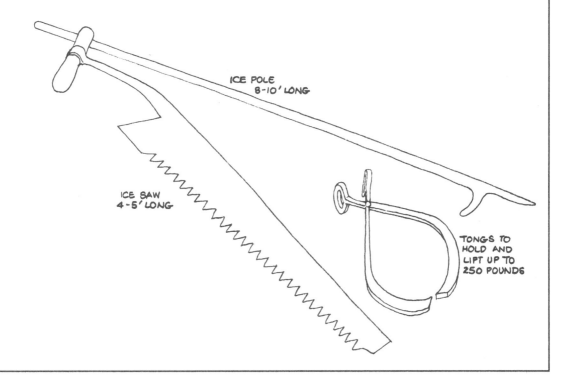

ICE POLE
8-10' LONG

ICE SAW
4-5' LONG

TONGS TO
HOLD AND
LIFT UP TO
250 POUNDS

youth worked just fine, too, and were beautiful enough that they are now collected as antiques.

A Wood-Heated Fruit Dryer

My son built a little solar fruit dryer one year—a half-box affair with a pane of glass over the front and vents on either side—a sort of tiny cold frame with vents. It worked fairly well for small amounts of fruit; we particularly liked the taste of dried strawberries even though they turned blackish and looked awful. But what we learned was that serious fruit drying took two hot, dry days to do a batch, and three days if the first two weren't perfectly sunny with low humidity. Various researchers have said as much (see *Home Food Systems*, Rodale Press, 1981).

Sun-drying food works well in hot, dry climates like the Southwest, but requires some luck with the weather in more humid parts of the country. What's more, fruit that sun-dries slowly over two to three days does not have the quality of that dried during a continuous 24-hour period with artificial heat.

If the people who dried common fruits commercially in the 1880s were around in the 1980s, they could have told us that. In the days before handy electric and oil heat, and before commercially canned and frozen foods were even dreamed of, large tonnages of dried fruit were sold—demand, says history, usually outran supply. Solar power was well understood in those days and used for many purposes, but drying fruit in humid climates was not one of them. Instead, methods of using only very small amounts of wood for heat were perfected— renewable, stored sunlight that could be more or less turned off and on as needed rather than relying on the slow passage of the sun from east to west and then time out for darkness.

Enthusiasts of alternative technologies today need to learn a lesson in this regard; direct sunlight is not going to solve the energy problem alone in the humid cold half of the country. Nature seems to know this even if we don't, and she has clothed this cold, most humid area with the most efficient forms of stored sunlight: white oak, white ash, hickory, locust, beech, and hard maple.

Adapting the Backyard Barbecue

Some of the earlier fruit dryers using wood heat were designed much like the barbecue-evaporator I described in Multiple Uses of Backyard Barbecues earlier in this chapter. But the masonry walls were extended up over the firebox and gradually arched inward to form a kiln or oven in which the fruit was dried. Should you wish to dry fruit in small quantities on your barbecue, you can buy or make a stovetop drying pan that has a reservoir of water in the lower half of it to distribute the heat evenly. Set it on the metal cover just as you would on your stove and start a small fire below. (Bumble Bee is the name of one such dryer that is distributed by S/A Distributors, 700 E. Water St., Suite 730, Midtown Plaza, Syracuse, NY 13210. Many hardware stores carry stovetop dryers or can order one for you.)

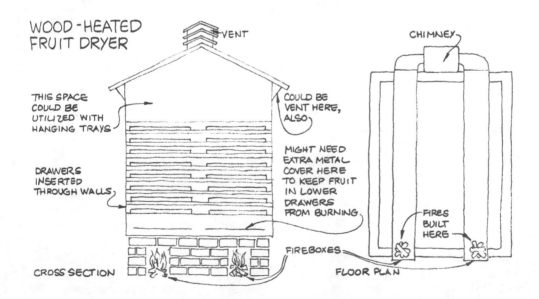

A Fancy Drying Hut

But much more efficient dryers evolved in those years before factory canning took away the commercial market for dried apples, strawberries, raspberries, peaches, pears, and so forth. These small buildings could be adapted today for backyard drying.

The Illustrated Annual Register of Rural Affairs for 1872, a yearly compendium that used to be published by Luther Tucker and Son, Albany, New York, describes a 7 by 10-foot drying shed capable of drying 20 *bushels* of raspberries in 24 hours with only two small fires. The little hut actually has two sets of shallow, long drawers that fit into openings on both sides of the building, rather than having a door for a person to enter.

Under the interchangeable drawers at one end of the building are two small fireboxes from which arched sheet-metal tunnels carry heat and smoke across the floor and to the chimney at the other end of the building. Even with a small fire a second flat piece of sheet metal is necessary over the tunnels to keep fruit in the lower drawers from burning. A cupola-style vent in the peak of the roof allows for good ventilation of the rising heat.

A Simpler Drying Hut

To make an even simpler drying hut for the backyard, use a 55-gallon barrel with the top cut out for a firebox, lay it on its side, and fill it about one-third full of sand. Build a stone foundation around the barrel and insert a metal stovepipe for a chimney at the back end of the barrel. Use the cutoff top of the barrel as a makeshift door on the front (unless you want something fancier, in which case there are plenty of kits on the market to make a barrel into a stove). Then build a wooden (or stone or brick or cement block) hut over the barrel, leaving slots in one side for a set of drawers. Drawer bottoms can be wood frames with hardware cloth stretched and nailed over them. They can be covered with muslin for cleanliness. Make sure the drawers are interchangeable so that if the fruit in the lower one gets too hot or dries sooner, you can switch the drawers around.

It goes without saying that the more fruit you dry in one batch, the more efficient your fire, since even the smallest fire is going to provide more heat than a small batch of fruit needs for drying.

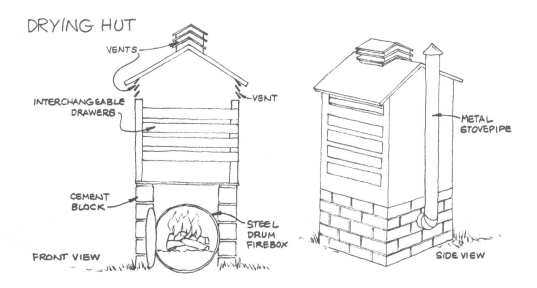

DRYING HUT

VENTS

INTERCHANGEABLE DRAWERS

VENT

CEMENT BLOCK

STEEL DRUM FIREBOX

FRONT VIEW

METAL STOVEPIPE

SIDE VIEW

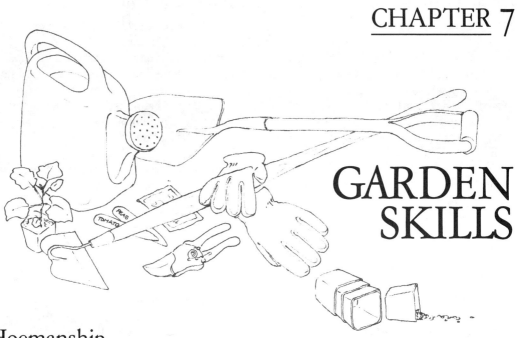

CHAPTER 7

GARDEN SKILLS

Hoemanship

In his fascinating book, *The Farm and the Village* (Faber Paperbacks, London, 1969), George Ewart Evans points out that the village blacksmith of the 6th to 17th centuries found himself very much in demand if he could make a hoe blade thinner than those of his competitors without sacrificing strength. The reason was simple enough. Not only would a thinner blade slice more easily into the soil, but more importantly, it would weigh less, by at least a couple of ounces. To people who hoed for 10 hours a day all week, a couple of ounces made a big difference.

I can appreciate that observation, since in addition to normal garden hoeing, I hoe ½ acre of corn twice during May and June, and I hoe dock, thistles, and other weeds routinely from an 8-acre pasture field. The only hoe I've been able to find to suit me is an ancient one I bought years ago for 50¢ at a farm sale. This hoe is so old that about a third of its original blade is worn completely away, and what is left is not half the thickness of a new hoe blade. Light, its edge sharpened well, the hoe does not tire me nearly as much as new ones, and the fact that the blade is smaller by a third means I can maneuver it between plants in the row much more easily.

I have bought three hoes since then, so that all the members of the family could join the weeding, but we all grab first for the old hoe. Two cheap hoes from the hardware store are, by comparison, almost repugnant to use, and everyone cheered when the handle on one of them broke. They are too heavy. The blades are too thick and blunt, requiring much grinding with a heavy-duty bench grinder to reshape the cutting edge properly. And after so much grinding you run the risk of ruining the temper in the blade. Most of all, the angle of the blade to the handle is all wrong; in drawing the hoe toward you, too much of the flat side of the blade breasts the soil, increasing the drag or draft needlessly.

242 ·

The best new hoe I have found, for my body anyway, is the "field hoe" sold by Smith and Hawken (68 Homer, Palo Alto, CA 94301). Though still heavier than my favorite old hoe, it is, at 2⅓ pounds, light compared to most hoes. Smith and Hawken's Scovil Pattern Hoe weighs 3 pounds 5 ounces and its American Pattern Hoe weighs 3 pounds 14 ounces. But at least it has a proper blade-to-handle angle. What's more, I like the way the blade fastens to the handle. The blade has a hole in it to receive the handle directly, making it what is called an "eye" hoe, or Scovil-type, after the principal manufacturer.

Most common hoes have a blade connected to the handle by a slender steel neck stuck into a ferrule and are called shank hoes, or (better) a one-piece neck and socket into which the handle fits, called a socket hoe. In both these cases, it is difficult to replace the handle. With eye hoes, however, it's easy to change handles, and the handle, being fatter at the blade end, is not as likely to break. Though the blade slips off easily, the action of the hoe in use binds it tightly to the end of the handle, requiring only a simple nail to hold it in place.

The hoe is one of man's most ancient tools, and true to its definition as a traditional tool, it is still commonly in use and always will be, as long as gardens are cultivated. Over the years many different hoe designs have been tried, the names proliferating almost as much as the hoes themselves: chopping hoe, hilling hoe, scuffle hoe, onion hoe, beet or nurserymen's hoe, Yankee hoe, Canterbury hoe, Dutch or double shanks hoe, grub hoe, Hazeltine hoe. The names are more colloquial and regional than standard, and you must look at the hoe first rather than the name it's been given.

Short-Handled Hoes

These are usually called hand weeders rather than hoes. They are for doing fine work between very small plants, down on your hands and knees. I've seldom found a hand weeder that will take the place of my fingers in good, loamy, humusy soils. The little three-pronged claw weeders are next to useless, although like most gardeners, I had to buy one before I was convinced. They *look* effective. I've never had a "Cape Cod" weeder, but John Withee, writing in *Farmstead* magazine ("Hoes for Hard Rows," Vol. 4, No. 2, 1977) says it is "an overrated, overpromoted, poorly designed toy." I have tried to use the short-handled, triangular wood scrapers that are somewhat like the Cape Cod, but these tools aren't very effective in the garden. (As a matter of fact, they aren't very effective on wood either, in my opinion.) The short-handled Hazeltine weeder, also called a hotbed weeder (sold among others by A. M. Leonard, Inc., Piqua, OH 45356) can be sharpened even on the outer tip edge, making it easy to work between little carrot and onion seedlings (but still not as easy as fingers).

Long-Handled Hoes

Many blades are made for long-handled hoes. The standard garden hoe may have square or rounded shoulders, or the blades may be square at the cutting corners or flared out a bit. Blades only half as long as the standard hoe blade, but as wide or wider, are called nurserymen's hoes or beet hoes, depending on who is using them. Hoes with even shorter blades, but still as wide, are called onion hoes, although in our part of the country, we tend to think of the real onion hoe as a very narrow but long-bladed hoe, or swoe.

Cultivating Hoes

Hoes with three or more prongs or tines for a blade, like Canterbury hoes and cultivating hoes, have been nearly as useless for me as the little claw weeders, but they may be of value in stonier soils. The heart-shaped, pointed hoes, called Warren or furrowing hoes, make nice little furrows to plant seed in. One kind, called

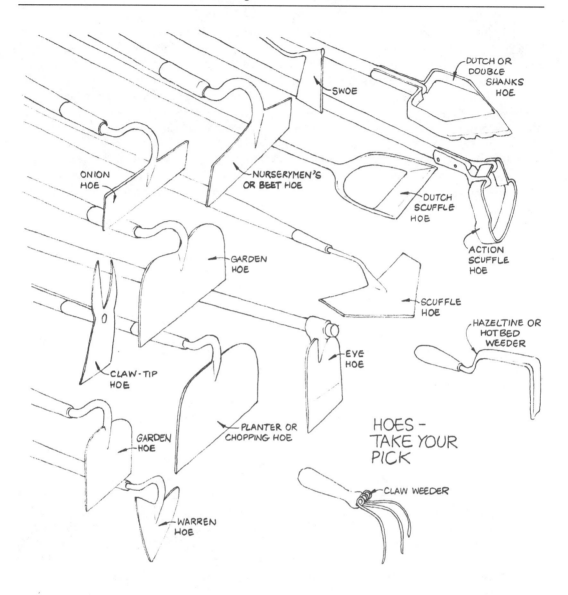

ONION HOE

NURSERYMEN'S OR BEET HOE

SWOE

DUTCH OR DOUBLE SHANKS HOE

DUTCH SCUFFLE HOE

ACTION SCUFFLE HOE

GARDEN HOE

SCUFFLE HOE

HAZELTINE OR HOT BED WEEDER

CLAW-TIP HOE

EYE HOE

GARDEN HOE

PLANTER OR CHOPPING HOE

HOES – TAKE YOUR PICK

WARREN HOE

CLAW WEEDER

the Swan hoe, has a long swan-shaped neck that enables one to pull the blade almost horizontally right under the soil surface, like the sweep-type blades on large motor-powered cultivators. I see no use for any of these hoes when a rotary tiller is used to cultivate between rows, or when a trusty old common hoe, half worn away, can be used for between-row weeding.

Scuffle Hoes

There are at least three distinct kinds of scuffle hoes. They are made to be pushed ahead of the hoer, not drawn toward him. The Dutch scuffle has two steel shanks running from handle to blade, which is pushed flat, just under the soil. The other common kind has only one shank

and socket connecting blade to handle. A third kind, rarely seen today, has the Dutch-type double shanks, but they are welded to the *middle* of the flat blade, not the back end of it. Thus, the blade could be scuffled backward *and* forward. Both ends had sharp edges, too, making this a much more useful and versatile tool than the other two. Other push hoes, like the Action scuffle hoe, have narrow looped blades of various shapes and can also be pushed or pulled. As Abraham Lincoln said humorously of other matters: "This is the very sort of thing that people who like this sort of thing are surely going to like."

Chopping Hoes

The regular garden hoe shape, when in extra large models, is often referred to as a chopping hoe or a planter hoe. The only person I've ever seen use one effectively is Harlan Hubbard, profiled in Practical Wild Foods in Chapter 5. Harlan avoids loud gas-guzzlers as much as possible, and he uses his big hoe as a primary tillage tool in his soft soil. But he does not "chop" with the hoe; in his hands it seems just to sink deeply into the soil, loosening it to perhaps 6 inches and breaking it up faster than I can do with a tiller, although not as finely.

Hoeing Know-How

The secret of using a hoe properly is that one should never actually "chop" with it, at least not to the point of raising it more than knee-high. If the blade is sharp and angled properly, you can set it on the soil, and, by pulling it toward you with a downward pressure of your arms, it will go into the soil well enough. In weeding, you need never raise the hoe more than a couple of inches above the surface on your backswing. As often as not, I let the hoe scrape or scuffle right on the surface as I push it ahead for the next draw, filling in with loose dirt where I have just hoed out weeds and the dirt around them.

Another trick to saving your energy is to use the hoe as a sort of cane when you are going to step ahead for the next draw-back. As you come to the end of the current draw-back, the hoe just ahead of your feet, lean on it as you step forward, then bring the hoe along. After half an acre, that leaning is luxury to your back.

If you learn to use the corners of your regular hoe skillfully, you won't need narrower onion hoes to remove weeds between close-growing crop plants. In using the corner, you do not try to draw the hoe toward you. Insert the corner tip of the hoe between two tiny onions (or whatever) and then *push* at a slight slant away from the row. The little weeds come right out, and because you have better control of the hoe, pushing the blade against the soil surface; there's much less chance that you will hoe out or cover the little crop plants. Besides, pushing in this way is somewhat restful after drawing the hoe toward you farther out from the row. And mixing the two actions keeps you from tiring too fast.

Hilling with the hoe can be artful, too. You have so much more immediate control of the hoe in your hands than you do with a power tiller. You can vary the amount of dirt you are pulling up to the row to suit the size of each crop plant in the row. You can hill up an inch going past one plant and, if the next plant needs 2 inches of dirt hilled up to it, you can immediately do so by applying a bit more muscle to the hoe. Hilling should be done straddling the row, the dirt rolled in from either side to bury little weeds much faster than you could hoe them out in any way.

In hoeing pasture weeds, the blade needs to be especially sharp, because if you do the job correctly, you will expend no more than one blow per weed, slicing through the sod to sever the taproot of the weed about 2 inches down, so it will not grow back up again. But even in this work, you should not swing from above your head with a mighty chop since all that energy is wasted, and you do not have good control of the hoe during such splendidly heroic swings. A "chop" from waist high will work better and is a lot easier on hoe handles. Even a bull thistle with a 1½-inch taproot should fall with one accurate blow of a sharp hoe. When I am cutting sour dock that has gone to seed, I like to use a hoe with a sawed-off handle, so I can swing it with one hand while grasping the dock seedhead in the other. When I get a handful I lay them in a bundle to carry from the field later. It is more difficult to be accurate with a one-handed swing—it's a little game I play to make the work more enjoyable.

A Low-Cost, Effective Glass Cloche to Force Plants in Springtime

My garden in May looks like the surface of the city dump. When frost threatens, I press every container I can get my hands on into service: buckets, baskets, sections of clay field tile, old rugs, and plastic containers of all kinds. My favorite plant protector is the ubiquitous gallon plastic jug, bottom cut out and lid in place. These let in sunlight and turn back a late light frost quite well. The lid can be removed for ventilation.

But those who are really serious about forcing early growth in their plants yearn for those neat glass cloches of various designs that

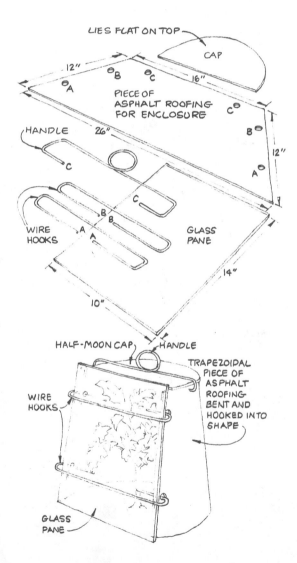

now seem to be popular again. The only problem is their expense. Everyone seems to have forgotten the cheap economy version of the glass cloche, popular in the early part of this century. Called a plant forcer or booster, this cloche was asphalt roofing on three sides and glass on the fourth, held together (rather shakily) by two wire hooks and a wire handle. Another small piece of roofing fitted on top as a cap.

This plant forcer can be made in any desirable size but is usually made to accommodate a pane of glass 8 by 10 inches or 10 by 14 inches. In the smaller size, the piece of roofing is cut in trapezoidal form 24 inches wide at the bottom, 14 inches wide at the top, and 9 inches high. In the larger size, the roofing is cut 12 inches high, 26 inches wide at the bottom, and 16 inches wide at the top. The trapezoidal shape produces an enclosure wider at the bottom than at the top for greater stability, although it can be cut nearly rectangular to accommodate a rectangular pane of glass better; the weight of the glass in place will hold the enclosure from falling over. In the design described here, the glass extends a bit out beyond the front edges of the piece of roofing. The fit is not exact and doesn't need to be.

Two wire hooks bent in the shape shown in the drawing hold the piece of roofing in the shape of a semicircular enclosure and at the same time hold the pane of glass in place. The two wires fit through holes poked in the roofing as indicated at A and B in the drawing. Holes C are for the top piece of wire, which is bent into the form shown to give you a handle for the forcer. But don't try to lift the whole forcer, glass and all, as the glass will usually slip right out. Set the forcer over the plant, then slide the glass pane in place, and then put the cap on. The cap is cut in the shape indicated, about an inch larger than the opening at the top, so the edge can be folded down between the top of the enclosure and the wire handle on both sides, thus securing it in place. When ventilation is necessary, the cap is, of course, removed, and a piece of screen of the same size as the cap can be placed over the top to keep out insects.

In use, the plant forcer is placed with the glass facing south. Heat coming through is absorbed and held by the dark roofing to be released during the nighttime hours. On hot days, the forcer is turned around, so that the glass faces north and the roofing shades the plant; the cap is removed or replaced with a screen vent. Users of this type of plant protector (like Benjamin F. Albaugh, *Home Vegetable Gardening*, Grosset and Dunlap, New York, 1915) claimed that the concentrated odor of the tar or asphalt did not harm the plants in the enclosure. They also claimed that if one used tobacco dust or mothballs to deter the striped cucumber beetle, the enclosed space strengthened the repellents' odors, making them more effective. I wonder if the odor of the asphalt didn't help, too.

Horse Manure Hotbeds

A hundred years ago, hotbeds were used profitably near large cities to grow two crops of lettuce through winter, and then a crop of bedding plants for setting out in the garden in spring. As long as horse manure was available, and of course it was in great quantities, these hotbeds produced lettuce at the rate of forty to fifty heads per 3 by 6-foot bed at far less cost than it takes today to ship lettuce from warm-winter states or raise it in greenhouses. Farmers near such cities as Boston and New York operated as many as a thousand beds, providing jobs for many people and making a good profit, with the expenditure of very little fossil fuel. The details of the design of a hotbed for practical winter use are seldom given in modern books, but they should be incorporated into *any* hotbed, even if used only for starting plants in spring, and even if an electric cable, rather than horse manure, is used for heat. But where horse manure is available, one can avoid the out-of-pocket cost of cable and electricity. This savings can be especially significant if one uses the hotbed all through the cold winter months. The cost savings is only part of it. Manure will also provide fertilizer for the hotbed plants and finished compost for the garden after its heat cycle has passed.

Building the Hotbed

But whatever you use for your source of heat, a good hotbed should satisfy the four following requirements:

1. With a manure hotbed, the soil in which the plants are growing is some several inches below the outside soil surface. Therefore, it must be built on a *high, well-drained location*. The foot of manure will give good drainage for ordinary watering or rains, but obviously, if this hotbed is built in a low place, it might very easily fill with water after heavy rains or thaws.

2. It must be *insulated from the soil around it*. Otherwise cold will move *through the soil and the frame of the hotbed* into the growing space. Just as insulation is now placed around foundations of houses, so it should be put around the "foundation" of a hotbed. Styrofoam or other kinds of rigid-board insulation work fine set at least a foot deep around the perimeter of the hotbed. Manure works fine, too, so long as you place it at least 6 inches wide on the outside of the frame, extend it down to the heating layer of manure below the hotbed, and heap it up around any of the frame exposed above the soil surface. For this reason the pit for the traditional 3 by 6-foot bed should be dug 3 by 7 feet wide, to allow room for the manure that is used for insulation.

3. The hotbed should be *protected from cold winds*. This is provided by putting it in a pit, or what is now often called a "grow-hole." The glass panes on top of the hotbed should

TRADITIONAL HOTBED

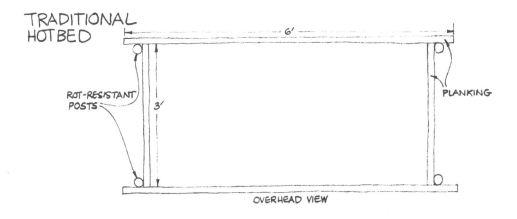

ROT-RESISTANT POSTS

6'

3'

PLANKING

OVERHEAD VIEW

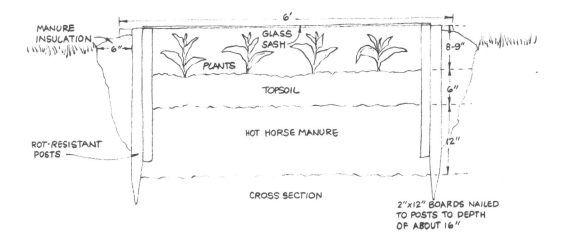

MANURE INSULATION

6"

6'

GLASS SASH

8-9"

PLANTS

TOPSOIL

6"

HOT HORSE MANURE

12"

ROT-RESISTANT POSTS

CROSS SECTION

2"x12" BOARDS NAILED TO POSTS TO DEPTH OF ABOUT 16"

be *only a few inches above the soil surface.* The surface of the loam in which the plants grow should be about 6 inches *below the outside soil surface.* Thus, the pit is dug a little more than 2 feet deep to accommodate a foot of manure, about 6 inches of topsoil, and then the plants, which then have about 8 or 9 inches of clearance under the glass.

The frame should be constructed with the *back board a few inches higher than the front* so that water drains easily off the glass, not, as so many think today, to allow better access to the sun. When the grow frame is built into the ground with the glass only a few inches above the soil surface, the slant does not allow any more sunlight in than a level glass pane would.

Next, the hotbed should be located to the lee side of prevailing winds; the south or east side of a building is excellent. If such protection is not available, a bit of board fence or a stone wall or several bales of hay or straw should be set up for wind protection.

4. Finally, and perhaps most important, the glass top should be *covered at night with some kind of insulation.* A piece of rigid-board insulation is ideal. A couple of straw bales work fine. Burlap sacks and old rugs will do. *Plants will not grow well when night temperatures in the hotbed are coolish, no matter how much sunshine they get during the day.* But on hot days, be sure to raise or remove the sash if inside temperatures rise much above 90°F. You'd be surprised how much the sun can heat a space under glass, even on a cool day if there are not clouds.

Packing in the Manure

Only horse manure is practical for hotbedding. Not only is it more available in quantity, but it heats up quicker and hotter than most other manures. The less straw or other bedding in it, the better, but mixed manure and bedding is adequate. The trick is to start the manure heating *only just before* you want to put it in the hotbed. This is easy if you have your own horse or access to a stable. Generally, the manure will not heat much as it lies in the stable (unless it gets quite deep). So, about three days before you want to start the hotbed, fork up the stable manure into a heap about 4 feet high and 4 feet in diameter, as if you were going to start a compost pile, which is exactly what you are doing. In a pile like this (larger is better if you can manage it) the manure will begin to heat right away, and in about three days it will be quite hot inside and really beginning to steam.

Wheelbarrow it to your hotbed hole (2 feet deep, 3 feet long, and 7 feet wide) and pack it in about a foot deep. For starting plants in spring, 8 inches may be enough if your hotbed is well-insulated as described, but 12 inches will be needed for winter heating and perhaps for spring, too. If the manure is quite dry, sprinkle

a little water on it, but the manure will heat better if it has been well-moistened with horse urine in the stable. You will have to watch carefully so that the manure does not overheat the soil during the first two weeks of intense microbial activity. Keep a soil thermometer in the hotbed, and if temperatures climb much above 90°F., open the glass sash a bit.

Pack manure around the outside of the frame, too, running it under the frame into the manure layer in the bed. The 2 by 12-inch frame planks are nailed to treated or rot-resistant posts at each corner, so it is easy to pack the manure around and under them.

Then place a 6-inch layer of soil over the manure. Water lightly if dry. You don't want it soggy. Place the glass sash over the bed and have insulative covering ready for night use. When the soil heats up to 70° to 75°F., plant your seeds. Regulate the temperature by raising and lowering the sash a bit.

Planting

For spring use, hotbeds should be started no earlier than March 20 in the north, and April 1 is better where plants cannot be set out until late May. The farther south, the earlier you can start, of course. If you contemplate experimenting with winter production of lettuce or similar crops, grow the first in November-December, then skip to February-March for the second, harvesting in time to grow bedding plants for setting out in the garden in spring. Skip the coldest times of the year: late December, January, and early February.

Growing Trees from Seed

A homeowner was complaining about the cost of the maple trees he had purchased and had planted along his driveway. The 12-foot trees had cost him $40 each, moving and planting included. Meanwhile, in the grove of trees behind his home, thousands of maple seedlings

year, another had died, but the three survivors were finally growing fairly well. In the meantime, the seedlings that received ample sunlight in the woods were 14 feet tall and growing strong, with stout, thick trunks and strong scaffold branches.

Not enough emphasis is placed on growing trees from seed in horticultural books. When information is available on the subject, it is couched in forbidding language that seems to imply the need of an advanced degree in plant science for success. The experts flaunt words like stratification and scarification, with much emphasis on seedcoat dormancy, storage temperature, and humidity. Few writers seem to remember that one of the most successful planters of trees since the beginning of the world has been the squirrel, and he cannot pronounce stratification, much less define it.

Trees native to your region will grow from seed quite successfully if you follow one the following steps:

1. Gather the seed when it is ripe and stick it just under the soil surface. (Seed is ripe when it is ready to fall from the tree. In the case of fruit trees, when the fruit is ripe.)
2. Gather the seed when it is ripe and store it in a cold, dry place until spring and then stick it in the ground.
3. Gather the seed when it is ripe and put it in a container of soil kept in a cold, dry place until spring. In spring set the container in a sunny spot until the seeds sprout and then stick the sprouting tree in the ground.

There are other ways to plant trees from seed. One year I threw a basket of rotten apples into the woods behind our house, and scores of little trees came up a year later. Another year, a pile of apple pomace left over from the fall cider pressing bristled in the spring with hundreds of little seedlings as thick as a two-day growth of whiskers. Cherry seeds dropped in the garden

were sprouting from seeds dropped by a mature maple growing there. There were even seedlings coming up every spring in his lawn—which he dutifully mowed off. Any of these little trees could have been moved in early spring to the sunny space along his driveway and in five years would most likely be as tall as his purchased $40 specimens, *if* the large trees lived. But he did not believe me. He had the typical American view: landscaping trees must be *bought* and bought *big*. It is part of our culture. After all, his purchased trees were Golden Mellow Sunset maples, or some such—said so right on the label. That the "wild" seedlings would also sport golden mellow sunset colors of fall foliage was lost on him.

One of his five $40 trees died the first summer despite much watering and wasted fertilizer. Two others had to be cut back severely to keep them alive. The other two sat there for two years, growing only half-size leaves and not increasing in height one bit. By the fifth by birds flying to and from the tree sprouted and grew up through the mulch.

Almost all North American trees need to go through a period of freezing or near-freezing weather before they will sprout. (Citrus trees are a notable exception.) White oak acorns sprout in the fall but do not grow as well if brought inside as they do when left out in the cold over winter, where they rest in semidormancy before beginning to grow strongly in the spring. To avoid all complexity in the matter, either plant the seeds in the fall, or, if you fear wild animals will eat them, store them where they get at least a couple of weeks of cold temperature—maybe an unheated garage or porch, under pots on the patio, even in the refrigerator or freezer. Then plant them out in the spring, or you can instead plant them in pots in the windowsill or greenhouse or other warm place protected from wildlife and set them outside later.

The disadvantage of planting trees from seed is that the seeds do not usually grow true to the parent variety. With ornamentals, this hardly matters, but for fruit and nut trees it can be an important disadvantage, though not always a problem. Occasionally, the seedling does resemble the parent tree in quality and sometimes is even better. Most of our favorite varieties today came from chance seedlings.

But even if seedlings do not produce high-quality fruit, they are most useful. If you learn how to graft (see Grafting Skills Anyone Can Learn next in this chapter), fruit and nut tree seedlings can be used as rootstock for grafting on any variety you wish, at great savings. What's more, in many soils, seedling roots grow much better than the dwarf Malling rootstocks that have seemed so popular over the last twenty-five years. Some of these rootstocks growing in heavy clay soil like mine require that the tree be braced or trellised. Most of these rootstocks keep sending up shoots from below the graft union that are difficult to control. And if you want to pasture livestock in the orchard—an excellent way to keep it mowed and keep fallen fruit cleaned up—the dwarfed trees are so short the livestock can ruin them. If you have room, you may find a full-size tree an advantage. Even without a lot of room, a full-size tree can be very efficient because you can graft several varieties on it. In addition, a full-size tree will take up no more room than several dwarf trees would take. Finally, you can prune full-size trees and keep them fairly low to the ground like dwarfs, if you wish.

An interesting practice, if you decide to grow your own seedling trees, is to graft a good variety to one side of each seedling and leave the other side to grow up as the seedling variety. If it is a good one, great. If not, at least you haven't lost the time of growing, since one side of the tree has a good variety on it.

Protecting Your Seeds

Since transplanting even a small seedling shocks the little tree unnecessarily, I like to plant my tree seeds where I want the tree permanently. For fruit tree seeds that usually are not bothered by mice, chipmunks, birds, or squirrels, I simply bury a couple of the fruits just under the soil or on top of it with a little compost.Or I drop a shovelful of pomace from fruit pressing on the spot I want a tree to grow. If more than one comes up, I let them all go a year, then keep the hardiest, most vigorous one.

Nuts and acorns require a little more concern in years when they are not abundant and so will be hunted out and eaten by the wild animals. One year I spent an afternoon planting acorns along a fence row only to discover that chipmunks followed my trail a few days later and dug up every one. In years of plenty, however, black walnuts can usually be planted carelessly this way: just walk along and drop the nuts, stabbing them slightly into the soft fall dirt with your heel.

But short year or abundant, white oak acorns, shingle oak (or northern live oak) acorns, hazelnuts, and hickory nuts invariably get eaten. So I hold them over winter, usually in the garage, in milk cartons full of dirt with a seed or two in each carton. Then toward spring I set the cartons on warm windowsills or in cold frames—anywhere I'm reasonably sure the animals can't get them—until they sprout and start growing. Then I set them out, carton and all, first being sure to cut the bottom out of the container so the roots can go on down into the ground. There are other methods of protecting seeds in the ground until they start growing, but I have found them to be more work than the milk cartons of dirt kept over winter in a cold but protected place.

Oaks, Hickories, Pecans, Papaw, Persimmon, and Sassafras

For deep-rooted trees that are very difficult to transplant, like oaks, hickories, and pecans, growing from seed is a practical alternative. Small papaw, persimmon, and sassafras trees found in the woods will very rarely transplant, since they are suckers from a mother tree without much root system of their own. Plant them from seed. Persimmon and papaw seeds have a very hard coat, as do locusts, coffee trees, and a few other seeds. It may take them two years to germinate. If these seeds pass through a body—man, bird, raccoon—the coat is softened and will more readily sprout. Putting the seeds in boiling water that is then allowed to cool gradually helps soften a hard seed, but so does the natural freezing and thawing of winter. If the entire fruit of the hard-coated seed is planted, acids in the rotting fruit pulp will also help soften the seed coat. A hard seed coat can be thinned by an abrasive—an emery wheel or sandpaper—to allow moisture to penetrate so that the seed splits open its coat more easily. This is the meaning of "scarification."

Evergreens and Frail Hardwoods

Another disadvantage of planting some trees from seed is that some little trees are so frail they can't compete with weeds, grass, and brush. This is rarely true of native hardwoods, which have evolved by fighting their way up through competing weeds and brush. But for evergreens and some hardwoods, you will be much farther ahead if you grow them in containers or in nursery beds and set them out when they are two years old. I plant small-seeded, fragile trees in a mixture of sand and soil in an old fish tank set in front of a south window. Even sycamores sprout by this method. When they are about 4 inches tall, transplant them in cardboard containers, and when they are about 8 inches tall, set them out. Evergreen trees that appear to need a more acid soil can be started in peat and sand and then set out. Once started, they grow quite well in soil they do not naturally reproduce in.

Collecting Seed

Gathering tree seeds can be in itself a rather fascinating hobby. While we are used to thinking of oaks having acorns, hickories having nuts, and maples having seeds, it almost comes as a surprise to discover that elms have seeds, too, if one but looks for them. And only this year did I find the seeds of sassafras, which do not seem to set very often here: a little blue fruit on a red stem.

The seed gatherer must sometimes race the birds to get seed. White oak acorns, being less bitter than acorns of the red-black oak family, are especially relished by animals and birds. Blue jays and woodpeckers like the small acorns of the shingle oak (or northern live oak) even more. These oaks do not bear consistently or abundantly, but the tree is one of our more desirable (though lesser known) lawn trees. The leaves stay green into mid-November and then hang brown through midwinter. This year I spotted some acorns on one tree, much to my delight. When harvesttime came, I pulled down the branch the acorns were on, only to find they had all been eaten out by birds.

Willows and Poplars

The seeds of willows and some poplars are very small and do not remain viable long in storage. But there is an easier way to plant seed from these trees. Cut branch pieces about 12 inches long and the thickness of your finger. Plant these in the ground, preferably in moist soil, leaving only about 4 inches of the branch above the soil surface. If the soil is kept moist, these cuttings will invariably root (see Trees, Flowers, Vines from Sticks later in this chapter).

Grafting Skills Anyone Can Learn

Grafting was already an ancient art fifteen centuries ago, and, as with all traditional skills, it is as useful today as ever. But whereas a couple of generations ago every farmer and gardener was expected to know the rudiments of grafting, we have, in an age of specialization, turned the skill into an occult science beyond the ken of ordinary people. We pay the special-

Patenting Mother Nature

Something sad happens when we decide to pay others to do something we might easily do ourselves. In the case of grafting, nurseries, in order to protect their large investment in time and labor, can now "patent" varieties, making it illegal for others to graft to increase varieties. This law could lead to all sorts of problems for judges to settle in the future. Let us say an orchardist finds a chance sport of Golden Delicious on one of his trees that appears to have some difference (real or imagined) from other strains of Golden Delicious. He gets it patented, if he has enough money. Another orchardist-nurseryman finds a sport on one of his Golden Delicious trees so much like the patented one, even an expert would have a hard time telling the difference. He increases and sells it. Nurseryman A sues nurseryman B. Lawyers get rich over the squabble. The nursery with the most money finally wins the case. But no one wins, because in the meantime everybody has decided they like Granny Smith green apples better anyway.

Far better the attitude of the past, where farmers and nurserymen exchanged scions of promising trees freely, creating the kind of diversity that encourages real progress. The main effort of marketing was not in hyped-up adjectives, but in getting to the customer trees with good root systems and accurate identification, which is precisely where the big mail-order nurseries in their frenzy for patented "new" varieties are failing the customer.

Fortunately, every action has an equal and opposite reaction, as the philosopher Hegel said. Organizations like the Northern Nut Growers Association and the North American Fruit Explorers have sprung up to help discriminating gardeners and horticultural adventurists in their pursuit of the more unusual or as yet undeveloped fruits, nuts, and other plants. Not surprisingly, the educational emphasis of these organizations is on grafting. If you have more than a casual interest in the art, and, more importantly, would like to put yourself in the flow of the nationwide and sometimes worldwide exchange of grafting material, join at least these two organizations (or similar but more local groups).

The North American Fruit Explorer's current address for new membership is NAFEX, 103 Smith Chapel Rd., Mount Olive, NC 28365; for the Northern Nut Growers Association, currently the address is NNGA, c/o Niagara College, P.O. Box 340, St. Catherines, ON L2R 6V6 Canada.

ist to do our grafting for us. As soon as this happens, a lot more than money is lost. Grafting, again like so many traditional skills, is fun as a backyard pastime, but it is extremely tedious done on a commercial scale, 8 hours a day, five days a week. Small nurserymen are forever complaining that good grafting help is hard to hire. Large nurseries serving mass markets can pay better wages. The result is that we have plenty of the commoner varieties of grafted fruit trees. But in nut trees where varietal improvement lags far behind fruits, good grafted trees are hard to buy; so also are selected, high-quality grafted specimens of wild fruits like persimmon and papaw.

Types of Grafts

The *splice graft* is generally used to graft where scion and stock are of the same size. The scion is cut diagonally from a tree and is matched to a similar diagonal cut on the stock. Since you will want to always graft close to the tree trunk (or on the trunk itself on 2-year-old trees), not out toward the ends of branches, the splice graft is normally used on small trees, especially to graft a variety scion onto a small seedling tree. On larger trees, the *cleft graft* (sometimes called the notch and wedge graft) is most always used. A branch is cut back to a stub close to the main trunk, the stub is split open on its face with a special grafting chisel (or most any thick-bladed chisel), and two small scions are wedged into opposite ends of the opening.

All grafts are a variant of one of these two basic techniques. If you learn them both, you know all you need to know. If you want to do some trickier forms, there are plenty of books and articles available. Robert J. Garner's *The Grafter's Handbook* (Oxford University Press,

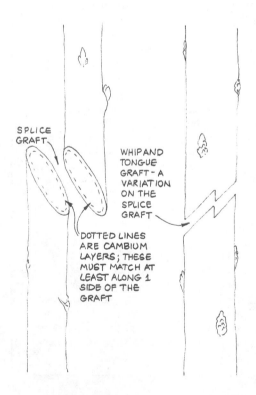

SPLICE GRAFT

WHIP AND TONGUE GRAFT - A VARIATION ON THE SPLICE GRAFT

DOTTED LINES ARE CAMBIUM LAYERS; THESE MUST MATCH AT LEAST ALONG 1 SIDE OF THE GRAFT

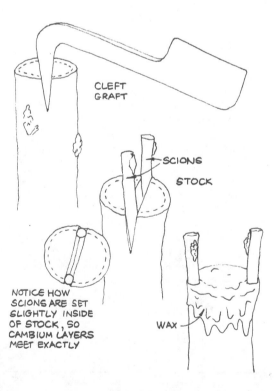

CLEFT GRAFT

SCIONS

STOCK

NOTICE HOW SCIONS ARE SET SLIGHTLY INSIDE OF STOCK, SO CAMBIUM LAYERS MEET EXACTLY

WAX

New York, 1979) is one. My *Organic Orcharding* (Rodale Press, 1981) is another.

All grafting embodies the same essential step, no matter what form it takes: At least a portion of the cambium layer of the cutting (called scion in grafting terms) must be placed precisely against a portion of the cambium layer of the tree limb (stock) onto which you are grafting. Although this essential step is repeated hundreds of times in horticultural books and articles, it takes time (I know from experience) before the beginner understands its plain, literal meaning. The cambium layers of the two surfaces can't be just very close to each other; *they have to match exactly.* Even $1/32$ of an inch off can cause the graft union to fail.

Before you're put off by this inflexibility of nature, let me quickly add that you can, with little effort, match cambium layers precisely because they are easy to see. The cambium layer is the thin green layer just inside the bark when you make a fresh cut across the branch. Here's the important detail: On a small branch or twig of, say, the thickness of your little finger, which is approximately the size of the scion used for splice grafting, the cambium layer is close to the bark. But on a larger branch, the cambium layer is in a little farther, maybe $1/8$ inch from the bark. In grafting a smaller twig to a larger branch as you do in common cleft grafting, the beginner's tendency is to set the scion in the cleft so that the exterior barks of the scion and stock are even. That's wrong. Instead, match the cambium layers, which means the scion will almost always have to set in a bit from the bark of the stock branch (see the drawing).

Splice grafting. Beginners usually have better luck starting with a splice graft, where both the scion and the stock are the same diameter. Then, when the cambium layers match, the outer bark usually matches also. But if you are splicing a scion that is slightly smaller than the stock (not the best idea, but OK if no other union is possible), place the cambium layer of *one side* of the scion directly over the cambium layer on *one side* of the stock. Don't try to put the scion evenly between cambium layers of the larger stock. And don't worry that the other side of the cambium layer on the scion does not match up with the cambium layer on the other side of the stock. Matching on one side is usually enough (see the drawing).

Next in importance after cambium layer contact is a very sharp knife. Some grafters use a surgeon's scalpel. The smoother the two faces of the graft union, the better contact the two cambium layers will make. And the sharper the knife, the smoother the face.

In splice grafting, either one or two buds are left on the scion (3 to 5 inches is the usual length). When one bud grows out, rub the other off. You can put a notch in the middle of both faces to hold the union more securely, in which case the graft is called a "whip and tongue." I have better luck with a simple diagonal cut.

The advantage of the splice graft is that you can wrap tape around it instead of sealing it with wax and get just as many "takes." Plain freezer tape or paper tape works well, wrapping from just below the union to just above it. To help make good contact between cambium layers, squeeze the two diagonal cuts together hard with finger and thumb of one hand while bringing around a wrap of tape. I overlap the tape to seal out air well, but in the process I actually get too much tape on the union and the constriction causes the plant tissues to bulge out as the graft heals over. So when I see the graft is taking well, I carefully cut away the tape to relieve the constriction. The bulge at the graft union is usually no problem.

Sometimes, after I have taped the graft, I put a plastic bag over the scion, holding the bag down below the graft with a rubber band. This makes a little greenhouse atmosphere around

GRAFTING ONTO A ROOTSTOCK: TWO WAYS

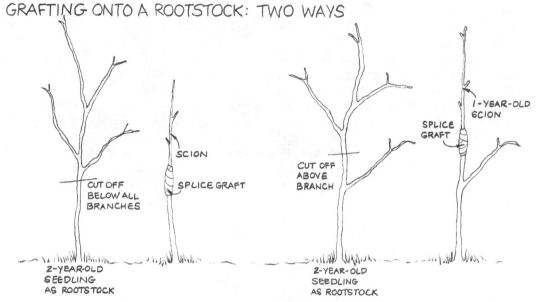

HERE YOU ARE SAVING THE ROOTSTOCK ONLY, ENSURING THAT THE STOCK WILL BE STRONGER AND WILL NOT SUCKER LIKE DWARFING ROOTSTOCK

YOU CAN ALSO LEAVE A BRANCH OF THE ROOTSTOCK INTACT AND GRAFT ANOTHER VARIETY ABOVE IT. THIS ALLOWS YOU TO SEE IF THE ROOTSTOCK VARIETY MAKES GOOD FRUIT <u>AND</u> YOU'LL HAVE FRUIT FROM THE GRAFTED VARIETY

the graft so it doesn't dry out. But if warm weather arrives, the bag should be removed or the temperature inside might get too high for the emerging bud.

I have the best luck with the splice graft when I use young, lush twigs for scions. Water sprouts make good scions. I tried for three years to graft a very ancient pear tree onto another pear tree in my orchard, without luck. The twigs were just not vigorous and lush enough. So I cut a somewhat large branch off the old tree. Lush water sprout branches grew just behind the cut the next year. These grafted easily.

Cleft grafting. As I described a bit earlier, the cleft graft is performed by wedging two small scions into a split stub held open with a grafting chisel. With this type of graft, you can use even smaller diameter twigs than you would for splicing, from close to the end of the tree branches; last year's wood that is still soft and lush enough to graft well is good. Cut the scion end into a wedge shape and fit it carefully into one side of the cleft so that the cambium layers match. Put a second scion on the other side in case one fails. (If both live, you can cut one off if you wish.) Now release your chisel, and the split closes tightly on the scions. Taping this irregular shape to keep out air is not practical. Seal the whole top of the stub and around the scions with grafting wax.

Timing

The proper time to graft is in spring just as or before the tree begins to bud out. For nut trees, a little earlier than that is better, but there are no hard and fast rules. The scion wood should be dormant when grafted on. The old-timers said scion wood would take better if cut in the late fall and kept in cold, moist

Waxes

When many trees are being grafted, commercial growers keep wax hot in a liquid state so they can quickly and easily brush it on, while not using too much in the process. But you can use a hand wax, making a wad of it pliable by working it with your fingers and then wrapping a rather thick gob all around the graft. Work it into every notch and cranny so no air can get to the union.

One more good reason to have bees is that the wax from the old hives can be melted down and later used for grafting, working it soft with your fingers and keeping it fairly warm in your fist. To make it go farther, you can mix it with half as much tallow and/or resin. Melt the ingredients, mix, then when still warm, work the wax into a pliable sealant as described. Grafting waxes are also available commercially from orchard supply firms.

surroundings over winter, often buried in the ground. But others claim the best luck with cutting scion wood in spring and grafting it directly to the stock. That way works for me. Keep overwinter scions in a refrigerator but don't let them dry out or get wet. I hold scion wood in plastic bags in the refrigerator, which seems to keep them moist enough, but not so moist as to mildew.

Having mastered these two grafts, you are ready to establish your own orchard (or arboretum for that matter) at very little cost. If you grow seedlings as described in the previous item, you can graft onto that 2- or 3-year-old seedling a scion from that great old tree down the road that bears nearly every year without spraying. Or you can rescue an ancient tree like I did the 100-year-old pear and graft it onto an existing tree in your orchard by cleft grafting. Having stood the test of time in your area, these trees will almost always perform better for you than the sensational new varieties from afar.

Shield Budding

Budding is a kind of grafting different enough to merit separate treatment. The most common kind of budding is called shield budding, so named by the shape of the bud that is cut and grafted onto the stock. Budding is supposed to work as well as grafting, but it doesn't for most beginners. The reason, at least if I may speak for myself, is that though the directions are plainly given in every horticultural book I've read, the words don't sink appropriately into the cranium. Not liking to think myself stupid, I blame that on writers who either know budding so well they take little details for granted, or have never budded anything themselves and know what they know only from reading what someone else has written. In either case, they do not emphasize the right details. The mechanics of shield budding are really quite easy to master. But at first, (for three years) I overlooked that part of the directions that explicitly said that budding works best *when the stock is no more than two or three years old*. I had been trying, vainly, to bud onto branches half as thick as my wrist and larger. That may be possible to do, but it is not very practical for beginners. Budding is best used in grafting onto very young nursery seedlings, which is how commercial nurseries do it.

Budding is particularly useful for grafting stone fruit trees—cherry, peach, apricot, and so forth, which are difficult to graft in other ways, than say, apple or pear. Budding is normally done in mid to late summer when the bark rind separates easily from the cambium layer. Although there are several ways to bud, shield budding is the most common and most practical for the backyarder.

Buds are cut, or rather sliced, from the current growth of wood out toward the end of

a branch. The best buds come from about 3 to 10 inches back from the branch tip. Every bud will have a leaf growing out right below it. Pinch off the leaf, but leave the leaf stem for a handle. With a sharp knife, begin to slice into the branch about ¾ inch above the bud, bringing the knife down and in behind the bud, hardly ³⁄₁₆ inch at the deepest part of the cut behind the bud, then back out gradually, to approximately ¾ inch below the bud. Be sure to keep your leaf handle attached to your bud. If you look at the back side of the little shield of bark you have sliced out, you will see an oval of cambium layer, and inside that a smaller oval of pithy wood. Budders and grafters argue about whether that tiny bit of wood should be removed or not, but if you are grafting the bud onto young wood like I believe you should be, you'll do just as well leaving that bit of wood on the bud. Don't worry about it.

With your shield bud in hand, proceed to the seedling tree or young branch you wish to graft. Make a vertical incision in the bark about 2 inches long and at the top of that cut, another horizontal one about ¼ inch wide. The incision should resemble a long T. Then, with the point of your knife, carefully pry up the bark, starting at the corners where the horizontal and vertical incisions meet. The bark, in mid to late summer, separates easily from the cambium layer. Now, with the bark opened slightly, grasp the shield bud between the thumb and forefinger of your hand (right hand for me) and slide it downward inside the incision. When the shield is about three-quarters of the way down, I cut the very tip off its top. This gives me a little firm edge at the top upon which I can place the flat side of the knife blade and continue pushing down the shield bud with a good deal more force than can be applied on the tender leaf handle. When the top of the shield passes just below the horizontal incision so that the top can be pressed down even with the bark above it, the bud is in place.

Then it must be wrapped. Some use rubber banding, some use raffia. Wind it around the stock branch above and below the bud, being careful not to cover the bud itself, just everything else around it. Then tie the wrapping behind the branch. Corn husk makes a good wrapping material and was used often in bygone times. If you grow any corn, this is another way to use this most versatile plant.

The bark around your newly grafted bud will continue to grow, although the bud usually stays dormant until the following spring. In about ten days you should remove the wrapping, which might otherwise constrict the bark too much. Then in the following spring, as soon as the bud shows the smallest sign of swelling life, cut the stock branch off 2 inches above the bud. Pinch off any other leaves that start to grow right above or below the grafted bud, so all the strength of the branch goes into the bud where you want it. If, on a seedling tree, the new bud wants to grow out rather than up, tie it gently to the 2-inch stub until it begins to grow straight. Then cut that stub off down to the new stem.

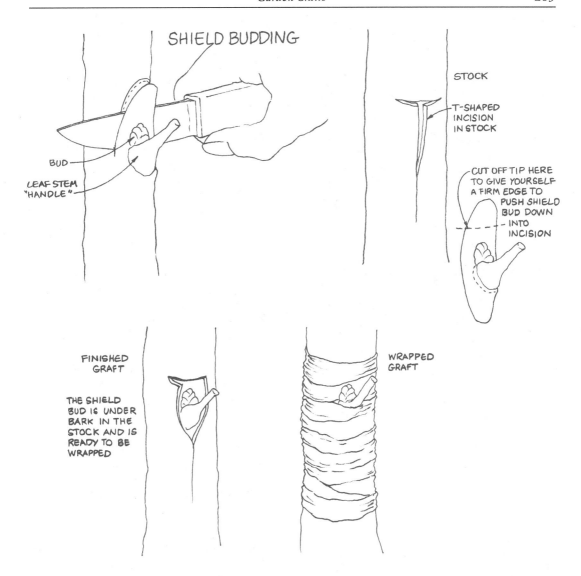

SHIELD BUDDING

BUD

LEAF STEM "HANDLE"

STOCK

T-SHAPED INCISION IN STOCK

CUT OFF TIP HERE TO GIVE YOURSELF A FIRM EDGE TO PUSH SHIELD BUD DOWN INTO INCISION

FINISHED GRAFT

THE SHIELD BUD IS UNDER BARK IN THE STOCK AND IS READY TO BE WRAPPED

WRAPPED GRAFT

Trees, Flowers, Vines from Sticks

We used to say that Aunt Stella had such a green thumb that if she stuck a broomstick in the ground it would grow. If the broomstick were a freshly cut length of willow branch, that might not be an exaggeration. A green willow shoot stuck into the ground will often root and grow if the soil is kept moist. I once cut a weeping willow branch about a foot long and the thickness of my little finger, just before it was about to leaf out. I removed little side twigs, and stuck it 6 inches into a depression in the yard where water stands after rains. That was seven years ago. It is now an 18 foot tree and growing rapidly.

Scientists have isolated a chemical in willow wood that enhances rooting in a proper environment. They believe that the chemical will make it possible to root fruit trees and those hardwoods that up to now have been almost impossible to get started this way. It seems that if you soak a cutting you wish to root in water where twigs of willow have been steeping for a month, you may get a response better than that from commercial rooting hormones now on the market. My father snorted when I told him about that discovery. "I knew that years ago," he said.

Many poplars will root readily from a green stick cut from a tree. Hybrid poplars such as those pioneered and sold by Miles Fry & Son in Ephrata, Pennsylvania root especially well, and the Frys have sold thousands of cuttings over the years. I've seen cuttings they stuck into poor, shaley soil banks in Pennsylvania root and grow against all odds. (But as Morton Fry reminds me, you are better off buying cuttings already rooted or root your own on good dirt, for transplanting on such barren soil.) A hybrid poplar cutting in good soil may root and grow 6 to 8 feet the first year. Fry makes a good case for planting an acre of them for fuel independence. In just four years you can start harvesting the wood, and in full production the acre will yield 5 cords a year indefinitely—about what it takes to heat a well-insulated house for one winter.

The grape is another useful plant easy to root from a stick. Take cuttings when the vines are dormant (when you're pruning) and make 18-inch pieces of vigorous, pencil-diameter sections. I make the pieces long enough so they include three joints, and I push the cutting deep enough into the ground so that two of the joints are beneath the surface. When collecting the cuttings, I always make a diagonal cut at the bottom (toward the trunk of the vine) and square across at the top. This keeps me from planting a cutting upside down (I don't know if it makes any difference) and also makes it easier to push the cutting deep into the soil. When the ground is hard, I make a hole first with a steel rod.

I've had cuttings root from fall plantings and from spring plantings. But the best luck comes from doing it the old-fashioned way. Make the cuttings in the fall, tie them in a bundle, and then bury them about a foot deep over winter. This allows the cut ends to callus over, and that seems to make the cuttings root easier. The oldest folklore says that the cuttings should be buried upside down, but I've had success with them just buried horizontally.

With any cutting, keep the soil around it moist. Even a short drought will likely kill it. And the more of an artificial environment of controlled humidity you can maintain around it, the better. My mother's way of getting a new rose was to stick a cutting in the ground in spring and cover it with a quart mason jar. The glass increased the humidity around the cutting, preventing it from drying out, and it often rooted. Another way to accomplish the same purpose is to fill a glass container halfway with sandy loam, stick the cutting into the loam, water well, and cover the top with a piece of plastic film. The plastic will hold in humidity very well; in fact, you will have to pull back the plastic regularly to allow the cutting to dry a bit, otherwise it will mold and mildew. In greenhouses, cuttings are rooted with misters on automatic timers going on and off frequently enough so the cuttings stay moist but not too wet.

Blueberries root fairly well in any of the above manners.

Tomatoes can be rooted readily from a cutting, though there is not much reason for you to do so. The old gardener across the road from us years ago often increased his tomatoes this way, just for fun, it seemed to me. He just stuck a green stem in the ground and kept it well watered.

Fruit and deep-rooted nut trees are, as I've said, difficult to root—almost impossible at our present level of knowledge. But these trees grow readily from seed. The rule doesn't apply to all fruits, however. History says that the Roman legions in their days of conquest inadvertently spread the olive tree by using branches to stake their horses at night. When they rode away, the stakes they left behind rooted and grew.

My Sister's Garden

I've been watching my sister's garden closely for ten years because it is the most successful organic garden I know of. I was originally intrigued because she has never had a problem with the striped cucumber beetle, which gives the rest of us in the neighborhood fits. Then I learned that she never has *any* insect or disease problem. Once she was plagued by slugs in her tomatoes. She offered to pay the neighborhood boys a dollar for each garter snake they brought her. They brought five. She grew her tomatoes on stakes the next year, rather than

sprawled out on the straw mulch. The slug problem vanished.

Ironically, my sister was gardening for fifteen years before she became aware of the word organic. She thought she was just doing what our mother had taught her. In fact she is still suspicious of people who call themselves organic gardeners and prefers not to have the word applied to her. Like most of the conservative people in the neighborhood, she lumps organic gardeners with socialism, animal rights, pasta, jogging, and all the other trends that she thinks run counter to common sense. Nevertheless, although she does spray her fruit trees with chemicals occasionally, her berry and vegetable gardens are totally organic, just as the gardens of her commonsense ancestors were. Why it works better for her than for most of us remains a mystery, but it seems to be a combination of the following characteristics:

1. The garden is located on land that was never farmed. It went from forest to sheep pasture gradually, starting about eighty years ago, and then twenty-five years ago became her garden. It has never been touched by the moldboard plow, never run over and compacted by heavy machinery, never chemicalized, never eroded. It is a naturally rich soil, level to gently sloping, with a heavy clay subsoil. This soil needs artificial drainage to perform well, and my sister's husband has run a tile line under part of the garden and plans to tile the other part eventually.

2. The nearest gardens (belonging to two other sisters) are about 1000 feet away. But adjacent to the garden is a commercial farm field that has been farmed hard with chemicals for ten years.

3. The garden is in three plots about 100 feet apart, about 2500 square feet altogether, on a 4-acre homestead that includes horses, chickens, a grove of evergreen trees, a bit of pasture, lots of lawn, and a great variety of ornamental plants and trees.

4. My sister grows all the common vegetables plus raspberries and strawberries in her garden, with grapes and fruit trees dotted around in various locations. No vegetable ever is planted in exactly the same place two years in a row. Rows of petunias, marigolds, and zinnias are interspersed with the vegetables. Why? "These are the only three kinds of flowers that do well in this soil," she says. "Mom always said, 'when in doubt, plant zinnias!'" Do the flowers have any beneficial companion effect on the vegetables? She thinks the marigolds might chase away some insects, but has no proof.

   At one end of the garden is a birdbath and several rows of herbs—oregano, chamomile, parsley, spearmint, basil. "The herbs do well because when I clean the water out of the birdbath, which is often full of bird manure, I water them with it," she says. She allows dill to grow like a weed all over the garden, reseeding itself each year. She hoes it out between the rows but lets it grow irregularly in the rows. We have theorized that the highly scented dill might be repugnant to cucumber beetles, but my other sisters have dill in their gardens, too, and the beetles still come.

5. The garden has been fertilized solely with horse manure—the chicken manure going only on the asparagus. Every winter, as time permits, she hauls the manure onto the garden, covering most of the area most years. Then in spring, she rototills it in. She has done this for about twenty years, every year.

6. She sprinkles rotenone on seedlings as a matter of course, sometimes before the seeds come out. But this has not helped the rest of us in our fight against the cucumber beetle. "I saw three of them last year," she says. "I blame myself. It was dry and I didn't get all my squash seedlings watered. The beetles were on the ones I didn't water. My theory is that insects don't hurt strong-growing plants."

7. She makes successive plantings wherever possible. There is rarely any space in the garden lying idle. Tomatoes, strawberries, and melons are straw-mulched.

8. If her gardening is unusual in any particular way, it is her fanaticism for keeping things tidy. The minute the last pea comes off a spent row, out come the old plants. I personally believe this is the key to her lack of insect and disease problems. The poor bugs and organisms never get a chance to settle in. Nor do weeds. And in the fall, when I'm inclined to let the straggling plants suffer into November for the meager pittance they still provide me, her garden is clean as a whistle and all rototilled for winter by the middle of October. She reminds me of those industrious housewives I used to watch with amazement in eastern Pennsylvania villages— out sweeping off the sidewalks at 7 o'clock in the morning. I wonder if they have cucumber beetles in *their* tidy gardens.

Raspberry Secrets

All gardening books (including my own, unfortunately) say that a raspberry planting should last seven to ten years, no ifs or buts about it. At the end of that time, the plants, in common parlance, "run out." They become weak and produce few berries, or they contract a disease, perhaps orange rust, or anthracnose, or what is airily dismissed as "mosaic." The term mosaic is a generality meant to cover a host of viral diseases not even plant scientists know too much about and all of which are largely incurable by any spray-can concoction. Some plantings do last seven to ten years or more in fair production, but more often a planting becomes diseased or weak in five years and even commercial growers, who should know

better, throw up their hands in defeat. Raspberries, they say, especially black ones, are too disease-prone for a long-term investment.

The main problem is that in the garden we ignore the raspberry's tactic for survival. A raspberry plant in nature *moves* and moves *every year*. Wild raspberries, even when infected with anthracnose, orange rust, and viral diseases, survive quite handsomely most of the time, producing good crops in spite of the dangers. Black and purple raspberries move by tip-rooting new plants, that is, the long canes bend over in late summer a good 3 feet or more away from the mother plant. The tip of the cane pierces the soil and roots. The next year that plant in *new*, uncrowded soil grows vigorously, while the cane from which it sprang produces fruit and dies. The new cane tips to the ground and

roots another plant. And so the patch of berries moves, like a flock of sheep in very slow motion. Red and yellow raspberries move also, not by tip-rooting, but by sending up new plants from lateral roots running out and away from the mother plant. After bearing, the old canes die. The new ones send roots on into new and uncrowded soil and more new plants follow.

In the garden, we try to stop the raspberry from this natural tendency. If we let all those brambles ramble, we'd end up with a weedy jungle, not a garden of well-trimmed and cultivated rows. So we keep them confined to rows. In three years, the berry roots become crowded in the row. If disease attacks, it easily spreads among the crowded, weak plants. If you prune old canes, thin new canes, discourage canes to tip-root, and fertilize properly, black raspberry roots will stay alive longer than they would in nature, but they will develop all sorts of cankers.

The answer is to begin treating raspberries the way we do strawberries. Begin a program of

continually setting out a new bed or row, not every year or every other year as with strawberries, but every third or fourth year. Raspberries are very easy to move.

In spring, dig or pull up the tip-rooted canes of black and purple varieties, first cutting off the new plant from the cane out of which it has sprung. Set the transplants in the new row about 18 inches apart—rather close together since you will not keep the row more than four years. These tip-rooted plants have a good root structure, formed in the preceding fall, and they will grow much, much faster than usual bare-rooted plants from a nursery. In the following year they will produce a partial crop. In the next year (the third) they will, from new shoots, produce a full crop, and possibly in the fourth year an even better crop. But in the third year, start another row. Allow only about every fifth cane in the row to root in the summer of the second year and prune the rest about 5 to 6 feet tall, so all their energy goes into berry production for the following year.

I follow the same program with red and yellow varieties, transplanting suckers in the spring that grew the previous summer and have developed a good root system. The cane you transplant is not so important but the new canes that sprout and henceforth grow from the root are. These will produce a partial crop the next summer, or if the variety is a fall and summer bearer, these canes will produce a few berries that fall and again the next summer. Be sure to make a new planting in the third year, so you always have a strong new planting coming on. The 4-year-old planting may get diseased and not produce so well. And even if it appears healthy at the end of four years, I think you should tear it out.

Rotating your raspberry rows around the garden has another advantage. You control weeds easier that way. Usually grass or hard-to-pull weeds invade a raspberry row by the third year and are exceedingly difficult to control otherwise.

With this method, one need not spend so much time thinning out the row in an effort to stop overcrowding. Nor is it quite so imperative to prune out the old canes as a way to prevent the spread of disease. The row just won't be there long enough to succumb to diseases.

Pruning and Trellising

My favorite red raspberry is Heritage, which produces a fall crop and then a summer one on the same canes. Often I do not leave the canes for that second crop, but mow them off after the fall crop and let new canes that come up in the spring make another big fall crop. This is an easy way to prune raspberries. If one row, or part of the row, is kept for a second summer crop, and another kept only for fall, there are berries to eat from late June until frost, not counting August, when the blackberries are in season.

I have tried every kind of trellis imaginable for raspberries. The red ones (Heritage) really

don't need any trellis, although some of the canes tend to fall over when heavy with fruit. For the blacks, I run a single wire over the row about 5 feet high and tie or wrap the canes I don't want to root around it. The cane tips have to be pruned off. In fertile ground, new tips often form and grow down to the ground anyway, as the plant tries desperately to move on to new territory. These second tips should be pruned off, too.

It is possible to prune the black raspberry canes to 4 feet to induce stout-branching growth that doesn't need a trellis. But then the side branches have to be pruned back, too, and the time spent gets to be considerable, with some loss of yield. In old books about black raspberry culture you will find engravings of plants pruned to the shape of small Christmas trees, no staking or trellis required. But I've found it nearly impossible to hold the canes in such rigorous bounds, the new growth induced by the pruning surging forth with amazing rapidity. The plants "know" they must flee the soil of their parents. The successful raspberry grower must know this too, above all else.

Is There a Proper Way to Spade a Garden?

Almost every gardener knows about Edward Faulkner's classic book *Plowman's Folly*, which in 1943 first questioned the practicality of the moldboard plow and pointed out its bad effects in terms of erosion, soil compaction, and exploitive farming. Now, some forty years later, much of what Faulkner insisted appears to be true, and farmers are learning various methods of "no-till" farming. However one might argue the pros and cons of the plow, it is certainly not a necessary condition for success in growing crops.

But what gardeners don't always know is that Faulkner's earliest experiments that led

Plants establish intakes, in the form of roots, for nutritive materials in the decaying fragments of last year's plants; and, left to themselves, they will use without loss every atom of the material that previously had been used in the dead plants. As farmers, we have not left the bodies of last year's plants where the roots of this season's crops could invade them. Instead, we have buried those decaying remains so deep that few roots could reach them. We have, by plowing, made it impossible for our farm crops to do their best. Obviously, it seems that the time has arrived for us to look into our methods of soil management, with a view to copying the surface situation we find in forest and field where the plow has not disturbed the soil. No crime is involved in plagiarizing nature's ways. Discovering the underlying principles involved and carrying them over for use on cultivated land violates no patents or copyrights. In fact, all that it is necessary to do—if we want a better agriculture—is to recharge the soil surface with materials that will rot. Natural processes will do the rest. The plant kingdom is organized to clothe the earth with greenery, and, wherever man does not disturb it, the entire surface usually is well covered.

Edward Faulkner, *Plowman's Folly*
(University of Oklahoma Press, 1943)

him to write his book were not done on a farm with a plow, but in his garden with a spade. He learned that spading was more or less useless work, and that as a way to bury organic matter to increase fertility for the plants it could even be harmful.

Filling the spaded trench full of leaves or other organic matter, as we are often tempted to do, and then covering it with 8 inches of loosened dirt, resulted, said Faulkner, in a barrier that blocked the capillary action of water up to the plants and drew down water from the surface, leaving the soil where the plants were actually growing too often dry and hard. Also, organic matter so buried does not always rot because oxygen can't get to it. It lies there in a sort of pickled state that does the plants no good, even if and when the feeder roots reach down to it. And with the organic matter 8 to 10 inches down, the soil surface is more vulnerable to erosion than if the organic matter were worked into the top layer of soil, where it belongs.

The spade certainly does not cause the problems in gardens that the plow has on farms. And Faulkner's low opinion of it will strike the French-intensive gardeners as heresy, but the fact is there are easier ways to "loosen" the soil than spading. First of all, a good hard winter freeze will serve quite well, which is probably why most champions of double-digging reside in the milder climes where one cannot take advantage of this freezing and thawing. Secondly, how loose do you want your soil? A loose raised bed is subject to drying out too much in the droughty Midwest, which is why many of the double-diggers, who don't get lots of rain, rely on irrigation, an energy-intensive practice that ought to be avoided when possible.

Thirdly, no garden ever becomes as compacted as soil run over by heavy farm machinery, or soil plowed too wet, or soil underlain with a hard pan caused by years of plowing. Farmers use huge subsoilers to break up this compacted soil—the agribusiness version of double-digging. But soil conservation workers tell me that a stand of sweet clover or even alfalfa will break up hardpan just as effectively and far cheaper. And in a problem garden soil, these deep-rooted plants will loosen soil even better, aided and abetted by a good earthworm population tunneling up and down in the soil.

And lastly, to the claim that double-digging increases garden production "incredibly," my answer is that with the care intensive gardeners give their plots, they would have incredible yields anyway, without wearing their lower back out of joint double-digging. And how many tomatoes or carrots do you really want? If I can raise all I need in the same space a double-digger does, why double-dig? And it makes no difference to me if the double-digger's carrots are 10 inches long in his soft soil and mine are only 8 inches.

I used to spade garden plots, especially when faced with heavy sod even a rotary tiller couldn't handle. Then I wised up. Instead of spading, I covered the sod plot with 8 inches of last year's leaves *after* the soil warmed up. Then every 3 feet in both directions I dug just enough of a little hole to insert a tomato plant in a peat pot. That was the entire extent of my cultivation that year, and the tomatoes did just as well

as previous conventional plantings had.

The next year, the grass was all more or less dead and the sod deteriorated. But instead of rotary tilling, I put on another 8 inches of leaves *after* the soil warmed up and inserted into little holes peat pots containing watermelon and muskmelon plants. Again a bumper crop. The next year I planted potatoes the same way. Not a big yield, but all we could handle.

The fourth spring I finally rototilled because I wanted to use that bed to plant the fine-seeded early vegetables—carrots, beets, radishes, lettuces, and so forth—and thought a fine seedbed was necessary. Actually, as I've learned since then, I can just dribble the seed into a tiny trench

made by my finger in the surface of sheet compost and press a bit of the compost over the seed (or just *walk* over the row, pressing the seeds down tightly) and get a better stand than planting into finely tilled soil. In this latter case, a rain on finely tilled soil that has clay in it results in a crust hard for tiny seedlings to come up in.

Use your spade to dig carrots.

There is too much preciousness exuded over the matter of planting seeds. In nature, seeds fall on top of the ground or in a bit of leaf mulch and, *when temperature and moisture are adequate*, they grow. In the same way, seedlings of last year's crops come up unbidden and uncared for in my garden. I've planted oak leaf lettuce only once. I let some of it go to seed, and it comes up year after year. I simply let a few plants grow, hoeing the rest out along with the weeds. This is how we "raise" cherry tomatoes, too. In fact, tomato seedlings are the chief "weed" in my garden. Volunteer muskmelons often produce as well as the ones I start in pots and coddle in the cold frame.

After the plants get started, it is still the top 4 to 6 inches of soil that make the vital difference, not the subsoil. Something dynamic, perhaps even mysterious, goes on right at the soil surface where soil and mulch are at work melding into each other. Worry about that, not about subsoil 2 feet down, which can be handled by deep-rooted plants.

Two miles from where I garden, there is a brickyard. Bricks are made there from our subsoil. This subsoil clay makes fairly good bricks just dried in the sun. Digging a posthole in my land in August is only a little easier than trying to dig through a blacktopped road. But this heavy subsoil has no bad effect on crops. In fact, its heaviness acts as a bulwark against drought. It can withstand more dry weather than light, sandy subsoil can. In one of my gardens in Pennsylvania years ago, the subsoil was not so hard, but 2 feet down was solid rock, which made the idea of loosening the subsoil above it almost laughable. But by gardening with mulch I grew good crops there anyway.

My experience on that land was a good example of shallow gardening, but the rain forests of South America are an even better locale; there giant trees and a dazzling variety of plants grow luxuriously in hardly any *deep* soil at all. The dynamism of growth mostly takes place near the soil surface.

Homemade Bug-Fighter
Cucumber Beetle Protection

Any translucent plastic container of a gallon or more in size makes a good protector for muskmelon, squash, and cucumber plants against the ravages of the striped cucumber beetle. The gallon milk or water jug is the handiest. Cut the bottom out and stick the jug, with lid in place, over the plants and into the ground an inch or so or heap a little dirt around the outer edge so the wind won't blow the jug away. In hot weather replace the lid with a bit of screen or drill tiny holes in it. Since cucumber beetles will burrow into loose soil around the tiny seedlings, stir the

How I Fool the Cucumber Beetle

A method I have found effective against the cucumber beetle wrecking my muskmelons (at least for four years) is to start the plants indoors or in a cold frame, then set them out in a row down the middle of the old strawberry bed that I plan to take out after the current harvest. I run the tiller down the middle of the bed first, to make a place for the melons. While picking the berries, one must be careful not to step on the melon plants, but that's the only drawback to this method. I don't know why this should fool the beetles, but the one year in the last five when I did not follow this plan, beetles infected the melons with wilt.

After the berry harvest, I mow off the berry plants carefully and then rototill, again being careful not to injure the melons. The melon vines then rapidly grow out and cover the whole bed. In addition to beetle protection, this is an excellent way to double-crop.

dirt with your hand before setting the jug in place, hopefully scaring away the bugs, if present. Beetles do the worst damage when muskmelon, cucumber, and squash are first coming up. Don't plant these seeds or set out plants until the soil has warmed to at least 70°F.

A second wave of beetles, when the plants have outgrown their plastic fortresses, usually do not harm the plants directly, but they may infect them with a wilt disease that kills vines later, just as they begin to blossom and form fruit. In former times, gardeners would build box frames about 2 feet square and cover all the tops with screening. These screen boxes were set over the plants until the vines started to runner out. Since the wilt disease is not a problem with squash, these were used on cucumber and muskmelon only.

An Easy Cutworm Collar

Save the cardboard cylinders from rolls of toilet paper and slice them into collars to put around young seedlings where cutworms may be a problem. Be sure to dig around a plant destroyed by cutworms regularly, using your fingers; the culprit is often lurking just under the soil close by.

Drown Those Coddling Moths

Because gardeners have the image of being kindly, patient souls, I was almost shocked at the language of an elderly gentleman whom I had spotted toiling in his garden and, on a whim, stopped to visit. Every noun he uttered was preceded by the vilest barnyard and back-alley adjectives imaginable, especially when the nouns were slug, coddling moth, robin in cherry trees, or cucumber beetle. Since he was otherwise kindly, polite, and amazingly well-read and articulate, his cussings and slangs evoked chuckles I could not suppress. He wanted to know what was so funny. So I told him. "Well," he replied, "after you have endured the #$%& coddling moth for ninety-two years, you'll refer to the #$%& thing that way too."

He had, however, in ninety-two years, found a way to control the coddling moth to some extent. The method was simplicity itself, and I have adopted it with fair to middling success. Fill a tin can halfway with a mixture of 1 part water and 1 part molasses and hang it in your

apple tree from just before blossoming to petal fall. Coddling moths are drawn to the sweet liquid and drown in it, the cans sometimes becoming literally clogged with their dead bodies. I use my own sorghum molasses. I assume any molasses will do, or possibly sugar water or honey water. Unfortunately, other moths that do you no harm, and occasionally mourning cloak butterflies, are also drowned in the can. The various brownish moths that jam together in the can are difficult to identify, but it seems reasonable to suspect that other pest moths that lay eggs in developing fruits are also controlled.

Vanquishing the Plum Curculio

A persistent pest of fruits, especially stone fruits, the plum curculio is difficult to control, with or without resorting to poisons. At the turn of the last century, the insect was even more pestiferous than today, and some seemingly novel control methods that didn't involve poisons were used then that could be of practical interest to a backyarder today.

The plum curculio can fly, but like most snout beetles, not too well. One theory had it that the insect rarely gets more than 5 or 6 feet off the ground. In the late 1800s, orchardists who built tight board fences 8 to 9 feet high around their plum trees claimed good curculio control in neighborhoods where whole orchards were badly infested. (See *The American Fruit Culturist* by John J. Thomas, William Wood & Co., New York, 1897.)

But the method universally claimed successful against the beetle was two-pronged: the orchardist literally knocked the curculios out of the tree onto a sheet and then destroyed them. He then followed up by penning hogs under the trees to eat the larva-infested fruit as fast as it fell, thus preventing the worms from moving from fruit to soil and pupating into adults. You could keep the fallen fruit cleaned up yourself, but it requires almost daily vigilance.

Knocking the curculios out of the trees was not as difficult as it sounds; in fact, the method used then is the same used now to harvest certain fruits mechanically. A hole was drilled in the trunk of the tree, or if a large tree, into each of the larger limbs. A large blunted nail or bolt was seated solidly in the hole. When the bolt was rapped sharply with a heavy hammer, the sudden jarring knocked the curculios out of the tree. Much experimentation was done, and no other jarring was found nearly as effective, and has been relearned in modern mechanical fruit harvesting. But for this method to be successful it had to be done early in the cool of the morning, when the curculios were more torpid. Later in the day, with warming temperatures, the insects were quicker to fly and more tenacious in their hold on the tree.

Muslin or cheesecloth was more often used as the sheeting to lay beneath the tree to catch the curculios. The cloth was tied to a framing of light poles or sticks, so that an expanse 3 by 6 feet could be carried quickly and easily from tree to tree. On most trees two or three frames were sufficient. The best frames were hinged in the middle so that they could be folded together and the insects then easily dumped into a bucket of used oil or kerosene.

The curculio lays an egg in a fruit just after it has formed—usually when the fruit is the size of a pea. It makes an incision on the fruit skin that is crescent shaped—a telltale sign of the curculio. Almost always the infected fruit, with the worm eating away inside, falls from the tree when only half its normal size. The worm soon leaves the fallen fruit and enters the soil. If hogs are about, they eat the fruit, thereby destroying the curculio's life cycle.

Composting

Some composters are so adept I would not be too surprised if one of them some day buried an old wood stove in a compost pile and turned it into rich loam in thirty-five days. On my compost piles, I am generally as disconsolate as Job on his dung hill. I love the idea of a compost pile, and I honor those proficient at coaxing them to heat up properly and change all that glucky stuff into rich humus. But under my care, organic matter becomes as inert as Plexiglas. So I have become something of a devil's advocate where compost heaps are concerned. To cover my failures, I claim that I'd rather do it nature's way—let the organic matter turn into humus on its own time, not mine.

In other words, I've become a champion supporter of sheet compostings—spreading straw, manure, leaves, grass clippings, or whatever in a thick layer around the garden plants and letting nature take her course. That's the way the woodland manages to build topsoil, and it seems to work out quite well in the garden. By year's end, the organic matter has mostly rotted away into humus, just as it does in the sanctified layers of the compost heap.

The viability of weed seeds is generally destroyed by the heat of the compost pile, and since there is no such intense heat in sheet composting, the result may be a herd of pigweed or a flock of lamb's-quarter in your garden. To keep weeds corralled, till under what remains of the sheet compost in the fall along with late-sprouting weeds. In spring, get in at least two good cultivations before applying compost and don't apply it until the soil has warmed up well and your garden is growing. Hand-pull the few weeds that come up early through the sheet compost in July. If you do it on a regular basis, the job does not take much time.

With leaves, there is less of a weed problem than with manure. But what do you do with the leaves between autumn and early summer? I "rake" my leaves into rough windrows with the mower, which saves half the raking time and also shreds the leaves to some extent. Then I simply make piles of them along the edge of the garden or tree grove and leave them until the following year. I like to use them *(continued on page 278)*

The Proper Feeding of a Compost Pile

A good compost pile is not just a heap of any old thing. At the heart of all composting is a complex group of microorganisms that behave a lot like one large beast. A compost pile has certain nutritional requirements. Some waste materials are consumed by decay very quickly, and others—say a piece of cardboard—rot slowly. But when a gardener brings materials together in a compost pile that match the food requirements of the decay organisms, and he gives the pile the right amount of air and water, the process begins to work at its optimum, composting nearly all plant and animal wastes (except wood chips and bone) quickly and efficiently.

Feeding a compost pile is simpler than feeding animals. The microorganisms require only a special blend of nitrogen (or protein) and carbon (or carbohydrate) sources, with about a 20:1 carbohydrate to protein ratio. High-nitrogen wastes are usually succulent green vegetation (kitchen garbage and grass clippings, to name two), pulverized seeds (like coffee grounds, soybean meal), and many animal by-products, including manure and urine.

Carbon-rich materials are almost exclusively dry, tough, fibrous former plant parts: leaves, straw, sawdust, paper, and the like. These contain complex carbohydrates, which the microbes digest for the energy they contain.

To digest all that food requires a lot of oxygen. A fast-acting pile will run out of the air it needs to sustain its optimum rate of digestion in about three days. Turning it is the only way of putting enough air back into it. By turning the pile every three days (and making sure the materials are in small pieces and not clumps or big masses so that air can circulate freely), you can have finished compost in about two weeks.

By the second turning, things should be steaming in the center of the pile. You should be turning as much of the material in the center as you can to the outer layer of the new pile. By the third turning, the pile

Gardeners are at their most creative when inventing compost bins—almost anything goes!

should reach its ultimate temperature, 150° to 160°F. If the pile doesn't get this hot, it requires more nitrogen. The other problem could be lack of water. Compost should be uniformly dishrag damp, not sopping. If there is a foul or rotten smell, the pile is probably too wet and there is not enough air getting into it. If it has a strong ammonia smell, you've put in too much nitrogen. Both problems can be corrected. Turn the pile frequently for the former and add more leaves, straw, paper, or sawdust for the latter.

After the last turning, the compost should rise to the high temperature range again. Then after a few days, it should drop to and stay about 110°F. for a while. At that point it is finished.

You can make excellent compost in any type of bin, or in no bin at all. The ideal setup is to have three bins side by side. One bin holds a full batch of compost in the making, another is ready for the batch you're making to be turned, and since compostable organic wastes tend to arrive in dribbles, it's useful to have a third bin to temporarily store them in.

The smallest workable bin is 3 feet square and 3 feet high. Seasoned composters say the heap should be at least that size if it is to retain ample heat and moisture for quick composting in mild weather. The bin can be wider or longer to suit you, but it shouldn't be taller than 6 feet. In addition to being hard to turn, piles over 6 feet will compact and exlude the air that is crucial to composting.

Adapted from *Make Compost in 14 Days* by the editors of *Organic Gardening* magazine (Rodale Press, 1982).

on strawberry and raspberry beds where annual weed cultivation is not possible.

With lots of strawy manure from my barn, I sheet-compost it around asparagus, potatoes, tomatoes, first-year strawberries, and if time permits, around the squashes. The other garden crops are rotated to the potato, tomato, and squash areas the following year, where they take advantage of the residual effect of the manure. Half the soil nutritives in manure are available the first year—roughly—and of the half that remains, half is available the next year. And so forth. I apply the sheet compost 4 to 6 inches deep, a very hefty application that could result in too much nitrogen, phosphorus, and potash if I treated the same plots that way every year. Few weeds will come up through such an application. And of course, soil moisture is well retained. If soil moisture is normal when the manure sheet-compost mulch is applied in June, the garden is virtually drought-proof the rest of the growing season. Compost heaps can't give you that insurance.

Grass clippings are another very good sheet-composting mulch if cut before they go to seed. I use them to keep mud off developing heads of lettuce because grass clippings are my cleanest mulch and I don't mind them coming into contact with food I'm going to eat. For the same reason I sometimes use them along the edges of the strawberry beds where the berries want to flop out over previous mulchings onto bare ground.

Sheet-composting has some disadvantages over the compost heap, but it takes a heap less time to manage, all things considered.

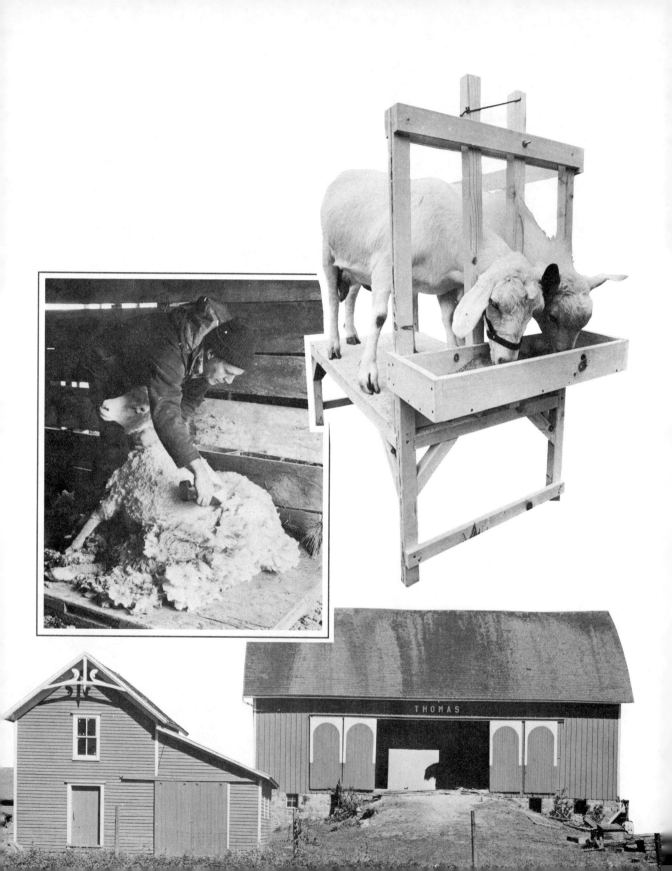

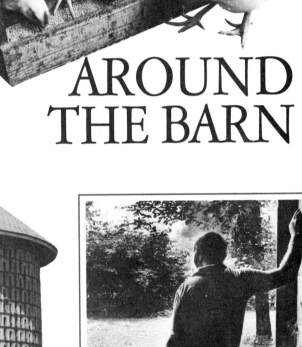

PART IV

AROUND
THE BARN

CHAPTER 8

CONSTRUCTION CONSIDERATIONS

Before You Start Building

Having built a 28 by 42-foot barn for my cows, horse, and sheep; a corncrib, a chicken coop, and two machinery sheds, I've come to believe that the most important part of construction is the thinking and decision-making you do before you start. As far as the actual building is concerned, whether pole construction, stud walls, or post and beam on a masonry foundation, there are immense amounts of information already available. (One of those information sources is *Build It Better Yourself,* from Rodale Press, 1977; it has some of the clearest-worded instruction for beginners of any book I know.) The basic principles of putting up a building are standard, easy to grasp, and within the capability of almost anyone. But there are other important considerations that affect the building but don't actually have to do with how to build—considerations that are important, even if you intend to hire someone else to do the actual work. Maybe even especially if you hire someone else.

The pointers here about barn building are things I or others learned the hard way; I seldom see them written about, and they are sometimes ignored by the experts. In fact, the experts don't always agree, as in my bias against concrete floors (see Number 6).

1. Water Protection. If your homestead is large enough so you have some choice about the location of your barn or outbuilding, give very careful thought to where you put it. Don't build at a place or in a manner that will allow water to run into the building after heavy rains or buildups of snow. Now that sounds obvious, I know, but the mistake is often made, though not so often as you might expect on sites where run-off threats are easily noted. In that case grading is usually necessary anyway, and the bulldozer operator will generally point out the need for grading water around the building, even if you aren't aware of the potential problem. The mis-

(continued on page 286)

How to Square Up the Outside Perimeter of a Building before Construction

To mark the corners of a building accurately, you need to apply a little basic geometry. On a right triangle, the sum of the two sides squared equals the square of the hypotenuse, or third side: $a^2 + b^2 = c^2$. Secondly, the diagonals of a square or rectangle are equal in length.

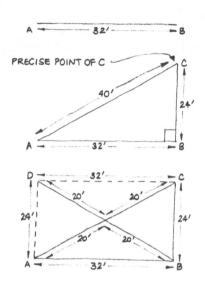

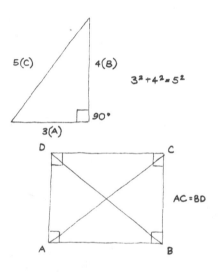

To lay out a building square with your property lines or "with the world," that is, straight east and west or north and south, you first measure in from the edge of your property or from another building properly positioned or use a compass or a level to locate one side of the building. Let us suppose the building is to be 24 by 32 feet, and the corners are identified A, B, C, and D.

1. Establish the first line, AB, which is 32 feet long, where you want it.

2. Then, to mark the corner C accurately so that it forms a right angle and is square, you need two tape measures (or a tape measure and a length of string marked at 24 feet). Having driven stakes at A and B with a nail in the top of each, hook one tape measure to the stake at A and the second to the stake at B, and form a triangle with them in the approximate area of corner C. Using the formula $a^2 + b^2 = c^2$ you know that $32^2 + 24^2 = 1600$, the square root of which is 40. Therefore AC will measure 40 feet. So where the two tapes cross at 40 feet and 24 feet is the accurate position of corner C. Drive a stake in with a nail on top at exactly the crossing.

3. You can find corner D by stretching tapes from AD and from BD, as you did for corner C. Or you can drive a stake along the diagonal AC, with a nail on top of the

stake, exactly at 20 feet on the tape. Then hook the tape on the nail at B and stretch it straight across the middle stake's nail. At 40 feet you should be at corner D. You may be off a wee bit this way, so double-check the sides and make sure all measurements are correct.

If the building is larger than your tape measure can reach, you can still use the right triangle formula (which builders refer to as the 3-4-5 ratio since $3^2 + 4^2 = 5^2$). Say you have only 50-foot tapes and the barn is 60 by 40 feet.

1. Establish the 60-foot line by measuring 50 feet, marking that point and measuring 10 feet more from there.

2. Then from B measure back 40 feet along AB and drive a stake at E.

3. Hook one tape to the nail on this stake, at E, and hook the other on the nail at B. Where the tape hooked on B crosses the tape hooked on E at 30 and 50 feet, you know you have a right triangle at B. Drive a stake, F, where the tapes cross at 30 feet and 50 feet.

4. Then pull the tape on out to 40 feet straight on that line BF, and you have located corner C.

5. Establish corner D the same way, working off of corner A. Check by measuring the diagonals to see if they are equal in length. Line EF should equal the new line GH.

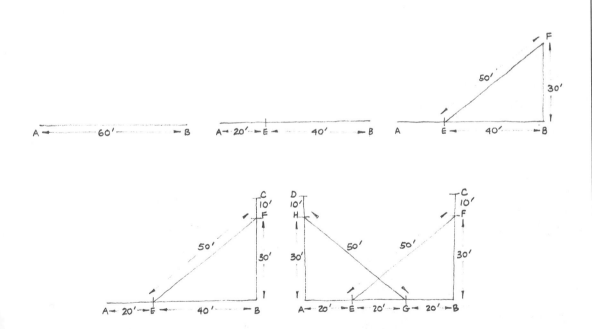

take occurs instead on sites that are very level or only a mite sloping, which lulls the amateur builder into thinking there will be no runoff problem. Therefore, he may be inclined not to bring the foundation up far enough above the surrounding ground level. If the site happens not to be quite the highest place in the immediate area, a heavy downpour, especially during spring thaw, will probably gather into running rivulets and gurgle into the barn. Let the foundation rise *at least* 8 to 12 inches above the natural ground level at its highest point. (Unless the site is perfectly level, the ground level will be higher on one end of the barn than the other.) Then grade soil up to the foundation top.

2. Wind Protection. If you can locate your barn buildings (not to mention your house) on the lee side of a woodlot or a really effective wind-break, your barn work and the lives of your livestock will be 100% more pleasant than in a windy location, even if you live in Canada—especially if you live in Canada. If you intend to make the activity of a barnyard a constant part of your life, the very best move you can make is to put it to the lee side of a woodlot. (Plant a woodlot immediately, if you don't have one.) The windbreak should stretch from the south-west to the northwest of your farmstead.

Wind protection is not only good for you and your animals, but for your roof, too. Aluminum roofing is so light to handle and easy to nail, but is quite fragile and will work loose in the wind, tear at the nail holes, and eventually blow away, piece by piece. Use galvanized steel if you can't get out of the wind.

Cattle barns that are open on one side should always have their opening facing east southeast. Our worst blizzards in this country come from the southwest, and a south-facing barn would catch them and fill with snow. Yes, occasionally there's a snowstorm from the east but never a combination of lots of snow, hard wind, and below-zero temperatures such as we get from the westerly directions.

3. Concrete Versus Pole Foundation. Speaking about foundations, this water problem doesn't crop up as much with concrete foundations as with pole barn construction, because there is no watertight foundation between the bottom of the pole barn wall and the ground. The water can easily run in if the floor of the barn is not high enough.

With a pole barn on fairly level ground, the general practice is to fill in with gravel, rather than grade the floor higher with dirt. To the inexperienced, this layer of gravel doesn't seem in the planning to amount to much, but on a building of any size, a necessary 2-foot layer at one end of the barn might become 3 to 4 feet of gravel to maintain level at the other end! Now, gravel is not expensive, generally speaking, but the hauling has become exorbitant. And when you start putting in gravel 3 to 4 feet deep, it takes a heap of stone. Budget for it. Pole barns are cheaper than barns with concrete foundations, but it may be that when you figure in *all* the costs, the concrete foundation is not so much more expensive than the less desirable pole construction.

4. Protection against Manure. While on the subject of concrete foundations that are used around a livestock barn, think about how you will handle the manure. I find letting it build up into a manure pack is advantageous. If the manure would build up higher than the foundation walls, it could cause the sills on the foundation to rot quicker. Use treated lumber, making sure it is treated with a preservative that won't harm cows licking it, or better, raise the foundation walls so they are at least 2 to 3 feet above the floor, allowing that much room for manure and bedding to build up. This may mean lowering the foundation walls at entrances, especially where you drive a tractor or manure spreader in and out.

5. Contracting Out the Foundation. Another point, and this is personal opinion: Unless you have lots of experience, you are probably better off having the foundation formed up and poured by professionals. Unless the job is very small, trying to mix all that concrete yourself is tedious and risky; it is better to get that whole foundation poured fast and at once. Also, forming up takes lots of wood. A contractor with scrap can usually do it cheaper. And he knows how to provide you with a good *square* foundation to work on. With lumber you can make mistakes and correct them. (My son calls me the carpenter who has to do everything twice, first my way and then the right way.) With concrete, you don't get a second chance.

6. *Concrete Floors Unnecessary.* Concrete floors in barns seem very nice, but they are rarely necessary, unless you are going to crowd a bunch of hogs into a small pen, or you are going to sell grade A milk. In the latter case, you are required by law to have concrete floors. In the uncrowded homestead barn, regular bed-

ding with clean straw has a lot more going for it. Concrete floors have the following disadvantages:

- They cost more money than dirt or hard-packed gravel.
- They get slippery and cows can injure themselves seriously.
- Neither horses nor cows ought to stand constantly on concrete in their stalls. It's hard on their legs.
- Because concrete seems to negate the need for lots of clean bedding, cows often lie on cold wet concrete, increasing their chance of contracting certain strains of mastitis.
- Concrete is easier to clean but must be cleaned all the time, while with regular bedding you can just let manure build up in a soft and warm pack and haul it out once a year.
- Urine and manure falling on concrete splatter all over.

- Concrete floors in small barns often crack.
- Worst of all, rats learn to tunnel under concrete floors where they can live safely from you and your cats.
- Even in machinery repair buildings, a fine gravel, packed down hard, makes as good a floor as concrete, and oil and gasoline soak in, rather than lie on the surface, demanding to be cleaned up.

7. *Winter Protection.* Study the style of barn that was favored between 1880 and 1940 in *your* area and build yours likewise. For example, in Minnesota, dairy barns invariably are bank barns with the cows on the partially underground lower floor. Very few such barns were built here in north-central Ohio, and when they were, like my great-grandfather's, they were built into a bank so that three sides of the lower barn were *above* ground. All the bank on the fourth side does is allow you to drive conveniently into the upper level. It provides some insulation and winter protection, but not as much as when three sides (south, west, and north, usually) are underground.

The reason for the difference in bank barn design is that a Minnesota winter is not only colder than an Ohio one, normally, it's also *drier.* Winters here are normally more wet than frigid cold, and the cellarlike environment of the bank barn stays so damp—aided by the moist breath and urine of the animals themselves—that pneumonia can become a problem, especially when temperatures are a bit above freezing. Ron Chacey, who raises sheep in southern Ohio, has quit lambing in his old quasi-bank barn because of this. He finds it healthier to put ewes in little *well-aerated* huts out on the hillside pasture. Even in Minnesota, most bank barns that are open only on one side have added air vents of one kind or another to reduce dampness.

The real moral of this story is that cold does not hurt animals; dampness and drafts do. It is nice, when the temperature is 10 below zero, to be able to milk in the warmth of the half-underground bank barn, but make sure you build so that at least *three sides* have windows and vents or doors that you can open for good cross-ventilation when the temperature rises above freezing. And a good, tight above-ground barn with a good windbreak to protect it is not so uncomfortable to milk in if the temperature rarely sinks below zero, and it is relatively dry.

Incidentally, bank barns built into hillsides are sometimes candidates for the water problem discussed in Number 1. Water runs into the lower floor in spring thaw time. Homesteaders in New England with livestock on the lower floor of these old barns know what I'm talking about. Often the farmers who built those barns did not keep cattle on the lower floor, only on the upper floor. The barn was banked only because there was no level place to put it and still be out of the wind.

8. Building with Wood. Do not paint wood siding the first year you nail it up. Wood is so green as it comes from the lumberyard these days, that it won't take paint well right away. Let it dry a season. If you put it on this summer, paint it next August.

And if you are building with hardwoods cut from your own woodlot, be advised that they will shrink upon drying. An 8-inch-wide white oak board will shrink ½ inch. Yet, if you wait until the wood is dry, it is hard to drive nails into it. You can compromise like the Amish do. Use the green hardwood boards and planks for inside stalls, hay racks, sills, pens, gates, beams, and loft floor boards (which seldom if ever need to be nailed down)—any use where shrinkage and some warpage are not critical. Then buy dry commercial softwood for siding. Another good compromise when using home-

sawed green lumber is to build outside walls in board and batten style. Shrinkage of green lumber is the reason board and batten came into popularity because the battens cover the cracks caused by shrinkage. Later it was found that boards in a vertical position seem to weather better than those in a horizontal position. And even later people decided board and batten was kind of folksy-pretty. It is also an easy way to build, since measurements are not critical—the battens can cover a multitude of sins.

9. *Roofing and Spouting.* Little details give big results. Extend the roof of your barn out over the wall about 2 feet in the so-called Dutch style. Besides looking pretty, the extension keeps most of the rain off the walls. The wood lasts longer and so does the paint. And in summer, the walls are better shaded and the barn remains cooler. The roofing should extend beyond the fascia board (the trim board over the butts of the rafters) ¾ inch and no less. If less, water will not drip *off* the roof, but slide back under the roof and down the fascia board, rotting it before its time.

Do not slight on the sheeting boards under metal roofing. An 8-foot panel should be nailed to at least four sheeting boards, especially if it is aluminum—and if you must use aluminum in a windy location, solid or nearly solid sheeting with eight rows of nails per panel is advisable.

Don't be in a hurry to add spouting to your barn. I have one side of mine spouted to catch the water for my animals. The other side is not spouted nor are my other buildings. I had intended to do it, but so far as I can see, especially with my roofs all extended well beyond the walls, the water is able to get away from the buildings quite well, so why should I add guttering? The money would be wasted.

10. *Bigger Is Probably Better.* No matter how big you build your barn or outbuilding, invariably you'll wish you had made it bigger. At least build large enough to house your animals very comfortably. My definition of very com-

fortably is to allow at least twice as much room per animal as the guidelines suggest for commercial operations. Or more. On a regular commercial farm, one of the names of the game is to crowd animals as closely together as possible without bringing on disease or other problems. The "space requirements" usually are based on the use of drugs, artificial ventilation, and automated cleaning devices of some kind. A chicken factory, and I use the word factory intentionally, may allow scarcely 1 square foot per hen. To keep the hen alive under such congested conditions requires so much additional equipment and energy that one wonders if the "efficiency" is really worth it. An electric outage of only 10 minutes caused the death of thousands of chickens in an Oklahoma factory a few years ago. And in 1983, disease swept through crowded Pennsylvania chicken factories, killing millions of chickens before it could be stopped.

On your homestead, where you intend to keep only a few animals, think big about space requirements and you'll never regret the extra construction costs. A 10 by 20-foot henhouse will conveniently house fifty chickens, but it is so much nicer for just twenty, as I explain in A Chicken Coop for a Small Flock, next.

A 15 by 15-foot stall for a horse is more than you actually need, but worth it. My two cows have a room 20 by 25 feet, plus the stanchion area where they eat. I wouldn't want it any smaller. A hog that you are raising to butcher doesn't need 100 square feet of space when it is confined, but give it that much or more anyway. Uncrowded, it will deposit its manure neatly in one place and keep the rest of the pen clean.

11. *The Barnyard.* Finally, give considerable thought to which side of the barn your animals will stand on while waiting to get into the barn. Even with only a few animals, this area can become muddy and full of manure if you are not careful. One old cow outside, pining for her calf inside the barn, can turn a wet lot into a

my barn has a gambrel roof, with more roof area than an ordinary gable roof. However, the livestock entrance to my barn is on the south end of the barn. Since water from the roof flows off on the east and west sides of the barn, I did not think I'd have a problem with water collecting on the south end. Little did I realize that the prevailing rains from the south and southwest would strike against the tall south *wall* of the barn, flow down the wall, and gather right where the animals stand. If my barn were built with the long sides facing north and south and the side where the animals enter facing *east,* that wall runoff would only occur during infrequent east rains. My only solution is to haul in a load of gravel occasionally to keep the south side of the barn firm and dry. A word to the wise . . .

A Chicken Coop for a Small Flock

A backyard henhouse for only a dozen or so chickens year-round should be commodious, a minimum of around 5 square feet of floor space per hen, which is much more than a commercial poultryman can afford. My henhouse design, based on what I've learned so far by building three coops of my own, differs from the standard designs in a few other ways, which you might find interesting to think about when building your own.

1. Predator Proofing. I would have preferred that my latest chicken coop be built on a concrete footing to make it more or less predator-proof. But pole construction was cheaper and easier. The bottom wall boards are of treated wood for rot resistance, and the wall is sunk into the ground 6 to 12 inches. Cats will not dig that far under to get in, and cats have always been my most troublesome predator—not my own, though, which I train not to bother chickens, but feral cats. I keep the dog tied next to the coop for further insurance.

hog wallow in one afternoon, just by pacing up and down. You can alleviate the problem considerably by not allowing livestock to stand in the barn lot. Either pen them out in the field or put them in the barn. But no matter how assiduously you try to follow that plan, the animals will occasionally spend enough time at the barn entrance to make it muddy. And just by going in and out of the barn, they will tend to drop a lot of manure in that area.

If, and this is an important detail to be aware of, rainwater from off the barn roof can collect in this area, you will have a mud problem, no matter what other precautions you take. I mentioned earlier that I had found spouting unnecessary on my barn. But if the cows stood on the side where the rain dripped off the roof, I very well would have to spout that roof to run the water away from that area—especially since

2. The Size. I knew that for part of the year I would house approximately forty-five to fifty chickens, although there would be less than twenty year-round. Every year we buy six Rhode Island Red chicks and about thirty White Rock broiler chicks, the latter for meat, the former to add to the laying flock. The broilers are butchered when about ten weeks old, and later on I'll butcher some old hens as they quit laying, so that the flock dwindles to around fifteen through winter. We buy chicks in June so have no need of brooder facilities. (The first few nights I might use a heat bulb on the chicks.) Anyhow, by my own idea of space requirement, a 10 by 20-foot building is more than ample. And it is tall enough so I can walk inside without hitting my head, as I did in the old coop.

3. The Roof. A slanted shed roof is adequate for a chicken coop, though if it pleases you, you can build a gable roof. The coop should face south with ample windows on that side for winter warmth. Ideally, the roof should extend out far enough over the windows to cast shade on the glass to keep out summer's piercing sun. On a slant roof, that means adding a cowllike extension on the front.

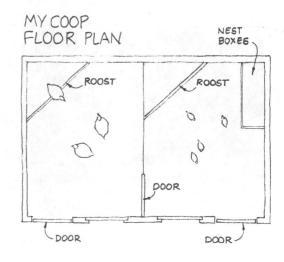

MY COOP FLOOR PLAN

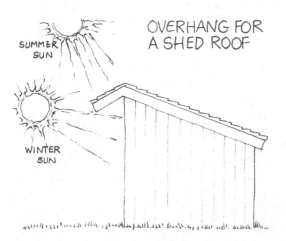

OVERHANG FOR A SHED ROOF

4. Divided into Two. The coop should be divided into two sections, with a door between, and a door for each section to the outside—three doors altogether. The division allows you to raise young chicks on one side separate from the adult hens on the other. Old hens drive young chickens away from the feeder, and so it is best to keep them apart. When the broilers are butchered and the pullets grown, I open the door between the two sections and let the chickens meld into one flock. The dividing wall is of chicken wire fencing only, so the two groups of chickens have had a long time getting used to each other—growing up across the fence from each other so to speak—and this cuts down on the ferocity with which the older hens establish a pecking order when the two flocks are joined.

The division of the coop is handy another way. Occasionally, a chicken will get out when you don't want it out. Then you can run the inside chickens all to one side, close the between door, open up the other outside door and run the errant hen back in, close the outside door, and then open up the between door again. Without the division there is no way to open an outside door without all the other hens running

out. You will find this feature very handy on occasion. You can also use one side in an emergency for other animals. I had a pair of quail in one section last spring. Occasionally I have had a need for a place to put a lamb or a pair of ducks.

5. *The Roosts.* I do not have catching boards for the manure from roosting hens to drop on. I don't need one, with all the space in the coop, and the small number of hens. Catching boards for manure are only necessary when you crowd hens into a coop at a ratio of something like one per square foot. My roosts are two 2 × 4s, one in each section, nailed across a corner of each section, hardly 2 feet off the ground and about 12 feet long. With plenty of bedding, the hens scratch the nightly manure deposit under the roosts into the straw, making of the whole a crumbly moist compost that does not stink. Catching boards, on the other hand, collect putrid piles of pure manure where flies can breed and disease infections begin, if not cleaned out often.

In a situation like mine, if the bedding gets wet and foul, you either aren't putting enough down or you have too many chickens for this system. I hardly use two bales of straw per month for bedding. If the coop were as small as customarily built, relative to the number of hens, I'd have to spread more straw than that, so with straw at $2 a bale, eventually my extra space will pay for itself. The compost the chickens make of the bedding is garden-ready for use every June—and the most effective fertilizer I know of.

6. *The Floor.* I have no floor in the coop other than the dirt nature put there. I strongly advise against floors in chicken coops (as I made clear, I hope, in the item Before You Start Building). Rats and mice get under wood or even concrete unless there is a good, deep footer around the concrete. Rats kill baby chicks. But the rodents will not live in coops without floors because there is no place for them to escape to when a hen takes out after them. My hens eat mice if they can catch them.

If you have to build up the floor above the surrounding ground level to keep it high and dry, I advise dirt rather than gravel. I made the mistake of putting limestone dust gravel in mine, and in summer the chickens scratch through the gravel, which sends clouds of dust into the air. And gravel is not the best material for hens to ruffle their feathers in to protect themselves from lice, either.

7. The Windows. The windows have to open for summer ventilation. Rather than installing elaborate sliding windows and screens, I used old windows I got for next to nothing—most builders have a supply they don't know what to do with. I made the openings in the wall a little larger than the size of the windows. Then I (actually my son did the work) built a frame on the outside of the wall that these old windows would fit against from the inside, the way a picture fits into its front frame. To hold the window vertically in place, all that is needed is a bit of sill on the bottom and two door knobs from scrap wood at the top. When I want to open the window for ventilation, I turn the knobs at the top and lean the window back about 6 inches. To hold it there, I either nail a board across the studs for the window to lean

on, or I attach two pieces of string or light chain between the window and wall. Very little rain can get in with windows tilted open in this fashion.

8. The Nest Boxes. Nest boxes need to be installed, of course, in one of the sections. Five-gallon buckets turned on their sides make nest boxes in a pinch. Nest boxes should be semidark inside to discourage hens from examining the eggs too closely and getting a notion to peck one open. We built our nests with slanting tops so the chickens can't roost on top of the nests, which they otherwise will invariably do. Our nest boxes are a little too open, as you see in the photo. If I run into problems of egg-eating, I will drape the fronts of the boxes halfway with pieces of burlap to make it darker

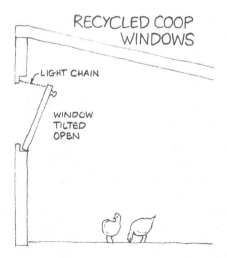

RECYCLED COOP WINDOWS

LIGHT CHAIN

WINDOW TILTED OPEN

Curing the Egg-Eating Hen

There are various folkways proposed for curing the egg-eating hen, the only foolproof one being to roast her for Sunday dinner. However, the problem is often solvable by other less drastic measures. Some hens, for example, will just quit eating eggs all of a sudden and then maybe start up again four months later. Hens usually get started on their addiction because of a soft-shelled or weak-shelled egg being laid by the sisterhood. As hens scramble in and out of the nest, such eggs break. Pecking at the yolk, the hens learn soon enough that they can break weak eggs easily with their beaks, too.

Therefore, to avoid the problem in the first place, it helps if the chickens are getting enough calcium in their diet—through good wholesome grains and greens (alfalfa hay) plus oyster shells or bonemeal. Bonemeal is one of the folk remedies for egg-eating hens. In my experience, it doesn't cure the addiction, but the increase in shell strength tends to cut down on egg eating or the incidence of broken eggs that leads to egg eating. By the same token, having enough nests so none are crowded with three hens at a time is helpful. And providing fine particles of sand or gravel, which allow the hen to digest her food better (and thereby makes nutrients like calcium more available to her body) is a part of the regimen for curing egg-eaters.

A neighbor says that bedding the nest with torn strips of newspaper will cure egg eating. The newsprint gives the eggs an odor hens dislike, so the theory goes, ruining their appetite. Newsprint often does that to me, so there may be some truth in this.

I haven't tried the newsprint remedy because I've found a couple of other ways that suffice. If hens can range outside, egg eating diminishes rapidly. Instead of standing around in the coop bored to death, the hens can chase flies and scratch for worms and get their minds off their addiction. Or perhaps they balance their diet better and have no urge for an egg.

Penned in the coop, a hen can be discouraged, if not cured, from egg eating by putting curtains (pieces of old burlap bag) over the front of the nests, or otherwise making the nest boxes dark. The explanation given is that hens can't see well enough in the dark to aim a good shell-cracking peck into a solid egg. But I'm not sure. I think the reason has more to do with psychology. The hen likes a dark, hidden corner for a nest, and it prompts her to act more according to her nature, which is not to eat eggs. And while she likes the darkness for laying eggs, she wants afterward to get back off the nest and out into the light of day quickly. Perhaps instinct still rules in such a situation, and the hen does not linger there so as not to draw the attention of predators to the nest. Or maybe she is a bit afraid of the dark.

A modification of the darkened nest box theory has proved to be my most effective way of curing egg eating. I discovered it by accident. One day I decided to move a 4 by 4-foot piece of plywood that was in the coop—left there from construction days for reasons I don't rightly recall. I started to carry it out of the coop, but it began raining and I didn't want to get the plywood wet. So I leaned it "temporarily" against the wall. It will probably stay there forever. What happened is that the hens loved that dark, narrow lean-to. Most of them began laying their eggs behind the plywood and avoided the nest boxes. And for unfathomable reasons, they do not eat these eggs. What's more, you can't build a faster, cheaper, or better set of nests than leaning a piece of plywood against a wall. Just tip it back and pick up the eggs.

in the nest. (Chickens have poor eyesight in the dark.) My nests are too big, too. Ten inches square is enough. I built these bigger as an experiment. It seemed to me that with only twelve to fifteen hens laying, more than three nests was ridiculous, but my hens, which continually remind me of people, all decide to do everything at the same time, including laying eggs. This resulted in two chickens trying to occupy the same space at the same time, which anyone who has taken physics knows is impossible. So I decided this time to build the nests big enough to accommodate two hens. The result? You guessed it. Three hens trying to occupy the same space at the same time. Whether they step on and break more eggs with a bigger nest than a smaller one I don't know, yet.

9. The Waterers and Feed Troughs. Waterers and feed troughs are needed, of course. You can spend money for a fancy waterer, but I prefer the bottom half of a plastic jug. One or two of these, refilled morning and night, suffice for a small flock. Such waterers are practically imperative for me in winter, since I think it is silly to go to the expense of a heated waterer for so few chickens. The water freezes in my plastic jug, but all I have to do is rap the container sharply on a solid surface and the ice cracks out. Simple and cheap. If the plastic cracks, I make a new container from another jug. For feeding

troughs, I have built some out of boards, with a broomstick above the trough, inserted by way of nails driven into each end into holes in the ends of the trough. The broomstick rolls over if a chicken tries to roost on it. But mostly, I use two metal troughs I've fallen heir to over the years that have wire covers over them. The larger one is handy not only for feeding but to set the container of water inside. Then the chickens can't spill the water.

My neighbor hangs his feed trough (and waterer) from the ceiling, regulating the height to the size of the chickens — chickens do not like to roost on a swinging perch. Also, as the layer of bedding builds up, you can raise the trough. Mostly though, the reason for a hanging feeder is to keep the hens from scratching bedding into it.

10. The Door. One goes in and out of a henhouse frequently, in most cases needing to close the door afterward. So a door latch is needed that can be worked from inside or out, but still be cheap and uncomplicated. My son built one that answers the requirements. It is a sliding bolt of wood, with a handle that extends on through a slot in the door so it can be worked from either side.

Designing a Small Barn for Easy Livestock Handling

You know the old saying: "You can lead a horse to water, but you can't make it drink." Even that first possibility is not true of cows, calves, goats, sheep, and hogs—at least not ordinarily. They don't lead, and they don't even drive very easily. On the small homestead, where you have a variety of animals that have to be moved in and out of the barn regularly and shuffled from one pen to another, you will learn many new cusswords while trying to lead or drive. You can't use logic to inform a 300-pound calf that you would like it to leave its mother now and go into that pen over yonder. And if you try to argue the point with muscle, the calf will always win.

The solution is very easy, but it took me two years to learn. You need a central aisle onto which the various rooms of the barn open, like motel rooms onto a central hallway. An aisle along one wall might work, but it is less convenient. The doors or gates to the various pens have to be wide enough so that when swung open, they block the aisle, leaving the animal no choice but to enter the pen. The aisle should be narrow enough so that the animals cannot turn around in it, or at least not turn around easily; that means it should be about 3 to 4 feet wide. It is amazing how obediently the animals will hustle up and down the aisle into the proper pen once they get used to this arrangement, and how balky and stupid they can be if you try to drive them into a pen without an aisle to guide them.

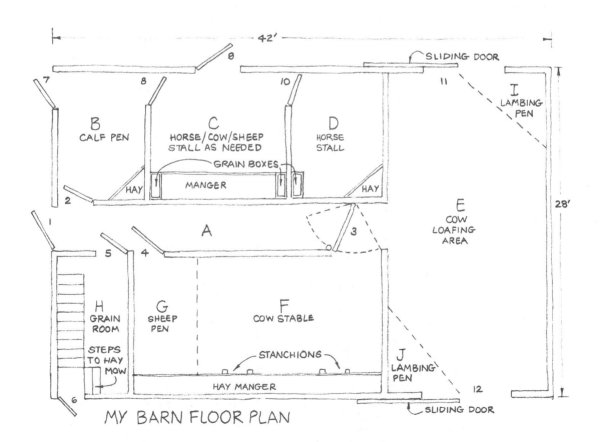

MY BARN FLOOR PLAN

In addition to this aisle, you need to develop the habit of always bringing the animals in the same door. Don't try to drive a cow in one door and her calf into another. Or the sheep in one door and the cows in another. Your animals, even of different species, like to herd together — cows, horses, sheep becoming one family, although not always a loving family. Ideally horses should not be pastured with cows and sheep — horses kick sheep and chase cows. But it would be impractical for most of us with limited space to separate them, and I have had no real problems keeping them together on my place. Anyway, your animal "family" feels more secure trooping into the barn by the same door. So let them.

The ground floor plan of my barn is not necessarily the one you will find best for you. I'd make some changes myself if I had to do it over. But I will use it as an example of how a central aisle makes handling livestock easy.

In the drawing, the solid lines indicate walls or nonmoving partition gates; the dash lines are gates put up for temporary sheep pens, the sheep staying in the barn only January through March, for lambing. Outside measurements are 28 by 42 feet, but the layout is not drawn to scale or exact dimensions.

As you can note, A represents the aisle running from door 1 down to gate 3, which can be swung open to allow access to rooms E and F; closed to allow access to, or exit from, neither; or closed to allow access to F only. If I need to allow access to E only, I can unwire the gate where it is held to the horse stall wall and bring it over to close off the F entrance. But rarely is this necessary because when the gate is closing off room E, the cows are in their stanchions in F and so cannot leave F anyway, even though the entrance to the aisle is open. There are outside doors at 1, 6, 7, 9, 11, and 12. The one at 6 is for humans only, the ones at 11 and 12 are to drive through with the manure spreader. The number 1 door is for the livestock to enter and exit. I never use door 7 anymore, except to shovel manure out of. Door 9 we use only for the horse

when she is being taken out while the other animals remain in.

To separate cow and calf into different pens, I first run them through door 1 with the calf following the cow. In this way the calf develops a lifetime habit of going through that door whenever I open it and indicate it should go in. Cow and calf then move down the aisle into the stable F, gate 3 being positioned to close off room E. Then I close door 1, open gate 2 up the aisle (blocking off exit back to door 1). Then, by stepping calmly between cow and calf in F (or putting the cow in her stanchion), I can easily nudge the calf back into the aisle and down into its pen, B. Then I close the gate to B, and the separation is complete. If the other cow has come into the barn with the first, or the sheep have scurried in, as they are liable to do, I can run the dry cow into E and pen her there, and run the sheep back down the aisle, having first opened gate 4, and they will run right into their pen.

If I want to separate the ewes, I can let one down the aisle into pen G, close it, drive the calf into room C temporarily, open gate 2 and run a second ewe into pen B. Then the three ewes are apart, and I can more easily get one into lambing pen I and another in J. For shearing, I can put the calf in E or F, run the sheep into B, and then one at a time into C, where we shear.

If rooms C and D opened onto the center aisle, animal control would be even more convenient, but when I built the barn I didn't realize that. To bring in the horse, which is always the first animal to come in on winter nights, I lead her through 1, 2, 8, and 10 to get to her stall. When we want to take the horse out alone to ride, we use door 9.

By opening and closing gates and switching pens, all sorts of maneuvers become easy. The method is crucial for my purposes, since I milk my cow while she is also nursing a calf. This gives me the freedom to milk or not milk as the situation demands, which would not be practical if I could not conveniently separate cow and calf almost daily (see How to Avoid Milking Your Cow Every Day in Chapter 9).

Hay Mangers and Grain Boxes That Waste the Least

Animals manage to waste hay out of the most cleverly designed mangers, but much less out of some than others. The most popular manger design is the most wasteful. This is the slatted, slanted manger that uses a stall wall for its back, or the V-shaped, slatted manger, doubled so that animals can feed from either side.

If there is no kind of shelf arrangement under the slats of the V, the manger is par-ticulary wasteful because most of the fine leaves of the hay, which contain most of the nutritional value, fall on the ground when the animals jerk a mouthful of hay from between the slats. One often sees such mangers, of metal, hanging on the walls of expensive horse stalls, where obviously money is no object. Even with catching boards under the slats, from which the animals can eat leaves that fall from the hay, these mangers are wasteful. The slats are too close together for the animal to get its head into the manger, which peeves it and causes it to jerk the hay out even more ferociously.

Secondly, we're talking about grazing animals who are designed, biologically speaking, to eat off the *ground*, not up in the air with their heads raised. When the animal does reach up

and gets a mouthful from a manger, its inclination is to drop its head down and away, and so some of the hay falls on the ground and is tramped into the manure before it is eaten.

Furthermore, V-shaped mangers are used most often for group feeding of flocks or herds, and there is rarely enough space at the feeder for all the animals at the same time. This leads to a lot of turmoil—animals grabbing a mouthful of hay and then being butted away from the manger by a hungrier companion. And animals tend to eat while milling around rather than standing over the feeder, and so they drop hay into the manure as they mill.

But worst of all, when sheep are fed from an overhead slatted manger, the hay chaff rains down on their wool. If you are producing wool for the premium hand spinning market, these mangers will quickly put you out of business because it is almost impossible to wash or brush certain kinds of chaff out of the wool.

The best manger for all animals that eat hay is a straight-sided container that sits on the floor or just above it, so the animals can stand

A Better Hay Manger for Sheep and Goats

Mary Stock, who spins her own wool, doesn't mind wasting a little hay if she can keep the chaff out of the wool. So she designed her own very unique hay manger. With angle irons, she attached a long shelf of 2 × 6s to the back wall of her barn, with short 2 by 6 uprights above and at right angles to the shelf. She spaced the uprights just far enough apart so that a slab from a hay bale fits between them. Then she stapled 2 by 4-inch turkey wire mesh over the whole front of the 2 by 6 arrangement. She slips slabs of hay bale into each section behind the mesh, and the sheep and goats can only barely nibble at the hay through the mesh. Little chaff gets in the wool. Note the long grain box under the manger.

with their heads *over* the hay and reach down to eat it.

Usually such a "container" takes the form of a rectilinear, boxlike feeder, just wide enough so that the animals can reach to the middle if feeding takes place from both sides, or to the opposite side if animals stand on only one side of the feeder. If there is enough room for all the animals at the feeder at the same time or if the animals have individual mangers or are held in stanchions with the manger in front of them, they will stand contentedly and eat over the manger most of the time. The manger should have a floor in it, the bottom of the floor raised a bit off the ground if the manger is outside, so it is not in contact with the wet earth. For horses and cows, the sides should be solid wood about 3 feet high, or at least no higher than the animals can reach from over the side. For sheep, the sides usually measure about 1 foot high, with slats above that for the sheep to stick their

heads between. The accompanying photo shows Ron Chacey's homemade manger—the one he prefers to use to keep chaff out of his sheep's wool (see Wool as a Cottage Industry in Chapter 9) and which he, like myself, feels is the least wasteful of hay. If you use plywood as Chacey has, and you feed outdoors, you may want to treat it against the effects of wet weather. (Be sure you use a nontoxic preservative.)

We built a straight-sided slatted manger for our horse on the wall of her stall about 3 feet off the floor and found it a bit too high. The slats were too close together for her to get her head in, and so she kept jerking hay out and dropping half of it on the floor. To remedy this we removed a center slat. Now she stands contentedly, her head *in* the manger, wasting much less hay.

The cow manger we built is not much of a manger at all. The wall of the barn is the back side of it. The front is really the stanchion fram-

ing, with the front side to hold the hay in the feeder scarcely a foot high. But since the cows mostly stand with their heads over the hay, they do not waste much. The floor of the manger is made of 1-inch boards. I can feed grain in the manger, too. (If you think you may sell grade A milk, a wooden-floored grain box is against the Grade A regulations in some areas. You need concrete, though the logic behind this regulation mystifies me and the dairy farmers I have asked about it.)

Small, octagonal or hexagonal mangers are often used for sheep and goats. The solid board floors in them allow feeding grain or hay. I like these mangers very much, but have learned not to leave them out where cows have access to them. The slats are spaced for sheep heads, not cows', and if you widen the slat spacing to a foot,

the manger doesn't hold baled hay quite as well as it should. If you don't widen the space, however, cows will persist in shoving their heads through the slats, rather than reaching over the top, and then they cannot pull back out again. At first it looks funny to see a cow jumping around with a manger for a hat, but when she breaks it up into little pieces in an effort to get it off, it isn't so funny.

Grain Boxes and Troughs

Grain boxes or troughs for animals have no critical design features except if you're building them for hogs or chickens. I've already described chicken trough designs that keep the hens from roosting on the feeders in A Chicken Coop for a Small Flock. Hogs will root the feed to the end of their troughs, and as it piles up there, they will root some of it right out of the troughs. If you nail a strip of board to all the top edges, extending the edge of the strip inward to form a lip, the hog cannot push the feed out with its nose.

A horse has a bit of a problem getting feed out of the corners of a straight-sided grain box. Adding quarter round inside the box all around where the bottom and sides meet helps.

Generally speaking, straight-sided troughs prevent feed from being pushed out and wasted better than V-sided troughs, although the latter are easier and cheaper to build. The V-sided are OK for sheep because they are rather dainty eaters. A good, practical design can be seen in the photo at left, again from Ron Chacey's farm.

How to Pin a Mortise-and-Tenon Joint to Hold for Centuries

The urge to write a book that would be a celebration of tradition, but a useful manual, too, first came over me when I was tearing down an old timber frame barn. The mortised-and-tenoned joints of that barn, over a century old, were as tight and solid as the day they were made (actually tighter), and the only way we could separate those beams was with a chain saw. I marveled at what secret skill must be involved in making such joints without nail, bolt, or glue.

Recently I was fortunate enough to observe exactly how these joints were made, watching the Amish build a barn using precisely the same traditional methods that have been handed down orally for 300 to 400 years. They did not even use blueprints. And to my surprise there was no special skill involved in pinning mortise and tenon together beyond being able to use a saw and a chisel accurately. The knowledge was traditional—accumulated over centuries of trial and error and reduced to a simplicity easy to grasp. The Amish boys standing around watching would grow up knowing how to do it as part of their upbringing, not even realizing what a wonderful education they had received.

The building of the barn was a perfect example of the real advances in civilization as opposed to the questionable advances of modern gadgetry. A tornado had ripped through the Amish farmland southeast of Wooster, Ohio, destroying four barns and a wide swath of timberland, where the huge trees of a good Amish woodlot lay in seeming ruins. *Within a month,* the trees were sawn into lumber and the four barns built anew, all with nineteenth-century methods. The barn I watched go up, said an outside contractor, would have cost him $100,000 to build, if he could find carpenters who knew how to do it. The Amish farmer told me it cost him about $30,000, much of that paid for by the Amish community's own brand of insurance. And when the people returned in the evening after the barn raising to have a party, they brought along enough livestock, free of charge, to replace the animals lost in the storm. Nothing even approaching this kind of cultural or technical progress can be matched by "modern" society.

After the foundation and cement floors of the lower level were in, the huge barn took only two days to build. On the first day, the main girders, beams, and posts of the lower floor were installed, some beams 16 inches thick, hoisted into place by Amish shoulders. All the pens, stalls, hay mangers of the lower floor were built that day, too, as was the floor of the upper level. The second day, the actual barn raising took place. At 6:30 in the morning there was nothing of that huge superstructure (it would end up a double barn) to see, but I was told that by noon it would be possible to put hay in the barn. I thought the Amish farmers were kidding me.

But by noon you *could* put hay in the barn, and I don't mean just a forkful. The hay track across the roof peak was in place, the ropes in their pulleys, the huge mows framed in hand-mortised beams—all in place. There was still a roof to go on and the back wing of the barn to complete, but by "chore time"—5:00 in the evening—the barn was complete. And not one of the more than 300 men seemed to work very hard, or even had to be told what to do. "Oh, we en-choy raisings," one man told me, amused by my awe.

The only other experience of my life (so far) that filled me with as much amazement, although in a totally different way, was standing in the grain pits at the Chicago Board of Trade when the day's trading began. That swarming group of screaming traders was unified by a frenzied greed; the results of their efforts were ephemeral, amoral, and often destructive. In contrast, the group of Amishmen moving about the barn was orderly and quiet, unified by a caring concern for a neighbor. The result of their work was a well-made building that would continue to be useful for centuries.

That the barn could be built without a blueprint was not so surprising once I understood what was going on. The way the barns go together has been more or less standardized over the generations. Once the overall dimensions are known, tradition supplies the sizes of the frame beams that are put together into "bents" on the ground, raised in place, and locked and braced together. The dimensional formulas are carried around in the master carpenters' heads and passed on to their successors, as well remembered as any carpenter's knowledge of how far a 2×4 ought to stretch without a support.

Once the bents are put together, they fit into the barn as preordained as the pieces of a puzzle. When they are in place, the siding, the rafters, and roofing all go on in the traditional way. Everything is done by a preset system. Every siding board, for example, is held by two nails at every point where the board rests against the frame beams. The boards are prepared on the ground—sawn to length, the nails driven partway at the proper spacings (the distances between the frame beams are already known). Then the boards are handed up the wall, as in a bucket brigade, to men clinging to the beams. *Bang! Bang!* Two blows on each nail drives them home into the beam. The boards seem almost to unroll across the face of the barn, so smoothly unified are the efforts of so many tradition-trained hands.

Mortise-and-Tenon Joints

The mortise-and-tenon joints might be called the basic building technique—the key to the strength and long life of the structure. Again, the whole operation is standardized. The dimensions of the mortises and tenons and the size of the white oak pins are standard. An Amishman, knowing the formulas being used on a particular barn, could cut a mortise in a beam while his neighbor a mile away was cutting a tenon on a beam, and when they brought the beams together the joint would fit.

But the detail that makes the fit solid and everlasting requires another step. Assuming that mortise and tenon have been cut, a hole must be bored through both, and the pin driven home. The tenon is cut with a saw and chisel. The mortise is first drilled with an auger bit, then the round hole is squared and cleaned up with a chisel. Supertightness is achieved by taking advantage of wood's natural tendency to expand and contract. The pins are dry wood; the beams are green wood. Green wood shrinks, but dry wood exposed to atmospheric moisture swells a little. During barn construction, the dry pins are heated in a little boilerlike receptacle with a fire underneath, kiln-drying them to superdryness, that is, drier than the air normally is. After being driven hot into the beam, they will absorb moisture from the air and swell a bit. The green beam, meanwhile, will shrink as it dries. Thus, the bond between pin and beam tightens irrevocably.

To make the joint even tighter, the hole for the pin is first bored through the mortise. Then the tenon is placed in the mortise, and the mark for the hole made just a bit less than ⅛ inch *back* (toward the shoulder of the tenon) from perfect alignment. The tenon is then withdrawn,

the hole drilled, and the tenon replaced. The tenon hole, slightly back from perfect alignment with the hole through the mortise, forces the pin, as it is driven through, to pull the tenon incredibly tight against its seat in the mortise.

It is no wonder that 100 years later, it will take a chain saw to separate the two beams. Or a tornado.

A Pigpen for the Backyard

Loose talk about pigpens in the yard will send the blood pressure soaring in the veins of local zoning officials, if not your neighbors. It's perfectly all right in our culture to keep a dog half the size of a cow in the yard, letting it bark all night and running all over town dropping manure in its wake. But a quiet, clean hog producing something useful like pork chops? Heaven forbid.

People think hogs are dirty because hogs will survive in crowded conditions. Because hogs will survive in crowded conditions, humans have always raised them that way, the better to make a buck. Try raising cats like we do hogs, and you'll know what dirt and stench are really like.

A neighbor woman has for twelve years raised a hog every summer in a pen in her yard. The pig and its pen are so clean I doubt close neighbors, if there were any, would know the pig was there unless she told them. The pen is simplicity itself. Sometimes she uses a simple V-shaped hut for a shelter. One side is a discarded tub once used for mixing cement in, and the other side consists of three 2 × 4s covered with roof paneling. At other times, she stacks some old hay bales together to make a warm, snug hut. The hay protects against the cool, moist drafts of spring and gives shade in summer, although plenty of shade is now supplied by trees that have grown up and over the pen.

The pen consists of an 8-foot-square platform of fifteen 2 × 6s, spaced ⅞ inch apart. The ⅞-inch crack between the floor planks is critical. If wider, the pig might get its foot

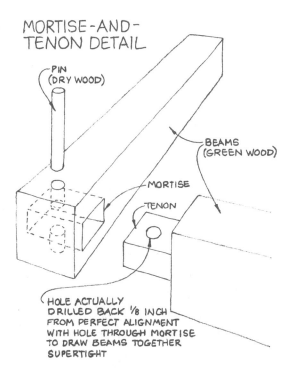

MORTISE-AND-
TENON DETAIL

PIN
(DRY WOOD)

BEAMS
(GREEN WOOD)

MORTISE

TENON

HOLE ACTUALLY
DRILLED BACK ⅛ INCH
FROM PERFECT ALIGNMENT
WITH HOLE THROUGH MORTISE
TO DRAW BEAMS TOGETHER
SUPERTIGHT

caught; if narrower, manure tends to build up on the floor rather than work its way through. The floor sits on a square frame of four 2×10s, with a fifth 2×10 down the middle. And the frame sits on cement blocks at each corner.

The pen sits on a slight slope. On the front side, the platform is nearly level with the ground, but on the other side it is about 2 feet above ground level, so it is easy to clean out the manure under the floor. To hold the pig in its pen, there are posts set into the ground at each corner of the pen to which picket fencing is wired. The fence is in two sections, 32 feet in all. A horizontal bar of 2×4s extends all around the bottom of the fence from post to post to strengthen the picket fencing. When the pig needs to be moved to a truck for hauling to the butcher, always a difficult job on a homestead, the neighbor lady and her husband unwire one of the picket fence sections and curl it around the pig. The pig is accustomed to being surrounded by the fence anyway, and by carrying the fence along as it surrounds the pig,

they can move the animal quite easily to the truck. Then they open the fence only enough so the hog has nowhere to go but up the ramp into the truck—or if the truck is backed against a bank (which is a much better way) the hog can walk right on without climbing a ramp. Or they can back a truck up to that side of the pen that is 2 feet above ground level. The picket fence can then be opened so that the hog can walk right onto the truck bed. In my own experience, this is the best way to load a hog easily: have its pen at the same height as the truck bed. Forcing hogs or any animal up a ramp is always difficult.

The neighbor's pigpen is surrounded by trees and bushes and so is barely noticeable as one walks across the yard toward it, unless the pig should squeal. It rarely does because it is the most contented pig in the world: overfed, shaded by trees, sprayed with water on hot days, and kept warm and dry on cool rainy days.

The neighbor buys her pig from a farmer in April, at weaning weight of about 40 pounds. She feeds it a commercial ration supplemented by homegrown corn, garden leftovers, and table scraps. She gets about 135 pounds of dressed meat and lard, at a cost of a little over a dollar a pound, counting all costs except her labor. But she says saving money is not her goal, and that she would go on raising her own hog even if it were costlier than buying pork from the grocery, which her husband says it is. Why? Quality. She says buying good lard at a store is almost out of the question, and that her own meat tastes so much better. She also knows it is not contaminated with drugs.

Designs of Traditional Corncribs

Cribs for ear corn in the traditional mold have a few things in common, although individual variations abound.

Wall Cracks for Ventilation

The walls are slatted with cracks of about 1 inch wide between the boards, the boards being anywhere from 2 to 6 inches wide. The cracks allow air into the crib in sufficient quantity to dry ear corn, even though it still contains as much as 20% moisture. If corn is dry enough in the field to husk out fairly well, it is dry enough to store in a slatted crib, where drying will safely continue until complete.

Novice farmers dealing with slatted corncribs for the first time fear that rain will get into the corn faster than the corn will dry out. But the normal amount of rain and snow that gets into the crib does not hurt ear corn; it is the inner moisture of the cob one must worry about, and that is cured out by the circulation of air through the cracks.

SIDE VIEW OF CORN CRIB

← 4' →

Bottom Width—4 Feet, Maximum

A second common feature is that the cribs are rarely more than 4 feet wide at the bottom. If any wider, air will not penetrate well enough to the center to keep corn from molding, especially in a wet fall. Some cribs have straight perpendicular walls, and some have walls that angle slightly outward. The latter hold a bit more corn safely (the top part of the crib can be wider than 4 feet because air can get down from above and also up into the corn from the sloping sides). The sloping wall also allows rainwater to drip down and out of the crib rather than running straight down perpendicular walls.

Rodent-Proof

The third feature traditional cribs have in common—or should have when built right—is that they are rodent-proof by one of several ingenious methods of making it impossible for the rats and mice to climb the supports that hold the crib above the ground. The earliest known of these posts were made of stone, actually two stones, and were shaped sort of like mushrooms. These were called staddles, and they date at least from the 1700s, when they were used as foundations for granaries. The bottom of the support was a truncated pyramid or a cone, the sides sloping inward, and then capped with a flat stone, either squarish or round (see the drawing). No rodent can negotiate the overhang of the capstone. Later, glass was used to cover the lower part of the staddle. These could be built easily today of concrete, or made from a concrete bottom and natural stone cap where flattish rocks are available.

Modern renditions of the old staddle are usually straight-sided and made of concrete or treated wood covered with strips of roofing metal, as mine is. My aluminum-sheathed posts seem to have worked so far—no mice or rats in five years, anyway. A straight concrete pillar might be negotiated by a stubborn rodent, however, and may not be as effective as having the overhanging capstone. A favorite innovation is clay drainage tiles filled with concrete. The clay tile, especially if it is vitreous, is too slippery for mice to climb. Another method is to sheathe the bottom of the crib between support and floor with a horizontal piece of tin wide enough so that no rodent can reach beyond it and gain a toehold up the wall or along the floorboards.

Essential in all these rodent barriers is the fact that they not only provide an insurmount-

CORN CRIB WITH STADDLE STONES

STADDLE STONES

Not your typical corncrib.

wide cracks allow cardinals and blue jays to peck corn easily off the ears inside to supplement their winter fare. If you wish to keep out birds, you will also have to staple wire mesh over the openings between roof rafters and side wall. I did that, but I left cracks more than an inch wide between the boards, which the sparrows soon found. However, I have lately rejoiced in my mistake because wrens have decided to nest in an old bucket I nailed to the wall inside the crib. The wrens keep the sparrows away in summer, and their cheerful singing is worth contending with the sparrows in winter.

Floor and Roof

The crib can be as long as one wishes to make it, but with the width limited to 4 feet, one must use common sense as to the height. If it is much taller than 12 feet, top heaviness in the wind could be a problem. To anchor my crib solidly to the supports, I notched the planks that the building rests on into the sides of the supporting posts and spiked the planks solidly to them. Floor joists that rest on these girder planks are also nailed to the posts, with the sloping wall studs nailed to the joists. Either a simple slant roof or gable roof is appropriate, but the slant roof is much easier to build.

Doors

At the top of the higher wall, I provided two small openings (large enough for the scoop shovel to fit through) with hinged doors through which to shovel corn into the crib. At the rear of the crib, at floor level, there is a small hinged door of the same size from which corn is removed. Cribs of this kind are normally filled completely with corn (I need only half the space for corn), and so doors all along the top of the higher wall would make loading the crib easier.

When the crib is completely filled, some sort of barricade is necessary at the entrance, otherwise corn will spill out when the door is

able barrier (hopefully), but that they raise the building off the ground. Rats are not inclined to stay in a building that is up off the ground, even if it is full of corn. How high the building ideally should be from the ground I don't know. (How high can a rat jump?) But by measuring existing cribs it seems that 18 to 24 inches is the norm today. In the past, 3 feet may have been common, since earlier cribs were often equipped with a short ladder on a hinge that swung down to the ground for entrance to the crib—a device that would not be necessary if the step up was less than 2 feet.

Don't Tempt the Birds

The cracks between the wallboards should not be more than an inch wide or English sparrows will get into the crib. They do not harm ear corn much, but a flock of them roosting on the crib means lots of bird droppings. And if you keep smaller grains or milled feed in the crib (as I do in the front of mine) the sparrows will feed on it voraciously. Also, the

Keeping the Snow Out

Snow is not as much of a problem in these cribs as might be expected. In December and January a crib is normally still a half or more full, and the corn itself partially blocks the snow from coming through the cracks. But an occasional blizzard can blow in enough snow on top of the corn to make removal a good idea. Some snow melting on the corn won't hurt it since by wintertime it should be quite dry. But a lot of snow would be undesirable for both corn and crib. Most of the snow can be removed from a small crib quite easily with a scoop shovel. Some homesteaders hang wide boards or pieces of plywood over the slats in periods of heavy snow.

Overall Size

The size of your crib depends of course on how much corn you use per year. It is a very good idea to use up the corn in the crib every year and put new corn in. Old corn is less tasty and less nutritious. And it may encourage weevil infestation. How much corn you need is a matter of experience. But if you are growing an acre, for example, your harvest should be between 80 to 120 bushels. A crib 8 feet long and 4 feet wide, filled to a depth of 8 feet will hold 102.4 bushels. (To find the number of bushels of ear corn in a rectangular crib, multiply length times width times height of corn in the crib, and then divide by 2½ or multiply by 0.4.)

opened. To provide a proper barricade, nail short pieces of board to the insides of the door frame to form grooves into which boards are slid at an angle down and inward toward the corn. As the crib fills, add more boards. Because of the slant of the boards, the ears of corn can neither work out between them, nor press so hard against them that the boards would be difficult to remove. The bottom board or two can be pulled out to remove corn—and shoved back in quickly if too much corn starts to tumble out at once.

Some cribs have slanted floors and small doors along the wall at the bottom of the slant. Such cribs are said to be "self-unloading" because the corn will slide out these small doors without the necessity of getting inside with a shovel and scooping it out.

Making Do: The Gentle Art of Coggling

I had just "repaired" a harrow (we call it Adam because it is so old) by replacing a broken link in one of the short chains that attaches to the drawbar with a few twists of baling wire. "Oh," a friend said, observing me. "I see you've learned how to coggle."

"Coggle" is not a word you will find in an ordinary dictionary. It's a folk word that, as far as I know, came out of the Kentucky hills where survival depended on the ability to coggle. It means to improvise a method of doing something when the proper tools or materials are not available. The word usually applies to a makeshift repair job. The idea is that one will redo the repair or improvisation properly when there is more time later—but such a time never arrives.

People who "come up the hard way," to use another folk expression, or who stubbornly refuse to come up at all, must become masters of the coggling art to survive. Hill people of southern Ohio, West Virginia, and Kentucky say that if the heater in your car doesn't work, heat up a rock or two on the stove and lay them on the floor under the dashboard, the way the Amish do in their buggies. That's coggling. A neighbor still heats a soapstone on the stove to keep her feet warm in bed. One hill man I know took coggling a bit too far, however. Wanting a convertible but being unable to afford one, he cut off the top of his car with a welding torch.

Farmers and homesteaders fail unless they learn to cultivate the coggling art. Your true farmer can do everything from keeping his boots buckled to keeping a $100,000 grain harvester running with a pair of pliers and baling wire. Take away baling wire and half the world would starve to death.

The true coggler values only the kind of coggling that saves money, but there is a lesser genre of the art where money is not the issue. One of my sisters dries her children's winter boots out with a blow dryer, and another defrosts her freezer with it. I have a third sister who washes her apples in the dishwasher, but that's another story.

Coggling from Stumps

A homesteader I know rolled one of those big wooden spools that originally held copper cable into his kitchen, set it on end, put a tablecloth on it, and christened it a table.

Another cut and split out a seat and back from a 4-foot length of log with chain saw and ax and had himself a serviceable lawn chair. The piece of coggling art of which I'm proudest is my milk stool. Originally it was four second-growth sprouts out of a small red elm stump. Red elm is harder to split than the atom. I sawed off the four sprouts, then sawed off the whole stump down closer to the ground. Turned upside down, I had a four-legged stool that has proven to be virtually indestructible. It took me about 30 seconds to "make" and has been in use now nine years.

Automatic Watering System

My watering system at the barn is pure coggle; I have fully intended to replace it with

something respectable for the last ten years. There is no electricity at the barn, no pumps, no automatic waterers, no well even. In earlier years when I was responsible for the well-being of a conventional farm, I used to have nightmares about automatic waterers that didn't turn off automatically and so flooded barn floors. I worried about other electrical gadgets that either didn't work like they should or worked too well, burning themselves out and the barn down. So when I built my own barn I solved the problem.

When I wake in the middle of the night or am off somewhere doing something else, I no longer worry about the barn. No switches have been left on because there are no switches. As for watering, the animals go to the creek daily, except in mud time or that rare day in winter when the weather is very, very cold.

To provide water for those days, and the little bit of water daily for the chickens and the ewes temporarily in maternity pens, I had planned a cistern filled with water spouted off

the barn. Or a well. Instead, I have contented myself with two barrels buried up to their rims in the ground, filled with water off the barn roof. They hold maybe a five days' supply, which is almost always enough, at least during mud time when it rains at least every five days, to refill the barrels. Only rarely must I carry water from the house. I rationalize that when the barrels rust out, as I suppose they eventually will, I'll build a cistern or a well with a windmill. But I have a hunch I will just put another barrel in the ground.

Even the way the water gets into the barrels is mostly coggling. The downspout is only loosely connected to the eave trough, held mostly by tension from the pressure of an old sawhorse against it. The sawhorse is another bit of coggling, nailed together very quickly years ago from lengths of tree sprouts. To direct the flow of water into one barrel or the other, I use the planks that normally cover the barrels, propping one or the other up so that the water runs down the board and into the barrel—another coggling trick.

A Barn Gate

Opportunities for successful coggling lurk everywhere, and one must develop an intuition for sensing them. On paper, the gate I needed in my barn aisle to separate animals into different pens (the gate 3 that I describe in Designing a Small Barn for Easy Livestock Handling) looked impossible to hinge at first. It can swing wide open (see drawing), and it can either close the aisle off from both loafing area and stable, or close off the loafing area only. And occasionally it needs to be removed from its normal position to close off the stable only. Obviously, this presents an engineering problem that might challenge the brains of an Einstein. But it's a snap for your everyday coggler.

I "installed" the gate by wiring it loosely to the horse stall wall with (what else?) baling wire. That's the gate's hinge, so to speak. When

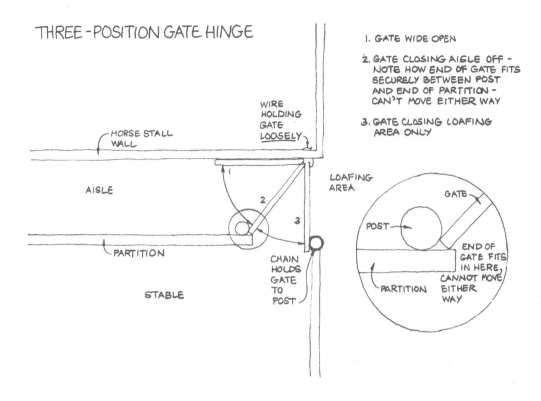

THREE-POSITION GATE HINGE

1. GATE WIDE OPEN

2. GATE CLOSING AISLE OFF – NOTE HOW END OF GATE FITS SECURELY BETWEEN POST AND END OF PARTITION – CAN'T MOVE EITHER WAY

3. GATE CLOSING LOAFING AREA ONLY

WIRE HOLDING GATE LOOSELY

HORSE STALL WALL

AISLE

PARTITION

STABLE

LOAFING AREA

CHAIN HOLDS GATE TO POST

POST

GATE

END OF GATE FITS IN HERE, CANNOT MOVE EITHER WAY

PARTITION

the gate is wide open, the wire holds it from falling over. When the gate closes off the aisle from both loafing area and stable, the wire holds one end, and the other end fits neatly into a sort of triangular slot formed (accidentally) by the partition and post at the stable entrance (see the drawing). When swung all the way over to close off the loafing area from aisle and stable, the wire is still holding its end, and a length of chain holds the other. The beauty of this piece of naturally occurring coggleship is that the gate is backed solidly by wall and post, which reinforces it when the animals that are blocked out of the loafing area press their weight against it. And when the gate is closing *in* the animals in both loafing area and stable, again it is backed solidly by wall and post in the other direction, so no cow can knock it over, despite the flimsy way it is held.

Instant Maternity Pens

When I needed small maternity pens for the ewes at lambing time, I wired gates across two corners of the cows' loafing area. The cows don't really use those corners anyway, and the instant pens did not cramp them for space.

My father and grandfather had their own version of the instant maternity pen, very handy for their flocks of 100 or so ewes. They took two gates, 8 to 10 feet long and 3 feet high, and hinged them together. Such a double gate could be opened to V-shape and set against the wall for a temporary pen or opened to an L-shape and set in the corner. Of, if you run out of corners and wall space, two such sets of double gates could be fitted L-shaped against each other and wired together to form a square pen anywhere.

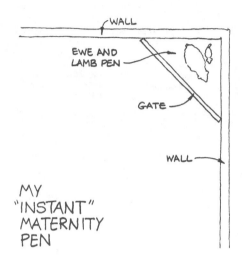

MY "INSTANT" MATERNITY PEN

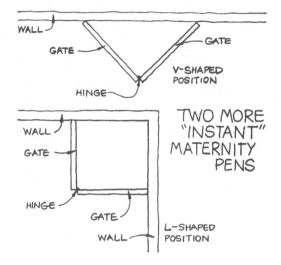

TWO MORE "INSTANT" MATERNITY PENS

Easing Equipment through Tight Spaces

We all know about the truck driver who lets air out of his tires to get under a low overpass on the highway—a great example of creative coggling. But do you know what to do when you have a piece of farm machinery that is just 2 or 3 inches wider at the axle or some other protruding point than the gateway? In the years when larger tractor machinery was being introduced to horse farms, this was a common problem. My father showed me a great trick to solve it sometimes, when the margin of victory

PLANKS TILT MACHINERY JUST ENOUGH SO IT CAN SQUEEZE BY

is only a few inches. He would pull the machine (the grain harvester usually) up to the gatepost it would not fit through, put a short plank or two or three beside the post where the harvester's tire would run, then slowly ease forward. As the tire rode up on the planks, the whole machine would tilt over a bit, just enough so the protruding pulleys higher up on the harvester could slide by the post unharmed.

Bracing Barn Doors Closed

One example of coggling around the barn has become enshrined in tradition—the "prop stick"—the boards used to brace large barn

doors solidly in place against the wind. Seeing these braces from the road, the outsider might wonder at such a "sloppy" way to keep the door closed, but a bit of thought or experience will prove that there is no better way. The doors at the big main entrances to barns do not have a post where the doors come together when closed. Such a post would be in the way of the hay wagons or other machinery entering the barn. So there is nothing solid to hook or knob the doors to at the center. A bar across the inside would work but is not operable from the outside. Stakes or heavy stones at the base of the doors would have to be moved out of the way of wagons. A concrete groove for the bottom of the door to run in fills with ice and dirt. A

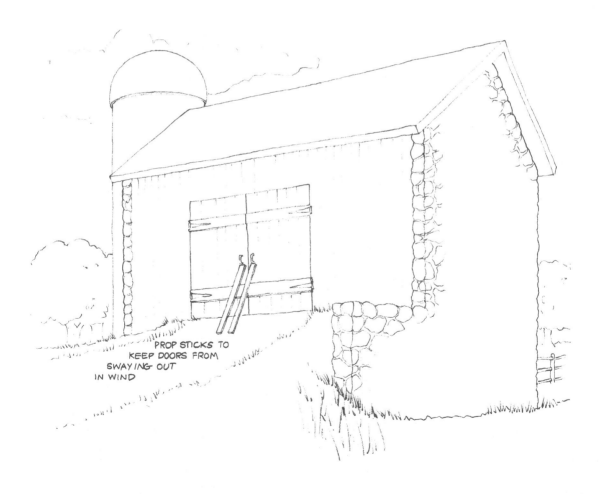

PROP STICKS TO
KEEP DOORS FROM
SWAYING OUT
IN WIND

prop stick is easier to move out of the way. The first farmer who hastily grabbed a post to brace his door so the wind would not lift it and bang it apart, was coggling . . . and starting a traditional method.

There is a way to avoid the use of a prop stick, as clever readers are by now leaping to their desks to write me. A bar of wood or iron, attached by brackets to the bottom of the door, can be fashioned to drop into a hole or depression in the ground or floor at the foot of the door at the center. Usually, such a bar was attached to a lever to raise and lower it.

In case of barn doors that *swung* open, rather than rolled aside, the lever-bar arrangement was made double, one to go down into the floor, the other to go up into the frame above the doors. One door was so fastened, and it lapped the other door with an extra vertical board on the outside. Then a simple knob on the inside held that door firmly to the one anchored above and below.

Making a Large Barn Door

Large barn doors that hang by rollers in overhead tracks need to be as light as possible and as strong as possible, which in a way, are conflicting characteristics. There may be more than one way to achieve the maximum of both, but sooner or later you'll conclude that the traditional method, perfected by trial and error, is the best. White pine is the best available wood, because of its lightness. The crosspieces need be spaced no closer than 4 feet — what you gain in strength by moving them closer, you lose in weight. And finally, there is the detail most often overlooked: the side edges of the door should be finished off with 1 by 2 strips to

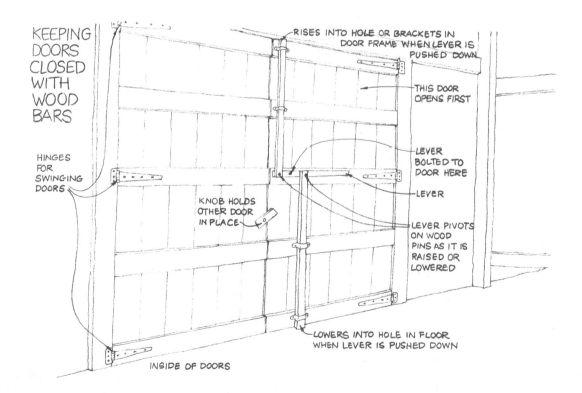

KEEPING DOORS CLOSED WITH WOOD BARS

RISES INTO HOLE OR BRACKETS IN DOOR FRAME WHEN LEVER IS PUSHED DOWN

THIS DOOR OPENS FIRST

HINGES FOR SWINGING DOORS

LEVER BOLTED TO DOOR HERE

LEVER

KNOB HOLDS OTHER DOOR IN PLACE

LEVER PIVOTS ON WOOD PINS AS IT IS RAISED OR LOWERED

LOWERS INTO HOLE IN FLOOR WHEN LEVER IS PUSHED DOWN

INSIDE OF DOORS

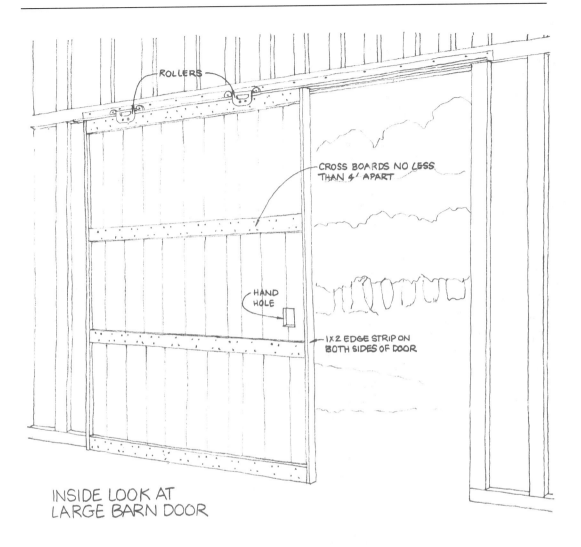

ROLLERS

CROSS BOARDS NO LESS THAN 4' APART

HAND HOLE

1 X 2 EDGE STRIP ON BOTH SIDES OF DOOR

INSIDE LOOK AT LARGE BARN DOOR

give the door greater rigidity and discourage end-to-end warping.

The boards of the door should run vertically, not horizontally. The reason is that the door is going to *hang.* If the boards were horizontal, the door would hang mostly from the top board, the weight eventually loosening it. With the boards running vertically, and a crosspiece on the top attached to all the vertical boards, the weight of the hanging is much more evenly distributed. Also, vertical boards

weather better than horizontal ones, all else being equal.

The width of the door boards is not crucial, although the wider they are, the fewer the cracks, which always widen a wee bit after the door is up awhile due to further drying and shrinking of the wood. Favor 1 × 12s unless they are more expensive per square foot than 1 × 10s or 1 × 8s. If the difference in price is only slight, stick with the wider boards. In some cases you will need boards of different widths to meet the dimension required by the door opening. If so, put the narrower ones to the inside and the widest to the outside.

Remembering that a door is in actuality part of the siding of the barn, use the driest wood you can get—especially if wide cracks from shrinkage would let in snow. Kiln-dried lumber is nice, but keep it under cover until used, and if you want a really tight door, do not build until the driest time of the year. Kiln-dried wood will reabsorb moisture and swell in wet weather. The "kiln-dried" lumber one sees stacked out in the rain getting soaked at a building site before it is used is sort of a joke.

The width of the crosspiece boards is not critical either, although the top one must be wide enough to accept all the bolts of the rollers that will be attached to it. Space the middle crosspieces equidistant from the top and bottom ones and from each other, trying to maintain the rule of thumb of about 4 feet apart.

Use galvanized nails that do not rust and run brown streaks down the door. Crosspieces go on the inside of the door, but nail them from the outside. Seven-penny nails are large enough. Drive at least three and preferably four nails where cross boards lap each vertical board. Clinch the nails well on the other side. In clinching, the temptation is to bend the nail over with the grain, since the bent-over part will sink so easily into pine wood that way. But often, the nail does not bend as sharply at the wood surface as it should; instead the whole nail sags over a bit before bending, which loosens it in the wood. Clinch at a *right angle* to the grain or at least 45 degrees to the grain. The last hammer blow of the clinch should be directed right at the point of the nail and at a slight angle rather than straight down, to drive that point firmly into the wood. If your last blow is at the bend of the nail, the point may stick out a bit above the wood surface and catch your coat when you brush by.

Finally nail on the 1 by 2 strips on both side edges of the door. Use nails with threaded or twisted shafts. Your tendency will be to close the doors by pulling on that 1 by 2 strip, and smooth nails there will pull out rather easily from pine. Put a nail through the strip into the board edge every foot and drive in extra nails at each crosspiece where you have a double edge to nail to.

Buy rollers with ball bearings and a track that is rustproof and weather-protected. Directions that come with the rollers and track tell you how to mount them. Usually holes in the track for mounting are situated every 18 inches —to match studs at that standard spacing—and attached with lag bolts. My barn's studs are spaced 2 feet apart, so I had to coggle. Where necessary I installed a 2×4 behind the siding between the studs, drilled holes all the way through it, and used bolts instead of lag screws to fasten on the track. Keep the roller bearings well oiled.

If barn owners don't use prop sticks to keep their doors from banging and swaying in the wind (and sometimes even if they do), they hook the doors to the doorway frame. When there is no smaller door handy for entering and exiting, a hole has to be cut into the big door

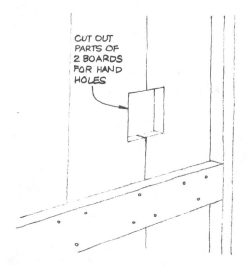

CUT OUT PARTS OF 2 BOARDS FOR HAND HOLES

near the hook so it can be latched and unlatched from the outside. The hole should be cut into the edges of *two* boards, not just through one, which could weaken that board too much. Particular farmers often cover the hole with a flap cut from a worn-out leather power-take-off belt or a stiff piece of rubber or a piece of board held loosely by a bolt. The board can be slid aside to open the hole, and then falls back in place over the hole again after you take out your hand.

The Great Barn— Then, and Now

When we use the word "barn," most of us think first of the great barns that were built between 1860 to 1920 and which are now, one by one, passing from the landscape. For those of us who grew up in them, the great barns never lost their enchantment, then or now. In winter they pulsated with life: lambs racing through the sheep shed playing tag; calves bawling from their pens for their mothers; pigs squealing; horses snuffling in their grain boxes; Old Rooster spending cold nights perched on top of Brown Girl the cow.

As soon as the corn fodder pile had been fed off the main barn floor (where it had been piled in November because there was no more room in the mows), Dad would lower the hay rope from the peak of the roof where it hung and we would swing on it—from the sheep shed mow at the far end of the main floor clear out into the sunshine through the open front doors. We were never allowed to play on the straw stack behind the barn, for Dad feared we would tear away the rain-shedding outer coat of straw he had so deftly arranged.

bales became practicable, spacious mows were necessary for storage of these forage crops. Moreover, hay and straw were the bulwark of the great barn economy: hay was the main feed for livestock other than hogs and chickens; straw (as bedding eventually mixed with the manure) was the main fertilizer. In Chapter 9, Livestock, I will discuss how hay at least should still be and can be the bulwark of the small farm-garden economy today, but for now here is one example.

But the hay mow, ah, that was our domain. Either diving into it from a beam above or simply lying in it, watching the hay dust dance in a shaft of sunlight streaming down through a crack in the wall or listening to the pigeons gossip to each other in low liquid gurgling noises, the big barn remained always as awesome as a cathedral.

I could give a good historical argument for the theory that the rise and decline of our rural society both culturally and economically paralleled the rise and decline of the great barns, but space does not allow me to. Be aware, however, that the kind of culture and economy those great barns supported has much in common with the aims and ideals of the modern small farmer-gardener seeking some degree of true self-sufficiency, and so those barns provide lessons that can be put to use again, albeit on a very small scale.

Unlike most commercial farms today, the great barns were huge because they sheltered a large variety of animals: workhorses, cows, a bull, steers, sheep, hogs, and sometimes more. The barns also had to be big because before the technology of compressing hay and straw into

The Great Barn Economy Reduced to Miniscale

You can raise all the food for a pair of rabbits and two broods of their young in a backyard—even if you have only one-quarter acre and a small shed to work with—when you understand the principles of the great barn economy. You will see the lawn as your "hay field," and a small part of your garden (or lawn) as your grain and roots fields, planting a strip of oats (the best grain for browsing nibble-grazers like rabbits, sheep, and goats), and a row or two of carrots. You will set your hutches in the shed in such a way that you can pile the 400 to 500 pounds of dry clover and grass clippings from the lawn and another separate stack of the unthreshed oat stalks (with grain still in the heads) over the hutches. You will dig a pit someplace nearby to store the carrots in. You will set up a rain barrel to catch the runoff from the shed roof to water the animals with. If you do not have room in your shed for all your "hay," you will stack it out in the open, first setting a pole into the ground and piling the lawn "hay" around it, combing down an outside cover of long-stranded grass so the stack will shed water fairly well. On a small hay stack, the center pole stabilizes the pile as the hay settles around it, enabling you to stack the hay up higher and narrower than you otherwise could. The higher and narrower the stack, the better it will cure and the better it will shed water. You will provide a pit under the hutches to catch the manure and pieces of oat stalk that fall through the hutches as the rabbits nibble out the grains and chew on the stalks. The manure and straw is your fertilizer for the next crop.

What you have done is re-create, on a tiny scale, the agricultural economy of the great barn era. You are, as far as rabbit meat production is concerned, self-sufficient. Although it is difficult to convince rabbit owners brainwashed to the convenience of commercial pelleted feeds, you will need no other food except garden leavings (like a bit of lettuce occasionally), unless, of course, you are a lousy haymaker and can't get your protein, calcium, and vitamin-rich clover from the lawn cured properly. (See Making Hay in Chapter 10.)

If you will study the barn plan here (from a barn built in the late 1800s) you will see that you have copied it quite faithfully, as far as you can go with only rabbits. The great barns almost always had a cistern (the equivalent of your rain barrel) to take advantage of the vast roof expanse

A DAIRY BARN

(FROM THE ILLUSTRATED ANNUAL REGISTER OF RURAL AFFAIRS FOR 1870, ALBANY, N.Y. LUTHER ZUCKER AND SONS. NO. 16)

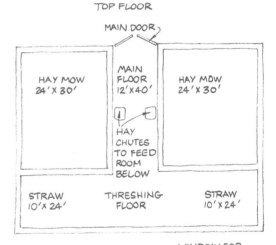

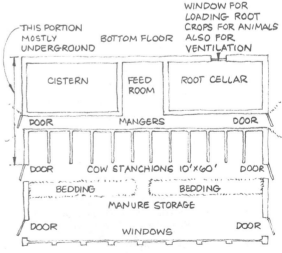

of the barns and because cisterns are usually cheaper than wells to install. The great barns always had their root cellars for the mangels and field beets that were a vital part of livestock fare in those days and still are in New Zealand, and may be again in this country. Your pit of carrots is your root cellar. Your pile of hay is your hay mow above your livestock, acting as insulation to keep the animals more comfortable just as it did in the big barns, and very handy to the rabbits' mangers right below it. Your stack of oats corresponds exactly to the big barn stacks. The difference here is in your advantage. The great barn farmers had to thresh their grain out. For you, the rabbits are going to do their own threshing. If you do want to thresh out a bit of grain, you will have a clean piece of plywood in your shed to lay on the floor, and with toy plastic bats as flails (for a small amount of grain these bats work adequately enough), you can mimic the great barn farmers flailing out their grain on the threshing floor.

In the process, you will have passed on to your children an experience and a cherished memory of how to fend for yourself—a lesson they will in their day pass on again in preparation for that time, sure to come, when the freedom to feed oneself may be tantamount to the freedom to *be* oneself.

Homestead-Size Great Barn

The size of your own version of the great barn will depend upon the number of acres and animals you decide to work with. The plan here was for a working dairy farm of maybe 80 acres—the kind of barn plan the Amish would use today although with a few more "modern" changes such as a windmill and well instead of a cistern, and the abandoning of the root storage bins in favor of more grain and/or silage. These big barns, like those of less specialized farms than in the above example, had room for horses and perhaps other animals. A typical modern

homesteader version of the great barn will be quite smaller, of course, but the hay mow will remain large in comparison to the animal quarters, and in fact its spaciousness may be even more important because the homesteader can't really afford a silo, may not desire a root cellar, and will probably not be able to afford a baler to compress the hay. (See Making Hay in Chapter 10, which discusses the economics favoring putting up hay "loose" rather than baled on very small homesteads.) Therefore, the part of the traditional barn that needs closest scrutiny from today's smallest farmers is the hay mow or loft. The characteristics you will want to copy as much as possible are: spaciousness, convenience of filling and feeding out of, and ventilation.

Spaciousness. This is achieved by either adding on another story to the upper barn structure, or by building a gambrel roof, which provides nearly as much space as a two-story superstructure.

For the small barn, and again I'll use my own for an example, the gambrel roof is the better choice because it gives you more room for the money spent and is easier to build with family labor. It is more difficult to go straight up with another story and then across with a slant roof. I had the half-trusses of the gambrel rafters put together at the lumberyard. After building the first-story animal quarters, we built the joists for the mow floor above and laid down some floorboards to walk on. Then we slid the gambrel half-trusses up on the floor, nailed them together at the peak with plywood gussets, and raised them with ropes and poles into position. The first two or three went up tensely and with difficulty, but after that the job was no harder than raising ordinary trusses into position. And it was certainly easier than framing up another story of perpendicular wall before adding on a roof.

Oddly enough, the angles and dimensions of gambrel roof planes are not standard. I

PUTTING A GAMBREL ROOF TOGETHER

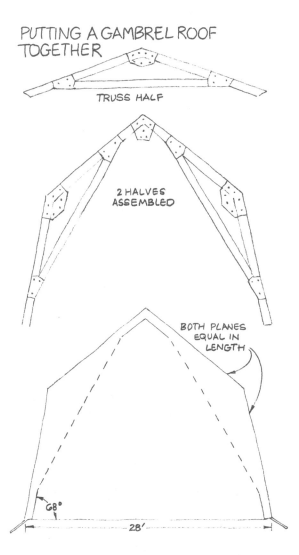

TRUSS HALF

2 HALVES ASSEMBLED

BOTH PLANES EQUAL IN LENGTH

68°

28'

measured scores of older barns before building mine and nearly all were different. So with one eye on a set of plans for a gambrel-roofed horse barn I had purchased, and the other eye on what looked like pleasing proportion to me, I settled on making both planes of the roof the same length, and the angle from floor level to the foot of the lower plane 68 degrees. This proportion pleases my eye on a barn 28 by 42 feet, especially after I added the "Dutch" overhang extensions at the edge of the roof line to direct water away from the wall.

Incidentally, it may be of some use to your planning to know that a mow 28 by 42 feet, with a gambrel roof as described, will hold enough *loose* (unbaled) hay, to feed the following menagerie for five winter months: a cow, a calf growing from 400 to 800 pounds, a horse, three ewes and their lambs, a ram, plus a small flock of hens and a pig that occasionally feeds on clover chaff from the hay. But the mow would have to be packed as full to the top as you could get it, and there would not be enough room left over to store all the loose straw you'd need to keep the animals bedded well for five months. Since I buy straw in bales and also buy some hay bales, I fill the mow about two-thirds with loose hay and the rest with baled hay and straw, and I do not use up all the hay in five months. If you store only bales, you need half or less of the space this mow provides to get you through five months with this number of animals.

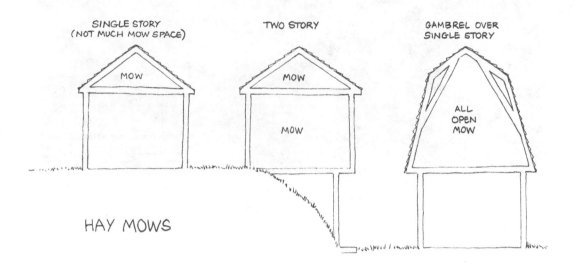

SINGLE STORY
(NOT MUCH MOW SPACE)

MOW

TWO STORY

MOW

MOW

GAMBREL OVER
SINGLE STORY

ALL
OPEN
MOW

HAY MOWS

Easy in, easy out. Earlier in this chapter I gave some cautionary observations on the use of bank barns in humid climates. If you solve the ventilation problems in the in-ground rooms of such barns, then a bank barn is the best answer to filling the mow in the most convenient way—especially a small barn the size of mine. In the great barns of yesterday's commercial farms, the huge high mows could not be filled by hand even when you could drive directly into the upper story. The hay was hoisted by rope and pulley and horsepower up to the hay rack, then over the mow area, and dropped into the mow. Of course, once in the mow, the hay was more easily fed to the animals by dropping it on the floor below. In the small bank barn where one can unload the pickup or wagon by hand on the same level as the mow, half of the work of that job is avoided. In my barn, *not* a bank barn, I must unload from ground level, *up* onto the mow floor, then as the level of hay in the mow rises, lift it up again. In a bank barn that entire first lift is eliminated.

In laying out the floor of your mow, remember to design the feed holes directly above the mangers. Not only does this make for convenience, but it saves hay. Every time you drop a forkful of dry hay, some of the nutritious leaves of the clover scatter out. If you can drop it directly in a manger, the animals can eat the chaff, not tramp it into the manure.

When filling the mow with hay, it is important to keep your hay holes (or bays as they are more properly called) uncovered. If you have extra room so you don't have to fill the whole mow, this is not a problem, but often a floor plan of a smaller barn requires a hay bay or two toward the middle of the mow, where it is very hard to keep from covering the bay when filling with loose hay. The traditional answer to this problem was to build a frame of boards around the bay as high as necessary, to keep the hole open. The frame was built in sections, or with large enough spaces in the side to shove hay down through it as the hay level receded. These frames were called hay chutes. Sometimes daydreaming boys up in the mow would fall through them.

Include in your barn plans a stairway, not just a vertical ladder, from the livestock area to the mow floor. You will go up and down between the floors many times, and those vertical ladders are harder—and more dangerous—to negotiate. You can usually squeeze a stairway in one end of the barn, between the first two floor joists, without taking up much room.

Ventilation. This is extremely important in hay mows. For the great barns, the danger was that hay, stowed away when not quite dry enough, would heat, catch on fire, and burn down the barn—which happened with tragic regularity. Good ventilation could lessen the instances of

Barn Painting

Here in central Ohio our great-great-grandfathers were bothered by hobgoblins. The hobgoblins followed them over from Germany where they were known to make cows go dry, to make sows eat their young, and ewes reject their lambs, and all sorts of other mischief. If the hobgoblins pester you, you must paint witch doors on your barn. With white paint you outline archways on the barn siding to look like real door openings. Hobgoblins are smart about some things, but dumb about fake doors. In semi-darkness, they will try to fly through the "opening." If the collision doesn't break their necks, it discourages them from misdeeds for the rest of that night, anyhow. And even if you aren't bothered by hobgoblins, those white arches accentuate and break up the mass of red barn siding in a most delightfully pleasant way.

Folklorists have argued for years over whether superstition motivated the hex signs on Pennsylvania Dutch barns, too and have concluded that they were put on "just for pretty." Not all the old farmers of these parts would agree with that, but the designs *are* pretty. Put one on your barn and perpetuate a nice custom. And, well, if there are any hobgoblins around . . .

Old Charlie Wentz, now gone from our county, had the likeness of his state champion Belgian stallion painted on his barn. Another nice decorative touch. But neighbors said Charlie hoped that if his mares saw the champion every time they went in and out of the barn, the sight might somehow influence them to birth other champions.

fire. Also, if the hay was not quite dry enough, but not so wet as to catch on fire, good ventilation helped it to dry without getting moldy. Since hay, like wood, will reabsorb moisture in humid weather, good ventilation will also let this reabsorption pass without harm to the hay.

The cupola was and is the most effective ventilator for a hay mow; those little turrets up on the roof aren't there "just for pretty." Eric Sloane, in his *Age of Barns* (Funk & Wagnalls, New York, 1966) advances the theory that some farmers favored cupolas not only for ventilation but also for lightning protection. A current

notion 100 years ago was that the heat of fresh hay curing in a mow attracted lightning, and so farmers who scoffed at the "heathenish belief" in lightning rods built cupolas instead. Cupolas make good ventilators because they are located in the right place: heat *rises.* But they can only work well if there are vents in the barn walls for air to enter. Windows that open in the gable ends or the long narrow slits in stone barns or the decorative grillwork in brick barns all serve that purpose. The big upper-story doors through which hay is loaded into some barns can also be left open in fair weather during the period the hay is curing to let air in.

Where hard driving snow is not a normal occurrence, the space between the rafters under the eaves can be left open to provide ventilation. Where the two planes meet on a gambrel roof barn, an opening can be left for ventilation. Snow will enter this crack, but only twice in ten years have I had to shovel snow out because it blew in too heavily. I also left an ample opening at the peak of the roof on both gable ends of my barn. Snow occasionally sifts in these openings, too, but when excessive, I can quickly sweep it out the hay doors below.

For the very small farm, mow ventilation is more important than even in the great barns. The reason is that the homesteader generally makes only a small amount of hay at any one time. I have learned that with good ventilation, I can spread a small amount of only half-cured hay in the mow—say a pickup truck load—and it will dry the rest of the way without spoiling or generating excessive heat. This greatly enhances my ability to make high-quality hay. I can bring it into the barn much sooner, thus escaping both possible rain damage and sun damage that might result if the hay were left in the field the "proper" length of time. (See Making Hay in Chapter 10.)

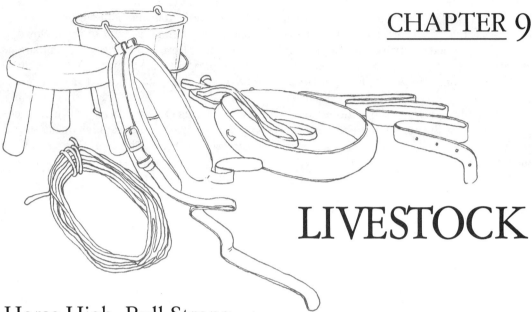

CHAPTER 9

LIVESTOCK

Horse High, Bull Strong, and Hog Tight

Country folk cringe whenever they see animals appear in the backyards of their new, eager, back-to-the-land neighbors. Experience has taught them that those animals will inevitably escape their confines, leaving paths of destruction wherever they roam. Reason? Beginners underestimate the importance of a good fence and/or do not know how to build one. The mistake can be more critical than just a ruined garden. Consider what might happen if your cow gets out on the highway. It could cause an accident.

Before you acquire livestock, build a fence that will be, as the old saying goes, "horse high, bull strong, and hog tight"—even if you don't intend to have a horse, bull, or hog. Stone fences and board fences are fine for small areas, but in most cases a wire fence is the most economical for a large area that is more than ¼ acre. A fence of three or more strands of barbed wire might serve the purpose out on the wide expanses of a lone prairie, but even with one or more of the wires electrified, this kind of fence is not very satisfactory for the small garden

A sturdy new wire fence provides the security; the old Virginia zigzag wooden one furnishes the beauty.

328 ·

Stopping Fence Jumpers

Farmers used to fashion wooden pokes for cattle that would prevent them from jumping over a fence or even leaning over for grass on the other side, thereby mashing down the fence. But it's much better to keep a good strong fence tight and high and topped by a strand of barbed wire.

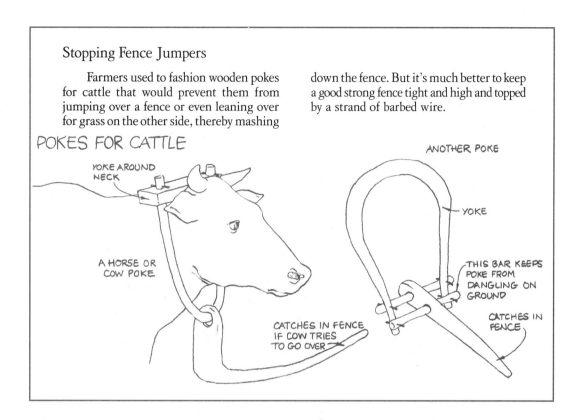

POKES FOR CATTLE

YOKE AROUND NECK

A HORSE OR COW POKE

CATCHES IN FENCE IF COW TRIES TO GO OVER

ANOTHER POKE

YOKE

THIS BAR KEEPS POKE FROM DANGLING ON GROUND

CATCHES IN FENCE

farmer—cows get their udders torn up on such fences and horses have been known to tangle in them and kill themselves. Little electric fences, especially the new kind that resemble netting, are excellent for temporary fences, as when dividing a pasture for rotational grazing, but they are not at all adequate for permanent fencing, especially boundary line fences. Take the advice of one who has chased cows for miles and miles: flimsy electric fences will let you down, I don't care how well you install them.

There are only two kinds of wire fence you should consider: a woven wire fence of the right gauge; or a four to five-strand high-tensile electrified fence—often called New Zealand fence (see High-Tensile Electric Fence in this chapter). The main advantage of New Zealand fence is that it is easier to stretch and costs a little less than woven wire. However, corner and end posts must be installed just as solidly for one as for the other since both kinds of fences must be stretched very tight. Setting and bracing the corner and end posts is half the labor, so my opinion is that except on very uneven rough ground, woven wire is the better choice. That's because, no matter what the salesman says, an electric fence will let you down, and the chances that it will do so increase proportionately to your distance away from home at the time.

In choosing woven wire fence, first consider which animals you are going to fence. If you are sure you are not going to raise horses or cows, you can install the standard 35 or 39-inch-high fence. But the difference in price between that and the standard 45 or 47-inch

Woven wire fence.

High-tensile electrified fence.

fence is about a dollar a rod, sometimes less. Occasionally good-quality 6-inch stay, 39-inch fence costs more than good-quality 12-inch stay, 47-inch fence. So you might as well put in the 47-inch and be done with it.

I notice with great alarm that the latest Montgomery Ward farm catalog carries an "extra heavyweight" standard 47-inch fence, only the kind with 10-gauge top and bottom wires and 12½-gauge line and stay wires. For the work you will put into installing the fence, a heavier gauge is much more desirable. Top and bottom wires should be 9-gauge (the smaller the number the thicker the gauge in wire) and line and stay wires no thinner than 11-gauge. This weight of fence in the 12-stay size (12 inches between vertical wires rather than 6 inches) is cheaper than the 10-gauge top and 12½-gauge line in 6-inch stay size, and a better buy in my experience. The 9/11-gauge fence in 6-inch stay is the stoutest and longest-lasting fence generally available today, but quite expensive. Where you intend to keep sheep, 6-inch stay wire is questionable anyway, since sheep will get their heads caught in it and, being too stupid to back out, starve to death if not found in time.

At farm sales and in the want ads of country newspapers, used woven wire is often offered. If it is still comparatively free of rust, you can save lots of money this way. Bend a strand of the wire back and forth. If it breaks fairly easily, the fence is too old. Sometimes older fence is better than new because the best quality had more copper in it than fences do today, and 9-gauge wire was the rule, not the exception. I've been able to buy forty rods of fence of *all* 9-gauge wire at a fraction of what new 9/11 costs. If you're buying new wire, go to a farm supply store and pick up the wire yourself to save money. For 9/11 wire in 12-inch stay, expect to pay around $100 for a twenty-rod roll (330 feet), although I believe some are priced as low as $88 a roll.

Line Posts, Corner Posts, and End Posts

Next you must choose your posts. Here is where a woodlot can prove its profitability. A treated end post or corner post from a farm store, 8 inches or more in diameter, can cost $12 or more, and line posts 4 to 5 inches in diameter cost more than $3 each. Steel posts of the quality and size to fit a 47-inch fence cost more than $3, too. The table Wood for Long-Lasting Fence Posts (see next page) lists woods that can be taken straight from the woodlot without needing a preservative treatment. These make longer-lasting fence posts than what you can buy.

Other woods make fairly good rot-resistant posts—sassafras, cypress, Cascara buckthorn in the Pacific Northwest, honey locust (but not

Fence Row Trees for Posts

Make use of fence row trees for posts, especially end posts, whenever possible. Timber buyers aren't going to buy fence row trees anyway. Just remember not to try to cut that wood up into firewood later on, as it will no doubt be full of nails and old fence. Trees grow right over wire wrapped around them, and, in young trees, quite rapidly. Trees will also grow out over electric fence insulators nailed to them, or force the insulator off the nail. To forestall that development as long as possible, use an extra long nail and attach the insulator so that it can slip on the nail. Don't drive it tight against the bark. Place boards between wire and tree trunk when attaching fence to trees. To have your cake and eat it too, prune fence row trees so they grow at least an 8-foot log *above* the height of the fence, safe from wire and nails.

One of the oft-repeated "lazy farmer" stories of our neighborhood tells of the fellow who stretched a fence to a tree. He

finished stapling the fence to the line posts, but was called away to matters of great importance at his local tavern. One thing led to another, planting season, harvesting, more business at the tavern, and the fence stretchers were forgotten. Five years later when there was no putting off building more fence, he searched high and low for the stretchers. When at last he found them, the tree had already gobbled up the chain and was starting in on the ratchet.

Wood for Long-Lasting Fence Posts	
Wood	**Life (years)**
Osage orange	30
Black locust	25
Catalpa	25
Northern white cedar	20
Red cedar	20
Bur oak	15
Red mulberry	15
White oak	12

nearly as good as black locust), and of course chestnut, now all but gone. A good preservative treatment adds a few years of life to any fence post, but it is a troublesome job to do in quantity.

The butt ends of used utility poles make excellent corner posts. Sometimes you have to saw off the lower end if it's beginning to rot, but utility companies usually replace their poles when there is still plenty of life in them. Discarded railroad ties suit the purpose fairly well, too, if they are still in good condition.

Covering the top of a corner post with tin or any rain shield will lengthen its life. At least saw the top at a slight angle so water runs off rather than soaks in.

Line posts ought to be approximately 5 inches in diameter. I use that circumlocution because a *round* line post of 4 to 5 inches—what you usually buy—indicates a young tree without much heartwood. A really good line post ought to be split out of a larger log. Instead of being round, it will be triangular in cross section.

Line posts for woven wire should be about 15 feet apart. Power augers for digging the holes are supposed to go fast and easy, but you've got to have $300 to $700 to spare. I use a hinge-type, hand-operated digger or, in our heavy clay soils, an ancient "spud" with a cylindrical blade. It is nearly 100 years old and still in perfect working order because there is nothing on it to break. I like to alternate a wood post

with a steel post because the latter drive in much faster, while I can take up any slack in a fence by stapling it around the sides of the wood posts. To drive steel posts you can buy or make a steel tube with a solid welded steel plug at one end. (You can buy used steel posts at farm sales.) The tube slides over the post and by briskly socking it down against the top of the post several times, the post goes quickly into the ground. In stony areas, such as in New England, cedar posts with sharpened ends are driven into the ground with a heavy wood mallet.

Posts should measure about 5 feet above the ground, leaving enough room for a strand

---

Prying Posts

To lift old posts out of the ground, avoid getting a hernia by using a pry rod and a short stay chain. First loosen the post by wiggling it back and forth. Then place your pry (a strong pole about 8 feet long, or, in a pinch, a steel fence post) on the ground next to the post so that it's perpendicular to the post. Wrap the short chain around it, cross the chain over and wrap it as tightly as you can around the post. Now lift up on the pry.

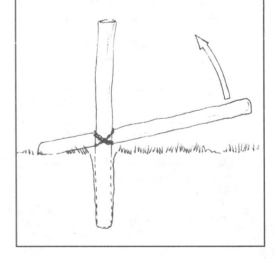

of barbed wire or electric fence to be attached above the woven wire. The end and corner posts should be sunk 3½ feet in the ground— altogether requiring an 8½-foot post, though you can squeak by with an 8-footer. If the post is set that deeply in the soil, and the soil tamped well around it from the bottom of the hole up, you will not need gravel or concrete around the post to make it solid. It's best, though, to set the corner posts and end posts a couple of months ahead of stretching the fence, so that they have time to settle firmly in the soil.

Line posts need to sit 2½ feet in the ground, so they need to be 7 to 7½ feet long. Keep the line as straight as possible between end posts by eyeing up each post from behind one end post to the other. If a post is out of line even a little, the fence might drag on it in the stretching.

End posts need to be braced. Brace designs vary with locality. Two good designs are the

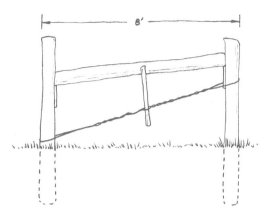

triangular brace and the double (or sometimes triple) post brace. In the first design, a post about half the length of the end post is braced against the end post on the diagonal, the bottom of the brace resting on a flat rock, the top notched into the end post. Then a double wire

is wrapped around the middle of the brace and the foot of the end post and twisted tight.

The second design, more expensive but better in my opinion, consists of a second post, 8 feet out from the end post, with a brace between them near the tops of both posts, but slanted back just a bit lower on the end post. Then a double strand of 9-gauge wire around the top of the brace post and the bottom of the end post is twisted tight with a stick that is then held against the brace to keep it from untwisting.

Stretching Woven Wire

To stretch woven wire you need a pair of chain ratchet fence stretchers (one is not usually sufficient for a heavyweight livestock fence) with two short chains that go with each, and a stretcher bar that fastens to the fence to give a solid place from which to pull evenly. One of the short chains fastens the stretcher to the end post and the other connects the stretcher bar to the ratchet of the stretcher. A stretcher kit contains all five of the necessary tools and costs about $200 new from farm supply stores. In most farming areas, you can borrow one. Or, now that building woven wire fences is becoming a lost art, you can buy an old kit at a farm sale or from a farmer at very low cost. I paid $35 for mine.

CHAIN RATCHET FENCE STRETCHER

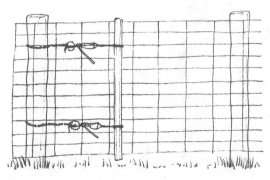

Unroll the wire, bottom end next to the posts and lay it flat on the ground. Attach the far end to the end post by wrapping it around the post and twisting each strand around itself on the inside of the post. Next, at the end post you will be stretching from, attach the stretchers to the end post, one near the top, the other near the bottom. Bolt the bar to the fence about even with the brace post, leaving approximately 5 feet of space to pull the fence—or the length of the chains connecting the bar to the ratchets. On the end post side of the stretcher bar, leave a "tail" of fence long enough to be wrapped around the end post and wired to itself after the stretching is complete. After you have done this once, you will know about where to bolt the stretcher bar, and until you do it once, the written word can be of only limited help.

Begin ratcheting up the fence after fitting the chains from the bar into the ratchet teeth. Bring both top and bottom of the fence along at the same time, working one stretcher a few pumps, then the other. As the fence tightens, the stretchers come up to a horizontal position and are easier to operate. As the fence begins to rise off the ground from the tightening, the tension will be enormous until the fence comes up to a vertical position. To alleviate this tension, walk along the fenceline and pull the fence up to about half vertical and attach it to the posts with short pieces of wire or twine every 50 feet or so. Then tighten some more. The fence will soon come vertical against the posts and you can take off the wire or twine. Keep checking along the fence as you tighten to make sure the fence is not catching on the posts. You almost need two people when stretching so that all goes smoothly.

If you have positioned the stretchers and bar correctly, the fence will be tight enough before you come to the end of your chain. It is only by experience that you know when the fence is tight. The little crooks in the horizontal wires should straighten about halfway—certainly no more. When tight, the fence will

STRETCHING A WIRE FENCE

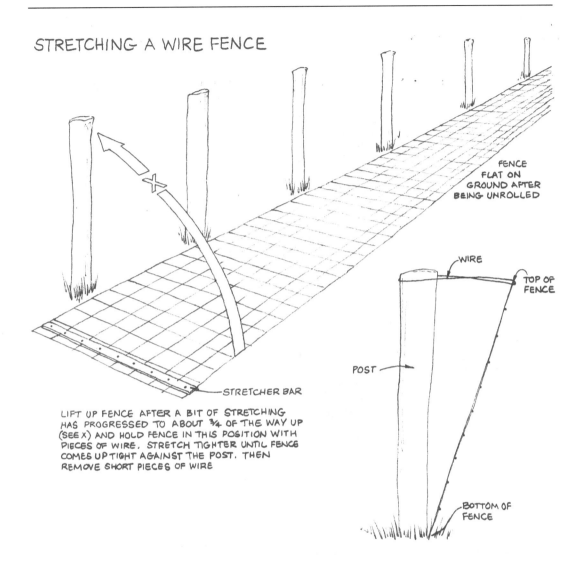

FENCE FLAT ON GROUND AFTER BEING UNROLLED

STRETCHER BAR

LIFT UP FENCE AFTER A BIT OF STRETCHING HAS PROGRESSED TO ABOUT ¾ OF THE WAY UP (SEE X) AND HOLD FENCE IN THIS POSITION WITH PIECES OF WIRE. STRETCH TIGHTER UNTIL FENCE COMES UP TIGHT AGAINST THE POST. THEN REMOVE SHORT PIECES OF WIRE

WIRE

TOP OF FENCE

POST

BOTTOM OF FENCE

have a vertical rigidity to it almost as if it were welded wire. If the line of fence traverses uneven ground, especially dips, you can't tighten it all the way with the stretchers because the fence will in the stretching rise above dips in the terrain and must be pulled down in the low spots and attached to the posts. If the fence is really tight, you won't be able to pull it down in the low spots. Semitight, you can pull it down, and the pulling down will complete the

tightening. If not enclosing hogs, you can leave the bottom wire a few inches above the ground to inhibit rusting.

When experimentation indicates the fence is tight enough, wrap the "tail" around the end post and wire each strand to itself on the inside of the post as you did at the other end. Then staple top and bottom wire and one or two equidistant middle ones at each post. (Staple all the strands at the end post.) If using steel or

Tightening Wire Solo

Old sagging fence can be tightened enough to last a few more years with several different kinds of one-person fence stretchers or tighteners, all available from farm supply stores. One simple device is little more than a strong wooden or steel handle of about 2 feet in length, with a slot or catch about 4 inches back from the end of it that will hold a strand of wire without slipping. You catch the wire in the slot, place the handle end against the end post, and by prying with the long end of the handle, you can lever a single strand amazingly tight. These stretchers are made especially for barbed wire, but will work fairly well to draw up slack even in a woven wire fence, if you pull on one horizontal strand at a time.

You can make one of these tighteners for barbed wire with a 20-inch length of 2 by 2-inch oak, shaved to a nice hand grip at one end. A narrow slot at the other end, through which the barbs of barbed wire will not slide, will serve as a catch, although at times the handle will twist in your hand as

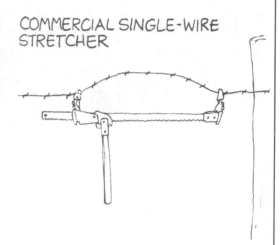

COMMERCIAL SINGLE-WIRE STRETCHER

you pry and the wire will slip out. With smooth wire, I just loop it around the far end of the pry rod, twist it back on itself, and then pry against the end post.

Another method for barbed wire is to bolt an old mower blade guard onto the handle. The slot in the guard through which the blade normally slides is narrow enough so the barbs on the barbed wire can't slide through. If the handle is curved to the curve of the guard, it won't twist so much in your hand when prying. To grip smooth or barbed wire anyplace along the line, you need to buy wire grips, or buy grips and handle already put together as a one-person stretcher mentioned above.

There are other small mechanical stretchers, or stretcher-splicers as they are called, which fasten to a strand of wire anywhere along the fence. By cranking or operating a lever, you can then pull the sagging line together, cut the extra wire, and resplice it tight. Do this on every other horizontal strand of a woven wire fence, about every 100 feet along the fence, to rejuvenate it.

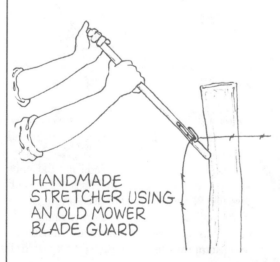

HANDMADE STRETCHER USING AN OLD MOWER BLADE GUARD

fiberglass posts, attach the fence with wire clips. When all is finished, release the stretchers.

One of the handiest fencing tools you can own costs less than a dollar. Called a wire splicer, this little 5-inch piece of steel is so shaped that it will bend a wire very tightly around another wire, even when you have only a short length of wire to bend. It is used in splicing two wires together, as when splicing one roll of fencing to the next, or to bend the wires at the end of a roll tightly around themselves when attaching the roll to the end posts.

WIRE
SPLICER

Finishing It Off

Traditionally a strand of barbed wire is stretched above the woven wire fence. Otherwise, horses and cows will simply bend the fence down while reaching over it for some morsel. Barbed wire is easy to stretch, but dangerous. If it breaks in your hand—I've seen it happen—it can mean a very nasty injury. Barbed wire in a roll will tend to twist when it is unreeled and pulled. Wear heavy gloves. What is called a "one-man wire stretcher" works fine to stretch barbed wire. A farm supply catalog like Nasco Farm & Ranch (901 Janesville Ave., Fort Atkinson, WI 53538) has them.

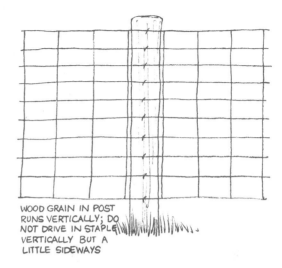

WOOD GRAIN IN POST
RUNS VERTICALLY; DO
NOT DRIVE IN STAPLE
VERTICALLY BUT A
LITTLE SIDEWAYS

If you really want to keep horses from ruining a fence, put the top barbed wire on insulators and electrify it. If this electric fence lets you down, you still have the security of the fence and the barb to keep the animals where they belong.

In stapling fence to posts, don't hammer the staple in a perfectly vertical position, because both prongs will penetrate the same grain of the wood and it will more easily work loose. Cock the staple sideways a bit so that each prong goes into a different grain. Do not pound the staple too hard against the wire, especially barbed wire, as the subsequent dent and crease in the wire sets up conditions for a break years later.

Fence building is slow, patient work. But done right, your fence may very well last the rest of your life.

High-Tensile Electric Fence

High-tensile steel wire fence, often called New Zealand fence, consists of individual strands of smooth spring steel wire, some or all of which are usually electrified, and therefore are strung on insulators or clipped to fiberglass posts. High-tensile wire is easier to install than woven wire and much safer to handle than

barbed wire. It is cheaper per foot than new woven wire, but the gap tends to narrow as more and better modifications and gadgets are added to the accessories.

End posts must be set as solidly as for woven wire—each strand of the wire should be stretched, according to general directions, to at least 250 pounds of tension. Stretching is accomplished by turning reel tighteners (called strainers), installed permanently at the end post on each strand. Experience will teach you how tightly to stretch the wire, but you can buy a gadget to measure 250 pounds or more, if you wish. The wire should be tight enough so it doesn't give more than a bit when a cow or sheep pushes against it. In turning the tighteners, much judgment is required if the fence stretches across uneven ground. If you turn the strainers too much, the fence will be too tight to pull down or up to posts on unlevel terrain. Stretch it a bit and check. It is nice to have a helper when building fence.

Don't try to unroll the reel of wire as you would woven wire. High-tensile wire is too springy. Manufacturers have various accessories to allow you to unwind the wire from a reel as you would from a fishing reel. Without such accessories, lay the spool flat on the ground, sit on the edge of it, and slowly pay out a loop at a time while your helper threads it through the insulators and pulls it on down the line.

You can't bend the wire easily because of its springiness. Special connectors are sold with high-tensile wire for making splices, and users say they are well worth the money.

Energizers for high-tensile wire generate higher voltage than ordinary electric fence chargers, but with low impedance. Thus the lines will not short out as easily as conventional electric fences, but the jolt will not harm you or your animals. On the other hand, neither you nor they are apt to forget it soon, either.

But all electric fencing, no matter how highly touted, requires regular maintenance checks. If the line does short out, animals have an uncanny way of finding out, usually in less than a week. On boundary fences, especially along roads, woven wire is better insurance.

Although they are fairly expensive, solar-powered energizers are now available for those fields far from regular electric outlets. Other modifications and new ideas are being incorporated into high-tensile fencing every year. When you buy the fence, you can get detailed instructions on the most up-to-date methods and accessories. Premier Fence Systems (Box 89, Washington, IA 52353) sells a 50-page manual. Check the ads in farm magazines, especially

A six-battery charger for an electric fence (left). It can also be powered by this solar panel (top).

magazines for small farmers like *New Farm* (Rodale Press) for a dealership near you. Many suppliers also carry Flexinet or other kinds of electric "twine" for temporary fencing.

An Easy Practical Farm Gate

Hundreds of gate designs have been devised to ease the passage in and out of fields and barnyards. Almost all of them depend on hinges to carry the weight of the gate swinging open or closed. The light aluminum gates today are the nicest but they carry a nice price tag, too. And even these will eventually suffer from the weakness of all large hinged gates—the weight is too great for the hinges. Even with a diagonal brace through the gate and up to the post above the hinge, these gates eventually sag and drag on the ground. To prevent the sagging, an enormously sturdy and solid hinge post must be set in the ground.

The simple board gate shown here avoids the problem and expense. To open, the gate is slid back on its bar hinge to about halfway, where it balances on the bar. Note that it can only open one way. Even if made of heavy boards

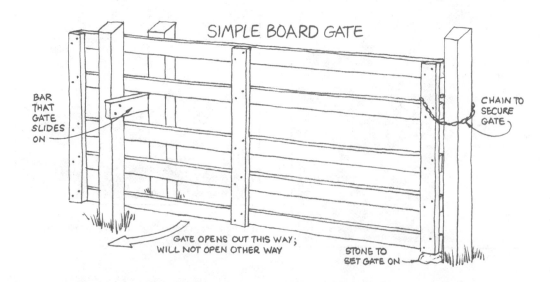

SIMPLE BOARD GATE

BAR THAT GATE SLIDES ON

CHAIN TO SECURE GATE

GATE OPENS OUT THIS WAY; WILL NOT OPEN OTHER WAY

STONE TO SET GATE ON

VARIATION ON BOARD GATE

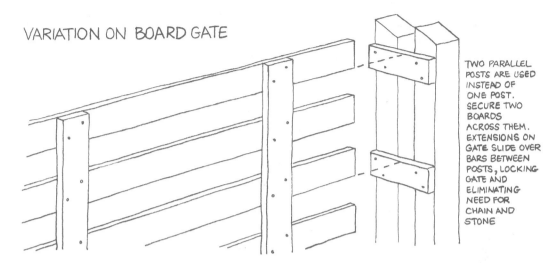

TWO PARALLEL POSTS ARE USED INSTEAD OF ONE POST. SECURE TWO BOARDS ACROSS THEM. EXTENSIONS ON GATE SLIDE OVER BARS BETWEEN POSTS, LOCKING GATE AND ELIMINATING NEED FOR CHAIN AND STONE

like oak, the gate is very easy to lift, open or closed. If grease is smeared on the slide bar occasionally, even a child can open it. The most durable wood is rough-cut hardwood from a sawmill. Red oak, being the longer lasting of commonly available cheaper woods, is preferred around where I live. If using softwoods like pine from the lumberyard, paint the gate after it has been left out to dry for a year. Most of the cheaper pine grades of lumber are now so inferior, they will not last ten years without protection. Some of the new penetrating stains are good, too, but they're somewhat expensive for live-stock gates. When using hardwoods, try to buy freshly sawed green wood, especially if the wood is oak, and make the gates right away. After the wood has dried, it is hard to nail.

The gate should be about 48 inches tall, made with five horizontal 1 by 6-inch boards. Nail the boards close together (3 inches) at the bottom if little pigs and lambs are to be penned. The gap between the boards can gradually widen to about 10 inches between the top two, as in the drawing. Uprights holding the boards together should be spaced 4 to 6 feet apart. Each juncture of upright and vertical should receive four 7-penny nails, or 8-penny if 1-inch-thick rough-sawn lumber is being used. Clinch each nail over well on the other side.

Set the gate between the two posts where the slide bar will be attached, raise the gate about 3 inches off the ground, and block it. Insert the slide bar under the second board from the top of the gate and nail it to the two posts.

Place a brick or flat stone on the ground by the single post to which the gate is fastened so the bottom board does not rest on the earth and begin rotting. To secure the gate at this end, a simple chain beats all the fancy catches and bars ever invented. Use a short length of light chain with a spring-loaded catch hook on the end—like the ones on lead ropes for horses. Bathe the chain and hook in used oil before putting them to use so they won't rust so fast.

If you use two posts at the closure of the gate, instead of the one I've just described, both the chain and the stone the gate rests on when closed can be eliminated. The two posts are set parallel to each other, hardly more than 3 inches apart. Nail two short pieces of board across them, one near the top and the other a little below the middle, both boards to coincide with the top and middle horizontal boards of the gate. The gate's upright at the end next to the closing posts is nailed to the horizontal boards *not* at the ends, but back from the ends about a foot. Thus the ends of the top and middle boards will slide right on the short boards between the two posts, closing the gate solidly and at the same time raising it off the ground.

Hurdle Gates from Saplings

Where woodland is growing up with vigorous second-growth saplings, you'll need to thin out many of the young trees, or they will die of their own accord when about 4 inches in diameter. These straight "sprouts," as woodsmen call them, can be split lengthwise and the halves used for making cheap but adequate fencing. The ones I make, of ash, last about eight years.

To make a gate of saplings, lay out three or four split halves (split them out with wedges) on the ground, flat side up, then place the uprights on the ends of the horizontals, about 4 feet apart, flat side down; then nail. You can add diagonal braces if the sprouts you are using are flimsy or if your uprights are more than 4 feet apart.

A gate of this kind will last much longer if you notch slots in the end uprights and sharpen the horizontal saplings so they fit tight in the holes, rather than relying totally on nails. *If you are very careful about kickback of the chain saw,* you can notch the slots with this saw. Don't

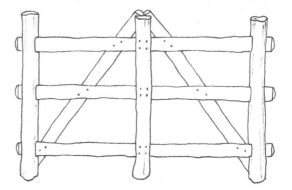

GATE MADE FROM SPLIT SAPLINGS NOTCHED AT ENDS WITH CHAIN SAW

Unsecured gates over creeks are more likely to be swept open than crashed by high waters, thereby staying intact.

try to go straight in with the nose of the saw, but hold it at about a 45-degree angle to the sapling. The slot will be bigger on the flat inside of the upright and smaller on the rounded outside, which is just what you want for driving the sharpened horizontal into the slot.

This type of gate is very much like the old English hurdle bygone shepherds used for penning their flocks temporarily, the uprights sharpened and stuck into the ground. I've never found this use of the hurdle practical on my place. Rather, I use them as a board gate or fence for cows, sheep, and large lambs (little ones can get right through my sapling fences). Since the gates are cheap and expendable, I use them mostly for floodgates across the creek, where the battering of ice, flood water, and driftwood makes mincemeat of gates in a few years, no matter how you make them.

Many elaborate designs for floodgates have evolved over the years to keep a permanent fence over a creek from being destroyed by high water and flotsam, but my experience is that the water humbles all of them, either wrecking the gates themselves in time, or washing the soil away from solidly set posts from which the gates are hung. After years of experimenting, I've found the simplest, flimsiest fence over a creek to be the best. I set the gates right in the water, well wired to posts at the bank but barely hooked to a post or two in the creek bed—just enough to fool the livestock (especially horses and sheep), which do not like wading in the water anyway. When high water comes, it sweeps the gates aside rather than smashing them to pieces, and when the water goes back down, I set the gates back across the current again. In winter I take them down completely to save them from the battering-ram force of floating ice, wood, and other debris.

Stanchions

Humans have invented many ways to restrain animals for milking, cleaning, and doctor-

SHEPHERD'S CROOK

ing. The oldest stanchion still in use is the shepherd's crook, strange as that may sound. It was the first device by which humans caught and held livestock by the neck. If you hold a sheep's head back so that its nose points up into the air a bit, the sheep is slightly paralyzed—it will stand more or less still. It didn't take ancient herdsmen long to figure out that with a long stick curved into a crook at one end, they could reach out and hook a sheep and hold it until they got close enough to grab it. Moderns are apt to think that the crook in a cane is for the convenience of the hand, but that was a later thought. Every time I see a bishop dressed in all his glory and holding his dazzling bejeweled crosier, I have to smile. The shepherd's crook has come a long, long way. You can still buy them—for hooking sheep by the neck. If you aren't as quick on your feet as you once were, a crook is handy.

The most amazing recent tool is a cage for sheep called a squeeze chute or a squeeze-and-tilt chute. A sheep is clamped in it helpless, and can be turned on either side or completely upside down so you can work on its hooves at your ease. Since they cost from $300 to more than $500, squeeze chutes are hardly economical for the small, noncommercial shepherd, but they certainly are handy. Of course, any reasonably

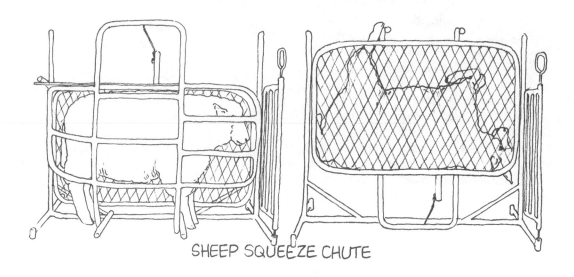

SHEEP SQUEEZE CHUTE

strong, healthy human can upend any smaller breed of sheep and hold the animal on its butt handily while trimming hooves, worming, or shearing. It is only now that we are breeding sheep larger and larger that we need mechanical restraints similar to what veterinarians need for cows and horses. And there is a good argument to show that the smaller, thriftier sheep bring in as much money as the large ones that eat grain like steers.

Holding an animal that is stronger than a human requires, of course, something strong. And so the stanchion as we know it today came into being for cows, goats, and perhaps sheep where the latter are milked for human food. When Whittier wrote in "Snowbound," "Impatient down the stanchion rows, / The cattle shake their walnut bows," he was describing the forerunner of today's neck yoke stanchion, although heaven knows we have "advanced" to the point where only the richest sheik could afford to make it out of walnut, the right wood for the job.

Cow Stanchions

The modern dairy stanchion, alas becoming obsolete itself, is the culmination of centu-

ries of trial and error in stanchion design. What was always desired was a neck yoke that would keep the animal from moving backward and forward too much, or sideways too much, in either case forcing the cow to drop manure in the gutter behind herself and not all over the immediate area. But it would also allow the cow the freedom of moving her head up and down enough so she could lie down. The modern dairy stanchion is flexible yet restraining enough to accomplish both ends adequately. But even in the dairy stanchion, and certainly in cruder wooden stanchions such as those I describe below, the cow should not remain for long periods of time without being freed so she can move around, exercise, lick herself, and so forth.

Because most of the modern dairy milking "parlors" dispense with stanchions altogether, the homesteader can easily find used ones in good shape hanging neglected in old barns, or for sale at farm auctions. My next-door neighbor fixed one up for his cow that serves the purpose admirably. He just set two wood posts in the ground and attached the stanchion to them, sides, top and bottom, with gates around to form a stall.

If you wish to go all the way with a stanchion stall like the ones in commercial stan-

chion height, 4½ feet; width of stanchion when closed on cow's neck, 7 to 9 inches depending on size of cow; manger, about 2½ feet wide. If you have room, the passageway in front of the manger can be 3 feet or whatever is convenient for you. I didn't have room for such a passageway, and with only two cows I did not really need one. I step up into the manger where it opens on my grain room and walk in if I need to carry grain down to the stanchions. I drop in hay from overhead.

The tendency now is to move away from stanchion-type neck holds to chains that afford the cow more freedom. Farm magazines present this trend as if it were something new, but chain ties were commonly used 100 years ago and for the same reason: to give cows that are not turned out every day more freedom of movement. The simplest of the traditional chain ties is a Y-shaped chain, the two arms of which fit around the cow's neck and join with a spring snap as on a horse's lead rope, with the tail of the Y attached to a large iron ring slipped over a round stanchion or manger post. The ring can slip up and down the post to give the cow lots of vertical head movement, and the length of chain allows her to move her body about a bit, lie down easily, and lick herself.

A simple stanchion just for holding the cow while milking can be made with a 2 × 4 pivoting on a bolt at the bottom of the manger

chion barns, you can put a gutter behind the place where the cow stands, concrete the floor, fence in the stanchion with side rails of steel or wood, and build a manger in front of the stanchion. Dimensions should approximate those in the drawing below. If you have a big Holstein cow, the length of the stall from manger to gutter should be 5 feet; otherwise, dimensions are: gutter, 2 feet wide, about 1 foot deep; cow's platform, 4½ feet long, about 4 feet wide; stan-

STANCHION STALL FOR COW

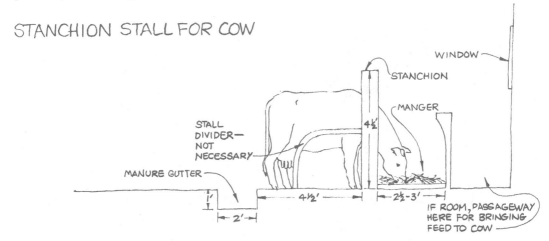

STALL DIVIDER— NOT NECESSARY

MANURE GUTTER

WINDOW

STANCHION

MANGER

4½'

1'

2'

4½'

2½-3'

IF ROOM, PASSAGEWAY HERE FOR BRINGING FEED TO COW

against a fixed upright post of the manger. On mine, the movable bar fits between double frame boards at top and bottom of the manger to hold it in position. When I push it against the cow's neck to hold her, I slip a bolt through holes in the top double frame boards to hold it. Pull out the bolt, and the bar falls back against its rest. Very simple and quite adequate. But a cow should not be kept in such a stanchion for very long, say overnight, because she can't lie down.

After cows get used to putting their heads into the manger to eat, it is not much trouble training them to the stanchion. The first time, I lure them into position with a choice bit of grain and quickly push the stanchion bar closed. Since it takes longer to get an older cow to tolerate having a chain or bar against her neck, it pays to tame your animals well from birth.

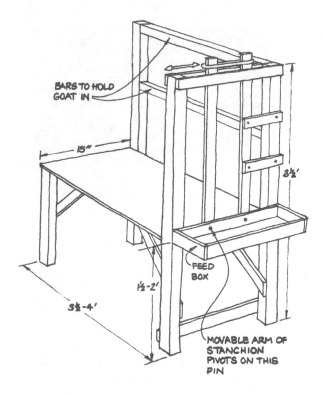

Goat Stanchions

Goat stanchions or milking stands can be smaller versions of cow stanchions. The closed

goat stanchion should allow 4 inches of neck space. The stanchion itself should be about 3½ feet tall. Make the platform the goat stands on 15 inches wide and about 3½ to 4 feet long— the length is not critical. The platform should be about 1½ to 2 feet off the ground. You don't need a ramp or step up to the platform—goats can jump much higher than that and love to. If the side of the platform opposite the side you milk from is not against a wall, build some kind of gate or bars to hold the goat in.

The "keyhole" stanchion is a very good restraint for goats, especially when used at their hay mangers because it keeps the animals from wasting hay. The keyhole stanchion has no moving parts, and it forms the side of the manger from which the goats eat. It has an 8-inch diameter hole at the top and a 4-inch-wide slit running down from the hole to the bottom of

KEYHOLE STANCHION

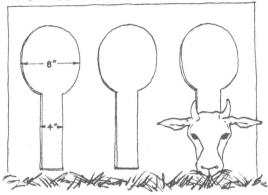

the manger. The goat sticks its head through the hole and then down to the hay. It can only back out by raising its head to the hole again, and so it is encouraged to keep its head in the manger instead of pulling hay out.

Horse Restraints

Horses are usually kept in box stalls and not restrained. They can be tied by a lead rope

to a manger, but they will invariably find a way to tangle up in it. The best way to restrain a horse for currying, harnessing, and so forth is with two lead ropes attached to the bridle, and then to walls on either side of the horse. The horse then cannot move its head to either side and has only limited movement backward and forward.

How to Avoid Milking Your Cow Every Day; or, How to Produce Your Own Tender Beef Cheaply

The first commandment of the farm is: Thou shalt milk thine cows twice a day—preferably at some early morning hour and then again in the evening when the rest of the world is enjoying itself. If you don't, the cow will dry up, or, if she is a heavy producer, she will develop udder problems and then dry up, perhaps permanently.

So, even though a cow can be the most profitable way to produce your own food on the homestead, it is the last to be adopted. Who wants to be tied down to a blamed cow?

Fortunately, you don't have to be, because you don't have to milk twice a day. Most of the year you don't even have to milk once a day, and for half the year, you need only milk when you feel like milking. The rest of the time, the cow's calf does the milking and for relieving you of the task, will present you, in six to eight months, with 300 to 400 pounds of the choicest beef you've ever eaten. Whether you want to call this getting your milk free or your beef free is up to you. All you need is 3 acres of good hay and pasture and about ¼ acre of corn. Even if you have to buy the hay and grain, you'll come out a little bit ahead.

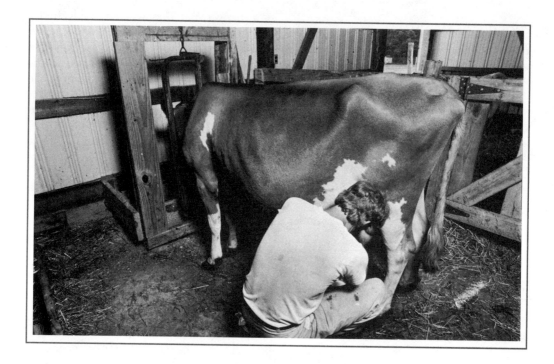

Low-Producing Cows Are Best

The key to avoiding milking every day is to get a cow that does *not* give so much milk. The typical cow today gives more milk than the typical family needs, unless a family can use it up making cottage cheese and butter, and feeding it to cats, dogs, chickens, and the family pig. Of course if you want milk for *all* those purposes on a daily basis, you may have to own a heavy producer and milk every day, at least once. But what if you want just your own milk and cream and occasionally a surplus for butter (we use our surplus cream mostly for ice cream), or for cheese? Then a cow like a Jersey or Guernsey that gives only about 3½ gallons of milk a day, but very rich milk, is a better choice than a high producer of milk with a low butterfat content. In fact, even if you *don't* want a low producer, I would still buy a Jersey or Guernsey

rather than a high-producing Holstein—the most popular commercial breed. (Around here we like to say that every dairy ought to have one Holstein—to put out fires with. But don't forget to put antifreeze in her for winter!) The dairy business is in poor economic shape today because of a worldwide surplus of milk, and yet the industry doggedly goes on wasting money shipping all that water around, instead of concentrating on butterfat and protein. A smaller amount of rich milk even fattens milk-fed beef better than a larger amount of watery milk, which is an observation I've never heard advanced anyplace except in my barn.

But whatever the merits of that argument, you should seek a rather low-producing cow rather than a high producer if you don't want to be "tied down" to milking. Since we use about

¾ gallon a day, a cow that averages 3½ gallons is just right—some for us and about 3 gallons for the calf. In practice, you can't be as precise as on paper, so you may find yourself at one time with too much milk and at other times with too little. We freeze cream during surplus times for use during times of scarcity.

Our cow is a Guernsey-Hereford cross, an unusual combination but perfect for our needs. The Hereford influence means even less milk than a Guernsey normally gives. Another advantage for us is that the cow is naturally polled (hornless), and none of its offspring have had horns. This characteristic has saved me the irksome chore of having to dehorn. In the small quarters of my barn, horns can be dangerous to other cows, if not to me. Even applying dehorning paste to calves just as the horn button appears under the skin is a job I'd just as soon avoid.

Setting Up a Milking Schedule

My milking schedule runs roughly like this: I like the calf to be born in early June, though some years it's May and some July. The cow has been bred to an Angus bull (artificially), and the calves are always black and stocky like Angus. Assuming a June 15 birth, I usually milk twice a day for about two weeks, making sure Betsy, the cow, gets milked out at least once a day during that time when the little calf won't drink all her milk. There is always more colostrum (first three-days' worth of milk) than the calf will drink, and this we freeze to use for orphaned or weak lambs that come in February.

In July and August I milk once a day, although in a pinch I can let the calf have all the milk. I wouldn't have to milk at all, but if I didn't, the cow would soon match her milk supply with calf demand, and my aim is to keep her giving a little more than the calf wants. For the first month to two months of the calf's life, I seldom separate them. I think this is important

to the health of both mother and offspring. The cow calves right out on pasture, and they remain together in the pasture, in woodland shade, or inside, when I bring them in together for milking. Young calves naturally nurse many times a day, and I believe it is important that they do so. They not only benefit from immunity to some diseases, but they also benefit emotionally.

In commercial herds, calves are taken from their mothers almost immediately. Mastitis problems plague the cows; scour problems devastate the calves. Much money is spent on antibiotics to control both diseases, and the administration of the drugs is often done improperly. I can't prove a direct connection between contented cows and calves that haven't been separated at birth and the absence of these diseases, but in ten years my cows have had no mastitis or scours, nor have I had to use any antibiotics to prevent these problems.

By fall, with pastures growing short, the cow's milk supply drops a bit, and I milk only once every other day. By this time I am usually penning the calf away from the cow during the heat of the day. Then in the evening there is milk for me, after which I turn the cow and calf out together. This means the calf is being cheated out of part of its milk supply, but it is getting plenty anyway and is by now eating grass, so there is no problem. If we have to be away for two or three days, I just leave them both out on pasture to fend for themselves.

Sometimes the calf begins at this age to overnurse, chewing on the teats and making them sore, even bloody. If that happens, I pen the calf up except for nursing until the teats heal. (Use Bag Balm for cuts and sores on udders and teats. It's available at all farm supply stores—even our drugstore has it. The salve is very good for chapped hands, too.)

Another little difficulty you might encounter: If you have been milking while the calf drinks during the first month, which occasionally is the case, and you pen up the calf in the

morning, mother may not let her milk down when you milk in the evening. So I just let the calf nurse on one side while I milk the other. After a week or so of this, I can usually milk alone, as Betsy gets used to the idea.

About the first of December, I put the animals in the barn more or less for the winter, letting them out only in the afternoons. In the normal course of farm events, the calf would be weaned by now. However, I keep it nursing because milk-fed baby beef is the cheapest and highest-quality beef I can raise. The calf nurses in the morning and is let out with the cow for afternoon exercise and water, and nurses again before I bring the animals all into their separate quarters for the night. (Now you see the impor-

tance of my aisle arrangement described in Designing a Small Barn for Easy Livestock Handling in Chapter 8.) When I milk, which is every second or third morning, the calf goes without that particular nursing. That doesn't hurt the big oaf at all, although it will complain some. It has plenty of hay to eat, and in January I begin to feed the calf a bit of ground corn. The calf will hardly eat the corn when it is nursing regularly, especially if it is getting high-quality hay.

By February, the calf is nearly as big as its mother. As mother's milk supply decreases in the latter half of its lactation, the calf starts to eat grain better, although I never give it more than 2 pounds per day. Around the first of

March we butcher. During March and early April, I dry the cow off, milking once a day for awhile, then once every other day, then once every third day. My aim is to have the cow dry about two months before she calves again. During those two months, the busiest time on the farm, I don't have to milk at all. We use the milk and cream we have frozen, and in a pinch buy some.

Costs and Savings

As far as I can figure, our cow produces about 8000 pounds of milk a year, or 1000 gallons. We use about 300 gallons of milk, and 150 to 200 pints of cream that we have skimmed off. (When milk is in surplus we sometimes skim off the cream and feed the milk to other animals.) The calf provides about 300 to 350 pounds of dressed meat. Cow and calf eat the hay we make at a very low out-of-pocket cost. The calf eats about 100 pounds of our own corn ground at the feed mill uptown. I add no protein supplements to it because the milk provides all that is necessary. The cow gets very little grain, hardly 500 pounds year, which is also our own—planted and harvested by cheap hand labor.

I could easily raise her milk production by feeding her more grain, as I have done experimentally on occasion, but I see no reason to do so. She eats about 3 to 4 tons of hay a year and pastures over 7 acres with the other animals, but I'd have the hay and pasture land anyway and don't know how to figure costs other than the small amount for gas, oil, and machinery use. It takes at least $100 worth of straw per year to bed her and the calf, but we get back some of the value of the straw in the manure, as fertilizer. We figure our out-of-pocket costs, including machinery, veterinarian, artificial insemination charges, and butchering, but not counting straw, at under $300. The meat, milk, and cream would cost us about $1300, if purchased retail.

The Gentle Approach to Animals Saves Time and Money

With a very small number of animals on a homestead, the whole tenor of livestock management differs from that of the commercial farm. You get to know your few animals well as individuals, and you become almost friends with them. Chore time becomes pleasurable. If you have hostile animals, you can get rid of them and buy others. And, if after a while you cannot find gentle animals, nature is telling you something. I have always believed that a good dairyman would be successful in any working relationship with humans because if you can get along well with a bunch of cows, you can get along well with anyone.

Animals are creatures of instinct. Do not think that what nature has taught them over the long, long centuries you can unteach in your puny little lifetime. Don't try. Observe instinct instead and learn from it. There is a wisdom to it far beyond the ken of humans.

Animals are creatures of habit, too. Domesticated, they will tolerate being trained to a routine somewhat foreign to their instincts, but once that routine is established, they do not look kindly upon an abrupt change. Change only confuses and alarms them. You must be patient, or suffer the consequences.

A totally gentled cow—the only animal I can talk about with conviction—is a pleasure to be around, more relaxing companionship than most people. She will not kick you when you are milking, if she considers you her friend, although she may fidget and raise her foot if she has a sore teat. Don't yell at her for that. She will let you trim her hooves when she is lying down—a job that otherwise you need a special (expensive) tool for, since a cow will not generally let you lift its foot up in your lap as a horse will.

Trimming Cow and Horse Hooves

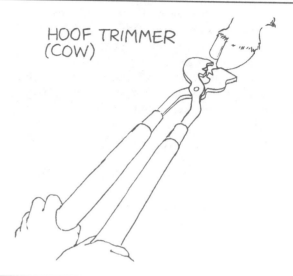

HOOF TRIMMER (COW)

If your cow won't let you trim her hooves with regular nippers while she lies down, you may need to resort to the special hoof trimmer shown here. Put the cow in her stanchion and then put a board under her hoof. She still may not want to stand still, but if you persist and don't lose your temper, eventually you will get the hooves trimmed. If you let the hooves grow too long in front, the cow cannot stand or walk properly, or the hoof will split back, causing a painful wound that could become infected.

Animal Talk

Animals can talk to you and they can understand most of what you need to communicate to them, so long as you do not get into anything as abstruse as the philosophy of Spinoza. Mostly they understand your tone of voice and will respond amazingly. I have a tone that they know

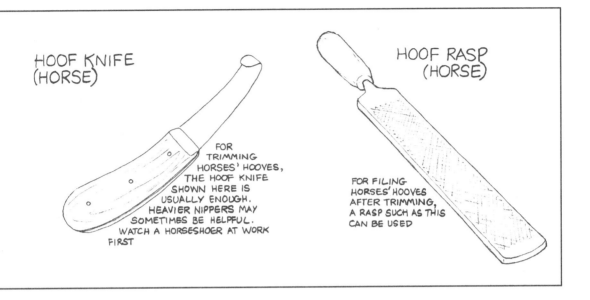

HOOF KNIFE
(HORSE)

FOR TRIMMING HORSES' HOOVES, THE HOOF KNIFE SHOWN HERE IS USUALLY ENOUGH. HEAVIER NIPPERS MAY SOMETIMES BE HELPFUL. WATCH A HORSESHOER AT WORK FIRST

HOOF RASP
(HORSE)

FOR FILING HORSES' HOOVES AFTER TRIMMING, A RASP SUCH AS THIS CAN BE USED

is angry; another they know is happy; another that means *please* go out the door, ma'am; and another that means Go! They know by my movement and my voice whether I'm just walking by or whether it is time to get up. If they don't want to get up, my cows lay their heads low to the floor and shake them in a very plain No! When they want to show me how pleased they are, they come up and lick me. When the horse is angry at me, she turns her rear end to my face.

Animals have many different sounds for communicating with each other. Knowing them can help you. Even if I couldn't see, I'd know when a ewe is going to accept her lamb—by the gurgling, almost inaudible sound she makes to it.

Body Language

Animals communicate with each other either by body language I can't always pick up or sounds I can't hear. The cow, for example, knows when the horse is going to chase her away from the water hole at the creek, and when the horse is going to sidle up in a friendly fashion—long before I can denote any flattening of the ears or baring of the teeth. If I could learn this language, I could communicate with them better. They in turn can occasionally sense my anger even before I think I have revealed it to them. They distinguish my different facial expressions. The horse and dog especially sense the slightest frown or smile and react accordingly.

This kind of intimacy makes work in the barn much more pleasant and easy. Hoof trimming is one example. Another is heat detection. On a homestead where there is only one cow, the novice homesteader has a difficult time knowing when his cow is ready to breed. (Cows will ride each other when in heat.) But if you are very familiar with your cow's character, you will know immediately when she is in heat, even before the telltale physical sign of excessive mucus issuing from the vagina. The cow will be noticeably belligerent, nervous, pushy, flighty—anything but her normal languidness.

Our horse taps gently on her stall gate when she wants out. If she gets no reaction from me, she taps louder. And louder. Finally I yell—to save the gate—and she stops. She knows at least that I've gotten the message. In the field she has a cunning way of continually walking in front of me and stopping. I finally realized she was trying to discourage me from leaving her.

Being gentle does not mean that you must be wishy-washy. I will whack, firmly, but not too hard, a balky cow that decides she just will *not* go out of the barn right now, thank you. Once whacked, she invariably moves with alacrity if I just wave the stick. The big calf will occasionally decide to keep on nursing after I tell it to go back to its pen. A prick with the fork changes its mind. But don't whack young animals until you have won them over completely with kindness. Until then, too much physical discipline will make them wary of you forever.

To gentle an animal to easy handling, I think you should start from birth. When I have bought an adult animal, I have never been able to instill in it the trust and understanding of home-raised stock. I started our flock of sheep with ewes raised elsewhere. They were wild beyond gentling, and they have passed their distrust of humans on to their young. Some day I will get rid of them and start over with bottle-raised lambs.

Stop to pet your animals as you pass their pens. Take a choice tidbit out to the field to feed them. I've never had any trouble catching the horse for work or riding, as seems to be the case on so many homesteads. The horse always comes up to me, associating my presence with something enjoyable. I always feed her a bit of oats when I first put her in the barn, for the same reason.

Nevertheless, there will probably be times

when you do lose your temper with animals. Be ashamed, but not discouraged. We all do, and always to disadvantage. It is sort of like smoking. Once you really resolve to stop it, you can. And like stopping smoking, the rewards are great. Around the barn, calmness pays in every way.

Training Cows

Training to Lead

It is not always necessary that a cow be trained to lead, but you will find that ability of great advantage, especially on the small homestead. Sometimes you have a field or lot not directly connected to the barn. It is easier to lead the cow there and back rather than try to drive her—especially if the route is over a public road or past a garden. Or you may wish to lead your cow to the neighbors' for breeding. The only way I think a cow or any animal can be trained to lead or do anything is to start when it is a young calf. But a mature cow is at least easier to train to lead than a mature horse, if the cow is one of the smaller breeds that is not much stronger than a man.

TRAINING
A COW
TO LEAD

In addition to a halter, put a safety rope around her neck (a rope alone will do) and run the rope through the ring of the halter. Be sure the rope is tied with a knot that will not slip tighter as the cow pulls. The trick is to pull the cow's head sideways against her flank when she gets rambunctious. You can keep her from exerting her full strength against you that way, perhaps going round and round in a circle until she begins to understand she must go where the rope beckons her. When she balks, don't try to outmuscle her—you can't. Pull her head sideways to get her moving again. If she absolutely refuses to move at all, tie her to a tree and let her stand still for a spell. A firm whack on the back (don't overdo it) sometimes chases away mulishness in a hurry, as does a light prick with a pitchfork. But soon—by the third day of training at least—she'll start following you on the lead rope. To help matters, take her over familiar ground, such as a path she has traveled routinely, during those training sessions. After training is complete, the safety rope is no longer necessary.

But you will have a far easier time training young calves to lead than you will cows. After they get used to the rope, you can even stake them out to graze, which will get them accustomed to obeying the rope, too.

Getting a Cow Used to Being Milked

If you wait until a cow freshens to start training her for milking, you will have a hard time of it for a few days. But if you have no choice, that is, if you hadn't had a chance to train her when she was a calf, start milking her *with her calf at her side, nursing at the same time.*

When the cow kicks a few times, don't give up and quit or the cow will think she has won the encounter. Stay in close to her flank where you are safer than if you try to stay far away and reach in. Milk with one hand and keep the other ready against her leg. If she moves the leg back, move your hand with it, so she never gets a good free swing going. If she lifts her leg, which is what she will normally do, hold your hand and arm against it, even pushing it back down. Hang in there. Don't try to milk into a bucket at first. Just milk onto the ground. Her kicking and fidgeting around would likely upset the bucket anyway, or she'd put her foot in it despite your hand blocking the way.

If she gives you a *vicious* sideways kick, it sometimes helps to give her one good firm whack right back, but no more than one per kick. Fidgety little kicks should be tolerated. Yes, you'll know the difference. The situation is made worse by the fact that the cow's bag usually is swollen when she is first fresh, and it is sore. If you can maneuver the calf over on the most swollen teats and you milk the one or two the calf has already nursed, so much the better that first time or two. Comfort yourself with the knowledge that if you keep a cow fifteen years, you won't have to "break" very many.

I'm dubious about devices cunning humans

have made to outwit kicking cows. If you must resort to leg hobbles or the back clamps that press against and deactivate muscles and nerves that control the cow's kicking mechanism, then it seems to me you have maybe won the battle but lost the war. When I was a kid we used leg hobbles on wayward cows. They would then jump up and down, both legs together, like a pile driver. Once I decided to fix an outlaw cow for good. I ran a rope tied to her one back leg around a solid post in the wall behind her and pulled her leg up off the ground. Standing on one leg, she could not possibly kick. With a triumphant air I sat down to milk in peace. The cow fell over on me.

The back clamps, usually called cattle controllers, really do work, I'm told, and may be of special use when a cow must be milked that has a badly cut teat. They are available from farm supply stores—by mail from Nasco, 901 Janesville Ave., Fort Atkinson, WI 53538.

My way of training a cow to milk is to start when she is a calf, periodically going through the motions of milking as she grows. She gets used to the idea long before she freshens, and milking goes smoothly from the start; rather smoothly anyway. Actually, it takes most of the first lactation to get the cow totally relaxed and comfortable with milking. And the older the cow gets, the easier the job becomes. Eventu-

Weaning

There are devices to fasten to a calf's nose, either by rings in the nostrils or by straps, to prevent it from nursing. Some have sharp points that jab either cow or calf to help dissuade them. I have never had any need for them. I let the calf nurse until it is butchered as baby beef. The few calves that I have raised to maturity have been kept on the cow until the end of her lactation period, then I have penned the grown calf in a different pasture or part of the barn until the cow had another calf. I've never had a yearling go back to nursing after being away from a cow that long, and after the cow has had a new calf. But some cows develop a habit of sucking themselves. If you do not wish to make hamburger of them, some kind of antisucking device might be appropriate. They're also available from Nasco, 901 Janesville Ave., Fort Atkinson, WI 53538.

HOMEMADE ANTISUCKING DEVICE

|← 8" →|

MADE FROM OAK BARREL STAVE

5"

HOMEMADE DEVICE, CIRCA 1870, TO KEEP A COW FROM SUCKING HERSELF. COW CAN EAT BUT NOT SUCK

NOSTRILS PRIED SIDEWAYS TO INSERT DEVICE (NOT PAINFUL TO COW)

ally she will as soon let her milk down for you as for her calf.

Some farmers try to "housebreak" cows by disciplining them from defecating in the milking stable. Big mistake. That's the first thing a scared or nervous cow will do. The calmer she is about coming into the stable and leaving, the less chance of manure in the stable. If cows are lying down when you come to put them in the milking stable, don't roust them up and run them in immediately. The first thing a cow wants to do after she has been lying down a while is defecate. Let her stand up and do so before walking her into the stable.

Training Horses

The term "breaking a horse" is unfortunate. If you take a wild horse off the range, or even a frisky colt that has been allowed to run on pasture without any human contact, I suppose you do have to "break" the animal to tame it for leading, riding, or pulling. But this is work for an expert. Maury Telleen, editor of *The Draft Horse Journal,* says that the last three things a horse owner needs to know how to do is break a horse, shoe a horse, or show a horse. Being able to do these things is not necessarily a mark of a good horseman any more than being able to put new piston sleeves in a car motor is a sign of a good driver.

I am personally not enchanted with the idea of training horses because if one wants to use animal power in place of a tractor, I'm prejudiced in favor of cows or oxen. Cows and oxen, I believe and shall try to show, are better geared to the smaller homestead farm. This belief is based partly on psychology rather than technology—I do not have the proper temperament to work horses (especially train them!), but I get along well with bovines. It so happens that my earliest recollections of fear come from three runaways involving horses—two I merely observed as a child, and one that I was the principal participant in. I have no romantic notions about horse farming. I have also been thrown from riding horses, one of which I was "breaking," so I have a dim view of horseback riding as a sport. It almost always turns out to be a luxury only the rich can really afford, if anyone can.

Nevertheless, I'm in the minority in this opinion, even on my own homestead. My son and my wife both are wonderfully adapted, psychologically, to work with horses, and they have been training a young Appaloosa named Teka that we hope eventually will be practical both for riding and pulling.

The way they have "broken" this horse to leading and riding is almost comical in its simplicity. From early age, the colt wore a halter at least some of the time. Her trainers, which later included a niece who had already trained a couple of horses herself, routinely led her around by it. The colt just grew up accustomed to the idea. When she was about two years old and by now a spoiled pet—perhaps too much so by some training standards—son, wife, and niece began to work with her in earnest. With a lead rope on the halter they led her about, teaching her the meaning of "whoa" and "giddyap." Son would say "whoa!" and step directly in front of the horse while pulling backward on the halter. Finally she learned to stop at the sound of the word alone.

Next she got used to a bit in her mouth. Everyone has a way to get a horse to open its mouth for the bit. My son holds the halter, pressing his thumb against her gums along one side of her mouth until she opens, then slips the bit in with the other hand and loops the bridle on over the horse's ears.

Next, he put a saddle on her back without cinching it. Teka did not seem to mind. The next day the saddle went on and was loosely buckled under her belly. No problem. Every day

he tightened the cinch a little more, until the saddle was ready for riding. Meanwhile, the leading had continued.

Teka was now ready for the big moment, though she hardly knew it. The saddle went on, the cinch tightened, and while my son stood in front of her, both hands on the bridle, courageous niece climbed aboard. For no more than 15 seconds Teka bucked furiously—or as furiously as she could with a muscular young man holding her head virtually motionless. My son says he doesn't think he could have managed this part if the horse were bigger—Teka is barely medium-size for a riding horse. At the end of the 15 seconds, she stood still, trembled all over, and her eyes rolled back into her head in a way I had never seen a horse do before. Then she straightened up and has never bucked or shown fear again.

Teaching a horse to neck-rein is easy. One way is to cross the reins so that when you pull on the right side of the bit, the rein presses against the left side of the neck. The other way is to have the reins in normal position, and (for turning right) pull on the right rein, but out far away from the neck so that the rein does not touch the neck at all, while at the same time laying the left rein against her neck with the

Rules of Thumb for
Training Workhorses

If you must train a workhorse, start it young. Tie it to the mother's traces when she is in harness so that it tags along, getting used to the sounds of harness and machinery at an early age. If the older colt is difficult to halterbreak, you can use the method adapted long ago for "halter pullers" —horses that pull against their halters until they break loose. Run a rope from the ring on the halter through a hole in a hitching post or manger and tie it to one of the horse's front feet just above the hoof. When the horse pulls back, it pulls its foot off the ground and because of its discomfort very quickly quits the bad habit. Some horsemen tie the rope around the horse's midriff, or around the tail rather than to the foot. In either method, the horse may associate the training with *all* backward movement and so resists backing up when in harness.

A new horse is usually harnessed with an old one to "break" it in or it is hitched to some kind of drag or breaking cart that will not easily be destroyed by wild training sessions. It is always best to pull some insignificant trifle behind the horse first, to see if the horse is going to be afraid of objects trailing behind it. Some are, some aren't, hence the use of blinders so the horse can't see what's behind it.

A neighbor, John Tschantz, raises, trains, and shows Morgan horses. He does not use blinders during training, so the horse can see behind it, but once the horse is trained, John puts the blinders on it because they are required in the show ring. He has the horse first pull a travois of branches he has quickly tied together. If the horse tears up the branches, there is little lost. Another neighbor, Jerome Frey, broke his last gelding after halterbreaking it when it was young, simply by hitching it up one day to a wagon out in the middle of the field—with no previous training sessions at all. But it behaved from the start; it did not really need to be trained gradually. "My only advice to draft horse owners is to keep geldings for a well-behaved team," he says. "A gelding is in the same mood every day. A mare during her heat period is nervous and flighty."

Never force a horse to pull more than it can. A horse must believe it can pull anything it is hitched to; otherwise, it may refuse to pull at all.

Treat a horse as if it had about as much intelligence as a 4-year-old kid—which is to say, quite a bit. Neither give in to it, nor overly punish it. Sometimes some horses need some physical discipline, but one swift sure blow or switch of the whip is enough. If the horse absolutely refuses to do what you want it to do and you can't make it

other hand. Soon the horse will associate the two actions, and begin reacting to the left rein alone against her neck. Horses are quite smart and quickly learn guiding.

The biggest problem with horses is that they are not ridden or worked enough. Reward and punishment is fine for training, but without repetition, the horse may "forget" why it was rewarded or punished. If the horse is not worked at least once a week (and much more often than that would be better), it is a good sign that the horse is not needed on the homestead for work or play and is only costing you money.

HEAD AND FOOT TIE FOR HORSE

change its mind at the time, make it do something else it doesn't want to do. Don't ever let it think it overwilled you. Don't yell at horses. They have extremely keen hearing and there is no sense getting laryngitis when a low gruff tone of displeasure will serve just as well. The calmer you are, the calmer your horses will be. And finally, never approach a horse without letting it know you are there, especially when walking into a stall from the rear of the horse.

For more on training draft horses, see *The Draft Horse Primer* by Maurice Telleen (Rodale Press, 1977).

Training Oxen

Any cow can be trained as a draft ox, although to be precise, an ox is a steer four years old or older. Bovines have some advantages over horses as draft animals. But rather than praise oxen in my own words, I shall bow in favor of that feisty old gadfly William Cobbett, who flourished (and I do mean flourished) from 1763 to 1835. Here is, briefly, his argument in favor of oxen (from *Cobbett's Country Book: An Anthology of William Cobbett's Writings on Country Matters,* edited by Richard Ingrams, [Schocken Books, New York, 1975]):

Harness, if harness be used and not yokes, is much less expensive and requires less strength than that which is to stand the jerking and the starting of a horse. (Yoking is cheaper, today, than horse harness.)

Food upon which a horse will not be able to work at all is quite sufficient for an ox.

One of the great plagues of the horse is the blacksmith . . . and loose shoes . . . . With oxen you have none of these plagues.

[With horses] there is the grease and the pole-evil and the glanders and the strangles and the fret and the coughs and the staggers and the botts and various other nasty and troublesome diseases. The ox knows none of these.

The first cost of the ox or steer, three years old is . . . less than half the sum for a horse the same age. (Quite true today, too.)

If from age, it be desirable to fat the ox, he may bring you one-third more than his first cost, if not double the amount . . . [whereas a horse in this regard] is a mere drug if it be old or out of condition. The ox is something to be eaten and has an intrinsic value. (And, I might add, cows trained as draft animals give milk as well as meat.)

We read in the Bible of war-horses; of horses drawing chariots. But we never find an allusion to horses employed in the tillage of the land; for which by their gentleness, by the nature of the food which they require, by their great docility, oxen seem to have been formed by nature.

And upon that, I will rest my case. Thank you, Mr. Cobbett.

That oxen were harnessed and not necessarily yoked in Cobbett's time is interesting in view of the fact that today yoking is the prevalent custom where oxen are used. My neighbor, Glen Kieffer, uses both a yoke and harness on his oxen, and his method, it seems to me, gives better results than either one or the other. He puts bridle and bit on his animals and guides them from the rear with reins, as with horses. But there is no other harness. Just the big wooden yoke over the animals' necks, to which the tongue of the implement being pulled is secured. Although oxen can be trained by voice and prod from a driver walking beside them, for precise work, as in pulling a binder down a row of corn as Kieffer is doing in the photo, the direct control from reins and bit seems far more prudent. I was impressed by the ease with which Kieffer handled the young Holstein steers, and the calm and placid way they worked. Should I switch to animal power on my farm, there's no doubt in my mind what I would choose—oxen, not horses.

Kieffer has several yokes of different sizes. He begins training when the oxen are calves, so that from an early age they grow accustomed to the work. Note that his homemade yokes are flat on the sides, cut from a beam, not carved round from a piece of wood with grain curving to the shape of the yoke. His yokes are therefore not the strongest, and might break with very heavy loads and huge oxen. But for the lighter work he does, such yokes are fine and easier to make.

A yoke can in fact be cut out with a chain saw, and the edges then rounded off with a drawknife. The bows are hickory or ash, steam-bent to shape. The implement tongue fits through a steel ring (not quite a round ring on Kieffer's yoke in the photo) and is fastened to it. That is all the hitching that is needed. For working in the woods, oxen are handier than horses, since there are no trace chains or whiffletree—just the chain going to the yoke.

Training the ox to gee and haw (go right and left), whoa and come up (stop and go), takes much time and patience. The first step is training the animal to lead as one would a cow or horse, then using ropes to back up the voice commands, over and over again until the ropes aren't needed. With rein and bit, the training goes faster. But to be able to guide only by voice is what makes ox driving so pleasant and handy, especially when dragging logs or loading a wagon, since your hands are thus free for working.

You can hitch up just one cow or ox alone. In years past, many a cow carted her milk to market. That is the kind of efficiency no modern technology can hope to match.

Feeding Farm Animals

Commercially Fed Chickens

The giant Ralston Purina Company, which both directly and indirectly aided the integration of the poultry business into a factory operation, has now discovered the backyard chicken grower. If the backyard chicken grower listens to the seductive murmurs of Purina Chow, he or she will go out of business, too, just like the farmers did. I suppose I should feel hopeful, not sarcastic, that after all these years agribusiness is finally recognizing the potent market force that we backyard and tiny farm producers represent. Nevertheless, seeing us as a market does not mean that they care about our welfare, however the officials of business protest. The millions of farmers now working in factories are ample evidence of that.

The article that the public relations department at Ralston Purina is distributing free to newspapers tells the backyarder how to raise twenty-five chickens for eggs or meat. It is a good article, on the whole, but like most such information, the advice is based on the experience of a commercial operation. Therefore, if you follow the methods given, in a few years you will conclude that producing your own eggs "doesn't pay," and you will be able to quote any number of agricultural researchers to back

you up. I can give you the reason quickly: 50 pounds of a commercial laying mash, which Purina advises you to feed to your chickens, costs about *$7.00 out-of-pocket cash*; 50 pounds of whole grain purchased from a farmer costs about *$3.50 out-of-pocket cash*; 50 pounds of grain raised in your backyard with hand methods costs about *$1.00 out-of-pocket cash* or *less* if you do it my way.

A rule of thumb among commercial egg producers says that 4.5 pounds of feed equals a dozen eggs (would that it were that simple!). So for about $10 worth of eggs you've already spent $7. If you get less than a dozen eggs per 4.5 pounds of feed, which is very possible, and the price of eggs slips to 80¢ a dozen, also very possible, you'll already be losing money, and you haven't even begun to count up your other expenses!

Of course if you just like to have your own good fresh eggs or like to work with chickens, fine. You've got yourself an expensive hobby—but not as expensive as golf.

But you *can* raise your own eggs, meat, and milk profitably on a very small scale for a very small out-of-pocket cost, and you do it by ignoring most of the admonitions of the commercial producers. If you want to make money (maybe) with $7-per-50-pounds feed, you have to have high volume. If you want to make money on low-volume production in the backyard, you have to drastically cut out-of-pocket expenses.

The Ralston Purina article and every so-called how-to book I've read assumes that chickens must be fed milled grains. Malarkey. Little chicks that cannot yet swallow whole grains need milled grains (unless they are following their mothers around the barnyard eating bugs and worms and bits of grass and tiny weed seeds). Hens and broilers do not. They will eat more if fed milled grains, which may mean a few more eggs and certainly more weight in a shorter period of time, but what do you care, in the backyard, if your broilers mature in ten weeks or twelve, or if your hens don't lay the absolute maximum they might be capable of?

Lights in the Henhouse

Here's the history behind this henhouse lighting business. Back when utility companies were stretching electric lines out into the country, there wasn't much money in rural electricity. To remedy this situation, the utilities went to all lengths to get farmers to increase the amount of electricity they used. (It took a great deal of social pressure just to get some farmers to "take the electric"—which is another of those facts the speechifiers of wonderful technological progress never mention in their biased histories. There was a whole class of country people who didn't particularly want electricity.) Since it was known that the egg-laying season in nature is influenced by the amount of available sunlight, wouldn't egg production increase if the chickens were kept awake longer in the shorter winter days? Agricultural researchers (with money from the utilities) leapt into the breach, and sure enough electric lights did increase egg production . . . for a while. So what if the hens suffered egg "burn-out"? Get new hens.

So egg production was increased at an increased cost in chickens, in electricity, and in feed because the hens ate more. The increase in egg production (which actually was more the result of up-breeding chickens) only made the price of eggs go down so badly after World War II that farmers sold their small commercial flocks because eggs "don't pay no more." Of course not. The poor farmer had been duped into spending his profit on off-farm supplies, including foolish things like lights in his henhouse.

You aren't on the commercial treadmill, working on 14% money, with expenses so high for all that automation that you have to scrape up every possible penny.

This brings up another of my pet peeves: Almost all books and articles on raising poultry will admonish you to keep a light on in your henhouse—that your hens will lay more eggs if the amount of light remains fairly constant for 14 hours per day. This practice is total absurdity for the backyard chicken grower. My chickens have never seen an electric light. We have never run out of eggs in eighteen years, never had more than twenty overwinter layers, usually less, and indeed have eggs to sell every month except December.

Home-Fed Chickens

Since chickens have a wonderful digestive system for grinding grains, you can just feed them whole grains as I do. But if you insist on grinding grain for chickens, you'll be way ahead if you take your grain to the mill and have it ground there instead of buying commercially ground grain. I hear you saying, well, my grains won't have all those vitamins and minerals and protein supplements in them, all scientifically mixed to give the chicken a "perfectly balanced" ration. I don't want to get into an argument about the relative merits of these "perfectly balanced" rations, but a few years ago there was arsenic in feeds to make the chickens eat more; and in some feeds there are still various antibiotics and drugs. Remember the mix-up in bagging feeds in Michigan a few years ago that led to the poisoning of thousands of animals, not to mention people?

If your hens have access to the outside at least a few hours every other day in nice weather, they will balance their own rations quite well with bugs and worms and grass and leaves (and your garden fruits if you aren't careful). If you can't let your chickens out for part of the day once in a while (the best way is to turn them out 2 hours before sunset—they won't stray far and

will come back to roost at dark), you can bring them grass clippings, table scraps, and garden surplus and provide them with a salt-mineral block, oyster shells, and water. Along with your grains, and in winter a bit of high-quality clover or alfalfa hay (you can dry the clover right off the lawn), you will have provided as balanced a ration as any you can buy. It may be a sight more balanced, in fact, because your egg yolks will have a rich orange-yellow color, denoting a higher carotene and vitamin C content than those pallid-yolked eggs from the egg factories.

If you are into grinding grains, the ration formulas you can use are myriad. The conventional mixture is invariably about ⅔ corn and ⅓ oats or wheat, or oats *and* wheat. Barley, wheat, and oats can all take the place of corn, but in larger amounts, because corn provides more energy. You can also mix in a bit of protein supplement. If you have good-quality alfalfa, you can feed that instead of the supplement. A protein supplement such as soybean meal usually is considered necessary for hogs because it makes them fatten faster, which, as I say, is not important in the backyard, except that it might make the meat a teensy-weensy bit more tender.

Here's what I feed my chickens: When there are eighteen chickens in the coop, they get six ears of corn per day, a pound or less of wheat, and four seed heads of sorghum, all grown and harvested on the place. If they don't clean that up, I reduce the ration a bit. In addition, they get a bit of leafy green alfalfa hay regularly in winter, plus lots of table scraps, garden surplus, scraps from butchering, and a bit of salt-mineral block and oyster shells. They roam the woods for part of the day for about 250 days of the year.

Chicks and young broilers get some ground corn alone, but every year I feed the broilers less ground feed and more whole grain, and they get fat just as well, only a bit slower. Speed of fattening is influenced by genetics, by the way. Some animals get fatter quicker no matter what you feed or don't feed them.

Feeding My Cow

I maintain the same irreverent attitude toward grinding feeds and fancy rations in feeding the other animals. My dairy cow's ration is as follows: from May 1 to December 1, pasture—a mixed pasture containing six different legumes, three grasses, and at least twenty kinds of weeds. Some of the pasture is on ground never farmed. I believe that the mixed herbage the pastures provide balance the cow's diet as far as vitamins and minerals are concerned, especially the latter. Many farmed soils in our area are low in selenium, causing problems more often with sheep than with cows. Since my animals show no mineral deficiencies, I assume something must be working right. I keep a common salt-mineral block in the field for them to lick on, too.

When pastures grow short, I feed the cow some corn. In late summer she gets the old sweet corn, sweet cornstalks, the stunted field cornstalks and their nubbins, which I cut out of the corn patch, and the big vigorous stalks that are still greenish after the ears are jerked from them. I feed her some of the ears, too, at milking time—the grains are still fairly soft and so are digested fairly well without grinding. Supplemental hay may also be necessary, at least in November.

From December to May the cow gets all the hay she will eat—mixed red clover, alfalfa, white clover, bird's-foot trefoil, timothy, orchard grass, June grass, and a variety of weeds mixed in, along with some very high quality alfalfa hay fed more sparingly. The alfalfa is, as I have said, the key to my feeding program. It has at least an 18% protein content, probably more. Don't think you must have a big farm to have high-quality, high-protein hay. Grow clover in your yard, cut and dry it carefully, and you'll have the same thing. Or rotate your garden with a plot of alfalfa.

In addition to the hay in winter, I feed the cow three ears of corn morning and night if she seems to taper off on milk production below the level I want to maintain. I usually do grind some corn in late winter, principally to feed the baby beef, but also to feed 2 pounds a day to the cow. Any milled corn left over after the beef is butchered and the cow is dried up is fed to the chicks. I have about 500 pounds of corn shelled and ground at our local feed mill. If I were feeding the ground corn *only* to cows, I'd grind it, cob and all. I wait until the end of January to grind because I don't need it sooner than that. I also want to be sure the corn has dried down to about 13% moisture in the crib before grinding, which it does by that time. If you grind corn with more moisture in it than that, it will cake and mold in storage.

Feeding My Sheep

The sheep go onto pasture in April and stay there until January. When pastures get short in December or earlier, I feed supplemental hay. In January, February, and March, penned in the barn, they each get a section of good alfalfa hay bale—about 8 inches thick—a day plus a pound of oats when they are nursing. During March I may increase that ration a bit because the lambs are eating, too. Once on pasture, no more grain. The lambs have always fattened wonderfully on brush pasture and nursing, though it takes them longer to get to 90 to 100 pounds than it takes the commercial lamb fed on grain. My lambs bring the top price because the buyer at the stockyard assumes they have been grain fed. The meat is excellent and tender. If a farmer is not in a hurry to sell his lambs, I cannot imagine why he would feed expensive grain to them if he could pasture them as I do. But I'm told that I have such good luck only because I don't stock the pasture too heavily—I have only eight to ten sheep and lambs on 3 acres. In eight years I have not wormed my sheep. They do not yet need to be wormed, and I think that is why they gain so well on so little feed. But why they do not need worming, I do not know.

Feeding My Horse

Our medium-size Appaloosa gets all the hay she can eat in winter, plus a pound of oats every day from about December to May. She also occasionally gets an apple or carrot. If she is being ridden hard or if the weather is very cold, I'll give her extra oats. Sometimes I give her an ear of corn, broken in three pieces. The oats, both for horse and sheep, would be better utilized, I suppose, if I crimped them, but a crimper is just one more expense I don't need.

Feeding My Pigs

A pig running on pasture or in woods can be fed as casually as I feed a horse or cow. The pig will graze quite efficiently even though it is not a ruminant animal and will also root up grubs, insects, acorns, and even snakes. When our creek dried up in August, as it often did, the hogs would slurp through the final water holes and eat all the fish they could catch. Hogs are death on water snakes, but I don't know about rattlers.

Penned up is the only way I'll keep a pig because I don't like to ring its nose to keep it from rooting up the pasture. Therefore, my hog needs about 12 bushels of corn to fatten to 200 pounds, or 15 to 20 bushels of wheat or barley or oats. Grinding the grain makes more sense with hogs, since whole grains tend to pass right through them. Or soak the grain in water till it's soft. If you have surplus milk, oats soaked in milk will fatten a pig very well.

The pig is one animal that will utilize a protein supplement well—especially soybean meal. But again, the main result is faster fattening. Are you in a big hurry? My father-in-law, who smoked the best hams in Kentucky, said that high-supplement feeding might make pork faster, but not good hams. He believed in fattening a hog slowly over eight or nine months, not four or five. He fed his hogs ear corn most of the time. In the classic book *Feeds and Feeding*

(Morrison Publishing Co., Ontario, 1961), F. B. Morrison says that for the first half of the feeding period, a market hog will do just as well on whole corn as ground corn. I have fattened hogs on soaked whole grains, high-quality alfalfa hay (for protein), garden surplus, and acorns. Feed a hog all it wants every day. It won't overeat on grains the way cows, horses, and sheep will if given a chance.

Summing up, it's important to grow a variety of foods to feed to your animals. Ruminants need good hay and, as research shows, high-quality alfalfa alone can supply the *entire* nutritional needs of a cow. For chickens and hogs, grain is more important than hay, but high-quality clover will provide protein and minerals and vitamins that may be lacking in the grain. Surplus milk and meat scraps (table scraps) are other good sources of protein and vitamins. Vitamin E, essential for chickens (a lack of it can cause them to peck bloody sores on each other) comes right out of the composting bedding in their coop. As a rule, the closer you can simulate natural conditions, especially allowing animals to graze or range, the better.

Feeding Goats

We don't have goats, but the same general principles apply as for sheep. A goat is a ruminant animal. The more hay you feed it and the less grain, the better off you are. Goats are great browsers of brush and can get many trace elements, minerals, and vitamins from tree and bush leaves.

Unconventional Methods for Small-Scale Sheep Management

A shepherd in our county raises, trains, and uses Border collies in handling his sheep.

He gave me a demonstration one evening that profoundly impressed me, since I have spent many agonizing episodes trying to chase sheep hither and yon. If you are serious about raising sheep, include good sheepdogs in the planning. They make handling a flock an easy pleasure and will even herd sheep into a trailer for you. Sources of trained collies can be found in the classified ads of sheep magazines.

Raising Lambs

Before lambs are born, pen the ewes in the barn separately. Keep close watch over the ewe but not too close. Some well-intentioned shepherds hover over the ewe at the first sign of labor and if nothing happens in half an hour, they panic and want to pull the lamb. When the lamb is born, they continue to hover over, trying to force the lamb to nurse. Both lamb and ewe are upset, and the shepherd is in a bloody sweat wondering why he ever decided to raise dumb woollies. I have only five or six lambs to contend with every year, but never yet have I had to pull one. If heavy labor lasts beyond an hour, your help *might* be needed. But lots of troubles can be avoided by just being patient. If you have never midwifed a birth, call the vet the first time and learn from him or her.

Of course lots of trouble can happen if you stay away too long, too. After the lamb is born it needs to be watched (from a distance). If it gets too weak while the mother is having a second lamb or because it is too cold or because mother has forgotten it in her concern over lamb number two, then you must be ready to supply the warmth and colostrum the lamb needs in its early hours. If the lamb gets too weak to find the mother's udder (almost always because of cold weather), we take the lamb to the house, warm it up by the wood stove, and give it a couple of ounces of cow colostrum that we have frozen and stored for this occasion. If the lamb is in a very bad way from low body temperature, we will immerse it in warm water a few minutes, then let it dry out in a box next to the stove.

This year we had twin lambs come on a ten-below-zero night, and both lambs did a stint by the stove. When I returned the first one to its mother, she did not like the smell of her laundered lamb and bucked it away. She had not cleaned herself of her placenta yet, so I took some of it and rubbed it over the lamb, particularly around its anus, which is where a ewe will smell and identify her lamb first. After that she was satisfied the lamb was hers. I remember my father would fool a ewe who had lost her lamb into adopting an orphan lamb by skinning the dead lamb and dropping the skin over the orphan.

You can raise an orphan lamb on a bottle —a big soft drink bottle with a lamb nipple on it. If you do not have colostrum to start the lamb on, try a pint of regular cow's milk with a beaten egg in it and some dark corn syrup. Don't try to force the lamb to drink more than a couple of ounces at a time. Some shepherds give weak lambs a little whiskey, which is probably a waste of good liquor.

Once warmed up and nursing regularly, a new lamb can stand below-zero temperatures if the pen is dry and out of the wind. The lamb will snuggle up to mother for warmth. Heat lamps are a waste of money. I know a lady who once warmed up a lamb by sticking a hair dryer through a hole in a box where the lamb was contained. A few hours beside a wood-burning stove is better, and cheaper.

A week after birth, the lambs are usually "docked"—that is, their tails are cut off. The reason for this is that heavy grain feeding or overly lush pastures can produce a mild diarrhea in sheep, causing the manure to build up on the underside of their tails. Maggots get into such buildups and cause problems. There is also a belief that a ewe without a tail is easier for the ram to breed, which is more malarkey. I have quit docking lambs that I intend to sell for market or to butcher. The way I feed they have no manure problems in the less than ten months they live. I may eventually quit docking the lambs I keep for ewes, too, just to prove a point. I get kidded as a greenhorn by the good old boys when my long-tailed lambs show up at market, but why do what you don't have to do?

When I do cut off tails, I cut about 2 inches out from the base of the tail. This also results in some kidding from conventional sheepmen because they all cut the tails closer to the body. My reason for not cutting shorter is that bleeding is less severe. To remove the tail, I first tie a piece of twine around the base of the tail very tight to act as a tourniquet. That's not usually done either. I cut off the tail with a pair of nippers that are not too sharp. (There's more bleeding with a sharp knife.) I heat the nipper blades first with a couple of lighted matches, not just for sterilization but to help cauterize the wound. I hold the lamb between my legs, tail end facing me, leaving both my hands free to work. After the tail is removed, I liberally apply a wound coagulant and sterilant and repeat the application an hour or so later. As distasteful as this job is, it doesn't seem to bother the lamb as much as I imagine. The lamb is bouncing playfully about the barn an hour later. The tail stub swells up but I've never had other problems. I remove the twine the next day and apply more wound dressing powder (available from drugstores here).

I do not castrate market lambs. This is another heresy, but a male lamb butchered at eight months or so tastes as good as a castrated one. Yet at market you get docked on price if your male lambs are not castrated. That's just the way life is—irrational.

Not castrating does lead to one problem, or can. The young rams at six months of age are fully able to breed mother, sister, or other ewes, so you should get them separated by late summer. If you don't separate them and you have the regular flock ram with the ewes, he *may* bully away the young pretenders to his throne and do the breeding himself, but you can never be sure. It's better to be safe and separate the young rams.

This brings up another difference of opinion—when to breed. I leave the ram with the ewes all summer and he generally breeds them "too soon" and the lambs are born in January—too soon by conventional standards in this area. I don't mind January lambs, since I have so few to contend with if the weather does get cold. February is better. But either January or February lambs can go out on pasture in April without harm from cold spring rains. Younger lambs would be more susceptible to pneumonia.

Shearing

I shear my three ewes and ram with hand shears, which no one is supposed to do anymore. I can't justify spending $80 to $100 for electric clippers for four sheep. In most cases I think it is practical to hire a professional sheep shearer. But if you are stubborn like me and do it yourself, you don't need to be told how to shear because you will learn all by yourself. I tried to learn to shear from reading instructions. A joke. I couldn't even learn from *watching* someone else. You just have to do it. You sit the sheep on its butt, more or less immobilizing it, and then start at the head and snip your way from flank, over back, down other flank, until you get to the rear

end. (There is no one method written in stone somewhere as to how you do this.) I have never quite mastered the professional art of turning the sheep far enough so I can reach clear to the other end of its body when shearing. I always employ a helper—my long-suffering wife or son. I snip off the belly wool separately and also the manury "tags" from around the anus, and throw this wool away. My wool usually goes to hand spinners who want only the cleanest wool to spin "in the grease." When you finish shearing, check the sheep's hooves. If they're too long or curled under, trim with a sharp pocketknife.

What can I say about shearing that will help you? If you're using hand shears, don't try to take too big a bite of wool. With clippers or hand shears, make as long a sweep or stroke as you can in cutting. Once past the neck, which is the hardest part for me, you can snip-snip a steady stroke from the flank on one side clear across the back and down the other, taking

hardly more than an inch of wool at a time. Keep the shears about half an inch away from the skin—don't try to cut down as close as you would when using clippers or you will inevitably cut into the skin. You will make cuts anyway while you learn how. Be very careful around ears and teats.

As the wool is sheared loose it rolls over and down the body, clinging together in one piece, as it should. When you have removed the whole fleece (you should be working on a clean tarp or raised shearing platform to keep dirt and chaff out of the wool) lay the fleece out, trim off dirty wool (you can leave some dirty wool on if going to conventional market), then bunch up the fleece inside out and tie it with *paper* twine. Do not use plastic twine—the fibers get into

the wool during processing and ruin it for manufacturing.

Another heresy I adhere to is shearing in December instead of early spring when most shearing is done, at least in this part of the country. Shearing when the sheep come in off the pasture means cleaner wool, free of bedding and hay chaff. Winter shearing doesn't leave the sheep too cold if they are inside, and the wool soon grows back enough to protect them. Some shepherds will argue that this means sheep go into summer with a heavier fleece. My argument is that the heavy wool that insulates against winter cold also insulates to some degree against summer heat. At any rate, my sheep have summer shade and endure hot weather as well as any sheep. Other shepherds who sell wool to hand spinners shear in early winter with good luck, too.

Protecting the Flock

A serious problem with sheep in more populated areas is the suburban dog that is not kept leashed. Dogs will run sheep, sometimes just for the fun of it, until the sheep drop dead from exhaustion. A few dogs turn killer. You are allowed to shoot dogs killing sheep but make sure you can prove it (wool caught in the dog's teeth is the traditional evidence), or the dog owner, who ought to be severely punished, can get *you* in trouble. Our topsy-turvy society gives loose-running useless dogs more sentimental support than valuable sheep. Guard dogs are being used to protect flocks (fight fire with fire) with some success, but guard dogs are not always reliable. An old tradition, still used, is to put a donkey in with sheep—the donkey will chase the dogs. Donkeys have also been known to kick and kill sheep, but that is a rare occurrence. Goats are not afraid to turn on dogs and a few in with sheep can be some protection. An owner of mouflon sheep tells me they will fearlessly protect their young from dogs. One of my ambitions in life is to breed dog-killing sheep, then turn them loose on my neighbors' properties, the way they let their dogs run on mine.

A Spinner's Flock of Sheep

The large-scale gardener or backyard farmer or modern homesteader (whatever term you wish to use to describe the newly emerging segment of American society for whom this book is written) wants to provide as much of his or her own food, clothing, and shelter as is possible and practical. This goal has been realized in terms of food production, as some 34 million gardeners and subsistence farmers have proven. Clothing and shelter, as "homemade" products, are still in the developmental stage,

relatively speaking, but progressing very rapidly from the raw materials of wool and wood. Wood as a cottage or home industry is making amazing strides. (See Treasures in Wood in Chapter 11.)

In the next generation we may again see a special room in the house for the preparation of fabrics for clothing—just as we now have the kitchen for the preparation of food—a return to the sitting rooms of yesterday where the spinning and weaving was done. In the modern "sitting" room, however, television and records will relieve the monotony, and there will be mechanical improvements in sewing machines, spinning wheels, looms, and so forth to make the work faster and easier. A surprising number of spinning wheels and looms are already back in business, some of the new ones much improved over the old. Knitting machines, in common use elsewhere as in Ireland where householders can knit two sweaters a day on such a machine, will eventually become popular here. Cottage industry carders for wool are now a reality—you don't have to find an old one rusting away somewhere.

Fred Zahradnik, writing in *New Farm* magazine, reports that Patrick Green is now making carders for $4900 (Patrick Green Carders Ltd., 48793 Chilliwack Lake Rd., Rt. No. 8, Sardis, BC, Canada V0X 1Y0) and has sold over thirty of them. One buyer, Donna Kennedy in Pennsylvania, is doing $700 worth of custom carding business a month, says Zahradnik, and figures that by carding her own wool into batting for quilting and blankets, and roving for spinning into yarn, she increases her income twenty times over just selling her fleeces on the market.

Wool is the longest-lasting fabric you can wear. And the source of wool, sheep, can be as near as your backyard or at least your neighborhood small-scale farmer. A mature sheep produces 12 pounds of wool a year easily. That's two sweaters' worth, sweaters that will last just about forever. The wool from eight sheep will be more than enough to keep you busy making something all year long in your spare time, and 2 acres of land is plenty for eight sheep. What you make is not going to wear out any time soon, so the results of the rather pleasant spare-time work are cumulative: a good woolen comforter, for example, will become an heirloom.

Wool as a Cottage Industry

Ron and Windsor Chacey in southern Ohio and Mary Stock in east-central Ohio exemplify the trend toward a wool cottage industry. The Chaceys breed sheep specifically for hand spinners. The crossbreeding of their Black Lincolns results in wool that is black, white, silvery, brownish black, and one they call ice blue. This wool hardly looks like wool, let alone undyed natural wool. It sells from $2 to $5 and (rarely) $8 a pound at a time when commercial wool with government incentive payment brings the farmer scarcely more than $1 a pound. Breeding stock sells for three times and up of what market lambs bring. The fat lambs they do market are first sheared at five months when the long-wooled Lincoln types already have a 4-inch growth. This amounts to 3 to 5 pounds of wool per lamb. Then, after the wool grows out in another two to three months, the lamb is butchered and sold to the Chaceys' own locker trade. They then have the hide tanned and it brings, in the more unique colors, as much as

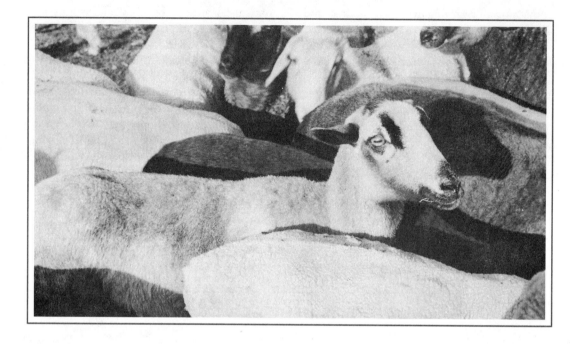

$110. Remember that the ordinary farmer gives the sheepskin away when he sells his lambs on the market.

Mary Stock keeps her sheep to supply her with wool for spinning and weaving in her shop, The Merrie Lamb. Mary is experimenting with various breeds of sheep in hopes of producing some unique natural-colored wool. She even has some Barbados and mouflon sheep. Colored wools bring more money right now than does white. Mary has a brownish ewe (brown is the most elusive color desired) that is one-quarter Karakul, one-quarter Southdown, and one-half mouflon.

My own somewhat brownish-grey ewe is Karakul crossed with Corriedale-Columbia, then inbred back to the same Karakul ram. The wool is a fairly unique brown—not just bleached-out black—but a bit coarse.

Coarse wool in commercial trade is considered low grade. But coarse means only thick-stranded, not harsh or itchy. The Chaceys' Lincolns have coarse wool, but it is as soft as down. Coarse wool is desirable in hand spinning because it spins faster. The fine wools, like merino, are rather tedious to hand spin. Incidentally, all naturally processed wool is soft and can be worn comfortably next to the skin. What makes wool itchy is the chemical treatments used commercially to dissolve dirt and foreign matter in the fleeces.

Choosing a breed for hand spinning wool is based mostly on personal preference. Variation within breeds rules out my making generalizations. Even some Suffolks, a meat breed, spin nicely, says Mary Stock.

Handling Sheep

Sheep are easy to handle—compared to cows and horses. And you are not likely to find them gamboling about on the roof of the barn, as you might find a goat some morning. I've described various ways of holding sheep, from shepherd's crooks to squeeze chutes, and how sheepdogs make driving sheep a pleasure.

Tending the Flock

Among the special efforts one needs to take with a "spinner's flock" are these:

1. Keep burs, thistles, chaff, and seeds out of the wool as much as possible. Burdock is the worst offender. In autumn its seed hulls catch in the wool and are almost impossible to comb out. Fleabane seeds and Spanish nettles won't come out, either. Small seeds of timothy and even bluegrass are pesky. Twice-a-year mowing of pastures solves the problem except in wooden or hilly terrain where mowing is not possible. Since burdock is an annual, chopping it a couple inches below the ground will kill it. But where the weed has had a chance to reseed many small plants, hoeing is tedious until the growth is reduced. If you can't get all the plants hoed out in one year, at least don't let any go to seed. Sheep will eat burdock, but only after there is little else available.

Keeping hay and bedding out of the wool is a must, too, as discussed in Hay Mangers and Grain Boxes That Waste the Least, in Chapter 8.

2. Healthy sheep produce healthy wool. Wool is mostly protein, so a well-balanced diet means a strong and lustrous wool. A sheep with a fever develops a weak spot in the wool at the skin. Shear a fevered sheep within two weeks and let the wool grow out again. Otherwise the weak spots in the wool strands grow out and ruin the fleece.

3. Use long-stranded straw for bedding. Chopped straw, sawdust, and wood chips work into the wool.

4. Second cuts when shearing leave short strands of wool that are hard to spin, and they make weak yarn. In shearing, if you cut too high by mistake in the first pass, don't make a second cut over the same area, or if you do, throw those short strands out.

5. Try not to shear in humid weather. Wool will be wet. Let wet fleeces dry before tying.

6. Discard belly, leg, and head wool, even neck wool if it is full of chaff. This is called "skirting" the fleece. The rest of the wool may be clean enough to spin in the grease, that is, before washing. If washing is necessary or desired, use warm water and a little mild detergent if you are not going to dye the wool. Sometimes warm water alone is enough. You want to keep some of the lanolin in the wool. If you are going to dye the wool, use more soap, because nearly all the lanolin must be removed for the dye to take. Let the wool dry. Store *loosely* in cardboard boxes or paper sacks. Do not store in plastic sacks.

Incidentally, without a dog you can get sheep to do anything, if you can persuade the flock leader (usually one of the old ewes rather than the ram) to do it. The rest will follow the leader into the very flames of perdition.

There are other handy ways to move sheep. You can lift a sheep into a pickup truck (try that with a horse) or a trailer, and you need racks scarcely 4 feet tall to contain it. When my neighbor brought me the ram I had purchased, he didn't have racks on his truck at all. He had put a halter on the ram and tied the halter rope into an iron ring he had affixed to the floor of the truck, hitching the rope up close so the ram couldn't go anywhere. Another simple way to transport a sheep is by dog-tying it. In all these handling procedures, it's advantageous to have small breeds of sheep, and small breeds, which make more efficient use of pasture, are better for the homesteader anyway (see Pasture: The Foundation of Garden Farming Success, in Chapter 10).

DOG-TYING A SHEEP

A LENGTH OF BALING TWINE TIED INTO A LOOP

SIT THE SHEEP UP AND SLIP ONE END OF THE LOOP OVER BOTH HIND LEGS. BRING THE OTHER END OF THE LOOP UP THROUGH IT AND OVER THE HEAD

Foot rot is endemic in sheep and serious, although a small flock on ample pasture should not bring a problem — I have had no foot rot in the ten years I've raised sheep. There are vac-cines being perfected to cure the disease, but with unpleasant side effects so far. There are medicines, which, along with keeping hooves trimmed neatly, are supposed to help, but traditionally sheep are run through a copper sulfate or formalin footbath as a protectant. (The only real protectant is a clean pasture.) If you have only a few sheep, you can slosh copper sulfate on their hooves with an old brush or administer an antibiotic. If you have more than a few, in sheep country you make use of a sheep-dipping service that comes to your place with a big vat and runs your flock through it. Or you can build a footbath trough quite simply. All you need is a wooden trough 1 foot wide, 6 inches high, and 16 feet long. Set gates on either side (3-foot-high gates are sufficient) tilted outward a bit to form a chute and run the sheep through. Here are plans for a typical portable footbath, although the sides do not need to be as elaborate as those shown.

PORTABLE FOOTBATH

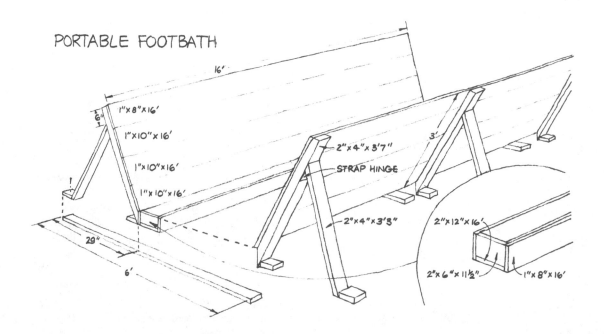

16'

1"x8"x16'

1"x10"x16'

1"x10"x16'

1"x10"x16'

29"

6'

2"x4"x3'7"

STRAP HINGE

3'

2"x4"x3'3"

2"x12"x16'

2"x6"x11½"

1"x8"x16'

PART V

ON THE LAND

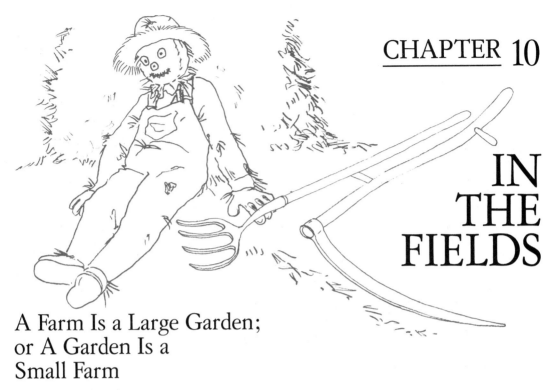

CHAPTER 10

IN THE FIELDS

A Farm Is a Large Garden; or A Garden Is a Small Farm

Homeowners who seriously seek to provide some of their own food, and perhaps some of their clothing, tools, and shelter, too, must first learn to view their enterprises within the proper economic framework, or perhaps I should say the proper *noneconomic* framework. They must understand that expanding their gardening to include some animal husbandry, forestry-orcharding, and home manufacturing is an *extension* of their gardening, not something new or different. What they propose to do might rightfully be called garden farming as opposed to factory farming, which is different from gardening. If they make the error of proceeding into small farming or a cottage industry of any kind using the expertise of factory economics, then what they will have is mostly an expensive hobby.

The differences between garden farming and factory farming are at least these eight, although characteristics tend to overlap:

1. Garden farming is craft work; factory farming is assembly-line production.
2. Garden farming is extremely diversified in production; factory farming tends toward specialization.
3. Garden farming is essentially noncommercial, that is, free to operate outside the structures and strictures that bind factory farming to definite criteria of profitability.
4. Garden farming is primarily an avocation; factory farming is primarily a job.
5. Garden farming is low-volume, low-cost production; factory farming is high-volume, high-cost production.
6. Garden farming arises out of the activity of willing individuals in social groups, usually the family; the work environment is therefore usually happy and positive. Factory farming sets up a dichotomy of boss-worker relationships, and work therefore proceeds in an environment of latent hostility.

7. Garden farming is the search for quality; factory farming seeks quantity.
8. In garden farming, time spent is part of the profit; in factory farming, time is money.

Garden Farming versus Factory Farming

To show in practice what those differences really mean, I will use as an example a comparison of two fields of corn. The first field is my ½-acre one, probably the smallest field of corn in the corn belt. The second will be an acre from a 1000-acre factory farm in this area.

My ½ acre makes no sense at all on its own. I can only talk about it by mentioning in the same breath that it is but a part of a small farm *system* that includes mostly hay and pasture, but also a small field of oats and wheat, an orchard, a planting of berries, a vegetable field and several "fields" of trees for nuts and wood. There is an interior diversity in the small cornfield, too. Small as it is, it includes several species and varieties of corn: enough sweet

corn for fresh and frozen table use, a bit of popcorn, and two rows of cane sorghum, which is a corn-related plant. Within the tiny section that is in field corn, there is still some diversity during some years—rows of hybrid corn alternating with twin rows of open-pollinated varieties. Also, there are melons growing in the early sweet corn, pumpkins at one end of the field and sunflowers at the other, and along one side, pole beans snaking up the cornstalks. Planting, weeding, and harvesting this field is mostly hand work, an hour here or an hour there in late afternoon, early morning, or evening— never becoming hard oppressive work, but, at least for me, generally pleasant unless the deerflies or mosquitoes are worse than usual.

I plow the clover sod for the corn planting in November. In the following spring I disk and harrow it. Even with a small ancient tractor, a small old disc, a plow, and harrow, the cultivation takes only 2 hours. For a planter I use my $30 Precision garden seeder. If I did all the planting at once, it would take the better part of the afternoon. I spread manure on the plot, too. I used to do that by hand, a 3 to 4-hour job done

over a weekend, but now, bowing to age I guess, I use the manure spreader. The corn is hoed two or three times, with various members of the family helping me out. This goes on continuously through May and June, a row or two or three in the evening, relaxing work for me away from the typewriter. By the first week in July, cultivation is over.

Harvest begins in August with the sweet corn. As quickly as we use it up or it becomes too old for us, I cut it, green stalks and all, for the cows and sheep whose pasture is beginning to fail in the dry spells we experience most Augusts. (Cutting this corn allows more sunshine in to the rapidly growing melons, too.) As quickly as the field corn dents in September, I begin to husk out the ears a few at a time and feed the still-green stalks to the cows. I will also cut stalks from a few rows, bind them into bundles, and make shocks to be husked out later (in November), feeding the fodder to the animals. My goal is to have half of the little field harvested by September 25, when the wheat planting season begins. This half then gets planted to wheat. This half also contains the popcorn and the cane sorghum, so these crops must also be harvested in September. The sorghum leaves are stripped from the stalks—my sister and her husband help in exchange for a portion of the molasses we later make, so the job scarcely takes an hour. We feed the leaves to the cows. I cut off the heads of the sorghum and dry them for chicken feed. We haul the stalks to the Amish sorghum press for processing.

In October I harvest the field corn from the other half of the field, jerking the ears from the stalks and tossing them on the truck, pleasant work when I do it a few rows at a time. I put the corn in the crib to finish drying. Then I shred the stalks that are still standing with the rotary mower, and the harvest is finished.

For the sake of simplicity of comparison, let us assume that the whole ½ acre is planted to field corn only, my yield being what it generally is, about 95 bushels per acre (small potatoes in this area) and corn selling at $3 a

bushel. My gross income from the corn would be $285 per acre. I've used about $7 worth of gas, oil, and fuel, including spreading the manure on my ½ acre, which works out to $14 per acre. Three or four sacks of wood ashes go on each load of manure for lime and potash, but these are free. The manure itself is free, as is the nitrogen from the plowed down clover sod. My hoe, the only herbicide I use, is for all practical purposes free, too—I paid 50¢ for it at a farm sale twenty-three years ago. I save the open-pollinated seed from the preceding year's crop. So my variable out-of-pocket costs per acre are $14—let's say $15 if I include the bit of hybrid seed I sometimes use.

Now let us look at the variable costs a factory farmer must pay, using figures for 1984 as budgeted by the agricultural economists at Ohio State University for a 150-bushel yield.

Factory Farming

Variable Costs	Cost per Acre ($)
Atrazine herbicide	4
Counter 15 G insecticide	13
Drying (fuel and electric only)	23
Fuel, oil, grease	19
Interest on operating capital	12
Lasso herbicide	11
Lime	8
Miscellaneous (utilities, crop insurance, etc.)	13
Nitrogen	42
Phosphorus	13
Potash	8
Repairs	18
Seed	24
Trucking (fuel only)	3
Total	**211**

Fixed Costs	
Labor	18
Land rental	110
Machinery	50
Management (5% of gross)	18
Total	**196**

Total Factory Farming Costs (Variable + Fixed)	**407**
Profit per Acre for $3/Bushel Corn	**43**

With corn at $3 a bushel, the factory farmer will gross $450 per acre, but after deducting variable costs, will have only $239. My 95-bushel-per-acre crop will have grossed $285, minus $15 in variable costs, to equal $270.

And what if the factory farmer did not hit his 150-bushel goal, which is entirely more possible than my not hitting my 95? In last year's bad drought, I still got 95 bushels, while the 150-bushel factory farmers were also getting 95, and some, just 2 miles away, were getting only 40 bushels.

But of course that's not all the factory farmer's costs. Fixed costs are also figured by the university.

If the price of corn averages $2.50 a bushel during 1984 (the university, in fact, projects only a $2.40 price), the factory farmer will have *lost* $32.00 per acre.

I don't have any fixed costs to speak of. On a farm of my size it is ludicrous to figure a land charge—no farmer is going to want to rent my ½ acre by itself. What's more, that land is paid for out of my regular job and would be there for me to enjoy whether I farmed it or not. Nor can I rightfully figure in a labor or management charge, as these are my pleasures, not costs. As for a machinery charge, my ancient equipment was either given to me for next to nothing, or, in the case of the tractor, is so old it is probably gaining value as an antique now, rather than costing me anything.

Nor does that tell the whole story. My corn is not marketed as such but is fed through animals at a "cost" of only my labor and thus the "profit" is increased several times. Then the food produced is consumed at home, not sold at wholesale, and so we can figure its value at the retail prices we'd have to pay if we bought rather than produced it ourselves.

Now you know why small and medium-size farms trying to operate the agribusiness way are going out of business, and why small farms like those of the Amish, where farmers are trying to do what I do but on a larger scale, are making very good money indeed.

The practice of garden farming, moreover, is not limited to rural areas of relatively large homesteads, either. It can be practiced in the suburbs and in the city. In fact, the inner city is especially ripe for it because there is plenty of human labor there to substitute for the expensive machinery and chemicals of factory farms. There are also tons (literally) of deteriorating buildings that could be recycled into barns and all sorts of wooden tools, furniture, and shelters. Those acres of crumbling buildings and rubbled ghetto lots could all blossom with tiny garden farms.

Tools for a "Handcrafted" Corn Crop

Obviously, using hand methods of corn production, the garden farmer can conveniently handle hardly more than an acre or two. With the aid of horses or oxen plus a two-row planter and a binder, farmers forty years ago could handle about 15 acres with family help alone, and the Amish farmers still do. I remember my father working very hard during corn harvest, but he will tell you, as most older farmers will, that he was every bit as happily employed as farmers today, if not more so. Mother drove the horses and binder while he set the bundles into shocks and tied them. Mother always sang as she drove, my baby brother asleep in a wooden box nailed to the tongue of the binder. We older children were sometimes allowed to ride the horses while she drove. More often we played Indian in the "tepee" shocks or hunted arrowheads in the bare ground between the corn rows. Our job was picking up ears of corn knocked loose from the stalks by the binder. I remember my parents in their weariness getting into giggling fits, and somehow I never got the impression that they were being bent and broken by "backbreaking" work, as the hucksters of a newer, debt-ridden technology like to say in describing those days. Mother would tell stories while we picked up corn. Dad showed us how to make cornstalk fiddles and dolls, and corn "rockets"—if you folded back the husk on an ear of corn and threw the ear into the air, it would always come down point first, the husk acting as a sort of parachute.

Among the devices that traditional farmers use to increase their "handcrafted" output with-

out significantly increasing their expenses, the corn shock itself is the cleverest. These shocks are not just subjects for pretty calendar pictures. Each shock is a corn dryer that operates without one penny's worth of expensive electricity or natural gas. More than that, each shock is a little barn, sheltering for future use the leaves and upper stalks of the corn plants for valuable animal feed. This fodder is not as nutritional as good legume hay, but does make good roughage for all livestock. Horses not working and beef cows not nursing can be wintered over almost entirely on corn fodder, and often are. The value of this roughage is not even figured into modern corn production budgets, since in large-scale farming, the fodder and stalks are simply plowed under after the grain is harvested. The fodder is not in this case wasted, since it will help increase organic matter, but the traditional farmer who feeds it first and then puts the manure on the cornfield draws that much more profit from his crop in exchange for his labor.

Making Corn Shocks

The method of erecting shocks differs with locality, and upon whether the whole field is to be harvested entirely by hand or with the aid of a binder. Assuming a smallish field entirely harvested by hand, the general rule is to include in each shock 144 hills of corn—12 hills square—or, for corn not planted in hills, an area about 40 feet square with the shock more or less at the center. In practical terms, a row of shocks 40 feet apart includes the corn from twelve 40-inch rows. The two center rows of those twelve will be where the shocks are erected. To start the shock, four stalks from 4 adjacent hills (or four stalks about 40 inches from each other) are bent over *uncut* and, together with an armload of stalks cut from the middle two rows, are tied together to form the center of the shock. The tie is made by twisting one of the *uncut* stalks around the other three uncut stalks and the armload of cut stocks, bending that tie-stalk in under itself as if you were making the first loop of

a square knot. Once the shock is begun, the farmer proceeds to cut the corn in the area around the shock, leaning the stalks against the shock forming a tepeelike structure. When all 144 hills (or 40 square feet) have been cut and placed in the shock, it is tied toward the top. Traditionally, a still-supple green stalk was used to tie, wrapping it around the shock and bending it over itself. With a little practice you can get the ties to hold quite well.

These drying shocks are quite small for good air penetration, but shed water fairly well. By November the corn is usually dry enough to crib and the fodder sufficiently dry to store in the barn. The farmer may let the shocks stand out in the weather all winter and husk out the ears as time permits. He can feed the fodder to livestock, often right on top of the snow. Sometimes when the shocks are taken apart for husking, the stalks are then shocked again. These "fodder" shocks are generally much larger than the original shocks and are retied using a

shock tightener—a rope with a metal loop or wooden or metal catch on one end. The rope is flung around the shock, run through the loop or catch, and pulled as tight as strength will allow, the catch holding the rope from slipping back. Then a length of twine is passed around the shock, tied, and the rope released. This rope tool may be used on the original shock and nearly always is used when shocking bundles behind the binder.

Shocks can be built from bundles without the uncut center stalks described above, but this is difficult to do, since the first few bundles you lean against each other will fall over while you are retrieving more bundles. To solve this problem, tradition invented the "corn horse," which looks like half of a sawhorse (see drawing). The bundles are leaned around the corn horse to keep them from falling over until they are tied. Then the corn horse is pulled out of the shock and dragged to the next shock site.

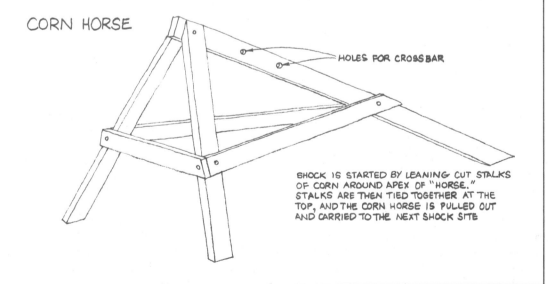

CORN HORSE

HOLES FOR CROSSBAR

SHOCK IS STARTED BY LEANING CUT STALKS OF CORN AROUND APEX OF "HORSE." STALKS ARE THEN TIED TOGETHER AT THE TOP, AND THE CORN HORSE IS PULLED OUT AND CARRIED TO THE NEXT SHOCK SITE

Planting Corn

Traditionally corn is planted in rows 40 inches apart because this was the minimum space a horse needed to walk between rows. If you are going to hoe weeds by hand or use a narrow tractor cultivator or tiller, you can set the rows to an appropriate narrower width, although the increased plant population demands a higher available fertility in the soil. Using organic methods—manure and legume rotations—the wider row widths are better. Certainly do not go any narrower than 30 inches apart.

Corn used to be planted in hills that formed rows in both directions so that mechanical cultivation could take place both lengthwise and widthwise. Most corn is now planted in a more continuous row, a plant every 6 to 12 inches, the latter decidedly better for organic farming or open-pollinated corn. As I've pointed out, yield is not as high, but the ears are generally bigger, and therefore much more efficient for *hand* harvesting. The opposite is true for modern corn combines (grain harvesters).

If one wishes to plant corn totally by hand, the stab planter (or jab planter) can be used. Old ones are fairly common at farm sales and new planters can be purchased from large farm supply firms because they are still used by scientists in small research plot work. They're also available from Lehman's Hardware and Appliance, Inc., Box 41, Kidron, OH 44636. For planting hills that line up in rows both ways, the common tool forty years ago was the horse-drawn, two-row check planter. A system of knotted wire stretched across the field tripped the planter to drop seed at every hill, 40 inches apart. Before these planters were available, farmers made simple drags with furrow markers set in a longitudinal beam every 40 inches. The drag was pulled by hand across the field lengthwise, then carefully widthwise. Where the little furrow marks crossed, the hills were planted with a stab planter.

The little push-type seeders (mine is a

Precision, commonly available from garden stores) follow a design in use many years, and are practical for planting as much as an acre a day. Similar but heavier seeders designed to be pulled by garden tractors or small farm tractors are available for somewhat faster planting.

Hoeing or mechanical cultivation should start as soon as the corn is up, since the secret of easy weeding is never to let the weeds get ahead of you. Hoeing in the rows, you can at the

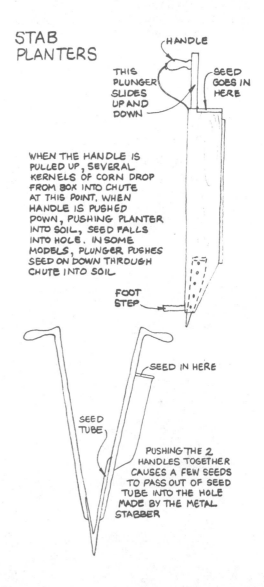

STAB PLANTERS

HANDLE

THIS PLUNGER SLIDES UP AND DOWN

SEED GOES IN HERE

WHEN THE HANDLE IS PULLED UP, SEVERAL KERNELS OF CORN DROP FROM BOX INTO CHUTE AT THIS POINT. WHEN HANDLE IS PUSHED DOWN, PUSHING PLANTER INTO SOIL, SEED FALLS INTO HOLE. IN SOME MODELS, PLUNGER PUSHES SEED ON DOWN THROUGH CHUTE INTO SOIL

FOOT STEP

SEED IN HERE

SEED TUBE

PUSHING THE 2 HANDLES TOGETHER CAUSES A FEW SEEDS TO PASS OUT OF SEED TUBE INTO THE HOLE MADE BY THE METAL STABBER

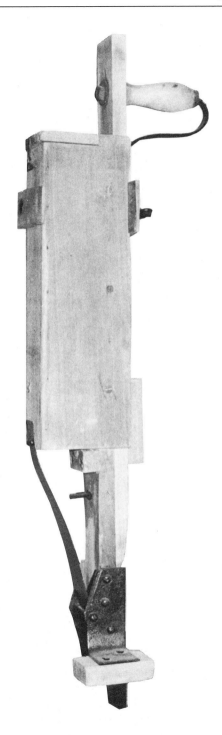

same time thin the corn to a desired stand. Rotary tillers do a good job of between-row cultivating, and there are scores of shovel cultivators for garden and small farm tractors. Or you can hoe between the rows as well as between the plants in the row. Since most gardeners have a tiller, this is by far the most practical alternative.

A traditional tool at corn planting not to be scorned is the scarecrow. Although not 100% effective, a couple of scarecrows in a small field of corn will prevent what can otherwise be a disaster in some years. Birds usually quit bothering corn after it is 3 inches tall. They like to eat the seeds right when they germinate. A scarecrow should move in the wind. And it helps if you make several trips to the vicinity of the scarecrow every day during that crucial germination week.

My scarecrows are very easy to make. I stick a steel fence post in the ground. Then I take a stick—any straight stick—about 3 feet

long and tie a string to each end so that the stick becomes a large clothes hanger. I put an old shirt on the "hanger" and hang it by the string to the top of the fence post. Then I pin an old pair of pants to the bottom of the shirt. At the cuff of each limp sleeve I pin a piece of aluminum foil. An old hat goes on top of the fence post, and I sometimes stick an aluminum foil disk or any shiny object of appropriate size under the hat as a kind of face. The arms of the scarecrow swing on the string hanger in the wind, and the aluminum "hands" wave and glint. I usually tie the trouser legs loosely around the stake at the bottom to anchor the scarecrow better.

Harvesting Corn

Harvesting and shocking the corn properly is a matter of timing. The corn kernels have to be dented, that is, hardened beyond the milky stage, though they will still give a bit to the pressure of your fingernail. The leaves and upper stalk should still be green, but not lush green. If you plant corn in the first part of May, it will be ready for shocking about Labor Day, as a general rule. If you let the corn go longer, until the green leaves are brown, you lose the nutritional value of the fodder. If you shock before the grain is dented, the ears will not finish maturing and drying properly in the shock. Favor the grain rather than the fodder when in doubt. Experience will soon teach you.

To cut corn by hand, there are several different kinds of corn knives: Some are more or less swordlike; others have sicklelike blades. The latter are called corn hooks, which are considered safer in that it is harder to cut yourself with the pulling action of the hook than with the chopping action of the machete types. Some Amish farmers use a unique corn knife that fits on one's shoe—a sort of stirrup under the shoe and a strap around the ankle, with the blade extending out the side of the shoe. With a stomping action of the leg, the

CORN KNIVES

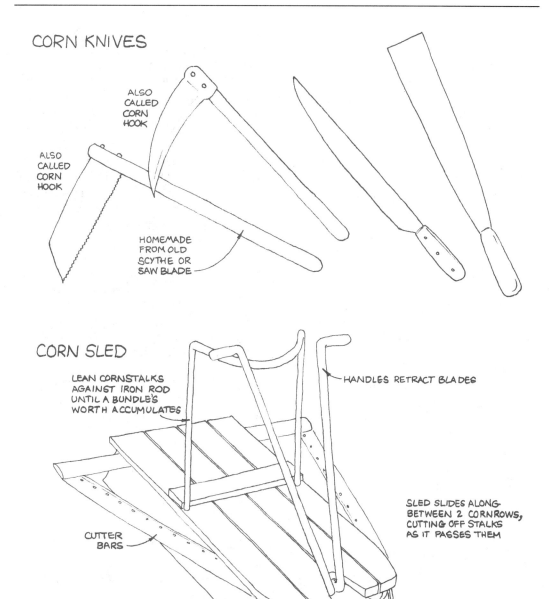

ALSO CALLED CORN HOOK

ALSO CALLED CORN HOOK

HOMEMADE FROM OLD SCYTHE OR SAW BLADE

CORN SLED

LEAN CORNSTALKS AGAINST IRON ROD UNTIL A BUNDLE'S WORTH ACCUMULATES

HANDLES RETRACT BLADES

SLED SLIDES ALONG BETWEEN 2 CORNROWS, CUTTING OFF STALKS AS IT PASSES THEM

CUTTER BARS

PULLED BY A HORSE

cornstalk is severed, and the harvester has both hands free to gather in the cut stalks.

A more elaborate corn cutter, still used by the Amish, predates the binder and greatly increases the efficiency of hand harvesting. This tool is a sled pulled by a horse. The sled has sharp blades extending at an angle from both sides. The sled just fits between two rows of corn and as it slides by the blades slice through the cornstalks. The farmer stands on the sled, gathering in the cut stalks and leaning them against the iron hoop in front of him until he has an armload. Then he places the armload into the nearest shock.

Husking Corn

A big mature ear of corn, loose inside the husk, can be quickly husked out without any tool at all. Grasp it tightly with one hand at the base. At the same time, reach inside the loose husk with the other hand, grab the ear, and twist or bend the ear between thumb and forefinger of the hand holding the ear at the base. The ear will pop right out. On badly formed

ears, nubbins, and immature ears, the husk still clings tightly around the kernels. Pulling it loose with the fingers is slow work, so farmers use a hand-held husking tool to rip through the husk. The earliest such tools were and still are called husking pegs, awllike in shape, of wood, bone, or metal, which are strapped to the fingers. Later, metal hooks sewn to leather that fit over the palm of the hand and strapped to the wrist became popular. Both can still be found in rural hardware stores or ordered from mail-order farm suppliers like Lehman's Hardware and Appliance, Inc., Box 41, Kidron, OH 44636. (Lehman's also sells corn knives and stab planters.) Both huskers rip and loosen the husk so that the hand can more easily strip it off the ear. The ear is then snapped from the husk as described above.

Once in the shock, corn can be husked during any spare time in the winter—an added advantage in spreading the work load out over a period of time when there is little else to do on the farm.

If high-quality fodder is not desired in a particular situation, corn can be husked directly from the standing stalks, and horses or beef

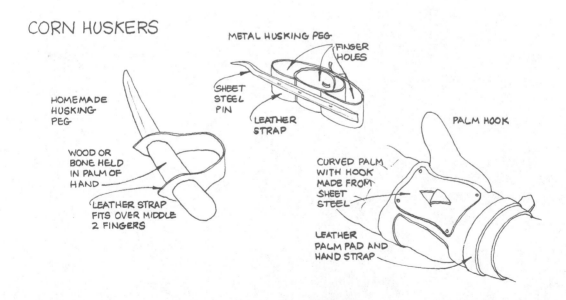

CORN HUSKERS

HOMEMADE HUSKING PEG

WOOD OR BONE HELD IN PALM OF HAND

LEATHER STRAP FITS OVER MIDDLE 2 FINGERS

METAL HUSKING PEG

FINGER HOLES

SHEET STEEL PIN

LEATHER STRAP

PALM HOOK

CURVED PALM WITH HOOK MADE FROM SHEET STEEL

LEATHER PALM PAD AND HAND STRAP

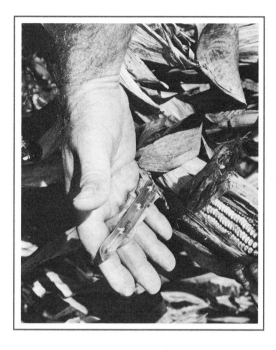

grain needs of a small farm population of livestock. With corn you really need no other grains but only plenty of good hay and pasture, which we'll talk about next.

Pasture: The Foundation of Garden Farming Success

A sure way to tell the direction you should take in garden farming is to watch the trend in commercial farming and then do the opposite. Commercial farming has de-emphasized—and all but ignored in the corn belt—pasture and tree crop farming because these types of agriculture lack the ability to return quick and high-gross profits. But as pointed out earlier, quick, high returns demand quick, high costs, so profit, if any, is possible only in large-scale enterprises.

On a small homestead there is no question that pasture will return more per dollar of cost than any cultivated grain crop. A pasture needs to be mowed, but there are no heavy fuel or machine costs from cultivation or planting. The grazing animals do all the work of harvesting and much of the fertilizing. There is no erosion. Hail and flood cannot really hurt grass. One of the saddest sights to see is an eager new homesteader plow his 10 acres and plant it to corn because that's what the large-scale farmers around him do. He's going to make that 10 acres pay, he declares. He grows the corn just like the pros do and nets very little. But he's out there on the tractor, tearing up the soil. He's a farmer now.

Developing a worn-out field into a good pasture is somewhat a matter of patience. If the cover on the field is nothing but weeds and brush, it might pay to go in and cultivate up a nice seedbed to plant to rye grass together with permanent grasses and legumes. But usually, and certainly in hilly terrain, it is far better to plant down through the existing ground cover with a no-till drill like a Tye, or to ruffle the

cows can be turned into the field later to winter on the dead stalks. Or the stalks can be chopped for mulch and ground cover.

A more modern though now obsolete way of husking corn involved a machine called a corn shredder, which resembled the old threshing rigs used for wheat and oats. The bundles of dried corn and fodder were fed into the shredder, which husked the ears and conveyed them to a wagon while it chopped up the fodder and blew it into a stack or into a barn mow. This method was appropriate for comparatively larger acreages, but questionable on 10 acres or less. Husking corn by hand alone in a cold winter field is not the most pleasant work. Yet husking out 25 bushels of corn a day is not particularly difficult, and with corn at $3 a bushel, it's not a bad little wage.

Summing up, the garden farmer needs to be convinced that where corn will grow, a relatively small acreage managed cheaply by hand methods can supply all or almost all the

This pasture is comprised of low-growing fern-leafed common ragweed, with taller foxtail grass. Both species are self-feeding annuals, which will disappear with good management.

ground up slightly with the disc set very shallow, and then broadcast seed by hand. Or if the ground is fairly bare, just broadcast with no tillage at all. In any of these cases, do the work in early spring when vegetation is dead so the seed has a better chance of coming into contact with the soil.

But before planting anything, apply 2 tons of lime per acre. You can take soil tests to determine the need for lime, but if nothing much is growing there except weeds, poverty grass, and scrub brush, you need lime. (If the soil was of the proper pasture pH, about 6.5 to 7, in all likelihood there would already be a nice growth of grass on it.) After liming, a heavy application of fertilizer will bring on both heavy grass and weed growth, if the soil has any latent fertility at all. But this application is not to the homesteader's advantage. It is expensive, for one thing. Usually it results in more grass than

Stands of grain rye tower over lower-growing sweet clover. Both are commonly planted, either in combination or individually, as a green manure crop for plowing under.

the homesteader really needs at one time. And on really barren, gullied hillsides, it may be mostly wasted.

When we moved here, my pasture had hillside areas totally devoid of any growth except for a few stunted weeds. In desperation I tried a quick fix of chemical nitrogen, phosphorus, and potash. Then I planted clover. Nothing happened. So I went back to garden methods. I spread manure and seeded again. On the worst part, I spread over the manure a layer of red clover hay a farmer friend had given me because rain had ruined it in the making. The clover seeds in the hay germinated after rain, and within a year, all the bare spots were marvelously covered with clover. Eventually the fixation of nitrogen by the clover (and the manure) enabled bluegrass to grow. This generally happens through the northeastern quarter of the United States, if not elsewhere—bluegrass and little Dutch white clover will eventually become the dominant plants. The clover fixes nitrogen for the bluegrass, and this symbiotic relationship continues, so long as mowing and grazing keep down taller plants.

On less problematic areas of the pasture, after liming, I lightly disked the soil surface and broadcast ladino clover, which looks just like little Dutch white clover but is twice as tall. The ladino covered the weedy, partially bare soil the first summer and was a solid lush stand the next year. I had no animals yet, fortunately for the soil, and all that growth rotted down into the ground. The next year bluegrass emerged, and in a year made a heavy sod that continues to this day.

On other sections of the pasture I broadcast orchard grass for late summer grazing (it also makes good hay). On one plot I broadcast bird's-foot trefoil and red clover without any soil preparation. Some of the seeds found their way down through the soil cover and sprouted, just as seeds in nature do. Now, every spring I sow more clover and try other grasses like timothy, which results in a very mixed herbage

Controlling Weeds

To control weeds, mow pastures in late July just as Canadian thistle and wild carrot are heading out, and then again about the last week of August, if necessary. Some weeds I cut by hand—sourdock, which can grow very thick, and burdock, whose big leaves shade out grass and whose burs get in the sheep's wool. Grazing sheep will eventually control such pesky weeds as wild carrot, and rich, fertile, well-limed heavy grass pastures tend to crowd out taprooted annual weeds, too. At any rate, a variety of weeds are desirable in the pasture as part of a healthful diet for the animals.

If pastures lie marshy and wet, tile drainage is necessary. Good legumes and grasses can't grow in wet ground, and the moisture could aggravate foot rot in sheep.

of legumes and grasses. Even wild strawberries and flowers like blue-eyed grass have grown there. I find endless pleasure in walking the pasture in summer when a rainbow of butterflies settles on the various clover and weed blossoms. A meadowlark nests in the pasture, as do several ground sparrows and bobolinks. Even if I had no animals, I'd keep a nice pasture just to walk in.

Healing a Gully

Where earlier farmers on my land had plowed straight down a hill, erosion had carved several gullies in the pasture hill. These scars have been difficult to heal. I have covered them with manure, filled them with cornstalks, and stopped them up with corncobs. The latter stop soil from washing away, although until they rot, grass is slow to grow up through them. Rocks judiciously dug into the gullies (not left high enough to catch the mower) slow the flow of water and prevent fill soil from washing away. But I have relied mostly on repeated applications of strawy manure, and slowly the gully bottoms have grown over with grass, although the scars are still visible. Deeper gullies need to be plowed shut, then stabilized with straw or perhaps tree branches and rocks. The straw can be held in place by pinning down a length of woven wire fence over it, but the fence should be removed before animals are let in to graze. Rolls of old wire fence are good for stabilizing large gullies, but if the rusty wire sticks above ground level, there is danger that cattle might ingest a piece.

A larger gully requires more drastic remedies. The cheapest practical method is simply to fence it off so livestock can't keep grazing away the grass and trees that would stabilize the gully. The fence should be set back from the gully bank a distance of about twice the depth of the gully, says the USDA Soil Conservation Service.

Where you wish to eliminate a large gully completely so that the area can be mowed, bulldozer work is often necessary. Some farmers have used a moldboard plow to close gullies or to at least shape them with shallow saucer banks rather than steep V ditches. When seeded down, the saucer-shaped sides spread out the water, weakening its ability to gouge out soil.

Once the gully has been filled or partially filled, a sod cover is imperative. Mulching over the seeding helps, especially if wire netting or a light covering of brush is laid over the mulch to keep it from washing away. Straw is good mulch; manure, of course, is better. Fescue is a good tough grass that will stand up to the rigors of an old gully's poor soil. But often grasses are slow to come until legumes first cover the bare soil and fix nitrogen. Sweet clover is not good for grazing, but as a pioneer plant to heal a gully, it is one of the best choices. On really rough gully land on steep slopes, black locust trees (a legume) will hold soil and encourage grass to make a stand. They also provide excellent fence posts.

Rotating Your Livestock

A pasture should be divided into at least two parts, and the livestock rotated from one side to the other. It is even better to have three or four paddocks (lots) for rotation. You can keep the animals on one until they have cleaned it up well, then move them to another, allowing a healthy regrowth. You not only avoid overgrazing, but if rotations are of at least thirty-five days' duration, you break the cycle of certain sheep worms. Paddocks also allow you to make hay from parts of the pasture in June when there is usually a surplus of grass. Manuring right after hay has been removed is a good practice, since less of the manure's value is lost in summer application. On frozen winter soil, when there are no growing plants to take up the manure's nutritive value, the manure may wash away rather than soak into the ground.

An acre of good pasture will carry a milk cow and baby beef for four months along with one sheep, unless the weather is excessively dry. Things work out nicely if you figure a cow and calf and ewe and lamb per 2 acres of pasture. An acre will support five to six sheep alone, although I know of some heavily fertilized pastures that carry fifteen sheep for three months. I keep seven sheep on 2 acres of poor pasture for five months. On only fair pasture, I keep two cows and calves and a horse on 8 acres for seven months, taking a cutting of hay off half that acreage in June. The sheep join the cows in October, and some grazing continues until December. The sheep, in fact, find some grazing even in winter on mild days. In the fall I feed some supplemental hay, along with that pasture. The carrying capacity of a pasture will differ from place to place, even year to year, depending on fertility and moisture.

But, says the town or suburban dweller, I can't have a pasture. Not so. Your lawn is a first-rate pasture. Most lawns have been fertilized either with chemicals or years of decomposed grass clippings, until the grass from an excess of nitrogen has a very high-protein content (for grass). If the lawn contains a good admixture of white clover, as lawns naturally do in many areas, you have a very good pasture indeed. My niece raised her pet lamb to butterball fatness on little more than her father's backyard. Although zoning often prohibits it, rabbits, chickens, ducks, geese, and small breeds of sheep and goats will utilize lawn pasture very well, and are practical animals to have *if* you do not keep more than a few. Stock a yard with only one-third to one-half the number of animals you might use in the country. Thus, two sheep to an acre. Their little hoof prints will not trample the lawn, and their little pellets of manure scattered about will not be offensive. Zoning ordinances against animals usually are enacted after someone has stocked an excessive number of animals and has not properly cared for them. Two or three hens roaming your yard and kept on your property will cause no problems, but a coopful getting out, their manure not handled prudently, or a rooster or two crowing at 5:00 A.M.—then you might expect trouble.

Pasture Rotation

The most common fault with small-scale livestock projects is overgrazing due to keeping animals too long on areas that are too small. In addition, the garden farmer, graduating to a small livestock enterprise, has not yet developed a sensitivity for the well-being of a sod grass surface, and he allows animals to trample their grazing lots into a quagmire during mud time. Both overgrazing and trampling can cause as much destruction and erosion as plowing.

Nobody's book can tell you how many animals an acre can support. Climate, weather, and soil fertility give a different answer for every field. An exceptionally fertile field with supplemental irrigation might support one cow per acre per year, while an eastern mountain pasture would support one cow per 4 acres per year, and in the dry western rangeland one cow

per 20 acres or more. As a rule of thumb in eastern humid regions, 2½ acres will support a cow and calf or a horse or five sheep or five goats, for one year. The garden farmer with another job should rarely stock any more densely than that, even if his neighbor farmer does. Denser stocking requires lots of fertilizer and sophisticated management. Sticking to the 2½ acres per cow or horse rule, the part-timer will generally accomplish better economies. An acre looks like a lot of land to a gardener, but a horse will ruin an acre if left continuously on it seven months or more a year, as often happens. Even at the 2½-acre rate, the land will provide good efficient food for the horse for the growing season and hay for winter, only if you remove the horse when the following conditions warrant:

1. When the ground is so soft the horse's hooves sink into it.
2. When the grass has not yet gotten a good start in spring.
3. When the grass gets less than 2 inches tall, especially during periods of drought.

On 3 acres, a horse (or cow or five sheep or five goats) does not need to be managed so carefully. With the extra room, it will not be as likely to overgraze or trample the soil into a mud hole. On the other hand, if the 3-acre field is at least moderately fertile, some grass will go to waste. If the grass gets over 6 inches tall, it is not being grazed intensively enough by farming standards. But this is not necessarily a problem for the noncommerical garden farmer—except that he is losing money. He could be making hay from part of the pasture.

To solve all the above problems, rotation grazing is a must. Even if you have but one goat on an acre, you would be wise to divide that acre into two parts. Rotation allows you to manage the grass successfully—keep it growing ahead of the animals, never less than 2 inches tall, never more than 6 inches. Shifting animals

from one plot to another (if the timing is by monthly intervals) breaks worm cycles. And during the period of flush pastures in May and June, rotation allows you to take a cutting of hay from part of the pasture.

Pasture rotation is an art with endless variations, depending on area, climate, type of grass or legume, and type of operation. A dairy farmer in Pennsylvania with 140 acres supporting forty-five milk cows divides grazing lands into four night pastures and eight day pastures, rotating the cows every few days from one to another and in dry weather onto yet other supplemental, nonpermanent pastures of rye, orchard grass, and Sudan. A rancher in West Virginia keeps beef cows on mountain pastures divided into three sections. In early April the herd goes onto the section that had not been grazed hard the fall before and therefore is growing quicker in the spring. In June, the cows are shifted onto the second pasture—the one that had been grazed hard the preceding fall. Finally, in August, the herd goes onto the third section, which had been used as winter pasture the previous year, but had all spring and summer to grow.

In my own case, I have three pastures, which I use in a sort of busy man's interpretation of rotation. In spring the animals go first on the 2½-acre pasture along the creek until about May 10 when I let them onto the 5-acre pasture, although they still have access to the smaller pasture. I take a cutting of hay from the 4-acre pasture in June. Then in July I turn the animals onto this pasture, too, after it has time to regrow a bit and after I have hauled manure on it to replace the nutrients taken with the hay. The animals still have access to the first two fields, which is not ideal but which fits my situation well enough. In November I turn them into a fourth field—clover plots that I rotate with grain on cultivated land.

Along with rotational grazing, mowing is necessary in most cases, whether hay is made or not. After a field is grazed down, there will still be some tall weeds left that the animals won't eat unless they're halfway starved. These remaining weeds need to be mowed to control them. And when pasture grows faster than the animals can eat, older grass also needs to be mowed to encourage new succulent and nutritional growth.

Experience (or a neighboring farmer) can teach you the best choices of pasture plants for rotational grazing in your climate. Bluegrass and white clover kept short are still probably the best for northern to central areas of the country, but bluegrass goes dormant in late

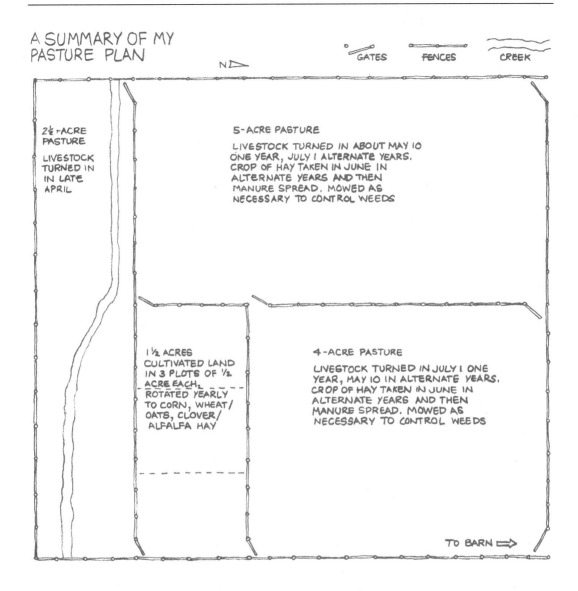

A SUMMARY OF MY PASTURE PLAN

N ▷

GATES FENCES CREEK

2½-ACRE PASTURE

LIVESTOCK TURNED IN IN LATE APRIL

5-ACRE PASTURE

LIVESTOCK TURNED IN ABOUT MAY 10 ONE YEAR, JULY 1 ALTERNATE YEARS. CROP OF HAY TAKEN IN JUNE IN ALTERNATE YEARS AND THEN MANURE SPREAD, MOWED AS NECESSARY TO CONTROL WEEDS

1½ ACRES CULTIVATED LAND IN 3 PLOTS OF ½ ACRE EACH, ROTATED YEARLY TO CORN, WHEAT/ OATS, CLOVER/ ALFALFA HAY

4-ACRE PASTURE

LIVESTOCK TURNED IN JULY 1 ONE YEAR, MAY 10 IN ALTERNATE YEARS. CROP OF HAY TAKEN IN JUNE IN ALTERNATE YEARS AND THEN MANURE SPREAD. MOWED AS NECESSARY TO CONTROL WEEDS

TO BARN ⇨

summer dry spells and does not produce the tonnage that red clover, alfalfa, timothy, and orchard grass do. Red clover and alfalfa do not persist in pastures the way white clover does, and lush stands will bloat cattle. The best way to graze these legumes is as regrowth after a crop of hay. Orchard grass and bromegrass are good dry-weather pastures but need to be planted regularly. They do not persist as well as bluegrass or native grasses. Fescue is less palatable but is used effectively as winter pasture in areas of moderate climate. A spring-planted red clover stand, allowed to grow ungrazed most of the summer, makes an excellent early-winter pasture. But the "one-goat" garden farmer can do no better than to maintain pasture as if it were a lawn of bluegrass and white clover, with perhaps some supplemental pasture plot of rye or timothy or even alfalfa rotated with his garden.

To give you a hint of what can be gained from rotational grazing, one of my neighbors farms 40 acres with sheep and hogs. He grows about 10 acres each of corn, hay, wheat/oats, and pasture. He turns the sheep into the permanent pasture in April. In July, following wheat harvest, he shifts them into the wheat stubble where they nibble on the new clover he interplanted in the spring, eat the weeds and grass in the fence row, and clean up the wheat that the combine missed. In a couple of weeks, he shifts them to the oats stubble after harvest where they clean up the field as they did in the wheat. Then the ewes go back on the permanent pasture and he turns the fat lambs into the cornfield where they eat off the lower leaves from the corn and the weeds not destroyed earlier, and again clean out the growth from the fence rows. The lambs finish fattening in late fall on the regrowth of the old hay field, while the ewes go into the harvested cornfield until late December to clean up fodder and ears missed by the picker.

As this method indicates, grazing need not necessarily be limited to pasturelands. When I was a kid, we sometimes "grazed" an entire field of corn. After the lambs fattened on the lower green leaves, Dad turned the hogs in to "hog off" the ears. When the hogs were fat and gone to market, dry beef cows, workhorses, or sheep could be turned in to winter on the fodder and ears of corn the hogs missed. The whole crop made money, not just the grain, and the animals spread their own manure in the bargain. Measured against the cost of machine combining, trucking, and drying corn today—around $50 to $60 per acre—such seemingly primitive methods begin to look very clever again.

Making Hay

Making hay sounds mysterious to the gardener who is branching into garden farming.

But anyone who has planted a lawn or has dried herbs is more than halfway there. Hay is a lucrative crop for the small-scale livestock enterprise—ask the person feeding $4 bales to a hungry horse. What's more, it is a crop that can be planted and harvested on a small scale with only the minimum of expense in tools. And most important of all, hay is one crop where the small producer has a decided advantage over the large producer. The former can more easily make high-quality hay and so is not obliged to buy expensive supplements and concentrates. The small operator, making a ton of hay or less at a time, can bring partially dry hay into the barn, scatter it out in a thin layer in the mow, and let it finish drying there. (Putting large piles of only half-cured hay in the barn can cause it to heat up and catch fire.) Or he can quickly stack the partially cured hay in the field in little "stooks" or what we call "doodles," which shed rain and which will then allow the hay to dry. Either method preserves the hay's nutrients. By the same token, the small-scale operator can get his limited amount of hay into the barn before it gets too dry.

Planting a grass or legume or mixture of both is basically the same operation as seeding a bare spot in your lawn—or seeding a whole lawn. You know that about all lawn seeding requires is to sprinkle the seed on the bare soil in the spring and wait for rain and warm weather to make it sprout and grow. You can plant a hay crop the same way. If you are seeding part of your vegetable garden to alfalfa for rabbit hay, you can just sprinkle on the seed by hand in the spring and rake a bit of dirt over the broadcast seed, if you wish. Weeds will grow with the hay crop, but if you mow the growth off in July, making hay of the weeds and all or leaving it for mulch, the alfalfa will grow back quicker than the weeds and shade most of the latter out. In the fall you can take a cutting of hay or leave it to make an even stronger growth the next spring. In the next May or June, you take a cutting of hay, perhaps a second in July and a third in August, depending on which legume you have

planted. Alfalfa will last on fertile, well-drained land seven or more years. It is a great destroyer of weeds—able to smother out even Canadian thistle—after several years of strong growth and three cuttings per year. Red clover gives two cuttings per year but lasts only two years.

If you use your lawn for livestock hay—for chickens, rabbits, geese, ducks, perhaps a goat —you can plant and encourage the most persistent perennial grasses and legumes for your region. Bluegrass and white clover are the most common throughout the country. Seeding rates for hay plants vary in pounds per acre because of the different weight and size of seeds. Alfalfa's rate is about 12 pounds per acre, red clover 8 pounds per acre, white clover 2 pounds, timothy 4 pounds, and orchard grass 6 pounds. Mixtures require some compromise. If you're planting red clover and timothy, an old standby in the north-central region, 7 pounds of clover and 2 pounds of timothy will work well. You can always ask the seed dealer, who usually has all kinds of guide charts. The best rule is the one

I've heard old-timers give: Scatter the seed evenly and thickly enough so that a silver dollar will almost always cover two seeds, but seldom more than three. This is a bit thick, actually, but a small portion of the seed won't germinate in any case, and when broadcast, not quite as many seeds will grow as when press-drilled into the soil. Nevertheless, broadcasting is a very adequate and far cheaper way to sow grass and legume seeds.

To ensure better germination, I used to wait patiently in spring till a freeze after a thaw formed an icy, honeycombed surface on the soil in March. Then I'd broadcast clover seed, believing that as the soil surface thawed, the tiny seeds would sink into the ground just a bit and sprout better. But now I get better results broadcasting on top of the ground in April because March-planted clover sometimes sprouts in a warm spell and then freezes to death in a cold snap.

For larger plots and fields of hay, you should invest in a handcranked broadcaster—the cheap-

A
HANDCRANKED
BROADCASTER

est ones are under $20 and will last a lifetime. These broadcasters strap over your shoulder and hang in front of you. You turn the crank to spin a propeller under the canvas and wood hopper. There's an opening in the bottom of the hopper you can adjust to the proper seeding rate. The broadcaster is a very satisfying little tool to operate as you walk along to the rhythm of springtime birdsong. The speed with which you crank determines the distance the propeller will scatter the seed. If you wish to plant a little thicker in one spot, all you have to do is walk or crank slower than your normal pace. I crank so as to seed a spot about 20 feet wide and, at a brisk walk, it takes no time at all to sow a few acres. My cousin routinely seeds 50 acres or more every spring with one of these marvelous little tools he paid less than $5 for years ago.

I use mine to broadcast both grass and legume seeds into my pastures and for inter-planting legumes in wheat and oats (see Crop Rotations later in this chapter). Most grasses are best planted in early fall so they get a start before winter, but will do fine if planted in the spring, too. Legumes are best planted in the spring, but if moisture is sufficient, August is also a good time. Any later than that and they do not get established well enough to endure the winter properly.

In the early fall when the weather and soil are often exceedingly dry, broadcasting is not a good way to sow legumes, since the seed may just lie there and not germinate until it's too late in the year. August-seeded legumes should be planted an inch or so into the soil. In a garden-size plot you can work the soil with your tiller, then run the tiller over lightly again after broadcasting, and rake smooth. In a larger area, disk a seedbed, broadcast, then disk and harrow lightly to work the seed into the ground. Or use a grass drill if one is available. Or be smart and sow only in the spring. For grasses, you can sow when it rains in early fall. My father liked to plant clover seed on snow in late winter so he could see if he skipped any spots—the dark seed showed up clearly on the snow.

Alfalfa is king of the hay field. Pound for pound, all else being equal, it is more nutritious than other hays, fixes more nitrogen in the soil, and produces more bulk. But alfalfa comes from the dry, sandy regions of Asia Minor and is not as well acclimated to humid climates of eastern America as is red clover. In the South, crimson clover is the most often planted legume, but it is not hardy in the North. Raised up with the agribusiness mentality, I was a great alfalfa champion in younger years. Now I grow red clover with a little timothy and alfalfa mixed in and raise more consistent, more trouble-free hay crops than when I planted alfalfa alone. The only real reason I include alfalfa anymore is that the occasional plants that do grow penetrate the subsoil better than red clover, increasing porosity.

Mowing Hay

The closer you can mimic herb drying, the better hay you will make. Legumes are at the peak of their nutritional content just as they begin to bloom, grasses just before they form seed heads. If you could cut sections of hay at this stage and dry them on screens or racks in a breezy building out of sunlight, you'd have the very best hay. And if you are making hay from your lawn for rabbits or chickens, you may be able to do just that. Legume hay made this way would contain almost all the vitamins and protein a grazing animal needs.

But even half an acre or an acre of hay would make this drying method rather impractical. At that size you have to begin to make hay like a regular farmer does, although not completely. You have to leave the hay out in the field until it is at least two-thirds cured. Then you can, if rain threatens, spread it in a thin (12-inch) layer in the hay mow, or any building where space allows, to finish drying.

A scythe can be used to cut small plots of hay. A sickle bar attachment on your lawn mower is nicer. Even the normal rotary mower

can be used, although it chops the hay a bit too fine and will choke up in taller stands. But for lawn hay, the mower will suffice. For larger fields, a tractor or horse-powered sickle bar mower is best, although flail and rotary mowers are OK. Old, used sickle bar mowers are best for small-scale farmers because they can be purchased relatively cheaply. The one I bought for my 30 h.p. tractor cost me $75.

When you have only a small amount of hay you can be picky about time of cutting. I never make more than ½ acre at a time, and usually only ¼ acre, unless I'm almost sure it won't rain for four days. I like to cut about 11:00 in the morning after most of the dew is gone. Then the cut hay will dry faster. I study weather maps and every folkloric sign I know of before deciding to mow. I want two days of sunny weather for sure, and hopefully three. If the signs point to rain the next day, I'll wait, even if it means the hay plants grow beyond their optimum nutritional peaks. It's better to have hay a bit overmature than ruined by rain. One hard rain on half-dried hay makes it practically worthless by my standards; hay not rained on is worth more to me than the asking price usually is. That's why when I need more hay than I can produce on my place, I pay a good farmer nearby $150 a ton for perfect alfalfa and consider it a bargain. Hay rained on even once in the drying may cost only $75 a ton, but to me it is a waste of money.

Raking and Windrowing

After hay has lain on the ground for about a day and is partially dried, it needs to be raked

into a windrow for curing. A standard 7-foot swath of the mower makes a nice windrow, although if the hay is very light you can windrow two swaths together. It is not overly taxing to rake up to ¼ acre of hay at a time by hand with a lawn rake. More than that is so easily done with an old side-delivery rake (I paid $25 for mine at a farm auction) that you should buy one at the first opportunity. I like to rake the hay into windrows the afternoon of the day after I mowed. The hay is still "tough" or green enough at this stage that few leaves shatter off the stems. Once in the windrow, most of the hay is off the ground, so it will dry better. At the same time, most of the hay is protected from direct sun, so it will not bleach out nutrients so much. If rain threatens the evening of the second day, I haul the hay into the barn, even if it is not as dry as it should be. Then, as I've described, spread it thinly in the mow until drying is complete. Or if there is not time even for that, I may pile the hay in the field in little "doodles" to protect it from rain. If rain does fall heavily on the windrows, I shred them with the stalk chopper, scattering the mulch back on the field where it will do more good than running it through my animals.

A heavy crop of hay will take much longer to dry in the windrow than a moderate to light stand will. So I do not put highly soluble fertilizers on my hay. Better a light crop of quality hay than a bumper crop of rained-on uselessness.

Storing the Cured Hay

The hay is dry enough to put in the barn two days after mowing, sometimes sooner in hot, dry weather, or later in humid weather. Only experience can teach you. Sufficiently dry hay has a raspy sound to it when you fork it on the wagon. A forkful is comparatively light. Hay not ready to be put in the barn is raggy and heavy. Hay too dry has very hard and brittle stems and if you shake a forkful, dry leaves rain out of it. If you put the hay in the barn at the right time, some curing and heating will still take place, so don't panic if the hay gets a *bit* hot in the barn. Farmers sometimes used to sprinkle salt on the hay as they layered it into the mow, supposedly to help it cure and not heat or mold,

but I've never found this practice necessary and wonder if it is scientifically sound.

We fork our hay loose, that is, not baled, on the pickup truck. For our ¼-acre and ½-acre dabs, a baler would be an extravagance. We can load the truck to a height of 10 feet from the ground, occasionally climbing up on the load and tramping the hay down. There is a bit of an art to stacking hay up straight and square without side rails to hold it in. We vie with each other over who can stack the straightest side so the work becomes more of a sport. When the truck is loaded, we stick our forks inside the tailgate of the truck, the handles pointing upward so they hold the hay back from sliding off when we zoom up the hill to the barn.

At the barn, one person forks hay from the truck into the barn mow and another stacks it up as high as possible, starting at the far end of the mow. Small garden farmers usually have small barns without enough space for a whole winter's supply of loose hay, and in that case bales solve a problem because more hay can be stored as bales in a given space than as loose hay. However (notice how I am always full of howevers?), where barn room is in short supply and a baler is out of the question, consider making a haystack outside. Years ago haystacks

were common on farms (for the same reason—lack of barn space). Hay keeps surprisingly well in stacks. John Vogelsburg, a large-scale organic farmer in Kansas who has gone back to field stacking, says the hay quality is better than barn-cured hay. Built with good rounded tops, a stack will shed water and only a little hay on the stack surface is ruined. And feeding the hay out of the stack right out in the field eliminates the treadmill of hauling hay to the barn and manure back out to the field.

I've tried building small stacks and have had good luck with them. I pile up the hay just as if I were loading up the truck, keeping the sides straight and filling in the middle as I build upward. I top off the square stack with a rounded bread-loaf shape. The stack settles into a fairly tight surface that rain penetrates only about 3 inches. When I break into the stack for feeding, it has a delicious cured-tobacco smell, better than the good smell of the barn-cured hay, and the animals love it. The trick is to feed out the stack without removing the rain-shedding top first. To do this, a hay saw is necessary. You can saw off about 12-inch layers from the side of the stack, forming a shear, vertical wall that rain does not penetrate. Hay saws were once very common on farms and almost always turn up at

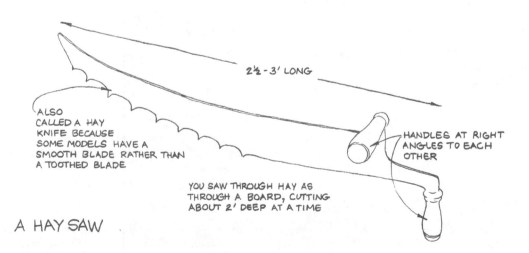

2½ - 3′ LONG

ALSO CALLED A HAY KNIFE BECAUSE SOME MODELS HAVE A SMOOTH BLADE RATHER THAN A TOOTHED BLADE

HANDLES AT RIGHT ANGLES TO EACH OTHER

YOU SAW THROUGH HAY AS THROUGH A BOARD, CUTTING ABOUT 2′ DEEP AT A TIME

A HAY SAW

auctions. If you can't find one, a one-man crosscut saw works pretty well, too. You don't think of hay as being easily sawed, but actually it saws easier than wood, when in a tight stack.

As I mentioned, with alfalfa you can get three cuttings, sometimes even four in one growing season. Red clover gives you two in its second year, after which it generally needs to be replanted. In meadows and pastures with wild and native grasses, you can usually get only one cutting. Orchard grass might give two on fertile soil, but generally only one, for many years, if fertility is kept up. Withdrawing hay regularly from a field requires that you return plenty of manure or other fertilizer—especially potash. On small plots, wood ashes are a practical potash fertilizer and contain the calcium hay plants need, too.

Crop Rotations

Most people view a farm as a fixed landscape—fields, forest, creek, barn, and house, immutable and unmovable, as in George Inness's painting *Peace and Plenty*. Actually, nearly everything on a farm is in dynamic motion. Even the creek in its meanders wanders from side to side in ever-widening loops through the centuries. The forest trees grow up, fall down, move out, retreat, sneak into the pasture, creep up the fence lines. Where proper rotations are kept, the various crops dance from field to field, season following season, year after year, the dance led by the farmer at planting, followed by him in the harvest. The "dance of the farm" is the key to its constant regeneration. Without rotation, there would be no "peace and plenty."

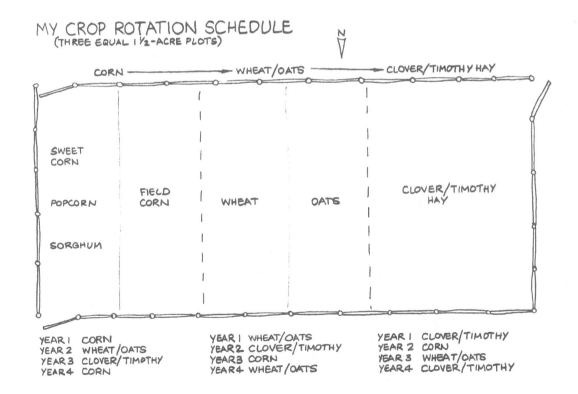

MY CROP ROTATION SCHEDULE
(THREE EQUAL 1½-ACRE PLOTS)

CORN ⟶ WHEAT/OATS ⟶ CLOVER/TIMOTHY HAY

SWEET CORN
POPCORN   FIELD CORN   WHEAT   OATS   CLOVER/TIMOTHY HAY
SORGHUM

YEAR 1 CORN
YEAR 2 WHEAT/OATS
YEAR 3 CLOVER/TIMOTHY
YEAR 4 CORN

YEAR 1 WHEAT/OATS
YEAR 2 CLOVER/TIMOTHY
YEAR 3 CORN
YEAR 4 WHEAT/OATS

YEAR 1 CLOVER/TIMOTHY
YEAR 2 CORN
YEAR 3 WHEAT/OATS
YEAR 4 CLOVER/TIMOTHY

Where the dance is not danced—in monoculture farming—disease, pests, and erosion do the dancing. Then follows a different dance, that of thousands of people leaving the land, leaving that which gave them dignity and equality: ownership and stewardship of a bountiful piece of earth.

Crop rotation in its simplest definition means not growing the same crop on the same land two years in a row. You can rotate just two crops, but three, four, or more will achieve the benefits of rotation more surely. Rotation keeps specific diseases, pests, and weeds from producing a population explosion. Residual benefits of one crop can be passed on to another that can use them. Therefore the general rule is to follow a crop with one quite different from it. Grains and grasses (all grains are actually grasses) should follow legumes (clovers and beans) because legumes fix surplus nitrogen for the nitrogen-hungry grasses. Root crops should follow leaf crops; row crops follow sod crops; vegetables follow berries. The classic exception is that of potatoes, tomatoes, eggplants, and peppers infected with verticillium root rot or wilt. Following them with berries, especially raspberries, will not break the disease cycle because raspberries are susceptible to the same strain of the disease.

Grains and Hay

In growing grains and hay in small fields, the overall rule is to follow, whenever possible, a legume with a grass and a sod crop with a row crop. In the north-central United States, you could do this simply with corn and alfalfa, or corn and red clover. The corn for grain and the clover or alfalfa for hay are the two crops most easily handled with cheaper tools and hand labor on the small garden farm. But it is difficult to get the legume planted in the corn in late summer, and so the land lies bare until spring when the legumes are seeded. The traditional farmer found that he could sow wheat in the fall, after the corn was harvested, and it would grow until cold weather, become dormant, and begin growing the following spring. A legume for hay or pasture could be broadcast into the wheat in spring, and after the wheat was harvested, the hay would grow vigorously. It could possibly be cut yet that fall, and then cut two to four more times the next year. So the traditional rotation of the corn belt came into existence.

But some farmers wanted oats to feed their livestock and so they split their wheat acreage in the rotation, letting part of it lie bare over winter (or sowing a temporary rye cover crop on it over winter) and put that part to oats in the spring. This was helpful from the standpoint of spreading labor—they did not have to harvest the entire corn crop preparatory to fall wheat planting, but only part, then plant the wheat, then go on and harvest the rest of the corn. So the rotation became corn, wheat/oats, hay. The hay was usually kept a second year, thus corn, wheat/oats, hay, hay. The real artists grew red clover for their hay and planted a grass (timothy) with it. Then in the fall of the seedling year, or in the fall of the first full year of growing hay, they would harvest not a second hay crop, but a clover seed crop. Red clover seed is expensive—$40 a bushel off the farm—and they could net from that crop possibly as much as from a normal grain crop because there was no cost involved that the preceding haying had not already paid for several times over. Then in the second year of the hay in rotation, if they chose not to put that field back in corn to start a new rotation, they might harvest a timothy seed crop, because this companion plant of clover would often grow strongly with diminishing competition from the fading red clover. A harvest of timothy seed might also net as much as a normal grain crop, since there was no planting or cultivation cost to deduct from it.

The only drawback to a small farmer practicing such arts and economies is lack of a harvester for small grains and grass seeds. Harvesting wheat and oats by hand is slow work, let alone clover and timothy. On tiny garden-size plots, these crops can be harvested with flails (a piece of rubber hose, doubled, makes a serviceable flail) for the small amount of grain you use in baking, or to feed a few hens or a pair of rabbits. For rabbits and hens, you need not thresh out the grain—just feed the whole plant and let the animals get out the grain.

For larger plots, like my ½-acre ones, a combine is the only practical answer. Sometimes you can get a farmer to custom harvest your grain, although farmers don't like to waste their time with such "small" plots. I bought a combine at a farm sale for $50—ancient, but still in working condition. It's an Allis Chalmers All Crop—it will harvest not only wheat, rye, barley, and oats, but small seeds like timothy and clover, although it has not been practical for me to harvest seed from the latter two hay crops.

The variations in rotations are endless. Soybeans, or field beans of any kind, can be planted satisfactorily after corn. Plant wheat or barley after the beans are harvested. This produces an excellent rotation where a legume always follows a nonlegume: corn, beans, wheat (barley, oats, or rye), clover, back to corn. Or you could translate that in terms of a backyard garden farm with a few rabbits and chickens: corn (including popcorn, sweet corn, and cane sorghum), beans (including garden beans and peas of all kinds), wheat/oats/rye (for humans and animals), and clover/grass for hay and lawn.

It is more important than ever to consider grains in your garden farming endeavors, now that it has become clear that large-scale storage of grains requires the use of potentially hazardous poisons. EDB's cancer-causing effects were known for years—protested since 1975 by certain environmental groups—but the government made no move to curtail its use until the stuff began to show up in drinking water. But its banning leaves a dilemma. It may be that there is no *cheap*, safe way to store large quantities of grain for long periods of time.

Handling Manure

My mother was fond of saying, somewhat facetiously, that manure was about the only profit in farming. Life on the farm has led me to believe that she was much more correct than she realized. I have noticed lately that the very large and progressive farmers who have decided that "manure is not worth hauling out" are the very ones the government has to bail out of financial trouble with huge subsidy payments. I can almost guarantee you that a farmer who is still hauling a lot of manure on his fields (unless he has been suckered into buying one of those expensive, modern new manure disposal systems) is a farmer still in good shape with his banker, if he has a banker at all.

But if you don't handle manure so that your soil gets the fullest possible benefit from its nutrients, then you might as well join the subsidy crowd and preach that manure is not worth the hauling, because it won't be. A common error of fastidious neophyte farmers is that they want to get manure out of the barn before it hardly hits the floor. They pile it outside in bad weather, behind the barn where they can't see it, or at least where the neighbors can't. If the ground is frozen, they dutifully haul it to the field. In either case, the manure leaches in the weather, and rain carries most of the valuable nitrogen, phosphorus, potash, and trace elements into the streams and lakes where they putrify the water.

Leave It in the Barn

In most cases, most of the time, you can let the manure build up in the barn and haul it out during the growing season when many more of the nutrients will go into the soil or be taken up by the plant immediately. Better yet, if you have only a few animals or you have lots of time, remove the manure and pile it under a roof where it can compost without leaching. In the late 19th century, at the zenith of the agrarian society, all good farms had manure sheds where the manure was stored until an optimum time arrived to spread it on the fields or in the garden.

Leaving the manure pack to build up in the barn requires adequate space (see Designing a Small Barn for Easy Livestock Handling in Chapter 8), of course. If a horse is boxed in an 8 by 6-foot stall all winter and the manure is not hauled out regularly, the poor horse's back will be rubbing on the overhead mow joists by spring. And its hide may be raw with urine burns.

Use Plenty of Bedding

Letting the manure pack build up all winter requires that you use bedding liberally. Straw is by far the best bedding, although it works even better if you can put a foot of sawdust down first. (Don't use walnut sawdust or chips in horse stalls—walnut can cause sore feet.) I've heard of farmers putting a layer of straw bales on their barn floors in early winter as a foundation for the manure pack. They claim the bedding never gets wet after that. I can't afford

to be that extravagant because straw is one material I have to buy. I begin by shaking out enough straw bales to make a loose layer of straw about 1 foot thick, if I've not put down a layer of sawdust. If I have, ½ foot of straw to start is sufficient.

The floors of my barn are all dirt—cement is an expensive nuisance, in my opinion. To keep the animals clean, I add fresh bedding on top whenever the old bedding begins to get squishy and smelly. At first this may mean bedding every three days until the pack gets some absorbent depth to it. With an underlay of sawdust, once-a-week bedding may be all that is necessary. Needless to say, if the stall or housing area is roomy, bedding is less frequent. In the cold of winter, less bedding is required because new manure usually freezes. Toward spring, much more frequent bedding becomes necessary. The idea is to maintain a dry, relatively clean surface at all times. But you can overdo it. Too much bedding is wasteful. I've learned that if two bales a week are sufficient for a given area, you will maintain a cleaner, drier floor

putting one bale down in the middle of the week and one at the end of the week, rather than both at the same time.

To scatter out a bale, stick your fork in one slab at a time and shake it into a fluffy layer. Bedding down is a pleasant job. In a few minutes you transform a manure-laden floor into a nice-smelling, dry bed for the animals. It gives you a good feeling knowing that you are making life comfortable for the animals and making yourself some valuable fertilizer in the bargain. The manure pack generates heat—nothing that you notice to the touch, but animals sleeping on it in winter are much more comfortable than sleeping on cold concrete, even if they have a bit of straw or a rubber mat between them and the concrete. Cows on a manure pack are much less likely to step on their teats, slip and injure themselves, or get certain strains of mastitis.

Horses are the hardest animals to winter on a manure pack. Their manure is high in ammonia, so horses can rather easily contract urine burns if you don't put down enough straw to soak up the liquid completely, or you can't let them out during the day. Since horses rarely have as much room as they really need, you may have to clean their stalls out once or twice a winter. But if you bed liberally, you don't have to clean the stable every day or even every week.

Cows respond nicely to a manure pack. Sheep and goats are even easier because their manure is drier, especially sheep manure, and so their pens stay drier with less bedding. Which brings up another point. If you are feeding cows good hay instead of that goopy silage that gives them continuous loose bowels, keeping the bedding dry will be much easier. Chickens are the best animals of all to raise on built-up litter, as they will scratch in it and compost it right there in the coop. Hogs are a special case—they are naturally housebroken to the extent that if they are not crowded, they will pick a certain corner of their pen for defecating. You can make a sort of litter box for them, built into the floor (not with sides they would have to climb over) and add sawdust to it, and keep the pen clean. It is all the rage to raise pigs on concrete with little or no bedding. This practice only intensifies the odor of hog manure—the most unpleasant-smelling barn manure in my opinion. Absorbing the manure with straw or sawdust cuts down on the odor and saves the value of the manure.

Rabbits can be kept in cramped cages only because their manure falls through onto various kinds of collecting shelves. There it stinks to high heaven in the absence of an absorbent bedding. Better to let the manure fall into a litter box on the floor into which straw or sawdust is added regularly. Some clever rabbit raisers put worms into these litter boxes to help turn the manure into compost—the compost for the garden, the worms to sell to fishermen.

Spreading the Manure

Small amounts of manure can be forked onto a wagon, cart, or pickup truck and scattered by hand over a field or as a mulch fertilizer around garden and orchard plants. For many years I did all my manure that way until I was able to buy an old spreader at a modest price. I still fork manure into the spreader by hand. Even if I could get a hydraulic front-end tractor loader into my stalls and pens, which mostly I can't, I'd still fork by hand. Old spreaders, made for hand loading, usually break down trying to disgorge the huge chunks of manure that a mechanical loader puts in them.

Spread manure, if you possibly can, during the growing season, especially if you are spreading it on top of the ground. Another good practice is to haul manure and then immediately incorporate it with disc, chisel plow, or rotary tiller into the surface soil. Burying it with a moldboard plow is not as beneficial, but it's better than leaving it on top over winter. In using fresh manure around garden plants, be careful not to get it close to or in contact with tender plants, if it is dripping wet. It will burn the plants brown. Usually plants so burned

recover and then grow faster than ever due to the nitrogen in the manure, but a bad burn might kill them. I put drippy manure around orchard trees and tall bushes, like raspberries. (When the manure is drippy, you know you weren't using enough bedding!)

Out in the field, I spread most of the manure on the pasture in May, June, and July. The grass responds to a summer application so much better than a winter application—I have tried both, side by side. I do not worry about covering some of the grass, even with a rather heavy application. The grass grows right up through it, and I use a fork to break up the occasional heavy chunk that drops off the spreader. I use the manure as a control tool for the grazing —spread it heavy where the animals are eating the grass too short. The manure dissuades them. I like to put the heaviest application where I have taken a cutting of hay, both to renew the nutrients lost to the soil in the hay crop and to

keep the animals from grazing that area until it grows back strong again.

I put an application of manure on my corn plot right after planting. The corn comes up through the manure, and when I rototill for weeds, I incorporate the manure into the soil.

How much manure is enough for a field? You never have enough, unfortunately, in a normal situation. But trying to reduce the value of manure to precise figures is difficult, if not impossible, unless you are testing and weighing every load you haul. The nutrient content of manure varies with the nutrient content of the food the animal ate, the nutrient content of the bedding (good, bright straw from a fertile field might have twice as much potash in it as rained-on straw or straw from a poor field), and the amount of nutrients lost to poor handling of the manure. Furthermore, nutrient content of manure is generally calculated by weight, but the weight of one load in the spreader might be quite different than another load, depending on how wet the manure is, how much bedding is in it, and so forth. Moreover, the amount of actual nitrogen, phosphorus, and potash in a given manure is not as significant as the figure would be for a precisely measured amount of soluble chemical fertilizer because only about half the nutrients in manure become available the first year, about half the remainder available the next year, and so forth. So if you are applying the same amount of manure yearly to a field, or even every other year, the effect is cumulative.

To quote F. B. Morrison's *Feeds and Feeding,* cited earlier, "Mixed [that is, from all farm animals mixed together] fresh manure, including bedding, contains on the average about 12 pounds of nitrogen, 5 pounds of phosphoric acid, and 12 pounds of potash, per ton." Chicken, rabbit, goat and sheep manure alone can be higher than that; cow, hog, and horse manure can be lower.

A practical rule of thumb is that an application of 10 tons of manure per acre on a field every other year, plus the green manure and legumes in rotation or interplanted in pasture, should maintain fertility with little or no additional fertilizer. That won't give you the highest yields in the county, to be sure, but more than likely the most profitable yields. Don't forget to figure in the manure the animals are themselves applying to the pasture during the summer. Remember, too, that urine contains more nutrients than solids. This is why using enough straw to absorb *all* the liquid is so important.

The amount of manure produced *per 1000 pounds of live weight* is: workhorses, 12 tons per year; dairy cows, 15 tons; fattening cattle, 9 tons; sheep, 9.8 tons; swine, 18.2 tons; and hens, 4.2 tons. *These figures include the bedding except for the hens,* which is why the dairy cows seem to produce more than the fattening cattle. These figures are from Morrison. Deducing from these figures, and extrapolating from others available, it is fairly safe to say that a 1000-pound cow or horse, or five hogs, or five sheep produce about 8 tons of manure and urine a year, not counting bedding. Stress the "about." If they are on pasture half the year, that would be about 4 tons per 1000 pounds of live weight the animals spread themselves.

Another detail of the art of farming: Since urine represents over half the value of manure (except in hogs) the more water your animals drink, the more urine and the more value in the manure. Animals do drink more water if the water tastes good. Thus, the purer the water, the more the intake, the more the urine. That equals dollars the agricomputers never count.

The Minimum Tools for Small-Time Garden Farming

One of the chief advantages of the small garden farm based on grassland farming with pasture and crop rotations is that only a small portion of the total farm is cultivated, and of that cultivated part, only an even smaller portion needs to be cultivated at any one time. To ascertain your power and tool requirements on such a farm, you do not look at total acreages, but rather the number of acres that necessarily have to be cultivated *in any one day.*

Tractors and Mowers

On a place such as mine with 23 total acres, approximately 10 are in woods, orchard, garden, house, barn and so on; 1½ are cultivated in rotation; and 11½ in pasture. At no time do I have to cultivate more than ½ acre per day and seldom do I *have* to mow more than ½ acre a day, either. Therefore, these are my points of maximum power and tool requirements. A walk-behind commercial two-wheeled tractor with tiller and attachments for mowing would suffice—would even have the power to pull one of those small manure spreaders now on the market. I'm speaking of the truly heavy-

duty two-wheeled tillers, like the Ferrari, the largest Mainline, or the Gem from Howard Rotavator. These are European models and there are others, plus some from Japan. They have not sold well in this country because Americans like to ride, even though for the privilege of a four-wheeled rider, they pay a couple thousand more dollars without necessarily gaining anything in performance. If you're not interested in saving money or the handy maneuverability of two-wheeled tractors, you need an 18 to 30 h.p. small farm tractor. Having gone that far, you are capable of farming quite a bit larger place on an 11½:1½ ratio of pasture to cultivated crops.

For example, because I was in a position to procure old equipment rather cheaply, I own an old 30 h.p. tractor, which can handle any of the following: an 8-foot disc dragging a 10-foot

harrow behind it, a two-bottom moldboard plow, a 7-foot sickle bar mower, a 5-foot rotary mower, a two-horse manure spreader, an 8-foot side-delivery rake, plus my 6-foot combine. These are the tools I find adequate for my cropping system. The reason I have both a sickle bar and a rotary mower is that I use the latter to keep open my lanes in the woods, to chop cornstalks, and to mow pastures after they have been grazed down and only rough weeds and dead grass remain. The sickle bar is for cutting hay. With these tools and tractor I could also farm more land than I presently do.

Since my equipment is capable of cultivating 5 acres a day without difficulty, I could handle, based on the 11½:1½ ratio of pasture to cultivated crops, a total farming area of 115 acres—100 in pasture and 15 in a cultivated field rotated to corn, wheat/oats, and hay. I would have to add a baler to my list of equip-

ment in that event, and hire help during the June hay-making period, since I might be faced with making a cutting of hay from nearly half of that pasture acreage. But even with this addition, contrary to what a machinery dealer would pencil out for conventional farming, grassland farming would require a comparatively low outlay of cash to equip a small commercial farm.

What does that translate to in terms of livestock and therefore profits? On my 11½:1½ farmed acres, I raise enough feed for 2 small cows and their calves, 10 sheep and lambs, and about 30 hens. At 115 acres, that translates roughly into ten times that number of animals or 20 cows and calves, 100 sheep and lambs, and 300 chickens. This is even without pushing for the highest fertility.

A year in my little fields sees my "least-cost" tools used in this manner. Starting in early spring, the first plantings are made with the little broadcast seeder, as described earlier, seeding clover and alfalfa on the new wheat and reseeding various legumes and grasses into the permanent pastures. Sometimes I've used the disc very lightly to scratch little furrows into the permanent pasture surface for the seeds to lodge in, but not usually. In late April as soon as the soil is dry enough, I disk the other half of last year's corn plot (half has already been planted the previous fall to wheat) and sow it to oats, again using the little broadcast seeder. The disking not only opens the soil a little for the seed, but kills the first wave of newly sprouting weeds in the soil. I interplant red clover and alfalfa with the oats. The next job is planting corn in the fall-plowed plot that was last year's hay plot. I use the tractor, disc, and harrow to prepare the seedbed, although occasionally, I have used the garden tiller instead. I then plant this ½ acre with a little hand-pushed row seeder, as described earlier. I use the garden tiller and hoe for weed cultivation. After corn harvest in the fall, I disk half of that plot and plant it to wheat with the broadcaster. After the last harvest on the hay plot, it is plowed, usually in November. That is the extent of the cultivation for the year.

Mowing and harvesting hay is, of course, the bigger part of the labor. From late May to about June 20 I am making hay, either in the hay plot of the cultivated crop area or out in the pasture field, more or less continuously during the clear weather between rains. I usually do not cut more than ½ acre at a time. On the hay plots, I will make hay again in August/September, or if the hay is mainly alfalfa, in July, again in August, and perhaps again in late September, although I like to turn under the last cutting for green manure.

Motor Hygiene

Your lawn and garden tractor dealer is secretly glad that human beings aren't half as concerned about the cleanliness of their machinery as they are about the cleanliness of their bodies. If they were, fewer machines would be sold each year because the old ones would last much longer. Dirt sells more new lawn mowers than advertising does. Dirt gets into the engine by way of dirty oil or a dirty air filter, and the subsequent abrasion wears out the engine. Dirt coating the exterior of the engine block makes the motor run too hot. Dirt accumulating on external movable parts makes them wear faster. We all know this, but nothing is easier to procrastinate about than motor hygiene. These simple steps will add years to your equipment and save you hundreds of dollars in a lifetime:

1. At least once a year, clean the engines of your tiller, mower, chain saw, and so forth, especially between the fins of the engine block. Those fins are there to help keep the block from getting too hot when the motor is running. Dirt between the fins negates their effectiveness. If you can take the housing off from around the motor, cleaning can be done fairly easily with a wire brush. If the housing is difficult to take off, work the dirt loose with an old, long-necked screwdriver, a piece of wire, or some similar utensil and then blow the dirt out. An air compressor is great for this purpose, if you have one. If you use a screwdriver or other tool, watch out for air governors and external coils.
2. On water-cooled engines, blow out any dirt that has accumulated on the radiator, too.
3. Wipe away excess grease or oil on exterior moving parts. Dirt collects in such spots and can cause problems over the years.
4. Carbon collects on some muffler ports and partially plugs them, causing the engine to lose power. Keep those ports all the way open.
5. Clean air filters as your maintenance manual directs. Don't shirk. A dirty filter shortens the lifetime of a motor, and if plugged with

dirt, will not allow the motor to run with the proper fuel-air mixture. This is particularly critical on chain saws. Clean those air intake filters often.

6. Change the oil every year or as the manual dictates. Running the motor a few minutes beforehand will heat the oil and cause it to drain out more completely. Drain the chassis, flush and refill with the proper weight and grade of oil. Before filling with new oil, install a new oil filter. Screw the new one on only hand-tight, like the directions say. If tightened too much, an oil filter becomes very difficult to remove a year hence. (There's a special tool you can buy now to loosen stubborn old oil filters.)

7. If the machine is not to be used over a long period of time (several months) drain out the old fuel. Remove the plug and screen from the bottom of the fuel tank and flush out the tank to remove those specks of dirt that always accumulate there. Make sure the breather hole in the cap is not plugged.

8. Again, if the machine is not to be used for several months, remove the spark plug(s) and pour a couple of tablespoons of oil into each cylinder. Turn the engine over by hand several times to spread the oil over the cylinder walls. Leave the piston at the very top position of its stroke or at the "fire" position so no valves are open. Carefully wire-brush away any carbon or corrosion on the spark plug tip before replacing it. Or buy a new one if the engine hasn't been starting as easily as it once did. The oil in the cylinder will cause the motor to smoke excessively for a minute or so when you take it out of storage and start it again. Don't be alarmed.

9. When replacing a patched or new tube in a tire, check the inside of the tire carefully for dirt or anything that might later wear a hole in the tube. Recently when I was mowing off some thorny bushes, a tire went flat. Before I replaced the patched tube I checked the inside surface of the tire. It looked clean.

But when I ran my fingers over the surface, I discovered five more thorns, just barely sticking through the tire. They were not easily visible from the tread side, either. They would have eventually worked on through and caused me no end of flat tires.

Getting the Most Out of a Farm or Garden Tractor

A novice to power farming or gardening is likely to think of a tractor as a machine to pull plows, discs, wagons, and so forth, not appreciating the many other uses it can be put to that greatly increase its value. Most of these capabilities are now being incorporated into garden tractors and even some rotary tillers, and a homeowner aware of the potential versatility of these tractors can save lots of money.

Beginning in the 1950s, hydraulic power systems began to appear on farm tractors with the capability of lifting implements mounted to or pulled by the tractor. Refined and combined today with three-point hitch arrangements, tractors of both farm and garden variety handily lift attachments for movement from field to field, or for precise turning and backing into small garden plots. But this ability only begins to show the versatility of hydraulic lift power. It also makes possible power lifting and lowering of manure scoops and small 'dozer blades.

Manure Scoops

As every livestock farmer knows, and every homesteader needs to know, there is no handier tool than a manure scoop—even if you don't have any manure to scoop. With it, you can lift just about anything; your tractor becomes a powerful, movable jack that can be raised about 15 feet (or more, depending on tractor size) in the air. The manure scoop can easily be slid under a log, for example, raising it for easy bucking or moving, or if it is not too large, lifting it onto a truck. Split wood can be carried on it to the truck and dumped in. The scoop is great for lifting and removing old fences and fence posts. It will hold a sagging barn beam up while you replace the supporting pillar. At butchering, it will carry the slaughtered hogs to the scalding barrel and can be used as the scaffold from which to hang the carcass for gutting. You can shovel away snow drifts and level gravel drives with it. It is great for dislodging large rocks and carrying them away, and for lifting an entire shock of corn and hauling it to the barn. It can replace a ladder because it can lift a human up into a tree or along a wall to be painted. And it is handy for lifting and moving balled and burlapped trees for transplanting.

If you have a farm tractor of from 30 to 50 h.p., made from the '50s on to the present, there is almost always a manure scoop made to fit it, and for sure a three-point hitch adapted to its drawbar. Check with the dealer who handles your tractor brand. If you have an old Oliver or Minneapolis-Moline (neither is manufactured any longer), talk to a White dealer, the company that bought out these models. If it's a Massey-Harris, see a Massey-Ferguson dealer. Before buying an old tractor, it is good to check to see if parts are generally available for it. Surprisingly, you can still buy new parts for many tractors thirty years old or more.

Air Compressors

A four-cylinder tractor can replace an air compressor with the addition of a little-known kit you can buy for about $10 at automotive supply stores. You remove one spark plug and insert a fake plug from the kit in its place. This fake plug does nothing but direct air pushed by the piston through it into an air hose attached to it. The hose has a pressure gauge on it. Start the motor and, though it doesn't run smoothly firing on only three cylinders, it is sufficient for the short lengths of time it takes to pump up tires or pump up the air pressure in a spray tank. Don't forget that there's gasoline

atomized in the air pumped this way. Spray painting with this air could cause some solvent incompatabilities.

Using the PTO Shaft

But by far the most useful by-product of a tractor's lugging power is its power-take-off (PTO) shaft, for which innumerable tools can be powered that otherwise would need their own motors. PTO capability is now built into most garden tractors and even some machines we tend to think of as tillers, especially those made in Europe. The Pasquali two-wheeled garden tractor has some seventy attachments, many of them for the PTO, which will do everything from shear sheep to saw wood (Pasquali USA, Verona, WI 53593).

Whether you have an old farm tractor or a new garden tractor, consider this partial listing of PTO-driven tools it can power: mowers, tillers, binders, seed harvesters, saws, hedge trimmers, electric generators, bale conveyors, post-hole diggers, broadcast seeders, lime and fertilizer spreaders, air compressors, sprayers, grinders, gristmills, cement mixers, mulch choppers, power brushes, grindstones, and snowblowers. By using your tractor fully as a power source, you save the cost of all the motors these tools would individually require.

A Diet for a Small Motor

Experience often proves that the reason for mechanical failure is simply a lack of proper lubrication. Next to keeping a motor clean, the most important maintenance rule is to keep it well fed. While that rule holds true for all engines, it is particularly true of the small, two-cycle engines normally found on lawn and garden tractors, chain saws, and other mechanized tools. These motors do not have separate gasoline and oil tanks; the gas is mixed with the oil to provide both fuel and lubricant. The standard mixture rate is 16 parts regular

leaded gas to 1 part two-cycle engine oil. Unless you have specific instructions to the contrary, no other ingredients will do. It is particularly important not to use regular car or four-cycle engine oil in the mix. It will jell the fuel in the heat of operation. The simplest way to get the right ratio of mix without having to measure every time is to use a gallon gas can and buy two-cycle oil in the handy half-pint cans. Fill the gas can half-full of gas, dump in a half-pint can of the oil, add the rest of the gas, and you have your 16 to 1 mixture, well mixed.

Some manufacturers of two-cycle motors make oil for their machines that require a 32 to 1 ratio or some other formula, although rarely. Follow the maintenance manual that comes with the motor.

You can get too particular in my opinion. I read in a popular chain saw book that refineries make a gasoline for summer that will not evaporate so easily and another gasoline for winter that is more volatile. The operator is instructed to use only summer gas in summer and winter gas in cold weather. I'd never heard of such a thing and so far, I can find no service station manager who has, either.

In four-cycle engines where oil and gas have their own separate tanks, regular leaded gas is the rule, and for oil, whatever the maintenance manual stipulates. Regular motor oil comes in various weights and classifications. Previously, a lighter oil was used in winter than summer, but the standard usually used today for summer and winter is an oil designated on the can 10W-30 or 10W-40. Follow the maintenance manual scrupulously.

In addition to engine oil, some small tractors and all large ones have transmission gear cases that need to be fed, too. Gear oil is much heavier than engine oil and also comes in various weights—80, 90, and more. Again, follow the maintenance manual. When a motor is new, it is a good time to check over the various oil reservoirs on it to familiarize yourself with the location of filler caps and drains. After the

Use That Used Oil!

Not only engines, transmissions, and bearings need the protection of lubrication. Wherever two pieces of metal rub against each other, oil will make operation tremendously smooth and easy. Keep a squirt oilcan handy and filled with the used oil left over from an oil change. Squirt it on drive chains (but use regular chain saw chain oil on saw chains) and on adjusting levers operated by hand. Occasionally I clean the inside bottom edge of my car body where the panels are more prone to rust and squirt on a coat of used oil.

Many other tools will benefit from a regular coating of used oil. My neighbor keeps a bucket of used oil handy by his toolshed. When he puts away a hoe, shovel, scythe, or any other such tool, he first dips it in the oil after cleaning off the dirt. Bare metal will otherwise rust quite quickly, making it much harder to work in soil. Cover sickle bar mower blades with used oil, too; I keep an old paintbrush in the bucket and slap a film of oil over guards, knife sections, and bar at the end of the mowing season. Otherwise these metal parts, shiny from dragging through the grass, will quickly rust. Garden cultivators and discs should be covered with oil for the same reason. Above all, the shiny moldboard of the plow should be kept either coated with grease or used oil between uses. Don't forget the back side of the plow point and the coulter ahead of the plow point. A rusty moldboard will not plow well and is *much* harder to pull than a shiny one.

motor is covered with dirt, it is easy to forget to check oil levels in transmissions.

Tiller and mower attachments on gear-driven tractors have their own transmission gear cases that must be kept adequately filled.

Bearings on tools are usually kept lubricated with grease. To grease them, locate the little metal grease fittings, slip the head of a grease gun over them, and pump. Usually a pump or two is sufficient, and it should be done on a regular basis. Some bearings nowadays are packed with grease at the factory and don't have fittings. Some of these are sealed and need no more attention; others need to be repacked occasionally. Even in reading the manual, you might overlook such a detail. I did.

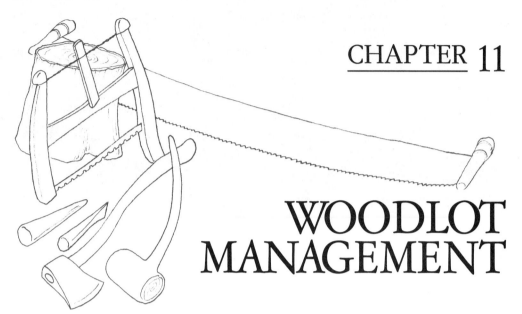

CHAPTER 11

WOODLOT MANAGEMENT

Why Even the Smallest Landowner Should Grow Trees

We are dutifully impressed by the benefits trees bring us, although too often not enough impressed to plant a few. Trees provide food and shade, stabilize soil and groundwater levels, provide a habitat for legions of animals and insects, act as windbreaks, and so forth. Now we're learning that trees are important for maintaining a balance of oxygen and carbon dioxide without which the so-called greenhouse effect could warm the earth too much—with catastrophic effects.

But there is a more practical, down-to-earth reason why you should plant trees. A proper "miniforest," even in the backyard, can produce more food than your garden, and with a most important by-product: wood. Of all the natural resources we manufacture into useful products, none is more versatile than wood—not iron, copper, rubber, coal, aluminum, or whatever. *Yet wood is the only one of these materials we can produce for ourselves on our own land at almost no cash cost.*

The first reason many homeowners resist the idea of a tree grove is that they feel they do not have enough room. But one good walnut tree could supply most of the furniture a house needs (after producing nuts for years). Orchard trees can be the source of quite valuable wood (see Treasures in Wood), after producing food. More wood can be produced on a small plot than the gardener imagines because trees use the space *above* your property. Morton Fry, a major supplier of hybrid poplar trees (Miles Fry and Son, Inc., Ephrata, PA 17522), says that 1 acre of his poplars (1200 trees per acre) will supply 5 cords of wood per year for sixteen to twenty years, which is enough to make the average home fuel-independent. The trees resprout from the stump—the old-world practice of coppicing.

On less than ½ acre, you can easily grow, in twenty-five years or less, enough white cedar trees for a log home. At least one log home supplier follows an innovative reforestation

program: They plant, in the name of every customer who buys a house, 100 seedlings to "repay the forest."

A second and more formidable reason gardeners and homeowners fail to see the practical investment opportunities in trees is that trees "take too long to mature." Commercial sawlogs do take 40 to 100 years to reach a marketable size, although on good soil some species may be ready, as in the case of southern pines, in 20 to 25 years. But trees on the homestead become useful much sooner than that. Fry's hybrid poplars, for example, are ready to harvest in only 4 years. Thinnings for

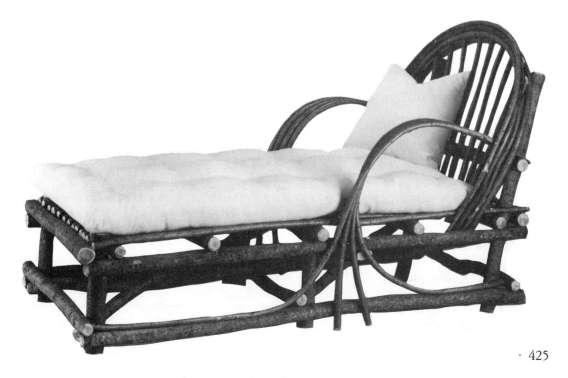

fuel wood can be taken from any timber stand in 8 to 10 years. Orchards begin to bear in about 5 years, and their fruit woods, harvested later, have special value for woodworkers. Young ash and hickory sprouts, less than 10 years old, make the best handles. Rustic furniture, fence work, creek bridges, lawn chairs, splints for weaving baskets, and such can all be made from trees less than 10 years old.

And as a long-term investment, a black walnut tree is hard to beat. In fifty years on good soil a black walnut planted from seed could be worth from $800 to several thousand dollars for veneer. (A 150-year-old black walnut sold recently by an Indiana farmer had a value of $20,000 for veneer.) Ten to twenty of these trees on the back of your lot could amount to a tidy little retirement nest egg. In the meantime, black walnut cake is not too hard to take.

Home-Cut Lumber

What makes home wood production more practical today than ever, even in residential areas, is not just the high price of wood, but the wide assortment of new home tools to "process" the wood. With a chain-saw mill, you can cut up a tree into lumber yourself. The guide and special blade used are inexpensive (under $200), and if you need a chain saw anyway it is not much of an added investment, and you save the high cost of hiring someone to move the log(s) to a sawmill and cut them up. (Who wants a big tractor dragging a log out of the backyard?) In fact, no commercial sawmill I know about will buy a backyard tree because of the risk of nails or wire being imbedded in it. If you cut into metal with your chain saw, the cost of resharpening or buying a new blade is minimal compared to the thousands of dollars it might cost a sawmill to repair one of its saws.

Chain-saw mills are practical for cutting out short bolts or thick beams, but not for milling boards to 1- or 2-inch thicknesses, except where only a tree or two is being cut up at a time. For such milling, another innovation is available to homeowners: the portable band-saw mill. These cost around $5000, within the price range of the small woodlot owner and farmer. Custom operators are beginning to offer their services to even small landowners like the backyarder. Blades for the band-saw mills cost as little as $20, and so the operators can risk running into a rusty nail in a yard tree. What most of them do is strike a bargain with the homeowner. The latter supplies the first blade and if the operator does not encounter metal, he refunds the homeowner the cost of that blade. Fair enough. And much hitherto "worthless" wood can now be turned into valuable lumber.

So in one unheralded little technological advancement, humans have opened up to commercial possibilities the whole "urban forest." Add, to these portable mills, the home shop power planers and resawing band saws, and it is now possible for the homeowner to prepare wood for woodworking almost as easily as he prepares food to eat.

Treasures in Wood

My brother made a gunstock out of a piece of curly black walnut wood that he got for free. Or rather, for having a keen eye for wood. Curly grain, sometimes referred to as curly figure, tiger-stripe, or fiddleback, has a spiral ribbon of darker wood running more or less at right

angles to the true grain. It is beautiful beyond words in finished wood, especially when the changing angle of light reflects off it and makes the wood seem to shimmer. Curly grain is usually found in maple, though even then it is rare. In black walnut, it is found so seldom that my brother's gunstock is more jewel than wood and makes his rifle extremely valuable.

Priceless Patterns in Freaks of Nature

Curly grain is found most often around the "bell" near the roots. It occurs because the longitudinal cell structure is stressed in some way there during growth. Most mills scrap this wood. If you watch for heavy slabs, you can pick up a good supply of curly wood very cheaply. My brother noticed the unusual shape of a scrap limb from a black walnut tree that was destined for firewood. A section of it unaccountably bulged outward from the normal diameter and then back in again, sort of like a burl, only encompassing the whole circumference of the limb rather than one side of the trunk as burls usually do. Since burl wood always contains a striking grain configuration, much in demand from cabinetmakers, my brother thought perhaps the limb might prove to be interesting. When he sawed it open lengthwise, carefully, with a circular saw, behold.

You can never tell for sure what you have in the way of wooden "jewels" until you saw the raw wood and plane the surface smooth. But there are sometimes hints. If you are splitting wood and it rives apart revealing a washboard-like, cross-grained surface, stop splitting. You probably have a piece of curly-grained wood worth much more than firewood, even in a short block. If you don't work wood yourself, someone who does will pay you well for it. (A good book to read is *Understanding Wood* by R. Bruce Hoadley, The Taunton Press, Newton,

Conn., 1980.) If the trunk surface of a maple is covered with pimply little swirls *under* the bark, you probably are looking at bird's-eye maple, another very valuable, exotic accident in wood.

Many jewels in wood are routinely burned in the stove. Only recently I learned that artistic cabinetmakers such as James Krenov prize white ash logs that have large diameters of dark heartwood in the centers. When such a log is slabbed out into matching panels, the configuration of dark heartwood bordered by white outer wood makes interesting and unusual patterns. I fed this kind of wood to the stove all last winter!

Another valuable part of the tree, especially in black walnut, is the underground portion of stump and the large roots leading directly from the stump. Crotch wood—where the trunk

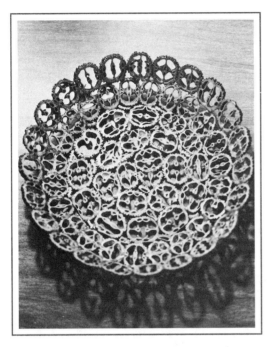

If you look closely, you'll notice that this unusual basket is crafted from sliced walnut hulls.

separates into two smaller trunks, or a trunk and a large limb—often reveals beautiful "feather grain" when cut longitudinally and planed. Since these pieces are hard to split anyway, save them for woodworkers.

When certain fungi attack wood, the beginnings of decay are accompanied by brown or black staining through the wood, which show up as well-defined, dark wavy lines on the surface of a sawn board. Varying shades of white, brown, and grey wood lie between the lines, somewhat marblelike in appearance. This phenomenon is called spalting, and spalted wood, before softening from rotting, is very desirable for turning into bowls or for plaques or other wood utensils. Don't burn it until you've shown it to woodworkers.

Woods Prized by Woodworkers

No fruit wood should be burned until its possibilities for other markets are explored. Red mulberry resists rot almost as well as black locust, which suggests numerous outdoor uses for it. Wood-carvers are always on the lookout for blocks of applewood. Artists who express their skills in handcarved woodcuts have a preference for endgrain of peach. We think of wild cherry as a cabinet wood second only to black walnut in desirability. Tame cherry wood is also beautiful, though its trunk affords only the smallest boards. Pearwood is a beautiful orange-yellow when finished and is used for expensive tool handles. Persimmon wood was once the preferred wood for golfers and clubs made of persimmon are still highly prized. A very large persimmon tree with a clear trunk is quite rare, though specimens still grow in the Ohio River valley. Such trees are very valuable and prized by the veneer factories of southern Indiana.

In fact, almost any tree that is very large for its species, especially if it is normally too small for woodworking, has extra value. Lilac is the preferred wood in the Scandinavian countries for rake tines, and you should save any lilac trunks that grow to 3 inches in diameter. Collectors and spoon makers would be most interested in getting such unusual wood. Often, large old Kieffer pear trees, planted by pioneers, are bulldozed thoughtlessly away when, in fact, woodworkers eagerly search for such large pieces of pear.

In the search for jewels in wood, the urban and suburban backyard may be as lucrative as the farthest wilderness woods because of the greater variety of unusual trees. Holly is a dense but lovely wood for carving, much favored by treenware makers. Dogwood can spend a lifetime beautifying a lawn, and then become valuable wood wherever impact stress is a factor;

Finds on the Tree, and Within

Not all wood jewels on trees are necessarily parts of the tree. Certain types of bracket fungi that grow on logs or tree trunks can be found in gift shops—dried, varnished, and sold as, well, jewelry. The "fairy stool," which grows on almost any rotting wood, is often used this way. "Artist's conk" grows in large semicircular shelves on tree trunks. The off-white underside of dried specimens scratches a darker color underneath, and artists sketch pictures on them. The fungus is then set on edge—where it had been fastened to the tree—to display the drawing. These fetch good prices.

dogwood is used for the shuttles in commercial looms. Honey locust has an unusual grain—pinkish brown and white—takes a high finish, and makes attractive furniture. But you never see honey locust furniture because lumbermen avoid it like the plague; the long thorns end up in the tires of their vehicles. But for twenty-five years now, thornless honey locust has been a favorite lawn tree, and as these specimens age and die or succumb to the mimosa webworm, the wood can be salvaged advantageously. It makes excellent firewood, too.

Nature's Curves and Bends

Naturally curved logs and limbs have special value for many woodworkers. Some wood can be steam-heated and bent, but why go to the extra labor if a curved piece can be found? Heavy brace beams and sled runners are beyond steam bending. In these cases, our grandparents saved trees that grew with a natural bend in the trunk and sawed them out for runners. They kept an eye out for multiforked branches and made pitchforks out of them. Chair rockers could be band sawn out of curved branches. Wooden arches could be pieced together from two pieces of curved trunk. One piece could make a curved plow beam or plow handles. Shipbuilders and barn builders of the 1700s used the tall forest timbers for straight one-piece spars or for main beams, but they highly prized the hedgerow oaks with many thick branches from which they could cut various curved and forked bracings and bulkheads. This artful skill

OLD HEDGEROW OAK TREE FOR CUTTING OUT BRACES AND CURVES

is as practical today as it was yesterday. A prize-winning mirror shown recently in *Fine Woodworking* magazine was oval in shape—made from three pieces of naturally curved wood artfully mortised together.

After all this extolling of fine wood, I have said nothing of the nuts, fruits, syrups, oils, gums, and honey that trees provide long before they are ever made into furniture. The basswood tree (linden) comes to mind. It has a very soft, but fine-grained wood and is today much sought after by carvers as a substitute for more expensive balsa. It is the wood from which piano keys are made. It grows fast. It produces fragrant blooms that bees turn into an excellent honey. Its young leaves are excellent in salads. What more could one ask of a plant?

Taking Care of Your Tree Grove

One of the most magnificent stands of timber left in our county, where most woodlots have been bulldozed away for surplus corn and soybeans, belongs to a man who has not much nice to say about modern "scientific" woodlot management. This man loves his trees as he loves his land; he is the only farmer I know who ever built benches along the creek edge of his pasture "for meditation purposes." He likes to point out that under "proper" scientific forest management we now have less lumber and more tree problems than ever.

He nods up at his trees as we walk through his woods. "The foresters insist that I cut down all those big trees because they are mature. But I've seen what happens under that kind of sharp management. All the good trees come down at once whether they need to or not. Then, after all that glorious talk about how he is releasing

young trees to grow more vigorously, the farmer realizes it will be thirty years until he has a timber sale again. He gives in to greed and bulldozes the whole woodlot into a cornfield."

The bottom line under modern commercial forest management is to get the most for the least, and that is how we have "managed" away so much of our forests. Some of what forestry science considers to be good management practice is rather pompously anthropocentric. The forest can manage for itself quite well without us. It will grow the right species on the right sites in the right climate. It will plant, thin, and prune itself into magnificent stands of trees the eye of man may never see again. All those brochures the Forest Service publishes to show how to thin trees and release the more valuable ones are so myopically generalized as to be worthless or downright harmful, as I learned from experience. The introduction of new species to an area ignores millions and millions of years of natural trial and error and invariably leads to tragic mistakes, like the colossal fiasco in Amazonia where Daniel K. Ludwig destroyed huge areas of rain forest and tried unsuccessfully to establish fast-growing *Gmelina arborea*.

Tree Care in an Established Rural Woodlot

First, wait. For awhile do nothing at all and let the trees instruct you. If the woodlot has been pastured, remove the livestock. Determine, after you have lived with the grove awhile, the best routes for logging and walking trails that skirt low-lying wet areas and avoid steep inclines and declines. Clear the trails. (Of course, if the land is very steep, making trails may be impossible, and logs and firewood may have to be sawed on site and carried or horsed out.)

Don't bother replanting. Do not waste time planting a whole bunch of trees in an established woodlot. The trees will replant themselves quite well once there are no livestock around and/or no owner who wants a park and so mows down what he considers to be the "brush" between the old trees.

Let the brush grow up. The thick brush that comes up is a sign that the woodland is doing its job. The brush may at first be thorny bushes and so-called weed trees, but very soon, seedlings of various native trees will sprout densely and grow up through the brush. In our area, maple, ash, and wild cherry grow best in this role because they are somewhat shade tolerant. Do not be alarmed that the "brush" makes walking impossible. You are not "letting the woods go to hell" as one person told me I was doing when I allowed my old sheep-pasture parklike woodland renew itself this way. In about eight years, the dense stand of new seedlings will thin itself and shade the ground well enough to stop the growth of weeds and thorns. In the meantime, walk on your logging trails.

Don't be too quick to thin. If you try to thin the tree stand to a more parklike environment, all you do is make it necessary to prune the saplings so they grow straight, tall, clear trunks. *In a dense stand they will grow this way of their own accord.* All those little trees are competing for available light—racing each other toward the sun. The one that gains a bit of advantage, because it is best adapted to that particular site, will grow slightly faster, and the trees around it will die, or weaken, and you can cut these for firewood. Don't rush the thinning, like I once did. Impatient with nature, I thinned a stand to one tree every 14 feet, or so as the forester advised, when the trees reached a trunk diameter of about 4 inches. I overdid it, he said later. All I accomplished was to let in too much light to the forest floor, encouraging undesirable low-branch growth on the trees that remained, and weed growth on the forest floor. Had I waited two more years, this stand would have mostly thinned itself, as the stand nearby did. In the woods, nature usually knows best.

The more variety the better. If you want to cut out crooked trees or less commercial species, go ahead. The foresters have tons of advice for you in this regard. But as pointed out in the previous item, it is these very trees that can supply you with wood you may not find elsewhere. And the more variety you have in the woods, the better the ecological health. Foresters tell us to cut the beech out of our woods because it has little commercial value, and the limbs tend to spread horizontally and shade valuable seedlings out. But beech wood is hard wood, good for flooring, joists, plates, rafters, thresholds, and many other uses. It's also excellent firewood. It produces nuts (mast) for wildlife, and old trees tend to be hollow in the tops, creating homes for a variety of wildlife important to the overall health of the woodland.

When to harvest. A tree will let you know when the time has come to harvest it. Crowded saplings will die quickly. An old tree dies back slowly, but you can see it happen by the dead limbs "balding" in the top. Fungi may grow on the trunk of a tree that looks quite alive. That is a sure sign that the tree is dying.

Starting a New Rural Woodlot from Scratch

Unlike the preceding situation, you are going to have to plant trees when starting a new woodlot. Actually, you wouldn't necessarily have to, since abandoned fields will revert to forest of their own accord from seeds windblown and bird-carried into the area from peripheral trees. But this method is unnecessarily slow, and the seedlings will not usually be thick enough to self-prune into a straight, tall stand.

Stick with species with proven track records. Plant species native to your area or at least those nonnatives known to grow well in your area. The forester can tell by analyzing soil types and nutrient levels in your proposed wood-

lot how thickly to plant the trees and when to plant what.

Plant seeds for hardwoods. For deep-rooted hardwoods it is much easier to plant seeds than seedlings. Gather acorns and nuts from good trees and plant them. But plant many, because wild rodents will likely eat most of them. Gather ash and maple seeds and scatter them on the field.

Weed control. If the trees are native, you need not worry too much about weed control or grass control because the trees will eventually dominate. But the field will look messy for several years. If you have planted Christmas trees where evergreens do not normally grow, you may have to mow to control weeds and grass. Your forester or local soil conservation office will have information galore in this regard.

Pruning special trees. In starting a brand-new woodlot, say of black walnut and white oak for the veneer market, you will usually have to do some hand pruning, since the dense seedling

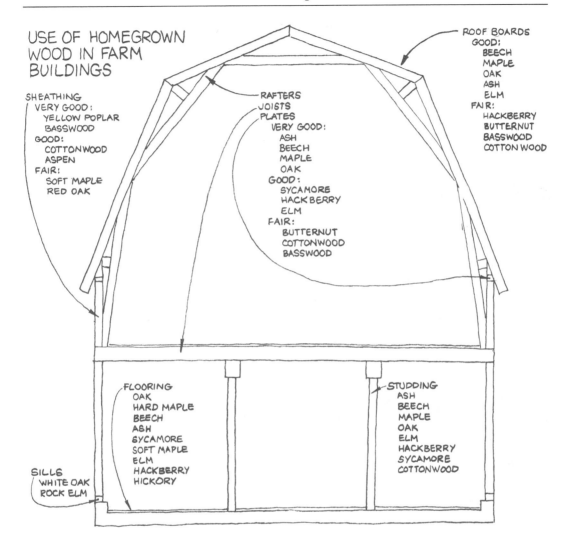

USE OF HOMEGROWN
WOOD IN FARM
BUILDINGS

SHEATHING
  VERY GOOD:
    YELLOW POPLAR
    BASSWOOD
  GOOD:
    COTTONWOOD
    ASPEN
  FAIR:
    SOFT MAPLE
    RED OAK

RAFTERS
JOISTS
PLATES
  VERY GOOD:
    ASH
    BEECH
    MAPLE
    OAK
  GOOD:
    SYCAMORE
    HACKBERRY
    ELM
  FAIR:
    BUTTERNUT
    COTTONWOOD
    BASSWOOD

ROOF BOARDS
  GOOD:
    BEECH
    MAPLE
    OAK
    ASH
    ELM
  FAIR:
    HACKBERRY
    BUTTERNUT
    BASSWOOD
    COTTONWOOD

FLOORING
  OAK
  HARD MAPLE
  BEECH
  ASH
  SYCAMORE
  SOFT MAPLE
  ELM
  HACKBERRY
  HICKORY

STUDDING
  ASH
  BEECH
  MAPLE
  OAK
  ELM
  HACKBERRY
  SYCAMORE
  COTTONWOOD

SILLS
  WHITE OAK
  ROCK ELM

environment of the naturally renewing forest is not present. In pruning young saplings for a tall, straight trunk, try to follow this rule: eliminate side branches before they are 2 inches in diameter and maintain about two-thirds of the lower trunk free of branches. This is not always easy to do because young trees in the open, especially walnut, tend to fork out rather than maintain a straight, single leader.

Smaller rather than larger. In starting a woodlot from scratch, stay small. An acre at a time will soak up about all the spare hours a person normally has available.

Starting and Caring for a Tree Grove in the Suburban Backyard

Most yards, or neighboring yards, have trees, and invariably, these trees are seeding new trees into neighboring lawns. You hardly ever notice these little seedlings because you mow them off every spring. If you start looking for them you will, in fact, find seedlings everywhere, including the spouting at the edge of your roof, if you have overhanging trees. If New York City were abandoned, trees would overwhelm it in a century.

Simply by allowing some seedlings to grow, or replanting them in appropriate spots, you can convert ¼ acre of backyard into a tree grove at little or no cost. On such a small grove, you can't let nature take its course as easily as you can in a rural woodlot of several acres or more. But how you prune or which bent trees you decide not to cut down (they're picturesque if nothing else) is entirely up to you. The usual rules of forest management don't really apply. Of course, if suburban homeowners were so inclined, they could treat their backyards collectively as an urban forest and manage them as such, selling the timber as a cooperative marketing effort.

In the backyard suburban environment, trees can be treated almost like individuals. Care of them entails protection from the kinds of injuries not so prevalent in rural settings. The trees in the "urban forest" are more often threatened by building and road construction, flooding, soil compaction, air pollution, injuries from lawn and garden equipment, chemicals, de-icing salt, and improper pruning and planting.

Construction. Fill dirt around a new home will injure or kill trees if it is piled up higher around the trunk than the soil level upon which the tree grew. A well around the trunk does *not* protect the roots from injury, and so the tree often dies anyway. Likewise, a driveway very close to a tree may cause root damage, or the roots will heave up the pavement. And a driveway near a tree invariably means a car gouging a wound in the tree, not to mention damage to the fender.

On construction sites, as in a subdivision, changes in drainage patterns often result in flooding where none occurred before. Water lying around trees that demand good drainage means dead trees. Ash, black gum, cottonwood, red maple, swamp oak (overcup oak), silver maple, sycamore, willows, white cedar, sweet gum, and certain elms will tolerate some flooding. Most pines, except loblolly, will not. Neither will red cedar (a juniper), white spruce, paper birch, hemlock, or most nut trees.

Compaction. Soil compaction injures urban trees, a problem more common on public land than in the backyard. Pedestrian and wheel travel should be designed to stay away from the root zones of trees.

Chemical pollution. Arborvitae, box elder, Douglas fir, English oak, magnolia, Norway maple, red oak, dogwood, and white spruce are relatively tolerant of the pollutants commonly associated with an urban environment—ozone and other oxidants from industrial and auto emissions. American elm, catalpa, jack pine, larch, Lombardy poplar, ponderosa pine, quaking aspen, Virginia pine, white pine, and willows are relatively intolerant. Saltwater runoff from de-icing streets and sidewalks is particularly harmful to basswood, Douglas fir, hemlock, ironwood, ponderosa pine, red maple, red pine, shagbark hickory, speckled alder, sugar maple, and white pine. Relatively tolerant of salt are Austrian pine, bigtooth aspen, the birches, black cherry, black locust, quaking aspen, red cedar, red oak, white ash, white oak, white spruce, and the yews.

Herbicides can injure and kill nearby trees, even when applied scrupulously according to label directions, because they drift away from the application area. Apricot trees and grapevines are extremely sensitive. I know of a case where apricot trees were killed when the owner applied a mulch of grass clippings that had come from a herbicide-treated lawn. If you decide to protect your trees from lawn mowers by keeping an area around the tree free of grass, don't try to kill the grass with chemicals.

Improper pruning. Every garden and lawn book tells you how to prune correctly: Undercut a

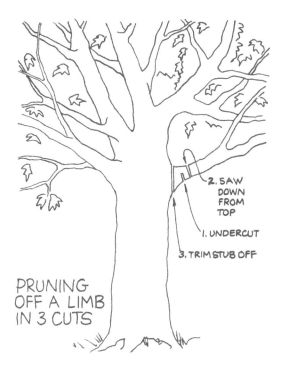

2. SAW DOWN FROM TOP

1. UNDERCUT

3. TRIM STUB OFF

PRUNING OFF A LIMB IN 3 CUTS

too. A small seedling will grow in five years to nearly the same height that a 10-foot transplant will. The latter usually suffers too much transplanting shock, even if balled and burlapped, to grow fast (if at all) during its first years.

Saws for Harvesting Wood

Most of us do not speak of the possibility of harvesting wood with the same expectancy that we speak of harvesting fruits and vegetables—mainly because we have preserved the art of the hoe and the rotary tiller better than the art of the ax and chain saw. With adequate knowledge and appropriate tools, the harvest of the tree grove is as practical as that of the garden.

Chain Saws

I have already discussed the use of the chain-saw mill and the band-saw mill—the only really new developments in home wood harvesting. The chain saw is, of course, most often

limb first, then saw down from the top, so that the limb falls free and does not peel down the side of the trunk. Then with a third cut, remove the stub flush with the trunk. Use a pruning saw to do this. If you try to use a bow saw, the metal handle above the blade will push the blade away from the tree and not give you a good flush cut.

Improper planting. Along with the trees they sell, every good nursery sends out detailed directions on how to plant them properly. Don't crowd the roots into too small a hole. Don't plant deeper or shallower than the depth the tree was growing before it was dug up and balled. Provide some fine, soft, absorbent humus in the hole around the roots but do not add fertilizer into the planting hole, and so forth. If you plant seeds or very small seedlings, as I urge you to do, you will not have too many planting worries. You will save time, work, and money,

used to fell trees and cut large logs or firewood, having for all practical purposes superseded the hand-operated log or crosscut saw, just as the rotary tiller has superseded the spade. This is not to say that the crosscut hasn't certain advantages, namely in money saved. In fact, skilled crosscutters can cut through a 12-inch log faster than chain saw users can, but they cannot keep up that speed all day. The crosscut must be very sharp and operated *lightly*, or it becomes a burden long before dinnertime.

But what is true of the old crosscut is also true of the chain saw. It, too, should be very sharp and operated *lightly*—a touch the modern woodcutter, not backgrounded in crosscutting, does not usually appreciate. He works twice as hard over his chain saw and makes twice as much noise. He is unaware of the pinching action of wood until his saw is hung up in a closed crack. And he spends most of his time waiting for his saw to be repaired

after wearing it out trying to force a dull blade through a log.

Sharpening a chain saw blade freehand with a file seldom yields good results. Even the rather elaborate little vise guides that almost force you to file in exactly the right direction are only partially effective. I have one and no longer use it. Take your blades to a professional saw sharpener who is equipped to sharpen blades almost as good as new. It's best to have several blades on hand. Take them all to the sharpener once a year. Use one until it starts to dull—until it no longer throws out those big, fat healthy flakes of wood that show it is cutting right. Then put on a new blade and take the dulled one to your sharpener. I make six blade changes each cutting season—about one blade per cord.

Don't try to saw with the grain of the wood unless you have a specially sharpened ripping blade. Cut across the grain or not at all to prevent dulling your blade. Don't let it run into the soil when cutting through a log, and don't cut through ice frozen on a log. All these can dull the blade, too.

Don't push down hard on the saw when cutting through a log. Go *lightly*. Let the blade do the work. If it won't, and throws out only puny amounts of sawdust powder, bearing down on the saw will only wear out you and the saw. In cutting through a large log, the chain saw will cut faster at the base, next to the motor, and slower out at the end. Rather than rocking the saw to try to force the far end of the blade to bite harder into the log, saw awhile on one side, then go around and saw awhile from the other side. On a log larger than the saw blade, you have to do this anyway. It's much easier on your saw—and you. Do not roar the engine excessively, especially when your saw is caught in a pinched log. You'll just ruin the clutch.

Don't buy a little $150 chain saw if you intend to seriously saw wood for home heat. Get at least a medium-size saw, with a 43, 44, or 45 cc engine. Lighter saws are only good for limbing, which you should rarely do with a chain saw anyway (see the next item).

The best use of the chain saw is to cut down trees larger than 3 to 4 inches in diameter. This seems apparent, but the temptation is to use it to cut down smaller sprouts, which is actually easier to do with a sharp bucksaw. Felling trees is a dangerous occupation. I have a good friend who is paralyzed from the waist down from a falling tree, and I think of him whenever I go to the woods. Dead trees, hollow trees, double-trunked trees, trees that lean decidedly, and trees on steep slopes are all especially hazardous to cut down. And the chain saw doesn't help because while it is roaring, you can't *hear* the tree beginning to crack loose, nor is it easy to watch the saw and look up at the same time to see if the tree is beginning its descent. Learn to very closely watch the crack you are sawing in. When it widens ¼ inch, the treetop is moving several feet and is probably on its way down.

Hollow, leaning, and double-trunked trees can split asunder as you saw and can kill you. Careful loggers wrap a short length of log chain around the tree trunk about head high to minimize this danger. Trees on steep slopes do not necessarily want to fall in the direction you think they should. I know of a case where the owners let the tenants cut wood from the lot but only where a tree fell down naturally. This is somewhat wasteful, but it is a very safe way to cut wood. Another caution: watch out for low horizontal limbs on the trunk. As the trunk

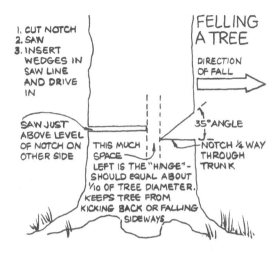

falls you may think you are clear, only to be struck dead by such a branch. That's why they are called widow-makers.

I never try to cut all the way through a tree. I reach the point at which only the "hinge" (see drawing) remains, and then I turn off the saw so I can hear. I drive wedges into the saw slot to tip the tree enough so that gravity pulls it on over. This is so much safer, since I can hear the tree begin to fall and have time to get away, without rushing away with a running chain saw in my hand. It is best to use wooden wedges rather than steel ones in case you have guessed wrong, and the tree is not sufficiently cut through for the wedges to finish the job. In such a case you have to saw a little more, and with steel wedges in the tree you might accidentally hit one of them, damaging your saw blade. Saw just a bit more. Stop the saw. Pull it out. Drive in the wedges again.

Power Cut-Off Saws

Though not as well heralded as the chain saw in the outer suburban world and countryside, the cut-off saw, usually powered by belt from the power take-off (PTO) of a smaller farm

tractor, is a very efficient way to cut up smaller limbs and logs (up to about 7 inches in diameter). New cut-off saws are still sold, and old ones generally sell at farm sales, which is where I got mine.

The cut-off saw is much faster than the chain saw. What my family and I generally do when working up a felled tree is to use a chain saw to cut the branches and small logs into lengths we can lift (4 to 8 feet, depending on the diameter of the piece). We pile up these lengths until a nice day in February or March, then saw up all the piles into stove-length wood with the cut-off saw in one day.

It takes two people to operate a cut-off efficiently. One lifts the wood to be cut onto the saw carriage and pushes it through the saw.

The other holds on to the pieces being cut off and tosses them onto a nearby pile or into a truck or wagon. Needless to say, working around a cut-off saw is potentially dangerous and demands utmost caution. Don't work more than 2 hours at a time without a break. Fatigue leads to haste, which leads to carelessness.

Limbing and Splitting with the Ax

When the tree is down, there is still great danger involved if big limbs hold the heavy log up off the ground. Study the situation very carefully. You may cut off a limb that is holding the log up on one side, only to have the log roll over, possibly on you. I came within 3 inches of being killed this way. Do most of the limbing (anything under 3 to 4 inches in diameter) with an ax. It is much safer, much faster, and much easier than using a chain saw. Except for those light inexpensive models, chain saws are too heavy for limbing.

Many chain saw accidents occur because the woodcutter gets tired and careless, or trips and falls in the debris of limbs and trunks. A man in our community was found dead, his throat cut by his chain saw, which he apparently fell on. Especially do not limb above your head, or in any other awkward position where the saw could fall against you. Use a bucksaw for overhead branches or a long-handled limb saw made for that purpose.

Most limbing work is best done with an ax. A sharp ax will cut through a 3-inch-thick green branch in one blow, if delivered correctly. Sever the branch on a slant, swinging *up* the log, not down. When possible, stand on one side of the log and cut the branches on the other side; in other words, keep the log between you and your ax when possible. It's safer that way and easier to cut most limbs from that position.

Common axes are straight-handled or curved—the latter referred to as a "fawn's foot" because of its shape. Which you should use is mostly a matter of preference. It is nice to have two axes, one with the fatter edge that axes come with for splitting, and one with a blade honed down to a thinner, sharp edge for limbing. Try to avoid axes with heads set in plastic. When the handle breaks, it's often difficult to get the wood out of the plastic-set heads to put in a new handle. Good axes use wood and metal wedges to hold the blade on tight; if the blade loosens a bit, soak the handle and head in water. (But don't do this too often; if you do, the handle will eventually rot.) To get metal wedges out of heads, drill holes in the wood around them and chisel or punch out waste wood and metal. If you try to burn out the head, the steel may lose its temper.

Use the ax for splitting straight-grained kindling. It is lighter and less tiring than the splitting maul. I think the ax works better in chopping out the slanting top of a notch when felling a tree, as the chain saw does not saw well when sawing partly with the grain. In chopping with the ax, the same advice holds as for most hand tools: let the ax do the work. If it is sharp, you should not have to swing it with all your might. Drop it more than swing it when

chopping. Use a little more force when splitting, but don't swing as hard as you can. Swinging hard may mean missing and hitting your foot.

Some wood will not split with a direct downward blow of the ax, but it will split if at the moment of striking the wood, the blade is twisted sideways a bit. This is called twirling.

Using a splitting block saves the ax from being dulled by thumping into the dirt. It's also safer. The lower your body is in relation to the wood to be split, the less chance of the ax missing or glancing off the wood and hitting your foot. That's why, when splitting a piece on the ground, the professional splitter will bend his knees as he brings the ax down on the wood.

Mauls and Other Assorted Useful—and Not So Useful—Tools

The value of traditional skill gained by trial and error over the centuries is nowhere more apparent than in wood-splitting tools. With the return of wood as a popular fuel, a rash of new products has filled the marketplace, purportedly to make wood splitting faster and

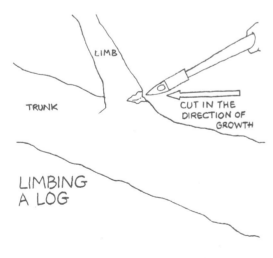

LIMB

TRUNK

CUT IN THE
DIRECTION OF
GROWTH

LIMBING
A LOG

easier. I've used some of these tools and observed others in use—everything from hydraulically powered mechanical splitters costing from $600 to $2000 and up; to metal screws that mount on a truck or car wheel; to heavy mauls that depend on sheer weight to split wood more "easily"; to innovative axes with spreading hinges built into the sides of the blade that help push the rending wood apart. All I can say is that the claims of faster and easier ain't necessarily so.

These tools will do all that the manufacturers claim on easy-splitting wood, but easy-splitting wood splits fast and easy with the traditional maul and wedge, too. Wood that is difficult to split is difficult to split with any splitter except the most powerful mechanical models that work off the hydraulic system of a large farm tractor or its equivalent. Most people can't afford these. Rental is over $30 a day, which is a cost higher than the price of a good splitting maul that should last you a lifetime.

Furthermore, feeding wood into a mechanical splitter and withdrawing the pieces makes for *more* physical labor, not less, than hand splitting. In some ways this work is more exhausting, since large log chunks must be lifted and one feels compelled to work as relentlessly and machinelike as the machine itself. The cheaper mechanical splitters are not worth the $600 or so you pay for them, in my opinion. You have the maintenance problems associated with all cheaper motors, and these machines will not split hard-splitting wood without breaking down anyway. I offered a pile of big, knotty white oak log chunks to an owner of one of these machines, since I could not split the stuff with my trusty hand tools without tremendous exertion. Although he needed wood badly, he turned down my offer. Said he'd learned from experience his splitter couldn't handle that kind of wood.

The Splitting Maul

Having reached the conclusion that my splitting maul, wedges, and a standard ax for

What Makes a Good Splitting Ax or Maul?

The blade is forged, not cast, held to the handle by wooden and steel wedges that can be removed if a handle needs replacing. The wood should be straight-grained in a straight handle, with the grain running directly up and down through the handle, not at a slant. If the handle is painted, suspect something is being hidden. You want to be able to see the grain. The preferred wood is seasoned white ash, but hickory is good, too.

If you want to get *really* choosy, you will investigate how the steel of your blade is forged. The old-fashioned blacksmith hammered the steel in an ax blade with repeated blows, which connoisseurs of such matters claim makes a stronger ax blade than the few high-pressure blows given to the hot metal in today's forged steel manufactory. At least one manufacturer (Hults Valley Works in Sweden, whose tools are sold in the United States by Smith and Hawken, 25 Corte Madera, Mill Valley, CA 94941) claims a better forged steel by using eccentric presses that imitate the blacksmith's repeated blows.

kindling were the cheapest and easiest tools for wood splitting, I was pleased to read in David Tresemer's book *Splitting Firewood* (Hand & Foot, Brattleboro, Vt., 1981) that he had made some rather scientific comparison tests of all the wood-splitting tools and arrived at the same conclusion. (Tresemer's books on various hand tools are excellent and charming reading for anyone who is intrigued by the traditional view taken in this book.) The splitting ax or maul with the aid of wedges when necessary, is, he says, "not only healthier and safer, but also more economical" than any of the other tools. What's more, in splitting one-fifth of a cord, the split-

A Wooden Maul

When using steel wedges, wear protective goggles to keep pieces of flying metal out of your eyes. The curled, worn tops of wedges should be ground off smooth to avoid this danger, but alas, I fear few people do it. I've "heard tell" of using a *wooden* maul, but I can't imagine one that would work effectively for splitting wood with steel wedges. My father-in-law used to describe a wooden maul he said would do the job—an "iron ball hickory" maul. To make one, the woodcutter would cut down a small red hickory sprout, about 4 to 6 inches in diameter. The base of the logs, the part right below the soil, would be the fattest part and the hardest. It had to be cut carefully out from the roots. Then the little log

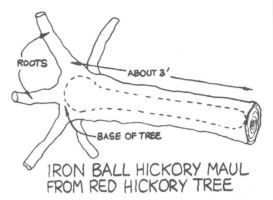

IRON BALL HICKORY MAUL
FROM RED HICKORY TREE

was cut to about 35 inches in length and shaved down with a drawknife into a round-ended maul. It was wonderful for driving wooden gluts and tough enough to stand blows on steel wedges . . . at least for a while.

---

ting ax or maul is faster than any of the other hand tools and only 2 minutes slower than a deluxe mechanical splitter.

Also interesting to traditionalists, Tresemer points out the advantages of *good* wood handles over metal and fiberglass ones. (He favors Snow and Nealley's "Our Best" splitting ax or maul.) Metal, unbreakable handles, besides being heavy, do not absorb much of the shock of the blow; your hands and arms absorb it. Fiberglass handles *will* break, he says, and are extremely difficult to replace. Nor, he says, can you slide your hand up and down the fiberglass handle as you swing. (The fiberglass gets rough as it wears, and the fiberglass splinters that result don't feel too good when they get stuck in your skin.) You must keep your hands on the rubber grip.

Tips for Hand Splitting

Splitting most wood, and any wood with knots, requires the use of the splitting maul,

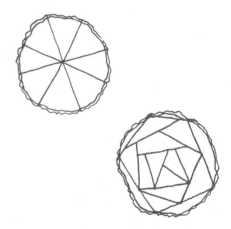

sometimes with the aid of wedges. There are two basic ways to split open a chunk of log: through the center, as in cutting a pie, or around the outside. Wood that resists the first method without a wedge can sometimes be rendered into stove-size pieces with the second

SMALL STONE
IN GROOVE
ALONGSIDE
WEDGE

Stacking Wood

Woodcutters tend to judge each other's character by the way they stack wood. My friend Dave Haferd is the neatest stacker this side of the Black Forest. He also is a most particular farmer, so his wood pile does tell something about him. My stacks are, by comparison, crude and apt to fall over when I stack them in the woods for a drying season or two. But I'm getting better. I've learned that I have a natural tendency to let the wood pile lean out toward the side I stand on when stacking, so now I take special pains to eye up the stack as I build it so it stays plumb. It is better to have a woodshed, or as Dave Haferd does, use a barn for wood. But wood will generally dry about as well out in the open, as it will indoors. Just put a piece of roofing over it to keep off most of the rain. Start a wood pile by laying down two fairly straight lines of limbs upon which to rank the wood, so it is off the ground. I stack between two trees whenever possible, although a good stacker can get by without any end brace, by boxing in the stack and laying the pieces in layers at right angles to each other on the ends of the pile.

Stacking wood is satisfying work. You learn to study each piece and fit it into the stack where it will lay the most level and so build the sturdiest pile with the least amount of air space. But if a fellow woodcutter remarks sarcastically that he can see the sun go down right through my wood pile, I have a smart remark ready in reply: the better to get the wood dry.

method. If neither works, use a wedge and proceed by the first method.

In very hard wood, the wedge may not stick when tapped into the wood preparatory to being hit with the sledgehammer or splitting maul. Or upon being hit hard, it pops back out of the wood instead of going in. An old trick in this circumstance is to place a small stone or piece of gravel alongside the wedge in the groove the wedge has made. The stone makes the wedge stick so it can be driven into the wood. Why this works, I'm not sure, but work it does.

Have two wedges handy, in case one gets stuck in the wood and won't come out. In splitting knotty, stubborn wood, you'll have

BOXING IN A
STACK OF
WOOD

better luck splitting against the direction of growth—down the tree trunk, not up. Frozen wood will split easier than thawed wood. Crotch pieces may split if you start the splitting line so it runs down through the fork branches.

A Peavey and a Cant Hook

A cant hook has a thick wooden handle about 30 inches long with a steel end to which is attached a hinged hook. If the steel end comes

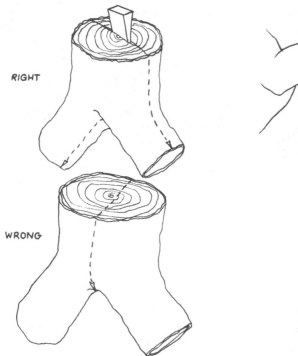

RIGHT

WRONG

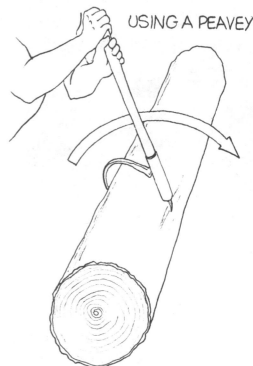

USING A PEAVEY

to a point, the tool is a peavey. With this tool you can roll fairly large logs with ease. Every woodcutter should have one.

With a peavey or cant hook, you can roll a log over to finish sawing it through. You can roll or twist a log to relieve a pinched saw. You can turn the log over on top of the peavey so you can saw a piece off without pinching. When a tree you are felling gets hung up in another tree, you can sometimes twist it free with the peavey, saving you the dangerous and laborious job of cutting short lengths off the butt until

the tree swings loose. With two people, each with a peavey hooked into the end of a log from opposite sides, you can lift and slide the log onto a truck bed—if, of course, it is not *too* large. Leverage built into the peavey's design allows one to roll logs that two or three people might not otherwise be able to budge.

There's another way to turn a log over without any tool. When limbing, let one stout limb stick out about 4 feet from the trunk. This limb becomes a handle with which to roll the log from side to side.

Photography Credits

Gene Logsdon: pp. xviii, top; 36; 54; 67; 78, top and left; 79, top; 94; 98-99; 101; 102; 108; 113; 129; 130-31; 135; 142-43; 144-45; 147, bottom left; 149; 150-51; 152; 154-55; 159; 162; 181; 186, left; 208-9; 212; 223; 265; 267; 268; 280, top left; 281, bottom right; 296, right; 299; 300-1; 302; 306-7; 311; 319; 328; 330; 331; 333; 338-39; 340; 342; 345; 363; 370; 372-73; 375; 376; 380, left; 381; 384-85; 387; 388; 391; 392; 395; 403; 404-5; 406-7; 416-17; 420; 429; 431; 440; 444.

Dennis Barnes: pp. xviii, bottom right; 64; 74; 79, bottom left and right; 105; 157; 183; 184-85; 187, left; 199; 213; 414.

Tom Gettings: pp. xix, bottom right; 18; 47; 127; 226; 262.

Mark Lenny: pp. xviii, left; xix, top; 11; 12-13; 15; 16; 22; 42-43; 115; 122-23; 256; 274; 320.

Mitch Mandel: pp. 2; 4; 136; 147, top; 280, bottom; 287; 323; 325; 348; 427; 445, top left.

Rodale Press Photography Department: pp. xix, left; 14; 23; 38; 57; 86; 92-93; 96-97; 107; 160; 170-71; 174; 177; 179; 186, top and bottom; 187, top and bottom; 192; 201; 205; 211; 214; 216; 229; 230; 245; 247; 248; 250; 253; 255; 264; 271; 272-73; 276-77; 280, top right; 281, top; 288-89; 291; 293; 294; 296, bottom left; 310; 312; 326; 346; 350; 352; 354-55; 359; 364; 366; 369; 380, bottom right; 396; 400; 412; 425, top; 430; 434; 438.

Additional photographs courtesy of

American Forestry Association: pp. 428; 432; 437; 445, bottom.

La Lune Collection: pp. 380, top; 425, bottom; 426, top.

The Library of Congress: pp. 78, bottom; 87; 118; 194; 238; 281, left; 309.

INDEX

Page numbers in italic indicate boxes, charts, and tables.